The Liberal Education of Charles Eliot Norton

The Liberal Education
of Charles Eliot Norton

James Turner

The Johns Hopkins University Press
Baltimore and London

© 1999 The Johns Hopkins University Press
All rights reserved. Published 1999
Printed in the United States of America on acid-free paper

2 4 6 8 9 7 5 3 1

The Johns Hopkins University Press
2715 North Charles Street
Baltimore, Maryland 21218–4363
www.press.jhu.edu

Library of Congress Cataloging-in-Publication Data will be found
at the end of this book.
A catalog record for this book is available from the British Library.

ISBN 0-8018-6147-0

Frontispiece: Charles Eliot Norton
at thirty, 1858.

All illustrations appear courtesy of
The Society for the Preservation of Antiquities, Boston.

For Julie

CHARLES ELIOT NORTON stood out, in the air of the place and time—which for that matter, I think, changed much as he changed, and couldn't change much beyond his own range of experiment—with a greater salience, granting his background, I should say, than I have ever known a human figure stand out with from any: an effect involved of course in the nature of the background as well as in that of the figure.

HENRY JAMES,
Notes of a Son and Brother, 1914

Why can't one speak truth sometimes, and call C. E. N. publicly and without apology the infernal old sinner and sham that he is.

WILLIAM JAMES
TO ALICE G. JAMES, 1888

My father's relation to the community he lived in was of a far more original nature than has, I think, been apprehended by most young men of Mr. Howe's generation. The very fact that my father's personality, his manner—dress, speech, were not of marked originality, led many an unthinking person to discount what was original in his contribution to his community. For instance, the *range* of his tastes and of his activities, promotion of the several Societies he was the founder of, or interested in, the new field of work he embarked in when he began to teach at Harvard, were all indicative of a trend of interest unlike that of his fellows working along other lines. And so it came about that he stimulated thought in many directions, which had been little referred to before in America.

This is what I mean by his originality. . . . I should say that without Ruskin's genius—and Ruskin's irrationality—my father had in some sort held the same relation to his time in America that Ruskin held in England. He opened windows through his teaching on new horizons.

SARA NORTON
TO CHARLES FRANCIS ADAMS JR., 1914

CONTENTS

Preface : xi

Acknowledgments : xiii

Illustrations following pages 134 and 306

THERE ARE NAMES known everywhere, it seems, at one point in time, then utterly forgotten within two or three decades. Charles Eliot Norton's is one of those. During the latter years of his life, almost all well-educated Americans could identify Norton, as could possibly most of their British equivalents. Knowing of Norton was in fact a touchstone of whether one *was* well educated. To Americans he was the great icon of the life of the mind; abroad, he counted as the most impressive exemplar of American high culture. Newspapers on both sides of the Atlantic treated his death in 1908 as a major event. Today, except among a handful of historians, his name evokes at best a kind of puzzled half recognition: people have seen it embalmed in the Charles Eliot Norton Lectures at Harvard, or they amalgamate it with that of his cousin, the Harvard president Charles Eliot. Such is the fate of an influence spread over many areas of endeavor rather than concentrated on one, of a temperament more generative than imperial, of an originality more organizational than intellectual.

Yet he ought not to be forgotten. From the Civil War through the century's end, no one touched the thinking of Americans in more diverse ways: in journalism, in letters, in academe. During the Civil War, Norton edited the North's most influential quarterly, the *North American Review;* near the war's end he cofounded the leading voice of American liberalism, the *Nation.* In the 1870s he became the first professor of art history in the United States. A few years later he created the Archaeological Institute of America, which evolved into the professional association for that discipline, and shortly thereafter the American School of Classical Studies at Athens, which became its chief training ground. He established Dante studies as an academic field in the United States, and his translation of the *Divina Commedia* was long standard. His volumes of the correspondence of Emerson, Carlyle, Ruskin, and Lowell helped to set a new norm of responsible editing. Almost incidentally, he wrote an article on the poet John Donne, which became seminal in modern Donne scholarship.

Norton's achievement can be stated bluntly: he was the most influential progenitor of the humanities in American education and scholarship. By the late 1880s he had also emerged as probably the preeminent cultural critic in the United States, an American analogue to John Ruskin and Matthew Arnold. Both of these men, along with other eminent Victorians, numbered among Norton's friends, for he was also a linchpin in the Anglo-American intellectual nexus that shaped high culture in Victorian America.

Norton was not a strikingly innovative thinker in the way of discursive writing; his originality lay in his adaptation of older intellectual practices to new purposes. His powerful influence endures, now mostly subterranean and unrecognized, in colleges and universities and hence in the life of the mind in America. This is true not because of particular works of scholarship or educational theory but because of institutions he invented and models he devised, mostly by inventive reworking of older materials.

In this accomplishment, he showed the force in American culture of a class with highly distinctive attributes: the now long-vanished Boston mercantile elite. From it Norton inherited a hierarchical ideal of culture and politics, an ideal in tension with the rising strength of mass democracy in the United States and with his own democratic commitments. In the chapters that follow I try to tell straightforwardly the story of his life from the point of view of his own prejudices and principles, not reducing his varied experience to any simple pattern. But I hope that the reader will see how Norton's upbringing in Boston's patrician world set him on a particular course in coping with this tension; how he adapted the ideas of that older world to try to nurture a democratic culture; how education and erudition eventually became his means to this end; how this larger goal resulted in a markedly new kind of teaching and research; and how the ultimate failure of Norton's democratic ambitions affected the future of learning and intellectual life in his country.

A BOOK THAT absorbs fifteen years in preparation amasses for its author a load of debt impossible even fully to confess. I cannot begin to count the scholars and other friends who contributed a helpful idea, a pointed criticism, a crucial reference. I may begin by acknowledging the most literal debts, the pecuniary sort. Funds to support travel to archives were provided by the American Council of Learned Societies; by the American Philosophical Society; by a Travel to Collections grant from the National Endowment for the Humanities; by a Beveridge Award from the American Historical Association; by former Dean Harold Attridge of the College of Arts and Letters, University of Notre Dame; and most steadily by the University of Michigan—through the Faculty Assistance Fund of the College of Literature, Science, and the Arts, through former Dean John D'Arms of the Horace Rackham Graduate School, and through the Office of the Vice President for Research. The History Department of the University of Michigan gave leave for research in 1989–90 and again for writing in the fall of 1994; Michigan's Institute for the Humanities provided congenial space for both in 1991–92.

Some of my thinking about Andrews and Charles Eliot Norton and about the history of higher education was tested in lectures and seminars at the University of Michigan, the Friedrich-Ebert Stiftung, the Isabella Stewart Gardner Museum, the University of Arizona, Duke University, the Russian State University for the Humanities, the University of Notre Dame, and the Ecole des Hautes Etudes en Sciences Sociales. I am grateful to all of these audiences for helpful criticism but especially to my colleagues Jean Heffer, François Weil, and Pap Ndiaye at the Centre d'Etudes Nord-américaines of EHESS for thoughtful comments during my visits there over the past several years: stays made more pleasant and productive by the helpful kindness of Caroline Beraud.

There would have been no ideas to try out were it not for the splendid assistance of the archivists at the more than one hundred institutions housing Norton papers in North America and Europe. Though grateful to all, I can hardly name every one; but I am happy at least to single out the archives on which I made the greatest demands and to whose staffs I am thus particularly indebted: the Archaeological Institute of America; the American Antiquarian Society; the Archivio di Stato di Siena; the Bodleian Library, Oxford University; the Boston Athenaeum; the Boston Public Library; the British Library; the Cambridge University Library; the Columbia University Library; the Isabella Stewart Gardner Museum; the Harvard University Archives; King's College, Cambridge; the Library of Congress; the Massachusetts Historical Society; the New York Public Library; the Pierpont Morgan Library; the Harry Ransom Humanities Research Center of the University of Texas at Austin; Trinity College, Cambridge; and the Sterling and Beinecke Libraries, Yale University. Librarians at the University of Massachusetts in Boston, the Harlan Hatcher Graduate Library of the University of Michigan, and the Pattee Library of Pennsylvania State University were helpful in obtaining printed sources. At the head of the list stands the Houghton Library of Harvard University, which houses the largest single collection of Norton papers as well as those of some of Norton's closest friends. The Houghton's staff was unfailingly generous with their time and expertise. More than anyone else, they made this book possible.

Several former colleagues at the University of Michigan obliged me with invaluable advice, including Raymond Grew on nineteenth-century Italy, Diane Owen Hughes on Italian medieval historiography, Thomas Trautmann on nineteenth-century India and on Indian historiography, and Nicholas Delbanco on narrative. Tom and Nick also read and criticized portions of an early draft. Another Michigan colleague, Richard Cándida Smith, contributed the phrase "invention of Western civilization" as a result of his own reading of Norton's lecture notes. Beyond these specific debts, I am grateful to friends at Michigan for a decade of animating intellectual life that very largely shaped this book. Other scholars contributed expert advice from their own special studies: Stephen G. Alter on William Dwight Whitney, John Bicknell on Leslie Stephen, Jane Turner Censer on Frederick Law Olmsted, Marjorie Cohn on the print collections at the Fogg Museum, Dayton Haskin on Donne scholarship, and Caroline Winterer on classical studies in nineteenth-century America.

Donald and Molly Robinson provided information on Norton's house in Ashfield. Gary Gallagher, chair of the Penn State History Department, arranged library privileges during my three-year part-time residence in State College. I thank Michael John and the president of Magdalen College, Oxford, and David Feldman and the master of Christ's College, Cambridge, for kindly arranging lodging during research trips; I owe the same debt to the master of Eliot House at Harvard and to Jack and Jane Censer. Barbara Ryan gave sage counsel. Torrin Finney at the University of Massachusetts at Boston and Paul Bernard and Siobhan Donnelly at the University of Michigan helped as research assistants.

The substantial volume in your hands was carved out of a first draft twice as long. Four good friends gave that behemoth a thorough critical reading, demonstrating not only affection but something approaching heroism. The diverse talents and expertise of Donald Fleming, Dan LeMahieu, Robert Sullivan, and Caroline Winterer made the second draft not only a good deal slimmer but infinitely more cogent and approachable. I cannot well say how grateful I am to all four. Jack Rakove's *Original Meanings* is one of the monuments of recent American historical writing. (A quarter of a century later, I can still recall Professor Bernard Bailyn saying after Jack's general exam that Rakove's meanings were nothing if not original.) Rakove read the second draft, and every subsequent reader ought to be as thankful to him as I am for his keen eye for obscurity and extravagance. Henry Tom, my editor at Johns Hopkins University Press, has worked with me longer than I have worked with Norton. He gave invaluable suggestions for final pruning of a manuscript whose author could not have been happier to make the last cut. The reader owes an even greater debt than I to Diane Hammond, whose careful editing of the manuscript clarified many obscurities.

The Liberal Education of Charles Eliot Norton was completed at the University of Notre Dame. In terms of intellectual stimulation and generosity of colleagues in sharing their knowledge, I cannot imagine a more propitious environment in which to bring this long work to a close.

I have lived with Charles Eliot Norton for fifteen years. I have lived with another person for twice as long, to my incalculably greater benefit. To her this book is dedicated.

The Liberal Education of Charles Eliot Norton

Prologue

The New England Clerisy

The gray-green waves of the south Atlantic broke tediously on the wooden hull; a sullen equatorial sun browned skins, bleached hair. It was 1849, late June. In the weeks since the ship had sailed from Boston the thrill of facing the unknown had faded; the young man—scarcely out of his teens—had little to do but think and read, watch for whales, stare at seabirds, read and think. Charley Norton did not much mind the monotony: he was given to reflection. His mind turned especially often to one person, the one who had shaped his judgments, his understanding of the world and of himself.

Andrews Norton had been a close and caring father, but Charley owed him much else besides. Andrews had given his son a thirst for knowledge that would eventually make Charley—Charles Eliot Norton—the most influential American scholar of his generation; a style of learning that the son would stamp on liberal education in the United States for generations to come; and a sense of obligation to others that would drive him through a life of service and reform until he grew into a revered critic of his nation's culture. Andrews had also given his son a sharp moral discrimination, a hierarchical idea of leadership, and a confidence in his own judgment that would leave him at the end, in a new imperialist mass democracy, a prophet reviled. The young East India merchant had not the slightest glimmer of any such future. Nor did he yet comprehend the extent to which Andrews's legacy was not solely a parent's gift but an inheritance from the community that had nurtured both father and son.

For us to grasp all this, to come to grips with the life of Charles Eliot Norton, is to understand different Americas—an America that once was and is no more, an America that once was dreamed but never was, an America that lingers still.

Aboard the little merchant ship furrowing its way toward the Cape of Good Hope and India beyond, musing steered the mind, not forward in the direction of an unknowable future, but backward toward home. Home meant Cambridge, Massachusetts, and the house there where Charles Norton was born, Shady Hill.

The whitewashed clapboard of Shady Hill preserved the Puritan simplicity of an older New England. Yet to walk from the capacious entrance hall into a dining room seating twenty-five was to enter a newer world, where ladies in Parisian gowns might gossip over green turtle soup and maraschino ice served on a table glittering with silver. At dinner any afternoon, though, gossip would soon give way to weightier matters: Polk and Webster, Wordsworth and Mrs. Hemans, Dante and Tasso, Schleiermacher and Eichhorn. And after the last of the Madeira, the guests crossed the hall to the library. There the aroma of leather bindings mingled with cigar fumes; on the walls hung monuments of European art; sunshine poured through the bay windows, warming impartially the Greek Fathers and Sir Walter Scott. Standing by one of the bookcases that lined the walls from floor to ceiling, an Italian refugee told bitter tales of Habsburg tyranny to a young poet and a learned matron. Other outrages—German biblical criticism, abolitionist radicalism—dominated conversation in the drawing room that spanned the back of the house.

Although the eminence from which Shady Hill took its name amounted to little more than a substantial rise, it still commanded the marshes, huckleberry pasture, and encroaching suburb around. When first built, the house had fronted toward Charlestown and the wharves of Boston harbor. Now, Shady Hill's avenue led down to Professors' Row, and the house faced west toward Harvard College. From the piazza one still looked east, out over the azalea and clethra, down to the tidal flats along the Charles River, and beyond to the statehouse's gilded dome crowning Beacon Hill and its merchants' houses. A small boy's imagination could gaze even farther, out to the masts crowding the wharves and on to Rio de Janeiro, Canton, and Madras.[1]

Voyages to such ports made possible Shady Hill and houses much grander. Their high ceilings and spacious parlors rose on foundations of furs and slaves, tea and sandalwood, lac and gunny carried in Boston bottoms. Sometimes the houses mirrored their origins: in the Nanking porcelain on the polished mahogany dining tables, the Madras shawls draped on the ladies' shoulders and the red carnelian necklaces around their necks, the oriental carpets on the floors instead of Aubusson or Wilton. More regularly, the wealth of Asia was domesticated in the handiwork of local craftsmen who turned the elaborate balusters and newel posts, carved the pilasters to set off the high arched doorways, molded the plaster reliefs above the mantel. The sofas themselves, the chairs and tables, were likely shipped from the workshops of Thomas Sheraton or another English craftsman. English, too, were the silver and the wall hangings. And here and there hung paintings bought in Paris or London during a European tour.

For the houses made palpable how far their masters had traveled from modest origins.[2] The beginnings of Boston's reigning merchant elite very nearly coincided with the century's. The American Revolution had shattered Boston's colonial upper crust, driving out Tories and bringing commercial upheaval. Revolutionary privateering enriched seafaring families from Salem and Newburyport and Boston; there followed a burgeoning intercourse with China and the carrying trade during the wars of the French Revolution, consolidating these fortunes, adding new ones. Ancillary dealings—wharfage, wholesale and retail traffic, lawyering, land speculation—made other men wealthy.[3] Commercial advantages, political connections, and the attractions of the metropolis lured the most opulent of these nouveaux riches to Boston.

The city drained off the elite of the towns ranging northward along the coast to Cape Ann, Portsmouth, and Portland. The Cabots—later alleged to speak only to God—and the Lowells—in that later era communicators only to Cabots—both came down to Boston from Essex County, just to the north.[4] Once arrived, they presumably spoke to at least Jacksons, Lees, and Higginsons, other Essex County families newly become Bostonians. They certainly married them and wed as well, though more hesitantly, into rising local mercantile clans like the Lymans and Perkinses.

These marriages did more than cement particular family alliances; they wove a dense web of cousins. The China trade made Thomas Handasyd Perkins (1764–1854) the richest of Boston merchants. Perkins and his wife, Sarah Elliot (whose own sister wed Perkins's partner James Magee), married off four daughters: Mary to another merchant's son, Thomas G. Cary (later taken into partnership by Perkins); Ann to another Cary; Caroline to a Gardiner, a scion of the Boston elite; and Eliza to the son of another Perkins partner, Samuel Cabot. Samuel Cabot's own brother and sister had wed a Higginson and a Lee. In the next generation, three Cabot sisters married three Jackson brothers. Marriage connected the prolific Jacksons, in turn, with the Gardiners, the Lees, the Higginsons, and the Lowells, these last themselves linked with the Cabots and the Higginsons. The Higginsons complete the circle: one of them married T. H. Perkins's younger brother Samuel. Other Perkins sisters (it was a big family) married other merchants: Forbes, Sturgis, Cushing. As this web grew thicker with every wedding banquet, there developed within it human relationships in which the personal, familial, economic, and political elements became not merely inseparable but indistinguishable.

Yet this great evolving cousinage did not close its doors to newcomers; nor did wealth alone provide a ticket of admission. Enterprise did. Isaac Appleton was a New Hampshire farmer able to offer his several boys only a sparse future at home. So his son Samuel (1766–1853) moved to Boston and set up in commerce. Presently, he brought his brother Nathan down to help, then brother Eben and cousin William. In short order, the Appleton clan became one of the richest in Boston. Marriages soon connected it with others: the Lymans, the Silsbees, the Coolidges. The Lawrences could tell a similar story. With a mortgage on the family farm as his stake, Amos Lawrence (1786–1852) left Groton, Massachusetts, opened a store in Boston dealing in imported goods, and took in his younger brother Abbott. The store prospered; the business expanded; the brothers grew wealthy. Abbott married one of his children to a Lowell—and Amos one of his to an Appleton.

These family connections provided mutual aid in launching ventures and a safety net when they failed, while openness to new blood fostered innovation: not a bad recipe for sustaining riches. Young Frederic Tudor (1783–1864) showed the most striking ingenuity, by creating tropical markets for an unheard-of commodity: ice. But far the most important innovation was the first integrated cotton mills, built at Waltham in 1813, then on a grander scale at the new town of Lowell in 1821. With this step the mercantile elite began to reduce its dependence on the notorious risks of foreign commerce.

Its wealth had already changed the face of Boston itself. In the 1790s the West End and South End began to fill with dwellings erected on mercantile money. On a former pasture on Beacon Hill, down from Bulfinch's new gold-domed statehouse, arose one great pile after another. By 1830 the Boston elite had consolidated itself within these residences: a cluster of perhaps forty families, willing to absorb the likeliest new members but mostly playing, going to school, marrying, dining, and doing business with each other. Their commodious homes carried themselves with the stateliness befitting the station their owners had attained. Mahagony spiral staircases rose past Palladian windows; on winter evenings the flickering light of silver candelabra reflected from gold-framed mirrors onto high-hung family portraits. This world of black-frock-coated gentlemen and their silk-robed ladies was one of ease, amplitude, often more. The monogrammed carriages implied something approaching opulence.

Yet these homes were not great mansions of aristocratic luxury. Compared to the palaces erected by the British peerage, they were small and simple things. The houses carried little or no external adornment; the servants wore no livery; the tables bore no golden flatware; the children shared bedchambers; the young ladies of the house shelled peas. Remarkably cosmopolitan in their travels, the Boston merchants remained squarely New England in their style of life. The privileged men and women who strolled the landscaped acres of a country estate in Brookline or chatted in the enclosed gardens on Beacon Hill enjoyed high bourgeois comfort but not the grandeur of unbounded wealth.

Even indulgence in the riches they did possess nagged at uneasy consciences. For the builders of these dwellings shared an ethic still recognizably Puritan in one respect: trade was honorable; ceaseless pursuit of wealth was not. Ancestral convictions imposed restraint. Piety, virtue, intellect outweighed profit, or were supposed to. Surprisingly often, they did, at least once the profit was secure. The families that had developed the China trade and the Lowell mills also built the Massachusetts General Hospital. Nathan Appleton insisted that moneymaking had never preoccupied him, and his brother Samuel proved the point by retiring at the age of sixty to devote his income to philanthropy. John Lowell Jr., at his death in 1836, endowed the Lowell Institute with more than $250,000 to inculcate "the truth of those moral and religious precepts, by which alone . . . men can be secure of happiness in this world and that to come."[5]

Along with moral and religious precepts went a high and hereditary regard for the clergy. There usually perched in the family tree, together with the sea captains, farmers, and cordwainers, at least one minister. The founder of the Eliot family fortune, Samuel (1739–1820), had a reverend Uncle Andrew who was a shining ornament of the prerevolutionary Boston clergy; and Samuel's sister Ruth married the equally distinguished Reverend Jeremy Belknap, pastor of Boston's prosperous Federal Street Church. Such eminence was naturally rare; the profession was not. Samuel Eliot believed no social gathering complete without a clergyman, stocking his dinner table with two or three after the monthly Thursday Lecture. Though few merchant princes pursued the clergy with Eliot's gusto, many had ties. Among the founders of Boston's greatest dynasties—scarcely more than a dozen men in all—John Lowell and Samuel Parkman gave sons to the ministry, while George Cabot, Peter Chardon Brooks, and Jonathan Jackson married daughters to clergymen.

These weddings linked the great families to intellect as well as religion. In the early nineteenth century the clergy still provided Boston's cultural leadership. In its earliest days this ministerial ascendancy had infused intellectual life with theology, but during the eighteenth century the ministers of eastern Massachusetts edged away from high-and-dry Calvinism toward a softer deity. Unitarianism became the orthodoxy of the best Bostonians, benevolence and refinement its earthly expression. So the clergy also drifted into a belletristic culture—still tinctured with theology, to be sure, but as deeply dyed with Addison, Pope, and Johnson. By the 1780s and 1790s the sermons of Boston ministers were more noted for sheen than depth, and even the sermons sometimes showed less polishing than the heroic couplets and occasional essays flowing from the same pens.

As religion shaded gently into learning, mercantile funds were transferred to the new account. The men who in 1805 clubbed together to found the Anthology Society and to edit the *Monthly Anthology* were not merchants but young ministers, doctors, and lawyers. Yet when, two years later, they transformed their projected Reading Room into the Boston Athenaeum, the list of subscribers comprised a directory of Boston's mercantile elite. And when, several years on, the Athenaeum needed a larger home, the China merchant James Perkins gave it his mansion in the South End.[6] In 1815, the *North American Review* took the place of the lapsed *Anthology;* its founding editor, William Tudor, had literary connections running back to the Anthology Society and mercantile connections direct to his brother Frederic, the Ice King.

In the pages of the *North American Review,* high Boston rehearsed its doctrines for the merchants and matrons whose subscriptions sustained the magazine. In the Athenaeum's library and art gallery, the writers who filled those pages hobnobbed with their readers on terms of easy familiarity. Nor was the distinction between merchant and writer hard-and-fast. Thomas G. Cary published a memoir of his father-in-law, Thomas Handasyd Perkins, and Nathan Appleton one of Abbott Lawrence. Appleton also printed a brief history of the Waltham and Lowell mills. Appleton and Lawrence both wrote as well on politics, John Lowell on travel and on theology, John Welles on asparagus. And the list could go on.

For the distinguishing characteristic of Boston's elite was the melding, achieved to perhaps a unique degree in American history, of the lives of the mind and of the countinghouse. The Massachusetts Historical Society and

the Provident Institution for Savings long shared a three-story granite building on Tremont Street; James Savage, officer of both, "had but a flight of
stairs" between his bank and his books. This detail was a metaphor for Boston. Samuel Eliot owned four thousand books, John Lowell Jr., ten thousand. By 1819, Boston money had created two of the three largest libraries in
America, Harvard's, with thirty thousand volumes, and the Athenaeum's,
with eighteen thousand. Private satisfactions became public benefit.[7]

Learning and literature fed not mere private delectation but the public
weal. James Perkins gave his house to the Athenaeum out of "a consideration of the importance of the diffusion of knowledge to the liberty and
happiness of any community."[8] Any community, he said; but in fact such
considerations weighed more heavily in Boston than elsewhere. The American Revolution had infused an afterglow of civic-mindedness throughout
the new nation: each republican owed active responsibility for public affairs.
Civic virtue shone no brighter in Massachusetts than in Virginia or Pennsylvania. But around Boston, republican virtue mixed with the special local
religious heritage of benevolence, the residue left when Unitarian preachers evaporated the theology from Puritanism. This moral impulse had no
American equivalent; even in Quaker Philadelphia, consciences worried
more about personal purity than communal duty.

Nor was community obligation a moral abstraction. Boston was a small
and homogeneous city; and at the moment when civic virtue congealed with
religious benevolence, it was a city falling under the sway of a brood of
intermarrying families. To them, "community" had faces: of aunts and uncles and siblings and cousins. Community had a depth, a vitality, a specificity—and thus a power to command—unique in the new United States. The
patrician families of Renaissance Florence must have gazed on their city
with similar possessing eyes. If the wishes of other Bostonians sometimes
ran counter to their own understanding of the common good, the great
families perhaps did not even notice. They certainly never questioned their
own right to decide.

Their notion of community was distinctly a hierarchical one. In religion,
they were Unitarian, with a minority of Episcopalians. In politics, they were
Federalist, with a horror of democracy. When, in the 1820s, Federalism
finally expired (lingering in Boston longer than almost anywhere else), they
necessarily changed their party—but not their minds. As their religion
taught them submission to an affable but dignified God, reverence for the
orderliness of the world that He had kindly created for them, and benevolence toward those of His creatures less fortunate than themselves, so their

politics taught them three analogous lessons: that the people ought to submit to the authority of the wisest and best, embodied in a cautiously ordered republican government; that the people ought to revere these natural leaders in the streets as well as in the state; and that the people were unlikely to do either to the extent they ought. But deficiencies in the people never excused failure in their rightful rulers to fulfill their own public duties.

These included steady effort, not only to bring the sagging populace up to the mark, but also to assuage its varied ills. To care for its bodies, the merchant families erected the Massachusetts General Hospital (1821); to aid the blind, the famed Perkins Institution (1832). The Massachusetts Historical Society (1791) guarded the community's past, the Massachusetts Horticultural Society (1829) its seed stock. The Massachusetts Society for Promoting Agriculture (1792) improved its farming, the Lowell Institute (1836) its minds. This network of civic institutions interlocked as densely as the mercantile cousinage that sustained it.

Even the distinction between public and private meant little. The Massachusetts Hospital Life Insurance Company (1823) steadily pumped out revenue for the Massachusetts General Hospital along with loans for the Lowell mill owners; it mixed the investments of rich Bostonians with those of the charities they ran. Doing good was no bar to doing well. Yet shady dealings were surprisingly rare, for this blurring of lines manifested, not the buccaneering of a marauding oligarchy, but, more simply, the hegemony of an elite that never separated its interests from Boston's.

And it was an obstinately Bostonian elite. To some extent a local orientation was still inevitable in the first decades of the nineteenth century. Poor roads, slow vessels, businesses centered on local markets, the lack of national newspapers or magazines, the absence of national universities or scientific societies all conspired to keep each city and its hinterland turned in on itself, whether in commerce or culture. But the Boston elite turned this rapidly fading reality into an enduring ideal. In the 1820s and 1830s, New York merchants underwrote reform societies with a national mission and structure, like the American Bible Society and the American Society for Promoting Temperance. Boston merchants, equally eager for improvement, organized resolutely local agencies, like the Boston Dispensary and the Massachusetts Horticultural Society. Philadelphians aspired (and failed) to create a national academy of art; Bostonians wanted a gallery for the Athenaeum.

Boston's elite deliberately elected to cultivate its own garden. Perhaps the defeat of Federalism and the concomitant triumph of democracy sealed the policy, for they doomed high Boston to national political irrelevance and condemned its social ideals to national obsolescence. Some Bostonians did choose to play parts on a national stage—the abolitionist William Lloyd Garrison, the universal reformer Lydia Maria Child—but they acted in a different drama, with a different cast, neither dining, traveling, nor marrying with the mercantile elite. Those who wed Lowells and Cabots appealed to their peers in self-consciously municipal terms. The founders of the Athenaeum reminded their fellow merchants that "we are not called upon for large contributions to national purposes" and urged them "to take advantage of the exemption, by taxing ourselves for those institutions, which will be attended with lasting and extensive benefit" for Boston.[9] That perennial Boston outsider, John Quincy Adams, called for a national university. The Appletons gave to Harvard.

Naturally—for Harvard provided a predictable center of mercantile philanthropy. Annually, Boston celebrated the ties between Beacon Hill and the college in the great seasonal festival of the Harvard commencement, when even the banks in Boston closed and their proprietors removed themselves to Cambridge for a day or two. Commencement reminded citizens of the enduring association of religion and learning, commerce and culture. The merchants had long taken interest in the advancement of arts and letters, and Boston's oldest institution of learning made the most obvious beneficiary. Their respect for learning grew in turn from a refined and secularized religion; at Unitarian Harvard this mixture of benevolent religion and polite letters more and more found its home. Both philanthropy and learning arose from a civic culture centered on Boston's great families; it was to Harvard that those families routinely sent their college-bound sons.

So the fathers routinely took charge of Harvard, as they had of the Athenaeum and the Massachusetts General. They could not do so as completely, for outsiders—ministers, state officials—sat ex officio on Harvard's Board of Overseers. But the small and self-perpetuating Corporation held the real reins of power, and it placed them firmly in the hands of the mercantile elite. Lowells, Jacksons, and Eliots alone composed almost a quarter of the members elected in the first half of the century.[10] In 1810 the merchants chose the Reverend John Thornton Kirkland, a founder of the Athenaeum, as president; when Kirkland retired in 1828 they named one of their own: Josiah Quincy, Harvard's first unordained president. The mercantile elite not only ran the college. Parkmans, Eliots, Searses, Phillipses, Thorndikes, Livermores, and Lawrences also showered it with their money.

The gifts of these patricians represented a sort of unknowing bequest to their posterity, whose lives would intertwine with Harvard. Samuel Eliot, building on a grocery business, had by 1810 or so amassed one of the largest fortunes in Boston. In the following decade, his three sons graduated from Harvard, and Samuel gave twenty thousand dollars to endow a Greek professorship. Two of his five daughters later married Harvard professors. His only son to survive into middle life served a decade on the Corporation, as Harvard's treasurer. One of Samuel's grandsons became a Harvard professor, another its president. Judge John Lowell (1743–1802) built up his family's fortune practicing law for the merchants. A Corporation member from 1784 until his death, he had three sons, all Harvard graduates; two of them served on the Corporation. The grandsons matriculated at Harvard by instinct, one of them later spending forty years on the Corporation; another of them, thirty-six as professor. The next generation produced merely an Overseer, but the following provided another Corporation member and a president. The names of other clans—Jackson, Cabot, Warren—likewise echoed into the twentieth century.

In such careers reverberated both the compunctions and the ideals of the families' progenitors. The founding generation passed its restless conscience along to its progeny. Just as the mercantile elite never doubted the dignity of its calling, so it never overestimated mere pursuit of wealth. "They say riches are a burden that harass the soul and lead into temptation," mused the son of Amos Lawrence in 1835 on the eve of his Harvard graduation; "so they are to the miser who is in constant fear of losing his acquisition." Young Lawrence did decide to be a merchant but "not a plodding, narrow-minded one pent up in a city, with my mind always in my counting room."[11] This ambivalence was a dearly bought luxury. A merchant in the dicey China trade or an entrepreneur in the uncertain early days of the textile industry (like Lawrence's father) needed to keep his mind always in his counting room.

Yet by such concentration he ensured that his offspring enjoyed broader options. The fathers had created Boston's wealth; they made their sons its stewards: trustees both legally and metaphorically. Manufacturing in New England, then the railroads that opened the West, provided that will-o'-the-wisp, a stable investment. Family funds sunk in such enterprises pumped out ample returns without constant attention. As a result, children coming to maturity after the 1820s, like young Lawrence, could eschew the temptations of avarice without risking the comforts of gentility. Encouraged by parents who had organized the Athenaeum and endowed chairs at Harvard, they indulged ambitions higher than commerce.

Someone had to hoe the family plot, even if only to cultivate a moderate increase; usually at least one son followed his father into trade. But as a rule the children pursued business less vigorously and devoted even more energy to Harvard or to politics than their fathers had done. Henry Lee Jr. (1817–98) followed his father into the East India trade, until it collapsed in the 1850s, and then went into a banking firm run by other relatives. But his affections centered on genealogy, on architecture—he was accomplished at both—and especially on the stage that he erected in his Brookline mansion, famous around Boston for its amateur theatricals.

Avocation became vocation for many sons of the mercantile elite. Three sons of the opulent merchant David Greenough cultivated the arts: the sculptors Horatio (1805–52) and Richard (1819–1904) and the painter and architect Henry (1807–83). Samuel Parkman also had three sons: the eldest a minister, the youngest a physician and Harvard professor. To abandon business for higher callings grew perhaps even more common in the third generation. Charles C. Perkins (1823–86), grandson of Thomas Handasyd Perkins, devoted his life to music and art. Charles W. Eliot (1834–1926) and Samuel Eliot (1821–98), both grandsons of the founding Samuel, became college presidents. Barely had the mercantile elite consolidated itself when it began to evolve into something more varied. The growth was smooth, natural, almost predestined, for the sons were realizing values that the parents had fostered.

The daughters realized them, if anything, earlier and more often. Francis Dana's daughter Martha married the painter Washington Allston. Peter Chardon Brooks's three daughters, Ann, Abigail, and Charlotte, married, respectively, Nathaniel Frothingham, Unitarian minister and belletrist; Edward Everett, possibly the first American to earn a German doctorate, professor of Greek at Harvard on Samuel Eliot's endowment, later politician and Harvard president; and Charles Francis Adams, lawyer, diplomat, and writer. George Cabot's daughter Elizabeth wed the Anthologist and Harvard president John Thornton Kirkland; brother Samuel Cabot's daughter Eliza married the German emigré and Harvard professor Karl Follen; Nathan Appleton's daughter Frances married the young poet and Harvard professor Henry Wadsworth Longfellow.

As sons of the mercantile elite began to take up intellectual careers, and as the daughters began to take up with intellectuals, a new sort of elite took shape—an aristocracy not of money but of mind. It grew organically out of the old, as family relations begat and nourished educational, literary, and artistic ones. It inherited the merchants' ethic of hard work and moral earnestness, though by no means all its members came from merchant blood or merchant money. Its borders resist clear demarcation: Emerson belonged (but uneasily); Thoreau never did (alien by birth and worldview); nor did Hawthorne (not in the family, though a welcome visitor). Yet, however foggy in definition, by midcentury this new caste was achieving self-consciousness: an awareness of its antecedents and commonality made tangible in institutions like the Saturday Club (1855)—loosely modelled on the Anthology Club—and the *Atlantic Monthly* (1857).

This intellectual elite, bred from the crossing of the Unitarian clergy with the merchant princes, inherited both the religious aura that surrounded learning in New England and an aristocratic sense of its own natural leadership for the public weal. To think of it in terms of Coleridge's ideal of a "clerisy"—adding the principle of hereditary succession—is not far-fetched. Just as Coleridge insisted a clerisy ought, it tried to encompass all the arts and sciences, and it aimed to promote the civilization of the community. And, above all, it achieved the broad cultural, if not properly spiritual, leadership envisioned by Coleridge for his "third estate" or "national church."[12]

The Boston clerisy dominated the fecund intellectual life of New England for the rest of the nineteenth century. As Boston's commerce in earlier days had drawn in merchants from up and down the New England coast, so its intellectual life attracted writers and scholars from the regional hinterland. Improvements in transportation alone would have promoted such an outcome, for New England was small, its population homogeneous, and Boston its center. But beyond this natural circulation, the prestige of Boston's writers and the power of its publishers gave its clerisy a further advantage over the rest of the region. Harvard added to it: almost half of the college-bred writers who matured in New England between 1770 and 1865 were graduated from Harvard.[13] Ambitious young savants arrived from throughout New England, from the "greater New England" settlement areas of upstate New York and the upper Midwest, and even from beyond. Henry Wadsworth Longfellow came down from Maine in the 1830s, Asa Gray up from New York in the 1840s, Arthur Hugh Clough west from England in the 1850s, William Dean Howells east from Ohio in the 1860s. The stream flowed steadily until after the Civil War, when New York elbowed Boston aside in publishing as it had long since done in commerce. Even then, the lure of Harvard remained, and the afterglow of the Hearthside Poets.

In its heyday—from 1840 to 1890—the Boston clerisy was New England's, and its reach extended far beyond. Just as it attracted aspirants to the life of the mind, so it transmitted a standard of mores and ideals: the "genteel tradition," to which middle-class Northerners broadly conformed and against which a few (like Thoreau and Whitman) self-consciously rebelled. One can imagine a series of rippling circles of influence, flowing out from Boston, interrupted here and there where the waves broke against the rocks of New Haven or Hartford or the great reef of New York, in all directions diminishing in strength with distance, yet eventually washing over most of America. And in the writings and persons of Emerson, Lowell, Norton, and Longfellow, the influence rolled across the Atlantic. The breakers still echo along unexpected stretches of the intellectual coast. As a class, no other group of American writers has achieved such resonance.

Yet the New England clerisy was by no means a self-sufficient estate of the professionally learned. Distinct yet inseparable from the mercantile elite, it always had members not easily classified into one world or the other, like the banker Henry Lee Higginson (1834–1919), founder of the Boston Symphony, who moved with equal authority in cultural and business circles. And business money, injected via continuing intermarriage, allowed other members to stay mostly within cultural realms. Seldom did the cash flow freely enough to sustain anything like grandeur. A pair of armchairs and a side table sufficed to crowd the entrance hall of even the amplest professorial house. Professor Andrews Norton's monogrammed carriage, the tangible sign of his wife's Eliot paternity, was enough of an oddity to last the century in Cambridge memory. But a wife's dowry or a husband's inheritance often meant silver on the table, a pipe of Madeira in the cellar, and rare editions in the library. More to the point, mercantile voyages founded the pecuniary independence that made possible intellectual voyaging.

And the clerisy's origin in this older elite brought it even more than money. Its cohesion came not so much from a shared worldview—though it certainly had strong elements of one—as from a shared world. The internal links of marriage tied the caste together: a network of bloodlines gave it a notoriously ingrown character and sustained its remarkable outreach. The communal shell of the social and cultural institutions of Boston fostered and protected the unity thus achieved. Shared families, shared education, shared work space produced a vigorous, tightly interlaced, and highly self-conscious tribe.

But it was far from a closed one. Like the mercantile elite, the cultural elite welcomed new talent; like that older elite, it bound these newcomers to itself at the altar. The great philologist Francis J. Child (1825–96) was a sailmaker's son. The boy's aptitude caught the attention of Epes Dixwell, principal of the Boston Latin School and unofficial talent scout for the clerisy. Dixwell found mercantile money to send Child to Harvard, where he graduated as first scholar in 1846. Harvard then made him a tutor and presently packed him off to the University of Göttingen, more Boston money in his pocket, to earn a doctorate. Child returned in 1851 to the Boylston Chair at Harvard and in 1860, by now naturalized into the clerisy, married Elizabeth Ellery Sedgwick, a daughter of the dominating clan of western Massachusetts and connected as well to the Danas and the Ellerys.[14] With his nuptials, Child acquired not only rich relations but also scribbling cousins.

Such a thicket of cerebral relatives was the rule. The Reverend William Ellery Channing (1780–1842) lives in literary myth as the prophet of American transcendentalism; but Emerson and Thoreau actually learned to write under his brother, Edward Tyrell Channing (1790–1856), Boylston Professor of Rhetoric at Harvard from 1819 to 1851. The third Channing brother, Walter (1786–1876), was dean of Harvard Medical School and a pioneer in anesthesia. Their sister, Ann, married Washington Allston. (Upon her death, Allston married Martha Dana, a cousin of the Channings, whose own brother was the poet and essayist Richard Henry Dana. William and Edward both married their own cousins.) William's son William Francis (1820–1901) achieved fame as an inventor; Edward's son William Henry (1810–84) became a prominent Unitarian clergyman and reformer; Walter's daughter Mary (1820–77) wed her second cousin Thomas Wentworth Higginson, minister, abolitionist, Civil War hero, copious author, and "discoverer" of Emily Dickinson; while Walter's son William Ellery II (1818–1901), himself a minor poet, married Margaret Fuller's sister. Children of this latter match included the Harvard historian Edward Channing (1856–1931) and the prominent alienist (psychiatrist, we would now say) Walter Channing (1849–1921).

The Channings were hardly the only intellectual dynasty. Joseph Story (1779–1845), professor of law at Harvard and justice of the United States Supreme Court, laid the foundations of both American equity jurisprudence and Harvard Law School. His daughter Mary (1817–48) wed a famed attorney, the constitutional historian (and counsel for plaintiff in the Dred Scott case) George Ticknor Curtis; and his son William Wetmore (1819–95) practiced law briefly and wrote two standard legal treatises. But William then expatriated himself to a career as a sculptor and writer on subjects Italian. William's son Julian Russell (1857–1919) became a well-known portraitist, his other son, Thomas Waldo, a sculptor. For a son to follow in a learned or artistic career, if not exactly his father's, thus seemed routine.

This tendency to filial imitation, when combined with common ancestry and continuing intermarriage, produced a sort of extended family of writers and teachers. A more intellectually various batch of characters can hardly be imagined than the pedantic though beloved classicist C. C. Felton (1807–62), the dilettante litterateur J. Elliot Cabot (1821–1903), the polymathic scientist Louis Agassiz (1807–73), the pioneer in women's education Elizabeth Cabot Cary Agassiz (1822–1907), and the prominent architect Edward Cabot (1818–1901). Yet all five could look back, through their mother or mother-in-law, to a common grandparent, the China merchant Thomas Handasyd Perkins. Agassiz exemplified the clerisy's capacity to absorb the right newcomers. When Harvard attracted the great Swiss scientist in 1847, Boston not only lionized him but married him to no less than Perkins's granddaughter.

Examples of such kinship ties—scarcely ever unrecognized—filled Harvard Yard. The Corporation that elected James Russell Lowell as Smith Professor in 1855 included his first cousin John Amory Lowell. President Eliot in 1874 appointed to the faculty his own first cousin Charles Eliot Norton and, a few years later, his brother-in-law Francis Greenwood Peabody. E. W. Gurney's brother-in-law Henry Adams followed him as professor of history, and Alexander Agassiz succeeded his father as curator of the Museum of Comparative Zoology. Such tales smack of nepotism: their real explanation was more innocent. So inbred was the clerisy that selection by merit (factoring in a bias toward local candidates) often pointed to a relative.

Yet undeniably the right relatives did give a young man an expansive sense of his own possibilities and, perhaps, more tangible aid. Barrett Wendell's kinship with Oliver Wendell Holmes, however distant, lent plausibility to his own literary aspirations. When Ellery Sedgwick matriculated at Harvard at the beginning of the nineties, his teachers included his uncle Francis J. Child and his third cousin Charles Eliot Norton; under their aegis he set out on a path that led to the editorship of the *Atlantic Monthly*. (Ellery had learned from his cradle the influence of kinship: his own parents were first cousins.) Samuel Eliot Morison arrived just too late—class of 1908—to benefit from his great-uncle Norton's teaching but did enjoy the last years of his great-uncle Eliot's presidency of Harvard, where Morison spent his own long and distinguished career as historian. Through such influences, perhaps impalpable but far from astral, did the New England clerisy draw its sons into the line of succession.

Still more salient were influences earlier and more personal. Where men carried out public duties that advanced the aims of the clerisy, women exercised domestic ones that reproduced the clerisy itself. Not a few women contented themselves with keeping a well-managed house and well-fed husband, bringing Christmas baskets to the poor Irish and good cheer to Cambridge's dinner tables, and teaching their children to read and write and practice the Ten Commandments. Good women, appreciated by their families and respected by their neighbors, they left book learning to others. They failed fully to do their job. For girls grew up not discouraged from intellectual duties but encouraged to a specialized version of them.

To fulfill this trust they required education. In the first half of the century, when custom denied girls higher schooling, parents, tutors, and older friends stepped into the breach. Thomas Wentworth Higginson (in later life a crusader for women's rights) grew up without "the slightest feeling that there was any distinction of sex in intellect. Why women did not go to college was a point which did not suggest itself; but one of my sisters studied German with Professor Charles Follen, while another took lessons in Latin and Italian from Professor Bachi and in geometry from Professor Benjamin Pierce."[15] Daughters born after the Civil War had wider opportunities for formal schooling, especially with the founding of the Harvard Annex, later Radcliffe College, in 1879. As adults, most were as likely to peruse a volume of Dante as a cookbook. Though usually unschooled in mathematics and classical languages, the women of the intellectual aristocracy sometimes equalled the men in knowledge of modern languages and literatures, natural and civil history, theology, painting, sculpture, and music. Women rarely mounted the podium but perpetually filled the audience; and a respectable diffidence about the public eye never cramped private intercourse.

Now and then, female intellect ventured into print. Before the Civil War, women who published inhabited mostly the abolitionist and transcendentalist fringe of the nascent intellectual elite. A less radical woman of that era might indulge literary hobbies; but if her work ever passed beyond a circle of friends, she cloaked it in decent anonymity. After the Civil War, a woman's name in print no longer seemed unrespectable among the clerisy, and by century's end even the most conventional woman had lost any trepidation about putting her name on a title page. Such women claimed a share in the clerisy's public role, but with diffidence.[16]

For the intellectual aristocracy did not mean to nourish career women. No one contributed more to the education of its daughters than Elizabeth Agassiz, the first president of Radcliffe College. But Mrs. Agassiz assumed that woman's nature made some careers impossible and any career an inferior option. Radcliffe existed not to prepare women for such eccentricity but to enhance their lives and thus make them better mothers. Mrs. Agassiz herself dreaded the public appearances required by her duties and regarded the college as secondary to her own family responsibilities. At the end of the century as at the beginning, the clerisy educated its daughters to converse knowledgeably about literature and natural history, not to pursue them. The women who resulted were cultivated rather than learned.

In the end, however, their cultivation proved a considerable force, for through it refracted the intellectual ideal of the clerisy. As mothers, these women understood themselves to bear a heavy obligation. They instilled with the alphabet the principles of manners and morals by which their class lived: the duty of seriousness, the style of unaffected civility, the obligation to the less fortunate, the mission of leadership. They guided children into the paths of learning and literature, bringing them as tots to delight in Bulfinch's *Mythology* and Aesop's *Fables,* Mrs. Hemans's poetry and Palgrave's *Golden Treasury.* They formed the rudiments of narrative and expository style with constant little epistles to aunts and cousins, which were as constantly if gently criticized. All this called for rounded learning, not deep. Traditional in their maternal role, the women of the clerisy thus modelled at home another tradition that the fathers illustrated in print: the Boston ideal of broad learning as against specialized erudition.

Traditional, too, were the subjects privileged in this notion of learning. From its dawn among genteel ministers, physicians, and lawyers, the intellectual aristocracy inherited a persisting bias toward belles lettres. Indeed, in its infancy the clerisy was distinctly literary rather than learned. Alone among his peers Sidney Willard, professor at the college and inveterate magazine scribbler, had taught himself to read German, and he passed this arcane lore along to young George Bancroft; but Willard had no clue as to pronunciation—with presumably disconcerting results for Bancroft when he arrived at Göttingen in 1818.[17] Of natural philosophy, philology, political economy, even painting and music, these early Bostonians knew little and cared less.

But their conception of literature was expansive, comprising history and the essay as well as poetry, criticism, and translation; and it remained so. In these genres the work of the clerisy endures: Emerson, Longfellow, Lowell, Motley, Parkman, Prescott. Novels, though read and admired, were seldom written; Melville, Stowe, even Hawthorne hovered only around the periphery of Boston. Theology, another early focus, evolved into philosophy after midcentury, Channing, Ware, and Andrews Norton giving way to Peirce and James. Of abstract political theory there never was much, though a good deal in the way of legal treatises and political pamphleteering. The great weakness for most of the century was natural science, partly compensated by imports like Asa Gray and Louis Agassiz, partly by hereditary strength in medicine and mathematics. The spiritual impress of the Anthology Society proved hard to evade.

Not so its physical locale. The clerisy was scarcely aware of itself before its center of gravity began to drift away from the Athenaeum and across the Charles River. By 1850 or so the pole was fixed at Cambridge, in or near Harvard Yard. Mercantile philanthropy to Harvard—amounting to almost a million dollars between 1827 and 1857—expanded the college faculty and made professorial life more attractive.[18] To be sure, major figures among the clerisy—old George Ticknor, Wendell Holmes—still lived in Boston; and meetings of the Historical Society or the Saturday Club, not to mention less formal socializing, brought Cantabrigians and Bostonians regularly together. The shift indeed brought no sudden transformation. Though the eastward parts of Cambridge had begun to bustle with manufactories and immigrants, Old Cambridge, around the college, remained a quiet, bookish, self-centered place. Cambridge's inhabitants still read faithfully the *North American Review*, knowing that each quarterly number was bound to include articles by their neighbors.

They also read the *Edinburgh Review*, holding its judgment in even greater regard. This reverence for British and European culture was hereditary. In 1806, Samuel Thacher averred that he "would cheerfully resign ten years of my life to be allowed to pass one in Europe." The tale is told that Mr. Justice Story, who never crossed the sea, astonished an English visitor by placing precisely a London street so obscure that the Englishman had never heard of it.[19]

What Thacher and Story coveted, later generations achieved. Progenitors of the clerisy like Ticknor and Edward Everett had ventured abroad on scholarly pilgrimages even before 1820; the advent of the transatlantic steamship made European travel an easier and, for the wealthier Cantabrigians by the 1850s, almost a regular thing. Their leisurely journeys led to fast friendships with English intellectuals and, occasionally, French or German. Little colonies of expatriate Bostonians settled in Rome, Florence, Paris, and London. The historian Motley went as United States minister to Vienna in 1861, then to London in 1869; the poet Lowell went as envoy to Madrid in 1877 and to London in 1880. It was far from unusual for a Harvard professor to feel more at home in London than in Chicago or even New York—and to have more friends there.

Provinciality also eroded in less obvious ways. The old Boston coterie, essentially literary with a theological subcurrent, was evolving after midcentury into a scholarly elite of wider interests, though still with a strong literary streak. It increasingly centered on Harvard, and Harvard itself grew steadily less parochial. The mere requirements of college teaching fostered some broadening of the narrowly literary focus of the Anthologists and the Athenaeum founders. The growing influx of outlanders into the faculty brought more. Contact with Britain and the Continent encouraged still more. And as Harvard developed from college into university in the second half of the century, its professors took as their audience less and less the ignorant youths in the classroom, more and more the scholars of Oxford, Berlin, and Johns Hopkins. Thus, as the clerisy became more academic, its range of interests grew more diverse, its publications more widely respected, its influence more extensive.

This proved fatal. Isolation and inbreeding had created the New England clerisy; wider intercourse and influence destroyed it. Authors who wrote regularly for *Harper's* and the *Nation* instead of only the *Atlantic* and the *North American Review* might end up in New York instead of Boston. Harvard professors who lectured at Johns Hopkins and Michigan might take jobs in Baltimore and Ann Arbor. Scholars whose acquaintance ran from Berkeley to Berlin might find their children marrying anywhere along the route. Such was the immediate human import of those twin abstractions, the professionalization of learning and the emergence of a national economy.

The New England clerisy did not vanish; rather, around the turn of the twentieth century, it dissipated. Although Amy Lowell and her brother A. Lawrence Lowell stayed in Boston, astronomical research eventually took their older brother Percival to Arizona. One of J. Elliott Cabot's sons, the pioneer of medical social work Richard Clarke Cabot, spent his career at Harvard; but his younger and even more consequential brother, the medical reformer Hugh Cabot, spent most of his at Michigan and Minnesota. Charles Eliot Norton's eldest son, Eliot, made a life as a New York lawyer; his youngest, Richard, pursued archaeology mostly in Europe; the medical career of the third, Rupert, centered in Johns Hopkins.

Even those who stayed around Boston—most of the clerisy's children— found their intellectual world less Bostonian. True, the Athenaeum was still there, and the Saturday Club. But to enclose oneself within the pleasant confines of either was now merely to indulge in provincial solipsism. Scions of the intellectual aristocracy might make their careers in Boston institutions—at Harvard, like Samuel Eliot Morison, or on the *Atlantic,* like Ellery Sedgwick—but the networks of scholarship or literature through which they perforce operated were largely national. Traces of the old elite lay everywhere: in the persistence of family names in Harvard's faculty, in the bookish clubs devoted to mediocre dinners and good conversation, in the concerts of the Boston Symphony and the classical artifacts at the Museum of Fine Arts.

But they were traces of a fading era. For half a century or more, the clerisy had sustained its Florentine Age. Nourished in the cradle of a thriving, locally rooted intellectual and communal life, it had self-consciously made this culture accessible to all well-educated persons and had conscientiously tried to make education accessible to all. Displaying its snobberies and its blindnesses, it had nevertheless left behind substantial and enduring monuments. Now, like the Medici, the New England clerisy had passed from the stage.

Yet in 1849 the curtain had just risen. The musing young India merchant who stared out over the endless Atlantic indeed realized only vaguely that such a thing as a New England clerisy existed. But he had been born into it. His mother, Catharine Eliot, linked him to Boston's declining commercial wealth, his father, Andrews Norton, to its rising wealth of learning.

ONE

Shady Hill, 1786–1842

The Eliots—or Elliots, Elliotts, Eliotts—were not an ancient family by New England standards. Only near the end of the 1660s did Andrew Eliot (1628–1704) leave East Coker, his Somerset birthplace, to settle in Beverly, north of Boston. A shoemaker, he prospered enough that his townsmen elected him to speak for them in the provincial assembly. (He served, too, as a juror in the Salem witch trials.) His grandson, also Andrew (1683–1749), removed to Boston, setting up as a merchant in Cornhill. The next generation moved further up in the world. Another Andrew (1718–78) became a celebrated Boston minister. His brother Samuel (1713–45) made a good living as a bookseller and published one of America's first magazines. The Boston traders with whom he dealt touched frequently at the West Indies; and in 1736 Samuel married a woman from there, Elizabeth Marshall. In short order they had six children. One son they named Samuel.[1]

His father's early death impoverished the family when this Samuel (1739–1820) was only six, but merchant friends and his reverend uncle Andrew kept an eye on the boy. Apprenticed to a prominent mercantile house, he soon rose to partner, then set up his own retail establishment in Dock Square. In 1765, he married the daughter of a Boston notable. But scarred by penury, Samuel never outgrew his "disposition to anxiety." Family legend has him during the Revolution shrewdly keeping both a Whig and a Tory clerk—and, consequently, customers of both stripes. He rose fast.[2]

One of his customers, Samuel Norton of Hingham, a town on the shore south of Boston, derived likewise from a background of moderate local achievement. The first Norton in Hingham, John (1651–1716), Ipswich-born and Harvard-bred, settled there in 1679 as pastor of the village church. His son, Captain John (1680–1721), held several town offices besides his militia captaincy before dying at age forty-one. A third John (1717–1750) died even younger, after siring Charles Norton's grandfather, Samuel (1744–1832). Samuel kept a shop, made money, and carried the burden of local service expected of a village leader: he was town clerk during the war years of 1776–78, a member of Hingham's revolutionary Committee of Correspondence, and later state representative and justice of the peace.[3]

His only known inner turmoil was religious. Raised a Calvinist, he so strongly reacted against his ancestors' stress on man's helpless depravity and God's relentless damnation that he nearly rebounded into "utter unbelief." But in Samuel's day the Reverend Ebenezer Gay preached in the Hingham pulpit a more comforting religion than old John Norton's. A rational God offered salvation to all, and all had the natural ability to take up the offer. In Gay's sermons was developing the Unitarianism soon to take its place as elite Boston's religion. Its intellectual foundation was the testing of belief by reason; its central dogma, the goodness of man; its perpetual beacon, the benevolence and rationality of God; its ruling axiom, the congruity of divine love and reason to human standards. The word "rational" became Samuel's talisman, and it led him back to "faith and peace."[4]

Certainly, the shopkeeper prospered, eventually buying bank stock and real estate in Boston. In 1772 he married Jane Andrews, who shared his solid Hingham ancestry though not his taste for books. By 1778 there were three children, John, Jane, and Samuel. After eight childless years, on New Year's Eve in 1786 came the last: Andrews.[5]

Samuel, intent on preparing Andrews for his role in the "great theater of the world," demanded much of the boy. He insisted that Andrews control his unruly temper. Yet Samuel gave his son fond attention, and Andrews responded with respect and affection that ripened into something like friendship. The relation had a high tone, for Samuel presided over a household both bookish and devout. His politics ran to High Federalism, his Augustan tastes to biography and theology. Andrews developed Romantic as well as Augustan sensibilities, feeling no war between them, for both were imbued with the piety of his father's mild and rational faith. By the time Andrews was ten, he was writing out for his father remarkably coherent précis of the sermons of Ebenezer Gay's successor, the equally liberal Henry Ware. Andrews was not destined to keep a shop. At the village's Derby Academy he prepared for Harvard College, the first of his family to do so since old Reverend John.[6]

Andrews was still a boy when he set out for Cambridge in 1801, and not a prepossessing boy at that. Even as an adult Andrews Norton never reached medium height; pale, delicate, slight in frame, inclined to melancholy, languid in "animal spirits," and reserved in temperament, with a piety shading into priggishness, he kept an uneasy distance between himself and the rambunctiousness of college life. Intellectual self-assurance overcompensated for social insecurity, and a sarcastic wit and tendency to arrogance stayed with him throughout life. On the whole, though, a basically gentle and generous nature healed occasional wounds inflicted by a tongue too quick and barbed; and his classmates liked him. Indeed, within a circle of like-minded friends, Andrews showed himself, boy and man, the furthest thing from a grim companion: actively sociable, downright amiable, always ready with a quip. A studious and dutiful boy, he became a favorite with his professors in those days of recitation and drill; and somehow he even learned to love learning. He fancied becoming "an *author by profession*" and dreamed of translating the classic Italian poets (a surprisingly cosmopolitan ambition in that time and place)—if only "I understood the language"! He did somehow get decent French.[7]

Along with ardor for polite letters there ripened the mild and rational religion inherited from Samuel. The two tastes were highly compatible and even suggested a career. Andrews's strictly scholarly enthusiasms led nowhere, vocationally speaking: not for another decade did it occur to any American to train for college teaching. But belles lettres and piety mixed easily among the liberal ministers to whom Boston had grown accustomed. Andrews Norton graduated in 1804 not only with a "high character for both scholarship and moral worth" but also with an idea of how to put these qualities to use.[8]

The road on which he set out was well marked but proved tortuous for Andrews. As a "resident graduate" at Harvard he read theology and practiced sermons under the new Hollis Professor of Divinity, his old Hingham pastor Henry Ware. The muses, however, still charmed him, and Norton joined the "society of gentlemen" who took charge of Boston's infant *Monthly Anthology* in 1805. He thus entered unselfconsciously into the patrician Federalism of the Boston mercantile elite, for which Samuel Norton had prepared him as best a provincial could. In America, warned Andrews in 1807, "where the spirit of democracy is every where diffused, we are exposed, as it were, to a poisonous atmosphere, which blasts every thing beautiful in nature and corrodes every thing elegant in art."[9]

This was pretty reactionary but not as reactionary as it later sounded. The specter of the Reign of Terror haunted Federalists; "democracy" evoked Jacobins, not the town meeting, and dripped blood. Boston Federalists distinguished an American idea of liberty from the French edition. They looked on their town as a latter-day Athens, where they, a collective Pericles, instructed a populace needing to be led. They were republicans with a bad case of nerves, verging on paranoia when it came to Thomas Jefferson with his lunatic sympathy for the French Revolution. But they *were* republicans, not—as Jefferson in his own cold shivers imagined—monarchists. They even shared with their American Robespierre a grudging respect for ordinary Americans' capacity for local self-governance as well as a fondness for education as a way of building a more reliably republican citizenry.

What they did not share with President Jefferson was optimism about those citizens. From 1800 onward the Federalists were in retreat on the national scene. Repeated electoral defeat damped the expectations of Norton and his new friends, confirming both the classical history they had read at Harvard, which taught them the political fickleness of the masses, and the Puritanism that they had incompletely shaken off, which catechized them in the moral weakness of the individual. Under these lights, the American Republic appeared a fortunate aberration, due more "to circumstances outside our control than to our constitution," as Josiah Quincy told the visiting Alexis de Tocqueville years later. The Revolution had not created freedom but had merely preserved it. Liberty had grown slowly over two centuries in New England, from seeds planted by "a completely republican religion" and by English resistance to Stuart tyranny. Through years of daily routine, citizens had absorbed habits of political discussion and built up institutions of government. This long past produced their happy present. History set the limits of the politically possible.[10]

Norton and his new friends sounded as if they had drunk Burke neat, but in fact there were earlier sources of their views. An appreciation of erratic development over time flowed from the common-law tradition, ubiquitous in English and American political thinking up to Norton's time, though he himself had no special acquaintance with it. He and his circle did know the writers of the Scottish Enlightenment; and it is a good guess that speculations like Adam Ferguson's on the slow "progress of civilization" shaped their understanding. The cake of custom crumbled readily. Unchecked passions, moral corruption, and unbridled greed could corrode in decades the achievement of centuries.

And just as moral corruption dissolved the ethical bonds that "feebly restrained" human passions, so intellectual debauchery dissolved the epistemological bonds that linked the mind with reality. To separate learning, religion, and politics was artificial: they were entwined by nature, and together they would fix the fate of the Republic. An institution like Harvard became, as Norton said, a bulwark of "the respectability and happiness of our country." "Very much must depend upon the tastes here cultivated, the sciences here taught, the principles here inculcated, and the views here opened to those, who are to go abroad into society, and be its teachers, guides, and governours." Such an outlook bred caution.[11]

Caution—but not inertia. Norton and his friends worked for progress, and they expected it. They looked to a reformed Harvard, for instance, to help to raise the moral and intellectual tone of the Republic, and even more hopefully to the churches. The "steady flame of pure and rational religion" seemed to them to burn brighter each year. Their complex and perhaps paradoxical worldview—its deeply historical conservatism, its admiration for the new American Republic, its faith in progress, its confidence in the application of reason to religion, even its hopes for Harvard—Andrews Norton would in due time inculcate in his son.[12]

Meanwhile, he was equipping himself to play a leading role in the clerisy to whom Boston entrusted its principles. Studying with Ware had solidified his learning; circulating among the Boston literati had added cosmopolitan polish. He moved with growing ease among Boston's elegant ministers and their propertied patrons.

Yet things were not falling into proper place. Norton's feeble voice and "preciseness of thought, statement, and utterance" suited a lecture room better than a pulpit. For several years he patched together a living out of occasional pulpits and college tutorships, supplemented by contributions from home. When, in the summer of 1811, chronic financial illness finally killed the *Anthology*, he saw an opening for his talents and started a more theologically oriented successor, the *General Repository and Review*. The journal sputtered out in little more than a year: leaden prose and esoteric erudition did not appeal even to patrician Boston's well-developed taste for theology, and the combativeness with which Norton flailed at orthodox trinitarian Calvinists worried liberal Unitarian leaders.[13]

Still, they could hardly deny his talents. In April 1813 Harvard made him Dexter Lecturer on biblical criticism and the college librarian; together, the posts would provide "something more than a support," Norton wrote to his doubtless relieved father. The lectureship developed more variously than its nominal subject suggested. The orthodox new Andover Seminary having invented a more thorough, more professional model of ministerial education than the slipshod program offered by the liberals, Harvard was scrambling to catch up when Norton came on board. He became in effect the dean of the new Harvard Divinity School and its intellectual center of gravity. In 1819 the university promoted him to Dexter Professor of Sacred Literature.[14]

Norton's views of the Bible and its interpretation were predictable. Like his father, Samuel, and his mentor, Henry Ware—and eventually like his son Charles—Norton regarded religious propositions as unworthy of credence if not rationally demonstrable from empirical evidence. There was nothing mysterious about the explication of Scripture: "the scriptures, both Jewish and Christian, are to be understood only through the same means of elucidation, as are applied to all other writings of similar or great antiquity." Knowledge of historical circumstances, of the biblical languages and their idioms, of the beliefs of the early Christians, and of "what is true and reasonable" allowed the modern reader to understand the meaning of the ancient writings. All this was the conventional doctrine of Boston's Unitarian liberals.[15]

More novel was Norton's deepening commitment to serious scholarship. Around Boston, ideas of learning were changing, and Germany was the Camelot of erudition. The awakening of learning in Germany, a phenomenon comparable in force to the Italian Renaissance, had only begun to attract sustained American attention. The few Harvard graduates lucky enough to study in Germany returned in awe of the monastic dedication of German scholars, who impressed them with the vastness of knowledge and the inability of anyone to master more than a small corner of it. George Ticknor, a young Federalist belletrist who had sailed to Göttingen, bitterly realized that, in building what passed for universities in the United States, Americans "think too much of convenience and comfort and luxury and show; and too little of real, laborious study and the means that will promote it." This fell little short of an outright attack on the Boston mode of literary elegance in behalf of the new Teutonic ideal, and Norton seconded it. By 1819, when he declared knowledge of German requisite for real scholarship—having just learned the language himself—he was offering practical advice but also articulating a new ideal.[16]

More specifically, this ideal promoted philology, the systematic study of texts and languages, as the model of erudition. To comprehend the real meaning of one of the Epistles, for instance, the scholar needed not only to grasp the precise connotations of every word, not only to know the intentions of the author, not only to understand the institutions and customs of the peoples of the ancient Mediterranean, but also to enter into their thinking, to discern the moral and intellectual patterns that defined a long dead civilization. History shaped every meaning. This philological approach was to define Charles Norton's scholarship even more decisively than his father's.[17]

Still, the Germans had their limits. However admirable their lexicons and their editions of ancient texts, to confuse this kind of useful pedantry with "the higher exertions of intellect" was "idle and mischievous." And "the extravagance of their speculation," especially about the Bible, threatened to corrode all belief and issue in blank atheism. So Norton conceived what was to be his magnum opus. In 1819 he began a "work on the genuineness of the gospels," which was to demonstrate on the basis of the latest researches the reliability of the Gospels as contemporaneous accounts of the words and doings of Jesus. The tools of German scholarship would refute the conjectures of German scholars.[18]

Growing immersion in scholarship led Norton to reassess his own role as teacher and writer; and behind this new self-image loomed the blurry outlines of a novel type, one that would both influence and trouble his son: the professional academic specialist. The scholar stood apart from other well-educated persons, distinguished by "much thought and much learning." He spoke with authority; nonspecialists, lacking knowledge to dispute his judgments, could only accede to them. But his authority flowed from his presumed erudition alone, not from birth, rank, or election; and unlike earlier forms of authority, it operated only within his field of expertise.[19]

The academic specialist's authority sprang from varied sources, but one of them was the professor's roots in the clergy. The traditional authority of the minister, already associated with learning, carried over to the professoriate. That this transference should have occurred in patrician Boston, where the clergy had long composed the core of the literati, seems natural. That it should have taken place more specifically in Harvard University, where most of the professors were ministers, seems even more logical. That it should have happened first in the Harvard Divinity School, where these professors trained other ministers, seems downright obvious. That the sole professor there who was *not* a minister should have first articulated the distinction between professorial and ministerial authority seems almost a foregone conclusion.

Yet the pull of belles lettres, and of the Renaissance-Enlightenment ideal of the learned amateur, remained strong. Norton wobbled between Teutonic scholar and *l'uomo universale*. For every pedantic footnote there flowed from his pen a line of maudlin verse. He bequeathed a confusing example to his Harvard successors, including Charles Norton. In some moods he foreshadowed the disciplinary specialist who emerged in the late nineteenth century. More often he presaged the great conundrum spawned by specialization: how to absorb professional scholarship into the older tradition of humane learning. The same ambivalence marked, the same dilemma preoccupied, his scholar son.

On 21 May 1821, Andrews Norton married Catharine Eliot, daughter of the recently deceased merchant prince Samuel Eliot, rumored to be "the richest man who has ever died in Boston." At five feet eight inches, Catharine had the stately bearing and calm self-assurance that seemed natural to her status and upbringing. Observant grey eyes looked out of an oval face framed by brown hair; her regular features, light complexion, smallish mouth and chin made her handsome by contemporary canons. Even "independent of her property," the twenty-six-year-old woman was thought "the finest match in Boston"; and Boston acknowledged Andrews a fit partner for her. If Catharine brought to the marriage wealth and the cachet of family, Norton brought cultural authority and the status it carried in Boston. His spare intensity set off her quietly elegant brunette beauty, and her literary interests and religious devotion harmonized with his own. The marriage was, as near as could be in its place and time, a partnership of equals.[20]

Still, her money changed his life. Shortly before the wedding, Catharine and Andrews bought the Cambridge mansion of Andrews's mentor, Henry Ware. Built in 1806 on a hill to the northeast of the university, the frame house sat amid thirty-five acres of bare ground stretching up to the Charlestown (now Somerville) line. Although it was adequate for Professor Ware, it was not for Samuel Eliot's daughter. While Catharine planned her wedding, her brother Samuel took charge of making the house grander. He put the front entrance where the back had been; added two bow windows and other improvements; landscaped the grounds in the naturalistic English mode, planting pines, maples, oaks, elms, and tupelos; and laid out a drive down to the estate's southern limit on Professors' Row (soon to be renamed Kirkland Street). The house was called Shady Hill.[21]

There Catharine gave birth on 21 January 1823 to the Nortons' first child, a daughter whom they named Louisa but called, more fondly, Louise. In October 1824 a second daughter arrived, Catherine Jane—Janie, later Jane.[22] Andrews gave his children hour after hour of his company and discovered that he enjoyed fatherhood. This was fortunate, since Catharine's pregnancies and baby care, combined with Andrews's studious habits and natural reserve, kept the Nortons much at home. At the same time, their Eliot connections and Andrews Norton's reputation made their home a center for the Harvard faculty and the more intellectually inclined of Boston's merchant elite.

Shady Hill emerged as one of the chief nuclei around which formed the New England clerisy; and the master of the house, along with his new brother-in-law George Ticknor, became its earliest arbiter of erudition. But never erudition alone. Perhaps responding to Catharine's interests, Andrews gave more time now than in many years to belles lettres, supervising between 1825 and 1828 three American editions of the English poet Felicia Hemans (best remembered for "The Boy on the Burning Deck") and beginning one of another British writer, Joanna Baillie. Meanwhile, there were learned commentaries on biblical topics in the *Christian Examiner* and a monograph on the Epistle to the Hebrews. Work went forward on the great book vindicating the genuineness of the Gospels. By German standards, Andrews produced nothing remarkable, but only one American scholar could match him. Boston looked to Shady Hill with something approaching awe.[23]

On 16 November 1827, a Friday, a third child was born. Catharine delivered about three o'clock in the afternoon "a fine little boy, apparently healthy and strong—a large child." The mother was fine, but the baby's sisters had whooping cough. While their new brother was held up at the end of one room, Louisa and Jane stood at the far end of another, peering at this distant curiosity through the doorway. The parents named the infant Charles Eliot Norton, after Catharine's deceased brother, who had also been Andrews's close friend. Four months later the new Charles was baptized by the same minister who had christened his father—Henry Ware.[24]

In the months after the baby's birth, Andrews, never healthy, collapsed under the strain of overwork. His doctor prescribed the common remedy for chronically ill but fiscally sound Americans: a sea voyage. On 1 May 1828 he and Catharine sailed out of Boston Harbor on the Liverpool packet. Louise and Janie stayed home under the care of servants and a cousin; five-month-old Charles, still at Catharine's breast, sailed with the grown-ups. He was "bright as a bird" when the ship hove into Liverpool four weeks later. Andrews, too, perked up as soon as they arrived in England.[25]

The country hardly seemed foreign. Its battlefields, its cathedrals, its literary monuments lived in novels and etchings. Lowells and Jacksons and Pickerings had dozens of British friends, to whom they commended their fellow patricians; ties between English and American Unitarians created another large circle within which Andrews Norton's name was well known; and his own writings had made smaller ones, theological and literary, wherein he himself was known by correspondence.

The family story runs that Wordsworth bounced little Charles on his Romantic knee and gave the babe his blessing. With Scott the Nortons dined at Abbotsford, having called on Southey en route. They visited the other standard monuments, literary and historical, flesh and stone. A few of the baby's celebrated new acquaintances would remember him when he returned to England as a young man. For now, the trip did Andrews a world of good. He disembarked in Boston at the end of October "a handsome man, in the prime of life, animated and imaginative."[26]

Return to the Harvard rut soon drained the animation. Andrews's health again sank; either his scholarship or his teaching had to give way. In 1830, aged forty-five, he retired to Shady Hill to pursue his biblical researches and literary aspirations full-time. He founded and, with a protégé, edited through 1833 and 1834 the *Select Journal of Foreign Periodical Literature,* which partly fulfilled his infant ambition of introducing Americans to foreign authors; and in 1834 there appeared his translation of Alessandro Manzoni's great novel *I promessi sposi.* His own poetry found a place in the day's anthologies. Pulling back not only from Harvard but from organized Unitarianism as well, Norton stood as independent critic, unbeholden to any institution. The role provided a model for the boy growing up at Shady Hill.

So, too, did his father's scholarly rigor. By dint of countless hours, Andrews made himself a specialist on the German model. Yet, as ever, specialized expertise seemed not enough. "The extent & accuracy of his knowledge in general literature, in history & biography were great," Charles remembered, "and his knowledge was always at command." The son also came to notice that in his father erudition sometimes defeated imagination, leading Andrews to underestimate the "variety in human nature" and the consequent "necessary diversity of men's opinions upon the most important subjects." For Andrews, as for Locke and the Scottish commonsense philosophers who provided his theory of knowledge, a fact could be only true or false, a logical argument from that fact only right or wrong. The insistent clarity that Andrews saw as a virtue the adult Charles came to regard as a limitation.[27]

For a small boy the shaping force of example works haltingly and unselfconsciously, but Andrews provided an unusually powerful model. Something of his public weight inevitably carried over into domestic life. An alert child noticed the deference of visitors; when he learned to read, he sometimes saw his father's name in books and newspapers. And Andrews was an unusually attentive parent—and always there, since Shady Hill was both home and workplace. When the boy peeked through the library doorway, he saw, surrounded by leatherbound tomes in German or Greek, his father at the table, pen in hand, filling page after page with his meticulous script.

A benevolent authority, but still an authority. In an era of patriarchal fathers, the habit of public pronouncement carried easily into domestic assertion, while the image of public importance (however vaguely focused in the children's eyes) reinforced authority within the family. As a rule, it was Andrews who instructed Charles and his sisters, especially as they grew older, in moral principle and social duty. Our life on this Earth, he would have told them, "is a state of discipline and preparation" for the afterlife. There, we will eternally delight in "social enjoyment and social duties," in the "proper exercise" of our "intellectual faculties," and in "continued progression and improvement." For now, the "characters that we may form in the present" will determine our future happiness.[28]

And—"being in so many respects but little more than portions of the society to which we belong"—we exercise our characters most essentially in fulfilling our duty of benevolence to others. As they grew older, the Norton children would notice how their father practiced these precepts: in his donations to certain philanthropies, especially those devoted to education or to relief of the poor; in his habit of making substantial loans to acquaintances in financial straits; in his interventions in religious or political debates. For the children in their earlier years, service was simply the law laid down by Andrews and seconded by Catharine. Unlike her husband, Catharine rarely taught the children explicit moral lessons, but her admiring words to them about their father reinforced him as ethical archetype.[29]

What Catharine herself gave Charles and his sisters was at once more diffuse and more complex. There was, most obviously, wealth: the most in Cambridge. Yet Charles learned not to overrate wealth, absorbing early the Boston lesson (visible in his own father) that neither birth nor wealth—but education and character—made a gentleman. And his mother's example even more than his father's precepts taught him to treat those less fortunate with generosity and respect; little information survives, for instance, about how his mother managed the servants, but they rarely left her employment. Catharine even wondered aloud (not to the servants) whether it was right for the Nortons to live so well, to gratify their tastes and indulge their children, when others suffered want. Yet live well they did, and privilege laid its easy assumptions among the deepest strata in Charles Norton's personality. A privileged family, the Nortons were also an unusually close one. As little Charley grew from toddler into boy, he knew stability, security, nurturing affection.[30]

But he early grew acquainted as well with illness, grief, and the tenuousness of life. It was not only his father's recurring sickness. From Charley's second birthday through the middle of his seventh year, his mother was as often pregnant as not, in an era when the late stage of pregnancy meant "confinement." In 1830 the two-year-old Charley got a new brother, William Eliot, named like himself after a favorite brother of Catharine. But late the next year that favorite brother, William Havard Eliot, died suddenly of influenza. And Charley himself also nearly died. His mother, shattered, pregnant again, slept only with morphine. In February 1832 she gave birth to a third sister, Mary Eliot. One month later, Charley's grandfather Norton died. A few months after that, scarlet fever carried off his little brother, Willie; six months later a "Brain affection" killed baby Mary. Within a year and a half a favorite uncle, a grandfather, a little brother, and a little sister had died, and he himself had teetered on the brink of death. There is no way to gauge the impact on a five-year-old boy. Andrews did report that Charley was, "for his years, much affected" by Willie's death.[31]

On 7 April 1834 Catharine gave birth to another child, baptized in November as Grace. Gracie completed the family. Catharine, past forty, eluded or prevented further pregnancies. Charley was six, and he now had two older sisters to look up to and a baby one to cuddle and torment. These three composed much of his world. Louise, eleven years old, took less part in childish affairs. Janie seems to have been something of the manager, one of the servants declaring that she "would make the best mistress of any of them." Gracie, pert, a bit spoiled, a little sassy, early the family comedian, made her mother throw up her hands, often to hide a smile.[32]

Charley seems to have glided happily through this female domain, a princeling to his older sisters. Since he could not yet write books as Father did, they helped him to paste little pictures on blank pages and sew them together. Perhaps the girls also helped him to make his "little museum" of seashells or to find creatures for his "ark." Together they fed Rover, played with Tobias the cat, pestered the cow. To imagine a child stretched out in the branches of a flowering apple tree, reading a *Rollo* novel, is perhaps cloying. It was also, like infant death and parental illness, a true picture of a child's life at Shady Hill and the more intensely colored one for Charley.[33]

Catharine, as custom assumed, took charge of the children's early education. This included reading and writing, which children of the Boston elite learned at home when quite young. Charley was reading and probably writing before he was four. Normal, too, was the children's literature he read: the *Juvenile Miscellany*, Maria Edgeworth's *Harry and Lucky,* and her *The Little Merchants* (an apt book for a Boston boy and one that gave Charley his "first impressions of Naples"). His first lessons in rhetoric came in his mother's letters, gently amending the lapses in her children's little missives to her. In bringing her children up to admire the written word, Catharine typified the mothers in her circle.[34]

Atypical was her own literary skill and sensitivity. In 1833 an Italian patriot, Piero Maroncelli, a refugee from the Austrians who ruled northern Italy, arrived in Boston; the previous year Maroncelli's comrade Silvio Pellico had published in Turin a memoir of their years in Habsburg dungeons, *Le mie prigioni*. With Maroncelli's aid Catharine set about translating the saga of Austrian tyrants and Italian heroes. Her vocabulary is simple, her sentences short and conversational, her rhetoric fluent and everyday, a style that Charley would soon absorb, in part from his mother.[35]

Maroncelli intensified an unusually strong taste for things Italian in Charley's family. Andrews was one of the two scholars in Boston "familiar enough with Italian poetry" to help the handful of Bostonians seriously engaged with Dante. Uncle Ticknor was the other; he corresponded with European Dantists and taught a Harvard course on the poet in the early 1830s. Even as a tyke, Charley was "very much at home" in the library of the Ticknor house, richly stocked even by Shady Hill standards and "one of the pleasantest rooms in the world" to a precociously literate child. Small wonder that the boy later turned his own eyes toward Italian literature.[36]

That was to come. Uncle Ticknor had expertise in "romps" as well as in Dante, and for now romps appealed more. Charley can hardly have begun to absorb the varied lessons of Shady Hill and its extended family when he toddled off, at the tender but customary age of four, to his first school. That he was already impressed with the importance of books and learning is as certain as speculation can be; if his parents' literary work did not yet affect the boy, the family's nightly recreation—reading aloud—would have done so. His first school was what was called a woman's school: "a place," one of his contemporaries recalled, "where a good-natured girl of twenty keeps thirty children reasonably happy for three hours in the morning and two in the afternoon."[37]

School also got Charley down the hill into the world beyond Shady Hill's gate. Although by the 1830s most of Cambridge's citizens no longer kept even vegetable gardens, the smells and sounds and sights in Charley's neighborhood still evoked a farm more than a modern city. Not a single house occupied Professors' Row on the side opposite Shady Hill—only marsh and huckleberry pasture, filled in spring and summer with blossoms:

roses where the Shady Hill avenue joined Professors' Row, rhexia by the woods, hibiscus standing high along the river that bore Charles's own Christian name, azalea and clethra in the marshes, honeysuckle, cardinal flowers, gentians. Charley began to collect flowers, an early hint of an aesthetic nature with a strongly visual bent.

As he grew older Charley ventured with new playmates farther from home. They walked the mile or so to the Market Place—later called Harvard Square—to watch the ox wagons pull up under the great elms with loads of hay or wood hauled in from the country; or the omnibus waiting in front of Willard's Tavern to pick up passengers for the hour-long trek to Boston. They followed the Harvard boys around, even learned their names. In summer Charley and his friends swam in the river; in winter they bundled up to skate on Craigie's Pond or, when a little older, on the black ice of Fresh Pond, way up along the Concord road. After school there was baseball and football, on Saturdays bowling in the tenpin alleys at Porter's Tavern, a mile north of the market. Life was not all boys. When Charley turned seven, he went to dancing school every Monday and Thursday afternoon with Louise and Janie. Best of all there were trips in July or August to Nahant, the spit of land north of Boston where a Greek temple had incongruously transported itself from Paestum or Athens to serve as Uncle Samuel Eliot's summerhouse. Here, Charley and his cousins chased each other along the gray sand beach, packed so hard by the waves that carriage wheels made no impression.

Cousins provided many of Charley's playmates. The favorite was Charley Guild, son of Catharine's sister Eliza, who had married Benjamin Guild. The boys, almost the same age, shared also the name "Charles Eliot." With houses on Beacon Hill and in Brookline just west of Boston, the Guilds lived inconveniently far; nonetheless, as "children of intimate sisters" the two boys shared from infancy many days, either at Shady Hill or in Brookline. Their parents were also much together, for the social world of Shady Hill was built around the Eliot connection. Catharine's sisters and their husbands—Guilds, Dwights, and Ticknors—all lived on Beacon Hill within steps of each other and of their brother Samuel A. Eliot.[38]

From family the web of affection extended out to enclose a few neighbors almost as close. The "merry and laughter-loving" Cornelius Felton, Harvard's erudite professor of Greek, regularly joined the Norton's dining table in the afternoon, even more frequently their card table in the evening. Another whist partner became, as Charley approached adolescence, perhaps the family's closest friend and, as he grew to adulthood, one of Charley's own. This was George Ticknor's successor as Smith Professor of Modern Languages, who wanted even more to be a poet than a professor, Henry Wadsworth Longfellow.[39]

These, with other acquaintances among the Boston elite and visitors to Boston, made up the varied crowd at Shady Hill. There were avuncular presences from the Divinity School, youthful wits from Boston. The young lawyer Charles Sumner argued politics, bringing the stresses of the Republic home to Charley with an immediacy no newspaper had. Writers of varied stripe crowded the table—the historian William Prescott, Andrews's meek protégé Charles Folsom, the versatile George Hillard—and naturally a spate of Harvard characters—the German refugee Karl Follen and his Cabot wife Eliza; Francis Bowen, only twelve years older than Louisa Norton but on the road to eminence in philosophy and political economy; Jared Sparks, making a name for himself by editing the writings of Washington and Franklin. None of these seemed individually to matter much to Charley; collectively they created for him a world in which affairs of intellect and public life were what weighed with real consequence.

When the Nortons sat down for dinner at two o'clock, some familiar guest commonly sat down with them. Or, if not, Longfellow or Sumner might appear for evening tea and a hand of whist. At more formal dinner parties, ten or twenty gathered round the "mighty bowls of hot stewed oysters." And always there was talk: talk of Paris and M. Guizot's school reform, talk of politics and the growing rifts within Massachusetts Whiggery over slavery, talk of Harvard and the new elective system that President Quincy had been persuaded to promote, talk of England and the Chartist agitation that threatened to unsettle Lord Melbourne's government. The talkers spoke from first-hand knowledge. Mr. Sumner had just returned from Paris; Uncle Samuel was mayor of Boston; Mr. Palfrey from next door edited the *North American Review*. Shady Hill's drawing room was a school for a precocious boy with open ears and a roving mind. Before he reached twelve Charley himself was "ready to talk upon all subjects and yet so modest and observant of others."[40]

Early in 1837 much of the talk was of the first volume of *The Evidences of the Genuineness of the Gospels*, published at last. Well received by reviewers both orthodox and liberal, and completed in two more volumes in 1844, it established Norton's reputation in Europe as a serious, if rather old-fashioned and derivative, scholar. Around Boston he looked both more impressive and more daring than this. Did not so great a scholar as Oxford's Henry Hart Milman tell George Ticknor that "no book in English, I might perhaps say in theological Literature" dealt "so satisfactorily" with the "great question" of "the antiquity and genuineness of the New Testament"? And Norton's handling of the Bible struck Bostonians as anything but fusty. His rejection as spurious of the first two chapters of Matthew gave one of the first great shocks to the understanding of the Bible traditional even among Unitarians—and showed that conservatism, for a Norton, did not imply subjection to received opinion.[41]

Nor had he closeted himself in erudition. Though steadily more the professional scholar, striving to satisfy German standards, Norton also wrote *Genuineness of the Gospels* for the ministers and merchants with whom he shared personal life as well as cultural principles, shunting into notes "what concerns scholars only." And Boston in turn admired "the ease with which real learning does its work without parade or pedantry, and quietly places the result of its researches within the reach of all." Even a nine-year-old, especially a bookish one, would take pride in such a father. Charley Norton was silently learning from him: learning to look for approval as much from one's own circle of cultivated friends as from European savants (but to seek it from both), learning to subject oneself to strict standards of scholarship but to bring erudition into service to general readers, learning to turn radical ideas to conservative ends.[42]

From both mother and father Charley was learning as well how smoothly literature blended with life, how permeable was the wall between parlor and study. Behind this lesson lay the Unitarian principle of self-culture, itself a democratic scion of the Renaissance idea of aristocratic self-fashioning embodied in the mirror-of-princes books. The Boston version asserted that we all have the power "of acting on, determining, and forming ourselves"; that "in a wise self-culture, all the principles of our nature grow at once by joint harmonious action"; that self-culture particularly perfects character and judgment; and that it depends especially on "intercourse with superior minds" through reading the best books. A Norton hardly needed to wait for Matthew Arnold to absorb this local commonplace.[43]

For life at Shady Hill revolved around the written word. Charley could listen to his father talk of negotiating with Macaulay over an American edition of his early essays; he could read in the *North American* about the "great care and fidelity" and the "natural and unaffected style" with which his mother had translated Pellico. His parents inducted Charley into literary business young. Devourers of books, the Nortons had informal agents purchasing for them as far away as Calcutta; Charley became one and, before he reached thirteen, was a practiced hand at Boston book sales, choosing and buying rare items for Andrews on his own initiative. By this time, too, he had started to collect his own, including a "beautiful" illuminated sixteenth-century manuscript given him by an older cousin.[44]

The visual arts, in fact, appealed to him with special power. As a twelve-year-old he already roamed the few galleries in Boston, but there was little to catch even a feebly trained eye. In May 1840, sent to an auction of French paintings to purchase one for "Cousin Mary" (Dwight?), Charley found himself gaping at "the most beautifully painted oil picture that I ever saw. The colors are laid on so evenly that it feels like planed wood." Even though Charley went often to concerts and learned to enjoy Beethoven, a violin never thrilled him as a picture could.[45]

His schooling was hardly calculated to thrill at all. Typically, after incubating them in a "woman's" school, Boston thrust its boys (at least those meant for college) at the age of seven or eight into a "man's," or classical, school. There they endured for eight years or so, gnawing on Latin, Greek, and math, garnished with geography and maybe a soupçon of history or French. Charley experienced three of these institutions. He started in 1834, at the precocious age of six, at a school just opened by Henry R. Cleveland; transferred two years later to the Cambridge Classical School, run by an "excellent classical scholar" and "pleasant youth" named Charles Stearns Wheeler; and finished (after Harvard snatched Wheeler away to make him Greek tutor) at an "excellent school" kept by D. G. Ingraham. At Wheeler's, Charley made a new friend, George Martin Lane, who would become his Harvard classmate and later colleague on the Harvard faculty and with whom he now vied for the highest marks, in deportment as well as studies. At "Old Ingy's," Charley ranked an uncontested first. At all three schools he was immersed in Latin and Greek for as much as four hours a day.[46]

In the course of this schooling he acquired fewer bruises from the master's cane and a much stronger grounding in classical languages than most of his age-mates. (To how many boys, even Cambridge boys, would a family friend give a seventeenth-century Latin translation from the Greek?) An attentive father, with formidable command of Latin and Greek, helped with lessons. The foundation thus laid proved essential in Charles Norton's career. But in other respects his schooling was by later standards pitiably weak. The English language got irregular attention, English literature none, modern foreign languages the briefest flirtation; mathematics ventured only timidly beyond arithmetic, history not at all beyond antiquity. Charley did learn geography: a Boston boy needed to know how to find Calcutta and the Canaries.[47]

Inevitably, the education of such a boy occurred largely outside of school, as the ideal of self-culture implied. For children as wealthy as the Nortons, even a lot of regular classes took place at home. Charley's sisters, whom custom excluded from classical school, got their schooling entirely there. Their father taught them Latin; his friend Charles Folsom, Italian; a Miss Giraud, French; and their mother, a good deal else. The record falls silent as to other teachers; but their neighbors the Higginson girls learned German from the Harvard professor Karl Follen and geometry from his colleague Benjamin Peirce, the most eminent mathematician in the United States. While Charley was parsing Greek under Old Ingy's eye, Janie was reading Vasari and Dante under Henry Longfellow's. Charley, too, learned modern languages in this way, sitting with his sisters in Miss Giraud's little class of nine neighborhood children, studying Italian and German with the help of parents or family friends. Even physical education, unheard of in school, Charley got in twice-weekly calisthenics classes.[48]

Yet classes provided a mere fraction of the culture essential to a gentleman, much more being absorbed than taught. Charley and his sisters grazed at will among the leather bindings that lined the library shelves at Shady Hill: Shakespeare's plays; the poems of Pope and Gray; the novels of Jane Austen, Maria Edgeworth, Walter Scott; works of history and travel; the *Edinburgh Review* and the *North American;* and (when they grew older) Scottish philosophy and German theology.

Civic Boston added to the education that friends and family provided. When southering geese flecked the skies, the birds passed over Bostonians flocking to evening lectures. During the winter of 1837–38, when Charley was just getting old enough for such things, at least twenty-six substantial series of lectures were delivered in the city, not to mention innumerable individual performances. As he entered his teens, Charley frequented them: "The Study of Shakespeare," Dr. Charles Jackson's series on mineralogy, the course on chemistry by Yale's distinguished Benjamin Silliman. Whether he also made use of the libraries at the Athenaeum and the Historical Society is not known; Shady Hill may have obviated the need. But the Nortons' next-door neighbor, John Gorham Palfrey, once speculated that the bias of those collections toward history turned Boston's writers in that direction, and Charles Norton certainly inherited the bias.[49]

For that matter, he inherited more than a bias toward history; the very history of the New England clerisy passed down to him in his own education, outlook, and principles. With it came an unusually solid edition of the classical education then common to English and American elites and an impressive acquaintance, for a fourteen-year-old, with samples of their literature and learning. His childhood had been cheerful, comfortable, secure. His parents, his older sisters, his aunts, uncles, and cousins had enfolded him in a warm cocoon of family.

As he began to emerge from it, his identity seemed as solid as his borning sense of duty: each indeed entailed the other. In most respects he resembled the other male children of privileged Boston, but he felt more strongly the mysterious lure of learning, and he had touched more often the European world toward which his parents and their friends genuflected. Many boys collected coins; not many had a friend in Marienberg who mailed them eighty-six Roman coins and the famous 1688 Drei Königs thaler of Cologne. It was hardly strange for a bookish fourteen-year-old to like Dickens; few shook his hand at their aunt's party. The wider world beckoned, but all the same it was not easy to leave Shady Hill.[50]

One day in March 1842, six months before he was to take the Harvard entrance examinations, Charley came home early from school with red, sore eyes. The "weakness" persisted until, in May, Andrews and Catharine put him on the train to New York for treatment by Samuel Elliott, a celebrated oculist much favored by Bostonians. Charley was soon home, though forbidden books for months and ordered to exercise in the open air as much as possible. The latter prescription hardly burdened a healthy boy in June, and by early August his eyes had improved enough that he was allowed to read for three hours a day. He did not miss the excitement when, in mid-July, a Harvard undergraduate bought two-and-a-half pounds of gunpowder and blew up a dormitory and a recitation room and damaged University Hall. President Quincy had improved discipline in the past decade but had not entirely squelched the high spirits of Harvard students.[51]

Charley was about to become one. At six o'clock on Monday morning, 22 August, he walked into the battered University Hall with seventy-five or so other youngsters. There for the next day and a half the faculty grilled them on the Greek vocabulary of the Gospel of John, the scansion of the Aeneid, the relative locations of London and Amsterdam. The afternoon of the second day the boys spent loitering in the yard, waiting to be called back to hear the result. In his turn Charley trudged up the steps of University Hall into the Corporation Room.

There Josiah Quincy and his professors, several of them habitués of Shady Hill, sat around the mahogany table. Charles bowed to the president and heard, surely without surprise, that Harvard had admitted him to the class of 1846. He was admitted "without conditions," a happy state achieved only by the best-prepared boys. Three days later he walked down to the steward's office to make the arrangements for admission, his fifteenth birthday still three months away.[52]

TWO

Cambridge and Boston, 1842–1849

Most Harvard freshmen found rooms in private homes near the college. Charley rented his in a big square three-story house (whitewashed, like everything else in Cambridge), just north of Harvard Yard and down Professors' Row from Shady Hill. Charley Guild joined him there. Even in a familiar house, with a familiar landlady to feed and look after them, the boys must have felt a thrill at being grown-up enough to live on their own—almost.[1]

A thrill but hardly anxiety. Harvard, with fewer than three hundred students, was not big enough to be scary: a dozen or so buildings, mostly red brick, straggling around the Old Cambridge Market.[2] Harvard had long since become chiefly an institution of the Boston mercantile elite, sustained to educate its own boys and to lift up specially talented ones among the less privileged. Only a few outlanders spiced the class. Charley's constant companion remained his cousin Charley; a few others of his classmates he knew from school; still others were Lawrences, Parkmans, Peabodys, whose parents—and maybe the lads themselves—he had met at Uncle Ticknor's. And for him even more than the other Cambridge boys, Harvard seemed extended family. Half the small faculty were used to dropping in at Shady Hill.

Charley sat down at Harvard's table as comfortably as to dinner at home, with the untroubled self-confidence of his kin. He had inherited Andrews's wit, which endeared him to some of his classmates, and Andrews's sarcasm, which did not to others. Sarcasm perhaps compensated for size, for Charley still awaited puberty and its growth spurt; indeed, at not yet fifteen, he and Charley Guild were two years younger than the average freshman and were soon good-naturedly christened the Babes in the Wood. Possibly it was diffidence arising from his young age that kept Charley from gorging on college social life. More likely his aloofness is to be laid to bookish habits, as Norton himself explained it, or to the hours he continued to spend at Shady

Hill. Regardless, he proved popular enough to be elected in January to the *second-best* elocutionary society. Harvard made him happy.[3]

Freshman studies can hardly have accounted for much of his joy. The college still retained the skeleton of the old classical curriculum, rattling around since the Renaissance. Meant originally to educate an elite for public life, at a time when public life still centered (at least in the fantasies of educators) around the Ciceronian orator, it was defended by Charley's teachers partly because they supposed ancient writings were favorable to American free institutions, much more because they believed that studying classical languages formed taste and style and that the requisite mental exertion would "sharpen and invigorate the faculties." The phrase "general culture" was also beginning to be heard.[4]

The culture was not excessively general nor the invigoration dangerously overstimulating. Yet, however dulling, Norton's college education mattered a great deal because decades later he profoundly influenced a radical reformation of liberal education in the United States. His experience as a Harvard student provided the model against which he reacted, with lasting consequences for millions of American collegians and their professors. The curriculum that Charley encountered (along with almost all other American college students in his time) stressed Latin and Greek, taught ponderously as grammar rather than literature. These, mixed with some algebra and geometry, yielded the basic curriculum of American colleges in the first half of the nineteenth century. These old bones had, especially in recent decades, put on softer flesh. But the padding was little evident to Harvard freshmen, except insofar as natural history and civil history (ancient, of course) cushioned the Latin, Greek, and math in their second term. The Nortons' neighbor John Palfrey declared in a sermon in the Harvard chapel that "a college, after a prison and a ship, is the dullest of all conceivable places to kill time in."[5]

The killing began early. Six days a week the two Charleys dragged themselves out of bed before daylight, threw on cap and pantaloons, grabbed their cloaks, and ran down to the dim, stuffy chapel on the second floor of University Hall. There student monitors took attendance; Dr. Francis from the Divinity School prayed; President Quincy rose in the front pew to protest the latest theft of the chapel Bible; smirking upperclassmen scraped their feet in derision. The whole ritual took ten minutes; then everyone gratefully wandered off to breakfast. Back in the reins at nine o'clock, the freshmen puzzled over geometry and algebra for an hour before facing up to the meat of their studies: three hours of drill in Latin and Greek. The Latin professor was a German martinet with a close-cropped skull, his Greek counterpart a kindly and befuddled Thessalonian with legendary pet chickens; but they were identical in their traditional obsession with conjugations and declensions.

This was much the same fare force-fed to the freshmen in their earlier lives as schoolboys. Indeed, in old age Norton recalled the Harvard College of his day as an "excellent high school."[6] The phrase implied a modicum of improvement over the 1820s, when Ticknor's great hope had been to turn Harvard into a good high school. And in several subjects, especially at the upper levels, contemporary accounts do suggest a higher standard of scholarship and more energetic teaching than twenty years earlier. Yet the dominant method of instruction remained recitation: the teacher asking a question about the day's assigned reading from the textbook, the pupil answering it, one boy after another. The system had altered remarkably little since the printing press put textbooks in students' hands. A curriculum so nasty, brutish, and dull naturally set boy against master; and animal spirits repressed in the recitation room inevitably exploded in what Uncle Samuel discreetly referred to as "occasional displays of a vivacious nature"—food fights, bonfires, firecrackers in chapel.[7]

The best that can be said for Harvard is that it left the boys plenty of free time. A medley of student organizations devoted themselves to diverse forms of self-culture: debating societies, an orchestra and glee club, literary magazines, a chemistry club. Charley's favorite was the Natural History Society, whose collections spread over two rooms in Massachusetts Hall; there, his hobbies of bird-watching and flower collecting acquired a scientific cast. As a Christmas gift during his freshman year, Andrews gave him a subscription to *The Naturalist's Magazine.*[8]

Reading, however, was becoming difficult for Charley, because by November his eye trouble had recurred. (Was there some underlying disease?) When term ended on 13 January, his parents took advantage of Harvard's six-week winter vacation to send him back to Dr. Elliott in New York. Under the supervision of Andrews's sister, Charley put up at a boarding house, where his stay turned out to be a long one, Elliott prescribing a three-month course of treatment. Andrews arranged with President Quincy for Charley to make up missed studies and rejoin his class without falling back; Mr. Longfellow sent letters of introduction to his New York literary friends and heartening words: "I know you will bear it like a hero, like a young Frithiof—and deserve to have a saga written about you (though you probably may not)." To a boy barely fifteen New York might well loom as epic.[9]

Andrews wrote to remind "Frithiof" that God intended life's suffering as "part of our discipline for the future life" and an "occasion for the higher virtues," for "the formation of our characters": "sufferings may be alleviated and made blessings by the qualities of character which they call into exercise." This was hardly news to Charley. Character formation provided the central dogma of Boston patrician upbringing and specifically of Boston's ideal of self-culture. Andrews's incantation, a litany going back to early childhood, etched "character" permanently into Charles Norton's aims of education; and, just as Harvard's drill of rote learning provided the negative template for Norton's later transformation of liberal education, so did the ideal of "character" provide much of its positive content. However, a merciful God did not appoint self-denial as part of a young Bostonian's character-shaping ordeal: Charley was not to worry about expenses in New York.[10]

Also in this practical line, Father delivered a correspondence course in social graces. When friends give you welcome, do not wear it out; time visits thoughtfully and keep them short; make yourself agreeable by good temper and good manners; stay alert for helps you can offer; bring little presents. New York offered a school for the uses of sociability. Andrews urged Charley to learn that not only books offered "*intellectual* improvement": "keep your eyes open and your attention awake." Explore the samples of life in and around New York. Visit the police courts. Piety did not require priggery; curiosity about the variousness of human beings was a quality Charley early acquired and never lost.[11]

Literary circles did interest him more than criminal ones. He visited bookshops and auctions, hunting for volumes that Andrews wanted, and captured a special prize, the seventeenth-century royalist classic *Eikon Basilike*. With an introduction from Longfellow to Rufus Griswold, New York's literary entrepreneur par excellence, Charley explored "the Literary *machinery*" of Manhattan, "the Editors' chambers, and publishers' dens." Another family friend, Charles Sumner, took him to see the eminent jurist Chancellor James Kent. He had tea with Theodore Sedgwick, distinguished writer on law and political economy. (On that particular evening, Charley, fond of little children, probably played with the Sedgwicks' six-year-old daughter Susan, who almost twenty years later would reenter his life in the most memorable way.) And he must have run into an aspiring poet from Boston, James Russell Lowell, also enduring Dr. Elliott's ministrations. Harvard offered no such course in the literary life.[12]

When, finally, Charley returned home toward the end of May, his eyes had grown stronger and so, his parents thought, had his character. On his own in New York, he had begun to form "habits of self-reliance, of trusting to one's own judgment, of being governed by one's own sense of right and wrong, of submitting patiently and cheerfully to disappointment and deprivation, and of controlling one's feelings." Andrews reminded him, as often, how favored the Nortons were in material circumstances; but even to a Norton life would bring suffering. "Happiness and virtue" lay in cultivating "a cheerful temper," in appreciating the good that befalls us rather than dwelling on misfortune—and above all, in remembering that "there is no happiness, nor permanent pleasure except in doing right." Leigh Hunt's "Abou Ben Adhem" became "a very great favorite" of Charley's. The honorable life, ultimately the only happy life, was one "of exertion and self-improvement." Even sister Louisa, from her elevated age of twenty years, impressed on her little brother these ruling ideals of patrician Boston. Charley would, she was sure, have many blessings "to be thankful for"—but also "accountable for." "From those to whom much is given much will be required."[13]

But not yet, and certainly not by Mother Harvard, to whose yielding bosom Charley returned for the fag end of freshman year. His months away had cost him no popularity among his fellows, for in June he was elected to the Institute of 1770, foremost of the student literary societies. Nor had they retarded his academic progress, for he caught up in Greek, Latin, and math, while Quincy let him make up freshman history in his sophomore year. Absence did disqualify him, when sophomore year began in August, for the Detur, a book prize awarded to students who had excelled in the preceding year. Charley coveted one; so President Quincy gave him "a prettily bound copy of Campbell's Poems" as a sort of unofficial personal Detur.[14]

Equally familial was his treatment by the faculty. Although as sophomores he and Charley Guild continued to board at the Stearns house, they often walked the mile to Shady Hill for dinner with professorial family friends like Cornelius Felton, Francis Bowen, and Asa Gray. Now, too, with Charley growing up and spending most of his hours away from Shady Hill, these elder friends began to treat the teenager as companionable in his own right. Felton had him to dinner, the Longfellows to tea. When a boy saw his professors as men who ate and drank and told jokes and played cards, he was far more likely to see what they taught as the real stuff of life. However ephemeral Professor Felton's harping on Greek grammar seemed, Charley knew that Felton also pursued scholarship of obvious substance.[15]

Even coursework, in the last three years at Harvard, faintly suggested that life flourished in learning. Between 1843 and 1846, Harvard College enjoyed, not springtime, but a January thaw. The old classical curriculum and the recitation system that went with it seemed about to melt away. In the 1820s, George Ticknor had tried to raise standards of instruction closer to German norms. Although his crusade foundered on the resistance of other professors, the seeds he planted sprouted in unanticipated forms. In 1833, Harvard made Benjamin Peirce, only twenty-four, University Professor of Mathematics and Natural Philosophy, on grounds of sheer genius. Immediately, Peirce ran headlong into the average Harvard student, whose distaste for mathematics equaled only the feebleness of his preparation in it. Peirce proposed a simple answer to this pedagogical conundrum: let the dullards opt out.

Simple but radical. Up to now, virtually all courses except modern languages were mandatory steps in a rigidly fixed curriculum. But from 1838 mathematics became optional after the freshman year. Soon, the classical professors decided to cut the Gordian knot—or cleanse the Augean stables—as Peirce had; in 1841, Greek and Latin became elective for sophomores, juniors, and seniors. These changes did not add up to a system of free election, but they did cut the core out of the old classical curriculum for students whose parents wanted them to have a more "useful" education. And in consequence students who did study calculus or Isocrates escaped intellectual sabotage by the resentful prisoners sharing their classroom. The experiment horrified traditionalists, and Quincy's successor quashed it—but not until Charley had graduated.[16]

These curricular innovations paralleled a new seriousness about scholarship among the faculty. There were nine professors at Harvard in Charley's day; of these, six staked a claim to competence in research (three of these to distinction) and another, Longfellow, to literary eminence.[17] These men brought into their classes an erudition that was deep if not always lively. Longfellow, copying the German mode of instruction imported by his predecessor, Ticknor, actually lectured on Dante and Cervantes rather than hearing pupils recite from a textbook; and he treated the boys like gentlemen, calling them Mr. Guild or Mr. Norton, an unheard-of practice. Jared Sparks lectured, too, on *modern* history; the great editor and biographer of the Founders demonstrated that history provided matter for scholarship as well as romance. Into Asa Gray's lectures on structural and cryptogamic botany filtered results of the most ambitious biological research program in America. The son of his father, Charley appreciated better than most of the fidgeting students the learning of Longfellow and Gray, Beck and Felton. Not only did their examples further mold the characteristic form of Norton's own later influential scholarship. He caught, too, glimpses of a new educational ideal, which in the quarter century after 1873 he played as large a role as anyone in establishing at the center of American academic life.

As yet, however, these were only momentary flashes of an unimagined model of education. Aside from languages and mathematics, the curriculum remained fixed: philosophy, rhetoric, history, and chemistry for sophomores; philosophy, rhetoric, history, and physics for juniors; more of the same for the seniors. The college's requirement that professors rate performance daily forced them back on recitations in most courses, cramping faculty research as much as student learning. Felton's scholarship eked out a flickering life amid endless hours of listening to students drone and of marking their exercise books. Trying to cross-examine every pupil every day frustrated his wish to teach broadly and systematically. When Greek became elective, he started to lecture on "Greek life and mythology" but wilted under the daily grading. Felton was the furthest thing from a philistine; it was he who first had students read entire Greek works rather than anthologized scraps, who nurtured a prophetic vision of education as humanistic cultivation. The recitation method would have forced Sophocles to reduce Greek to grammatical calisthenics.[18]

In such patchy pastures Charley browsed. College records indicate where he grazed but cannot say what he digested. Did he take anything away, for instance, from the stultifying lectures on chemistry that Dr. John Webster came over from the Medical School to deliver to the sophomores in a "dank, dark, almost slimy" lecture room? Or from Joseph Lovering's junior physics course, which covered a great mass of technical astronomical detail (which the boys merely recited from open books) while neglecting Newton's laws? Not "specially industrious" by his own account—not above resorting to a pony to puzzle out Aristophanes—Charley nevertheless turned out a good student.[19]

Like most of his classmates, he continued with Greek and Latin; unlike most, he mastered both well enough to read with fair ease for the rest of his life. He also kept nibbling at the modern languages begun under private tutors: German certainly, Italian and French probably. The college's scattershot and superficial teaching would have added little. Without quite realizing what he was up to, he was laying a broad foundation on which could later rise real command of Western European languages.

For now, English was the language most occupying attention. Charley's prose came under the unsparing eye of Edward Tyrell Channing, professor of rhetoric since 1819, who had sharpened the pens of Emerson and Thoreau, Holmes and Lowell, Motley and Parkman. Catharine had already schooled him to attend to description when he wrote family letters, while years of Greek and Latin had drilled him in grammar, instilling a feeling for structure: even his college compositions had a strong skeleton. Channing's exercises tightened the musculature and developed suppleness and speed. He excoriated slang as savagely as pomposity and, while thinning their verbiage, instructed the boys to form phrases stately and strong, to balance sentences, to harmonize sounds. He taught them to write for a miscellaneous audience, as Catharine had in *My Prisons*, Andrews in *Genuineness of the Gospels*. And he trained them to write with the fluency that enabled a Boston merchant to turn out a magazine article in a few evenings. This "art of easy writing" Charles Norton came greatly to value. Above all, Channing proclaimed that "the first requisite of Style" is intelligibility; fogginess, the writer's worst offense, a warning that must have carried home to a boy who read with filial admiration the "studied preciseness" of Andrews's prose and poetry.[20]

Indeed, in many ways Harvard's teaching codified what Charley absorbed from Shady Hill and Boston. The classical bias of education had long encouraged the American elite to think of their Republic by analogy with Greece and Rome; Charley's history books explained how growing corruption and extremes of wealth and poverty destroyed Roman liberty: a moral tale central to American republicanism. But Harvard gave republicanism a Boston spin, stressing continuity between British and American political experience, affinities outweighing ancient animosity. Newer theories of the state also got smuggled into the curriculum from Germany; these projected a more active role for government than republicans might normally abide but one congenial to Boston traditions of philanthropy.[21]

Courses in ethics, metaphysics, and theological apologetics likewise spoke in a familiar accent. They echoed the Scottish common sense school, of which Thomas Reid was the stellar intellect, Dugald Stewart the great popularizer, and Boston's clerisy the devout admirers. Besides confirming a lasting taste for philosophical reasoning, Charley got down pat doctrines he had heard in everyday snatches of dinner table discussion. Morally, he learned that slavery was an evil but one to be corrected by gradual legislation and the "mild diffusion" of the "light" of Christianity; that the "principal province" of religion is "promoting the happiness of our inferiors"; and that property is a conditional right, justified only by the good it does. Philosophically, he learned that all knowledge derives from "the impressions made on our senses by external objects," processed by innate powers implanted by

God in all human minds: clarity and precision being epistemological as well as literary obligata. Theologically, he learned that we know Christianity to be true from just this sort of logically construed empirical knowledge: from the study of nature and from the historical testimony of Jesus's miracles—as his own father had helped to demonstrate. As an adult, Norton would push these principles of knowledge to conclusions about religion that would have staggered his teachers and Andrews.[22]

Charley also read that knowledge did not exhaust understanding. Music filled Uncle Ticknor's drawing rooms; poetry lounged round the table at Shady Hill. The Scottish doctrine of the imagination explained their influence: not "a simple power of the mind," imagination comprises "a combination of various faculties"; its strength and range thus depends on cultivation, on "acquired habits." Imagination profoundly affects "human character and happiness," making us empathize with the pains and joys of others, overcome selfishness, "partake with a more lively interest" in our community. So it became clearer why, in well-ordered Boston, benevolence and the arts walked arm-in-arm and why, conversely, a perverted poet infected the state. Decades later, this doctrine of imagination, reworked, would provide the core of Norton's own pedagogy.[23]

History, too, depended on imagination, as other courses taught. The historian, Professor Sparks explained, had to enter imaginatively into past lives in order to recreate a dead era. The early history of Rome, Charley read, survived only in the imaginative realm of mythology. Customary institutions such as oracles and games had embodied and preserved "the character of the Greek nation"; works of art expressed Greek life and values; the "culture of the Greeks" traced back to their "thoroughly poetical" popular religion. There floated around Harvard College, at least in germ, an idea that grasped this teenager: that an act of historical imagination could extract the animating principles of any civilization from arid parchment and crumbling stone. Here echoed Andrews's familiar insistence on understanding the meanings of the Gospel texts by placing them in the mental world of antiquity. But here also emerged a more sophisticated melding of this philological method with the Scottish doctrine of the imagination and with German historicism. It would not be far from the mark to say that the seeds of Norton's lifelong intellectual project were germinating.[24]

Charley was an unusually reflective adolescent. All these ideas brought to fuller consciousness principles that suffused his milieu. He turned them over in his mind, now and for years to come, adjusting them to novel concepts he would encounter, growing aware of internal tensions and contradictions, drawing out conclusions that would in some cases take him far from his parents' world, though always following a compass set there.

He was growing up in other ways. In the summer of 1844, Charley took two excursions with a friend—and without adult accompaniment. One was to western Massachusetts and Connecticut, the other was through Vermont to Montreal then back via Ticonderoga and Lake George. When college reopened at the end of August, the two Charleys moved into rooms on the second floor of Holworthy Hall, the poshest of Harvard dorms and reserved mostly for seniors. Their ample sitting room, the neatly arrayed volumes of the *Encyclopedia Americana* lining the bookshelves, surveyed the heart of the yard, and each boy's chamber commanded a view of the countryside to the north: "the best room in the College, and the pleasantest," young Norton thought. Here they lived the two years until graduation.[25]

Situated now in the midst of college life, Charley expanded his circle. Since freshman year he had been good friends with a couple of intellectually inclined lads a class ahead, Edward Pringle of South Carolina and Manning Force of Washington. During his last two years Charley grew into a larger and more diverse acquaintance, becoming appreciative of "good company," beginning to notice that his family's friends "knew how to converse," developing an unusual capacity to empathize with widely different personalities. One of them was another neighbor in Holworthy, Francis Child. A working-class boy forwarded to Harvard on merchant largesse, Child was understandably "shy and diffident." Charley's mother and sisters were, Frank said, almost the first real ladies he had ever seen. Yet Child—"Stubby," after his physique—turned out "the best writer, the best speaker and the best mathematician, the most accomplished person in his knowledge of general literature in the class." These qualities appealed to a Norton, and during senior year Frank's round face and curly hair were more and more by Charley's side.[26]

Growing up never meant growing away from his family. Charley remained as much a fixture of Shady Hill as Tobias, the cat, curled up in the rocking chair. Charley took tea at the Palfreys' house across the fence; he rode with Jane and got lost. At home, his sisters were growing up, too, and growing into charming young women. With them and Mother he regularly attended Aunt Ticknor's sparkling receptions, hobnobbing with local celebrities like Daniel Webster and meeting foreign eminences like Charles Lyell and William Thackeray. Father usually preferred to stay home, but this by no means made him a recluse, for Shady Hill remained the center of Cambridge society. Within the concentric circles rippling out from his home, more than within the sphere of the college, Charley matured socially as well as intellectually.

Table talk at Shady Hill stretched the mind, and in these years it more and more turned to politics. The Nortons shared the Boston elite's untroubled assumption of its duty to lead, perched atop an unofficial hierarchy, guiding a legal democracy. But belief in hierarchy implied neither contempt for American republicanism nor enthusiasm for European aristocracy: quite the reverse. The domination of "rank and wealth" over even the "freest country of Europe"—the otherwise beloved England—mocked the formal equal protection of the law, producing poverty, misery, "intellectual debasement & vice." America escaped these evils because of "our political and civil institutions," including most notably general access to education, the staircase by which any citizen might rise. Late in 1844, Andrews (often housebound by illness these days) began an extensive comparative inquiry into poverty and its problems in Britain and the United States. His son gave him *The Wrongs of Women,* a "small book" on "the condition of the poor in England," which Andrews found "too *terribly* true" for Catharine to read. Yet relative prosperity was not the "first and fundamental difference" marking American exceptionalism; the crux rather was "that the laborer with us feels that he is a *man* and a *citizen.*"[27]

In this light, slavery appeared a cancer on the Republic. Yet even so grave a disease needed gradual healing, lest too drastic a treatment jolt republican institutions themselves and the orderly habits and property rights on which they rested. During Charley's senior year war broke out with Mexico: a war, the Nortons believed, fought to extend slavery. Moderation in the extirpation of evil was one thing; a war that would push the Republic deeper into the embrace of slavery quite another—and was "abominable."[28] These convictions the Nortons shared with most of the mercantile elite.

Yet his family continued to bend Charley's twig in directions oblique to the Boston norm: most obviously toward scholarship, as distinct from journalism. Uncle Ticknor's great *History of Spanish Literature* was inching closer to publication; and at the end of 1843 Andrews actually completed *Evidences of the Genuineness of the Gospels,* to New England's solemn admiration. And not just New England's: Charles Darwin read it, with (and probably prompted by) his devout wife Emma. For an American work, *Genuineness* was impressive in erudition, even daring in conclusions. Andrews indeed printed only "a very small edition," not wishing to "force" his unconventional views on the public. "If they are true they will gradually make their way." The patient accumulation of learning; the slow incubation of research; the blending of radical opinions into an essentially conservative outlook; the reach for a general readership but qualified by a reticence in pushing conclusions on unprepared readers and an unconcern about immediate acceptance: there was a particular ethic of scholarship here. Charley absorbed it, slowly, unconsciously, inevitably.[29]

He began even to display it. As one of the highest ranking members of his class during junior and senior years, Charley won a role in the College Exhibitions. Thrice annually he strutted in a black silk gown before family and friends gathered in the chapel—"great days," he later recalled, "for the undergraduates who took part in them." At first he delivered only a translation, but in July 1845 graduated to his own treatise, "The Recently Discovered Remains of the Ancient Etruscans." The topic reflected his deep interest in Italy, and Charley ransacked the library for material. The finished piece, largely descriptive (only a couple of tremolos of mystery thrown in for effect), showed real flair for detailed evocation of buildings and artifacts.[30]

Even the best behaved senior got restless. During February vacation Charley took a trip with his cousin Ned Dwight to Baltimore and Washington: dancing at balls till wee hours; hearing Congress debate the Oregon question; shaking the hand of General Winfield Scott, hero of the Mexican War; seeing an actual "slave pen" in the District of Columbia. In Baltimore he visited the newly built German Catholic church of Saint Alphonsus, designed in the Gothic style by the noted local architect Robert Carey Long Jr. Charley had seen Gothic-influenced structures before; this was his first thoroughly Gothic building—inside, "the most beautiful church I ever saw." It gave him "new ideas of the effect of architecture." The columns rose "with the most exquisite grace to meet the roof," fifty feet high in the nave, "and the light coming through beautifully stained glass windows, was mellowed and softened deliciously." Yet Charley already gazed with critical eye. He observed that the crowded-in pews compromised the openness of the nave, while the exuberantly gilded ornamentation clashed with the soft interior light (although he guessed that the gilding "when it becomes tarnished may relieve the dead color of the interior"). Marveling, he returned to Harvard with lessons that New England had yet no means to teach but that profoundly influenced his own cohering interests.[31]

In Cambridge, senior tedium was dissolving into anticipation, Charley drifting toward a serious choice. The ethic of Boston and of the Nortons demanded a useful career. Charley's varied talents and inclinations might have nudged in any direction, but no obvious vocation called. Andrews had long advised against following his own path into a clerical or a "merely literary" career; measuring his life against those of his wife's merchant relatives, Andrews suggested that Charley emulate them. The "business of the world" would prove more useful to others, more enjoyable to himself; and a career in commerce hardly ruled out literary activity. Indeed, "if he have talent as a literary man," the man of business "may secure time for its exercise" and, unwearied by study, "enjoy the pleasures of literature and knowledge with the keenest relish."[32]

The necessity of employment seems scarcely to have crossed Charley's mind until the approach of commencement forced the issue, but Andrews's advice made sense to him. He was a young man, eighteen now, who enjoyed life. He admired his father but had inherited his mother's gregarious temperament. Neither as self-centered nor as self-conscious as most males his age, he had a lot of friends. Granted, most came from his own little world, but he rubbed along well with others and with strangers, too. He had some taste for adventure. He enjoyed books and paintings, but they hardly filled his life. The tang of the salt sea begin to twitch his nostrils. Uncle Samuel Eliot reported that Henry Lee, partner in the East India house of Bullard & Lee, was seeking "a young man of merit to learn the theory & practice of that important profession which is vulgarly called 'business.'" Charles called at No. 39 India Wharf.[33]

On 16 July, Class Day arrived. The whole college gathered round the Liberty Tree near Holden Chapel to applaud the class of forty-six's upcoming liberation. "I have passed four most happy years here," Charley told his classmates, "happier than I ought to expect any other years of my life to be." He only regretted that the allure of Shady Hill, "joined with a natural taste for books, which has led me to seek for friends in them, has prevented me from being as much with you as I should have liked." Too late now; on 25 August the seniors attended their class dinner. If custom held, they drank more than they ate.[34]

The next morning the young men marched, or staggered, under a downpour to the new meetinghouse, where the bell that for four years had tolled them to chapel now foretold their commencement. "With dignity & grace" the new president, Edward Everett, assumed his seat in the three-legged president's chair, older than Massachusetts Hall. William Ladd Ropes (not Billy today) began the twenty-five senior speeches with a Latin salutatory oration. Charles Eliot Norton, ranking tenth in the class, earned a seven-minute "dissertation." Sounding a motif becoming characteristic of Norton, he evoked major actors of the Italian Renaissance—Dante, Michelangelo, Machiavelli, Galileo, Alfieri—in an imagined tour of their monuments in the Florentine church of Santa Croce. At last Francis James Child, first scholar of the class of 1846, arose to tumultuous applause to pronounce the valedictory oration: "Here we played a little, and there we slept a good deal, till finally we awoke, and found ourselves walking somewhat blindly on." On that ambiguous note, President Everett donned his academic cap and handed the graduates their degrees.[35]

Entering a countinghouse must have seemed as natural to Charles as going to Harvard. Both his grandfathers had been merchants, one on a noteworthy scale. His closest uncle, Samuel Eliot, belonged to the brotherhood; so did Uncle Edmund Dwight, out in Springfield, and Uncle Thomas Wigglesworth, practically round the corner from Charles's new employers. Uncle Thomas (married to Andrews's sister) had made a fortune in exactly Charley's new line, trading to India.

Making a fortune, though, was not the main thing. Just as his family tied Charles to Boston's merchants, so, too, they instilled in him the values animating that elite. And money getting was no proper goal of life. As he entered Bullard & Lee's countinghouse in September 1846, Charles recorded in his commonplace book two lines from Coleridge:

What wouldst thou have a great good man obtain?
Place—titles—salary—a gilded chain?

The anxiety may have weighed especially heavily on Charles. His parents, even his older sisters, had repeatedly impressed on him that duty grew heavier in proportion to privilege, that only public usefulness could justify private wealth. Uncle Samuel reported that some of Boston's "damsels" indeed wondered that "a young man of so much delicacy of mind should choose to give up literary pursuits, & go into the rough intercourse of the world, & the seemingly meaner pursuits of commerce."[36]

Seemingly. It came down to how one pursued commerce and to what end. Charley chewed these worries, as had countless Boston merchants from the days of John Winthrop. On one hand, to devote oneself to making money was morally dubious, mentally dulling. On the other, commerce offered as wide a scope for intellect as for profit. Uncle Samuel assured Charley that a merchant in foreign trade had opportunities to exercise his mind in no way inferior to those of "the scientific or literary man." True, an apprentice would hardly guess this; learning the tools of the trade entailed a good deal of "very odious labor." But so did acquiring the tools of German-model scholarship, as Stubby Child had set out to do. Samuel urged his nephew to regard the tedium as like "fagging at the grammar & dictionary of a new language."[37]

If the initiation was wearying, the fraternity was noble. Charles Norton entered Bullard & Lee at the start of the most prosperous decade in Massachusetts's maritime history. And of all Bay State traders, the East India merchant carried his head highest. In Boston he "possessed social *kudos* to which no cotton millionaire could pretend"; Cape Codders complimented a young woman by calling her "good enough to marry an East-India Cap'n." The trade with British India, begun in the commercial chaos that followed the outbreak of the French revolutionary wars, had nearly gone extinct when British commerce revived after Napoleon's defeat. It was saved by a Yankee commodity that Great Britain could not produce: ice. By 1846, the trade flourished on the export not only of ice but also of an ingenious miscellany besides and of the import of hides, linseed, shellac, saltpeter, gunny bags to pack Ohio's corn, gunny cloth to bale Alabama's cotton, indigo to dye New England's textiles, and jute for rope to tie it all together. Seldom, though, was an East India merchant so imprudent as to cast his fortunes exclusively on the markets of Calcutta and Madras. Bullard & Lee, for instance, also kept a hand in the South American trade. To Buenos Aires and Rio went pine boards from Maine and cotton sheeting from Lowell; there came back wool, hides, sheepskins, tallow, and sixteen million pounds of coffee.[38]

All these goods and more crammed the warehouses of India Wharf, a great brick block extending hundreds of yards out into Boston Harbor. On ground level were thirty-two stores, with counting rooms and warehouses occupying the three stories above; smells of saltwater, hemp, and tar, aromas of cinnamon, pepper, and coffee tickled Norton's nose when he arrived at No. 39. His bosses there made an oddly matched pair. Henry Lee Jr. was "a Bostonian *pur sang,*" William Bullard not even a New Englander—"a strain of Southern blood," Norton believed. Orphaned young, Bullard turned up penniless in Boston, where a family took him in, got him schooling, and placed him in the India trade. By the time Norton met him, he stood on equal footing with his patrician partner. Both were "comparatively" young in 1846, and Charles liked them both. Lee's ardent love for the theater may have stoked Charles's enthusiasm for drama, which warmed noticeably during the countinghouse years. Yet Bullard attracted him more. A "man of fine character, delicate, sensitive, strong," somewhat withdrawn, intellectually serious, given to metaphysical speculation, Bullard read widely, despite lack of a college education. Charles may have sensed in him experiences and feelings akin to some of his own.[39]

Mostly, for now, he sensed in him a boss. By nine o'clock every morning except Sunday, a passerby might notice through the small-paned windows Charles's pale oval face bent over a calfbound ledger, "casting up columns of figures, or copying mercantile letters." He riffled through wooden chests, each holding the carefully filed records of a single vessel. He learned to make up accounts, to draw up bills of lading, to write invoices. It was probably a welcome break when Lee or Bullard sent him to settle some payment with the customhouse. A slack hour might find him perched on a high stool, his left hand pushing dark brown hair back from his high forehead while his right slowly turned the pages of a treatise on bookkeeping. He perfected more than the merchant's legible hand. Stroke by stroke, Norton forged habits of accuracy and attention to detail, essential in commerce, perduring through life.[40]

This routine was shattered whenever a bluff-bowed, three-masted East Indiaman docked for Bullard & Lee. That winter, Charles learned how it felt to shiver on the wharf, dawn to dark, accounting for each bag of coffee and bale of goatskins as the ship's hold disgorged them in rapid succession. In summer he sweltered over boxes of indigo and bales of gunny, trying to keep his brain alert. A single missed box, and he would find himself inside a steaming storeroom, going over the whole shipment, "often tearing down the piles that had been carefully made," to determine whether the mistake was his or the shipper's.[41]

Shady Hill seemed more welcome than ever. Charley boarded the horse-drawn omnibus in Boston, crossed the long causeway over the Charles, and rode two miles farther to "the village," as Harvard Square was then known. Only forty-five minutes in good weather, the journey could last twice as long when the horses had to struggle through dirt roads made mires by rain. When Charley climbed down from the 'bus in the village, he walked home up Kirkland Street past the familiar smells of wild azalea, apple blossoms, and the manure of Shady Hill's cows.[42]

There was no question of Charley moving out on his own. He and his family behaved as if he would never leave and as if only marriage could tear his sisters from Shady Hill. Nor did starting a career make independence even a theoretical possibility. The nominal salary paid an apprentice by Bullard & Lee—plus the cash Charles picked up now and then by selling samples and damaged goods on his own account—did not begin to cover expenses. These varied wildly but averaged around $50 a month: meals out, a play or a concert, clothes, and above all (a third of his outlay) books, magazines, and the *Daily Whig*. Andrews provided an allowance of $25 per month; Catharine was generous with odd sums here and there; and room and board came free. Nonetheless, starting out with $33 in assets in September 1846, Charley was down to $15.64 at the end of 1847.[43]

India Wharf did not monopolize his hours. Except when a ship berthed, Charles's workday allowed him to return to Shady Hill in time for the leisurely family dinner around three o'clock. There were long, relaxed family evenings around the fire in Andrews's study, Gracie or Jane reading aloud from the new number of *Living Age,* Magnus curled in canine content on the carpet, a servant bearing in a supper of cheese and crackers or a dish of oysters to end the night. Charley also frequented concerts, performances of Shakespeare, the perpetual lectures, sometimes accompanying Catharine and his sisters, sometimes taking Frank Child, sometimes escorting President Everett's pretty daughter Charlotte, with whom he seems to have had an on-again, off-again relationship. Even the lectures were a social as much as an intellectual occasion, Norton and his companion strolling in half an hour before the speaker started, wandering from seat to seat, chatting with old acquaintances, meeting new ones. Afterward, some friend would ask them home for supper and more conversation.

Almost imperceptibly, Charles was loosening the bonds to his family. Andrews's growing feebleness strengthened his son's autonomy. Neither adult enough to assume the headship of the household nor child enough to take great satisfaction in the ever more female atmosphere of Shady Hill, Charles found interests elsewhere. In one sense, he was only maturing, as other young men did. For him, though, the home ties that restrained ripening were unusually strong. Andrews's decline weakened the force field of a magnetic and much-admired father, an embracing and much-loved home, and freed Charles not to reject Andrews and Shady Hill but to incorporate them into a persona increasingly formed by his own hands.

Charley was not cutting his ties, only stretching them. He still enjoyed seeing the Shady Hill friends: his old Greek professor Cornelius Felton, Henry Longfellow and his bride Fanny, and the rest. He still traveled up the North Shore to Manchester to stay with the Ticknors at their summer house, The Cliffs. His oldest friend, Charley Guild, he saw almost daily. But one of his newest, Stubby Child, shared Norton's more enduring literary interests; in the lengthening autumn evenings, they kept their Greek in shape by reading the *Odyssey* together. Frank's round face and unruly curls became almost a part of the furnishings of Shady Hill. Charles Mills, a member of Norton's infinite cousinage and a fellow businessman in Boston, also spent many free hours with Norton; welcomed at Shady Hill, he still was, like Child, much more Charles's friend than the family's. Even more so was another business acquaintance, George Livermore, who rarely set foot in Cambridge. Livermore was "a devoted lover of good books, & an accomplished collector of them"; it was perhaps under his tutelage that Norton's fascination with old editions began to ripen into expertise.[44]

For, consonant with the Boston ideal, the countinghouse left ample room for the pursuit of culture. In James Perkins's old mansion on Pearl Street, Norton had available the resources of the Boston Athenaeum. The substantial library there may have mattered less to him than the Athenaeum's permanent art gallery and its yearly exhibitions, for Charles's curiosity about the visual arts was expanding. Boston owned a few "first class paintings" and possibly the best collection of statuary in the country (mostly casts of European works). Among Charles's regular expenditures from 1846 on was a monthly payment to the Art Union.[45]

A passive gaze did not satisfy Norton. When the countinghouse relaxed for the summer of 1847, Charles geared up for his first effort at publication. Appearing in print was normal for a Boston merchant of his inclinations; and Francis Bowen, the family friend then editing the *North American,* may well have encouraged him. The only question was the subject. Norton had acquired Coleridge's *Table Talk* just before graduation and, with it, a horrified fascination with Coleridgean doctrine. "Folly" and "Silly" peppered the margins of his copy. Coleridge's Trinitarian Christianity irritated Charles's Unitarianism, and his transcendentalist metaphysics seemed as fuzzy to Charley as to his Harvard teachers and his father. Still, somehow it drew Charles in; and respect for Coleridge's powers mitigated inherited scorn for his philosophy.[46]

Under the usual pretext of an anonymous book review, Norton composed a forty-page critical biography of the poet, which appeared in the *North American* for October 1847. He was not quite twenty. The article showed assiduous reading of the Coleridgean corpus and of a mass of memoirs of the poet: diligence displayed in Harvard exhibitions had ripened in the countinghouse. (Norton evidently missed, however, the keenest assessment, John Stuart Mill's in the March 1840 *Westminster Review.* The radical *Westminster* did not hobnob with the *Edinburgh* on proper Boston's drawing room tables.) But thoroughness in research was less striking than authority in tone, Charles adopting an authorial posture as commanding as his father's. But where Andrews reasoned, Charles pronounced. "The criticism on Wordsworth's poetry in the Biographia Literaria seems to us in many respects exceedingly happy." Period. Keen readers may have suspected camouflage, imperiousness of utterance disguising poverty of analysis. That skill, after all, had formed no part of his education. Perhaps this explains why Norton devoted far more pages to describing the life than to commenting on the works.[47]

Most of his dicta were predictable, but not all. Coleridge's early discipleship to "metaphysical and theological writers" who wallowed in "obscure speculations" had "bewildered and unsettled a mind originally not well balanced." Charley had heard the grim story from Andrews: a youngster experiments with a little Kant, ends an opium eater. Unstable in principles, fickle in purpose, Coleridge became an awful warning of the perils of the hyperactive imagination. Yet Norton, too, was eager to dabble in some new views. Flatly astonishing for Andrews's son, he gave high marks to *Aids to Reflection*, a farrago of Germanic "obscure speculations" if ever there was one. Fickle principles seemed at least as much Norton's problem as Coleridge's, though fickleness may, in Charles's case, have been less apt a term than youth.[48]

His opinion of the biographer's art, however, was as fixedly Bostonian as his understanding of the imagination's role was fluid.

> The highest interest and the only value which biography can possess must consist in its truth. The lights and the shades should be set off one against another, the springs of action should be shown; and when the whole has been told, the judgment may well be left to others, with an assured belief that time will bring about a righteous verdict. We would not be understood here as recommending that minute scrutiny of a man's life which would bring to light those details which can only gratify a malicious spirit or a childish curiosity. . . . What we would urge is, that there should be no concealment of that which is of real importance in forming a true estimate of the character.

And, in the article's concluding judgment, Norton ringingly reaffirmed the New England clerisy's version of noblesse oblige. Every man must account to his fellows for the talents entrusted to his care. "The greater those talents, the greater becomes his responsibility."[49]

Pace his puzzling respect for *Aids to Reflection*, Charles judged Coleridge by pretty nearly his father's standard. The criterion was very much before him as he wrote. Frail health had not stayed Andrews's scholarship, only forced him to hire an assistant, a former student named Ezra Abbot. Probably in the summer of 1847, Andrews began both a supplementary volume to *Genuineness* (proving the Gospels' authenticity from internal evidence) and an actual translation of the Gospels meant to achieve unprecedented verbal precision. Father's new work went hand in hand with his son's contempt for Coleridge's intuitionist metaphysic. Did not Unitarianism teach that exact reasoning from carefully weighed evidence gave the only warrant for religious belief?[50]

And religion mattered to Charley. The entries in his commonplace book in these years suggest aspiration to Unitarian sainthood. A high-minded, conventionally religious young man, he sought anxiously to do good to others, even (or especially) at pain to himself. He prized duty and character but understood both as oriented toward helpfulness: here sounded the New England Calvinist doctrine of "benevolence" retuned in an anthropocentric Unitarian key. A gentleness infused his ideals; his duty was not the muscular sort, preached famously in this period by Charles Kingsley. At one point he quoted Coleridge: "A feminine tenderness, and almost maidenly purity of feeling, and above all a deep moral earnestness." He showed mild ambition for an honored name, none for wealth and power. (A luxury he could afford.) But all remained vague, even abstract, in a slightly troubling way. A note of soft anxiety haunted these pages. *How* was his life to be useful? This was the key question that his ancestral religion posed for Charley. And religion could hardly *not* matter to a son of Andrews and Catharine Norton.[51]

Nor could it fail to form a locus of recurrent intellectual inquiry. The question was what form the inquiry would take. Andrews seems to have provided Charles "sufficient reasons" to convince him of Christianity's truth. Although Charles wrote a poem about this time treating the wreck of faith in the wake of personal tragedy, he was almost certainly only aping the literature of doubt then being written by celebrated English authors. The "waves of doubt" in Charley's verses had not yet washed over him.[52] One thing, though, did set him a little apart from his parents: references to the afterlife are sparser in Charley's correspondence and private scribblings than in their letters. He had inherited a full measure of the Unitarian moral striving for earthly good, but this somehow seemed to push the transcendent into more remote geography. Charles was anxious to write for the *North American*. The *Christian Examiner* never figured in his aspirations.

Duty to the less fortunate always did. The distressed Irish pouring into Boston formed just then a subject of concern at Shady Hill; so Norton perhaps took special note when the *North American* in January 1847 commended to the attention of "the 'merchant princes' of Boston" an "excellent report" on improved tenements for the poor.[53] In any case, he got the notion somewhere; and it took root, to flower in a few years. Other evils, though farther from hand, now pressed more urgently.

First among them was the controversy over slavery. The issue was not its right or wrong. Patrician Boston agreed that moral progress rendered enslavement indefensible. The question was what to do about it. In their zeal to put wrong right, a growing abolitionist faction was willing to risk tearing the Republic apart and, the Nortons feared, rending the fabric of their own community irreparably. Better to let slavery be slowly corroded by its own inefficiencies and the spread of enlightened morals. These characteristically cautious views, widely shared among the Boston elite, fitted its conservative reformism and its Scottish theories of the evolution of civilization. Now the Mexican War was altering the terms of debate. Should slavery, that relic of less civilized times, extend to lands wrested from Mexico? Even respectable citizens began to waver under the Free-Soilers' persuasions, including the Nortons' neighbor John Gorham Palfrey and their talented young friend Charles Sumner, who had shown much kindness to Charley. But Free-Soiler "philanthropy" reminded Andrews of "the days of Robespierre," "rabid and ferocious," exciting "the feelings of the community," unsettling good order.[54]

Such revulsion from abolitionist tactics was visceral, welling up from Boston's native brand of utopianism, hearkening back to the Puritan ideal voiced by John Winthrop on board the *Arbella:* "that every man might have need of other, and from hence they might be all knit more nearly together in the bounds of brotherly affection." This organicist conservatism in its latter-day republican and Unitarian avatar, rooted in a Federalist past, persisting into the Whig present, overheard by a child at Shady Hill, and expounded at Harvard College, set Charles's stance toward the slavery question and to other disturbances in the state. Leaving India Wharf on 18 March 1848, he heard an *Evening Traveller* newsboy crying of revolution in France; Chartist agitation was already roiling Britain. For no sort of agitators did he have much sympathy; but he shivered at "the enormous inequalities of rank & condition, the grinding oppression worse often than slavery, & the horrid suffering connected with all this, which exists in England." He was "almost ready to believe that no change, however violent, could bring about a worse state of things."[55]

Yet, ideally, change altered habits and institutions by imperceptible evolution, of the sort that the Scottish writers had explicated. Thus had generations of town-meeting government turned monarchist Englishmen into republican New Englanders; thus had eons of wind and water reshaped the face of the Earth. (Fifteen years earlier Sir Charles Lyell—whom Charley had met during an 1841 lecture tour—had proved this latter fact in his

Principles of Geology. The analogy was exact and demonstrated the congruity of all nature's laws, material and moral.) The commonwealth was no "encampment of tents on the great prairie, pitched at sundown, and struck to the sharp crack of the rifle next morning." Just as present grew from past, so a shared history nurtured ties of mutual obligation, thickened them with years, binding the citizenry to each other in an organic whole. To rip these tendrils was to shred the growth of centuries, to inflict a wound that could heal only with decades—if then.[56]

Even in 1848, Charles's attention naturally centered less often on the barricades in Paris or the Halls of Montezuma than on India Wharf. The judgment on his apprenticeship lay many months away yet. Interim accounting indicated progress. Charles still lived principally on his twenty-five-dollar monthly allowance from Andrews and Catharine's supplements to it; but he was now pulling in a little more from "the store": ten to fifteen dollars a month on average in 1848.[57]

That bit of cash represented a big step in his training as a merchant. After sixteen months of tutelage, he began trading with India on his own account. Apprenticeship was not over by a long shot. Prosperity in the trade depended on amassing the knowledge and honing the judgment needed to assess both the quality of and the market for a bewildering variety of goods. Success also required developing reliable contacts with, and personal reputation among, both bankers and factors: the former usually British firms, the latter on the spot in Calcutta or Madras. All this required years, not months, of learning.

Learning to steer on his own advanced Norton to a crucial stage in that training. While his mundane duties at Bullard & Lee continued, he now had his own bankers to provide credit and to exchange bills (Baring Brothers of London for foreign transactions; the Boston Bank for domestic ones); his own agent to advise him on Indian markets and complete transactions for him there (Richard Lewis of Calcutta); and his own accounts to keep. True, the bankers and the agent were passed along from Bullard & Lee; and in other ways, too, Charles sailed in his masters' wake, benefiting from their advice in his maiden enterprises, getting better prices in Calcutta because Lewis lumped his "interest" with theirs. A partner or two was normal in Boston's East India trade, especially for younger and less substantial merchants, to provide more capital and spread the risk—still considerable, despite marine insurance and improved navigation. Sometimes Norton pooled resources with Bullard or Richard Lewis but, most often in these first ventures, with his old chum Charles Guild. He imported indigo and "lac dye";

saltpeter; linseed; straw rugs; jute, hemp, and twine; cow, buffalo, and goat hides; and—greatest in volume—gunny cloth and gunny bags. Small-scale, but the real thing.[58]

Yet it was far from all-consuming. Charles found time to write a sarcastic notice of Raffaele Capobianco's *Breve Racconto delle Cose Chiesastiche più Importanti, occorse nel Viaggio fatto sulla Real Fregate Urania, dal 15 Agosto, 1844, al 4 Marzo, 1846* for the January 1848 *North American*, making fun of Capobianco's confusions about Boston, displaying Norton's own orthodox anti-Catholicism, and proving that his Italian was up to snuff. The same issue of the *North American* introduced Norton to an eccentric book by a young English art critic named John Ruskin. The "strange opinions" voiced in *Modern Painters* astounded the reviewer, but Charles went out and bought it. On a brief visit to New York City with Jane and Louisa that spring, he negotiated a rather more substantial book purchase: a number of volumes from George Washington's library. Andrews and Jared Sparks, Charley's old history professor, had set about raising five thousand dollars to get them for the Athenaeum. The effort succeeded, and Charles and George Livermore then prepared a catalogue of them, intending to produce "the best specimen of a work of the kind that has ever been printed in this country."[59]

This was far from his only literary project. Taken with Sir Arthur Helps's *Friends in Council*, published in 1847 in London, Norton got Helps's permission and arranged an American edition. And it was likely Norton the bibliophile who helped Frank Child lay hands on the extremely rare 1820 Roxburghe Club printing of four sixteenth-century plays; Child added a powerful critical apparatus and published the whole as *Four Old Plays* in 1848. The work, unlike any done before in America, established Child "as a scholar of more than usual competence of learning and sobriety of judgment." Harvard was grooming Stubby to succeed the aging Edward Channing and would soon send him to study in Germany.[60]

Another Frank, a newer friend four years older than Charley, called on his literary skill more directly. Charles must have earlier crossed paths with Francis Parkman, but perhaps their mutual cousin Ned Dwight really brought them together now. In any case, Charley's "extraordinary, almost feminine talent for intimacy" quickly made him Frank's closest confidante. Parkman, recently returned from the Far West, was casting his adventures into *The Oregon Trail*. As fall 1848 turned into winter 1849, many an evening found the two friends huddled together on a pair of high stools "in the solitary counting room" revising Parkman's proofs. Charles toned down the saga to fit Boston taste (as Parkman wished), reducing the whiskey and the sex. Parkman in turn aided Charles by example: his gift for dramatic narrative fed into Charles's own sense of history, mightily exemplifying Jared Sparks's doctrine of imagination and afforcing Charley's aspirations.[61]

The latest expression of these aspirations was an article for the October *North American* on the English reformer William Tyndale. With Child's example before him, Charles threw himself into research, reading modern biographies and Reformation-era writings from Latimer to More. He emerged with a straightforward thirty-page biography of Tyndale, supplying a capsule history of the English Reformation. The article displayed what was becoming Norton's characteristic mode as biographer and historian: a chronological narrative built around long quotations from original sources, especially letters and similar documents, and meant to show great ideas and events in a small mirror. It did *not* display the "pepper and allspice" that Frank Parkman was urging him to add to his writing.[62]

Mildness of expression implied no blandness of taste. Norton's latest enthusiasm, American archaeology, seemed spicy enough for Boston. Probably Parkman had put him onto the work of E. G. Squier, a rough-edged character who in 1847 had explored with care and intelligence the vestiges of the mysterious Mound Builder Indians in the Ohio Valley. By November, Norton was spending his evenings—at least those not demanded by Bullard & Lee or devoted to Shakespeare or Charlotte Everett—writing about Mound Builders.

Such hobbies did not interfere with his real career. On 22 February, William Bullard presented Charles with that most Bostonian of gifts, a share in the Athenaeum, "in evidence of my unqualified approbation of your conduct in our counting house."[63] Only one step remained before the apprentice became a master. In the East India trade—as in most commerce in those days—merchants relied on counterparts across the seas. Traders in Calcutta and Madras provided their opposite numbers in Boston with current information and informed predictions about Indian markets. A merchant's success thus depended heavily on his personal knowledge of both Indian merchants and Indian markets. Whose judgment could you trust, and how should you interpret it?

Norton's finishing lessons as a merchant, then, must take place in India. Bullard & Lee arranged to send him as supercargo on the East Indiaman *Milton*, chartered by the firm to sail in May. As supercargo, his job was to oversee the cargo and its eventual sale and, as advanced apprentice, to acquaint himself with local merchants and markets. Norton meant the trip to

be educational in another way. Curious about India, its peoples, its governance, its gods, its books, its monuments, he planned to take several months
"to look about him in the East."[64] And more conventionally, he would not
pass up the chance to go on to Europe and see the places and pictures and
churches and statues about which he had so long read and heard.

First came a shorter trip. Toward the end of February, he set out for
Washington to witness Zachary Taylor's inauguration. On the way he
stopped in New York to talk with Parkman's publisher about the engravings
for *The Oregon Trail*—and to meet the intriguing Squier. Parkman feared
that Norton, with his "strict and precise" education, could hardly get on well
with so flamboyant a character as Squier, but Parkman underestimated the
capaciousness of Norton's talent for friendship. The two crammed weeks of
talk into a couple of days—talk about Indian remains, to be sure, but talk,
too, about Squier's unorthodox life and religious skepticism. "His whole
appearance & manner is that of a man of excitable temperament, perhaps of
genius." Charles dug into "a body of his mss on the subject of American
Archaeology"; the similarities Squier pointed out between the religious
symbols of American Indians and those of the ancient civilizations of the
Old World amazed him. When Norton finally had to leave on the evening
of the twenty-sixth, he wrote his father to request the *North American* "to
defer the printing of my article till I return. With the knowledge I have
gained here I can make it much better, more worthy of the Review."[65]

The huzzahs and parties surrounding the presidential inauguration were
almost an anticlimax; back home, Charles hurried to finish the Squier article for the April *North American* before his big journey began. All of his
excitement ended in what he called "a mere abstract" of *Ancient Monuments
of the Mississippi Valley*. This digest ended with a patriotic flourish. The
infant "science of Ethnology" will reap its "richest harvest" in America; for
there "the interesting and anomalous civilization of its ancient inhabitants"
coexisted with a present ethnic diversity found "nowhere else." "Highly
important conclusions" about "the distribution and progress of our race"
hung in the balance. Norton urged the country's "historical" and "literary"
societies to join in financing a great collaborative investigation.[66]

This suggestion withered on rocky ground, but Norton's encounter with
archaeology did fertilize his own thinking, nurturing ideas already planted.
Squier's ethnological investigations fitted within a conventional Scottish
Enlightenment view of the "progress of civilization" up from savagery; more
specifically, he accepted the historicist principle that specifics of time and
place shaped ideas and institutions. All this Norton had earlier learned, both

at home and at Harvard. But Squier showed him concretely how archaeology provided tools for deeper understanding of the slow evolution of civilization and how, in turn, this evolution itself gave universal meaning and form to archaeology. Archaeology, as an ethnological or cultural science, could become the great revealer of humanity's upward path. The Mound Builders receded into Norton's past, but this conception of archaeology endured in his thinking, with eventual consequences far from anything Squier imagined.

Meanwhile, Squier's ideas about the place of religion in the progress of civilization set Charles to thinking. This was no surprise; any American planning a trek across India in 1849 would have had "primitive religion" on his mind. Squier assumed that religion, like other facets of civilization, evolved from primitive to advanced forms. Again, so far, nothing new; the Scots had suggested the same thing a century earlier. Boston Unitarianism defined itself on this schema: first Judaism then Christianity had shaken off successive layers of primitive superstition until finally emerged the pure truth proclaimed by Andrews Norton. But Squier evidently carried familiar logic a dangerous step further. Might the progress of intellect leave Christianity itself behind? A scattering of English writers had already decided that it had, as Charles well knew; and so had a few of New England's fuzzy-minded Transcendentalists. But Squier was neither a name on a page nor a mystagogue; he was an actual friend and a clear-thinking man of science.

He had given Charles a lot to ponder, but for the time being India demanded full attention. Trunks appeared at Shady Hill, to be crammed with clothes, utensils, and oddments for two winters and two summers in two antipodal climates. He would have a companion on the *Milton*—a classmate, Montgomery Ritchie, sailing for his own mercantile seasoning— but also endless hours on shipboard, slow travel across the subcontinent, lone nights in Europe. Books went into the boxes: and ink and paper, for, as Uncle Samuel reminded him, a traveler wanted to record all the novelties he encountered. His mission of self-education required letters of introduction. Uncle Ticknor, whose friends ranged from Metternich to King John of Saxony, could alone have filled his nephew's European calendar. The secretary of the evangelical American Board of Commissioners of Foreign Missions supplied a letter to the board's missionaries (an odd document for a Unitarian to carry); the American Oriental Society, an introduction to the Emperor of Delhi.[67]

On 27 April 1849 he got his passport. Friends sent gifts: a writing kit, a traveling case, books. Frank Parkman gave him a great bone-handled hunting knife, Uncle Samuel the pocket edition of Virgil that he himself had carried to Europe twenty-eight years before.[68] Charley was excited but sober. He would not return for at least two years. Travel was dangerous, disease deadly: he might not return at all. He gave his parents a bound volume of his own published writings: "What I have done is yours, what I have to do is yours." He said farewell to Charlotte.[69]

Late in the morning of 21 May, cargo secured, masts creaking, friends waving from the dock, the *Milton* slipped away from India Wharf. By half past noon she was six miles out, ready to leave her pilot and Boston Harbor.[70] Andrews had given him a letter to open at sea:

> I feel how blessed we both are, that you are entering on this new era of your life under circumstances so peculiarly favorable. . . . You leave behind you also an unsullied reputation, and a belief common to all who know you, that you have more than common power of doing good.
>
> These are not things to make one vain. On the contrary, their true tendency is to produce that deep sense of responsibility,—of what we owe to God, to our friends, and to our fellow men—, which is wholly inconsistent with presumption and vanity.[71]

In his old age Charles Norton considered that, until that May morning, he had "led a narrow life, in a sense, of domestic seclusion in Cambridge,— pleasant, good for a foundation,—but the circumstances were fortunate which finally took me out of it and enlarged my vision of the world." A few months before sailing, he had jotted in his commonplace book some lines of Washington Irving: "As I saw the last blue line of my native land fade away like a cloud in the horizon, it seemed as if I had closed one volume of the world & its concerns, & had time for meditation before I opened another."[72]

THREE

The World, 1849–1851

Time for meditation he would have aplenty, but first Charles savored the novelty of life at sea. The *Milton* was no Leviathan—around five hundred tons burthen, maybe 140 feet long and 30 abeam. But she could carry a sky full of Lowell cotton duck on her three tall masts and "tack in a pint o' water." It followed that she rolled and tossed in even a moderate sea. Norton discovered with relief an immunity to seasickness. The fifteen or so crew members struck him as able, the captain intelligent and kindhearted, the *Milton* herself "an excellent ship." Fair winds had her halfway to Africa by 1 June.[1]

Norton's days settled into routine. Along with his classmate Montgomery Ritchie and the first mate, he took his meals at the captain's "excellently supplied" table. As supercargo, Norton had on shipboard the status of an officer and the substance of a wraith. Entirely responsible for cargo in port, he had no duties at sea. The steward woke him at half past six. After breakfast (at half past seven), Norton and Ritchie dawdled on deck for half an hour; after dinner (half past twelve), a cigar absorbed another half hour; after tea (six o'clock) they strolled the weather deck till dark, then lay down there "on our plaids to talk together, or to think of home." "By nine we are in our berths."[2]

Charles got stimulation from long hours reading in his cabin or, in fair weather, on deck. He exercised his German on Alexander von Humboldt's *Kosmos,* his French on Victor Jacquemont's travels, his Latin and Greek on Horace and Herodotus. He honed his powers of observation and narrative in lengthy letters home and a journal of the voyage. His "light reading" included Milton, Shakespeare, most often "some Eastern traveller." Austen Layard's account of the recent discovery of Nineveh fascinated the archaeologist in him; Norton planned to see the excavations for himself. A well-informed selection of books on India prepared him for more immediate encounters: Mountstuart Elphinstone's *History of India* prior to the British conquest; James Mill's *History of British India;* Edmund Burke's speeches on India and Bishop Reginald Heber's travels through it; the Koran and the *Laws of Manu.*[3]

What Charles extracted from this Indian mélange is hard to say except for two points: the low state of India, the lofty destiny of his own country. Even fairly sympathetic British observers thought that Indian civilization, once high, now lay sunk in ignorance, superstition, and immorality. His reading implicitly confirmed that he had left behind "the country which is the happiest on earth," but one with "responsibilities" commensurate with its great privileges. As to whether India's misery was "the fault of the people or of the government," Norton felt uncertain. And he "missed more than anything else" his father's "advice and judgement" upon such doubtful points, feeling constantly how much he "owed to the principles of thought and judgement" that Andrews had imparted.[4]

Such musings were set against a flat infinity of sky and water. Week after monotonous week slipped by. When even his leather-bound tomes grew heavy, Charles amused himself by observing seabirds. The *Milton* plowed southward; the air chilled. By 22 July the ship was rounding the Cape of Good Hope. Five days later a gale lashed her with "immense waves" that sent the fore topgallant mast crashing down. Charley reported himself not terrified but exhilarated: a young man's taste for adventure. After repairs, a cool Antarctic wind blew the ship north. On the afternoon of 29 August the watch at the masthead spied Ceylon to the west. An offshore breeze blew sweetly fragrant: Charles imagined walking past a bed of violets or lilies of the valley. On Saturday morning, 1 September, the *Milton* hove to off Madras, anchoring opposite the great white Ice House. She had made the fastest passage from Boston to Madras on record, 102 days.[5]

Arrival at Madras tried a supercargo's nerves. The city lacked a harbor for a ship to dock, so within half an hour *masoolah* boats built like a huge "transverse section of a pear or pumpkin" had crowded the *Milton's* decks with "black & naked natives" who "knew few English words but 'money' & 'eat.'" Norton sent a message to Bainbridge & Co., the British house engaged to handle the *Milton's* business, introducing himself and requesting the long-awaited letters from home sent via London over the faster overland route. Three hours later a boat from Bainbridge arrived—but no letters from Shady Hill. "I never before had such a disappointment." There was nothing for it. Norton and Ritchie ordered their trunks into Bainbridge's *masoolah*

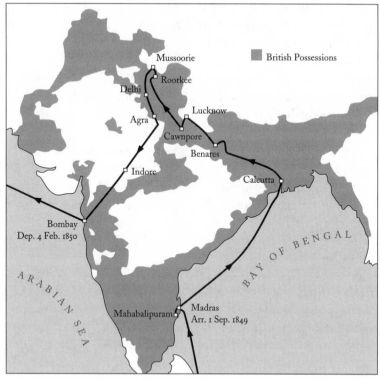

Norton's Route across India, 1849–1850.

boat. Their feet dangling helplessly from planks laid across the high thwarts to serve as seats, an awning shielding them from relentless sun, the two Harvard boys met India.[6]

Bainbridge's head invited Norton to stay with him at his house three miles in the country. Already, Charles "had learned enough of Indian customs" to hire a servant, who awaited in his chamber: a room fifty feet by twenty-five, with a ceiling twenty feet high (to let the heat rise) and a bathroom attached. The servant kept the *punkah* going. Norton was learning Anglo-Indian ways.[7]

In this strange new world Europeans enjoyed privilege in inverse proportion to their tiny numbers. The Honourable East India Company dominated the subcontinent. Its directors in London appointed both the soldiers who commanded the company's mainly Indian troops and the "civilians" who staffed its bureaucracy and administered European justice. (The term "civilian" applied in India only to these company officials.) Fewer than forty thousand British troops and scarcely more than a thousand civilians ruled a hundred million people directly and kept on a short leash another fifty million in "independent" principalities. A few thousand merchants, planters, missionaries, and miscellaneous others made up the rest of the European population. They lived, for the most part, in proconsular luxury that made the affluence of Shady Hill seem downright democratic. Norton discovered that, when a horse pulled a carriage, its groom had to run alongside, no matter how hot the sun, no matter how far or fast the travel. To Charley Guild he deplored the "things of this sort, & of much worse character in the treatment of the natives." To his hosts he said nothing. He was there to make money and "to look about him."[8]

Making money left plenty of time to look about—to visit the mint, to investigate the noxious slums of Black Town (the Indian quarter), to dine with the artillery officers at nearby Saint Thomas Mount. Several days after arriving, Norton and Ritchie traveled the forty miles south to Mahabalipuram, ancient City of Seven Pagodas. To escape the wilting daytime sun, they set out in the evening, carried in palanquins, each borne by two alternating teams of six men apiece. They arrived at six o'clock in the morning and camped for the day in a deserted temple. The great *rathas*—the "pagodas"—with their complex scenes of Hindu mythology carved out of massive outcroppings of rock reduced Norton to puzzled admiration. Each temple "deserved the study of hours rather than the hasty glance of a tired traveller on a hot & sultry morning." The traveler could identify a few gods, but the world they inhabited eluded his empathy. He sat and read Southey's faux-Hindu "Curse of Kehama" (set partly at Mahabalipuram) and meditated on the "fallen gods" of Hinduism.[9]

For the "fallen power" of "Brahmin" religion that he perceived in Mahabalipuram's *rathas* gave the solidity of reality to the abstract schema of human history he had received. Charley's education had taught him to look through such artifacts for the ideas and feelings, the rituals and customs, of the people who had carved them. But education—and recently Squier—had also taught him that these ancients belonged to the infancy of civilization. At best, Norton could bring to Mahabalipuram the appreciation of a man who reveres his ancestors but also sees how far they have been surpassed. And any reverence owed the carvers of Mahabalipuram was strictly limited, for their relatively primitive beliefs lay far behind the higher civilization of the Greeks, not to mention that of the divinely endowed Hebrews. Latter-day Hindus could at best excite pity. They were not, strictly speaking, "savages" (never risen above the state of nature) but miserable, degraded relics of a decayed civilization. Better the clean death that Nineveh had met.[10]

Yet no degree of Indian degradation justified British brutality. All his reading had not prepared Norton for so many scenes "painful" to him "not merely as a republican but as [a] man." He had expected better of the British. Anglo-Indians routinely treated "the natives" only as "useful for immediate objects." This "short-sighted" attitude puzzled him, "for the native character seems to be such that it will advance with the most extreme slowness unless under the most direct influence of persons of a superior civilization." Norton (forgetting American slavery) rejoiced "that his country is free from such evils." Still, given "the influence of example" and the "apparently so degraded" character of the Indians, he wondered if "I should become a tyrant if I were to remain here long."[11]

He was not tempted. Letters from Shady Hill had finally arrived. Except for word that his father had again taken ill—hardly unexpected these days—the news was reassuring; and, business done, Norton had no further reason to linger in Madras. Filling the newly empty spaces in the *Milton's* hold took some time, and rain delayed loading. But in dark of night on 15 September the sails were set to a fair wind across the Bay of Bengal.[12]

Calcutta, the City of Palaces, was not only British India's most elegant city but its largest and busiest. In the interstices of a European population of several thousands dwelt hundreds of thousands of Indians. On the ghat, Norton stepped into an exotic bustle he had not seen in comparatively sleepy Madras. His palanquin wended its way through crowded streets to the office of Bullard & Lee's agent, Richard Lewis; there, he devoured letters and newspapers and, for an hour, was back home. The outcry in the United States to annex Canada alarmed him; but he took a less "desponding" view than his father of the European situation following the revolutions of 1848: amid the continent's "war and misery & want of principle," the "great mass of the nations are darkly groping for something better than they have had."[13]

Only after this longed-for draught of home did he settle into his rooms in Spence's Hotel (the best in Calcutta, though "very inferior" by American standards) and turn to business. The *Milton* had to be unloaded, her goods sold, and new merchandise bought for the return voyage. As Bullard & Lee's agent, Richard Lewis handled much of the work that had fallen to Norton in Madras, the more willingly as Charles's talent for companionship quickly made him "a dear friend." Norton himself scoured the bazaars and in two days got much of his buying out of the way.[14]

Business then elided into "looking about." Norton had been in Calcutta scarcely three days when he set about learning what he could of Hindustani, meeting each morning with a "moonshee" he hired for the purpose. Soon he was spending hours in the collections of the Asiatic Society. On 1 October, Norton and Ritchie called on Aushootas Day, a wealthy Indian merchant. Day's full-length portrait of Washington and his European style of entertainment (calculated to appeal to Americans, Charles assumed) disappointed. Norton wanted India, not Boston.[15]

Calcutta offered it raw. Even Madras had not inured Norton to seeing the "greatest wealth" jostling the "most miserable poverty." The "low mud hovels of the natives" crowding "between the large and often handsome houses of the English" ruined European Calcutta, the City of Palaces. Government House shared in the general blight; the dirt, neglect, and shabbiness of its spacious rooms shocked him. His business in the bazaars, located in "the wholly native parts of the city," disoriented his sensibilities: "dirty"—but—"picturesque." Open drains "filthy beyond description" separated streets so narrow as to be "mere lanes" from "low and very damp" windowless mud houses lining them.[16]

Darkest shadow and brightest light mingled in the most confusing ways. Charles had the luck to arrive amid Durga Puja, a festival celebrating the triumph of good over evil. He watched the people parade their "images of the goddess Durja [Durga]" amid "the most horrid noise of drums, cymbals and buffaloe [sic] horns," then "carry them down to the bank of the river and drown them." That evening he drove through the streets, his eyes riveted by the brightly dressed statues of the goddess and her attendants, set against the masses of dark Hindus, they set in turn against their white garments. To Boston correspondents he waved away the whole show as ignorant superstition, but perfunctory dismissal joined with suspiciously fervid description. His pen found words, many of them; his Protestant imagination, no effective categories. In the end he could only contrast the spectacle with a Fourth of July crowd![17]

The Anglo-Indians puzzled him less and pleased him little. Norton's letters of introduction set in train a month of lunches, dinners, and housestays—with an army surgeon, a barrister, other "civilians," a celebrated mesmeric doctor, Calcutta's chief newspaper editor, the American consul. On 18 October, at a town hall meeting to discuss which Boston firm Calcutta should buy its ice from, Norton observed the Anglo-Indian population en masse. He found them unedifying. Experience quickly taught him the loose construction of "Calcutta honesty"; and Company officials proved no better than the merchants. Both treated Indians with harshness and caprice, paying "not the least attention" to "the feelings of the lower classes, very little to those of men who are superior in manner at least to those who slight &

wound them." There were exceptions, such as Hugh Falconer, distinguished botanist and paleontologist, with whom Norton stayed for three days at the famous botanical gardens down the Hooghly. A cultivated bachelor of "gentlemanly bearing," Falconer respected Indian feelings and took a broad view of India's current state and future prospects—subjects on which Charles pumped him for hours. No wonder, Norton wrote home, that a man of Falconer's fastidiousness eschewed Anglo-Indian society. Charles himself gravitated to "the best native society"—"an infinitely more curious circle."[18]

He slaked his curiosity in long visits to Rajah Apurva Krishna Bahadur, the "Poet Laureate of Delhi," to another Indian man of letters, Juggernath Persaud Mullich, and to Prince Ghoolam Mahommad, son of Tippoo Sultan. But only the merchant and physician Rajinder Dutt commanded his respect. Their business began with cashmere shawls; it soon ran to very different matters. Norton thought Dutt "by far the most intelligent and cultivated Hindu" he had met, "very remarkable for having struggled successfully against immense disadvantages of position." They shared "very long and interesting" conversations covering religion, Dutt's family, his aspirations, his sufferings. Like most Europeans, Dutt judged traditional Hinduism "Brahmanical thraldom [sic]." At the same time, he defended other Indian ways, asserted the talents of his people, and deplored Anglo-Indian prejudice.[19]

"My dear Norton Sahib" became a regular guest in the Dutt household, headed by old Doorga Chara Dutt. Norton aimed to treat the Dutts as equals (simply behaving as a gentleman, he said, which "few do"); and the family welcomed him, "the more so as they see that I am interested in the Hindus & desirous to see all that I can of their characteristic customs and habits." He sat with the Dutts on their second-story verandah and tried to comprehend an "opera" (evidently based on a story from the *Mahabharata)* in the torch-lit courtyard below. He watched Doorga Chara Dutt sacrifice three goats to the goddess Juggudchatri. (Although "very glad" to see the ceremony, Charles nonetheless thought it odd in a family conversant with "the literature and science and, more than all, the religion of the West.") When the Dutts staged a spectacular *nautch* (an entertainment by professional dancing girls) nominally closed to Europeans, Rajinder outfitted Charles with Indian clothing—loose white muslin trousers, pink satin vest, muslin gown buttoned at the waist, "a round high cap of Cashmere"—and the nom de guerre "Nondolal Shan" (chosen to sound like "Norton").[20]

For Charles was a terrier, scratching up information about India; all told, his conclusions were cheerless. Ordinary Indians seemed to him superstitious, fawning, devious, ignorant: debasement he explained as a result partly of British abuse but also of "native character." Yet Norton distinguished between a lower and higher type of Indian. The demarcation hinged, not on wealth or even on education as such, but on whether privileged Hindus used "their education and intelligence" to "raise the character of their people." Of those who did, like Rajinder Dutt, there seemed hardly a saving remnant; and even they aped English culture instead of revitalizing Indian. No one had filled the place of the great reformer Rammohun Roy, dead for sixteen years. Only by unchaining their country from "the most revolting superstition that human imagination ever concocted" could Indians set it on the road to progress; yet the grip of custom and fear of losing caste induced even "the most intelligent Hindus" publicly to approve "superstition" that they privately reviled. India's potential leaders failed to summon the needed mental independence and moral courage. "Opposition to change" formed "one of the most striking features of the Hindu character."[21]

To alter that character would require shifting the weight of India's history off its peoples' shoulders. Lacking education, imprisoned within the caste system, "ruled as a conquered nation," subject to "an enervating climate," deprived of "animating examples" and "glorious aspirations," Indians could not possibly develop "patriotism" and a "manly spirit." One could hardly expect "the nobler qualities among a people without any moral guide"; their religion itself dissolved "common sympathies" and "united objects." Yet Norton's calculations did not point to despair, for it never occurred to him (as it did to some of his contemporaries) that biology had condemned an Indian "race" to unalterable degradation. True, British railroads and irrigation projects could never remove "the great drawback" to India's prosperity, "the want of energy among her people"; nor could a horde of missionaries eradicate the superstition chiefly to blame for this inertia, Christian doctrine being "utterly incomprehensible" to the Hindu mind. The "only hope" lay in gradually overcoming India's history by "diffusing education" among its people.[22]

This insistence on the primacy of a people's moral condition in fixing their political and economic state, this stress on the rootedness of that moral condition deep in the people's history, and this faith in education as the only long-term cure for moral feebleness—these principles flowed directly from Norton's Boston background; they would flow out into every phase of his adult thinking. India helped to channel that stream.

Norton hoped to learn more farther upcountry; but to "look about him" in Calcutta or Madras was one thing, in the interior quite another. Hotels were nonexistent, and the *dak* bungalows maintained by the company for its mail relays made a wretched substitute. The wayfarer might shelter there against the heat of the day, but he needed to carry everything: food, bedding, his own interpreter. The India Post Office aided travelers by arranging relays of bearers for palanquins and supplies, but it disclaimed responsibility for "the Misfortunes and disappointments which are inseparable from Dâk Travelling." In Ritchie, Norton at least had a fellow sufferer in misfortunes and disappointments. Meanwhile, from Calcutta friends he collected letters of introduction to civilians and officers upcountry: men who could teach him more of India.[23]

On 5 November, Norton held a reception for his Indian acquaintances. Rajinder gave him "a complete Hindu dress" as a going-away gift. Palanquins were purchased, trunks shipped round to Bombay, business settled for the *Milton's* departure. On Thursday, 8 November 1849, Charles handed Lewis his last letters for home; and around half past three he and Ritchie climbed into their palanquins. Charles hoped that the scenery, disappointing so far, would improve. Where was "the splendor of tropical vegetation"?[24]

Not in the first leg. They followed the new Grand Trunk Road northwest into the dull and dusty plains of Bihar. Scenery failing, Norton watched the passing cavalcade: "Men showily dressed riding on horses covered with red or blue hangings, others traveling in jingling, gaudy, awkward square carts with a high covering over them, disbanded Sepoys, way worn travellers with their worldly goods tied up in one end of their turbans hanging at their side, haggard and horrible old women, white bearded old men, venerable and stooping, bands of fettered criminals working on the road." Once they passed a fakir measuring the road with his body—throwing himself down full-length, rising, walking as far as his hands had reached, then flinging himself down again.[25]

Covering fifty miles a night, they came to Sasaram in the darkness of 14–15 November. Norton and Ritchie breakfasted at sunrise on "thin & tough chicken" then set off to see the ruined splendor of the Mughal ruler Sher Shah. From a high mound they stared down on a scene "one of the most striking I have ever looked at." A vast open stone-lined pool stretched out before them. Around it lay "many sculptured tombs and scattered bits of sandstone that had once formed the sepulchres of some of the Faithful." And from its midst arose the great sandstone mausoleum of Sher Shah himself, a five-layered hexagon towering 150 feet to a huge dome. A younger Charley had marveled at it in a volume of the *Oriental Annual*. Now he waded fifty yards through waist-high water and clambered up its broken base to study the "faded colors" of the paintings, the "arabesque" carving of the arches, the "graceful stone tracery" of the walls. These "delicate beauties" were "well worth twice the trouble that we had taken to see them."[26]

West of Sasaram they cut north, reaching the sacred Ganges at daybreak on 16 November, Charley's twenty-second birthday and, as he wrote to his family, the first "ever spent away from you." "Am I, I frequently incline to question myself, the same youth to whom India Wharf was a year ago so familiar, am I the same, whom dearest Shady Hill with all its peace and pleasantness, nourished in unadventurous and delightful quiet." He could hardly believe so. "But you may trust that caelum non animum mutat qui trans mare currit."[27]

Now he crossed only the river, a half-mile wide, to Ghazipur. There his Harvard classmate Fitzedward Hall had settled to study Indian languages and literature, beginning a distinguished career in philological scholarship. Hall drained Norton of news from Harvard and home, while Norton squeezed from Hall information about India. Norton and Ritchie also saw the sights of Ghazipur, streets cleaner, houses more commodious, bazaars more flourishing than among the Bengalis. The company's local "collector" (magistrate) gave them dinner before sending them on their way around midnight, equipped with a letter of introduction to a fellow magistrate in Benares.[28]

Benares fascinated Charles—its naked beggars and well-fed Brahmins, its ghats where corpses burned and lingams stood along the sacred Ganges, its labyrinth of streets so narrow he could almost touch the houses from his *tonjon* (a kind of sedan chair), its hundreds of temples where wandering bulls munched undisturbed the marigold wreaths bedecking the gods while Brahmins passed out sacred water and tended the holy fire. The ruins of the observatory impressed him with the advanced state of Indian science three centuries earlier. Norton was discovering an India deeper than it had seemed in Calcutta.[29]

He was also discovering more palatable Anglo-Indians. In St. George Tucker, a Benares magistrate scarcely older than himself, Norton found "one of the most agreeable, intelligent and public spirited men that I have met in India." The attraction proved mutual. "I am usually very slow in forming friendships," Tucker wrote after Norton had left, "but your open & unreserved manner convinced me from the first that you can be as sincere a friend as you are a pleasant acquaintance." Letters from home also awaited in Benares, but these turned expectancy to anxiety. Andrews had fallen seriously ill again in early September. All Charley could do was to try to turn his mind to other thoughts.[30]

India made this easier. For two weeks, Norton and Ritchie used Benares as their base, riding on elephants to see the nearby caravanserai, traveling upriver to visit the British fort at Chunar, stalking deer on the rajah of Benares's hunting estate. On 30 November, traveling separately, Norton and Ritchie set off for Lucknow. Two nights later, Norton's bearers deserted; brandishing a pistol only sped their flight. A passing party of sepoys scoured the area without result; but messages sent into the vicinity, promising great baksheesh, lured replacements in several hours.[31]

The country now turned rougher, for Norton had entered the shakily independent Moslem kingdom of Oudh. The land was less cultivated, dotted with mango groves instead of fields: tropical vegetation at last. Almost everyone Norton saw carried sabrelike swords, ancient matchlocks, or iron-tipped bamboo spears. At Lucknow, Oudh's capital, Norton reconnected with Ritchie. Lucknow was "full of interest," "by far the most Oriental" and the "most Mahommedan" city yet seen. The architecture captivated Norton, and he arranged for his Anglo-Indian host to hire a draughtsman to make drawings for him. Then, clattering down the new paved road—the first in Oudh, secured against highwaymen only weeks earlier—the travelers crossed the Ganges and, some twelve hours later, arrived in Cawnpore, back in British India. From Cawnpore, again leaving Ritchie to follow, Charles struck out for one of his main goals: the Upper Ganges Canal, under construction in the Northwest Provinces. Its irrigation would open vast new acreage for agriculture. Here, a merchant's eye could see what British rule might do for India's prosperity.[32]

On 15 December, Charles arrived in Roorkee, a small settlement on the canal, the Himalayan foothills visible in the distance. The authorities gave him a room in the new engineering college, set up to train English superintendents and Indian foremen. By the seventeenth he had "seen all the works to the greatest advantage" and recorded a mass of data in his journal. Around midnight, his palanquin—with Norton bundled against the cold in "a thick wadded suit," a coat over it, his "plaid" on top, and "a thin native blanket" around his feet—left for Haridwar, at the head of the canal. There he bought two brass statues of Hindu deities, dipped them in the sacred Ganges, and then headed for the mountains. At Dehra Dun he met Ritchie, abandoned the palanquin for a horse, and rode up the steep road to the white cottages of Mussoorie, "scattered like sheep about the summits." The two Americans got someone to open the little summer hotel for them; bought firewood, milk, eggs, and bread; cooked themselves a meal of sorts; and brewed tea over their fire. They rose early to climb to Landour peak, nine hundred feet above Mussoorie.[33]

As they ascended the hill's southern flank, "a sudden turn in the path opened to us one of the most splendid views I have ever seen." A "sea of hills" spread before them, "stretching for miles after miles on every side, till they were bounded by the snowy peaks of the highest range of the Himmilayas which rose towering above them bright and beautiful in the light." Charles's "heart beat quick." Of all he saw in India, this was and remained the view he "would first choose" to see again. The "sublimity and the beauty of the scene" defeated his "powers of description"—and made him hungry for the Alps.[34]

There was more of India to see first. Delhi's modern buildings, reached just before Christmas, Norton thought beautiful but not so impressive as the "dark remains of palaces, of forts, and of tombs" that lay "in splendid desolation around the wall which encloses the gilded mosques, the gay houses, the crowded streets of the present town." The preference was characteristic. Qutb Minar, just outside Delhi, remained Norton's surpassingly lovely memory of India. A red stone column over six centuries old, it towered nearly 250 feet into the sky, "surrounded by ruins of various & exquisite beauty." Qutb Minar summed up India in other ways as well. From its top Norton looked out over "many miles of mouldering ruins." Without question, there was "something very impressive in a scene like this," strewn "with the memorials of many generations." Yet—though "the fate of nations have [sic] been decided" on this ground—"it is unconsecrated by actions the memory of which might be honored & cherished through age after age. It has not one stirring association connected with noble deeds; it is barren of all history that might awaken any high ambition, & one turns away from it only with a sigh."[35]

Norton had stored up not only impressive views and romantic sighs. His experience traveling across India had reinforced lessons learned in Madras and Calcutta. Among the company rulers he had seen abuse of power and "great oppression." Among the Indian ruled he had perceived "a very small minority of them advancing under the influence & example of the English," the overwhelming majority uniting "the vices of barbarism & civilization."[36] All this had fortified the opinions with which he had arrived: the dangers of aristocratic power and the value of republican institutions; the determining hand of history in shaping a people's institutions and underlying culture; the heavy weight of culture, especially religion in its ethical dimensions, in constraining or undergirding progress; the dependence of progress primarily on a people's moral character; and the strengthening of a people's character as a glacially slow achievement chiefly through education.

Yet India did not merely confirm received views. It connected them with reality, deepened their complexity, made them into tools for deciphering actuality rather than only abstract schemata. It planted a developmental scheme of history firmly in Norton's worldview. And it stretched the twenty-two-year-old's mind. It made him sensitive to wider ranges of personalities and cultural backgrounds; it unsettled some expectations and questioned some easy Boston answers; its exotic and mind-expanding scenes opened an already receptive young man to new experiences and novel worlds. He would subsequently see even Europe with eyes wider open than those of most Bostonians.

Around eight in the morning on 2 January 1850, his bearers carried Norton's palanquin up to the *dak* bungalow at Agra, where Ritchie awaited. Charley immediately sent for an expected packet of letters; the most recent, written on 24 October by William Bullard, had followed him from stop to stop until finally catching him in Agra. Andrews's condition had deteriorated. He might not live.[37]

At once Charley wrote to Bombay to book passage on the Suez steamer. The 750 miles from Agra to Bombay ran through native states and sparsely settled areas. There was no regular *dak;* he could be two hundred miles from an Englishman if his bearers deserted. He hired twenty-five of them and a cook, sent word to Indore (halfway along and with a British Resident) to have fresh bearers ready, saw the Taj Mahal, bid farewell to Ritchie, and on Friday morning, 4 January, supported "by that faith in GOD, in his infinite goodness, in our constant connection through him" that he "felt sure" was supporting his family as well, set out for home.[38]

On 30 January his train walked into Bombay. The "excellent set of fellows" had averaged almost thirty miles a day. A "large batch of letters" awaited, which Richard Lewis had received in Calcutta on 18 December with Bullard & Lee's request to forward them as rapidly as possible. Charles unwrapped the packet, found the letter with the latest postmark, ripped it open, and "with a thrill of happiness & gratitude" read: "'All well.'" "I felt twenty years younger than I had two minutes before." Bullard's alarming note had, it turned out, been sent at the crisis of Andrews's illness. By early December improvement surpassed even Charley's hopes; and he could feel easy traveling in Europe, where communication with home was fast. He did

.

cancel plans to see Syria, Palestine, and Constantinople; he would not, he assured his parents, regret what he had not seen, only be "glad that I had seen so much." "You know," he wrote them, "that my only desire is to do that which will really please you best, & my chief hope is to prove my affection to you by doing all that lies in my power for you."[39]

There was time in Bombay to take account of its flourishing market and the popularity of American textiles: "an excellent opportunity" for "establishing an American House." Norton also arranged to talk with the celebrated merchant Sir Jamsetjee Jeejeebhoy, adding the resulting data about Parsees to his "famous journal." He sent off some "Caubur preserves" to Mrs. Everett, packed the tiger skin sent by one of his hunting companions, and on 4 February 1850 boarded the steamer *Victoria* bound for Suez.[40]

From Suez a cramped horse-drawn van carried him across the desert— with a view of the pyramids that thrilled him—to Cairo. A night steamer down the Nile took him to Alexandria and the boat to Europe. His ship called at Smyrna (giving him time for a twenty-five-mile ride through robber-infested hills to see a "monument of Sisostris") and Corfu before docking at Trieste on Tuesday, 19 March.[41]

Then Venice floated around Charles, a golden dream. By day a gondola wafted him through its watery lace; by night his footsteps echoed solemnly on the stone bridges that arched each little *rio*. From atop the campanile in Piazza San Marco he looked out over the island-flecked *laguna*. He wandered the narrow streets, where buildings four or five stories high closed him in; it was like walking through high canyons, tunnels back into time. Entering the "glorious churches," standing "in the Place of St. Mark," Charles luxuriated in "the associations of the past." He half expected to encounter at the next turning "some new triumph of the art of Titian or of Sansovino" and did find bits of fresco by Giorgione and Tintoretto still clinging to palazzo walls.[42]

An entire frescoed ceiling crowned the capacious rooms that Norton engaged at his own palazzo, the Guistiniani, reduced by 1850 to playing Hôtel de l'Europe. He stood at his windows, looking out at the Isola della Giudecca, which Canaletto engravings hanging at Shady Hill had made "a familiar and friendly place." But to look at a copy was one thing; another altogether was to see the glorious original. A cast of a statue might represent it fairly; no engraving could reproduce a church or do justice to a painting. Wandering through the Accademia gallery Norton saw color and light and shadow as he had never imagined. Titian's *Assumption of the Virgin* hung

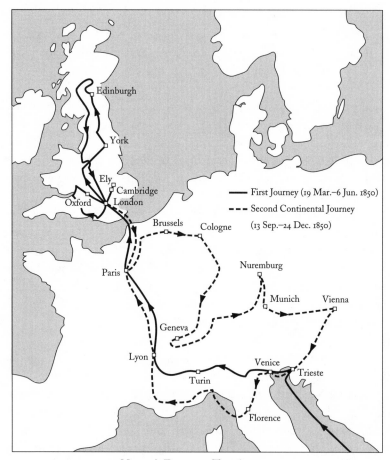

Norton's European Travels, 1850.

before him like the door into an unknown country: "until I saw it I had no idea of the powers of painting in these respects." For in Boston's third-hand culture, Norton had mostly learned about art not even from casts and engravings but from books.[43]

Yet, even with Venice glowing before him, a pale imagining come to full-blooded life, he still saw it through books. His Venice was a Shakespearean city of history and "associations." He wandered for two days through the Palazzo Ducale, where "the gratitude of Petrarch" lived on in the library and "the beheading of Marino Faliero" cast a pall over the courtyard—references revealing the visitor's considerable interest in Italian history.[44] Perhaps this leaning explains why Venice's historic buildings fascinated Norton even more than its paintings, why the architectural merits of the palace evoked less emotion than its "wonderful associations." "At each step you stop to look at some object which awakens a new train of thoughts." Or at least you did if you had read as much about Italy as Norton had. He wanted to wander alone through the grand and solemn rooms—with a book for a companion.[45]

Yet he also saw what he could not have read. He gazed in wonderment at the "great variety and beauty of the coloring" of San Marco, at the Palladian harmonies of the Redentore. His eye, trained by flower collecting, now admired the "exquisite finish which is carried into the innumerable details" of the Doges' Palace, such as the way in which "a running pattern of leaves giv[es] a general similarity" to the array of pillars, while a unique capital made each distinct. He was haphazardly starting to teach himself—the Boston path of self-culture—how to look at buildings.[46]

He took Italy seriously; Italy in turn, while validating and enriching his inherited assumptions, also nibbled, very quietly, on them. The traces of erosion came more from how he saw than from what he heard, for Norton's "powers of conversation in Italian" were still "of the most limited kind." On 29 March he went to San Marco for Good Friday services; he had, it appears, never witnessed a Roman Catholic liturgy. He found it "very strange and very painful," a "theatrical display" that "travestied" the "most sacred history" commemorated in Holy Week. Never had the "simpler creed" of Boston "seemed so precious."[47]

He returned for Holy Saturday. A Boston allergy to incense blinded Charley to his own confusions. "Theatrical display" repelled when wearing vestments but not, somehow, when wearing marble: Norton thought San Marco "a treasure house of beauties," and on every visit he felt the basilica's glories more deeply.[48]

Norton repressed these contradictions with the aid of the Unitarian version of history. Of course, gems of truth glittered under the putrescent crust of Catholicism. After all, Luther, Calvin, and their Unitarian improvers like Andrews Norton had not invented Christianity; they had only scraped away superstitions that distorted the message of Jesus, a message so bright that even the "corruptions and the evils of the Roman Catholic creed" had not entirely obscured it. Catholicism certainly clogged the wheels of progress. (Hence, Norton was convinced, educated Italians only kept up a pretense of Catholic faith.) But Romanists were not trapped in a blind alley as Hindus were, for Catholics glimpsed dimly the living truth that Unitarians saw clearly.[49]

Yet the fact that papist Neanderthals were directly ancestral to *Homo sapiens nortonensis* did not clear up all the mysteries. How could these be-nighted souls have glued together mosaics infinitely more beautiful than anything in enlightened Boston? The Unitarian story of the progress of religion—man slowly learning to understand a divine truth revealed to primitive Hebrews—did not answer the question. Neither did the Scot-tish Enlightenment account of the progress of civilization—man slowly rising from barbarism pure and simple. (Nor, for that matter, did these two tales themselves jibe, though Andrews and Harvard had taught both.) And neither fitted with the Boston conviction that *might* explain San Marco: the idea that great art embodied timeless beauty, so that a young Unitarian seeing a mosaic in 1850 resonated to it in the same key as the Catholic who had designed it in 1250.

On 5 April, Norton climbed the campanile in Piazza San Marco "to take a farewell look." The coach carried him first to Padua, where Giotto's frescoes crowded the Arena Chapel: most Americans did not bother to see them; Norton did. Then he was off to Vicenza and its Palladian villas. Their "fine" proportions and "elegant" details impressed Norton more than Giotto had. In the Biblioteca Capitolare at Verona he searched for "some unedited poems of Dante," found instead "a splendid collection of early editions" of the Tuscan poet and some magnificent ancient and medieval manuscripts. Philology was bred in Norton's bones. Everywhere he regret-ted his ignorance, wished some great scholar were accompanying him. At Mantua he gave himself another lesson in critical vision. The frescoes in the Palazzo del Te were "very striking"; but, he concluded, they lacked "that beauty which interests the feelings and affects the imagination." "The color-ing is violent, and the designs though full of force are wanting in grace"; and the mixture of pagan and Christian symbolism "jars upon the taste,—either alone would be striking,—the combination of the two is bad." Lacking some great scholar as his guide, he was haphazardly educating himself.[50]

The education involved more than frescoes and villas. The misery of Italy's governance sounded persistent counterpoint, in Norton's scoring, to the splendor of its art. These strains were hardly surprising from any Ameri-can, almost inevitable from a Norton. At Shady Hill, little Charley had half comprehendingly heard Italian refugees fume at Austrian tyranny. When he was older he had scanned his mother's translation of the memoirs of one of them. Still later, he had rushed to Uncle Ticknor with the heady news of the revolutions of 1848. That revolutionary heat had given birth to a Venetian republic, but it fell to the old Habsburg master only months before Norton's arrival. Charles believed that "oppression" had only "forced back into its crater to boil" an inevitable "eruption" of liberty. Eventually, Italian hatred would smash Austrian guns. What then?[51]

Norton saw issues here transcending Italy. He understood himself to be studying European politics from a perspective precisely the reverse of that from which he studied European art: gazing up at the Old Masters from the lowlands of American art; peering down at the swamp of continental politics from the alps of American republicanism. In paintings and buildings, European antiquity implied ripened beauty; in government, merely ancient oppression. Only in the happy Kingdom of Piedmont, of all Italy, did republican institutions flourish, forming ramparts against tyranny and "red republicanism" alike. But a more telling case study lay down the road.[52]

Norton picked up his pace, hoping to reach Paris in time for the French elections on 28 April. From Turin the post road climbed through dramatic Alpine views up Mount Cenis Pass, before winding down into France. A brief stay in Lyon showed Norton a threat to republicanism more insidious than Habsburg tyranny: radical silk weavers on the Left and reactionary Jesuits on the Right pinned the city between "two great elements of danger." (He also found in a shop some "curious old engravings by Albert Durer" and "etchings by Rembrandt," the whole lot for fifteen francs. His thirst for collecting was at last finding chances to slake itself.) From Lyon, an icy nine-hour voyage up the Saône, followed by a chilly night's diligence ride and a cold railroad train, brought Charles into Paris on Friday, 26 April.[53]

Bone tired, he did nothing that afternoon but read the waiting mail. The next day, he ran into a young Boston lawyer named Burlingame, the first person he had recognized since leaving Ritchie in Agra. Paris was full of familiar faces. On Sunday, Charles saw Edward Cabot and Tom Appleton; on Monday, Eliza Follen and Miss Cabot; on Tuesday he was reunited with Frank Child, en route to join their classmate George Lane at the University of Göttingen. The long foreign winter had suddenly thawed.[54]

But Norton's business lay with France, not Boston. As tallies from Sunday's election dribbled in, Norton tried to read in these entrails the destiny of France's infant republic. Eighteen-forty-eight had broken down the old principles of order; no new ones seemed to be emerging. The *Journal des Debats* announced the triumph of anarchism. Norton found the *Journal* hysterical, the state of politics not quite so bad as he had expected. The voting, at least, had gone off "with the most entire and perfect quiet." "From what I can learn," the election seemed a qualified victory "of the friends of the republic over the friends of reaction."[55]

Behind Norton's interest in France's politics lay concern about America's. As, twenty years earlier, the young Frenchman Tocqueville had studied the United States to infer the future of democracy in Europe, so the young American now scrutinized France to decipher the prospects of republican government in the United States. For, at moments in the spring of 1850, his own nation seemed to teeter on the brink of dissolution. It had been pushed there by conflict over whether slavery should expand into territory recently wrested from Mexico in the odious war that most New Englanders had decried as the dirty work of slaveowners. Charles, far from home, worried about his country; from home, Mr. Longfellow reassured him. Politics were "raging furiously" but would not rip the Union apart. His father, too, wrote calmly; the compromise supported by Webster would "restore the peace of the country." But that compromise included a law requiring Northerners to aid in recapturing fugitive slaves, and this appalled Andrews. Charley was young. He read American omens in the cheeriest light. "Everything," he felt sure, "will work out for good in our republic."[56]

In Europe the story might end differently. Charley expected that a desperate political struggle would engulf France within a year or two. (It turned out to be Louis Napoleon's coup d'état.) Andrews advised him to hope for nothing from the "bloody revolutions" to which the continent seemed prone, for they "do not touch the seat of the evils that pervade society in Europe"—principally "the long continued want of true religious faith," which "alone can bind man to his fellowmen in a community of feeling, as members of the same immortal family." Absent religion, "gross selfishness springs up in its place; and becomes the only restraint on what it prompts men to do—to prey upon each other." France did not need another revolution; it needed "moral renovation of the character of communities." Italian and French postrevolutionary politics were a furnace. In its intense glare Charles was beginning to see his inherited republicanism more sharply; in its blazing heat, to refine his ideas.[57]

In Paris, though, he meant to study more than politics. He was well prepared. Patrician Boston had long-standing commercial ties with France and routinely tutored its children in French; its fledglings felt more at home in Paris than in Berlin or Venice. Uncle Ticknor's cosmopolitan influence left Charles, even by Boston standards, exceptionally well connected in Paris, unusually receptive to it. With his inbred seriousness of approach, Norton set out to bolster these advantages: in Calcutta he had hired a tutor to teach him Hindi; in Paris he engaged one to improve his ragged French. But first he had to find a tailor, "for to confess the truth I reached Paris completely out of clothes."[58]

On 30 April, Charles encountered Joseph Coolidge, a friend of Andrews and Catharine's, strolling one of the boulevards. This chance meeting proved a happy one; for Coolidge, who "knows the persons who are worth knowing" in Parisian society, offered his services as cicerone. The next day he escorted Charles to meet Uncle Ticknor's great friend Adolphe, comte de Circourt. "I have rarely heard a man who talked better." His vast "fund of knowledge," coined in striking turns of phrase, spread its wealth "upon any subject that may come up." Circourt's salon became a haunt of Norton's, always stocked with a surfeit of duchesses and a few luminaries like Alfred de Vigny.[59]

The comte metaphorically on one arm, Coolidge on the other, Norton hardly needed his packet of introductions. He soon moved to Coolidge's quiet little hotel on the rue de la Paix, just north of the Place Vendôme. Together, they visited the Jardin des Plantes and the Museum of Morbid Anatomy, attended the opera, shopped for furniture for Coolidge's new Boston house ("an excellent opportunity for cultivating my taste in these articles of household decoration"). With Coolidge's son Algernon, Norton heard the Assemblée Nationale debate at the Palais Bourbon; the "republican simplicity" of its hall pleased him. Norton found other comrades among the Bostonians swarming Paris, predictable ones, such as solid John Lowell and William Bullard's brother Stephen, but also less likely companions, like Thomas Appleton and William Story. Both Tom and William were a little too flippant, a little too bon vivant, a little too ardent about painting and sculpture to be entirely approved by Andrews and even, perhaps, by his son.[60]

Charles was learning to taste what he could not quite swallow. On 9 May he visited one of the celebrated soirées of the Virginia expatriate Mrs. Edward Lee Childe. He found her "a woman completely denationalized, & very little to my taste." He also found himself thereafter much in her presence. He did not (he assured Mother and Father) admire her frivolous worldliness; but being abroad "for the sake of seeing the world in all its sides," he was "glad to have made Mrs. C's acquaintance."[61]

Other acquaintances, famous rather than risqué, proved heady to meet, occasionally interesting to talk with: Alexis de Tocqueville, Alphonse de Lamartine, Nassau Senior. The last was one of many Britons in Paris with whom Norton dined. (Charles was, after all, George Ticknor's nephew.) Lady Elgin, widow of the Scottish earl who had hijacked the Parthenon frieze, turned out "rather a dull old lady" but one with a charming daughter, twenty-seven-year-old Lady Augusta Bruce. The Elgins invited Charles to

stay with them in Scotland later that summer. Richard Monckton Milnes—
"Dicky" Milnes, with his fizzy reputation as wit, poet, raconteur, patron of
young writers, and reforming politician—had Charles to breakfast. Norton
did not much like him. Milnes, in contrast, found the young American
intriguing enough to cultivate.[62]

The greatest treat was visiting the house of the fashionable painter Ary
Scheffer, on the southern edge of Montmartre. On 11 May, after examining
with Coolidge an exhibit of Sèvres porcelain and Gobelin tapestries at the
Palais Royale, Charles called on Sophie Scheffer, two months earlier converted from mistress to wife. (The liaison did not ruffle Norton: the French,
like the Hindus, had their own ways.) Mme Scheffer ushered him into "a
studio most tastefully arranged & hung with the finest of Scheffer's paintings." "My heart beat quick at seeing the works of so great an artist and with
which I had so many tender associations." Scheffer's *Saint Augustin et Sainte
Monique* showed saint and mother sitting side by side and hand in hand,
staring worshipfully and vacuously toward the upper right of the picture.
Norton gazed at the canvas as reverently as Augustine and Monica gazed
into the empyrean. Mme Scheffer took Charles into her husband's working
atelier. The great man, who knew a rich American when he saw one, laid
down his brush to receive Charles "most kindly." Norton was not duped, but
two nights later he happily came back to dine. These were the first of several
visits to "the most delightful place in Paris."[63]

Charles was realizing how deep was his fondness for pictures and evolving his own sense of what mattered in them. Scheffer painted the deepest
feelings of the heart better than "any other"; "in point of expression" his
Christus Consolator seemed the finest picture Norton had ever seen, better
than Titian. But Charles gave himself plenty of chances to compare. Mme
de Circourt took him to "a fine gallery of modern painting"; he viewed
contemporary French paintings in the Luxembourg; twice he visited the
Louvre. The lighting there was bad, the paintings in disrepair, good pictures
swamped in a sea of bad ones; and he had seen enough in Italy to realize that
the "greatest Italian masters are without exception badly represented." Still,
the Louvre's "chief treasures"—which he thought its Murillos, Van Dycks,
and some of the Rembrandts—merited careful study. "How I wish," he
wrote home, "that you could see the fine galleries of pictures in Europe with
me; for I am sure that your admiration of paintings would grow with mine.
It is to me an unexpected and entirely new pleasure to find these works of art
so beautiful."[64]

Buildings, too, as in Venice, he observed with interest, pleasure, and growing sophistication. Notre Dame impressed him as "by far the finest specimen of the florid French Gothic architecture that I have seen," with "some very beautiful points and peculiarities." And like San Marco, "it is full of interest from its antiquity and from the events of which it has been the scene." The Pantheon, however, suffered in Norton's opinion: spiritually, from the relics of Rousseau and Voltaire (the Federalist in him shuddered); materially, from the disharmony of its exterior elements and the breaking up of its interior space by "overornamented pillars[,] pilasters and vaultings." Despite a fine dome and portico, "the grandeur of its size and proportions is quite lost." His eye was still only a tourist's but keener and more active than most.[65]

When not peering at a pilaster, he was apt to be watching Racine. The days Norton had spent in the countinghouse with that fanatic of the footlights Henry Lee can only have sharpened the taste for theater cultivated at Shady Hill. But where American managers staged plays to showcase some well-known actor, Parisian theaters, Norton learned, did not depend on "one star to light the whole performance." The "completeness" of Paris performances enthralled him, with their "attention to the minute details by which the illusion & the effect of the acting is wonderfully increased." He attended at least six performances by the Alsatian actress Rachel Félix, including *Virginie, Phèdre,* and *Adrienne Lecouvreur,* "her greatest role." The waifish Rachel clearly gave him a sexual frisson. But, much more, Norton's fondness for dramatic expression was shaping the way he conceived history, literature, and even painting, a tendency abetted by the setting of all these plays in the historic past.[66]

Some of them he saw with Quincy Shaw, a young New Yorker on the homeward leg of eighteen months abroad. When they dined together on 29 May at the Café de Paris, Shaw brought along "his traveling companion, a young man from New York named Curtis"—George William Curtis. For all three, the time approached to leave Paris, and they decided to travel together.[67]

Charles was ready to go. The more he saw of French "high society," the more he thought it "very frivolous and very selfish." (A hint of self-reproach? Was Norton pulling back from a side of himself that he had recognized with a guilty start in the salons and theaters and cafés?) Even the comte de Circourt's judgments depended "more upon his temporary state of feeling than upon any fixed rules." True, Paris charmed. What delight to live in one of the high-roofed, narrow-windowed, red-brick houses in the Place Royale, where everything "bears the marks of age and freedom from change"! But even this "air of quiet and repose" would grow malodorous when aristocratic titles mattered more than personal character. Perhaps, Charles mused, it was only because Europe "has been presented to us so often in glowing, not to say, exaggerated colors, that the dark side strikes me the more forcibly." In any case he was "delighted & almost surprised to find that in all the comparisons which I draw the result is favorable to our own country." His travels were teaching him that Americans had "cause for an increase of self respect": "just now the great deficiency of our people as a nation."[68]

The boat train left Paris on the morning of 6 June; Charles pulled into London fifteen hours later. London seemed to Charles "not in appearance so gay as Paris," hardly a surprise considering that it was nearly midnight. Next morning, the city appeared no gayer. At least his rooms at Fenton's Hotel, between Pall Mall and Piccadilly, put fashionable London within a few minutes' walk. Fenton's was also convenient to Russell and Julia Sturgis's house on Harley Street, where Norton went the evening after his arrival to meet "all the Americans who are in town." In this case, "America" extended about as far west as the Back Bay, for Russell Sturgis was an old Boston merchant settled in London.[69]

The web of acquaintance enveloping Charley in London made his Paris connections look skimpy. He was about to experience the thickness of Boston's transatlantic network, as scientific and literary London opened wide to him. Hensleigh Wedgwood, philologist and London official, cousin and intellectual companion of Charles Darwin, entertained him. The distinguished geologist and public man Leonard Horner had him to dine with the mathematician Charles Babbage (even then tinkering with his analytical engine) and the historian Henry Hallam. The still more eminent geologist Charles Lyell (a friend of Uncle Ticknor) invited him to a party where he met Henry Rawlinson, the army major who had deciphered Darius's cuneiform inscription at Behistun, and John Ruskin, the young art critic whose surprising *Modern Painters* Charles had read. Another old friend of Ticknor, the amiable John Kenyon, gave Charles a series of meals to meet the older generation of literary London. Ticknor also provided entree to Earl Fitzwilliam's more aristocratic table, at which Charles dined with Lord Brougham, "who talked a great deal, almost always about himself."[70]

The young Bostonian proved capable also of opening doors for himself, though whether they would have swung so wide had he not been "the nephew of Mr. Ticknor" is open to question. Norton got himself invited to a party given by old Joseph Hume, Bentham's disciple, where he chatted at length with Richard Cobden. Richard Monckton Milnes turned out far "pleasanter in London than in Paris"; and at Milnes's famous breakfasts Norton met Prosper Merimée, Louis Blanc, Arthur Penryn Stanley, a German called Dr. Waagen "with a profound knowledge of art" (or so Norton then thought), and "a young Tennysonian poet" with the Tennysonian name of Coventry Patmore. The Prussian scholar-diplomat Christian Bunsen asked him to a "family dinner." London was looking much gayer. With George Curtis he visited the tourist spots in and around the metropolis. Curtis was becoming a constant companion, as were William and Emelyn Story. The four of them took to lunching together almost every day at the Sturgises'.[71]

Norton was immensely enjoying this vast and growing acquaintance; he was also putting it to use. For London, like Paris and Venice and Calcutta, he conceived as a stage of his education. Sometimes the learning was low keyed, incidental. Dinner conversation with Babbage, a long talk with Cobden, gave some expert insight into scientific work or practical political economy; a day at the London docks, a morning at the Bank of England, added to his own mercantile expertise. But Charles also pursued knowledge self-consciously, drawing on his connections. He toured Westminster Abbey under the expert guidance of the ecclesiastical historian Henry Hart Milman. Thousands of tourists in 1850 gaped at the monumental winged bulls with men's heads, at the great stone reliefs of battles and sacrifices, newly dug up at Nineveh and put on display in the British Museum; but not many had the Assyriologist Henry Rawlinson to explain what they were staring at.[72]

More to the point, Norton stood prepared to take advantage of his advantages. He had read Austen Layard's book on the discovery of Nineveh (and probably discussed it with its two Boston reviewers) before he met Rawlinson. And his growing fascination with such diverse products of the human imagination as Assyrian palace ornaments and hammer-beam roofs impelled him to spend hours trying to comprehend them. He put in a long morning at the British Museum studying the Elgin Marbles; he stood silently in the British Institution's gallery, his protruding eyes searching the paintings; he secured an invitation to see "Lord Ashburton's splendid collection of pictures." Two weeks after Milman escorted him through Westminster Abbey, he returned for a morning alone.[73]

The many hours produced results. On 28 June, with Julia Sturgis, Curtis, and the Storys, he made a second trip to Windsor to see the castle gallery and chapel. He assessed the Van Dyck portraits with a confidence and specificity inconceivable three months before: "I doubt if any painter has been superior to him in taking expressive and animated likenesses." Saint George's Chapel—"one of the most highly finished and complete specimens of Gothic architecture I have seen"—interested him as "belonging to the same style as Henry the VIIth's Chapel at Westminster Abbey." He took George Curtis to visit the medieval Westminster Hall; its hammer-beam ceiling he declared "the finest roof I have seen in England." He was on target. Norton's was not an expert eye, but it was becoming an informed one. Yet it remained one that saw "stirring memories" in a building as readily as fine woodwork.[74]

Art, archaeology, and architecture competed for attention with politics, political economy, and the many faces of power. The exact relation of culture to polity, past to present, imagination to action remained foggy in Norton's mind. But that all somehow cohered in his self-tutelage he did not doubt.

Norton had (as Francis Parkman observed) "too much sense to be bitten by the John Bull mania which is the prevailing disease of Boston." His "first strong impression of the English" was that they fawned on "rank and position"; the drawing rooms teeming with "white cravatted flunkeys" and "snobbish looking men" disgusted him. This reflex was normal in Americans. Even among Boston Anglophiles, republican distrust of aristocracy had long complicated admiration of English culture, ancestral hostility to the British Lion confounding pseudonostalgia for the Old Home. Norton's months in India had heightened these reflexes. In all his use of the word "race," he attached scant importance to somatic differences among human beings: even as the Victorian intellectual consensus began to shift toward stressing the gravity of physical ancestry, Norton did not budge from his certainty of the determining force of cultural descent. As he saw it, the English benefited from a superior culture; the weight of an inferior one bore down the Indians. These fortunes of history gave no one a moral warrant to lord it over others. But most Anglo-Indians behaved as if they held one.[75]

That same swagger, and the sycophancy that was its obverse, he saw in Lord Ashburton's drawing rooms—where, Norton noted acidly, Ashburton had mounted a Murillo showing "St. Thomas dividing his garment among the poor beggar children." Charles quoted a mot of John Kenyon: "In France there has always been social liberty and political servitude, in England there has been political liberty & social servitude." "For my part," Norton added, "I don't know which is the worse." He had no problem with the principle that a superior class should govern, an inferior follow. How else did his own relatives see their duty in Boston? Yet it was quite another matter, a wholesale violation of Christian ethics and the Boston ethos, to treat the unfortunate as means to gratify the pride and desires of the powerful.[76]

The unfortunate were properly subjects for improvement; and Charles followed closely English discussions of the social question, collecting official reports on schooling and attending a Commons debate on the subject. While conceding that the "great questions for England of national education and the relief of pauperism" excited "as usual" some public attention, Norton thought the attention "quite inadequate to the demands." Housing schemes for "workmen & laborers" caught his eye as especially promising, but the "bigotry" and "selfishness" of the English aristocracy augured ill for any reform.[77]

Charles's own education was getting more delightful by the day. On 29 June he, Emelyn Story, and the Sturgises took the train for Cambridge, to join there Emelyn's husband William, George Curtis, and "a pleasant, intelligent Englishman," C. C. Black. After walking about the colleges, they "sat up till one o'clock discussing various pleasant subjects of art and literature" with "a young fellow of Pembroke, Mr. Brown." An excursion to Ely provided "a splendid study" for Norton, the cathedral there combining "all the styles of English Gothic architecture." The restoration then under way, moreover, was being carried out "with uncommon taste." Charles had, he told his family, "grown very fond of architecture" since arriving in Europe. "I have been reading a good deal about it so as to look at fine buildings with some intelligence, & to be able to carry away with me a more distinct impression of their beauties."[78]

Norton returned to London on 1 July to spend a couple more weeks of sightseeing, socializing, and indulging his passion for old-book shops. His new friend C. C. Black gave him dinner, and there he met Richard Baird Smith, an engineer on the Ganges project that had so interested Charles. Baird Smith told Norton of plans to visit the United States in 1851 to see American public works. Sir Arthur Helps, whose *Friends in Council* Norton had got published in America, also sought him out.[79]

Into these overfilled last days in London broke startling news from Shady Hill. William Bullard had asked Louisa to marry him. Her brother seemed taken entirely by surprise; and Louisa herself needed convincing that a man raised under circumstances so different from Shady Hill, accustomed more to the countinghouse than the library, too shy to banter easily in a crowded drawing room, wanting in "that intellectual cultivation and development" to which Louisa was used, would make her the ideal husband. Perhaps she only needed assurance that life could go on outside the gates of Shady Hill. Charley believed it could, at least for Louisa, and repeated his "great respect and esteem for Bullard."[80]

While his sister fretted, Charley packed. He bid reluctant farewell to George Curtis, whose friendship had blossomed into the "warmest love," and on 17 July set out to see the rest of Britain on the standard tourist route. Along it, he delighted in historic "associations" and Van Dycks, lamented the poverty of the country folk on which such wealth depended, marveled at the quiet uncomplaining way in which they bore their oppression. He arrived in Edinburgh just in time for the annual meeting of the British Association for the Advancement of Science, where the Ethnological Section intrigued him, another sign of the bent of his mind toward the forces shaping behavior and mores. Edinburgh also brought a reunion with Lady Elgin's daughter, Augusta Bruce. The "very warm intimacy" that continued between the two indicated how Charles's friendliness could negotiate even the Victorian delicacies of gender. Two weeks touring the Highlands—where he ran into Captain Baird Smith again (it was shooting season)—were followed by the conventional pilgrimage to the Lake District: "oh, shades of Scott and of ye Lake Poets how do ye preside over this wild vale."[81]

By 6 September, Charles was back in London, preparing to return to the Continent. He did find time to go with Julia Sturgis to Tottenham to see the Windus collection of Turners: the one "which gave Ruskin his enthusiastic admiration for the painter." In declaring Turner's watercolors "beyond all comparison finer than any other landscapes I remember having seen in truth to nature," Norton was probably paraphrasing Ruskin.[82]

Yet possibly not, for day after day of comparing pictures and buildings had built up a store of artistic and architectural knowledge that approached the beginnings of expertise. Expertise, not original insight: like most cultivated Americans, Charles favored Renaissance masters in painting (Scheffer and J. M. W. Turner being the exceptions) and Gothic construction in architecture. His intellectual growth had not been limited to the arts. Although Europe had not altered his inherited principles of social order, confrontation with aristocratic hauteur and grinding poverty had enlarged his knowledge and honed his belief in America's superiority. American republicanism represented a new and higher stage of human political development—even while American artistic and literary culture limped behind its European parents. Travel had also taught him something about personal qualities. He realized how rare were the "great and undisturbable aimiability [*sic*] and thoughtfulness for others" that he admired in Russell and Julia Sturgis. But the rarity in others of these attributes so admired at Shady Hill only emphasized the need to cultivate them in oneself.[83]

Norton stayed in Paris only long enough to get a dentist to drill an aching tooth and to pick up the winter clothes he had stored there. On the Rhine steamer between Bonn and Koblenz, he met a "thorough specimen of a Cockney" who waxed persistent on the superiority of the Thames to the Rhine. Eventually the man conceded, "It's very remarkable that the Rhine always runs one way, isn't it?" To this observation, Charles said, "one naturally assented."[84]

Mostly, however, Norton absorbed the splendors of the great Gothic cathedrals along his route. He tried to grasp what he was seeing, but growing experience made him realize how deep was his "ignorance."

> I know so little about what I see compared to what is to be known, there are such treasures of history, & of romance, such studies of art and of life which I have never even approached, & which I long to unfold. I know enough to awaken my enthusiasm and my admiration, but I feel as if it were a waste of opportunities to see so much and not to know more.

He could scarcely realize—no American could, least of all a twenty-two-year-old—how much he had to learn. He decided to give up northern Germany rather than to see both it and Italy "superficially."[85]

Switzerland and Bavaria intervened. For three days, with a guide, Charles walked and rode among the mountains and glaciers under the shadow of Mont Blanc. In a hut on the summit of La Flegere he found William Bullard's and another friend's names in the "book of visitors." He proceeded alone, by mule and foot, over the Gemmi Pass to Interlaken and then hiked the Brünig Pass to Lungern: a lot of Alps, a lot of mileage on his boots. At Lucerne on 11 October he reentered the world of newsprint and learned with gratitude that America's political "trouble has been got over." Clouds still dotted the Republic's horizon, but "on the whole our future is very bright." "GOD grant that it may continue so, for our country is the hope of the world. Religion and education are its only safeguards."[86]

As he passed through the massive city gates of Nuremberg on 17 October, the Middle Ages grabbed him with a force not felt since his first sight of Venice. Nuremberg's "treasures of art & antiquity"—Peter Vischer's bronzes, Adam Kraft's sculptures, Albrecht Dürer's engravings—could have held him "for weeks." (Norton's admiration of Dürer lasted a lifetime.) Yet what ignited Charles in Nuremberg was not the city's array of great pieces of art but its gestalt. Nuremberg endured as if the Middle Ages had never faded. The thick, stern miles of grayish-brown stone wall girding the city, the "thousands of traditions & pleasant histories" clustering round it, its finely detailed Gothic churches, the very house in which Dürer lived, all this came together to plunge Charles imaginatively into the Middle Ages, "a period which seems to me little known & understood." Somehow, in two days in Nuremberg all his experience of art and of history since Venice fused in a kind of epiphany. "I have not been so sorry to leave any place, where the parting was unconnected with saying farewell to friends, as I was to bid good bye to Nuremberg this afternoon."[87]

He never really would say goodbye. His fascination with the "little known & understood" Middle Ages—already kindled perhaps in his Harvard dissertation on Santa Croce, fanned by Venice, but bursting into full flame in Nuremberg—formed a leitmotif of his career.

Arriving in Munich on 19 October, Charles learned that Louisa had at last decided to hand her vacillating heart over to William Bullard (who, Catharine said, "has gained our confidence, our esteem and our affection"). Charley, though eighteen months away from the nest physically, had never flown Shady Hill emotionally. His letter home gushed with happiness and family sympathy. The only shadow cast by Louisa's engagement was that it "must in some part alter that familiar course in which our lives have run most happy and unchanged for so long." He wished "with all my heart" to be with his family now.[88]

To tell the truth, a good part of his heart wished to be in Italy. He arrived there at the beginning of November. Having traveled Europe, Norton feared that Venice on second acquaintance would have lost its original luster. His "fears were vain": "all is picturesque, all belongs to the past, and all is tinged with melancholy that adds to its loveliness." Still, he could spare only four days there. He took a few hours in Padua to revisit the Giottos in the Arena Chapel, liking them much better this time for understanding how they compared with other works of the kind and with the limits and efforts of the artist. Interest in Giotto indicated in 1850 an advanced taste, almost avant-garde.[89]

Within the medieval walls of Florence, Charles planned to settle for the winter. Amid peddlers crying "Signori miei! Un' paolo soltanto!" he set out to find lodging. For twelve dollars a month he got three rooms and a servant in a house on the central Piazza di Santa Maria Novella; with breakfast for fifteen cents at the Café Doney and dinner at "the table d'hote of one of the hotels where I shall meet the strangers who are in town," this scheme would be cheaper than living in a hotel. The saving would buy books and engravings. It also helped to pay for an Italian tutor.[90]

Indeed, he seemed now more student than tourist, working at Italian for hours each day, much of the rest of the time immersing himself in the galleries. He spent the morning of 16 November, his twenty-third birthday (his second abroad), at the Uffizi, struck especially by "the first efforts of Cimabue and Giotto, in which the desire of expression is checked by the want of knowledge." The same want depressed him, and he came away "half sorrowful because there was so much to know and I knew so little." On the way back to his rooms he stopped by a bookstore, gave himself a birthday present of Vasari and Machiavelli. The next day he visited the Franciscan church of Santa Croce, laying eyes at last on the monuments that he had limned in his Harvard commencement dissertation. Four long years had passed since that Cambridge morning, yet he seemed barely to have begun.[91]

Two days after his arrival, his London acquaintance C. C. Black knocked on the door of his rooms: a pleasant surprise followed shortly by a call from the poet Robert Browning, to whom Norton had addressed one of his infinite letters of introduction. For the next weeks the Blacks and the Brownings formed the poles of his social world. When not in the Uffizi or Pitti galleries or the studios of the American sculptors Horatio Greenough and Hiram Powers, Norton was apt to be at Robert and Elizabeth Browning's, discussing Italian liberalism and Catholic superstition, or driving out into the olive-covered hills to talk with Black (something of an authority on Italian art) about painters. These were the pleasantest of classrooms.[92]

Norton's lease expired on 14 December. He planned to spend then a leisurely week traveling to Rome via Siena and Perugia. But in early December letters from home arrived with news of Louisa's wedding plans. Charley took an hour's walk and made up his mind. "The pleasure or advantage" of a few more months in Europe could not compare "with the happiness of being with you, dearest Louisa, at your wedding, and with you, dearest Father and Mother, after Louisa, Jane & William are gone." He hoped eventually that Louisa and William would build a house on the grounds of Shady Hill.[93]

Now he booked his own passage home. A week in Paris gave him time to buy gifts, to revisit the salons of the Circourts and Mrs. Childe, and to worship again Rachel Félix. He returned to Ary Scheffer's studio to commission a painting (at nine thousand francs) as a wedding gift for William and Louisa. In London the season was over, and most of Norton's friends had vacated the city. But Charles had "a little pleasant talk" with Dickens ("sobered somewhat in his dress and manner since I saw him in America"), met Mrs. Gaskell and Edwin Landseer, dined again with Sturgis and Babbage. On 4 January the *Asia* steamed from Liverpool, carrying a musing Charles Norton.[94]

With a hundred passengers chattering away in the first-class salon, meals gave little chance to think; nor did the promenade deck encourage meditation in a North Atlantic winter. But in the ship's little library and his own tiny cabin Charles could mull over what had passed. One conclusion needed no thought. Italy was his beloved, Venice its chiefest jewel: "no other city is half so peculiar, half so beautiful." Italy meant frescoes, churches, statues, oils, medallions. What had surprised him there was more in himself than in the land: a passion of unforeseen depth for the astonishingly various incarnations of art, a capacious love that had grown with his knowledge.[95]

England, in contrast, land of "selfishness and flunkeyism," had chilled his inherited Anglophilia. Even Paris, for all its superficiality, for all the looseness of its mores and morals, he preferred to London. Possibly New England even had something to learn from Paris salons, where not only men talked of diplomacy, history, politics. "I wish our ladies would so far follow this Parisian fashion as to allow themselves to be addressed about something more than the Opera, a sleighride, or the last novel." He did not mean the ladies at Shady Hill, for in this happy respect they were more Parisian than American.[96]

Norton had also found in Paris a model for himself, one that did not displace Andrews but expanded and elaborated the paternal pattern. The comte de Circourt impressed Charles "as the most remarkable man I have ever seen for the variety, the extent, the readiness of his knowledge, combined with natural talent & esprit." Someone averred that Europe had not known his equal since Pico della Mirandola, and Charles was ready to believe it. One afternoon in Scheffer's atelier "in the course of half an hour" Circourt had

> quoted Homer, Petrarch, & our President's message, analyzed the characteristics of the Venetian school of painting, referred to some of the technical difficulties of art, told Madame Scheffer where Washington Irving lived, gave her an account of [Sir James] Stephen the new History professor at Cambridge, and said that he had been all the forenoon on duty as a National Guard.[97]

Circourt lacked some of Andrews's best qualities; his morals were Parisian, his judgments fickle. That was not the point. Boston had outfitted Charles with solidity and earnestness to last a lifetime. What Circourt supplied—and in this Circourt stood for the Continent, draped in a frock coat of specially elegant cut—was a fuller idea of what might arise on such a foundation. The comte stretched Charles's imagination; the mind's eye saw an Andrews Norton more polished, more variously learned, more sophisticated in taste, more at ease in the wide world. Charles was imagining himself, though surely not very self-consciously. He was barely twenty-three, wriggling out of his chrysalis.

FOUR

A Merchant in the Unmaking,
1851–1855

For now, wriggling back into Shady Hill was what Charley longed for. When the *Asia* docked in New York on 18 January 1851, his cousin Charles Mills stood on the wharf, a first glimpse of home. Norton had already asked his family to have William Bullard meet the train alone in Boston. "Do not let anyone else be at the cars, I would rather see you all at home where I left you nineteen months ago."[1]

The past would not submit to recapture. Shady Hill bustled with arrangements for William and Louisa's wedding, only days off. A couple of weeks later, the newlyweds left for an eight-month wedding tour of Europe, taking Jane with them. Otherwise, on the surface, home life glided along as if Charley had dreamed the two years abroad. A new railroad on the northern side of Shady Hill, houses springing up along Kirkland Street to the south, scarcely yet encroached on "the pleasures of seclusion." The Longfellows still came in the evenings for rhyming games and family theatricals; Charles Mills dropped in to dabble with Charley and Grace in the latest fad, spirit rapping; Mrs. Stewart, the new cook, was turning out a great relief: her predecessor had proved a disaster.[2]

Yet, beneath apparently changeless cycles, Shady Hill had altered and not chiefly because Jane and Louisa had left: the larger reason was Andrews's decline. Though only sixty-four years old in 1851, Andrews had for fifteen years thought of himself as "a feeble old man"; his nearly fatal illness in the fall of 1849 had left him one in fact. As the running of the household slowly slipped from his hands, his son took increasing charge.[3]

Charles himself was older now, more widely traveled than his parents, with his own experiences, his own tastes, his own diversions, subtly diverging from Andrews and Catharine's criteria. His new friend George Curtis visited from New York for a few days, to compare memories of the Sphinx and the Pyramids. "Il tuo Giorgio" was fop enough to nettle fastidious Norton sensibilities, but "Carlo caro" did not care. In April, Charles had

James Russell Lowell to dinner. Lowell hardly qualified as outré, his *Fable for Critics* and *Biglow Papers* only now and then tweaking Nortonian propriety; but he did write for the abolitionist *Anti-Slavery Standard* and thereby qualified at Shady Hill as a dangerous radical. Moreover, both Lowell and Curtis had once fluttered around the Transcendentalists, Andrews's bêtes noires. Lowell was as yet only a friendly acquaintance, but Curtis was well on his way to becoming an intimate. The elder Nortons' placid courtesy rarely wavered, but Charles was starting to redecorate Shady Hill intellectually to his own taste.[4]

For this, he had plenty of time. His premature return from Europe had stranded him with no business, and a depressed market did not immediately bring any his way. By April, however, he was lending Henry Lee a hand on India Wharf and "quite enjoying," his youngest sister observed, "the little return to his old habits and business." Soon he moved into his own counting room at No. 34 Central Wharf, sharing space with Franklin Story, an erstwhile fellow apprentice. There, for the next four years, Norton clambered about among linseed, dyes, gunny sacks and cloth, jute, hemp, twine, straw rugs. He chartered ships in partnership with Story or Charles Guild, Bullard or Richard Lewis. He bought and sold in London and Liverpool, Boston and Calcutta, sometimes for cash, sometimes for a six-month note. He dunned textile manufacturers in upstate New York, and he turned a profit.[5]

The profit was never large. In 1851 "extreme *pressure* in the money market" (the worst since the Panic of '37, Norton believed) "diminished the value of all mdze." In 1852 the *Seth Sprague* ran into foul weather, missed the height of the Calcutta market, and lost a bundle for Norton. Merchants had always played a chancy hand. But Boston now grappled with a deeper and persisting problem. The burgeoning port of New York was siphoning off her trade, turning the ups and downs of commerce into steady decline. In 1852, Bullard and Lee gave up. Norton hung on, but commerce occupied fewer hours than ever. Trade had always competed for Norton's loyalty with other interests; its power to command him was slackening.[6]

A throng of new-made friendships partly filled the open hours: Rajinder Dutt and George Sim in India, Richard Milnes and John Kenyon in London, the Scheffers and the Circourts in Paris: letters flowed on and on. This stream of mail eroded the old boundaries of Norton's world. He now heard directly of people, events, and opinions across the seas, especially in Britain; now he found himself receiving letters of introduction for traveling Englishmen.

Such individual acquaintanceships supplied the cement of cultural activity in the days before professional organizations and specialized journals. Intellectually inclined travelers learned to know like-minded individuals across the country or across the sea; and they thereby linked together local cultural webs centered on cities as different as Boston and Charleston, Edinburgh and London. In this way, on the basis of common language and intertwined histories, a great North Atlantic matrix melded diverse regional cultures into a single cosmopolitan Anglo-American world of ideas, itself overlapping Continental European networks. Like Uncle Ticknor before him, Charles entered the thick array of personal familiarity binding together British and American intellectual elites. Within two decades his place in it would make Ticknor look provincial.

For the time being, his role was still largely defined by the broad limits of greater Boston; and with two years' pent-up energy Norton returned to the local literary scene. In early April, Frank Parkman submitted to Norton's editorial pencil rough proofs of his new book on Pontiac's conspiracy; Charles had not finished working them over before Francis Bowen, who wanted *Pontiac* "favorably introduced to the public," asked him to review it for the *North American Review*—which Charles did with the gravity of a newly elected corresponding member of the American Ethnological Society. While helping to launch *Pontiac*, Charles was also supervising American reprints for his new English friend Sir Arthur Helps.[7]

He still found ample time to grind his own literary mill, his Indian experience providing good grist. For the July 1851 *North American* Norton wrote an account of Jamsetjee Jeejeebhoy, the wealthy Parsee merchant he had met in Bombay, whose stupendous charities earned him the first knighthood awarded an Indian. A swift sketch of Bombay introduced the piece. Norton made the city vivid by imagining exotic peoples jostling together in its streets, each character brought to life by a detail of dress or physiognomy ("the Chinese sailor, with his blue trowsers, his straw hat, and his long tail of braided hair"). This word painting concluded with the purple brimless hat and spotless white dress of a Parsee, the "most interesting figure" in the procession. A quick overview of Parsee culture followed, this in turn framing a detailed account of Jamsetjee's benevolences, drawn from documents acquired in Bombay.[8]

In this triple movement, Norton worked out a narrative technique suited to both his characteristic materials and his presumed audience. The putative reader came to Norton's topic with no special curiosity; so Charles tried first to arrest the mind's eye with a visual, kinetic dramatic scene. (Behind the pictures and actions in Norton's prose worked Edward Channing's teaching of rhetoric and his own months in galleries, lessons sharpened by the hours poring over Parkman's writing.) A splash of local color served a second function: readying the reader for concise summation of whatever foreign culture, political theory, or religious system Norton had in view. This précis in turn made understandable a wealth of documentary detail that composed the meat of the piece. Norton would ring changes on this formula for decades, shifting the components around but never deserting the triune relation. And in the same happy experiment he found a subject with éclat; writing and lecturing on India became for a while a Norton speciality.

But India still interested him less in itself than as a laboratory for testing permutations of Boston principles. Like Alexis de Tocqueville seeking France's future in the American present, Norton always pondered foreign cultures with an eye to elucidating his own. Parsees prowling the pages of the *North American* became a case study of the natural interweaving of religion, literature and the arts, and individual moral formation: a Nortonian experiment with general ideas about the relationship of art and national character, later to be applied to the United States. Because "no divinely gifted poet has sung to them, and no hero has arisen among them whose glories have been handed down by any pious narrator," the Parsees had no "literature of their own." Hence, they also lacked the "nobler qualities of character, those alone which can give a people an honorable place in the history of the world." Their religion exemplified the historicist principles by which Unitarians explained religious development, in this case the corruption of belief into "superstition." Parsees, Norton suggested, must once have venerated the sun as a symbol of deity; and as "so often" in "the history of religious beliefs, the symbol, from being regarded only as a sign of the Supreme and Holy Being, is now reverenced by the vulgar and uneducated as the visible God himself."[9]

With more urgency, Sir Jamsetjee Jeejeebhoy's benevolences presented an object lesson for Americans. Although Americans "speak proudly" of their charities, Norton insisted that they had "little real reason" for complacency. "We have forgotten that we are the most prosperous community that the world ever saw, and that we should be more blameworthy than any other people were we less liberal." Moving beyond ancestral High Federalism, Norton took the United States, rather than New England, as his native land. But he transferred to this vaster theater of political action the Boston notions of community and of a corresponding web of human obligation.

Such obligations ran deeper than the formal rules governing the polity. Norton's upbringing in Scottish Enlightenment historicism taught him to relativize human institutions. Legal systems were no more than mutable outgrowths of historical evolution, and the progress of civilization had yet far to go. To bridge the gap between imperfect governments and inevitable human needs, voluntary effort had to come into play: to ease injustices, assuage oppressions, ameliorate the defects of underdeveloped laws. The horrors of poverty in Britain—and the insouciance of British aristocrats—had burned into him a lesson he never forgot: "benevolence is not simply a duty, it is a necessity," so long as "the laws which regulate the acquisition and the possession of property are so ill understood as they at present are all the world over."

Paradoxically, although America had fewer of such ills than Europe, it had yet more need of benevolence; for a republic's survival depended on the moral health and political intelligence of its citizens. Not only altruistic "virtue" but also "the most refined selfishness" called Americans to work to improve conditions of life for the least fortunate among them: a vocation reinforced by sentiments implanted deep in human nature by a benevolent God. "We have learnt that expensive schools are the cheapest institution of the state; we have yet to learn that the prevention of pauperism, at any cost, is cheaper than the care of it when it exists; we have yet to learn that the truest pleasure which wealth can afford is in spending it so as to promote the happiness of others." Benevolence obliged not only the rich. Most Americans could afford charity; and the "duty is the same to every man, to give to others according to his means." An ancillary obligation evidently fell on some: exhorting others to do their duty, a mantle comfortable on the shoulders of Andrews Norton's son.[10]

For, out of raw materials bequeathed him, Charles was forging an author, alter ego to the young merchant. In December, Longfellow reported to a London friend that Norton kept "one eye upon books and another upon the sails of Canton ships. Which will carry the day is doubtful." Norton's writings, however, bore no resemblance to the playful, precious *Nile Notes* that his friend Curtis had just published, a lateborn child of the Knickerbocker school of New York literature. New England seriousness simmered under even Norton's lighter pages; he aimed at instruction more than entertainment and at moral formation more than either. The question now chiefly nagging at him was how communities ordered human relations. This quandary owed much to two concurrent though unrelated crises, the great Irish immigration and the expansion of slavery. But Norton was exploring basic principles as well as particular problems.[11]

He had in mind a book to bring under the searching light of Boston principles the radical social theories that had animated Italian rebels and piqued Circourt's salon. When this idea came into his head is impossible to say—maybe on the evening in Florence when he and the Brownings talked Italian politics and Robert handed him a copy of Mazzini's *Foi et Avenir*. By April 1851 he was "reading and studying much" in preparation for "a short essay on Republicanism in Europe, which I mean to print as a pledge to that small portion of the world who care anything about it, that I do not spend my time idly, and that I still claim Literature as a love who is not to be supplanted in my affections by any other." He enlisted George Curtis, with his New York publishing connections, and Frank Child, in Paris on his way home from Göttingen, to buy "republican pamphlets" for him, and alerted other friends to keep an eye open for tidbits of Continental politics.[12]

The address for such deliveries shifted in June to Newport, Rhode Island, where the Nortons had decided to spend their summers. The physicians had prescribed Newport's milder climate for Andrews, but the therapy hardly inconvenienced his family. Grace, always her own woman, did turn out an "unbeliever in Newport," but her parents and siblings found the island resort nearly Edenic. A "gay crowd," many from New York and the South, filled the town itself; but over the rest of the island, Charles felt, "broods a spirit of repose." Literary work went on, with occasional attention to the countinghouse; but he also enjoyed long strolls along the shore and through the pastures, varied by bowling parties and visits from old friends. Newport recommended itself as a permanent annex to Shady Hill, and before they left in October the Nortons decided to build a house there. Charles managed this business; he had taken over from his ailing father supervision of all the family finances, which he oversaw along with his own investments in the India trade. At twenty-five, he had reached financial maturity.[13]

Business mingled with a remarkable miscellany of other involvements in the early 1850s. Norton took to the lyceum circuit in a small way, lecturing on India. Always good with children, he taught a Sunday school class at the First Parish in Cambridge, soon becoming the school's superintendent. (It was probably for the Sunday school that he printed the pamphlet *Five Christmas Hymns:* New England was learning to celebrate that suspect papist feast.) Harvard (appreciating his "bonne prononciation") appointed him to its Committee of Examination in Modern Languages and, in October 1851, called him to cover the classes of a French instructor who had died suddenly. In January 1852 the Athenaeum elected Norton a trustee.[14]

Adulthood crept up stealthily on Norton, as it does on most of us, but with a Boston twist. This mélange of tasks carried local meaning: Charles was assuming his civic toga virilis, taking on, a little more conscientiously than most of his peers, the adult responsibilities that befell his station. There would come to Norton over many decades hundreds of the routine jobs that oiled Boston institutions.

He was at the same time taking on out-of-the-ordinary duties. Not every Boston patrician paid more than lip service to the local ethos of community obligation, but the Nortons' wealth cohabited with sensitive consciences. As Catharine said, one must work "to aid the struggling and forlorn." In that spirit, Andrews had helped to raise funds to relieve the great Irish famine in the later 1840s. Charles confronted its aftermath, his own sensibilities heightened by misery seen in India and Britain. The famine had driven millions from Ireland, thousands of them to Boston. In 1845, Cambridge counted scarcely a thousand Irish among its 12,000 souls; ten years later the city had swelled to over 20,000, nearly a quarter Irish. The conditions under which they had to live sickened a sensitive spirit. But what did duty enjoin?[15]

The standard republican prescription to make citizens safe for democracy was also patrician Boston's favored therapy for uplifting the poor: education. In his article on Jamsetjee Jeejeebhoy, Norton had called "expensive schools" the "cheapest institution of the state." They appeared a special bargain in present circumstances. The Irish had arrived in such numbers and in such disadvantaged conditions as to "form almost a nation by themselves." Unlike earlier immigrants, they could neither "rapidly amalgamate with our native population" nor "speedily adapt themselves to our institutions"; yet Massachusetts law quickly gave them the "full rights of citizens." Americans never should and never would "send them back to starve," whatever "the consequence to us"; but, if anyone needed uplifting, these immigrants did.[16]

Norton persuaded the School Committee to let him use a schoolhouse near Harvard, then enlisted among his friends a corps of "excellent volunteer assistants." In mid-November an evening school opened for men and boys "too occupied during the day or too poor to attend our day schools": the first such institution in Cambridge, perhaps in the state. It operated only two evenings a week for a four-month term, and Norton had to fight a parsimonious School Committee to keep it going that long. He himself feared that the twenty-odd students got no "direct beneficial results." But at least one ten-year-old orphan, after learning to read under Norton's "gentle kindness," frequently visited Shady Hill, where he got "choice books to read, with instructions on how to read carefully"; eventually, he entered Harvard Law School and ended as mayor of Providence, Rhode Island.[17]

In any case, the evening school idea prospered around Boston. Norton's cousin Charles Eliot taught in one across the river; his one-time playmate Thomas Wentworth Higginson organized another in Newburyport; and in 1854 the pastor of Saint John's Catholic Church in East Cambridge opened one for Irish men. How much these owed to Norton's experiment is no longer knowable, but the evening school did reaffirm and shape his own commitment to Boston's indigent. A principle became a practicality. Measures to equip the poor to improve themselves, to fit them better to the community in which they dwelt, had become for Charles a lived reality, one in which he could play a part.[18]

It remained a reality in striking counterpoint to most of his activities. Germania Society concerts, Jenny Lind, *Don Giovanni*—how did Mozart mesh with the evening school? Chuckling with the Longfellows over one of Tom Appleton's bons mots as they strolled out of a performance of *The Crown Diamonds*—did Mme Thillon's singing echo on the highway verges where that Irish orphan boy eked out a "precarious livelihood" tending other people's cows? Such questions the Nortons had cultured themselves to ask.[19]

And Shady Hill remained Charley's lodestone. By early December, winter had crept into Boston. It was the best of times for Louisa, William, and Jane to return from their European travels and inspirit the household. The closeness of the Norton family is hard to exaggerate, its substantiality to Charles impossible to ignore. As Andrews weakened and Louisa moved to a new home on Beacon Hill, he perhaps grew even more conscious of the salience of his family. Jane, nearest to him in age, was closest emotionally. "Your precious note written on my birthday," she told him, "has given me a great deal of happiness today and every word of love and affection that it contains I respond to from the very bottom of my heart." As siblings do, they sometimes quarreled; and Jane was not above mocking the affection between *"my precious brother," "our dear sister* Grace," and herself. None of this loosened their attachment. "We are very important to each other and let us see that we are faithful to our trust. Let us see that we do justice to our real love."[20]

The emotional center of Charles's life being at Shady Hill, it was natural that his deeper friendships flourished there, notably—in the early 1850s— that with Frank Child. "I value as you would have me all your love," Charles wrote Frank at New Year, with the open affection easy to Victorians, "and will try always to be faithful to it,—faithful not only in loving you but in making myself more worthy of your affection." It was equally natural that Frank become an intimate of the whole family. After studies in Göttingen and Berlin, he had succeeded Edward Channing as Boylston Professor of Rhetoric (thanks in small part to Charley's lobbying); and, living nearby, he fell into the habit of spending Thursday and Sunday evenings at Shady Hill, talking and reading with Charley, submitting to Gracie's ragging, playing music with Jane, before walking back to his digs at ten or eleven o'clock.[21]

Some evenings Frank and Charley worked rather than played. Child, with intermittent help from his best friend, was overseeing for a Boston publisher a series of standard British poets. He undertook Spenser himself, a solid scholarly edition in five volumes; and he later added for the series an eight-volume collection of ballads, which Norton admired as "far superior to any preceding similar work." Most Boston patricians with a taste for publishing were dilettantes; Child refused to edit Chaucer, on the ground that materials for a tolerably accurate version could not be had in America. Working with Frank kept alive for Charley an ideal of scholarship exceeding even his father's in fidelity to the austere norms of German erudition.[22]

In the winter of 1851–52, Frank and Charley surely talked also about an article of very different character that Norton was writing. "Schools and Dwellings for the Poor" appeared in the April 1852 *North American*. Norton began by noting in "the literature of the present age" a new concern for "that portion of society which is generally called 'the lower classes'"; "the common ties of human sympathy binding together the highest and the lowest are now more readily acknowledged, the rights of the ignorant and the suffering are now more warmly asserted, and the duties of all classes towards each other are now more strongly urged." He thought it "the visible sign of the influence of the spirit of Christianity, and the progress of Christian principles" that concern for the poor sprang from "a sense of the claims of man as man," from "a true brotherhood." This opinion marked his own progress beyond his ancestors' High Federalism: Norton scorning the idea that charity should rest "on the belief that the poor are the dependents of the rich, & have the claims of dependance." Norton conceded that eradication of pauperism was "utterly impossible," since "society is at present organized" on the basis of "unjust inequalities." But this unhappy state of affairs only made more urgent "doing the much that may be done to diminish it."[23]

First among things needful was "improvement of the dwellings of the poor." On this hinged the success of "all other measures," for bad housing was the "primary source" of vice and misery. In the "low, disgusting haunts of poverty," the "very ideas of neatness, of prudence, of sobriety, of chastity, of self-respect, are lost." Where lay the remedy? Government ought not supply housing but should regulate and inspect it, ensuring proper ventilation, drainage, and so forth. Private hands should erect the needed buildings—but not "as a matter of gratuitous charity." For "interference with the usual laws which govern men's dealings with each other" would in the end frustrate reform: tenement owners would rise in opposition, and the poor would lose "self-reliance and self-respect." Instead, "benevolent associations" should take the lead by building model tenements to provide decent housing for the poor along with a decent return for investors. Norton had bought these ideas wholesale from English reformers, and he detailed projects in London that had turned a profit on good, cheap housing.[24]

The second essential was to combat the ignorance that mired people in pauperism. An allusion on the first page to "the rights of the ignorant" suggests Norton's attitude: ignorance was a deprivation, not a vice, demanding redress, not reprobation. Americans could find excellent models in the French *salles d'asile* for very young children and the English "ragged schools" for older ones. Norton wanted the former appended to American common-school systems; the latter corresponded to the "Evening Schools" recently established, devoting "chief attention" to "the poorest and most depraved." He admitted that the job was complex, the teaching "by no means a simple process of cultivating the intellect." "The affections are to be developed by sympathy and kindness; the moral truths taught by words are to be illustrated in conduct, and the progress of the intellect is to be based on the cultivation of the heart."[25]

Although Charles here spoke from experience, he echoed his upbringing and education. Invocation of "sympathy" as key to pedagogy recalled Scottish psychology of the moral sentiments and the imagination as developed by Francis Hutcheson and Adam Smith, as appropriated by Andrews Norton, and as taught to Charles at Harvard. Dependence of "intellect" on "heart" reflected not only this Scottish heritage but also more recent American stress on building "character"—on developing an interior moral compass to guide the mind's judgments—as a chief aim of education. Finally, the reference to "cultivation" recalls Unitarian Boston's ideal of "self-culture": the continuing formation of intellect, will, and affections by self-immersion in learning and the fine arts. From these materials, Charles was constructing understandings of education, its relations to personal morality, its salience for citizenship. His ideas were slightly bewildered infants; they would mature in the 1870s and 1880s into a new model of higher education.

Already, his practical proposals attracted readers. The article and the evening school gave Norton a small reputation as an urban reformer, of a "thoughtful" rather than "ardent nature." With commerce occupying only a fraction of his hours, with no clear alternate vocation in view, Norton's moral inheritance pushed him toward social activism: yet another career beckoned to a young man unsure of his direction in life. As the *North American*'s editor saw, "literary attempts" had become "subservient to other & higher aims." "Schools and Dwellings for the Poor" put Norton in contact with reformers in New York and London, but a local contact had more consequence. On 15 April, Henry B. Rogers, a friend of Bullard's, wrote to say that he, too, had been looking into English model dwellings. Norton had mused about turning exhortations into bricks and mortar; so, when Rogers asked if he knew "of any persons disposed to enter upon an enterprise of this sort," Charles leapt at the bait, agreeing to take on the organizational work himself.[26]

This had to wait a month or two. Central Wharf and Harvard duties prevented him from settling into Newport until the end of June; and, there, work on the lodging houses sometimes took second place to interests of a less public-spirited nature. South Carolinians escaping torrid summers favored Newport; and with one of these families, Oliver Middleton's, a particularly warm acquaintance grew. His daughters Matilda and Eleanor, a few years younger than Charles, became fast friends of Jane and Grace and, later, occasional guests at Shady Hill. One of them attracted Charles, though the Victorian practice of referring to ladies only by surname prevents us from knowing which one. *The* Miss Middleton sailed with him on idyllic afternoons, romanced with him on moonlit evenings.[27]

Even so, Newport was far from paradise that summer. As Andrews's health fluctuated between bad and worse, the psychological burden on all the family grew. Business required Charles to shuttle to Boston; even when in Newport, the building of the new house and the planning of the model lodging house competed with Miss Middleton for his hours. And, with Father often abed, Charles was helping Andrews's assistant, Ezra Abbot, to edit the elder Norton's collected *Tracts on Christianity*.

Another literary project involved interests more characteristic. Harriet Beecher Stowe's *Uncle Tom's Cabin,* published in March, had set the Anglo-American world to talking—even Calcutta was abuzz. Norton, detesting slavery even more than abolitionism and considering *Uncle Tom's Cabin* "a work of uncommon power," posted a copy to his English friend Arthur Helps; he also persuaded his college friend Edward Pringle, a member of the Carolinian summer diaspora in Newport, to read it. Unsurprisingly, Edward and Charley argued; and at Norton's behest Pringle wrote out a refutation of the book and defense of slavery. A few weeks later a long letter arrived from Helps endorsing the book and attacking slavery. Norton believed that Northerners needed to hear Southern voices; Pringle's he thought a cogent and high-minded one. Helps meanwhile encouraged Norton to publish *his* letter in the United States. So, as summer ended, Charles found himself a small-time moderator of the great debate. He paid a Cambridge printer to run up copies of Pringle's *Slavery at the South* and Helps's *Letter on Uncle Tom's Cabin*. (Tactfully, he sent Stowe only Helps's tract.) *Fraser's*, the magazine that had initially printed Helps's *Letter* in England, reprinted *Slavery at the South;* then Littell issued it as a pamphlet. Norton got out of all this the novel satisfaction of intellectual arbitrage, far from his last.[28]

Another consequence was a new acquaintance. Helps asked Charles to transmit a copy of his *Letter* to Ralph Waldo Emerson, with whom Helps had become friendly in England. Communicating with the celebrated transcendentalist would not otherwise have occurred to Norton; for, in the 1830s, Andrews had violently assailed him as American avatar of German mystagogy, and inherited mistrust lingered on. Emerson, however, unexpectedly took the occasion of acknowledging Helps's pamphlet to wish for "new opportunities of establishing my acquaintance" with the younger Norton. These would soon come, as opportunities for other new friendships already had. William Porcher Miles, another Carolinian in Newport, shared Norton's interests in education; when the two met, they hit it off immediately. Captain Richard Baird Smith, the Ganges Canal engineer whom Charles had met in Britain, dined with the Nortons in early August 1852. An ugly little man, "very agreeable & intelligent," he and Charles became such warm friends that two decades later Norton, who never laid eyes on Baird Smith again, named a son after him.[29]

Norton had indeed a remarkable gift for making friends—and, as matters turned out, for keeping them. William Miles regarded his "brief" acquaintance "as one of the warm and bright things of my life." Henry Arthur Bright, a young Englishman on an American tour after graduating from Cambridge, visited Norton hurriedly in 1852 yet returned home regarding him as a comrade for life. Norton's talent for friendship was often remarked upon. It was in everyday talk that he won much of the admiration that contemporaries expressed for him, resembling Coleridge in this if in little else. And this fact is key to understanding both Norton's influence and the failure of later generations to comprehend it, for with ephemeral words vanished much of the reason for the respect accorded him.[30]

The sources of Norton's capacity for friendship lie now partly hidden, but six elements at least played a part. First came a material precondition: Norton possessed the means to entertain and the residences in which to do it agreeably. But rich boors abound—Norton, secondly, had (as a younger contemporary who knew him well recalled) a "desire for constant self-improvement" that engendered "zeal for the best intellectual companionship." This urge probably related to his omnivorous curiosity; though in the course of things he met persons whom he disliked, Norton (thirdly) rarely encountered anyone who failed to interest him. Curiosity went along with, fourth, a tolerance for personal disagreement, even for moral disagreeableness in individual persons, remarkable in a man so strongly principled and, indeed, censorious as Norton in the abstract. Fifth was the undemanding, offhanded generosity that his parents had formed in him—noblesse oblige without the condescension: "He is the kindest creature in the shape of a young man of 25 that ever befriended an emigrant stranger anywhere."[31]

Finally, sixth, Norton had a knack for talk: not for throwing off witticisms but for sustaining engaging conversation. One could chat for hours and go off to bed reluctantly. That same younger friend, looking back on a lifetime spent in literary and intellectual circles, recalled that Norton filled Shady Hill with "more pleasant conversation of an original sort" than he had known "in any other house." The secret lay not only in Norton's own discourse but in his talent as "a good listener," his knack for turning talk toward fertile topics, his ability to draw out interlocutors. Yet the depth of Norton's closer friendships, the intellectual caliber of those friends, and the permanence of his influence on them testified to something deeper, to a tougher fiber running through his conversation, giving Norton a highly personal authority. He never hesitated to criticize his friends' work bluntly and face-to-face, and they heeded. They accepted his competence, "felt him to be one of them," understood his candor as proof of love and admiration, Norton's frankness flowing as it did from "a curious simplicity of character in him, careless of and blind to suspicion which it knew to be unwarranted." Accepting another person with full and unself-regarding seriousness is a powerfully alluring compliment.[32]

In 1852 this force attracted Miss Middleton, at least until October interrupted their moonlit romance. She returned to the plantation, the Nortons to Shady Hill, and Charles to his varied duties. The India trade was picking up; Sunday school started again; so also did Norton's occasional lyceum lectures on India—and so did the evening school, requiring from Charles not only hours in the classroom but a fight for its survival in the city council chamber. Now, too, with Boston's patricians home from their varied summer shores, Norton organized with Bullard and Rogers a subscription to raise funds for the proposed model lodging house, then persuaded architects to volunteer to design the building. Fall also brought its forms of relaxation: pleasant family parties at Shady Hill, opera with family or friends, the annual dinner of Charles's Harvard class, and just after Christmas an agreeable evening party where Charles met again the little girl he had played with at Theodore Sedgwick's in New York ten years earlier. At sixteen Sue Sedgwick had begun to attract a different caliber of attention.[33]

Charles's social life, however, now revolved around another guest at that evening's party: a young Englishman named Arthur Hugh Clough, in Boston hunting a job. Clough had started a promising Oxford career but, coming to doubt the truth of Christianity, had resigned his fellowship. (Oxford still required adherence to the Church of England: a statement of belief not always taken seriously by those who subscribed to it. The delicacy of Clough's conscience awoke fellow feeling in Norton.) He now needed some other way to support the woman he wished to marry. Soured on hidebound, class-ridden England, Clough looked to America with hope for humanity's future as well as his own. Literate Boston already knew him for a poem widely noticed in 1848, "The Bothie of Toper-na-Fuosich"; and he had struck up a friendship with Emerson when the latter was in Britain that year; then, on the steamer to Boston, Clough fell in with James Russell Lowell. He also carried a letter of introduction from an English friend to Charles Eliot Norton.[34]

Clough arrived on 12 November 1852, a Friday evening; on Monday morning he met "young Norton" and, after three hours of walking and talking through Boston, swore "eternal friendship." Clough took to Cambridge almost as quickly, finding "in its intellectual atmosphere a repose which recalls that of grand old Oxford." Cambridge reciprocated by liking him, "with his gentleness, and his bewildered look, and his half-closed eyes." Longfellow entertained him; Lowell became a good friend; but Norton and Clough were inseparable. Clough, though, was the first confidant to call him "Charles" rather than "Charley": a sign of a subtle but self-conscious maturation in Norton.[35]

Clough became, like Frank Child, a shadow resident of Shady Hill, fond of Andrews and Catharine, "a fine venerable old fellow, rather infirm," and "a most good, kind, maternal woman." Charles helped Arthur look for work, and it may have been Norton who arranged a commission from Ticknor and Fields to revise the so-called Dryden translation of Plutarch's *Lives*. "Your kindness quite makes me ashamed," Clough mumbled. But he in turn stretched Norton's world. When they talked, as incessantly they did, religious faith formed a prime topic. Clough, though still clinging to a vague theism, had cast off every shred of credence in historic Christianity. His sincere and almost reverential unbelief immensely impressed his pious Unitarian friend, raising questions, fostering doubts, abetting trains of speculation that would ripen over the next decade. Friendship with Clough may well have been the turning point on the road that eventually led Norton away from Christianity into agnosticism, profoundly affecting his thinking on everything from the ends of politics to the means of education.[36]

For now, Clough provided a haven from the too-many projects Norton juggled: Calcutta and Madras, the house under way in Newport, two model lodging houses rising in Boston, the evening school, the book on social theories he was trying to write. Even for a young man, it became exhausting. In early March, Charles took a few days off to visit George Curtis and other friends in New York. Curtis, just made assistant editor of the new *Putnam's Magazine*, took advantage of Charley's stay to add to his friend's workload— a little something for the magazine.[37]

Norton responded in ten days with a characteristic piece: an attack on the consciences of *Putnam's* middle-class readers, cast in the form of a miniature memoir of his visit to New York. Its three pages contrasted the "tasteless display, and lavish, reckless wastefulness" of a posh dinner at the new Saint Nicholas Hotel with the selfless devotion of a clergyman who had set up a House of Industry amid the "confusion, dirt and misery" of the Five Points slum. The article also relived a moment in Pisa, evoking the shabby gentility of a palazzo there to puncture the Saint Nicholas's brand-new pretensions. "Magnificence, to be complete, needs a glory which comes only with antiquity and the associations that belong to age," for "beauty lies much in the imagination." Charles did not lecture only in the lyceum.[38]

While dashing this off for Curtis, Norton put the last touches on the book that he had been preparing since returning from Europe. Finished in mid-April 1853, *Considerations on Some Recent Social Theories* appeared in the first days of May, anonymously. In Boston anonymity protected modesty rather than identity. Norton himself made no secret, sending a copy to every acquaintance suspected of a whiff of interest in political ideas on all three continents he had trod.

For, as he told Arthur Helps, recent ideas about liberty, republican government, and social reorganization "seemed to me to be ground for much confusion of thought," and Norton wanted "not to lose the chance of doing even the least to turn the current in the right direction." He was realist enough to cherish little hope of effect. Diffusion of education in the United States, wide but shallow, imbued Americans with "a certain pride of intellect," which led them "to form strong opinions upon the most difficult questions." It befell "those favored by education or circumstances to use their best efforts[,] however feeble, in helping the formation and the spread of right views."[39]

Right views were urgently wanted. The Fugitive Slave Law, appended to the so-called Compromise of 1850, had inflamed nerves on both sides of the Mason-Dixon Line. The law required Northerners to assist in recapturing escaped slaves; this produced an explosion of Yankee outrage that Southerners took as direct insult. Norton saw in the sectional shouting a "growing danger," a "disposition towards 'nullification' in all parts of the country." Even Andrews, long churlish toward abolitionists, urged fellow citizens to resist the Fugitive Slave Law by every legal means. Charles was not so sure. Experience of Europe had strengthened his conviction of "the absolute necessity" of "cultivating the spirit of obedience" to properly constituted laws. ("Properly constituted" was a key phrase: Italian resistance to Austrian tyranny seemed legitimate.) While no man of principle should want to help to enforce the Fugitive Slave Law, Charles deemed that a judge's duty might require "unwilling assistance" and that even a private citizen ought to protect from mob violence a slaveholder trying to recover a slave.[40]

The United States enjoyed the best and stablest government on Earth, but its endurance depended "on the spirit of obedience among the people to the laws." Substituting a "right of private judgment" for the "duty of obeying the laws as they stand" would "unsettle the foundation" of the Republic—"or of any government whatsoever." Americans must wait for "educated public opinion" to "correct bad laws without disobedience to them while they remain on the statute book."[41]

Norton's views can appear the staunchest conservatism, if not downright authoritarian. But he echoed here the republicanism of the Founders: because voters can change laws, in a republican government the need for extralegal resistance disappears. Charles's confidence in education also bespoke an enduring Enlightenment faith in the plasticity of human nature; he remained in this respect truer to Boston's Unitarian principles than Andrews.

With the crisis of American slavery lying behind *Considerations on Some Recent Social Theories*, it seems odd that Norton chose to school his half-educated countrymen in *European* political thinking. Perhaps it was not. Norton was no American exceptionalist. He saw his country and Europe as wrestling with the same deeply rooted problems. And—like Tocqueville turned round—he believed that America must ultimately come to terms with the forces and ideas convulsing Europe. It therefore behooved Americans to develop right views of liberty, republicanism, and socialism.

Recent Social Theories began by identifying what Norton perceived as the toxic illusion of republicans like Mazzini, Kossuth, and Louis Blanc. Their "speculations" disregarded the real "differences in nations, both in character and in natural and material position." Their "cry for Universal Liberty, for the establishment of Republics, and for the direct government of the people by itself," while "dazzling" to the oppressed nations of Europe, ignored the fact that in most countries the people was far from ready to govern itself. The American Republic showed "the fairest prospect ever open to any people," a great step forward in "the progress of mankind"; but the success of the United States reflected exceptionally favorable historic circumstances. Of all the large countries of Europe, only Britain gave the least hope of carrying through in the foreseeable future the "necessary reforms" to undergird popular government.[42]

In an age of utopias Norton was an anti-utopian political thinker, subscribing to neither the liberal utopianism of the market nor the socialist utopianism of the state. He held the stunted doctrine of the state typical of Americans, mirroring the fear of government power engrained in American republicanism; and, for a theorist of his time and place, he paid slight attention to the laws of political economy. In fact, he saw both governments and economies as reflecting particularities of history rather than as embodying some world historical trend. Disregard of both state and market perhaps owed most to Norton's appreciation of human community. He located the animating principle of social order neither in formal institutions nor in abstract universals but in human beings individually aware of ties binding them together.

He did share one dogma of the progressives' faith: that "the rights of all men will at last be vindicated and acknowledged," for he believed "those rights to be the care of divine as well as of human power." But, although "in the long stretch of time, the progress of the world is assured," progress comes slowly, "not visible from year to year, and only with difficulty to be seen from century to century." "Rashness and inconsideration" would simply delay the "advance of freedom, and the elevation of the oppressed and suffering." More specifically, only by ignoring the realities of history could revolutionaries come to the fatal assumption "that wisdom and power are derived directly and immediately from the people,—that is, from the great mass of any nation; and, consequently, that political liberty is an inherent right of mankind, and that a republic is necessarily the best form of government."[43]

Norton's view was profoundly historical and flatly pragmatic: a wise Solon diagnosed a people's state of development before prescribing its rights, judged who *could* govern before declaring who should. The "final object of government" was "to secure the fullest enjoyment" of liberty to the governed; and the form of government "best fitted for this object"— monarchy, republic, whatever—depended on a nation's quantum of "enlightenment and virtue." No people had yet grown "so wise that it can know, or so calm that it can choose, what is best for itself." Few were ready for self-government, and a pious absolute monarch would secure more liberty than an impious republic. The people—"misled, troubled, and exasperated"— needed guidance from "the few who have been blessed with the opportunities, and the rare genius, fitting them to lead."[44]

This was venerable Boston doctrine; but it was more than that, as became clear when Norton discussed liberty. The simplest definition of liberty, he wrote, is freedom "from restraint of whatever kind." But this conception falls apart "the instant that we connect with the term Liberty any moral idea," the "instant that it becomes to us . . . the aim of our highest and steadiest pursuit on earth." So Norton offered a definition, "based on the primitive meaning of the word," that shall "answer to that Liberty for which the best men of all time have lived, toiled, and died." Liberty, in this "nobler signification," is freedom "from all restraints which may prevent the doing of what is right. In other words, Liberty is the possession of the power to do the will of God."[45]

Norton's linkage of liberty and virtue grew out of the intertwining of different traditions of thought. It echoed the Reformation notion of "Christian liberty," which the Puritans instilled in New England's political theory and which lived on feebly in the conservative Unitarianism of Andrews Norton's generation and still twitched in the footnote where his son quoted Tyndale's *Obedience of a Christian Man*. More immediately, liberty's "nobler signification" evoked the ideology of the American Revolution, the belief that a republic's safety depended on the virtue of its citizens; this conviction, reinforced in Norton's classical education, still counted as conventional wisdom in the 1850s, though smacking more of bourgeois Protestantism than of Sparta.[46]

Another of Norton's arguments pointed in yet a third direction. Unchecked freedom permitted man's "savageness and wildness" to "tyrannize" over him, making "impossible the full development of his character." This claim led to a final refinement in the definition of liberty in "its social or political" meaning: "that state in which a man is not deprived of the power of doing what is best for himself or others by the interference of another." Norton readily conceded the evils flowing from economic inequality and political injustice, and he urged that socialist and other schemes to remedy them be judged on practical effect (about which he was pessimistic). But he also insisted that institutional reforms could never cut deeply enough; permanent improvement "could only come from a change in the characters" of individuals, such as lessening the selfishness of the rich and privileged. This way of thinking about liberty had affinities directly to the Boston idea of self-culture and more remotely to German post-Kantian conceptions of human self-development, notably Wilhelm von Humboldt's *Bildung* ideal.[47]

All three lines of thinking had a more ancient ancestor in Stoicism. Norton's education had exposed him to what was plausibly the *fons et origo* of Stoic political science in Cicero. Three teachings loomed large in that tradition: first, the axiom that human beings are naturally social, inclined to bind themselves by duties to others and to find their fulfillment in such relations; second, the understanding that this fulfillment came through an individual's growth in virtue, conceived chiefly as control over oneself; third, the counsel that a virtuous person submit patiently to apparent vagaries of fortune beyond human control, knowing the universe to be divinely ordered and providential.

Very early in the Italian Renaissance, Ciceronian principles revived in a Christian Stoicism. Dante's political writings took a Ciceronian view of an individual's duty to the community's welfare; this Dantean tradition grew into later Florentine civic republicanism, which ultimately influenced the thinking of the American Founders. Moreover, neo-Stoicism in the northern Renaissance independently infused Ciceronian ideas into the Calvinist political theory inherited by, among others, Boston Unitarians. Meanwhile, Petrarch had developed the Stoic idea of growth in virtue into something resembling self-culture (*virtú* being a more flexible notion for the Florentines than virtue became for the Victorians). This Renaissance conception of self-fashioning in turn evolved into both Boston's ideal of self-culture and Berlin's of *Bildung*.

Norton did not need to read Dante or Petrarch (though he had) to absorb their points of view, for Stoicism and neo-Stoicism so infused the worldview he inherited as to be, practically speaking, ineluctable even when unrecognized. Norton's conviction of the inevitable progress of liberty ultimately grew from an essentially Stoic idea of the divine ordering of the cosmos, a belief to which the element of progress later adhered. His patient submission to the slow creeping of that progress had the same source. So did his emphasis on society as a voluntaristic community of mutual obligation and his corresponding inattention to constitutionalism and formal arrangements of power. And his idea of liberty as a school of virtue, a precondition for the gradual self-improvement of individuals and the race—to be limited and regulated for that purpose—also flowed from the Stoic tradition.

> All that is wrong in a single heart, or in society, or in the laws, is opposed to Liberty. But, on the other hand, every advance in intelligence; every evil overcome; every new spread of sound, upright thought; every gain, however slow or however small in the progress of right principle, is the gain and the fresh strength of Liberty. As long as human nature remains as God has created it, a struggle between good and evil must exist in the world. Restraint of what is wrong will be needed, and not until men become perfect will full and perfect Liberty be known. Such Liberty is the heritage of angels, and not of men. But as men become more and more enlightened and virtuous, Liberty will more and more gain possession of the world. Her progress will be slow, for the improvement of mankind is very gradual; but her progress is certain, because that improvement is assured.[48]

In these views Charles Norton would not, over the next half century, find cause to waver. Nor would there ever disappear from his thinking the intimate connection between the development of character through self-culture and the development of a people for republican self-government. "The first duty, the first necessity, is to help them to gain possession of their intellectual and moral natures."[49]

Now, at least, most of his circle agreed with him. Felton praised Charles's "admirable" vivisection of "the doctrines of the reformers": the book "will not only do good, but will bring you honor." And Bowen went "along with you very heartily"—though at first thinking Charles "too hopeful"! Friends elsewhere generally approved Norton's views as well. Only that defender of slavery Edward Pringle thought Charles went too far in denying inherent superiority to the republican form of government: Southerners often stuck closer to the old republicanism of the American Revolution than did other Americans in the 1850s.[50]

The book finished, there remained projects enough to overfill Norton's days and talks with Clough late into the night. From late April, Charles ricocheted between the new house in Newport and Shady Hill (where Clough had transferred himself during the Nortons' absence), attending to business on Central Wharf, escorting Clough to a farewell dinner for Nathaniel Hawthorne (off to become United States consul in Liverpool), entertaining at the Somerset Club a touring nineteen-year-old Englishman called Sir John Dahlberg Acton. Norton took Acton to the Massachusetts Constitutional Convention then meeting, to show him "the way in which we manage a revolution." The future Lord Acton impressed Charles, and vice versa. Norton believed he had never seen "a more intelligent young man"; Acton thought *Recent Social Theories* "very good." A lifelong friend-ship began.[51]

Norton's far more intimate friendship with Clough, however, suffered abrupt interruption. On 28 June, Arthur got letters from England urging immediate return: a job in the Education Office had opened, which might enable him at last to marry. The next day, he boarded the ship for home. He left behind an edition-in-progress of *Plutarch's Lives,* which he asked Nor-ton and Child to help in completing. Charles's most tempting reason for shuttling to Shady Hill had vanished literally overnight.[52]

A far graver loss loomed. Returning to Newport on 1 July, Norton found his father sinking. (No medical records survive, but symptoms during his later years suggest heart disease.) Charley remained to keep vigil, finding distraction in writing a series of newspaper essays on poverty in Cambridge and an article for the *North American* on the Ganges Canal. In early August, Andrews got a bit better, and Frank Child came down for three or four days. The improvement proved transitory. Toward the end of August, Louisa gave birth to Andrews and Catharine's first grandchild, a boy named Wil-liam Norton Bullard. By September, Andrews could no longer leave his room, though his mind remained clear. On Sunday afternoon, 18 Septem-ber, his breathing quickened, became difficult, and "about eight o'clock it ceased without a struggle." The family traveled to Cambridge for the funeral on Tuesday, 20 September, returning to Newport the next day. The funeral was held in the library at Shady Hill, "where my Father's presence seemed still to be with us."[53]

His presence never left Charles. Andrews's intellect, conscience, and personality had shaped his son in so many ways that the impress could not fade: fastidiousness of taste; priggishness in morals; rigidity about truth; compunction about duty; the strong sense of community and its entail-ments; the deep commitment to family and its comforts; the high opinion of self, shading into self-righteousness; the generosity toward others, in dollars and in hours—the list went on and on. A former student wrote that news of Andrews's death came "as it might to a sailor who had heard that a great light on a dangerous coast had been extinguished"; Andrews's physician, a man with a doctor's experience of death and no disposition to gush, doubted that he had "ever known a family where the father's loss would be greater." How must Charles have felt? In November he printed privately a collection of his father's verses to give family and friends. He set about editing, with Ezra Abbot, Andrews's translation of the New Testament and other scholarly remains.[54]

Yet Andrews gave his son a beginning, not an end. Charles moved on, reworking his father's moral and intellectual legacy, dropping elements, adding new ones. Already, the younger Norton's attitudes had drifted some distance from his father's: Charles had grown even more deeply impressed than Andrews by history's shaping power on humanity; he was less insistent on the universal despotism of logical rationality, more tolerant of talk and behavior that raised the eyebrows of proper Bostonians, more curious about the arts. On the remarkably broad and solid foundation gently but firmly imposed by Andrews, his son would ultimately erect an edifice that would have surprised and not entirely pleased the father. In this sense, Charles's great loss in the autumn of 1853 also freed him or, more precisely, made easier the self-manumission already quietly under way. At the same time, so deeply did Charles's roots sink in the culture of Unitarian Boston that Andrews's world seemed not merely normal but normative. Self-manumission was always partial, never more than adaptive.[55]

So there was no sharp break. In the months after his father's death, Charles returned to teaching Sunday school (even printing a book of hymns for the children's use); he supervised the opening of the model lodging houses; he struggled to keep the evening school running. In all this he was surpassing his father in his father's own line. Yet Charles also became treasurer of a new School of Design for Women. Andrews would not have disapproved, just yawned. As yet, Charles's artistic interests remained, for all the ardor aroused in Europe, unfocused and subordinate to his reforming commitments; but they marked out his own place beyond his father's long shadow.

Friends also drew Charles away from the world that Andrews had inhabited. Charles was seeing more of Boston's wittiest bon vivant, Tom Appleton, of George Curtis, and of a Philadelphian called John Field—"the only good fellow from that tedious place I ever knew." They were all good fellows—but not in the old Shady Hill vein. They were a little too frivolous,

a little too witty, a little too fond of extravagant prose, a little too involved with painters and sculptors. No whiff of scandal, just a faint scent of
bohemia. Norton strolled with them through Newport; they came to stay at
Shady Hill. Partly through them—and maybe through Frank Child's Sedgwick friends in New York—Charles met more artists. He grew especially
amicable with the landscape painter John Frederick Kensett; at Newport,
Charles sat on the rocks and talked as Kensett sketched. For now, Norton's
passion for art mainly expressed itself through friendship.[56]

Of these newer friends, James Russell Lowell mattered most. Just when
they met, who can now say? In Cambridge everyone knew everyone else.
Charles had dined with him a few times since returning from Europe in 1851,
evidently liked him, and owing to their mutual friendship with Clough, had
seen him a good deal in the winter and spring of 1853. But Lowell's brush
with transcendentalism in the 1830s and 1840s and his continuing links to
abolitionists surely raised Andrews's hackles. Andrews was gone now; and in
late October, Lowell's wife Maria also died, rather suddenly. One evening
shortly afterward, Charles walked to Lowell's home, Elmwood, a mile or so
on the other side of the college from Shady Hill. Loneliness had devastated
Lowell; Norton's own recent loss made him even more sympathetic than
usual. They quickly became close. (It helped that Lowell was eight years
older. Every man with whom Charles had really hit it off was his senior:
Clough, Baird Smith, Kensett, even Child and Curtis by two or three years.
Perhaps Norton sought in friends something of his father; perhaps he was
simply mature beyond his years.) For the next year and a half, Norton and
Lowell were much together. Lowell came "constantly" to Shady Hill, and
the friendship soon grew to embrace "the whole family."[57]

All added up. Looking back, Norton realized that his travels in India
and Europe, then the "summers at Newport" and the "new friendships" had
"gradually" worked "a great change in my character." These influences "finally took me out" of a life of "domestic seclusion in Cambridge" and
"enlarged my vision of the world."[58]

"Gradually." There was no sharp break in Norton's outlook or routine: sharpness was not in his repertoire. New friends did not displace old;
through 1854 and into 1855, Charles dined regularly with a little group calling itself the Beefsteak Club, which included Frank Child, their classmate
George Martin Lane (now, like Frank, a Harvard professor), and a Ticknor
daughter. He kept pecking away at the literary craft. *Putnam's* turned down a
couple of submissions; then, in June 1854, it published a sketch of his palanquin travels (a recycled lyceum lecture). And he still balanced the merchant's

trade with civic duties, serving in the winter of 1854–55 on the Athenaeum's Library Committee and the Cambridge School Committee while simultaneously struggling to keep the evening school afloat.[59]

Externally, indeed, Norton's life continued much as it had since 1851. Good citizen; amateur author in the Boston mold; tolerably successful merchant: he even contemplated a second voyage to Calcutta. Yet sometimes he felt himself adrift, wondering where his compass pointed. Cryptic lines appeared in his most private notebook:

Sancta Maria, ora pro me!
17th April 1854.
De profundis clamavi.

"Holy Mary, pray for me! From the depths I cried aloud." From what depths he might have been crying, no clue survives.[60]

Perhaps exhausted by too busy a life, Charles was certainly feeling poorly physically. The Middletons had invited their Newport friends to visit; relaxation in coastal Carolina's balmy climate must have seemed a fine idea. In early March, Charles and Jane set out, arriving in Charleston on the fifteenth. The city reminded him of Italy: "a fine air of age, & dusty decay which invests whole streets with the venerableness of the past." He visited his Newport friend William Miles at the College of Charleston, searching there for signs of intellectual life, finding none. After several days, Charles and Jane removed to Oliver Middleton's plantation on Edisto Island, a short ride from Charleston, to loll in "perfect summer."[61]

Lolling did not drain Norton of curiosity: above all, he observed slavery, talking frankly "with all sorts of persons" about it. What distressed him most was not physical suffering (of which he saw little, and that no worse than the poor endured in Northern cities) but mental and moral neglect. Slaveholders abandoned their slaves to what Charles saw as a degraded and brutish condition, with no effort to educate, to elevate. Oliver Middleton was a considerate master; but, for just that reason, on his plantation Norton felt "most bitterly the inherent evils of the system." One of its "worst effects" was "to deaden the moral feelings and to obscure the intellects of the masters." (Focus on the slaveholder was common among white Northerners, who found it easier to identify with masters of their own race than slaves of another.) Norton heard "men of character & cultivation" utter "with utmost honesty of feeling" patent "fallacies and monstrous principles." The women proved better, "clear-sighted in regard to the wrong," but helpless; their "eyes fill with tears when you talk with them about it." He found particularly alarming the drift in public opinion. The great majority of the men, at least, had over the last few years come to think slavery a positive good for both black and white.[62]

Where lay a remedy? Norton saw none "but the gradual & slow progress of the true spirit of Christianity, bringing together black & white, quickening common sympathies, and by degrees elevating both classes"—the one from "ignorance & brutality," the other from "indifference" and "blindness of mind." But this must be "a work of ages," sighed the author of *Recent Social Theories*. No "immediate, compulsory measures" seemed likely to help either blacks or whites. All the more important, then, to stop bolstering the system. Seeing slavery at firsthand deepened Norton's long-standing hostility to any national measure that propped up slavery or encouraged its spread.[63]

By 1 May the Nortons were reunited at Shady Hill, and Charles was back at work. His new best friend, however, was gone: James Lowell had taken off to Europe for a year, to prepare himself to succeed Mr. Longfellow as Smith Professor of Modern Languages and Belles Lettres. Norton found solace for Lowell's absence in William James Stillman, only a year younger than Norton and recently arrived in Cambridge from New York to solicit contributions for his new art weekly, the *Crayon*. Stillman was also preoccupied with other business: extricating himself from orthodox Christianity, quarreling with his family about religion, mooning over a suspicious female protégée, and doing all with Weltschmerz of Alpine proportions. The *Crayon* appealed to Charles; so did Stillman's earnestness. Something in Norton responded to the emotionally hungry. Perhaps whatever impulse drove him to succor the poor in body—to take seriously that command of his religion often treated by others as nominal—drew him to needy and questing spirits. He had developed, from nurture or nature, from upbringing or genes, and probably from both, the personality of a caregiver. It was not coincidence when, years later, he took up the vocation of teacher. And Stillman was only one of a long series of informal protégés—most, like Stillman, from poor backgrounds—whose broader education Norton enabled.[64]

Stillman noticed that Charles was suffering his own worries: "You have walked with Pilgrims and become weary and bewildered, I know." The only pilgrim Charles had strolled with recently was Stillman, but he did seem tired and uncertain. The India trade continued its desultory course, Norton taking "gloomy views" of its future. He planned to edit more of his father's work, probably to write a memoir; but that was not a career. He dabbled in other literary business—an American edition of a recent English novel of life in India; a quick piece for the *North American* on the opening of the Ganges Canal; a brief and surprisingly favorable notice for *Putnam's* of "a curious and lawless collection of poems" by "a kosmos" named Walt Whitman. But dabbling was all this was. There was no big new project; no sense of how literature would fit with commerce, or commerce with reform, in his days to come; no direction. His father's death had made him head of the household, but whose house did he head? The birth of Louisa and William's second child in August underlined Charley's failure to find his own moorings.[65]

By that time his health had worsened again. In early July he suffered some sort of physical collapse in Cambridge. He returned to Newport to take it easy, reading a little Greek, riding horseback, "trying to win back a quicker pulse." He did not recover; "a too long walk" or "too much writing" would exhaust him for a couple of days. The ailment was mysterious; the doctors, convinced that Norton had overworked himself, prescribed a vacation: he could stay home if he wished or try the panacea of Victorian medicine, a change of climate. Charles thought he would find it embarrassing to remain at home, looking tolerably healthy but living like a drone. By mid-September he had decided that a "few months" in Europe were the answer; a week later, Mother, Jane, and Grace resolved to go with him. After autumn in England, they would spend winter in Rome, then rescue Lowell from his studies in Germany. Norton handed over the model lodging houses to Martin Brimmer, his business affairs to William Bullard.[66]

On 10 October 1855 the family sailed for Liverpool. Charles was a few weeks short of twenty-eight, but illness made him look older; his acquaintances believed his life to be ebbing away. They "had nearly given up hope" that he would return.[67]

FIVE

Adrift, 1855–1857

Twelve days later, at dawn, the ship docked in Liverpool. There were still "wearisome hours" on the sloppy upper deck before Her Majesty's Customs allowed passengers to disembark around eleven o'clock. The Nortons made for Boston's usual oasis, the Adelphi Hotel, to eat a second breakfast and allow Catharine a few hours' rest "on a bed which neither pitched, rolled, or palpitated."[1]

A letter awaited from James Lowell. He was soldiering on in Dresden, wallowing in the German language like "a learned pig." ("To learn German in Germany," Norton thought, "must be like having an intellectual slow fever for six months.") Lowell now ranked among Charles's closest friends—rumors even floated that James meant to marry Jane—and he half promised a rendezvous in Italy. At half past three in the afternoon, the family departed for London "in the comfortable English cars," reaching Euston Square at ten o'clock. Within a couple of hours Charles was asleep in the familiar accommodations of Fenton's Hotel, where the Nortons had booked a parlor, a dining room, and three bedrooms.[2]

For the next fortnight they happily reacquainted themselves—Grace acquainted herself—with London. For twenty-one-year-old Grace the trip was meant to bring "improvements" as well as "enjoyments." She was, any-way, an adventurer; and Charles often took her roving while Jane, ten years older, stayed "in the most perfectly quiet, domestic way" with Mother. The first morning, Charles and Grace drove out to find his Philadelphia friend, John Field, then in London with his wife, and to visit the Lyells; they came back with Arthur Clough. Clough, "astonished and delighted at once to see Shady Hill reposing it[self] in St. James's Street," invited the Nortons to tea that evening. Charles liked Arthur's new wife; Arthur decided that Charles did not look ill at all. The next few days were 1850 all over again and a delight—breakfasts, dinners, long talks with old friends.[3]

A week or so after arriving, having bought a copy of John Ruskin's

Modern Painters to carry with him to Rome, Charles wrote to its author, whom he had met briefly in 1850, for permission to view his pictures. Three days later, Norton went to Ruskin's house on Denmark Hill to spend an afternoon, look over his Turners, and listen to Ruskin "lecture" about them: not "ex cathedra, but in the most agreeable, unpretending, and kindly way." Ruskin "specially pleased" Norton—"no pretence nor affectation," only the "pleasant ease of a well-bred gentleman." Norton admired the Turners as well; several, he wrote Lowell, he preferred to any other landscapes in the world.[4]

Right now, though, the landscape looming in Norton's imagination lay hundreds of miles southeast of Denmark Hill, London being only a staging post for the journey to Rome and the mild Mediterranean winter. Charles's health remained precarious, and his mother was also looking peaked. The Nortons encamped briefly in Paris on the Rue de Rivoli, their hotel windows overlooking the Tuileries. The view had changed since 1850, for Napoleon III had begun his great rebuilding of the city. Charles found the effect splendid but characteristically missed the "old historic localities" and "picturesque bits of dirty tumble-down streets" (though he did succumb to the allure of the new gallery of the Ecole des Beaux Arts). The friends of 1850 remained; Charles dined with the Scheffers, where by pleasant coincidence Charles Dickens greeted him again, and crossed paths with the Brownings, who, like the Nortons, were en route to Italy.[5]

The rail line from Paris to Marseilles not yet open, the Nortons hired "a traveling carriage of the utmost comfort," four good horses, and a factotum known as a courier. Shortly after mid-November a carriage laden with trunks and Nortons rolled out of Paris. Avignon's "narrow, crooked, steep, and ill-paved" streets had disgruntled Petrarch but (from all appearances unimproved since 1326) charmed Norton. As Italy neared, his health steadily improved. Jane reported to Louisa that his "spirits" were "more equable" and his "special trouble" was gone. What she meant by the last phrase remains a mystery, but he had clearly "gained flesh and color."[6]

His strength flowing back, Norton took to journalism once more. While traveling in 1849 and 1850, he had posted home voluminous, sharply detailed letters, usually composed at speed in whatever time he could snatch while on the road or before sleep ended a busy day. The descriptive and narrative skills honed in those letters he now turned on whatever came before him, with an eye to a broader audience than friends and relations. William Stillman needed copy for his struggling *Crayon;* and, in early December, Charles began to send sketches of scenes and events the family encountered in

Italy. Some of these reflected a pleasant week in Florence, where Norton renewed friendship with the duomo, Santa Croce, the Giottos, the Cimabues
and with Mr. and Mrs. Black and their children. From Florence the road
roamed through hill towns: craggy, forbidding, medieval Arezzo, Cortona,
Orvieto. Chill rainstorms turned the highway to mud; not till Christmas
Eve did the carriage roll into the Eternal City.[7]

The only city that ever surprised him upon entering it, Charles told
Lowell, was Benares. If not a surprise, Rome at least impressed: "all & far
more than I believed." Norton thought that he had never seen a place where
Nature smiled "so kindly" on "the works of men," hiding their flaws and
uniting them "in one combination of beauty with her own perfect self." Yet,
as he took almost no time to realize, Rome was also "far less" than he
had believed, "the city of hypocrites and pretenses"—or more exactly, of
priests and pope. The "worship of the Virgin" was increasingly displacing the "worship of God," just as Bernini and Borromini had supplanted
Michelangelo.[8]

The Americans and English had not quite supplanted the Romans but
were doing their best. The attractions of Rome's mild winter, its art and
antiquities, its exotic religious spectacles drew them by the thousands, especially during Carnival, when mobs jammed the Via del Corso and jostled
out into the side streets, and as Holy Week approached. At solemn celebra-
tions in the great churches, English speakers crowded out the Romans.
When spring came, Norton discovered, even hiring a horse to go riding in
the Campagna could prove impossible. The Nortons did find rooms in Casa
Dies on the Via Gregoriana, a favored street of wealthy visitors since the
seventeenth century, but on the "4th piano, 96 stairs up." Their Italian tutor
fortunately turned out to double as a helpful guide to the city.[9]

Not that they lacked for friends to help them find their way around. The
Ticknors were in town, staying on the Via Condotti, just across the Piazza
di Spagna. (The English and Americans almost all lived within a few blocks
of the piazza.) Uncle Ticknor was greyer now, at age sixty-four, but well
preserved and enjoying Rome. John Field had also come; and the painter
William Page, a close friend of Lowell's and probably also acquainted with
Norton, had lived in Rome since 1852. Painters cast a spell on Norton; before
January was half gone Charles had seen Page several times. Norton also
sought out Charles Hemans, a noted writer on Roman antiquities and son
of the British poet Felicia Hemans, whose American editor Andrews had
been. The younger Hemans had turned Catholic ("very sincere though

liberal," Jane reported in exculpation) and settled in Rome. He shared with Norton boyhood memories of Andrews and Catharine's visit to England.[10]

As a member of the city's large English Catholic community, Hemans became Norton's entrée to Catholic Rome. On the second Sunday after the family's arrival, he escorted Charles to mass. A week later, he got Norton a ticket to the crowded annual Festa delle Lingue at the Propaganda Fide, where future missionaries from all over the world recited compositions in Hebrew, Chaldee, Gaelic, Arabic, Georgian, Chinese, Bengali, and thirty other of their native languages. It was probably Hemans who took him, on the following Sunday, to see the blessing of the animals at a *festa* of Sant' Antonio and, a week later, to watch a Benedictine postulant take the veil at Santa Cecilia. Catholicism, the ancient snake, had power to fascinate even a New Englander well dosed with antivenom. Norton expiated his guilt by restoring Keats's grave in the Protestant cemetery.[11]

Rome was, as prescribed, restoring his health—but just as effectively draining the family coffers. Though still afflicted by "variations of strength," Jane wrote, "Charles is gaining all the time." Yet traveling cost at least $1,000 a month, and Charles now expected the family's expenses for 1856 to outstrip income by not less than $7,500. He had money invested in two Calcutta voyages, and Frank Story's reports gave him hope of making $3,000 or $4,000 on each. In the interim, Norton asked William Bullard to borrow $5,000, to be repaid "at intervals after our return." The loan "may enforce upon us some strict economies after we get home," but Europe was worth the price.[12]

Careful budgeting did not exactly amount to cramping poverty. One of Norton's first pieces of Roman business was to commission, for $500, a portrait of Catharine from William Page. Charles thought Page's portraits not only "striking likenesses" but "artistically" superior to "those of any other living painter." (This was not necessarily high praise; Norton had seen "few things of interest in modern art" at Rome "except Page's pictures.") A month later, the family laid down an equal sum for a second picture by Page, perhaps a landscape. Desire to subsidize a worthy but impecunious artist probably influenced this purchase: a mode of charity typical of Norton throughout his life. But charity had nothing to do with Charles, Jane, and Grace spending $275 from their grandmother's legacy on a "splendid French work upon the discoveries of Art in the Catacombs"—"much below the original price," they said.[13]

This six-volume *Catacombes de Rome*—the report of the French commission that explored the catacombs after French troops occupied Rome in 1849—held the story that most intrigued Charles that Roman winter. Late in February, Father George Doane, stepbrother of an old friend of the Nortons and thus practically the family papist, invited them to visit the Lateran Museum's collection of paleo-Christian art. Pius IX had founded the museum two years earlier to house artifacts from the Roman catacombs. (These ancient Christian burial places, their location long forgotten, had been rediscovered by accident in 1578 when a collapse along the Via Salaria Nuova revealed subterranean chambers; but modern excavation began in earnest only in the 1840s.) As their guide, Doane enlisted the Reverend J. Spencer Northcote, another of what Norton called "the learned band of converts from Oxford to Rome." Northcote worked closely with G. B. de Rossi, principal archaeologist of the catacombs, and was himself preparing the first book in English on the investigations. Soon, he was sitting in the Nortons' parlor on the Via Gregoriana.[14]

Even the catacombs could not exhaust Charles's taste for art and "associations." The Via Gregoriana ended in the piazza before Trinità dei Monti, which became one of his favorite churches in Rome, perhaps owing to its late Gothic interior, which was more to Norton's taste than the baroque that littered the city. Sometimes holding his nose, he did pass a good deal of time in Saint Peter's and even in the despised Borromini's Santa Carlo alle Quattro Fontane. But it was a relief to find "the little chapel of Nicholas V., in the Vatican," its walls frescoed by Fra Angelico. Here, amid the "general wreck" wrought by the Counter-Reformation popes, survived the art of one of those early "masters who regarded their art as a sacred calling, and worked not for the sake of applause or gain, but for the love and in the fear of God." Norton lamented, too, the virtual disappearance of ancient Rome and pursued its traces among the ruins of the Campagna.[15]

All this left him with mixed and unsettled feelings, the sort of tension often an impetus toward new ways of thinking. Norton grew truly fond of Rome, where beauties of nature and associations of history reinforced the beauties of art. The catacombs opened for him a new window on antique art and, indeed, on the significance of archaeology for the study of art, a connection that decisively informed his later career. He could not but admire—and learn from—the glories of building, sculpture, and painting that dotted the city. Yet most of them aimed no higher than "worldly pomp and selfish display." Michelangelo's genius had fitted papal splendor; but Rome had decayed from there, Bernini expressing in stone its "weakness and decline." Pius IX seemed even "to like a gaudy show"; his numerous restorations of churches merely meant (as "restoration" did usually, Norton was coming to believe) "destroying the original character." Yet what else did one expect from a pope?[16]

Catholicism was, after all, a religion of empty show, of "idols & images." Norton conceded the sincere desire of most Catholics to know and teach the truth; and at times he appreciated the appeal of Roman ritual to the feelings: nuns sweetly singing vespers in Trinità dei Monti "touched my heart." But Catholics were far from understanding that the essence of Christianity lay in love for other human beings, not in superstitious ritual or barbarous asceticism. Simply "being a Catholic" lowered the Nortons' opinion of someone's brains. That was one of the kindlier reactions. "I think I could roast a Franciscan with pleasure," Charles informed Lowell, "and it would need only a tolerable opportunity to make me stab a Cardinal in the dark." The political corruption endemic in Rome appeared the natural outcome of religious hypocrisy. The author of *Considerations on Some Recent Social Theories* could now see the advantages of revolution: Rome "battered down" and "depopulated" would be a price worth paying to "get rid of these churches and these priests."[17]

Charles would happily postpone the revolution, however; for James Lowell was coming to Italy. The plan was to meet in Orvieto, whose cathedral Charles wished to visit. James proposed that Norton leave Rome right after Palm Sunday (to give Charles time "to see the English perverts march in the auto da fé with candles in their hands"); then they could get back by Holy Thursday when "the Holy Father washes the unholy feet." Lowell's friends Page and Field accompanied Norton; and, on Tuesday afternoon, 18 March, in the old Etruscan hill town towering over its deep, narrow valley, Charles embraced his comrade. For a day or so they walked together the "dark and dirty streets" of the little city, shrunken within its haughtier medieval walls, Norton attending in loving detail to the great duomo, his first genuine Gothic church since December. Back in Rome, James and Charles delighted in exploring Rome and its environs—ranging as far as the Benedictine abbey at Subiaco to the east—but chiefly delighted in each other's company. "Charles is enjoying his companionship most entirely," Jane reported to Louisa, "and is so strong that the slight addition of excitement and fatigue it brings does not affect him injuriously." And, with Field and Page, Norton and Lowell made a high-spirited *quattro*.[18]

Page's own spirits could use lifting: his experiments on canvas appealed to entirely too select an audience. Norton had joined that audience but with qualified enthusiasm. He believed Page, though conscientious and gifted, to lack "judgement," a "sense of relative proportions both in art & life." Without that, he would never paint "works of the highest genius": a revealing glimpse into Norton's enduring aesthetic standards and their moral basis. He never subscribed to the Byronic ideal of the untrammeled Romantic individual; he would eventually play a large part in propagating the cult of classical Greek balance and order.[19]

Still, Page did paint to a high standard; and, perhaps more important to Norton, he had, like William Stillman, passed through the refining fire of "sorrows & trials," personal and spiritual, with great integrity and high purpose. Page's "creed" was

> his own, worked out by himself for himself, not built up on other men's facts, not deduced from other men's arguments, but the pure conclusion of the honest truthful & earnest thought of a whole life. And with all this independence, this force, & originality, there is joined a love of truth far greater than the love of his own opinions, and a tenderness & charity for others, and a regard to their views which few men possess even when without opinions themselves.

How much insight into Page this paean gives is hard to judge. It gives a great deal into Norton.[20]

That spring, Page was putting the finishing touches on a Venus. A later viewer finds little to admire in the painting except the goddess's skill in keeping her poise while holding a very awkward stance on a dangerously unbalanced scallop shell. Contemporaries were more apt to notice her alluring if not downright lurid pose and her nonexistent wardrobe. The Salon in Paris, the Royal Academy in London, and the National Academy in New York successively rejected the painting for indecency; the *Crayon* called it "a disgusting insult to Christian delicacy." Full frontal nudity did not ruffle Norton. He decided that *Venus* should hang in the Boston Athenaeum and undertook a subscription to raise the purchase price—which, not incidentally, made a handy way of putting bread on his friend's table. Racy Grace insisted that Page "has presented to us the most beautiful work of God's hand"; "to the pure in heart it is freed from all association with social conventionalities." At times, even Nortons felt more at home in Italy than New England.[21]

Now the literally sultrier end of the peninsula beckoned. By mid-April, Nortons, Fields, and Lowell were all in Naples, along with C. C. Black, come down from Florence. Naples offered an unintentionally hilarious ballet (*Shakespeare, Ballo in Quattro Parti*); Sorrento, its orange groves; Pompeii, its ruins. Not a cloud marred the sky; Bullard had even reported that

Charles's mercantile profits would likely balance the costs of their European travel. Charles, continuing to gain in health, was by now "not nearly so liable to variations of strength."[22]

So well did he feel that on 21 April, leaving sisters and mother in Sorrento, he set off with Lowell, Field, and Black to trek across Sicily. They sailed to Palermo, where they admired "the earliest specimens of Greek sculpture" and hired mules and a guide to convey them cross-country. Muleback over broken terrain proved agonizing; "armies of fleas" occupied the inns; and it was wonderful. Flowers in exuberant variety colored the landscape; the ruins of Greek temples, Norman churches with fantastic Moorish embellishment, welcomed exploration. The return to Sorrento shortly after mid-May was pure anticlimax.[23]

For Don Carlos and the Hospodar—as Norton and Lowell jeered at each other on muleback—these weeks tightened the cords of intimacy. The two had come to share a "deep and tranquil sentiment" like that uniting Charles with Frank Child, while literary and artistic interests joined Charles and James at even more points of connection. Frequent letters when apart, the faint penumbra of endless conversation when together, composed a dialogue spanning decades, littered with puns and jokes, books and paintings, writers and artists. They often disagreed, exchanging explanations and justifications that honed the critical judgment and expanded the knowledge of both. Through everything flowed currents of sympathy that enabled mutual exploration with scarcely a reservation. So it would endure.[24]

Now James had to drag himself back to Dresden, the Nortons to Rome. From there, on 2 June 1856, the family set out northward. In Cortona, a "very beautiful" Greek picture of a muse had "a grace & refinement hardly to be found in any of the Pompeian pictures" that Norton and Lowell had admired together. Comparing it with what they had seen in Sicily and with the Madonnas in Italian galleries set him thinking aloud to James.

> How much farther Greek civilization was developed than ours yet is! With the basis that we have got we must in time have finer results than any the world has yet seen,—but how slowly they come, & how far off our hopes have to stretch forward. Compare Sicily under the Greeks,—its temples, its poetry, its coins, its vases, with Sicily under the Bourbons. One might suppose the world has been running backwards.

This idea of great life cycles of civilization, evolving from the remains of earlier ones, would one day mature into a powerfully influential motif of Norton's work. Now, for ten days, Ruskin's recently published *Stones of*

Venice guided the Nortons through that city. But travel in Italy's summer swelter was proving wearing; with a sigh, they took the road to Switzerland's cooler air.[25]

Returning one day by boat from Vevey to Geneva, Norton spied a familiar face across the table in the little cabin of the paddle wheeler. It was John Ruskin, traveling with his parents. Charles rose and, as Ruskin recalled it thirty years later, "with the sweetest quiet smile I ever saw on any face" walked over to ask permission to introduce his mother and sisters. The two families talked till the boat docked in Geneva and, before saying farewell, agreed to meet again in Saint Martin. There for a couple of days Norton and Ruskin enjoyed long walks and talks together.[26]

The American's "bright eyes" and "melodious voice" charmed Ruskin; Charles in turn was attracted by Ruskin's "pleasant readiness of sympathy" and cordiality of manner ("rare to find in any Englishman"). The "over-confident & dogmatic tone" that marred his books showed not at all in his conversation.

> I was struck as one would expect to be after reading his books, with the fineness of his powers of observation, and their great cultivation, but in general his talk was not so much that of a sound thinker, or of a clear headed man with an equable temperament, as of a man sensitive to all external impressions, & likely to change, not his principles, but his judgments & his opinions according as one point of view or another came most distinctly before him.

This was a discriminating assessment. Ruskin's emotional and intellectual instability raised no barrier to friendship with—or learning from—him. Ruskin had found "my second friend" and "first real tutor"; Charles, a soul mate and mentor.[27]

At the time Charles and he formed their friendship, Ruskin was on the verge of becoming, if he had not already become, the foremost critic—and prophet—of art in the Victorian world. With his vindication in *Modern Painters* of the artist's immediate recourse to nature as against imitation of the classical tradition running from Michelangelo to Claude Lorraine, with his championing of both the contemporary Turner and the early Italians who preceded Raphael as against this Renaissance classical canon, with his elevation of the role of ideas in painting, with his insistence in *The Stones of Venice* that the highest art perfused an entire society and arose from its inner being, Ruskin had flung down the gauntlet before the British art establishment—and had awakened the enthusiastic assent and lively admiration of Charles Norton.

Andrews Norton. Bust by Shobal Vail Clevenger,
circa 1839.

Catharine Eliot Norton, date unknown.

Shady Hill.

Jane Norton, in the 1850s.

Grace Norton, probably in the 1860s.

Charley Norton and Frank Child, shortly before or after
Norton's 1849-1851 travels in India and Europe.

James Russell Lowell, date unknown.

Charles Norton, November 1861.

The Locusts, Ashfield.

Villa Spannocchi, Siena.

The Norton children, 1872. From left, in rear, Eliot, Elizabeth, Sara; in front, Margaret, Richard (infant), Rupert.

Susan Ridley Sedgwick Norton, circa 1871.

It is natural to assume that so powerful an influence as Ruskin determined the thinking of his younger friend. Yet exactly what Norton got from Ruskin is elusive, their affinities mostly antedating their friendship. Norton's taste for things medieval went back to his college days, if not to his childhood love of Sir Walter Scott's novels. His belief in an intimate linkage between art and morality could hardly have been avoided in the Boston of his upbringing. Perhaps the connection of art and spirituality did owe something to Ruskin's teaching, though Norton could have got that principle, too, closer to home. His conviction that the arts must subserve education in ethics was likewise learned in youth. And his correlative notion that the arts expressed the animating beliefs of the culture that produced them flowed from the philological axioms underlying his father's biblical scholarship. Certain sites for applying these doctrines came from Ruskin: probably Norton's enthusiasm for trecento and quattrocento Italian painters and churches; certainly, his admiration of Turner, his orientation in Venice. Others equally significant—Dante, classical archaeology, American prehistory, Indian antiquity—had entirely other sources.

Perhaps it is best to speak of nothing resembling discipleship but instead of intimate intellectual friendship. This was founded both on shared creeds and on adverse but complementary personalities. Ruskin bolstered his younger friend's existing beliefs, supplied him with a more supple, more compelling vocabulary, and spurred him toward lifelong study of medieval church building and painting. Norton gave his volatile older friend what might almost be called psychological counseling and urged (and exemplified) an intellectual solidity much needed by Ruskin, though in these respects Norton's effect proved palliative at best. He also turned Ruskin toward deeper engagement with classical antiquity. For the next quarter century, until Ruskin's final mental collapse, the two men loved, goaded, informed, inspired each other. That July, parting in Switzerland, Ruskin entreated Charles to visit him before leaving England.

To see Ruskin or anything else in England, the Nortons needed to hurry, having booked passage from Liverpool on 11 October 1856. Charles, "debilitated" by the heat and the fatigue of travel, needed a fortnight in Paris to recover. By 22 August, the family had settled again in Fenton's Hotel. "London is so familiar to me I can hardly believe I know any other city better." Certainly, familiar friends abounded; and through Clough, Norton made a new one, Matthew Arnold. Ruskin gave the family lunch and a tour of his Turners.[28]

Yet Norton's health, though slightly improved since Paris, continued fretful. He had by no means sunk as low as in 1855, but his body remained weak, affected by "trifles." His mother worried. Accepting that he would never be "robust," she yet believed that by learning "to manage himself wisely" he could recover his old level of strength. They began to discuss Charles staying in Europe for another winter. He preferred to go home with his family but agreed to consult Sir James Clarke, the physician of a cousin who lived in London. Sir James could put his finger on nothing definite; but Norton was certainly "feeble," his pulse "still too low."[29]

The nature of Norton's illness remains uncertain, for it was not one of the diseases subject to clear diagnosis in nineteenth-century medicine. (It was *not* neurasthenia, the "nervous exhaustion" that began to be diagnosed about this time. Although neurasthenia became almost fashionable in the decades after the Civil War, with doctors blithely applying the label to all sorts of puzzling cases, it never appeared in connection with Norton.) The scant evidence indicates spinal problems, difficulty in walking, exhaustion. Stress, physical or mental—even "a tiresome succession of people to be talked to"— evidently aggravated the illness. These symptoms, especially when combined with Norton's lifelong susceptibility to eye inflammations, hint perhaps at a rheumatoid ailment.[30] Most rheumatoid diseases, however, do not involve the digestive problems that also afflicted Norton (though some are associated with chronic intestinal illness). There may have been more than one ailment. The possibility that he picked up a tropical parasite or disease during his travels in India and the Middle East certainly cannot be discounted. Whatever his illness or illnesses, Norton would never recover health. His mother was right. He would have to learn "to manage himself wisely."

Sir James Clarke "unhesitatingly and absolutely" prescribed "another winter in the south of Europe"; John Ware, the family physician at home, concurred via mail. By happy coincidence the Nortons' neighbor John Gorham Palfrey was booked on their steamer from Liverpool; he could look after Charles's mother and sisters on the return trip.[31]

A reluctant Charles conceded. He had looked forward to playing a small part in "the political revolution" under way in the United States, where the "great final question" of slavery looked to him on its way to solution. The new Republican party had nominated for president an antislavery candidate, John Fremont; and Norton gave him a clear shot at victory. Southerners had bloodied Kansas Territory and even the Senate chamber in Washington, where a South Carolina congressman had severely beaten the Nortons' old friend Charles Sumner. The violence seemed to Charles a great boost for

Fremont. "Real fighting about slavery," he wrote to Palfrey, must spell its end. Having to sit out the campaign disappointed Norton, but he took consolation in the prospect of seeing and learning more in Italy.[32]

An ambling four-week tour circling through the West Country, the Lake District, and East Anglia filled most of September. ("What a Titian there is at Longford Castle, what portraits at Warwick!") Charles deteriorated, sicker than at any time since leaving home. At York "an attack of pain in his bowels" put him in bed.[33]

On the eighteenth he wrote to William Bullard to wrap up his business affairs. Charles did not expect to regain the strength to carry on regularly as a merchant when he returned. That being the case, he wanted to devote his working hours to editing his father's writings and preparing a memoir of Andrews's life. This would absorb two or three years. Afterward, he preferred to achieve "power for good" through means other than business. The family had enough property to live on without Charles adding to it. The last wisps of dreams ambivalently dreamed ten years earlier at No. 39 India Wharf faded into the autumn sky. Late in September, the family returned to London; Charles escorted his mother and sisters to Liverpool, embraced them, and commended them to Dr. Palfrey's care.[34]

On his own now, Norton wandered London a bit more ad libitum, studying again the relics of Nineveh in the British Museum, visiting Thomas Baring's collection of Dutch and Flemish old masters, spending a couple of hours with Augusta Bruce, the charming friend from 1850, strolling through Westminster Abbey. The Brownings also lingered in London, and Robert introduced a poet and painter just a few months younger than Norton, Dante Gabriel Rossetti, a member of the Pre-Raphaelite brotherhood championed by Ruskin. Norton warmed to Rossetti, talking with him about his pictures from the *Vita Nuova*, admiring a "study of Giotto painting a picture of Dante" (a subject calculated to stir Norton), returning to talk more, predicting renown. Also through the Brownings, Norton met "two young fellows lately from Oxford names Morris & Jones," both in their early twenties but already friendly with the Pre-Raphaelites. William Morris would remain on amicable if fairly distant terms with Norton; Edward Burne-Jones would in later years become one of his most intimate friends. Charles saw Ruskin himself several times—buying on the latter's advice his first Turner: a "vignette" of Scott's house in Edinburgh, purchased for forty guineas at White's in Bond Street. Norton was settling congenially into the company of artists, as he had in Newport.[35]

And he was as usual fretting about politics. A month in London revived his contempt for shallow, class-ridden English social life. At best, the rich saw the poor as dependents, not brothers. Norton listened to the old Chartist orator Ernest Jones address a working-class meeting at Saint Martin's Hall. But he thought the "dirty & ill looking audience," "the thin, sickly excitable workmen," to be "a bitterer denunciation of the social system than anything which Mr. E. Jones or any other ranting orator" could say. The transatlantic situation looked differently grim. Hope for Fremont's election was slipping away. If Buchanan won the presidency and expanded the territory open to slavery, then Norton wanted "the whole North" to secede—but griped that the "Southern North" lacked New England's "principle and courage." "The real opponents of slavery (not the 'abolitionists')," he feared, "are going to have a hard time.[36]

The weather was growing as cold as the political prospect—and damp, to boot. Norton shared a last dinner with the Cloughs on 13 November 1856 then boarded the boat train to Calais. For the first four days in Paris, Norton's mouth was besieged by Dr. Gage, the American dentist. Charles lingered for four more days mainly to keep company with his "good old friend and tutor" Henry Torrey, just named professor of history at the college, who was laid up with a bad knee. Torrey hoped to see Norton in Rome. The Storys, too, were in Paris, en route to Rome; and Norton decided to travel with William, Emelyn, and their children.[37]

At Marseilles, rough seas pinned their little steamer to port for a week. Story took advantage of the delay "to make an intolerably bad drawing of me." Finally, with even Norton fighting seasickness, they made Civita Vecchia on 4 December. The next day they drove through the wide Campagna, passing "shepherds leaning on their long staffs, the wooden plough, the white cattle, the grey mud-covered buffaloes, the jingling wine cart," and at the eleventh milestone from Rome caught sight of the great dome of Saint Peter's. Just after sunset, through the Piazza of Saint Peter's, Norton reentered the papal city. The cast of characters had scarcely changed: the Ticknors, the Fields, Page. And Rome itself was "the same dirty old place— damp, mouldy, sunny and delightful—that it ever was." And as crowded. After a long search Charles found four sunny rooms at the top of a house where the sculptor Thorwaldsen had once lived; a balcony overlooked the Piazza di Spagna. Charles wrote to Paris to offer Henry Torrey the fourth room; and, shortly after New Year, Torrey arrived: sensible and witty, a good talker who knew when to be quiet.[38]

Norton could use quiet and not only for his health. He had settled down to concentrated intellectual effort, his first since leaving America. Open on his worktable lay a copy of Dante's *Vita Nuova* and, next to it, the latest translation of the *Divina Commedia,* a painstakingly accurate prose version by Lamennais, the introduction to which Norton read with care. "I have amused myself," he told his mother, "with beginning a translation of the Vita Nuova." He hoped to make one "that may preserve the spirit of the original in its simplicity, sweetness, tenderness & delicacy."[39]

As Catharine would have known, her son's effort at least had the appeal of novelty. English translations of the *Divina Commedia* abounded; and Charles Lyell's father (also called Charles) had published a translation of the *Vita Nuova*'s poems in 1835. But the only published English translation of the whole work, Joseph Garrow's, printed obscurely in Florence just ten years earlier, had sunk from view.[40]

What inspired Norton to try his hand is equally obscure. A cult of Dante had flourished around Shady Hill for longer than Charles could remember—Uncle Ticknor, Dr. Parsons, Mr. Longfellow, and Father himself were connoisseurs—but familiarity does not necessarily breed translation. Norton's engrossment in the visual art of Dante's Italy (evident in his growing admiration of Giotto) put him in the right milieu but wrong medium. That latter-day Dante, Rossetti, possibly gave Norton the push that sent him from frescoes into canzoni. Rossetti not only painted scenes from the *Vita Nuova* but had also translated pieces of it; and he bubbled over with theories about Beatrice (an inheritance from his father, the Dante scholar Gabriele Rossetti). Did Dante Rossetti plant the seed in Norton's brain during their talks in London that germinated two months later in the sunny rooms on the Piazza di Spagna?[41]

Whatever the inspiration, the task daunted. Pietro Fraticelli's 1834 edition of the text was the best available, and Norton perforce relied on it, knowing all the while that it was "notoriously defective": simply nailing down the Italian words could puzzle. Then ensued the struggle to find English ones adequate to Dante's sometimes elusively allegorical intentions, English diction resonant with his *dolce stil nuovo.* And the thicket of scholarship surrounding Dante was vast and tangled: by February, Norton was working his way through Milman's *History of Latin Christianity*. He began to collect Dante books to bring home. He did enjoy it all. As he grew more familiar with the *Vita Nuova,* he wrote to Lowell, the lovelier it became to him. "One can hardly appreciate rightly the Divina Commedia without knowing this first." Lowell agreed, but *cui bono?* If Norton cherished any ambition beyond amusing himself, he kept it quiet.[42]

The same was true of his deepening immersion in art and archaeology.

He haunted the galleries, learning most notably to look with an exacter eye at Rome's speciality, antique sculpture. But to what end? He renewed his acquaintance with the "wonderful learning" and "clear-minded enthusiasm" of Giovanni Battista de Rossi, the expert on the Roman catacombs; in February he had that *cavaliere* and Uncle Ticknor to dinner with Torrey and himself, and the four talked classical archaeology late into the evening. De Rossi came back to talk more. Torrey, equipped with "accurate & intelligent scholarship," was proving invaluable in investigations medieval and ancient.[43]

To one aspect of the Roman present Norton kept recurring, like a dog worrying a sore: the legion of English-speaking converts to Catholicism. Only a few days after Charles arrived, John Field introduced him to the writer Aubrey de Vere, whose volume of Greek travels rested on a shelf at Shady Hill. De Vere proved "very much better than his poetry"; and Norton was soon seeing a lot of him. De Vere brought to Norton's rooms Henry Manning, former Anglican archdeacon, future cardinal-archbishop: impressive in person if suspect in doctrine. Norton's friendship of last winter with Father George Doane also renewed itself. Faced with men such as these, Norton uneasily conceded "*some* true growth of purity, charity, and holiness" in Catholicism—but precious little. So he reflexively attributed the surge of conversions to Catholicism, "especially among the English," to "a great wave of superstition" sweeping Europe. No other explanation made sense, given his inherited view of the pope's minions.[44]

The trouble was that this one made no sense of the men who lounged in his parlor on the Piazza di Spagna, chatting about poetry and archaeology. They were not ignorant peasants but men of culture and learning equal to any Unitarian's. Yet they had tumbled backward on the path of progress and chosen Rome; in no calculus known to Boston did this compute. Norton threw up his hands and tried to convince himself that the "liberal & clever" de Vere became "blind" and "illogical" as soon as religion came up. Manning (known in Rome as "the Apostle to the Genteels") he dismissed as "a wily and soft dialectician." Very slowly, Norton's conception of religion would evolve in a subtle way that reduced these dissonances—but not yet.[45]

They did not much rattle him anyway, for he was in a phase more of absorbing than of reflecting on experience. Ironically, poor health pushed him further into the social whirl of anglophone Rome. A regimen of horseback rides in the Campagna, suggested by an English physician, was doing little good. A patient who could still smack his lips over a frittata in "a memorable little trattoria" near the Piazza Navona was not knocking at death's door; but John Field was worried enough to introduce Charles to a Philadelphia doctor who was visiting Rome. This consultant, inferring that "the too active condition" of Norton's nerves "sometimes exhausted" his body, recommended "perfect indolence": "literally trying to do nothing, as much as possible in the open air." Thus ended the long, lone horseback rides in the countryside; thus began a Rome of easy strolls and carriage rides.[46]

Perfect indolence was not in Norton's line. When Carnival came, he did sedately watch the happy milling mob from the Ticknors' balcony on the Via Condotti—but kept dashing into the crowds, coming back covered with confetti. A week later, zigzagging through the crowd in the Storys' street, Charles grabbed some confetti that a woman was dangling from their balcony. "Oh look what a charming face," the woman cried; William Story replied, "Oh that's Charles Norton"; and "a chorus of welcome" bid him "come up."[47]

The woman was Elizabeth Gaskell, whom Charles had met briefly in 1850. Her novels were family favorites; Andrews had listened to *Cranford* during his last illness. Now she and her two daughters, aged seventeen and eighteen, were on their first trip to Rome, staying with the Storys—and so, once again, the tight little world of anglophone intellectual culture in which Norton dwelt offered another of the threads from which he wove his thick fabric of transatlantic friendship. He soon discovered in Mrs. Gaskell "a truly delightful person": sweet in heart, abundant in intelligence, lively in humor, quick in perception, ready in sympathy. Especially after Torrey departed in mid-March, Norton saw much of her and her daughters; with time on his hands and a fund of local lore picked up in roaming Rome, he made the perfect cicerone. As his hour to depart Rome drew near, he decided to travel with the Gaskells: the spectacle of Holy Week over, they too were headed back to England. Norton packed his trunks, fuller now with Dante books and a good-sized collection of photographs of works of art.[48]

For, having arrived in Rome a well-informed amateur, Norton was leaving as something like a scholar. True, he had not apprenticed himself in the German workshops of erudition; and even in comparison with the best British scholars, his reading had been scattered and unsystematic. His knowledge of painting and architecture, in particular, probably came mostly from personal observation, informed and framed more by conversation with men like Ruskin and Rossetti, de Rossi and Northcote, than by study of learned literature. Still, by American standards he stood out: one of fewer than a half dozen of his compatriots seriously acquainted with Dante scholarship, as competent as any to comment on Italian painting, best informed of all about the art of Christian antiquity. Boston, *faute de mieux,* gave him a reputation as art expert before he earned it. Francis Gray, bequeathing his "beautiful prints" to Harvard in 1856, hoped that Norton would become the collection's curator.[49]

In retrospect, his intellectual growth seems organic. The bookish boy from Shady Hill had branched out in college to add art to inherited interests in literature and history. Travels in 1850 had nourished these seedlings with direct exposure to European art and architecture, in the course of which Norton refined his historical and aesthetic frameworks to organize and understand better what he saw. Travels with his mother and sisters in 1855–56 fostered another spurt of growth. Then, left in the Roman hothouse of Italian art and history, responsible for no one's time but his own, fed by the erudition lying at hand, forced by the doctors' prescription of quiet, Norton had blossomed. Rome had set him squarely on the path that would lead, albeit through two decades of twists and turns—themselves decisive in refining the character and purpose of his scholarship—to his position as the leader of American humane learning.

Yet he was not sad to leave Rome. He loved the Campagna and had enjoyed the outings to Frascati, to Veii, to Hadrian's Villa. But his eyes were worn out "with the tawdriness & shams & pretenses" of Rome's Jesuit and baroque churches; he yearned for the bluff candor of home. He and the Gaskells haggled with a *vetturino* to get them to Siena; they offered sixty scudi, settled on sixty-five. Norton said good-bye to his constant companions of the past four months: Story, Field, de Vere. De Vere gave Charles a book of his poems, "which I am really pleased to have I like him so much." On Wednesday morning, 15 April 1857, the carriage rolled out of Rome.[50]

In Siena, Norton sought out "some special pictures that I knew of as being precious," a few Sodomas in particular. "I went to the gallery knowing Sodoma to be a great painter, & I left it thinking him one of the very greatest of all": a judgment putting Norton on the leading edge of Anglo-American connoisseurship. Two hours in the Arena Chapel at Padua on 27 April sent an already unconventionally high opinion of Giotto to dizzying altitude. "No painter has ever succeeded in telling a story with such distinctness & such simple truth as he. I set him side by side with Dante." That same afternoon he and the Gaskells arrived in Venice.[51]

Venice was where in March 1850 art had baptized Charles, and the city still bathed him in unique glory. His eyes, "unsatisfied with the blank whites & browns" of the duomo in Florence and "the tasteless show" of the basilica of Sant'Antonio in Padua, "rested & rejoiced" in the sight of San Marco. In "the beauty of the design, the exquisiteness of the finish, the preciousness of the material, the harmony of the color," in its "pervading thoroughness & completeness," it remained to Norton the "most impressive of Italian cathedrals"—but not only for these reasons. Beauty still impressed him most when most deeply embedded in historic associations, in human drama; and San Marco was "all Venice in a church; her pride, her faith, her adventure, her art, her conquests & her fall." Charles with his philological approach read her walls like "the illuminated pages of a chronicle." Yet he also observed with mounting distress the effect on Venice of "restorers & modernizers," those "cankerworms and caterpillars" who stuck cast-iron stovepipes in the exquisite arches of a loggia and polished the Tintorettos in the Accademia.[52]

Until the Gaskells left for their Manchester home on 5 May, Norton served as their cicerone; then he took *The Stones of Venice* in hand and set out to reabsorb the city himself. Ruskin's topography largely became Norton's. Seeing through his new friend's eyes, he fell in love with the little island of Torcello, remote in the *laguna*, its shallow canal with "green crumbling banks," its lonely "old church & campanile" on the dirt piazza. Or perhaps he fell in love with its romance as related by Ruskin: a tale of refugees fleeing the Lombard invaders, huddling for safety on the tiny island that grew into great Venice, cobbling together with scraps of marble salvaged from the mainland a cathedral to honor and plead with the Virgin who protected them. Certainly, the great powerful mosaic of the Madonna, Porta Salutatis, Gate of Salvation, Haven of Safety, set an imagination as sensitive as Norton's ablaze. But, in the end, he remained faithful to San Marco. Even Giotto's Arena Chapel finished second to it on the list of Norton's favorite places in Italy.[53]

Places, however, absorbed less time than pictures, even in Venice. And he was not only looking at, but for the first time buying, old paintings. After indecision and haggling, Norton purchased three, for five hundred dollars: two Tintorettos—an Adoration of the Shepherds and a portrait head of an old man—and a Giorgione of a woman sitting on a green bank, her hands stretched forward to bend the stem of a small tree. It was a beginning.[54]

But nearly the end for Italy, reluctantly. Around 16 May, Charles left for Verona, planning on Ruskin's advice to stay there several days before rapidly passing through Germany. Compared to Italy, Germany was dull now, "the brewery against the vineyard." Even picturesque Nuremberg, apple of his twenty-two-year-old eye, let down his better-informed self; "the art is far below what uninstructed I had fancied when here before." By the standard Rhine route to Cologne, he reached Paris on 15 June 1857.[55]

A letter awaited from James Lowell, announcing that he was to edit a new Boston magazine. It would be called the *Atlantic Monthly*, its title self-consciously naming the Anglo-American intellectual culture of which the New England clerisy formed the western pole. James wanted Charles to write up the discoveries in the catacombs for it and also to get a story or sketch from Mrs. Gaskell: "our *heavy* batteries are tolerably well mounted, & we want something of smaller bore." Norton solicited Clough as well.[56]

When Charles arrived in London on 25 June, news of the Sepoy Revolt (the Indian Mutiny, as the British called it) was shaking the city. Memories flooded back. Norton lamented the English dead—happily for him, only a few turned out to be people he had met—and equally dreaded the savage retribution that he knew would befall the Indians. Time allowed just a few days in London; and Norton saw few people but Clough, but him almost daily. He did go to a small private exhibition of Pre-Raphaelite paintings; though not bowling him over, the pictures impressed him as the most promising of contemporary art, a shrewd enough judgment. He also took the opportunity to pry a poem out of Dante Rossetti for Lowell's new magazine. The next afternoon, Charles made "a most pleasant visit" to Ruskin at Denmark Hill. Ruskin was about to set out for Oxford to deliver a series of lectures on the political economy of art. The heat in London so distressed Norton that he himself immediately took the train to Oxford.[57]

His health was crumbling again. The next day, Monday, 29 June, he boarded the train for Manchester. He made it only as far as Leamington before becoming so ill that he stopped. The next morning he crept back to Oxford. There, Ruskin sent Charles to Henry Acland, a close friend and distinguished physician. Under his care, Norton stayed quietly in Oxford for the next ten days, seeing much of Ruskin and finding a new friend as well in Acland. His condition, however, can only have increased his longing for Shady Hill. Ruskin's departure on 9 July left nothing to keep him in Oxford. Charles returned to London, organized himself for departure, collected a few manuscripts for the new magazine, said his farewells, and on 16 July took the train to Manchester.

The Gaskells had invited him to stay with them, and he wanted anyway to see the great Manchester Art Treasures Exhibition. The center table in the Gaskell drawing room laden with "books & work," the "landscape over the fireplace," the flowers "blooming in the little conservatory," the dog

Lion keeping guard over all touched Charles's strong domestic instinct, sharpened his longing for his own parlor. The Exhibition Hall was the furthest thing from cozy, Norton's "first impression" being of a "vast space filled with light and rich with color"—his second of the sharp contrast between the ugly, cutthroat industrial city outside and the beautiful, harmonious world of art within. The exhibition provided a gallery of British portraits, some six hundred paintings of "the British School" from around 1700 to the present, and a substantial survey of European painting as represented in British collections (therefore heavy on Netherlandish, German, and Spanish works). Norton came away more impressed with what was barely represented than with what abounded, more convinced than ever of the supremacy of early Italian painters over any after 1500 except Turner and of the Pre-Raphaelites over their contemporaries, and more firmly aligned with Ruskin against the art establishment.[58]

After stopping at Ambleside to see the Cloughs one last time, Norton embarked at Liverpool on 25 July on the steamer *Persia*. Europe had reminded him that the "grandeur" of American "opportunities is proportioned to the immensity of our deficiencies." He "rejoice[d] to be an American even while seeing how far we fall short in many ways of what is accomplished elsewhere, & how much we have to do." To be "contented" in America, he felt, "one must work." But at what? In a few months, Norton would turn thirty. He had ample wealth but little health, no vocation, the obscurest of prospects.[59]

He landed in New York at the end of the first week in August. One trunk had somehow disappeared and, with it, the manuscripts Charles had garnered for the new *Atlantic Monthly;* but not even this disaster dented his joy at being home. The ocean voyage had again restored his strength, Jane reported; yet a few hours' "fatigue" in New York proved "too much for him."[60]

SIX

A Literary Invalid, 1857–1861

Norton's return to Shady Hill passed in a blur. His mother and sisters came down there to greet Charley from William and Louisa's summerhouse at Lenox in western Massachusetts, where all the Nortons were evading the August heat; back to the cool of the Berkshire hills they immediately carted their worn-out son and brother. Charles had come home tanned, Jane reported, "so bright and animated that every body congratulates us on his looking so well"; but beneath the deceptive bronze his health was "only tolerable."[1]

Jane soon lost her own brightness. On 21 August, James Lowell announced his engagement to his daughter's governess, Frances Dunlap. "We were all disappointed," sniffed Mrs. Longfellow, "and regret all the more that he did not marry Jane Norton." Any awkwardness passed soon enough; and by autumn Charles was assuring friends that James had done "a very wise thing." Still, Lenox proved a blessing for Jane, who did not have to walk the lanes of Cambridge while tongues wagged.[2]

In the event, Cambridge saw the Nortons only briefly that fall. Charles tried to work at Shady Hill but found his health "so delicate"—or the invalidism of a healthy-looking man so embarrassing—that he decided to winter in the milder climate and quieter environs of Newport. "Agriculture, dullness, & tranquility," sawing wood and taking short walks with a sister or two suited him. By late November he felt less feeble and through the winter slowly strengthened.[3]

The family's financial health, however, took a sudden turn for the worse. A decade of economic expansion and financial overextension in the United States had inflated a bubble that burst soon after Norton's return from Europe. By mid-October 1857 banks everywhere had suspended specie payments. On Friday, 23 October, Charles was urgently called to Boston; the following Monday found him sitting in a countinghouse opposite the Merchant's Exchange, a "suspended bank" under his feet, sorting through the wreckage. He had always favored safe investments, and modest retrench-ment cleared up the Nortons' troubles. The extended family fared worse; Uncle Samuel Eliot—once mayor of Boston and treasurer of Harvard—actually went bankrupt. The Nortons did what they could to soften his enforced retirement. Samuel's son Charles had become an assistant pro-fessor at Harvard, and Catharine transferred to this nephew a parcel of Shady Hill acreage to build a house for his destitute parents.[4]

Otherwise, the crisis did not greatly ruffle the tranquil household at Newport. William Stillman came to visit, having abandoned the evanescent *Crayon* but having become himself a permanent Norton project and occa-sional drain on the treasury. He tried to draw Charles but could not keep his friend's bulging eyes from looking *"lobsterish"* ("very kindly attributing it to the bad light"). Frank Child was one of the few other visitors that quiet winter and spring, once bringing Lowell with him. Frank had engaged himself to Elizabeth Sedgwick, daughter of the western Massachusetts clan that oscillated between Lenox and New York City; but this new relationship cramped not at all his intimacy with the Nortons. Grace, he teased; Charles, he loved with a "deep and tranquil" affection, "tried so long that I am sure it is all pure gold and will stand the fires of the last day." No man could be more loveable than Child himself. "*How* good he is!" Lowell shook his head; "I smell sulphur about myself when I am with him."[5]

Catharine presided placidly over the few servants; Jane and Grace car-ried on their timeless routine: neighbors to visit, notes and letters to write, household tasks to assist in. As Catharine aged (sixty-four now), Jane slipped into a quasi-maternal role: "The General Blessing," Grace called her. Gracie herself, "the Last & Least," still played family jester. In the evening they read aloud to each other—*Modern Painters* or the new *Atlantic Monthly*—or, on Sunday, sang hymns. When Charles's Tintorettos arrived in February, hanging them made a great event. A visit to Cambridge almost counted as a foreign journey. In December the Nortons bought a ten-gallon glass tank and filled it with seawater, soldier crabs, sticklebacks, sea anemo-nes, little pink starfish, and a pair of oysters. Charles sat and watched for hours; in May he added a "young seaserpent." By then he was also gar-dening. At every season, more than anything, he sat and read. "Books are like virtues,—the more one has the more one wants."[6]

Yet merely idle reading came close to vice. In Europe, Charles could "pass an indolent existence" (or what passed for indolence in his mind) without distress of soul. But he had not been home two weeks before he began to impose on himself the pressure of "public responsibilities." These duties, he knew, his health kept him from meeting—"& there comes the difficulty of content." The generic Victorian compulsion of duty had evolved in the Boston species its sharpest claws. Semiconsciously, Norton may have fled to Newport partly to elude the hunting eyes of responsibility. But for him there was never any real escape.[7]

The psychological problem was to reconcile public obligation, personal enjoyment, and intermittent health; the answer, Norton soon concluded, was literary work. He could pursue it when strength permitted; he enjoyed reading and found satisfaction in writing; and he could regard writing—his own or that he aided—as doing good by entertaining and educating readers, even if this did not exactly equal the evening school or the model lodging houses. Norton fully articulated neither problem nor solution; perhaps he never clearly saw his dilemma nor consciously realized how he had resolved it. But he discovered a way of both doing what he wanted and satisfying his guilty conscience—or holding it at bay. If not quite a vocation, literary odd jobs postponed any pressing need for one.

Norton began to wield again the editorial pen that he had sharpened on Frank Parkman's and George Curtis's manuscripts. John Gorham Palfrey, next-neighbor to Shady Hill, started in October to send Charles for comment and revision proof sheets of his gargantuan *History of New England*, a stream of paper that for years flowed on like the Mississippi. Proofs of Richard Grant White's multivolume scholarly edition of Shakespeare began arriving several weeks after Palfrey's, interrupted briefly by a plea for a loan to enable White to finish the work. Norton spent his time (and money) wisely: both Palfrey's and White's projects counted as major American contributions to scholarship.[8]

Far more of his effort poured into "the Maga," as Lowell and Norton called the *Atlantic Monthly*. Though grudging the time that editing it stole from Lowell's writing, Norton never stinted his own hours: scouting out additional contributors among English writers whom he knew, suggesting others whom he did not for the publisher to solicit directly (notably "Mr. George Eliot," whose *Adam Bede* greatly impressed Norton), scrounging puffs from transatlantic friends like Ruskin and de Vere. Miraculously, in April the prodigal steamer trunk showed up in a second-rate New York hotel, "unopened and uninjured," with its cargo of copy for "the Maga," including William Story's *Roba di Roma*. Norton filled more pages with his own contributions, ranging from frequent book reviews to an old India hand's report on the Sepoy Revolt. In January he asked James to raise his pay from five dollars a page. Charles was getting the hang of journalism.[9]

Some of his articles suggested a role more weighty and concentrated than journalist. The first such was an account of the celebrated Manchester fine arts exhibition in the *Atlantic*'s inaugural issue of November 1857. In what was becoming his stock technique, he helped readers to visualize a visit like his own three months earlier, leading them from the bleak industrial city into the "vast space" of the exhibition hall, marching them through its different sections, pausing occasionally to draw their attention to particular paintings. But Norton was not merely guiding a tour; he was guiding his readers' tastes and understandings, as they well knew.

Fanny Longfellow, for one, judged his article "a little à la Ruskin, not in style but in theory." And why not? Ruskin's idea of beauty as a kind of theophany, a bodying forth of God's love for the world, appealed almost instinctively to the pious and Romantic son of Andrews Norton. Besides, Ruskin had become friend as well as teacher. His mark showed in Norton's belief that Fra Angelico's "pure, clear colors" reflected "his tranquil life and his reverential soul"; in his judgment that after 1500 painting sank in quality because "religion almost disappears from Art"; in his praise of Turner as the "great leader" of "the lovers of Nature as seen in the external world"; in his identification of Pre-Raphaelitism as the great promise in contemporary painting. Norton was more than "a little à la Ruskin."[10]

But far from Ruskin's ape. Norton's thumbnail sketches of individual artists relied on his own substantial firsthand acquaintance with drawing and color, acquired in galleries across Europe. Moreover, he paid far greater attention than Ruskin to portraits; and he read them differently, less as composition and color, more as expression of personal qualities and evidence of cultural history. Thirty years later, Henry James would flatly aver that "there is no greater work of art than a great portrait"—which for a novelist may be true. James could have got this attitude from Norton (quite possibly did); for Norton advised his readers that they would learn as much "of Venetian men and of their lives from the pencil of Titian and of Tintoret as from the pens of contemporary chroniclers." Norton believed that every nation's art opened a window onto its mental interior, especially on the moral and spiritual state of a culture. Ruskin, sharing the conviction, must have encouraged Norton's thinking along these lines.[11]

Yet in this matter Norton was more master than student—and possibly this is what Ruskin meant when he called Norton "my first real tutor." Charles's early and repeated immersion in the Scottish Enlightenment had fixed in his brain, long before he read Ruskin, the key idea that the customs and writings, paintings and architecture, of a "civilization" (later generations would say "a culture") reflected its stage of development. No surprise here: by 1857 this notion had settled comfortably into truism. But Norton's awareness of historical criticism of the Bible infused the truism with philological specificity. He had gained this understanding over his father's shoulder then solidified it in editing his father's work. To comprehend any text, the interpreter read it in light of available information about its author's culture. The text, thus illuminated, itself cast brighter light on that culture—leading then to still better grasp of the text, and so on, in a version of what later became famous as "the hermeneutic circle."

Norton's historical approach to art evolved out of philology; and, though barely breathed in "The Manchester Exhibition," it was nonetheless pregnant with possibilities of new knowledge. In contrast, Ruskin's notion of art as spiritual diagnostic was too vague and inchoate to be fertile for learning. Ruskin, the ripening prophet, increasingly treated art as a path to spiritual rebirth. Norton, the budding scholar, shared the spiritual concern; but he also had a methodology of erudition to incarnate spirit in historical flesh, one that was to provide the animating principle of his mature work.

Furthermore, the authorial habits inculcated by Edward Channing made for more efficient lessons than Ruskin's. Norton wrote with greater concision and composed in clearer order than his friend, though with nothing like Ruskin's genius. In four swift pages Norton trotted the *Atlantic*'s audience through a coherent history of Italian art. He warned them off the post-1500 painters (who until "very recently" had "been more loudly praised") and told them to admire instead those from Giotto to Bellini. In equally brief compass and fluent sentences, he laid out the differing strengths of individual Pre-Raphaelite painters, their generic virtues, and the vices that crippled their collective promise. He spoke with the authority of one who had "made a thoughtful study of Art."[12]

In short—very short—"The Manchester Exhibition" presented Norton in a new persona. From his childish fascination with the pictures in the Athenaeum to his recent roamings through the galleries of Rome, Munich, Paris, and London, he had amassed a trove of information about paintings, statues, drawings, and buildings. Out of this he had distilled, using Ruskin's alembic more often than not, a degree of expertise about art. To Fanny Longfellow he might still be "Charley Norton." But he had, more or less officially (America had no one to lay on hands), donned the mantle of art expert.[13]

He wore it again in the report "The Catacombs of Rome," which he had promised Lowell before leaving Europe. At New Year, Norton was reading about nothing else, fretting for books only available in Italy. By then the digest had burgeoned into a five-article series. Lowell figured the subject to have enough éclat that he used the first instalment to lead off the March 1858 *Atlantic*. Much of Norton's knowledge of the catacombs came direct from the mouths of Spencer Northcote and Giovanni Battista de Rossi; but he also relied heavily on the seventeen parts of the uncompleted *Monumenti delle Arti Cristiane Primitive nella Metropoli dei Cristianesmo*, published in 1844 by Padre Marchi, the catacombs' pioneering explorer; on the six volumes of *Catacombes de Rome* printed between 1851 and 1855 by the French commission established to excavate the catacombs; and on still unpublished writings of the cavaliere de Rossi. This material he fleshed out with a handful of medieval Latin sources.

Out of it all he shaped a study melding entertainment with erudition. The general frame was a sturdy Protestant assurance that the catacombs revealed the pure Christianity of the age of the martyrs, not yet corrupted by popery. However, half realizing that this horse had been dead long enough to putrefy, he beat it only lightly, showing far livelier interest in Catholic legends surrounding the catacombs and in the paleo-Christian art within them. Antique legend had obvious dramatic appeal, and Norton mined that vein in an article devoted to the stories of Saint Cecilia. General readers might have expected details of paleo-Christian art to offer a chance for an after-dinner nap, but Norton worked even mortuary inscriptions into a tolerably engaging story of the transformation of pagan into Christian culture. The inscriptions, he took occasion to note, provided no evidence for any distinctively Roman Catholic doctrines or for Trinitarianism. He also took occasion learnedly to criticize errors in the French commission's reproduction of certain murals.

For "The Catacombs of Rome" was a learned work, though hardly erudite by the standards of Göttingen or Berlin. Norton's interest in the physical remains of ancient peoples had drifted from Squier's Mound Builders to Mahabalipuram to desolate Greek temples in Sicily. Italy in 1856 and 1857 had focused this romance with archaeology more tightly on classical antiquity, and Norton's dalliance had grown into a more serious relationship. "Catacombs" rested on critically alert awareness of the best recent scholarship and the original sources. Moreover, the articles had some importance as the first work to acquaint Americans with the discoveries in the catacombs. In all, the scholarly achievement was substantial enough that Norton considered publishing it as a small book.[14]

Yet in making himself into a scholar he did not suppress the fascination with the larger human story that had enticed him into archaeology in the first place. Norton understood that some of his more arcane writings would interest only a limited class of readers. But he laced the *Atlantic* articles with dramatic touches calculated to intrigue a general reader; he deployed the minutiae of erudition to illuminate broadly the evolution of both Christian history and ancient art; he conveyed a sense of recovering from their long burial in the catacombs human meanings important to anyone. All came together as a scene in the great drama of human self-forming, of universal history: all, therefore, of a piece with Bellini's painting or Dante's *Vita Nuova*. Norton wrote from this vast perspective, not simply because he aimed to please general readers, but also because he remained one himself.

Yet he was decidedly a scholar, too, and of a type that needs explication. With his father's example before him, Norton filled his solitude at Newport (as he had many days past in Rome and would many to come at Shady Hill) with reading, much of it arcane, much got from booksellers in New York, London, and Paris with whom he now regularly dealt. The boxes arrived, and Norton pored over their contents. The French medievalist Antoine Frédéric Ozanam's *Documents inédits* contained "some curious things." "As usual" with Italian commentaries on Dante, "nine tenths of Picchioni's book is worthless"—but the other tenth stuck. In "the life of Virgil which used to be ascribed to Donatus," Charles recognized the germ of one of Boccaccio's tales.[15]

He sharpened his learning (and claws) in book reviews: of J. C. Peabody's plagiarizing "translation" of the *Inferno;* of John S. Harford's incompetent biography of Michelangelo; of the famous German art authority G. F. Waagen's careless and fawning survey of recent additions to British art collections. By the time he came to review J. S. Brewer's Latin edition of Roger Bacon's works in 1860, Norton had a pretty sure grasp of the past half century's scholarship on scholastic philosophy, the best of it French: Hareau's *De la philosophie scolastique,* Jourdain's *Recherches sur les traductions latines d'Aristote,* and more. He thought that George Bancroft "ought to be flayed alive" for omitting reference notes from his American history. A few decades later American students would undergo this sort of indoctrination in doctoral programs; ill health was Norton's graduate school.[16]

Yet in one crucial respect he did not resemble at all an expert cut according to the standard pattern of the great German universities. A student of Florentine painting *might* dabble in Dante, but he was not supposed to write about paleo-Christian inscriptions nor to join the American Oriental Society. Norton's comrade Frank Child makes an instructive contrast. "The

Professor"—one of Frank's nicknames among the Nortons—did hold a Göttingen Ph.D.; and from the start of his career he concentrated his research exclusively on late medieval and early modern English philology. About the time his sick friend was leaving for Europe, he published a five-volume edition of Spenser. When Charles was wandering in print from Michelangelo to the catacombs, Frank was working on a seminal essay on Chaucer's language (1862) and preparing an eight-volume collection of British popular ballads (1857–58). That last work proved prolegomenon to a more thorough edition that would absorb virtually all his scholarly energies for forty years. In thus contracting his range, Child was the very model of a modern professional scholar. Yet Norton never understood his own scholarship as different in kind from Child's, nor vice versa (and indeed they shared key assumptions drawn from philology), even while Charles stubbornly refused to settle in one field or even to see his different subjects as essentially distinct.[17]

Still, like Child, Norton was acquiring the authority that attached to learning. Or, more precisely, he was assuming it in his writings; and his readers were granting it. The very possibility was recent. As late as 1825 or so, cultural authority of this sort—authority to pronounce what ought to be believed and felt—belonged in America not to expertise but to religion, not to scholars as such but to the settled clergy. (This is not to say that lay people paid more attention then to ministers than they did later to professors.) Norton's father could claim that such authority belonged to him *as a scholar,* at least as far as pronouncing on the Bible. Andrews's success in attaching clerical authority to his new scholarly persona had owed a lot to his own straddling of the line between minister and lay expert. Occasional preacher, professor of divinity, biblical scholar: people commonly mistook him as "Reverend."

His son moved that authority more clearly into the lay domain. In Charles's case, the right to pronounce derived transparently from expertise, not ordination. Norton had "made a thoughtful study of Art"; he never entered Holy Orders, except perhaps metaphorically. Yet the religious origins of the cultural authority he was acquiring showed in the tone of "The Manchester Exhibition" and his book reviews: he spoke as a preacher would, expounding truth and exposing falsehood to his invisible congregation. These roots showed, too, in the spiritual quality that Norton assigned to the experiences of art and literature about which he wrote. In this passing of the scepter from clergyman to secular expert, Norton helped to foster a mutation that altered irrevocably the cultural structure of the Anglo-American world.

And it was very much an Anglo-American world in which he played his new part. The *Atlantic Monthly* had given itself its watery name precisely to insist that the ocean bridged, not divided. Britain and America, or at least New England and Old, were supposed to share a single "Anglo-Saxon" culture. When one remembers the great Irish immigration to New England and the class divisions that rent both nations (but especially England), this claim begins to appear as (hoist on its own metaphor) a fog of wishful thinking and willful blindness rising from an ocean of truism. Be that as it may, the Boston intellectual elite certainly did now cohabit, more intimately than ever before, with their counterparts in London: with the writers and scientists, mostly from middle-class dissenting or evangelical families, who had come to dominate the British quarterlies, run the scientific establishment, and write the popular novels. In this conjoint world Norton was emerging as a matchmaker.

For, in returning to America, Charles scarcely left Europe. His transatlantic friendships flourished in correspondence, as after his 1850 trip, but with a notable difference. Growing in number, they contracted in geography. Virtually all his European correspondents now were English: Mrs. Gaskell, Richard Baird Smith, Arthur Helps, Dante Rossetti, Lady Augusta Bruce. By 1860, Charles could no longer provide friends with letters of introduction for the Continent, so stale had his acquaintance grown there. Even for news of Italy he relied on Aubrey de Vere or the expatriate Storys.

The thickness of English connections more than offset the atrophy of links to the Continent. Indeed, so well connected was Norton that, when the *Origin of Species* was published in 1859, he had the first copy in Boston.[18] Clough's monthly letters amounted to a newsmagazine of British intellectual life: which recent articles merited attention (and who had written them), which books were stirring controversy, which issues were agitating politics. Mrs. Gaskell's were similar, though predictably more attentive to fiction. Charles reciprocated and also tried to secure American attention for British authors and artists whom he admired, like the Pre-Raphaelites.

He also performed more immediately practical services, becoming an unpaid literary agent (as he had for Arthur Helps in 1849 and again in the early 1850s): transactions made tricky—and often embarrassing for Norton and other cosmopolitan Americans—by the United States government's refusal to recognize foreign copyright. Besides dealing in Mrs. Gaskell's behalf with the Maga, he negotiated with the Boston firm of Ticknor and Fields for the right to publish authorized editions of her work in the United States. For Clough, he oversaw the publication of the Plutarch translation (completed at last in 1859); then reviewed it in the *Atlantic*; negotiated and edited an American edition of the poems; even invested for Clough his American royalties. In comparison to these labors, arranging the American reprint of James Spedding's seven-volume edition of Francis Bacon's works was a breeze.[19]

The dominant note in these transatlantic relations was friendship, not business. Norton's intimacy with Ruskin in particular steadily deepened. Ruskin encouraged Charles in his writing. ("Still I think your talk is better than your writing—at least it is more above other peoples talk than your writing is above their writing": one more hint of the elusive qualities that made Norton such a force person-to-person.) As his own mind grew more turbulent, the older man increasingly relied on Charles emotionally; by August 1859, Ruskin was avowing that "you are almost the only friend I have left. I mean the only friend who understands or feels with me." The next spring he sent Charles a painting by Dante Rossetti, *Beatrice at a Marriage-Feast*. It was the most thoughtful of gifts. No other subject, no other living artist, could Norton have valued more deeply. He thought the picture "exquisite."[20]

Norton's health remained far from exquisite, "strong some days, & not very strong on others"; yet he had regained enough of it to move back to Shady Hill in November 1858 and to resume tentatively a part in civic affairs. With Kansas still bleeding and the great question of slavery coming to a head, his conscience would scarcely let him rest. Norton thought James Buchanan's South-leaning administration "the worst we have had" and Buchanan himself weak and unprincipled. Norton expected the next president to be "a Northern man" not just in residence but also "in principle." But who? After William Seward delivered a fiery speech declaring the quarrel over slavery an "irrepressible conflict," Norton declared the senator from New York to be "not merely the best statesman in the country, but the most available man for the Republican party." He urged Lowell to have the *Atlantic* push him for president. And as the new year began, Norton was working his European contacts for all they were worth, promoting a scheme to settle German colonists in Missouri in hope of building a free-soil majority in that key border state.[21]

The crusade against slavery did not dominate Norton's winter. His health permitted a little more sociability—Charles even organized a dinner at Parker's restaurant to celebrate Lowell's fortieth birthday on 22 February—and there was more of Mr. Palfrey's *History of New England* to revise. Mostly, though, Norton used his hours of well-being to read and write. In April the *North American* carried a deprecatory article by him on the native rulers of India; this (and a brief review in the *Atlantic* several months later) turned out to be Norton's farewell to his long literary affair with the subcontinent. Italy now preoccupied him; he had in mind expanding the *Crayon* sketches into a book.

First, however, came Dante. Norton continued to pore over volumes of commentary, ancient and modern, and to tinker with the translation of the *Vita Nuova* that he had begun in Rome "to amuse himself." During the summer of 1858 he had read "with some care" Dante's *Convito* and "all I could get" about Dante's friend and fellow poet Guido Cavalcanti; more and more firmly Norton believed "the intellectual & spiritual development of Italy" to culminate in "Dante & Giotto." Unknown—astonishingly—to Norton, Dante Rossetti had also translated the *Vita Nuova* and was preparing to publish it. Early in the fall Rossetti mailed proofs to his fellow enthusiast. Norton "at once" wrote back that he would withhold his own translation from full publication but that he wished "to print some parts of it" before Rossetti's appeared, "so that the independent work I gave to it may be plain."[22]

By October, Charles was working on a pair of articles on the *Vita Nuova,* "to be interspersed with translations." In the event, "'The New Life' of Dante" turned into three articles, published in the *Atlantic* in January, February, and March of 1859. The first offered a historical-biographical-critical introduction to the *Vita Nuova* for readers who knew little of Dante but the name. The second and third summarized the work, while providing a running commentary and pointing out connections to Dante's later writings. All three were larded with large chunks of Norton's translation, including snippets from other writings by Dante. Remarkably, these articles made the first effort to introduce the *Vita Nuova* to American readers. As serious scholarship by European standards, they counted little; as learned *haute vulgarisation*, they distinguished themselves by any measure. And they immediately established Norton in the forefront of American Dante scholars. After reading them, Longfellow volunteered to hand over to Norton his long-meditated project for an anthology of source materials and criticism introductory to the study of Dante.[23]

Norton massaged these essays for the next several months, for he meant to have them privately printed as a book. Longfellow loaned him more commentaries; Lowell, just then publishing his own first article on Dante, advised on translation. This was—like Andrews's rendering of the gospels— as literal as Charles could manage, consistent with fluency and his desire to capture Dante's tone. James urged him "to archaize the language a little" to suit "the matter & the date." That made sense; but Norton dismissed as almost "vain" any effort by a modern "to seek the interior & intention" of Dante's poetry, "owing to the completely different intellectual conditions under which we are." In mid-May specimen proofs from the printer followed Charles to Newport. Norton fretted about the typeface, the number of lines on the page, the tint of the paper. His fastidiousness in bookmaking never weakened.[24]

Otherwise, life in Newport was busy but scarcely anxiety laden. Artist friends, including Stillman, came to visit, as did Lowell and a couple of Eliot cousins. (Child had gone to Europe with his ailing fiancée.) In July the Harvard alumni approved his scheme to have William Story sculpt a statue of ex-President Quincy; that would entail a flurry of organizing and fundraising. He sent the manuscript of his Italian sketches off to Ticknor and Fields, revising further, with Lowell's help, as the proofs came back. Norton's once-phenomenal energy seemed to be flowing again—despite hair turning gray at thirty-one. It was James he worried about: between editing the Maga and professing belles lettres in the college, Lowell's own writing was being squeezed thin.[25]

Then Norton's body turned on him. On the night of 29 August 1859, the rest of the household already asleep, Charles fainted on the entry floor. How long he lay there, no one knew; not long, Charles guessed. But for two days he was too weak even to try to write a letter. For days afterward in a blue funk, he muttered that his Italian book "will not be good enough to suit me." James bucked him up, told him not to "feel at all bashful" about his book. "*I* find it very interesting & I am a much harder person to please than most folks"; the book would give Charles repute among "the truly judicious—which is all that is worth having." The spell passed, but it reminded Norton that he could not rely on recovery.[26]

His stamina returned quickly enough for Norton to take command in a new campaign early that fall. James Jackson Jarves, a wealthy native of Boston, had settled in Florence in 1852, assembling there a collection of paintings to illustrate the development of Italian art from Giotto to the cinquecento. Wanting the collection to rest in his natal city, Jarves approached—no surprise by now—Norton. Even less surprisingly, the idea appealed to Charles. After getting his Anglo-Florentine friend C. C. Black to vet the pictures, Norton set about raising the twenty thousand dollars Jarves asked. In late September he prepared a pamphlet testifying to the collection's value and began quietly circulating it among wealthy Bostonians "interested to obtain such a gallery for Boston." His principal target was the Athenaeum trustees, who owned Boston's existing art gallery; in October they voted to contribute a quarter of the money, appointing Norton and four others as a committee to raise the rest.[27]

Norton was simultaneously in charge of raising funds for the statue of Josiah Quincy at Harvard—and in both cases learning how little good "printed circulars" did. Prying cash out of people's fingers required "personal effort & solicitation." That became possible when Norton returned from Newport on 1 November, but he found most fists clenched. Rumors floated that the pictures were third-rate. The truth was that few Bostonians "value[d] the works of the old masters," despite Norton's efforts in the *Atlantic* to enlighten them; "the most cultivated part of the public" understood neither the importance of "'old' pictures" to "modern artists" nor "their essential value as representing the past thoughts and habits of men." Jarves's deadline arrived on 1 January 1860; the money did not. (Yale finally bought the collection in 1871.) Even the campaign for President Quincy's statue—the least controversial act of Bostonian pietas imaginable—was proving frustrating. Norton was gaining painful experience in organizing and fund-raising that he would later put to remarkably effective use.[28]

His Dante work ended more happily. At Christmas, Norton mailed to friends and scholars on both sides of the Atlantic a hundred privately printed copies of *"The New Life" of Dante*. "The book," he wrote, "has at least the merit of rarity." Running scarcely a hundred pages, it was a miniature triumph of the bookmaker's art. Richard Grant White, who knew whereof he spoke, thought it "exquisite"—the title page "a jewel," the "tint & surface of your paper & your press work" alluringly beautiful—*tout à fait* "the most beautiful" book "that has appeared in America." And it included a genuine nugget of original scholarship: an appendix bringing to public attention for the first time the *Vita Nuova*'s structural symmetry, an ordering of the poems that gave its symbolism a dimension previously unobserved. This was hardly an extravagant feat of erudition, but Norton's discussions as a whole did add up to the first serious American contribution to Dante studies.[29]

Only two months later his "Italian book" came out. This one actually was published, by Ticknor and Fields as *Notes of Travel and Study in Italy*, an erratic and curious composition. Most of the first half comprised the sketches, largely unrevised, that Norton had written for the *Crayon* from December 1855 through early July 1856: a mishmash of scenic description, art commentary, quaint tales, accounts of Italian politics, and revulsion at things Catholic. Added to them were two substantial sections comprising well over half the book's 320 pages. The first was a 60-page account of Orvieto's great duomo and its history, drawn partly from Norton's observations of the cathedral in March 1856, partly from secondary accounts, partly from published medieval documents. The second was an assortment of pieces written during his second stay in Rome, from December 1856 through April 1857. Several were swift sketches—a picturesque scene, a repellent ritual—no different from those he had tossed off for the *Crayon.*

But Norton filled most of these pages with longer or shorter bits of cultural and social history, culled from his reading in old books: a mode of narrative by no means absent from the earlier sketches but swelled very considerably in these later ones. An attack on papal indulgences did not stop with a few anecdotes calculated to horrify Unitarians, as it would have in 1856; rather, it segued into three pages carefully explaining the doctrine, then ten pages examining with a Protestant eye the history of the controversy surrounding it. What started as a depiction of a picturesque medieval tower on the Quirinal devolved into a twenty-page essay on Dante and Rome. The book concluded with a broad-gauged but compact essay on art and society in the cinquecento, analyzing what Norton took to be the fifteenth-century crisis and subsequent decline of Italy.[30]

This was Norton practicing the mode of writing that he had learned to manage best. Themes becoming familiar to his readers ran through it: that buildings and paintings must be seen in light of their times; that they in turn illumine those times, since art expresses the ruling ideas of its era; that great art must be true both to nature and to some spiritual conception; and that only an age of faith can produce the highest art, just as the most spiritual artist in any age will create the most spiritual art. The method of approach was also becoming familiar. Norton anchored his essays in broad (though not yet deep) command of musty sources and of centuries of learned commentary on them. Yet he conjured from cracked parchment living human beings for his readers. He achieved this not just because he had picked up tricks of vivid scene painting and arresting anecdote but also because he saw in the past lessons for the present: the dangers of superstition, the importance of free government, the evils of corruption, the struggle of spiritual values against a material age.

For Norton's ideal as historian was to paint with broad brush strokes yet precise pigments, to expand moral horizons yet stick scrupulously to the historical record. The analogy to the Ruskinian ideal of art is revealing, but revealing of why Ruskin attracted Norton rather than of where Charles got his ideas. Norton's model was one of humane learning derived from Boston principles, his own father, and fellow Cantabrigian writers like Longfellow and Lowell. Lowell expressed the archetype in reviewing *Notes of Travel and Study in Italy:* "When, as in the present instance, scholarship is united with a deep and active interest in whatever concerns the practical well-being of man, we have one of the best results of our modern civilization."[31]

In 1859, Norton still groped to name this mode of scholarship. It was, he understood, the alternative to the model of knowledge represented in the natural sciences. But, writing of university education, he could find no better antonym for "the pursuits of science" than "what are called classical studies"—the tentativeness of the phrase showing his dissatisfaction with it. "Learning, so called" and "learned studies" hardly worked better.[32]

Whatever the name, America stinted it.

> The temper of our people, the wide field for their energies, the development of the so-called practical traits of character under the stimulus of our political and social institutions, the solitary dissociation of America from the history and the achievements of the Old World, the melancholy absence of monuments of past greatness and worth,—these and many other circumstances peculiar to our position all serve to weaken the general interest in what are called classical studies, and to direct the attention of the most ambitious and active minds far too exclusively to the pursuits of science.

Norton held no brief against science, but he called for "balance." Americans more than the peoples of Europe, he said, needed to read literature other than "newspapers and magazines," "to entertain as familiars" great writers of old. For "our birthrights in the past are imperfect; we are born into the present alone" and live "but half a life": "by living also in the past we learn to value the present at its worth."[33]

Among "learned studies" Americans underrated in particular textual philology. Even love for great writers "of other times and other tongues" did not "stimulate the ardor of students to the thorough examination of their thoughts and words." Norton admitted that philology bore some blame, too often nit-picking at boring questions; such "useless inquiries" betrayed "its true end." Here, his father's son spoke, explicitly citing the relation between scholarship on the text of the *Divina Commedia* and on "the text of more ancient works, as, for instance, that of the Gospels." Charles ranked "verbal criticism" high among studies because it treated "the instruments of human power" best fitted to express spirit: "words as the symbols of thought." Philological scholarship "makes thought accurate, and perception fine." For writers it "adds truth to the creations of imagination by teaching the modes by which they may be best expressed"; and for readers it "leads to fuller and more appreciative understanding and enjoyment" of past masterpieces. "There can, indeed, be no thorough culture without it."[34]

His own erudition elevated Norton, still a middling scholar by European gauge, to the highest levels of learning in New England. Thomas Parsons greeted *"New Life"* with a sonnet putting Norton's name "on the scroll of sacred scholars"; Thomas Appleton, whom Boston credited with a sharp critical eye, thought *Notes of Travel and Study* "distinguished and superior," the Orvieto chapter "famous." Indeed, the book stayed in print for half a century; and, as late as 1897, Houghton Mifflin planned to include a selection in its *Library of the World's Best Literature, Ancient and Modern.* In understanding the enthusiasm for his writings, the twenty-first-century reader needs not only to remember how few Americans worked the ground that Norton did but also to appreciate the frequent acuity and prescience of his judgments on the artists and critics of his era.[35]

As his city metaphorically ordained him, Norton's actual religious beliefs were drifting toward the outer reaches of Boston Harbor. Over the past few years, religion had often preoccupied him. He had caught from Andrews the germ of an uneasiness with institutional religion. Encounters with papal Rome had raised it to fever, for there he saw the church's stultifying effect (so he judged) on English Catholics whom he otherwise liked and admired. True, no Boston Unitarian expected better from—well, no longer the Whore, but still the Lady of Uncertain Virtue, of Babylon. But his friend Clough, after wrestling long and hard to harmonize his conscience with the capacious Church of England, had in the end saved his self-respect only by abandoning the church and, ultimately, giving up Christianity *tout court.* The long evenings together at Shady Hill in 1852–53 and their more recent talks in London can hardly have omitted Clough's intellectual struggle with organized religion.

Charles increasingly suspected repression and conformism to be inevitable in any church. This was no great leap for a Unitarian suckled on the rhetoric of liberty of conscience, and Norton's belief in the spiritual role of the artist encouraged him to take it. To achieve spiritual insight one must throw off the shackles of tradition. How else to reconcile admiration for Giotto and Fra Angelico with contempt for their church? Moreover, his deepening historicism led Norton to see all religious institutions as secondary to whatever endured in Christianity: every church was the fleeting product of a particular age, destined to evolve into something new. Norton still taught Sunday school but stressed "the spirit of the Gospels" over the letter of doctrine; and the best thing that he could wish for his students was "the formation of an independent religious character."[36]

He observed with close attention the "struggle for faith," which Clough had foreshadowed and which now shook the British intellectual class and spilled over into the United States. Unitarian leaders attributed it to "the absence of faith & the prevalence of skepticism." Norton disagreed, blaming loss of faith in Christianity rather on "absence of independence of judgment," the result of "long training of men's minds within the limits of formulas & creeds." Real Christianity, he thought, "has never yet been fairly tried." "Enlightened and liberal men," independent thinkers like Clough and the British authors of the controversial *Essays and Reviews* (which Norton reviewed approvingly), were in actual fact struggling to draw Christianity "from its chrysalis." In the "new age, soon to come," the church would cease being "the guardian of faith" and become merely "the external, social expression of the presence & rule of the Holy Spirit in the hearts & lives of each individual."[37]

Norton still called himself Christian, but he had shaken off commitment to any particular beliefs, concluding that "the Christian religion is no fixed and formalized set of doctrines, but an expansive and fluent faith, adapting itself to the new needs of every generation and of each individual." It is impossible to guess who, besides Clough, may have encouraged him to think along these particular lines. Norton knew of Ruskin's "unconversion" from evangelicalism; had they talked of his deeper skepticism about Christianity? Had Charles read Thomas Carlyle's unsettling *Sartor Resartus* (first published as a book, after all, not in Britain but in Boston in 1836)? or pondered the contention of Andrews's old adversary Theodore Parker that historic Christianity was "transient"? or discussed such questions with his new friend Emerson? The only thing obvious is the congruence of Norton's new view of religion, as evolving through changing forms in changing cultures, with his old philologically rooted historicism. It is equally hard to pin down specific articles of his own "fluent faith" at this stage. But closest to its heart seemed to be the "gradual improvement in human nature" and "gradual increase of human happiness upon the earth."[38]

To this religion he did commit himself. He cast his scholarship in a mold meant to foster just such "gradual improvements"; and, though still at times an invalid, he took no mean part in civic life. In 1860 he felt able both to rejoin the board of the Model Lodging House Association and to publish a long article in the *Atlantic* encouraging its imitation.

Increasingly, though, the impending crisis over slavery turned Norton away from Boston's problems and focused his attention on the nation's. He was beginning to shift his primary sense of citizenship from Massachusetts and New England to the United States. In this, Norton enacted a broader American transition induced by the clash between North and South; for Charles, as for many others, the pivotal moment can be specified almost to the date. On the night of 16 October 1859 a radical abolitionist named John Brown, at the head of eighteen men, captured an undefended federal arsenal at Harper's Ferry, Virginia, hoping against hope to raise a slave rebellion that would bring the hated institution to a fiery end. The notion was bizarre, the attack suicidal. Thirty-six hours later Brown was in irons, most of his raiders dead. In the South crowds screamed for his blood. In the North some acclaimed him as a hero, more denounced him as a scoundrel, most tried to sort out the laudable from the damnable in this strange crisis and stranger man.

Norton belonged to the majority, struggling to form a "dispassionate judgment." No doubt Brown was legally a traitor, and Virginia had a constitutional right to hang him (which it did on 2 December). But Norton, deploring Brown's course of action, admired his "strong love of liberty"; and the fanaticism with which the South responded to Brown's raid appalled him, raising to a higher pitch his hostility to slavery. Brown himself seemed to Norton a magnificent "anachronism," an "enthusiast" reminiscent of "the Scottish Covenanters and the English regicides"; yet he deeply admired his courage in the face of the gallows—and knew that his posture as a martyr "increased daily the sympathy which was already strong." He also knew that, North and South, Brown had stretched nerves already taut. Talk grew, he informed English friends, of a Republican victory in the upcoming presidential election and, in that event, of Southern secession. Charles also told them that the South was too weak to make secession stick. In ten years the slavery debate would be over, Republican policies in place: no extension of slavery into the territories, no slaves in the District of Columbia, no Fugitive Slave Law. In these views, Norton sounded like many moderate Republicans.[39]

He differed from most, however, in seeing the crisis of slavery as an episode in an epic transcending America and the nineteenth century. Garibaldi's Red Shirts, Boston's model lodging houses, even Lord Vernon's recent republication of the first four editions of the *Divina Commedia* belonged to the same saga: the story of the "gradual improvement in human nature" and "gradual increase in human happiness." At times, surveying "the state of Europe and of our own country," Norton found "more need for faith than ground of hope." But usually not. His confidence in progress grew "firmer" as his knowledge of events widened. Yet he could hardly be called a Pollyanna, for—"heavy as the sadness of the world is and disappointing as men are"—he expected improvement to creep with glacial slowness, amid confusions and setbacks. The recent "admirable patience & steadiness" of the Italians "in their struggle for national existence" almost startled him.[40]

His own country's role in the drama enacted a grand motif: popular government. Like Tocqueville, Norton saw America as a laboratory of democracy for the entire Western world; going beyond Tocqueville, he regarded the experiment more broadly as an episode in the evolution of human nature. For instance, because democracy tended "to destroy privacy & seclusion," Americans had a hard time sustaining "independence of character" and had to solve in a new way the age-old problem of leading "a double but not divided life," "in the world but apart from it." The most severe immediate stress came from slavery; but immigration, schools, literature, slums, mores all had tested and would test the system. In art and literature America humbly followed its European parent; in politics and government the United States painfully carved out a new and higher path. "The real course which affairs are taking," Norton wrote to Aubrey de Vere in February 1860, "can only be seen by watching the undercurrents" in the "untracked seas" on which America was setting out. He deemed "the prospect before us" encouraging: "looking forward for some centuries I seem to see a social condition different from any which the world has known, & better & happier than any that has gone before." The Scottish Enlightenment had never imagined "the progress of civilization" in terms at once so fluid and so encompassing.[41]

The vastness of these "untracked seas" never distracted Norton's gaze from his tiny duties in their navigation. With George Curtis he thrashed out what national politics demanded, on one of Curtis's rare visits to Shady Hill in January 1860; but the Maga framed a lot of Norton's social existence now. At the center stood Lowell. The *Atlantic* also brought Norton into regular contact with Oliver Wendell Holmes, the physician-poet who figured in its pages as the Autocrat of the Breakfast Table. Holmes came to spend a few days with Norton at Newport, departed calling him Cousin Charles. In the spring of 1860, Cousin Charles was elected to the Saturday Club, brought together around the *Atlantic*'s writers a few years earlier. Emerson was one of the regulars. By now, Charles had buried deep his father's animosity to the mystagogue of Concord, even commissioning a picture of Emerson that hung at Shady Hill; Emerson for his part was saying "the pleasantest things" of Charles. The Saturday Club took its name from its monthly eating habit;

and there Norton dined convivially with very old friends like Longfellow, Felton, and Benjamin Peirce, merely old ones like Lowell and Tom Appleton, newer ones like Holmes and Emerson, but only two really new ones, the poet John Greenleaf Whittier and the railroad entrepreneur John Murray Forbes. Boston, after all, was Boston.[42]

Newport was still, in that era, pretty much Boston, too. The Nortons went down in May as usual, soon joined by the summer medley of visitors—James Lowell, then Ezra Abbot; Uncle and Aunt Ticknor; a stray artist or two; and, when the American Association for the Advancement of Science met in Newport at the end of July, Mr. Felton and Louis and Elizabeth Agassiz. Charles, the woodsman, cut his leg with a hatchet while opening a case of wine, immobilizing himself for two weeks. He was agile by early August, when he and Jane left with the Lowells, Stillman, and some other artist friends to spend a fortnight in the Adirondack mountain wilderness. Norton never got past Lake Saranac. "Knocked up by the heat of the weather & some overfatigue," he collapsed in the apt village of North Elba. There "the General Blessing" nursed her brother while their friends forged ahead. From his chair Charles fell in love with the Adirondacks, "constantly & deeply" feeling "the presence of God." But Lowell was the one who got to fish. On the twenty-first, they limped back into Newport, reminded anew that Norton could still not count on his body.[43]

A day or two later, a letter arrived from Frank Child. He and Lizzie, back from Europe and holed up at Sedgwick headquarters in Lenox, had married there on 20 August. All of Norton's intimate male friends—Lowell, Curtis, Clough, Ruskin, now Child—had embarked on marriage. Charles alone remained in the pupal stage, an ailing man well into his thirties with no real career. Whatever emotions his inability to mature evoked he kept to himself. He simply rejoiced with Frank, probably, and rightly, expecting to see nearly as much of him as ever.[44]

Autumn grew grimmer. As October faded into November, the fate of the Republic and perhaps of slavery hung in the balance. Though preferring William Seward for president, Norton had grown tolerably comfortable with the more moderate Abraham Lincoln. The important thing was to get a Republican president, and Charles felt reasonably confident of that. He was far less sure of a Republican majority in Congress. Both opinions give strong evidence merely that he read the newspapers.[45]

If Lincoln's election on 6 November did not surprise Norton, the speed with which the Gulf states moved to secede did. He had calculated that Republican victory would provoke secession, slaveholders realizing that the steadily growing majority of Yankee voters had "forever" deprived the slave states of the political power to protect their institution. But he had not guessed so quick a move and blamed the "rash bravado" of Southern leaders on the corruption of "their characters" by their own system: slavery "has produced a generation of men of hasty temper, of arrogant & tyrannical disposition, of narrow minds."[46]

That was superficial; the true origin of secession lay "deep in principles, & remote in time." The American Republic had always formed "a Union of incompatibilities." Still deploying the Aristotelian categories of classical republican theory—terms familiar to the Founders—Norton described the slave states as "more or less completely oligarchical," the free states "almost pure democracies." The Constitution had manufactured "an alliance" between "these two conflicting systems"; but the "divergence of moral sentiment" between them inevitably widened, especially after the South persuaded itself that slavery benefited both masters and slaves. Rather than "indulging in dreams" of perpetual Union, "we ought to have been preparing for its inevitable rupture."[47]

This came on 20 December when South Carolina voted to secede. Two days later, Norton wrote to a Charleston friend who had taken a leading part in the movement. "Shall we laugh or cry? Let us do both." South Carolina did right, Norton said, to wait for "no compromises or concessions, for we have none to offer or to make." He did not lament "the destruction of a nominal Union"; yet he remained "utterly sceptical as to the success of your experiment": "higher laws than the Constitution and higher ordinances than those of Conventions" would operate so as to "save the country from destruction and preserve all that is worth preserving in our Republic." "Spite of all your decrees you & I will not be foreigners to each other": through rising sectional tensions, through the secession winter, Charles kept on cordial terms with Southern friends. He even felt "sorrow & compassion" for the South as a whole, given "the retribution that they are preparing for themselves." "The harvest they must reap is one of inevitable desolation."[48]

He felt less charity toward Northerners. His "chief fear" as Christmas approached was that "we of the North should fail to see that the time has come when the dispute between the North & the South can be settled finally." The North must cast away "timid counsels" and "compromises & concessions." Like many, maybe most, antislavery Northerners, he was at first willing to let the South go in peace, believing that the slave system, unprotected by the Union, would crumble before the moral revulsion of the world. If conflict did come to rifle and sword, Northern might would bring slavery to a bloody end. "New England is stronger than New Africa."[49]

Meanwhile, the "whole country," Norton wrote to Aubrey de Vere, itched for 4 March when "we shall be relieved from the imbecility of Mr. Buchanan." Lincoln he believed "an honest, straightforward, courageous man." Still better, the new president would presumably heed the advice of Secretary of State William Seward, more than honest and brave, "a statesman of a high order." Lincoln's inaugural address impressed Norton as "manly & straightforward"; he rejoiced to see "the dignity & force of the government once more asserted."[50]

He also rejoiced to hear that Lincoln had appointed George Perkins Marsh of Vermont, with whom Norton had chanced to dine in early December, as United States minister to the new Kingdom of Italy. The erudite Marsh shared Norton's philological interests; he could provide a congenial superior, even a scholarly collaborator, while residence in Italy could offer a wonderful opportunity for Norton's studies. Norton wrote to Senator Charles Sumner, suddenly a man of influence, asking "to be considered a candidate for the post of Secretary of Legation." He took no other steps, "for I do not wish to place myself in the position of a beggar for office." In political patronage, beggars are usually choosers; and the job went to a more assiduous scrounger.[51]

This was a disappointment; but far darker clouds closed in, both personal and national. Arthur Clough had fallen ill that winter; in mid-March the Nortons learned that the disease was consumption. South Carolina's noose around the federal fort in Charleston Harbor strengthened; so did Lincoln's determination to break the stranglehold. In early April, Charles and Jane journeyed to Hartford to witness another inauguration, their cousin Samuel Eliot's as president of Trinity College. On 12 April, as the predawn darkness softened over Charleston Harbor, the battery of the Palmetto Guard opened fire on Fort Sumter.[52]

SEVEN

Toward "A Science of Ideal Politics," 1861–1865

The shelling of Sumter ignited outrage throughout the North. Massachusetts had never seen "so strong and so fervent an outburst of popular sentiment," Charles wrote to George Curtis. Southerners reacted in kind. On 17 April, Virginia voted to join the Deep South in the Confederate States of America; Arkansas, North Carolina, and Tennessee quickly followed. The secession of the border states dashed Lincoln's hope of dividing the slave power and fulfilled Norton's opposite desire, for it defined with "undeniable distinctness" the "lines between liberty & slavery, between support of authority & anarchy." Lincoln—timidly, Norton thought—proclaimed a war only to preserve the Union; Norton wanted one to end slavery. Any thought of letting the South go in peace had vanished from Norton's mind, as from the minds of many other Yankees.[1]

His rationale appeared in the yoking of "liberty" with "support of authority," set against the linkage of "slavery" and "anarchy." Republican dogma insisted that slavery corrupted the slave owner. In most antislavery propaganda such "corruption" equaled brutality and lasciviousness. But Norton, staying closer to the politics of eighteenth-century republicans than to the moralism of nineteenth-century evangelicals, worried more about sapping *public* virtue than debauching *personal* morals. By giving masters leeway to indulge their inconstant moods, slavery fostered license, the toxic simulacrum of liberty. Plantation habits shaped political behavior. With self-restraint and civic duty enfeebled, public order in the South became as volatile as its fickle guardians. And without a stable and well-ordered polity, liberty itself could not long survive. Boston patrician conservatism, ironically, made Norton an antislavery radical. No wonder he longed "to do or to give something for a cause which has my heart as this has."[2]

A man in Charles's health could hardly answer the president's call for volunteers, but the outbreak of war did induce a decisive shift in Norton's orientation. The fluctuating balance in his commitments between literary interests and civic duty, leaning to the literary during the last several years of ill health, now tilted sharply toward the civic. The change did not occur overnight. However military Norton's fantasy life, his external one in that summer of 1861 remained bookish. He passed his time "reading & writing on the old Commentators of the D[ivina]. C[ommedia]": writing "of some use to myself" but "of very little interest to anybody else in America." "Besides these old books & the newspapers," he read "scarcely anything else." The only army he joined was the great corps of readers combing old volumes to find illustrations of word usage for the London Philological Society's new dictionary (Private Norton being assigned to *Morte d'Arthur)*. The only attack he launched was a slashing assault in the May *Atlantic* on a pretended "translation" of the fourteenth-century Dante commentary of Benvenuto da Imola. And the only military manual he read was Xenophon's *Anabasis*, in the course of helping Sam and Anna Ward's son Tom cram Greek for the Harvard entrance examination.[3]

Along with neighbors' children to tutor there was an occasional English visitor to entertain; to these rites of transatlantic hospitality, routine for Norton, the war added a new tension. Relations with Britain had turned critical and sensitive; British alliance with the Confederacy could tip the balance, mere British recognition strengthen the Southern cause. Most of Norton's friends in England favored the North (Aubrey de Vere opened the war with a drum-beating "Sonnet to Charles Eliot Norton"); but they were a minority in their own country. In these circumstances, cultivating well-placed British visitors had become a patriotic duty.[4]

And patriotism needed encouragement. In July the fresh Union army marched from Washington to capture a key railway junction at Manassas in northern Virginia. On the morning of the twenty-first, a cocky audience of Yankee reporters and congressmen cheering them on, Federal troops attacked the Confederate defenses behind a creek called Bull Run. By late afternoon guns and packs littered the banks of Bull Run, tossed aside by eighteen thousand Union soldiers running as fast as they could toward the District of Columbia. It would not be wrong to say that the Civil War began in earnest at Manassas Junction. The four years that followed transformed the lives of countless Americans.

To Charles Norton's life, the war brought tighter focus and clearer purpose. Bull Run, he actually welcomed. By making peace more remote, the defeat made peace "more likely, when achieved, to be satisfactory"; for the debacle had "forced men to sounder reflection as to the causes & objects of the war." Despite Lincoln's foot-dragging on emancipation, the "connection of slavery with the war is becoming more & more evident." (These views identified Norton yet more clearly with the radical wing of the Republican party.) Norton looked for, and wished for, a prolonged war. He had no "gloomy" views about the ultimate outcome: "the people will save the country and the gov^t in spite of all the weakness & mismanagement and corruption at Washington." But too quick a victory would leave slavery in place. Moreover, "our public men" needed a "longer training of adversity" to overcome "the feebleness of character" that forty years of "so-called prosperity" had bred in them, while only a protracted struggle would force the people at large to realize that the real goal of the war was "the civilizing of the Southern States."[5]

A literary man might help them to come to that realization. Certainly, the Lincoln administration had "wholly failed to concentrate & invigorate public opinion." Norton saw himself as now charged with a duty to impress on the public some home truths: that "war really meant *war*" and that slavery was not only "the real cause of the rebellion" but "incompatible with the existence of a democratic republican form of government." The smoke had barely lifted from Bull Run before he wrote for the *Atlantic* an article entitled "The Advantages of Defeat." He urged on readers chivalric dedication to a holy war to root out slavery—*"sans peur et sans reproche."* "Honor and courage are part of our religion"; "let there be no unmanly or unwomanly fear of bloodshed." Fear of bloodshed was not a serious temptation for a semi-invalid four hundred miles north of the battle lines, but Norton apparently felt no irony. His Anglo-Indian comrade Richard Baird Smith had learned about blood during the Sepoy Revolt, and he now warned Charles, "God help the poor people to whose homesteads it shall come." His words fell on rocky soil. His friend's new gospel was writ in burnished rows of steel.[6]

No emergency could put steel in Norton's bones, however. Summer crises of health were becoming predictable. When Charles collapsed this time, about the third week of August, Lowell happened to be visiting. He stayed to keep the invalid company; then, when James left, John Field arrived from Philadelphia; so it was not a lonely convalescence. Nor was it a difficult one: a week after falling ill, Norton agreed to write for distribution to Unitarian soldiers a tract on "the purpose and feeling with which they should go into the war." He had *The Soldier of the Good Cause* in the American Unitarian Association's hands on 16 September. Though still weak, he expected to "get back to my common level of strength"—not exactly Herculean—as the autumn weather grew cooler.[7]

With the autumn inflow of strength, the flow of ink from Norton's pen increased. One essay contended that the general welfare clause of the Constitution gave Congress power to emancipate slaves, but this ambitious claim sank without a trace when a lawyer friend pointed out that it utterly lacked warrant. An article on Tocqueville in the November *Atlantic Monthly* drew more plausible lessons for Americans. Norton naturally called attention to the Tocquevillian insight that "democratic equality" was "the dominating principle in the modern development of society." But he also linked Tocqueville's political wisdom with his "character"; and he pointedly quoted him on the existence of "two distinct divisions in morals" and the need to resurrect a zeal for *public* virtue now evident mostly in *private* morals. In Norton's eyes, at least, the Civil War showed how much value old-fashioned republican values retained in the age of "democratic equality."[8]

The war was nearing home; indeed, in all forms death stalked Charles's friends that fall. On 25 October an anguished note came from Lowell. At Ball's Bluff a beloved nephew had fallen; another lay gravely wounded; so did Wendell Holmes's son. In summer, Arthur Clough's illness had seemed to require a long recovery; by mid-November his body lay beneath the cypresses in the Protestant cemetery at Florence. Richard Baird Smith fell ill in India; he died in early December on the steamer carrying him home. By then Charles had learned that his favorite uncle and now next-neighbor, Samuel Eliot, was terminally ill; he died in January, not yet sixty-five.[9]

Other friendships flourished under tribulation. Charles saw James Lowell more frequently than ever; for James had thrown off the burden of editing the *Atlantic* and, following his father's death, had moved into the family home, Elmwood, on the other side of Harvard from Shady Hill, not far past Mr. Longfellow's house. The walk through the village to his two friends became for Charles a stroll as delightful as frequent.[10] Longfellow needed company. In July his wife Fanny had burned to death in an accident that reduced Cambridge to stunned horror. Longfellow's "Christian resignation and fortitude" under his sorrow, Charles said, "taught me to love and respect him more than ever." Frank Child had thrown himself into local pro-war politics, forging another bond with Charles. George Curtis was traveling the Northeast to give political lectures, making his visits to Shady Hill more frequent. A newer acquaintance, Chauncey Wright—amateur philosopher, part-time calculator for the *Nautical Almanac,* often taciturn but always worth hearing—Charles found as "sweet" of temper as acute of intellect; occasional meetings blossomed into friendship. Only Ruskin, wallowing in emotional turmoil, his heart "cracked—beaten in, kicked about old corridors," brought gloom, awkward and pitiable at once.[11]

A new friend compensated. This was Susan Ridley Sedgwick, the little girl with whom Charley had played at her parents' house in New York in 1842, the charming young lady seen again at a holiday party in 1852. Her father, Theodore, was a scion of the Sedgwick clan of western Massachusetts, into which Frank Child had married; but her mother, Sara Ashburner, was Anglo-Indian by birth. Susan had grown up partly in New York, where her father was the first editor of *Harper's Weekly,* partly in the Sedgwicks' ancestral Stockbridge. In 1856 her mother died; three years later, her father. Their deaths orphaned not only Susan, then twenty-one, but her sisters Sara, nineteen, and Theodora, only eight, and her sixteen-year-old brother, Arthur. When Arthur entered Harvard in 1860, his three sisters moved to Cambridge with their unmarried Ashburner aunts, Anne and Grace. Second cousin to Frank Child's Lizzie, Susan impressed Frank with her kind heart. Shady Hill became involved with the Sedgwick-Ashburner ménage only after the Nortons returned from Newport in late October 1861. By December, Susan and her sister Sara were on first-name terms with Grace and Jane.

In that month, Sara formed part of a Norton expedition south. Frank Palfrey, son of the Nortons' neighbors, commanded the twentieth Massachusetts Volunteers; and he invited Charley to present the regimental flag. Besides family ties, the honor presumably recognized literary distinction and patriotic blood lust. (A year or so later, Nathaniel Hawthorne commented that he "would not give much for a rebel's life if he came within a sword's length" of Norton.) On Thursday morning, 12 December, at the head of a little troop that included Grace and Sam Ward as well as Sara Sedgwick, Norton set out from Providence Station, his objective Camp Benton, outside Washington.[12]

He made it as far as New York before another physical collapse stopped him. Ward escorted the "young ladies" on to the ceremony, where on Christmas Day, John Palfrey read Norton's speech, not exactly dripping Christmas spirit, to his son's regiment. Norton vicariously exhorted the regiment to return their new banner stained with "blood & smoke." He himself was just then reclining beside a Christmas tree on Staten Island, where he had gone to convalesce with George Curtis and his family (his first visit there after many by George to Shady Hill). "Dis Grace," as Jane had taken to calling her sister, rejoined him there; and the day after Christmas they hobbled homeward.[13]

A deadening winter rain was falling when they arrived the next evening, but Shady Hill bustled with a new project of Jane's. Her "managing and fascinating faculties" at full force, she had launched a scheme to set to work the poor women of Cambridge, superintended by its ladies, to make shirts for the army. Sue Sedgwick became her "energetic" assistant, "constantly" at Shady Hill. A project of "so *public* a nature" also required "the help of some man"; and Charles found himself signing a contract and a five-thousand-dollar bond with the United States quartermaster general. He also found himself daily with Sue Sedgwick. Besides Susan's attendance at thrice-weekly meetings at City Hall of the shirt-making detail, she was frequently invited by Jane to dinner at the Nortons. Charles himself invited Miss Sedgwick to join the four or five "young ladies" who met with him every Tuesday and Friday to read *Paradiso* in the library at Shady Hill.[14]

Death also became a nearer acquaintance that winter. Charles's beloved cousin Ellen Twisleton wasted away in England; then at the end of February a heart attack killed his Harvard teacher Cornelius Felton, "as old & as faithful a friend as we had in Cambridge," just as Norton was preparing a memoir of Clough for the *Atlantic Monthly.* "These last months are the most memorable ones in my life for the number of friends they have taken from us." "It is still deep winter with us," Charles wrote to George on Wednesday, 19 March—but "tempered by the singing of the impatient robins."[15]

The next evening he proposed to Sue Sedgwick. She did not ask time to think it over, nor should she have. She and Charles made an ideal match. Both had grown up in prominent families with a bent toward intellectual activity and a tradition of public service. Both were used to considerable comfort though not, by the standards of the 1860s, riches. Both were "entirely *refined,*" as Grace put it, "by nature by education & by taste." He played whist; she played chess; each could probably manage the other's game.[16]

Susan, "tall & slight, usually pale," with a narrow nose too big for her face, was no Aphrodite. But then neither was her fiancé Apollo: small for a man, also pale and thin, nose just as prominent, eyes protruding, and now hair disappearing. But Charles, "studious-looking" and wearing these days a pale brown moustache and side-whiskers, did have physical dignity. And Susan had the female equivalent, physical grace, enhanced by big dark eyes, rich dark hair, and an elegant forehead. She liked to wear black and shuddered at "anything showy or striking in her dress." Longfellow thought her "very lovely," nose or no.[17]

A nose stands out when a face draws back from it; and their shared thinness and paleness pointed to another source of the lovers' compatibility: chronic ill health. Susan's diagnosis is as uncertain as Charles's. Evidently, in her very late teens a breakdown occurred, attributed, not implausibly, to the strain of nursing sick parents while helping to manage household and siblings. She also suffered periodically from "fever & ague," apparently from malaria contracted on Long Island in childhood, and frequently from "neuralgia." Nevertheless, "though not strong" as the wedding approached, she was "nothing of an invalid." The same could have been said of her soon-to-be husband. It is not implausible to speculate that both found it easier to enter marriage with a spouse who could empathize with the other's need to retreat often to bedchamber or couch.[18]

For Charles, his fiancée's lack of parents was perhaps not so much deprivation as attraction. For nearly thirty-five years he had orbited Shady Hill. Marriage would bring "no change of home" to Charles, "only added happiness to this old home, which was so happy before." Shady Hill could absorb Susan easily; after all, although she enjoyed a pleasant web of relations (and Charles would enjoy them, too), she had no mother or father, no real family home, no competing center of gravity. The Nortons fitted up a big room at the back of the house as Susan's drawing room, and she fitted herself into Shady Hill, taking her place, as her Aunt Catharine put it, "in the temple of the Boston aristocracy."[19]

Susan certainly fitted Charles. In temperament she was calm, even reserved, not given to romantic enthusiasms. In humor she was bright and witty, a match to friends like James and Frank. Like Charles she enjoyed books, pictures, intellectual conversation. And possibly as important as anything else, given the particularities of Charles's deeply moral persona, he admired her. To Frank Child, who knew Sue well, her engagement to Charles was "an unspeakable happiness." Mrs. Gaskell, who did not but who knew Charles, rejoiced for him: Norton better appreciated women than any other man she knew and in consequence most needed, "along with your masculine friendships, the sympathetic companionship of a good gracious woman." Only an increasingly cranky and self-absorbed Ruskin groused, complaining that Susan would take Charles away from him.[20]

Charles and Susan wanted a home wedding, but realism dictated the college chapel. There, on Wednesday, 21 May 1862, they were wed. The fifty or sixty guests retired to Shady Hill to toast the newlyweds. James gave them a rare old-folio Dante; Longfellow, a Roman mosaic. Susan was not well enough to travel, so they made their honeymoon at Shady Hill. Catharine, Jane, and Grace tactfully retreated to William and Louisa's Lenox house for the summer.

To luxuriate long was not in Charles, even with a new bride. He had been invited to give a course of Lowell Lectures the next winter, and by early June he was hard at work "on the characteristics of the 13th century."[21]

There were anxious distractions as summer wore on. Susan needed care; by mid-July she was recovering from her neuralgia but only slowly gaining strength. Lowell needed comfort. In the Seven Days at the end of June, Robert E. Lee's army had turned aside George McClellan's advance on Richmond; and a rebel bullet had taken Jem Lowell, just recovered from his wound at Ball's Bluff. James remembered in tears the four little nephews who used to have snowball fights on the lawn at Elmwood; one dead in Italy, two killed in Virginia, "Charlie only is left." Charles Russell Lowell, dashing "Beau Sabreur," would die the next year at Cedar Creek.[22]

Through it all, Norton stuck to his desk—but cautiously. He had learned his body well enough to know that overwork risked overload, then collapse. He gave up making extracts from *Morte d'Arthur* for the Philological Society's new dictionary. He begged off criticizing the new chapters of Mr. Palfrey's history of New England. By autumn he was deep into Saint Dominic and Saint Francis and Saint Thomas, "the Art & the Science" of the thirteenth century, "so full of moral energy & intellectual activity." There were two things he could not postpone. One was his edition of Clough's poems, which fate had made a memorial to his late friend and which occupied many hours through the fall.[23]

The other was the war. Except for Clough's poems and his memoir of Clough, Norton published nothing unrelated to the war between November 1861 and January 1864. In July, Lincoln replaced the ineffectual McClellan with Henry Halleck as general in chief ("Little Mac" remaining in command of the Army of the Potomac); and Congress authorized the enlistment of African American soldiers (a measure "radicals" like Norton had urged from the outset). Neither move worked a miracle. At the end of August, Lee's outgunned troops met the Union army near Manassas again, again drove it back onto Washington. Something like panic spread through the North; Curtis wrote Norton that the rebels might well capture Washington, putting the Union in "mortal peril." The British government seemed on the verge of recognizing the Confederacy.[24]

During this summer of disaster, when "the incompetence of our generals & the vacillation of our administration" nearly disheartened even the unflappable Norton, Charles trudged on with patriotic odds and ends. "As I cannot go with the army, I must do my part at home." He gave money to support the Cambridge Volunteers, assisted in setting up a War Claims

Association to protect the financial rights of Union soldiers and sailors, helped to publish and publicize a "Historical Research" by his old friend George Livermore advocating full acceptance of blacks as citizens and soldiers. A "Negro army," Norton wrote to Curtis a little later, "is the need beyond all others of this moment." When shortly thereafter black regiments did take the field, they inspired in Norton "the completest confidence in the capacity of the blacks for service in war"; and he came to look on "military training" as "an unequalled school for educating them to the position & rights of freemen."[25]

His thoughts were veering in new directions politically. The dragging out of the war, the piling up of suffering and setbacks, had, he thought, produced "a great gain." Even before the disasters of the Seven Days and Second Manassas, Norton perceived among Northerners a new "consciousness of national existence." In earlier days Norton had, like his father, spoken almost exclusively the vocabulary of old republicanism and seen himself primarily as a New Englander. But his transatlantic friends received him mostly as "American," and the war immensely deepened that identity.[26]

It also moved "the nation," as a locus of meaning and value, to the forefront of his political thinking—and, he believed, that of Northerners generally. (He was at least right that a majority of the politically alert shared in the transformation.) Nationalism did not *displace* republicanism in Norton's politics (as it did for many other Yankees); the recurring motif of public virtue and its answering theme of ordered liberty still sounded loudly. But the new centrality of "the nation" did jar republican axioms and revise republican forecasts. Where this shift would lead, Norton could hardly say in 1863; but that it "promises the most important results in the future" he felt sure. Not only for eradicating slavery, then, but also for building "a true sense of national life, & national honour, & national duty," he, like other radical Republicans, welcomed the protraction of the war—and its painful costs.[27]

These were rising and not abstract. On 17 September, around Antietam Creek in Maryland, McClellan botched his battle plan and spilled a river of his soldiers' blood. But Confederate troops also suffered huge casualties (more Americans died on that day than in the War of 1812, the Mexican War, and the Spanish War combined); and McClellan turned back Lee's invasion of Maryland. The crisis had passed. Antietam was the closest thing to a major victory that the Union had seen for a long time, and President Lincoln took advantage of it to issue five days later an Emancipation Proclamation: on 1 January 1863 all slaves living in states then still in rebellion would become free. "God be praised! I can hardly see to write"—the note Charles dashed off to George Curtis—"for when I think of this great act of Freedom, and all it implies, my heart and my eyes overflow with the deepest, most serious gladness. I think today that this world is glorified by the spirit of Christ."[28]

Norton continued to regard Lincoln as a well-meaning "domestic cat" when "a Bengal tiger" was needed; but he threw himself into the fall election campaign with renewed confidence in the Republican cause: with emancipation in sight, the "war is paid for." Still the price rose. Although, in November, Lincoln finally relieved McClellan of command, a month later Lee mauled his successor at Fredericksburg. In the battle George Curtis's brother fell leading his regiment.[29]

Amid death, life. As autumn turned to winter, Susan discovered that she was pregnant. The prospect of a child affected Charles as it does most new fathers, putting in longer perspective the daily round of mundane tasks.

His current daily task, preparing the Lowell Lectures, in turn, put the war into its "just relations to the past & the future." "It is, indeed, by acquaintance with the past, that one learns to estimate present things justly, and to see, indistinctly it is true but with continually increasing certainty and clearness, the meaning of history, the relation of past times to the present, the unity not only of nature but of development of the human race." The note sounded here would echo through all Norton's years to come. Just *how* "Innocent III and Heresy" or the "Poetry of the Franciscan Order" clarified the meaning of the blood flowing down Antietam Creek into the Potomac, he did not now specify. Perhaps "The Last Crusade" cast some light.[30]

There were twelve lectures in all, two each week, beginning on Tuesday evening, 2 December 1862, and concluding (with, no surprise, "Dante") on Friday, 9 January. "Roger Bacon and Experimental Philosophy" took advantage of Norton's long review for the *Atlantic* in 1860 of Bacon's works. "St. Louis and Chivalry" laid the groundwork for a later article in the *North American Review*. "Cathedral Building" took off from the Orvieto chapter in *Travel and Study in Italy* and launched an enduring line of research. The whole series showed Norton's fragmentary scholarship on the High Middle Ages achieving new density and coherence. The "many pleasant expressions" afterward also showed him a "decidedly successful" lecturer—and one rather pleased with himself.[31]

Still, he was happy to be done with them. He had more time now for Susan, whom neuralgia still made miserable two or three days a week; and he could turn his own "never very strong" energies to postponed literary tasks. He went back to reading Palfrey's proofs with at least interest; and he took "real pleasure" in commenting on Longfellow's translation of the *Paradiso*—"delighted that you, who first taught me to love Dante should continue thus to be my master and guide." There was time now to chair an Athenaeum committee, to hear Henry Ward Beecher lecture at the Music Hall. He and Susan began to talk of European travel when the war ended. In February, Mrs. Gaskell dedicated the American edition of her new novel *Sylvia's Lovers* to Charles and Susan together.[32]

The jointure was apt, for Norton's wife had added to his life a new sort of happiness, on which her pregnancy set the seal. This addition entailed more than intellectual companionship, romantic affection, and sexual gratification, though doubtless those played their parts. More primally, in his marriage Norton achieved familial tranquillity of a sort idealized in the world-view of Unitarian Boston, of a sort experienced in his unusually happy childhood and youth, of a sort modeled in Andrews's relationship with Catharine and their children, of a sort symbolized in Shady Hill itself. To say that Norton was "domestic" in temperament, while true, does not convey the temporal depth, social salience, or psychological weight—in the world as he felt it—of wife and children. Susan filled this need remarkably well. Charles treated her brother Arthur as a son even before she gave him his own; and the rest of the Sedgwick-Ashburner household soon moored alongside Shady Hill, in a house built on a piece of the estate along Kirkland Street.

Yet for Norton—and this fact is key to how "family" structured his life—his home reached out to connect him with the world, rather than closing in to shelter him from it. Nor did only cousins and aunts belong to "home." Lowell and Curtis were as integral to Shady Hill as Uncle Ticknor or Charley Guild had ever been. In 1863, on a lot carved out of the Norton estate (next door to Charles Eliot), Frank Child built a house for Lizzie and himself.

In this little world Charles and Susan flourished together. Late in life, he wrote inside a portfolio of papers from 1863: "The year was one of the happiest of my private life." It also became the busiest yet of his public life. Where the Civil War trained haler Americans in small arms and artillery, it drilled Norton in the strategy and tactics of organizing. As the year began, he was working with other Bostonians to set up a Union Club.[33]

Toward the end of January, John Murray Forbes, a one-time China merchant who had made a fortune building railroads, enlisted Norton in a more ambitious scheme. Forbes worried that Northern public opinion was growing soft. Early in 1863 he hatched a plan for a "club" to shore it up by mailing to editors of small-town newspapers—always on the lookout for reprintable copy—bracing editorials from big antislavery dailies like the *New York Evening Post* and *Boston Daily Advertiser*. Either Charles Norton or James Lowell seemed to him ideal as editor—Boston already thought of them as a literary pair.[34]

Norton got the call. By the end of January he was sending out "slips" provided by metropolitan dailies. (These newspapers reprinted articles onto slips of newsprint from type already set for the paper itself.) He also helped Forbes, Sam Ward, and Martin Brimmer (a fellow trustee of the Athenaeum) make the rounds of Boston's patricians, ending in a meeting at Brimmer's house on 10 March, at which a dozen or so civic leaders took "steps for the formation of a Society for the publication and distribution of sound doctrine and information upon public affairs." Forbes became president of this New England Loyal Publication Society; Norton became editor and managed the money. Of the active members of the executive committee, all except Forbes and Ward were within four years of Norton's age, those two only a decade older. A new generation was taking its place at the forefront of Boston's civic life.[35]

After Lee in early May 1863 mauled the Union army at Chancellorsville, the Loyal Publication Society's greatest concern was to cement loyalty in Illinois, Indiana, and Ohio, where a lot of inhabitants shared Southern roots and sympathies and, even more, suspected New Yorkers and New Englanders of giving Western needs short shrift. So in that region the society—by the end of May reaching 585 newspapers in twenty-three states—concentrated its propaganda. Norton, experienced in working with printers, soon came to think the slips too easy to overlook and too difficult to copy; he began to collect "articles of good sense & strong expression" into twice-weekly "broadsides," printed in better type on better stock. He wrote many broadsides himself; and he extended their circulation to editors in Britain and France, hoping to dent dangerous pro-Southern sentiment abroad.[36]

Norton's transatlantic links brought that problem close to home. Lord Palmerston's government swayed perilously close to diplomatic recognition of the rebels, and meanwhile Liverpool shipyards turned out Confederate raiders to prey on Yankee commerce. Norton's blood boiled at what amounted, in his view, to perfidious Albion abetting piracy; and most of his English friends simmered in sympathy. The large exception was Ruskin, as obnoxious about the war as he was about Susan ("If she's not jealous of me, I am of her"). For the war's last two years, he mostly shut up, which inexplicably tactful silence, together with Charles's patience, may have saved their friendship.[37]

When opportunity presented itself, Norton tried to make clear to leaders of British opinion the depth of Northern fury and to persuade them that anger had legitimate ground. Now and then, an English friend would clip a telling passage from one of Norton's letters, to send to an English review or to lay before a cabinet minister. In May, Norton himself wrote to the sympathetic Liberal member of parliament John Bright that war could be avoided so long as the United States kept any "hasty naval commander" on a leash and Parliament checked "its unreasonable temper." But he insisted that "the spirit shown in the [British] governing classes,—the aristocracy and the commercial class,—toward the North, have excited a feeling throughout this country of deep resentment, as natural as it is to be regretted"; "the coals of anger against England" would, he predicted, continue to sear relations long after the war ended. Later that summer, he delivered much the same message to Henry Yates Thompson, a reporter in Boston for the *Times* of London. Thompson found Norton "very decided as to our iniquities on the pirate question."[38]

Norton's growing literary reputation made it natural that a journalist would seek his views. Several months earlier, the New York Infirmary for Women and Children had solicited him to join nineteen other luminaries of the pen in contributing a jeu d'esprit to a gift book being printed for the dispensary's benefit. The success of his Lowell Lectures solidified and extended his standing. Strangers were beginning to write to him as "Professor Norton."[39]

It was hardly a surprise that, when Harvard's new president Thomas Hill decided in March 1863 to institute University Lectures for graduates, he asked Norton to deliver a course. Norton's lectures, "On some Characteristics of the Medieval Revival of Learning," began in Andrews's old haunt, Divinity Hall, on Tuesday, 7 April, and continued, one a week, into early June. Like Norton's Lowell Lectures (which they probably largely reprised), they were "esteemed of great value" by the sixty-four auditors (an odd lot of Harvard law and divinity students, schoolteachers, and America's most distinguished scientist, Louis Agassiz). President Hill hoped that Charles would lecture again the following term or "meet with & direct the studies of a class of graduates."[40]

War work precluded that degree of commitment, but Norton did undertake a new Dante project. Learning in April of Florence's plan to celebrate the six-hundredth anniversary of Dante's birth two years hence, he and

Lowell concocted a "literary contribution from America" for the *festa*: an edition of Benvenuto da Imola's well known early "Comment" on the *Divina Commedia*. Though it had, in Norton's opinion, "a value beyond that of any other of the fourteenth century commentators," the "Comment" had never been printed. There were two good manuscripts in the Laurentian Library, and Norton enlisted George Marsh in Florence to find a competent copyist. This "work of scholarship" was meant to show "that such studies were not neglected" in the United States "even under the pressure of civil war."[41]

Yet the press of war work more and more squeezed scholarship to the margins of Norton's life. Like most radicals, he viewed the conflict with a hard-edged, ruthless optimism. Never doubting the Union's final victory, he was far from deflated by temporary defeats. Indeed, he judged the "moral condition of public affairs" in the spring of 1863 "far more satisfactory" than at any time since the war began. "Hard experience" had "knocked out of the nation" a "great deal of nonsense," of "shallowness of thought & shallowness of feeling." The speedy enlistment of black soldiers, the employment for wages of freedmen in Louisiana, "are both most certain agencies for the destruction of slavery." And the "mass of the people" were finally coming to understand the need "for a long war" to push the rebels into "unconditional submission." "We must thoroughly subjugate & if necessary exterminate the slaveholding class, leaving them no power politically or socially, & this is not a quick process." Did he think of Middletons and Pringles?[42]

He or Jane must certainly have written to Matilda that, on 1 July at half past ten at night, Susan gave birth to a son, Eliot. A few days later, the Union army defeated Lee's troops at Gettysburg.

The tide of the war had turned, but Norton struggled to win Yankee minds and hearts to the radicals' program. Usually alert to historical novelty, he was apparently too busy to realize that he was helping in a small way to perfect the concept of public opinion and to devise the correlate strategy of propaganda. As the Loyal Publication Society's circulation mounted, Norton now regularly produced two broadsides a week, despite his "great difficulty" in finding enough "good *democratic* doctrine." Nor were broadsides his only outlet. He used the October *North American* to plug a new quarterly "written by colored persons" at a private "Manual Labor School" in Spartanburg, Indiana—and to swipe at white Indianans for barring African Americans from public schools. The "public welfare" required educating every "class of citizens"; in any case, "all distinctions dependent merely on color or race, should be as far as possible avoided."[43]

This black magazine had reached Norton through its white printer and editorial advisor, Jonathan Baxter Harrison, whose own story was Lincolnesque. Child of a backwoods Indiana family, he had scant schooling, worked till age twenty as a farm laborer, studied "at night by firelight" because his family could not afford candles, and "read everything I could find." He had kept school, sold books, preached to Methodists, lectured to anyone, laid rails, served in the Union army till invalided, and now edited a country weekly in Winchester, Indiana. The Loyal Publication Society connected him with Norton.[44]

Norton thought Harrison's paper the most interesting "of the local papers I see" and reprinted Harrison's "Conditions of National Success" in a broadside. He thought its editor a man meriting attention and urged Harrison to try to find "some time for quiet reading & reflection," naming a few authors for him to chew on: Plato, Dante, Shakespeare, Bacon. Harrison hungered for learning, a man starving in the Sahara, and gulped Norton's advice. He had read some Shakespeare, had peered at Dante in "the bookstores in the big cities," but knew of Plato and Bacon only by hearsay.[45]

Before winter, the two editors had settled down as teacher and student. Norton sent Harrison a hodgepodge of books: Andrews's version of the Gospels, John Stuart Mill's *Political Economy*, John Carlyle's translation of the *Inferno*, Clough's poems. Harrison sent in return his religious perplexities. He grew so voracious for guidance that Norton worried.

> I shall be glad to help you,—but as I write the word I feel that help in any common sense is not what you want. I shall be glad to be your friend,—that is better,—and to do for you what I can as a friend. It would be a bad result of friendship were you to lose by its means any of your own independence, or to find yourself weaker because of it. If it can serve you to build yourself up from strength to strength then make use of it, but if you find yourself leaning upon it to the diminution of your own resolution & vigor then say Goodbye to it.

Harrison never said goodbye.[46]

Norton's war work, it proved, never interfered with Norton's powers of friend making but only provided a new arena in which to exercise them. The English historian and polemicist Goldwin Smith was another lifelong comrade met through the Loyal Publication Society, while constant association in its activities turned casual friendships with Sam Ward and Martin Brimmer into enduring ones. And older poles of attraction still operated, notably Harvard. Charles Eliot had lost his post teaching chemistry there; but the college had appreciated him more for administrative genius than scientific brilliance, anyway; and he left to study universities in Europe. His cousin fed him "crumbs of College news" and asked about lodgings for the poor in Paris. One of Eliot's Harvard students, twenty-one-year-old William James, took to dropping in at Shady Hill from time to time; probably his brother Henry did, too, having audited Norton's Harvard lectures.[47]

In Shady Hill's library—now a silo storing fodder for Loyal Publication Society broadsides—Norton read hundreds of articles, argued with Forbes, and gauged the reactions of distant editors. Time for systematic reflection was out of the question; nonetheless, Charles had immersed himself, without intending it, in a medium nourishing his evolving political thought. He began even to think that Lincoln was growing in wisdom. The coincidence of increase in wisdom and convergence with Norton's opinions is striking, but later historians would concur that Lincoln's thought deepened as the war ground on. Norton believed that his recent letters belonged to "the rarest class of political documents, arguments seriously addressed by one in power to the conscience & reason of the citizens of the commonwealth."[48]

Here, Norton spoke in the once familiar accents of old republicanism, a dialect fast becoming archaic beyond Shady Hill. When slavery or race was at issue, however, he called himself a radical. But the "Negro question," though vastly important, was not the only one; and by 1863, Norton had come to view the Civil War as more than a war to end slavery; it was equally "a war for liberal ideas and for the establishment of liberal principles." Still, he cautioned, the past held "much more that is good & precious" than "our people" understood, including "some good things" in the United States "which men have not attained elsewhere"; so "let us also be Conservatives."[49]

Confusion of tongues suggests ideas in transition, but the contradictions were far less serious than they appear to later eyes. The republicanism of the American Revolution, with its stress on communal self-government and civic virtue, does look at first glance diametrically opposed to nineteenth-century liberalism, with its emphasis on individualism and personal freedom. But John Stuart Mill—who virtually defined liberalism for mid-Victorians like Norton—understood liberalism precisely as a program of moral education, individual freedom being in his view the only sure way for human beings to develop their higher capacities. Far from being antithetical to a politics of virtue, liberalism was supposed to produce a kind of virtue (though admittedly not the civic virtue of such a latter-day Spartan as the American revolutionary Samuel Adams). It was not, after all, so hard for

Norton—who tightly linked liberty and virtue from his earliest political writing, *Considerations on Some Recent Social Theories*—to blend a modified liberalism with his republicanism.

Mill's educative liberalism also fitted reasonably well with the Unitarian ideal of self-culture that Norton's teacher Felton had begun to transform into a program of liberal education. Far from contradicting Norton's republicanism, then, liberalism, suitably adapted, could actually serve as a bridge between his political thinking, his cultural work (with its conservative bent for recovering the past), and, later, his own matured educational program.

Hardly wallowing in confusion, Norton was actually beginning creatively to meld disparate but not necessarily hostile ideas. As the reference to unique "good things" achieved in the United States hinted, these competing voices somehow harmonized around one category completely foreign to the older republicanism from which Norton sprang yet increasingly crucial to his political thinking: the idea of the democratic nation—a nation defined neither by language nor by race but by principles and their history. "Every day convinces me more and more of the soundness of the main principles on which our nationality is founded." And its founding *on* principles set the American nation an ocean apart from, say, England: "No man in a country of class distinctions & political privileges feels safe when a general abstract political proposition is set loose." In the United States, in contrast, "a strong government" could safely coexist "with entire & immediate dependence upon & direct appeal to the people."[50]

For the United States was the single country "where political principles are fairly understood." On its territory alone "a science of ideal politics" might apply "its conclusions to actual conditions." The Civil War, "the most useful of commentaries on our democratic institutions," had convinced Norton of this possibility. The present challenge was to give "to our people a truer sense of what is meant by American principles"—to make "them recognize the rights of man"; to impress on them "the responsibilities & duties that are involved in our immense privileges"; to develop "in them faith in liberty & equality as principles of universal application." Then that "strong government" immediately dependent on the people could carry national principles into daily application.[51]

To this broader end of political education the Loyal Publication Society increasingly directed its efforts. By late 1863 more than eight hundred American newspapers received the broadsides, as did hundreds of strategically placed individuals and foreign papers. Norton thereby reached several hundred thousand readers each week, his contributions to "the local press of the northern States for the last two years of the war" far exceeding (as Edward Everett Hale later pointed out) "those of any other single man." Norton thought the "intelligent progress of public opinion" as swift in the latter half of 1863 as ever during the war; and the Loyal Publication Society was his heaviest engine for speeding it.[52]

He never regarded it as his only one, and a promising new possibility appeared on his doorstep in late September in the person of Edwin L. Godkin. Godkin, an expatriate Irish journalist of self-consciously English mien, carried a letter of introduction from Frederick Law Olmsted, the New York reformer and architect of Central Park, whom Norton had known casually for over a decade. Godkin and Olmsted had drawn up plans for a weekly journal aimed at advancing the postwar agenda shared by Norton and Curtis as much as by Olmsted and Godkin. Now Olmsted had gone to California, leaving Godkin to carry on alone. Olmsted had urged him to call on Norton, as the man best placed to secure backers in Boston for the proposed paper. Charles liked the idea, liked Godkin, and introduced both to his Loyal Publication Society associates and other useful acquaintances. On the verge of success, a competing weekly, the *Round Table,* appeared, bringing Godkin's plan "for the present to a standstill." It did not take Norton long to conclude that the *Round Table* fell "very far" short both of Godkin's idea "& of what is required by the times." The standstill would prove temporary.[53]

A couple of weeks after Godkin's arrival, James Lowell brought Charles another refugee from the United Kingdom, traveling in the United States to survey wartime American democracy. His name was Leslie Stephen; and he belonged to the same stratum of English society—roughly, a bourgeois intelligentsia—represented in the Lyells, Ruskin, and Clough. Like Clough, having lost faith in Christianity, he had thrown over an academic career rather than swear that he believed in a creed he did not. Stephen was at first "shy and reserved"; but reticence melted under Nortonian hospitality. Soon, the two men were deep in talk about "certain points of religion."[54]

Religion had occupied Norton's mind a good deal in the last few years. The editor of Clough's poems could scarcely avoid it (so heterodox a thinker as Emerson advised Charles to suppress Clough's "Easter Day, Naples" on the ground that its negations were "a little too rude" for "the young public"); and the funeral bells tolling for Lowell's nephews and Curtis's brother persistently asked eternal questions. Norton still believed in a God, even an afterlife; but a mist obscured any specifics. A "real religious life and spirit" seemed to him the thing needful, any particular creed—even Romanism— almost incidental.[55]

Two invitations in the fall of 1863 concentrated his thinking. On 14 October he rode to Springfield, Massachusetts, to address the Unitarians' convention on "American Ideas Applied to Religion and Politics." Then on Sunday, 8 November, he preached to the late Theodore Parker's congregation in Boston. Parker's repudiation of historic Christianity for a diaphanous theism had infuriated Andrews; it now came pretty near his son's adoctrinal "Christianity." No record of what Charles preached in Boston survives, but he told the Unitarians assembled at Springfield that the essence of their religion was "liberty in religion."[56]

This was hardly Andrews's idea of Unitarianism, but Charles did follow his father's logic in two respects. First, Andrews and the other founders of the denomination had insisted, against the orthodox, on the centrality of freedom of thought—at least until transcendentalism took off. It was hardly bizarre for Charles to deduce that the proper direction of American religion (as of American politics) was "more and more democratic." Second, the Unitarian Fathers found noisome the evangelical habit of dwelling in public on all the emotional ups and downs of an individual's religious experience; Andrews flatly declared it "offensive to a man of correct mind to make his deepest feelings and his strongest affections a subject of common discourse." Why were one's most intimate *convictions* any less private? Andrews did put doctrine squarely in the public realm, as Emerson and Parker learned to some discomfort. Still, when the experiential core of religion grew private, shrank from public scrutiny, religion *tout court* drifted away from objective fact toward individual sensibility. Charles did not *entirely* betray his lineage when he decided that Christianity depended, not on creeds or doctrines or public truth claims of any sort, but on each individual's "real religious life and spirit."[57]

To say that Norton had settled his religious puzzles would be far from true, but he had started down a path that he found comfortably "in conformity with American principles in politics and society." The tenets of "individual responsibilities & duties," of "liberty & equality," had indeed become in his hands "principles of universal application."[58]

A reputation as a powerful advocate of American principles had by late 1863 attached itself to Norton, extending beyond Boston, amplifying the more modest standing he had achieved before the war as scholar and man of letters. And, having learned to regulate his erratic health, he had proved himself in the Loyal Publication Society an efficient and effective editor. He certainly had nothing approaching the celebrity of Longfellow or even of Lowell, with whom Boston naturally paired him; but he had a certain éclat, and he inspired considerable confidence.

In October, Crosby and Nichols, publishers of the *North American Review,* approached Norton and Lowell. The *North American* remained the most respected American exemplar of what Russians called "the thick journals," the fat quarterly reviews like the *Edinburgh* and the *Westminster.* But its gravitas owed as much now to stodginess as to authority, and its heavily New England authorship put it at a further disadvantage in a new era of national monthlies. The *Atlantic Monthly* and New York's *Harper's* churned past it like Cunard steamers leaving behind a weltering merchantman. James wondered whether "the day of the quarterlies is gone by," and "those megatheria of letters" were "withdrawing to their last swamps to die in peace." Charles thought at least the *North American* "nearly extinct."⁵⁹

Yet perhaps it was "capable of reinvigoration." Crosby and Nichols wanted Norton and Lowell to try. It was understood that the bulk of the editorial labor would fall to Charles. James would help with that, write a good deal, and wield his fame in attracting authors. There was some jockeying about pay, both the editors' and the contributors'. Crosby and Nichols gave a little ground; and, on 23 October, Charles and James signed a contract. Charles believed "we can put some life into the old dry bones." He even dared to hope that the *North American* could "be made of some use in influencing public opinion correctly."⁶⁰

Eighteen sixty-three ended amid a scurrying of editors. Crosby and Nichols needed copy in hand for the January number well before the first of the month, and contributors suiting the *North American's* fresh look had to be found. Norton worked connections in all corners of his life: fellow journalists, Harvard professors, Washington acquaintances, Loyal Publication Society colleagues, Unitarian leaders, family friends. George Curtis visited in early December; filled with magazine experience, just named political editor of *Harper's Weekly,* he presumably had authors to suggest. Tactfully warding off old contributors mattered as much as securing new ones, since the last thing Norton and Lowell wanted was for the frumpy *North American* to continue her tired old tune.

Charles sounded the fresh notes more distinctly than James, but their intentions fully harmonized. The first need was to escape New England provinciality, the second to expel the stale thinking of late Federalist Boston that still hobbled the *North American.* "We hope to be able to 'nationalize' it," Norton wrote to Senator Charles Sumner, "& secure for it contributions that shall truly represent the best & most advanced thought of America on questions of politics & literature." When Norton talked of "influencing public opinion," he conceived the project broadly. He meant the *North American* to weigh heavily not only in debates over wartime and postwar policy but also in scholarship, literature, and the arts.[61]

Policy makers would listen only if the magazine's writers could speak with authority. So, for an account of the Sanitary Commission (the army medical auxiliary that functioned as the chief civilian war agency), Norton enlisted the Reverend Henry Bellows, the New York minister who founded and led it. To write on the Union navy he got Charles H. Davis, chief of its Bureau of Navigation. From Senator Sumner, high in Republican councils, he solicited other Washington contributors. But, while recognizing that famous names sold magazines, Norton and Lowell put expertise first, not prestige. Ignoring their publisher's obvious salivating, the editors shunned a strategy of larding the *North American* with celebrities. Norton's aversion to "flunkeyism" was not limited to London.

Believing that power of argument gave force to opinion, they refused to let reputation displace advanced ideas and acuity as criteria for choosing authors. Edward Atkinson wrote about cotton as a weapon of economic warfare, and Edwin L. Godkin became Norton's mainstay for constitutional and political theory. Neither was well known then. But both would rise to distinction after the war, Atkinson as an industrial economist, Godkin as the greatest American political journalist of his era. (Godkin, too, was quickly growing into a friend.) These unfamiliar writers were meant to push fresh thinking. The *North American*'s radical Republicanism and Millian liberalism could not but startle some of its old readers. Still, in method of argument, the political cut-and-thrust that Norton and Lowell fostered was hardly novel.

Norton's version of *literary* journalism was anything but familiar; indeed, the cultural agenda he propounded for the *North American* even Lowell had scarcely conceived (though happily adopted). Norton meant to use the magazine as a whetstone to sharpen American standards in scholarship, literature, and art. One of the first of his own articles ridiculed the lurid, best-selling "dime novels" put out by the New York publisher Beadle and Co., then went on to argue (from the firm's own sales records, naively provided by the hapless Beadle) that cheap editions of "popular masterpieces of English literature" would outsell *Buck Taylor, King of the Cowboys* or even *Lariat Lil.* And by peddling Shakespeare and Jane Austen instead of Ned Buntline,

Beadle would discharge the "serious responsibility" owed by a mass-market publisher who wielded "an instrument of immense power in education and civilization." It may be doubted that he really expected Beadle and Co. to see the sweetness and light, but this exhortation foreshadowed Norton's own later efforts at popularization.[62]

He hoped for real effect in more elevated regions of national intellect. The "shallow quality of much that passes for learning and scholarship in America" appalled him. By publishing the "ripest learning of the country," Norton meant to set a new criterion for "high culture in America." The first step was to establish a serious standard of criticism, to replace "indiscriminate eulogy" with "just severity of judgment." If critics cared little for truth, neither would authors. *Finding* competent critics in the United States was a job for Diogenes but also "a patriotic duty"; and Norton put himself to it. Some of his own book notices applied enough severity to gratify the most demanding patriot.[63]

Besides sorting erudite wheat from counterfeit chaff, the magazine needed to teach readers "what is meant by scholarship" by providing from time to time "a genuine piece of learning." The *North American* could "hardly do a more important work." Norton enlisted in it most of the North's few real *érudits* and several of its first-rate intellects: men of the stamp of William Dwight Whitney, doyen of Sanskritists and theoretical linguists; Chauncey Wright, the most acute philosopher of his generation; Eugene Schuyler, America's first Ph.D. and first translator of Turgenev; Richard Grant White, the country's ablest Shakespeare scholar. Norton aimed very self-consciously—evidently the first American editor to do so— to "represent the best American scholarship."[64]

The search for it pulled him into a national network of expertise, which in the third quarter of the century was beginning to spin threads tying Boston and Cambridge to New Haven to New York to Princeton to Philadelphia, reaching south to Washington, even west to Cincinnati and Ann Arbor and Saint Louis. The old capitals of locally oriented culture, each serving its region as Boston served New England, were starting to blur into a more diffused and more diffuse national culture, blended of popular and academic ingredients—compounded of, to make the matter concrete, both *Harper's Weekly* and the American Philological Association. *(Harper's Weekly* began publishing in 1857; the American Philological Association, first of the disciplinary and university-oriented learned societies, was founded in 1869.) The Philological Association, at least, gazed toward Germany and England as often as toward Cincinnati and Ann Arbor; and thickening American connections with European intellectual life helped to bring American scholars and writers to a consciousness of each other.

When Norton needed a review of an anthropological work or a learned article on geography, his Harvard connections steered him toward experts at other universities. Self-conscious connection with this still embryonic national intelligentsia undergirded his renovation of the *North American*—and the magazine thus became one of the many midwives bringing it to birth. His political nationalism paralleled a cultural nationalism, as politics and culture always connected in Norton. But networks of expertise were yet frail and partial in the 1860s, and more often than not Norton ended by relying on a Boston writer. Several of his nonresident experts (Whitney, Grant White, Davis, Bellows, for instance) he secured through personal or family friendship rather than professional advice. And a remarkable proportion of scholars recommended by Harvard professors lived down the road in New Haven.

Not even these more considerable oases in the Great American Desert had a surfeit of the sort of author wanted: one too fastidious to assume learning he did not actually command. The search was often frustrating. Norton's attempt to secure an article on Jacob Grimm's philology turned into a comedy of musical chairs, each besought scholar pleading incompetence and pointing to the next. Repeatedly, Norton had to settle for amateurs; he himself reviewed books on Egypt, musical scales, Arctic exploration, marksmanship. Yet he persisted. He freely admitted to a hopeful author that her "Chinese Classics" would "fill a gap" for "the mass of readers" and, further, that probably no American could write a "thoroughly learned treatment." He still turned her down: "if I print an article on such a subject I print it not for the mass but for Professor Whitney, Mr. Marsh, and two or three others."[65]

For in scholarship (as in the political work of the *North American*) Norton aimed at a limited but defined audience. He saw clearly that a revolution had transformed journalism within the past fifteen years, that the rise of mass-circulation monthlies and weeklies had forever changed the rules of the game. He knew the *North American* would never reach the crowds Curtis preached to from his *Harper's* pulpit. He realized that few Americans had time or patience for "the careful essay" on a question "already discussed and settled by the daily or monthly press." Yet there remained readers "not averse to serious thought," wanting to "be instructed by men who have made a study of special subjects." So the old quarterly still had "a definite place to fill, and a valuable work to perform," speaking to "the limited, though still large class in the community, who are themselves the leaders and formers of popular opinion." Put succinctly, when mass journalism consolidated the modern version of public opinion, the opinion leader emerged. And the opinion leader was the magazine's real target, whether denouncing slapdash learning or lenience to rebels.[66]

The *North American* scored a direct hit. The big New York dailies sat up and took notice: the "brilliant promise" of the January issue "presages a brighter day for our oldest literary periodical." America's most consequential opinion leader, Abraham Lincoln, wrote to praise (and slightly emend) Lowell's article on "The President's Policy"—a piece that the *Boston Transcript* recognized "as a palpable force in forming or confirming opinion on the acts of the present administration." High in the Andes, Norton's old ethnological friend Squier, "broiling and lunching" among Inca ruins, read of the *North American* on the scrap of newspaper that wrapped his sandwiches. Conservative papers groused at the journal's "abolition management" (the image of Norton as "wild doctrinaire" must have had Cambridge in stitches); evangelicals bemoaned its defection to "the lowest school of humanitarian Unitarians." The journal had made the impression Norton wanted, where he wanted it.[67]

After a "brilliant" April number, the *New York Evening Post* decided that "under its new editorial management the *North American* is evidently to take its stand foremost among the quarterlies in the English language." Given his skepticism about critical standards in the United States, Norton may have refrained from leaping in glee. But from Yale, Daniel Coit Gilman reported the *North American*'s rapid gain "in influence & favor" among the right sort. In the wake of the October issue, Octavius Frothingham (a certifiable member of "the lowest school of humanitarian Unitarians") informed Charles that "till the North American has uttered its voice nothing authoritative has been spoken." "Four such successive numbers as yours of this year," William Dwight Whitney declared, "I do not think any American review ever had to show before."[68]

Justly, it was to Norton that Whitney said this; for the credit accrued mostly to him. Lowell usually wrote the "political article" for each issue, reviewed a few books—and handed his contributions in late. (No matter; the pair got on famously.) The shaping of the journal was Charles's. After Ticknor and Fields purchased the *North American* in October 1864, they adjusted the editors' salaries to recognize this: Norton's going up to twelve hundred dollars, Lowell's down to four hundred dollars. Like James, Charles wrote an article and a few reviews for most numbers. But he also solicited contributors, patted disgruntled authors on the head, dealt with the printer, and wielded the editorial scissors.[69]

By most accounts, he wielded well. Years of practice on friends' manuscripts, and his own, paid dividends. Norton seems to have done the usual things—tightened arguments, deleted excurses and technical material not needed for general readers, suppressed flowery language—but to have done them unusually well. Emerson, Lowell, and Parkman were not the only students to take to heart Edward Channing's lessons. So fastidious an author as Henry Adams told Norton that his "omissions" were "decided improvements." Perhaps authors remained genial because their editor cut with such suavity that they failed to notice the blood. Norton's tact showed, too, in a knack for guiding writers toward crafting articles both better informed and more appealing to a general audience.[70]

He had a knack, too, for cultivating young writers: there was always something of the teacher in Norton. In 1864 a restless Harvard law student, Henry James, sent a book notice that impressed Norton. The editor encouraged more; and, in December 1864, Norton asked James to review all the novels of the quarter in a lump. The "offered cup of editorial sweetness" entailed an invitation to Shady Hill. In the spacious library there, "where the winter sunshine touched serene bookshelves and arrayed pictures" with "golden light of promise," Norton chatted to young James of books and pictures and principles of criticism. In memory, this half hour became the novelist's "positive consecration to letters." His was far from the only experience of the sort.[71]

Whatever so impressed impressionable young men has slipped away past recovering. High ideals served with a refined blend of tea? a compound of erudition with grace? a bestowal of a sense of worthy belonging, a fellowship of aspiration? an appeal to intellectual haughtiness, an invitation to an exclusive club? Whatever transpired must be remembered even as it eludes specification. For those ephemeral essences of personality, character, and intellect provide a key (there is more than one) to unlocking the puzzle of Norton's vast appeal to, and consequent influence on, not only this young man and thousands of later ones but also on riper souls as different as John Ruskin from Elizabeth Gaskell, Jonathan Harrison from James Lowell.

In 1864, this quiet charisma provided but one ingredient of an unusually able editor. It took another editor (looking back) fully to appreciate Norton's "strong editorial sense" and to see how he had "really breathed a new life into the North American Review after it had become very nearly a corpse."

The resuscitation involved, inter alia, modernizing the magazine's form. Over the next few years, Norton abandoned the old pretense of heading every article with a list of books nominally reviewed therein. In 1868, he began to print the names of authors. The cleaner look enhanced the *North American*'s appeal to contemporary readers; well-known names helped to sell it in a national market, where not every reader was a Boston patrician who knew the authors without being told.[72]

That Norton had saved the *North American* from its grave went without question; how long it would breathe did not. For the journal was, as its editors knew, a life-form from an earlier epoch struggling to survive in a harsh modern environment. The new national magazines like *Harper's Weekly* and the *Atlantic Monthly* not only provided lighter fare for busy readers but, by virtue of larger circulation, also could afford to pay authors much bigger fees. Norton grappled with both challenges, targeting the *North American* to what would later be called a niche market, trying to squeeze out of his publishers more money for his writers. Ticknor and Fields sympathized but drew the line. Publishing the *North American* brought honor without profit, and "we must not put too much expensive powder and shot into a cannon that refuses to go off." It was Indian summer for the *North American,* if a glorious one.[73]

EIGHT

The North American, the Nation, and the Nation, 1865–1868

For the *North American*'s principal editor the season was high summer. Not yet forty, Norton found himself directing the nation's leading journal of serious thought. For the first time since shrugging off the East India trade, he had a defined public role—while enjoying a satisfying private one. Oddly, editorship seems not so much to have exorcized the ghost of his vocational quandary (marriage and family had already expelled any urgency) as to have put the question of vocation aside. Charles never regarded journalism as a settled career: he and Susan still talked of sailing to Europe after the national crisis had passed. And, though the *North American* occupied the largest block of his time, it hardly exhausted it. He still edited the Loyal Publication Society's broadsides, still helped English friends with American publishers, still pulled his oars in Boston's flotilla of civic institutions.

Such public duties floated on a tranquil private sea in the spring of 1864. A second child was on the way. Another of George Curtis's whirlwind lecture tours brought him to visit; Frank Child cracked jokes; Mr. Longfellow came on weekends to study Dante. The new friend, Chauncey Wright, spent more and more time at Shady Hill, his quick mind, ingenious talk, and thoughtful attentiveness making him a favorite with Jane and Grace as well as Sue and Charles. In early May, the Battle of the Wilderness ended in indecisive blood; the Spotsylvania campaign began.

A few weeks later, as the Republicans set about renominating Lincoln, Charles made a tour through western Massachusetts, seeking a house in "some quiet, pleasant village among the hills" to rent for the summer. He needed to guard his health—and Susan's, whose "old enemy fever & ague" had "pulled her down very much" the past winter. Why Newport fell from favor as summer retreat is a mystery. Perhaps it disagreed with Sue; perhaps Catharine wanted to be closer to Louisa and William in Lenox; most likely Charles recoiled from the influx of swaggering New York plutocrats. In any case, the Nortons never went back. Charles located a replacement in Ashfield, an isolated village in northwestern Massachusetts, some fifteen miles west of the Connecticut River and not much farther south of New Hampshire, reachable by a two-stage rail journey plus twelve miles of bad road. He returned to Cambridge to watch Sue's younger brother Arthur celebrate his Harvard Class Day on 24 June. The next day, Arthur left for Virginia to take up a commission in the Twentieth Massachusetts Volunteers.[1]

A week or two later the Norton clan moved into the "good old-fashioned farm house" Charles had rented in Ashfield. "Embosomed in the hills" thirteen hundred feet above sea level, amid beech and hemlock forests broken by moors, Ashfield romantically mingled in Norton's eyes "fresh wild nature" with "cheerful farms." All reminded Charles of the Lake District in England, "on a smaller scale." In Norton's pastoral, the townsfolk lived in solid New England comfort, with only three poor people blemishing the idyll ("& they are very old"). In prosaic fact, rural poverty was endemic in central Massachusetts; Ashfield rose to Norton's fancy by isolating its "loafers & drunkards" in a little settlement called Tin Pot two miles from the main village.[2]

At Ashfield, Charles edited the *North American*, though at long distance, followed national politics and the war, and, with July turning into August, welcomed George Curtis for a visit. As George came, so did bad news: the rebels had captured Arthur Sedgwick while on picket duty. A worried and very pregnant Susan was perhaps ready to return to Shady Hill. Before leaving, Charles arranged to buy the farmstead they had rented. That done, and after sitting five hours in the station at Greenfield awaiting a late train, the Nortons arrived exhausted at Shady Hill on the evening of 1 September.[3]

Ten days later Charles and Susan's first daughter, Sara (called Sally) after Susan's mother, arrived. A couple of weeks later another welcome arrival appeared: Susan's brother. Released in a prisoner exchange, Arthur came home exhausted, feverish with malaria, and anxious to return to his regiment.

Beyond the family the great thing that fall was the election. Norton, by now fully converted to Curtis's admiration for Lincoln, groused at the "extreme radicals" opposing the president and rejoiced at his renomination. In August the Democrats chose McClellan as a peace candidate, making radical Republicans such as Norton fear that war-weary voters would abort the Northern crusade before it had smashed the slave system. Like all his close friends, he threw himself into the campaign. Child canceled classes on Election Day, 8 November, so that he could stand all day in front of Lyceum Hall handing out Republican ballots.[4]

The result was a triumph, a "solemn and momentous day" in Norton's eyes. The president swept back into office, and the Republicans (renamed the Union party) got a hammerlock on Congress and the state governments. The election seemed to Norton (hardly eccentric in this) to assure Union victory and to secure Lincoln's status as greatest of American statesmen. "Of the people" by upbringing, Lincoln's great strength was his full confidence *in* the people—and in "the political principles which are distinctively American": "the political equality of men, their right to equal justice and freedom, their right to self-government, their right to every means of self-development consistent with the general welfare." Norton had always fretted less about victory in war than about the principles of peace; for many months he had dwelt on the vital importance of bringing the freed slaves fully into "the American system of democracy."[5]

That it now seemed possible to do so showed how much "these years have changed us"—including, one might add, Norton. The Civil War appeared to him a transforming event of greater power than "all our past." Its "stern tuition" had schooled Americans in their own political axioms as well as nurturing their "sense of nationality." Certainly an awareness of the United States as a nation, more than a federated republic, had grasped Norton. He used the *North American* and the Loyal Publication Society specifically as "means of developing the nation, of stimulating its better sense, of setting before it and holding up to it its own ideal." When, on 3 March 1865, Congress created the Freedmen's Bureau, Norton believed that the nation had taken a large step toward realizing "its own ideal." In late February he lectured his new friend Godkin pretty severely: the latter's inclination to withhold suffrage from the freed slaves clashed "not only with my political creed but with my sense of right, if the two are not merely forms of one and the same thing."[6]

Taking the correct line mattered more now than ever, for the war was winding down. Charles still hoped to "see our army before peace comes," wanting to "hear a gun fired in earnest, & to stand at least once under a hot fire." The only hot lead he would approach was at Bigelow and Welch's print shop. On 9 April, at Appomattox Court House, Lee surrendered the Army of Northern Virginia. The "new world," Norton crowed, had triumphed "over the old," the "future over the past."[7]

Then, on 14 April, John Wilkes Booth fired his pistol. Lincoln's death threw Reconstruction into the doubtful hands of Andrew Johnson. Ipso facto, the assassination threw into confusion the war to secure democratic principles.

Norton was in those weeks helping to forge a new weapon for the radicals. Near the end of March, the Philadelphia abolitionist James McKim came to Boston soliciting support for a national weekly to be devoted to "the condition & position of the black race." Norton thought the projected *Nation* (as it was to be called) a "good scheme" and took charge of raising Boston's half of the needed capital of a hundred thousand dollars. Norton himself subscribed a thousand; other Bostonians supplied the rest.[8]

With this much money at stake, the *Nation's* stockholders insisted on a more experienced hand at the editorial helm than McKim's. Norton, now chief organizer, failed to talk Curtis into the job and turned to Godkin. Godkin envisioned in the *Nation* a broad-gauged journal of politics and literature, not a freedman's advocate. Lukewarm on black rights, he was, however, willing to commit the new weekly to "true democratic principles" as Norton understood them. Godkin's talent impressed Norton, and Godkin's idea of the *Nation* fitted better than McKim's into Norton's broad program of educating the American public: Godkin's weekly almost sounding like a affiliate of Norton's quarterly. By 4 May, Godkin was installed as editor, with McKim and his son-in-law Wendell Phillips Garrison "as assistants in the Freedman's Department." The first number appeared on 5 July. The freedmen got due attention in it; but so did Richard Grant White's edition of Shakespeare—from Norton's hands.[9]

Norton provided Godkin with other assets. Half the *Nation's* original roster of authors, including Longfellow, Lowell, Child, William Dwight Whitney, and both Henry Jameses, came out of his stable; in December he enlisted Charles Eliot to write a regular summary of scientific news. He recruited two young Harvard graduates who became mainstays of the magazine, J. R. Dennett and Susan's brother, Arthur Sedgwick; and he supplied a stream of copy in his own neat hand. Without Norton the *Nation* might never have appeared or, appearing, survived. The energy that he poured into the venture stretches credibility when one recalls that this far from robust man was simultaneously editing the *North American* and Loyal Publication Society broadsides.

And keeping an eye cocked on Dante. The weight of Norton's editorial labors never crushed his interest in letters. Reviewing books on art, literature, and history for the *North American* and the *Nation* kept his critical edge honed; and during these years he developed an intimacy with William Blake, whose "unworldliness" touched him. But Dante engaged him most deeply. The scheme to print Benvenuto da Imola's commentary having foundered, Norton prepared a little essay, *On the Original Portraits of Dante*, to travel to Florence in May 1865 "in onore della festa per il sesto centenario di Dante." In this libretto Charles claimed to authenticate an alleged death mask of Dante by comparing it with the putative Giotto portrait of supposed Dante in the Bargello. The exercise was a triumph of hope over evidence. Arguably the feeblest scholarship Norton ever produced, *Original Portraits* can charitably be taken as testifying to the distractions of war and editorial work. That his Dantist friends failed to squelch him shows how far American learning still had to go.[10]

Yet these very Dantists, whatever their limitations, were pushing it along. The substantial American contribution to Dante's birthday party was a preliminary printing of the *Inferno* from Longfellow's unpublished blank-verse translation of the *Divina Commedia*. For some time, Longfellow had been reading his cantos for Norton's critical response; by 1865 the two of them were deep into *Purgatorio*. That fall Longfellow turned occasional readings into a Dante Club. It met for the first time on 25 October at Longfellow's home, with "the XXV Purgatorio" chased by oysters and one of the "elect vintages" that Longfellow savored. Almost every Wednesday evening thereafter—save summer recess—Norton and Lowell spent at Craigie House over a canto and supper. Other visitors took to dropping in to hear the reading and discussion. Dante far from dominated the suppers; but Longfellow's white-paneled study, its round table piled high with books, did incubate organized Dante scholarship in the United States.[11]

Why Americans should have taken such interest in Dante is a curious question, with possibly revealing answers. Milton's *Paradise Lost* offered a more accessible epic, and a more obvious one, especially for New Englanders with a Puritan ancestry that writers like Norton were beginning to celebrate as the origin of American democracy. Yet, for that very reason, there was need to put distance between themselves and other aspects of Puritanism: notably its uncompromising Calvinism and its supposed hostility to the fine arts central to Victorian ideals of high culture. In Norton's circle, Puritan politics seemed admirable if primitive, Puritan religion and intellectual culture simply appalling. (The doctrine that historical origins explain present conditions almost demanded some such binary view of the Puritans; for in 1865, America's *polity* seemed to a Norton unquestionably superior to Europe's, its *culture* just as obviously inferior.) Had Dante's religion been remotely plausible intellectually to the New England clerisy, he could not have played the role he did; but Norton and his intimates could not begin to take Catholicism seriously in that way.

So Dante could provide, on a cultural plane, needed alternatives to the Puritan ancestors whose hand always lay heavy on at least Norton's shoulder.

The aesthetic beauty that he extracted from Catholicism (even understood as in some sense its enduring essence) proved by contrast the feebleness of Calvinism (however fruitful a germ of democracy) as a faith for modern life, a basis for culture. Dante's grand intellectual synthesis of Catholic faith in the *Divina Commedia,* precisely because incredible as knowledge but compelling as poetry, became perforce a metaphorical spirituality deeply human and immensely appealing to a man drifting away from his Unitarian moorings. And Dante supplied a cosmopolitan bridge to the lush and ancient culture of the richly imagined Continent for an American who looked around him and saw the impoverished culture of his own raw new land. That some such urges powered the growing vogue of Dante among educated Americans, particularly New Englanders, seems likely; for Norton, almost certain.

Yet he found only odd hours for Dante in these years. War's end brought no discharge from civic duty, only new postings. The *North American* still swallowed whole days; now the *Nation,* too. At least John Forbes was taking on more of the Loyal Publication Society editing.

Inevitably, Harvard put Norton on the alumni committee to plan a Civil War memorial building; inevitably, he found the architects wanting. Norton did not doubt the "merit and dignity" of Ware and Van Brunt's Gothic design; he did doubt whether it had the "first requisite of great architecture": "unity and simplicity of organization." For Norton, like Ruskin, a "great and noble building," as "the material representative and expression of great and noble thought, imagination, and moral sense," must be "beautiful in every part, and absolutely thorough in execution." Not all buildings needed to be great and noble. But the one at hand did, because American colleges were "utterly destitute of noble architecture," a failing as much pedagogical as aesthetic. The Memorial Hall should begin to remedy that defect. As a reminder of the noble dead, the structure should work "upon the hearts and imaginations of the future generations of youth," cultivate "those sympathies and associations which fine architecture is fitted to evoke, and which enlarge, illustrate and dignify the lessons drawn from books." Norton sounded more like professor than alumnus. Ruskin would have applauded— had Memorial Hall not involved the sore subject of the Civil War (though with the war ended, Ruskin felt himself able to talk to Norton, "a little").[12]

Not till the middle of June 1865 did the Nortons manage to get back to what was now their own house in Ashfield. Eliot left Shady Hill with a fever, from teething they thought. The boy rapidly worsened in Ashfield; within days he had grown "dangerously ill." The crisis passed around

28 June, but for weeks Eliot required constant care.[13] Charles also was "far from well" before leaving Cambridge and remained weak and sickly through most of the summer. The familiar pattern of overwork and collapse was repeating itself but now, too, was the tonic effect of mixing physical with intellectual work at Ashfield. Bringing in the hay balanced getting out the *North American,* and, by late August, Norton was "gaining strength." Having George and Nan Curtis as neighbors helped at least to keep him happy. Godkin also came to visit, as did Chauncey Wright. In mid-September, three years a wife, Susan became pregnant with her third child. Such rapid-fire childbearing would have strained a stronger woman than she; but it was not unusual; and, if she regarded pregnancy with more distress than delight, there is no sign. In late October the Nortons left Ashfield.[14]

As 1865 wound down, *Nation* business took Norton to New York to confabulate with Godkin, Sam Ward (who had just moved to the city for business reasons), and the rest of the *Nation's* leadership. Susan went with him, and they stayed with Edwin and Fanny Godkin, making around the *Nation* meeting a little vacation, "far the pleasantest days" Charles had ever spent in New York, "& Susan enjoyed them as much as I did." While there, Norton met a young contributor to the *North American,* then writing for the *Nation,* whose work he much admired, William Dean Howells. He also renewed ties with Frederick Olmsted, who was pitching in with the *Nation* while practicing landscape architecture. Both men entered Norton's permanent inner circle, if never quite becoming intimates. The Nortons had barely got home when a "sharp attack" of neuralgia sent Susan to bed. Her husband stayed up, putting the *North American* to bed. The overload phase of the cycle was starting again.[15]

Under these pressures—perhaps, in part, owing to them—Norton was articulating a newly coherent vision of the nation and its future. Heated arguments over Reconstruction became the furnace in which Norton refined his politics. President Johnson's laxity toward the defeated South alarmed Norton; like other radicals, he believed a social revolution necessary to root out the system of "class privileges" founded on slavery. Readmitting an unreconstructed South to the Union would allow "an aristocracy still imbued with the slaveholding spirit" to regain national power. Then would ensue, Norton warned, "degradation for the blacks, worse political corruption in the North, & probable foreign war." He was understandably relieved when Congress reassembled at the end of 1865 and the radical Republicans wrested Reconstruction from the president's hands. But he still feared that

Congress would falter, or Johnson circumvent it, handing the South back to its old leaders.[16]

The pivot for Norton was African American suffrage. He refused even to print any article concluding against it in the *North American*, a censorship imposed on no other topic; for only by eradicating "the evils of a caste system" could the Union raze the system of "spurious aristocracy" in the South. And, as a practical matter, enfranchising the freedmen provided "our only safety" for the immediate future: African Americans formed "the majority of loyal men" in the South; if they could not vote, their former masters would sweep back into power as soon as the Confederate states reentered the Union. For this pragmatic reason, Norton by early 1866 had ruled out any educational test for voting in the South. In principle, requiring voters to have appropriate skills seemed to him "eminently wise"; and he freely admitted that slavery was scarcely training for republican citizenship. But a literacy test would induce the Southern "ruling class" to "keep the blacks ignorant." Without the ballot, the "late slaves will be practically held as serfs"; with it, "the negro will not only have an inducement to learn, but his relation to his late master will be radically changed."[17]

Yet far more than expedience made Norton sneer at what he called "the feeble sophism, 'This is a white man's country.'" He insisted on the freed slaves becoming citizens because "our democratic principles" demanded it. Norton even doubted whether a state that made political rights depend on "descent or color" qualified as a republican form of government, as required by Article IV of the Constitution; Yankees had no more right than ex-Rebels to deny suffrage to African Americans. For "political equality" formed a foundation stone of the "free political community" that was the United States. Previous failure to recognize this principle was obvious in the "atrocities of slavery," which Norton saw as an unnatural distortion of "our system." But the Civil War had initiated a new phase of that system's evolution, a phase in which "distinctively American" political principles were "to have fuller scope and development."[18]

This development would, he thought, make citizens not only of black men but of all women. Anyone growing up in patrician Boston would have noticed that women discussed politics as cogently as men, but it may have been John Stuart Mill who pushed Norton to draw the theoretical conclusion from daily life: after reading one of Norton's political essays, Mill urged him to extend the principle of civil equality from race to sex. In any case, Norton did not advance the rationale common among American feminists that, if African Americans voted, so should white women, by virtue of racial superiority; he simply asserted that no ground existed for political inequality between the sexes. Surprisingly for a Victorian, Norton did not even see a variance in nature between men and women that might produce differing political behavior. Segregating women from politics appeared to him now—in the wake of war-driven rethinking—like the "Turkish" practice of veiling women: a result of "inherited prejudices," not essential difference. And such timeworn biases were collapsing all around.[19]

For the war had "led to a clearer understanding of the nature and worth of the principles embodied in our institutions." "A democracy in name, in form, in externals" was growing, fertilized by blood, into "a democracy in reality." That many Americans still resisted American principles, Norton well knew; that a "vigorous contest" awaited, he fully expected; but that these tenets would one day reign "supreme and unopposed," he had little doubt. Norton examined the country's political evolution in a long essay, "American Political Ideas," in the October 1865 *North American*. John Stuart Mill greeted it warmly, suggesting how solid had become the consensus of Anglo-American liberal intellectuals. But this attempt to comprehend immediate political disputes within a sweeping historical context was also a classically Nortonian performance.[20]

The American "commonwealth" had no proper founding, he insisted; it grew organically and "undiscerned" from the "instincts, desires, and efforts" of the Puritan settlers of New England. United solely by conscience, they gave their colony "a moral rather than a political foundation," thus transferring into "practical politics" an "order of ideas" previously "relegated to the domain of theory." Theirs was the "first historical application of the truth, that politics are a branch of ethics"; and it led to a "wholly unanticipated" result—"the dawn of modern political civilization." Political modernity germinated from a seminal fact: that in morals each individual stands equal and independent. Basing politics on ethics therefore required the Puritans, without intending any such thing, to replace "king and priest and noble" with *"the People."*[21]

Conditions of life in colonial New England fostered this individualism but fostered, too, a parallel "habit of combined action in the community." And although New England was "the mother of *ideas,*" similar *conditions* molded all the colonies. The Revolution then "welded" the colonies together; and the Constitution embodied the "long lessons of Colonial experience" in its animating actors, *"We, the people."* But—and here is the key that springs the lock on Norton's politics—"the people" meant "not a political body forming a state" but "a moral community, already organized and governed by moral principles." Or more fully: "a civilized community spontaneously organized to promote the general welfare, and actuated by the moral forces which civilization has ingrained in the habits of a race, and which are derived from the Divine order of the universe."[22]

Individualism and community thus did not contradict but rather reinforced each other. An individual's moral responsibility included the community's welfare, a conviction every Boston patrician had imbibed with his mother's milk and father's Madeira. Equally familiar was Norton's explanation of "the crimes, the wrongs, the miseries which deface the ideal of our state": slavery, corruption, "the selfishness of materialism, the mass of ignorance." These were "excrescences" that time would remove, "so that the actual commonwealth should assume slowly, imperfectly always, but ever more and more nearly, the image of the ideal." Perhaps there echoed here Scottish Enlightenment notions of the progress of civilization; but there sounded more distinctly the smug Unitarian view of church history, revamped to fit the polity.[23]

Undergirding Norton's optimism about "the perpetual beneficent progress" of American principles was unfailing confidence in the moral capacity of the people. This trust, too, appealed to history. Equality, freedom, and moral responsibility had produced in America, Norton thought, "a new type of character," nobler than anything in Greece or Rome. It had emerged into visibility only in the last generation, at its finest in the self-denying heroism of Union troops. The United States was "maturing a national character"; that is, a "distinct moral nationality."[24]

This historical conviction powered Norton's new enthusiasm for "the nation." In the 1860s "nation" largely displaced "republic" in his taxonomy of American politics. He understood nationality as "the sum of the differences" that separate one people from every other and make it conscious of itself "as a community"; these distinctions eventually "modify the character" of individuals and produce "the traits of national character." Though all too easily perverted, "the sentiment of nationality" at its best lifted people "out of narrow and selfish individualism into a region where they behold their duties as members one of another, and as partakers of the general life of humanity." The Revolution separated Americans politically from England but did not create a nation, nationality not being "the growth of a night." The war for the Union had congealed American experiences into national consciousness, "separating us as a nation, not only from our own past, but also from the Old World."[25]

For the American nation was a breakthrough, without "parallel or exemplar" in the past—though pregnant for the future. Its uniqueness lay in the source and glue of American nationality: not language, not race, not a feudal past, but republican institutions, democratic principles, moral responsibility, and "true community." Even in Europe, the "distinctive principles" of this new American nation posed "the greatest question in the art and science of government," for European polities tended "plainly" toward democracy. America's republican example formed "a persistent revolutionary fact," its "moral influence" a "standing menace to Europe." So much for the cliché that Southern rebellion soured Northern intellectuals on revolutions abroad.[26]

Implications for the United States concerned Norton more. The "constant interaction of the moral order of society and of the governmental order" required a morally sensitive and sturdy citizenry. Here again, his partial absorption of a Millian version of liberalism as moral education developed, rather than contradicted, his classical republican linkage of liberty and civic virtue. Happily for the nation, the absence of fractious class divisions, the prevalence of egalitarian ideals, and the very experience of citizenly cooperation worked to generate "mutual confidence and helpfulness." American democracy thus fostered the moral improvement of its people: the "kindliness, sympathy, and humanity" of its citizens distinguishing the United States from other polities (or so Norton alleged). Such genial folk, he went on, resulted naturally and inevitably from America's "politico-religious faith." If the essence of Christianity was moral amelioration, then "the American system" was "the political expression of Christian ideas." Conversely, "the doctrine of equality," having such results, seemed to him "in its nature a religious doctrine."[27]

This understanding of American nationality left Norton both at ease and anxious. On the one hand, defining the nation as a moral cooperative fitted into habitual patterns of thought. The vision of a republic striving to attain "the true brotherhood of man" could have come—probably did— straight out of High Boston Unitarianism. After all, Boston's edition of Unitarianism was itself a kind of democratized moral Federalism; and by its tenets each individual was supposed to "find his completeness and perfection, his worth and his happiness, in the recognized relations of mutual dependence existing between himself and the community of which he forms an integral and essential part." That this image owed a good deal to Romantic notions of fragmented modern man rooting around after primal wholeness is no surprise. That this communitarian ideal was claimed as American republican principle (and the words do come from Norton's "American Political Ideas") is at first startling—on reflection, perhaps not so jarring. For Norton's new nationalism absorbed without strain two key elements in his (and Boston's) older politics: the Stoic stress on civic duty and mutual obligation; the classical republican insistence on public virtue as the health of the polity.[28]

On the other hand, his idea of nationalism posed Norton a problem. If America were to lead Europe along the path to democracy, if American principles were to realize the "fuller scope and development" he forecast, then the American people must progress intellectually as well as morally. They must grow in both understanding of and commitment to democratic axioms. And this firmer grasp of fundamentals must edify their social life as well as their political institutions, for each depended on the other. Yet Norton (like Tocqueville) believed that, while democracy tended to bring "the mass of men up to a comparatively high level" (which he suspected that Americans had pretty nearly reached), it sapped "the means for the highest culture."[29]

In brief, democracy made mediocrities—delightfully exemplified at the moment in the "very good-natured" but "very uncivilized" Phineas T. Barnum. Where but in America did one find "The Paradise of Mediocrities," as Norton called his nation in his *Nation?* England might be flunkey-ridden, but it shamed America in the "art of social morals." The good news was that Old World mores rested on "false postulates"; the bad news was that, however much "finer in promise," America was sparse in achievement. "We have lost the ancient grace, the fine trained sense of moral relations in purely conventional society, and have not yet gained the true modern grace which"— Norton whistled in the dark—"is hereafter to model our lives & manners in its own form." America's cultural feebleness unexpectedly turned out to threaten its political superiority.[30]

The true modern grace involved more than knowing which fork to use (though Norton was never inclined to underrate the implications of that). It entailed grasping fully why African Americans and women should have ballots in their hands; why a dirty Irish boy represented a duty not a threat; why the state must not wriggle out of financial commitments by diluting the currency; why struggling with Dante's obscurities befitted a democrat better than gaping over one of Beadle's dime novels. Mere practice of democratic forms, sheer persistence in the well-worn grooves of social cooperation, would not likely bring the American nation to these realizations.

Education could. It became the pivot of Norton's political writings as

Civil War became Reconstruction. This stress showed not merely the instincts of a teacher but the principles of a democrat. Most immediately, the North must impress on Southern whites ("essentially opposed to modern civilization") the basic principles of equality and justice on which American democracy rested. Norton knew that "the process of educating the South to become an integral part of a Democratic community, is not likely to be finished in our day." But his whole approach to Reconstruction flowed from his broad conception of the history of American democracy, a history that clarified democracy's defects and prescribed remedies. Anyone who grasped this history must realize that the North needed to take an unyielding grip on the old Confederacy, to revolutionize its social structure and institutions, to clear the roadblocks to its tutelage in democracy. At the same time, Norton knew that the South could not be held indefinitely "as a conquered dependency": all the more reason for a long-term regimen of education.[31]

Not only the South needed teaching. Though further along in school, the North, too, required "steady, unwearied efforts" to "educate the people to a true sense of their responsibilities as a free & selfgoverning people." Education had been a leitmotif in Norton's writings of the 1850s on amelioration of poverty, a theory brought to practice in his evening school. He now pressed further in insisting on compulsory schooling as mandatory for a democracy, proposing "an invariable and fundamental political rule" that "every extension of the elective franchise should be accompanied with or preceded by an increase of the means of popular instruction." "Education," he instructed his friend and tutee Harrison in Indiana, "lies at the foundation of democracy."[32]

"Not the education of the intellect alone" but "of the moral nature as well." And Norton construed "the means of popular instruction" with a breadth befitting this wide aim. This was why (believing literature "one of the great instruments of education") he deployed the *North American* against critical sloppiness and intellectual slackness. This was why he deprecated both the "exclusive classical and mathematical training" of English public schools and the utilitarian and scientific bias that he detected in American schooling. He wanted schools to nurture the whole person, to offer a liberal education that would widen human sympathies, refine taste, cultivate imagination, discipline the soul as well as the mind, and enlarge man's conception of himself and of his destiny by bringing him into communion with the spirits of men long dead and creating in him a sense of the historic continuity and perpetuity of the race and of the intimate responsibility and relation of every generation, however remote, to those that succeed it upon

Earth. This was also why he wanted Harvard to have a noble Memorial Hall and New York City to have first-rate architecture, generous public works, spacious parks: all "among the most effective instructors of the public." And this, too, was why he saw no conflict between, but instead the essential interpenetration of, politics and learning, culture and democracy. After the 1860s, Norton was never again able really to think of politics apart from education nor to think of education without considering its ramifications for democracy.[33]

Positions staked out between 1864 and 1866, their acuities, their blindnesses, remained the framework within which Norton understood politics—that is, within which he conceived democracy and its relation to culture—for the rest of his life.

The friends on whom Norton most often tried out these political views were George Curtis and Edwin Godkin. Not even Lowell proved as useful a sounding board as these two: Curtis as weather vane of current politics, Godkin as skeptic of all democratic enthusiasms. George was back at Shady Hill "off & on" for a week in January 1866; Edwin during that first postwar winter stuck close to New York, wrestling with the *Nation*. He got an earful at long distance—much of which qualified as political only in Norton's expansive sense, including a review for the *Nation* of Charles Perkins's *Tuscan Sculptors*, in which Charles insisted that only insofar as "the study of art" investigates the broad conditions shaping an art form does it deserve "the attention of serious thinkers interested in the progress of the race." *Ars gratia historiae—et republicae.*[34]

The review was a moment snatched for art in a busy and not entirely pleasant winter. Charles did find spare hours to begin translating Dante's *Convito*; son Eliot got his first sled; and in February that young writer whom Charles admired, William Dean Howells, moved to Cambridge, hired away from the *Nation* to edit the *Atlantic Monthly*. Sue and Charles helped Howells and his wife Elinor navigate the local tradesmen and find a house (Charles got his brother-in-law Bullard to provide a mortgage). Howells evinced even more enthusiasm for Norton than Charles for him; their friendship took fast and lasting root. Meanwhile, neuralgia was making the pregnant "poor Susan" miserable. A short trip to Washington with Godkin in April supplied welcome diversion. Not long after returning, Charles himself fell ill, remaining "poorly" for three or four weeks though able to drag himself and the household to Ashfield in late May.[35]

There on 12 June, Sue gave birth. They named the baby Elizabeth Gaskell Norton, after Charles's English friend, recently and unexpectedly deceased. At first, Susan seemed to recover quickly; but then her malaria recurred, and a painful abscess developed in a breast. These ills and general "disability & languor" confined her to her chamber through much of June and July, getting worse in the latter half of July. She did not seem dangerously ill, but for a woman to die in the weeks after childbirth was not unusual.[36]

It is easy to imagine Charles's anxiety that summer, but all evidence has vanished. Private relations he held private; and before his death he put the most intimate of all under unbreakable seal, destroying all direct evidence of his and Susan's love. All indirect evidence points to much happiness taken in each other, to emotional and intellectual communion of unusual warmth and delicacy. One can only guess about the summer of 1866, but one guesses at sleepless nights and anxious days through June and July.

By early August, Sue was downstairs, by the middle of the month almost as strong as usual; and both Nortons could enjoy the continuing Curtises and the occasional houseguests: Lowell, Chauncey Wright, Sue's brother, her Ashburner aunts. An aunt or sister was a standard fixture around Ashfield, for the Norton family remained a sturdily extended one. Shady Hill to Cantabrigians never implied Charles and Susan alone but "the ladies of the master's family" as well. The Bullard estate in Lenox provided an alternate residence for Charles's mother and sisters; and they seem to have used it, especially in summer, to give Charles and Susan breathing room. Catharine approached her seventy-third birthday with solid health and habitual quiet dignity: unchanging type of an older Boston.[37]

In contrast, his sisters' personalities were defining themselves more distinctly as the two women matured. Jane, past forty now, had settled definitively into the role of General Blessing, "distill[ing] civility and sympathy and charm," as Henry James recalled. She was the one for whom the family's closest friends seem to have felt the warmer affection, though the word "service" did spring to mind in connection with her. She seemed entirely contented in her place. Grace did not, entirely. There is no reason to think Grace brighter, but she was developing a more definite passion for intellectual life. Perhaps not so great a favorite as Jane with most of the Nortons' older friends, she was forging closer ties with younger ones such as Henry James. Grace seemed a tad more anxious to step beyond the household's doors. Yet to suggest discontent on Grace's part or any breach between the sisters would be extravagant error, and both took lively part in the household's robust and sometimes rambunctious intellectual life.[38]

Into that arena entered perhaps its acutest and most avid player when Chauncey Wright took to visiting the Nortons. Not that Wright was overbearing; to the contrary, Charles described him as free of egoism, free of pettiness, a delight as a friend. But he lived for ideas—and, unhappily, for drink, alcoholism manifesting itself as binge drinking. This seemed under control in the mid-sixties, when he bubbled over philosophically with his friends, keeping them up past midnight. Wright and Norton wrestled for hours with a subject of absorbing interest to them both: "what religion is."[39]

In between Wright's visits that summer came a man with whom Norton had exchanged long letters: Jonathan Harrison from Indiana. Norton admired Harrison and had begun to furnish him with journalistic commissions as well as books, both practices lasting the rest of Harrison's life. "One of the homeliest men I have ever seen," Harrison's craggy ugliness and palpable poverty made it even easier to think of him, at twenty-five, as a young Lincoln. He brought frank and vigorous talk, much of it about religious uncertainties shared with his cultivated mentor: a subject on which Norton was thinking more and more.[40]

Religion, however, was far from his most urgent concern. With congressional elections looming in November, Charles grew more and more upset with President Johnson's pliancy toward the South. "So thick skulled & thin skinned a demagogue" needed the "lesson" of a severe thrashing at the polls. Norton joined his friends in doing their part to give him one. Curtis was chairing the platform committee of the New York Union (Republican) party. In late August, Godkin was visiting Ashfield; and Frederick Olmsted and Samuel Bowles, editor of the influential Springfield (Massachusetts) *Republican,* made a flying trip there. On a rainy Saturday, the five men sat down in Norton's study and wrote the Republican platform, duly adopted at the New York convention a few days later. It offered the president no shred of comfort. Neither did the Loyal Publication Society broadsides Norton was editing, which, in September, he stepped up again to weekly publication.[41]

There were also local civic involvements as summer turned to fall. On Tuesday, 25 September, Charles and George Curtis began a series of four benefit lectures at the old church in Ashfield, to raise money to start a library. Norton had come to see the town as another of his projects. That Ashfield was in decline admitted no doubt—its population drifting away, its academy standing abandoned and dilapidated. Norton saw something worth saving. Perhaps Ashfield replaced in imagination the lost hometown of his boyhood, the bucolic Cambridge now hidden somewhere inside a city quintupled in population and revolutionized in topography. But there was a more current, less nostalgic reason.

Ashfield represented to Norton an ideal of republican village existence. Its homogeneous folk, its life rooted in the soil, its rough village equality, its prosperless but independent people, its artless literacy, its sturdy moralism— all contrasted, on one side, with the pullulating cities of a newer America, a more European America, where poverty and ignorance, class strife and ethnic strain, put unprecedented stresses on the Republic, on its culture as on its politics. But, on another side, Ashfield's country health stood in contrast to rural degradation: to the ignorant farmers Norton imagined in Alabama, the debased peasants he had seen in Italy, both warning how rustic blight could endanger democracy as much as any urban ill.

To save Ashfield was to vindicate the Nortonian saga of democracy as a New England community writ large. Norton threw himself into the town's life as if he personally had to prove the possibility of educating and elevating American democracy. His founding of the Ashfield Library Association was the first in decades of civic projects. And, despite part-time residence, Norton contrived to behave as civic leader more than social worker, "entering with zest and wisdom" as one resident recalled "into nearly every local activity," making real friends in the village as well as finding cases there. One bright if perhaps bemused Ashfield boy found himself spending "stimulating evenings" at the Norton house, carrying home books calculated to enlarge the animation. And, whether the fact testifies to Norton's suavity or the townsfolk's deference, there is no evidence at all that sudden intrusion of improvement from Olympus irritated Ashfield's citizens. They kept the library going when the Nortons trekked back to Shady Hill toward the end of October 1866.[42]

Before leaving Ashfield, Sue was pregnant again, though presumably that information remained unknown for several weeks. Charles came home "to a heap of work" and within twenty-four hours found himself "rather cross internally—the way in which I feel fatigue." At least he had learned by now how to parcel out overloads so as to avoid full collapse. Moreover, Republican triumph in the November elections brought not only elation but easing of his duties; for, with a radical majority in Congress large enough to override Johnson's veto, the New England Loyal Publication Society ceased publishing.[43]

This left Sue and Charles with a few more hours in which to enjoy friends. They went to New York in December to see the Godkins, and, in January, George Curtis visited Shady Hill. In the Cambridge circle, James and Fanny Lowell and Frank and Lizzie Child were as much about as always but were now joined by the "very pleasant" Will and Elinor Howells. Even

Sam Ward, expatriated in New York, showed up for dinner in December—though that was a formal one and, like all such affairs, "rather fatiguing to me with their responsibilities."[44]

This particular dinner was for Donald MacKay, a Dutch-bred Briton then staying at Shady Hill: a Scottish baron in the Netherlands diplomatic service. MacKay arrived in mid-December; and Norton discovered "one of the pleasantest men I have known": "a man of uncommon sweetness & uncommon strength of character," easygoing, "well-mannered," and filled "with the best information." By the time MacKay left in early January 1867, Norton's inner circle had another member, his transatlantic network another link.[45]

Maintaining so hospitable and so substantial an establishment did not come cheaply, and the inflation produced by the Civil War was putting the Nortons' fisc under strain. "Those of us who are dependent on fixed incomes," Charles explained to George Marsh in Florence, "are obliged to diminish our expenses & to practise a pretty strict economy." Years as a merchant had ingrained in Norton a care for balancing the books. War taxes worsened the plight. By early 1864, he even had to curtail his philanthropy. Despite fifteen hundred or so a year from the *North American*, the gap between income and expenses yawned wider; before 1866 ended, Norton could see no choice but to sell some of Shady Hill's thirty-five acres.[46]

Even in carrying out this grim necessity, he wished to set an example for the community. Norton meant to subdivide the bulk of the property, but he decided to reduce the house lots in size in order to save ten or twelve acres to lay out as a "pleasure ground" for the estate's residents, the Nortons included. (Shady Hill already furnished the neighborhood children their favored sledding slope.) Conveniently, Norton numbered among his friends the country's best-known practitioner of the new speciality of landscape architecture, Frederick Law Olmsted; and Olmsted drew up a plan meant to perpetuate around Shady Hill "the more agreeable rural characteristics of a New England Village." The design cost Norton. Setting aside acres for a park reduced his profit, and he feared that this common might be "misused by the low population of the neighborhood & of Boston." This price he was willing to pay in order to reproduce Ashfield in Cambridge—or his old Cambridge in the new one. In the event, Cambridge, Somerville, and Harvard (on all of which Shady Hill encroached) had to agree to preparatory drainage work; and years passed before subdivision began. But Norton's vision of an environment designed to nurture moral health in its residents carried, like much of his civic work, an almost religious charge.[47]

His faith in anything like traditional religion, however, continued to fade. Norton was his father's son, and religion could hardly fail to occupy his mind. Nor, for that matter, could other Unitarians keep their eyes off Andrews Norton's heir, "the Elisha upon whom the mantle of the father had fallen." Harvard Divinity School had in 1865 elected him to its directing board, and invitations to speak to Unitarian congregations came his way occasionally. All the while, Elisha wandered farther from ancestral allegiance.[48]

Who waved him onward is hard to say. Arthur Clough may have "led the way to independence" for Norton; Norton said he had for many others. Possibly Norton's conversations in 1863 with that other British freethinker, Leslie Stephen, encouraged deeper skepticism. Friendship with Emerson perhaps played a part; by 1867, Charles had come to see him, like Clough, as "a forerunner and a prophet." Probably, however, long conversations with Chauncey Wright abetted Norton's drift from Unitarianism more than any other single influence. Yet no single influence is needed to explain adherence to a movement of thought widespread among Victorian intellectuals and shared by friends as close as Godkin, Olmsted, and Curtis. Norton himself thought that he rode the crest of the wave of the future. The Civil War— dissolving "many prejudices & many superstitions," showing that freedom in one matter required liberty in all—had, he said, opened the door in America for a "new style of religious life." "Creeds" and "authority" would yield to "liberty" and "the spirit."[49]

Andrews would have wondered what brand of spirits his son had been taking liberties with. To Charles, Unitarianism seemed "to have nearly done its work," insofar as it stood for "liberalism in theology & as a protest against dogma & creed." Insofar as it made "religion an affair of the church," it seemed to him retrograde; for the deepest and wisest thinking about religion, in his view, now went on outside of any church. The thing now needed was "a free Church" in which private judgment ruled supreme and doctrine gave way entirely to nurturing of "religious life." In February 1867, Norton took part in launching a new Free Religious Association, "paving the way for my 'church of the future'"—though soon he drew back even from that, on grounds that the less organization, the better. In April, appalling the ghost of Andrews, he preached his new religion at (Theodore) Parker Fraternity Hall. That same month he published in the *North American* an article titled "Religious Liberty," followed a year later by one called "The Church and Religion." The evangelical *New York Observer* denounced him as an infidel.[50]

There could not be much argument about that. Norton had left anything resembling Christianity far behind. He now made only the feeblest snatches at the name, though still thinking himself faithful to the spirit of Christ's teaching. Norton was not anxious to hurt "tender & pious souls," but he feared that "bewildered ones" needed help. This he wrote to supply.[51]

True religion, he insisted, had nothing to do with "definite beliefs." As recently as 1864, he had approved as the basis of "rational religion" two closely related doctrines. First was a teaching at the very heart of his father's Unitarianism (as Norton recognized): "that the Human Morality is identical with the Divine." The second followed from the first: "that the moral nature of man points truly, though remotely, to that of God." By 1867 even these thin doctrines had evaporated from religion as Norton understood it. Part of the reason was that religion comprised "the most private and personal part of the life of every man"; it was thus "a new, a different, a peculiar thing for each separate soul." Hence, no creed could possibly be "broad enough to serve as the exact statement of the religion of two souls."[52]

But this act of Emersonian faith was Norton's more superficial reason for evacuating belief from religion; more profoundly, he had decided that religion was in essence "an attitude of the will," having little or nothing to do with any commitment of the intellect. Norton drew this opinion explicitly from John Stuart Mill, but it had actually seized Charles while he and Chauncey Wright together wrestled with Mill's writings. Norton now defined religion "as a man's devotion—that is, the complete assent and concentration of his will—to any object which he acknowledges to have a right to his entire service, and to supreme control over his life."[53]

Why should Norton have divorced will and intellect, traditionally thought by theologians to rub along rather well together except when sin intervened?[54] Paradoxically, he needed to make this move to remain faithful to his father's teaching. Andrews, as an admirer remembered, "was a sceptic by nature and by habit." "He repudiated intuition as a ground of belief, could not tolerate mysticism, and had so little appetency for the supernatural that he could admit it only on compulsion." To weigh the evidence for Christian beliefs incautiously, to assent to doctrine "where positive proof was wanting," seemed to him "weak credulity." His son took an equally rigorous line, insisting equally that evidence be assessed by scientific canons. "True religion has always been on the side of science, and science is always on the side of religion."[55]

Yet, to Charles, evidence for Christianity seemed to be fraying. Darwin had turned natural theology on its head; the authors of *Essays and Reviews* had gnawed at the authority of scripture; John Mill questioned the very logic of belief. The "application of the scientific method—the method of all true knowledge, that of induction from the facts of particular observation—to the investigation of religious truths" was eroding "belief in creeds." Norton applied to religious doctrine an essentially positivistic canon of knowledge, inherited from Andrews if honed by Mill and Chauncey Wright.[56]

Yet in his writings on history, art, and culture he deployed a quite different notion of knowledge—also inherited from Andrews though honed on different whetstones—a conception of knowledge more holistic, probabilistic, historicist. Where did Charles stand? Was knowledge to be understood as achieved through analytic generalization, from "induction from the facts of particular observation" to a precisely specifiable conclusion? Or was knowledge most securely founded in a textured, multiplicitous grasping of an entire *Lebenswelt?* Was he scientist or hermeneut? There was probably some unrecognized inconsistency here—but also good reason why he failed to recognize it.

For Norton's historicism, too, damped the guttering flame of Christianity in him. He had read Emerson and, one suspects, Parker; whether he had also paged through Schleiermacher, Lessing, Carlyle, no one knows. It hardly mattered. Charles had heard from youth the saga of man's long ascent from papist superstition to Unitarian light. Why should enlightenment stop with Unitarianism? A man might well ask that question if he had studied the Mound Builders, experienced India, and learned that the rise from an orthodox Christianity to a liberal one hardly exhausted the human story. Why doubt that Christianity, too, would turn out to be only a stage in the progress of the race—especially when "the progress of political liberty" was steadily sapping "the authority of the churches"? "In the Church, as nowhere else at the present day," Norton lectured the *North American*'s readers, "are to be found the still-flourishing relics of the childish elder world." (Norton conceded that the anachronism was felt chiefly by "the most intelligent portion of society"; but he still oddly failed to notice that churches in America flourished in his day as never before.) Moreover, Victorian orthodoxy christened modern science as the latest and highest stage in that intellectual advance: so historicism reinforced the whittling away of Christian beliefs by scientific canons.[57]

If, then, doctrine had lost its grounding, what remained of religion? For a Unitarian, the answer was morality, which in any case had always seemed the point of Christianity in patrician Boston (Boston in this respect only exaggerating a general Victorian tendency). So for Charles Norton religion devolved into duty—the most elevated aspect of duty—and the feelings that braced a person to do it. Religion had nothing to do with reasoning, except insofar as there are "*reasons* for our sentiments, & thus reason used rightly will purify our religion." "Faith & reason," he assured Jonathan Harrison, "are in conflict only among the theologians. There is nothing irrational, as there is nothing strictly rational, in a sentiment or emotion."[58]

Norton had pulled off a feat his father would have regarded as beyond miraculous, because oxymoronic: he had reconciled Andrews and Emerson. He had adopted both Emerson's view of religion as an irreducibly individual intuition and Andrews's insistence that religious truth could rest only on universally received standards of knowledge. Charles held on to Andrews's epistemology by denying that religion constituted knowledge; he reconciled this epistemology with Emerson's intuitionism by further denying that intuition provided knowledge; and he followed both in insisting that religion rightly commanded man's life. What of substance remained after this tour de force is another question.

At least in 1867, Charles still clung to "a deep faith" in a personal God. He also believed, more hesitantly, in personal immortality. And he retained enough respect for historic forms of religion to have Lily christened late in 1866—though the ceremony seemed a slightly embarrassed afterthought to an unanticipated visit from the Nortons' old Newport pastor. That was about it. Sometime prior to early 1866, Norton had concluded that "it is impossible to attain to definite beliefs" about God other than "his own existence and his goodness and omnipotence." "We only know," he wrote Mrs. Gaskell's daughter, "that the love we feel in our own hearts must be but a faint image of the love of God."[59]

This last wisp of supernatural knowledge lacked warrant in Norton's system, and one suspects that only hope or habit now sustained his theism. But "the heart is never a positivist," he reminded Godkin,

> & we have not reached the last word & final truth of philosophy till we have succeeded in reconciling the seemingly conflicting claims of the intellect and the affections. As men come to love each other not only more but better in this world, as we succeed in overcoming the selfishness of common love, which makes so great a part of what men & women call love, I think we shall care less about those things [he meant supernatural beliefs] which now rack our hearts, & test the constancy of our souls.

Charles had come to see religion as "the striving to realize the ideal of our own nature." "The only way in which I can truly worship God is by trying to serve man." The Choir Invisible began to hum.[60]

So it made sense that he paid attention to Congress rather than to God; and, as a body, senators pleased him more than theologians. Congressional passage of the Reconstruction Acts in March 1867, along with the steady decline of President Johnson's power and will to resist, put public affairs on a sounder footing than for a year past. Still, looking farther down the road, Norton saw a clouded prospect. Educational problems, labor strife, demands for tariff protection, the clamoring of Civil War veterans for a place at the public trough: all threatened national progress. Norton remained enough of an old republican to worry that these controversies opened the way "for the practice of the arts of demagogues"—and enough of a Norton to fear that "the material progress of the country is so rapid compared with its intellectual & moral advance that there is a constantly larger infusion of ignorance & what might be called uncivilization in our councils." Still, he trusted to "the weight and steadiness of the sober sense of the great community."[61]

He took the long view—a very long one. Comparison with George Curtis is striking. The two hardly differed at all in political principles; but Norton felt that his friend's "peculiar sensitiveness to what might be called the atmospheric currents of popular opinion" made him a different animal. Though Curtis's maxims never wavered, "his feelings & his opinions as to modes of action & courses of policy vary with the popular weather." This barometric effect made Curtis, in Norton's view, "an excellent & useful political writer & actor in such a country as ours & at such a time as this." But it did not make him a statesman of the first order (not that America "just now" had any of those). Norton, in contrast, was always jumping beyond the here and now into the long course of history or the rarefied air of political axioms. (He deemed himself a poor newspaper writer for just these reasons.) He assessed, say, the expediency of expanding public schools by examining the role of education in the evolution of democracy rather than by asking whether voters wanted more schools, whether the treasury could pay for them, or whether teachers existed to staff them. Ability to get elected being more or less prerequisite to the role of statesman, it may be doubted whether his approach would ever have made Norton one. It *was* making him a philosophic historian and a sometimes penetrating political and cultural critic.[62]

In these circumstances, it was predictable that he kept wandering from present politics back to such fixations as Dante. Norton's library, indeed, by now housed the country's most formidable Dante collection, including all important editions of the *Vita Nuova*, many of the *Divina Commedia*, and massive critical apparatus, constantly augmented. (He was not building for himself alone but planned eventually to give the collection to Harvard.) By March of 1867 the Dante Club had added to its Wednesday soirées a weekly Saturday conclave at Shady Hill. Perhaps inspired by Longfellow's work on the *Divina Commedia*, Norton had pulled his translation of the *Vita Nuova* from its drawer and begun to revise it; it was now getting the same collective going-over as Longfellow's more ambitious project. The Dante Club adjourned in May when the Nortons retired to Ashfield; but there Charles continued to tinker with the *Vita Nuova* in hours spared him by exuberant infants, pregnant wife, the *Nation*, and the *North American*.

And his own protesting body. In early June, *Nation* business took him to New York for a few days; although careful to avoid even "pleasant fatigue" while there, he still was "under the weather" for two weeks after his return, "quite unfit for doing anything more active than lying on the sofa reading the newspapers." By the time the Curtises arrived in early July, he was in better shape and withstood the freshet of summer visitors without serious setback. So did Sue, a new nurse for the children reducing her burden as pregnancy neared its end. During the spring she had felt "better & gayer" than for years, and the birth of a "fine, large, vigorous" boy on 21 July caused no problems. They named him Rupert—apparently, this time, after no one. Sue was back downstairs within three weeks.[63]

At the beginning of October, the Nortons returned to Shady Hill—and Charles to "a sharp attack" that laid him low for a week or two. Even when up and about, he grew weary with too many letters to write, too many dinners to smile through. He and Sue began to talk more seriously about going abroad, "if only for a month to get freshened up, and have the wrinkles of wear smoothed out of my mind." A package from Ruskin arrived to remind them of the advantages of European treatment for wrinkles. It contained fourteen plates from Turner's *Liber Studiorum*, along with a series of the artist's sketches, "full of astonishing power."[64]

Meanwhile, the calendar filled, sometimes pleasantly: toward the end of autumn Charles Dickens, whom Norton had not seen since Paris in 1855, arrived in Boston to begin an American tour. He and Norton hobnobbed a good deal, shared dinner at Shady Hill, grew into real friends. Mostly, though, "the bondage of society" was slowly wearing Norton down. One November week began with a Monday morning meeting in Boston of the directors of the Model Lodging Association and a party at Shady Hill that evening for a friend of Sara Sedgwick's; continued on Tuesday with a dinner party at the Nortons' for Lord Amberley, son of the British prime minister, and his wife, Kate Stanley Russell; persisted on Wednesday with a publisher's dinner honoring Longfellow; then took Norton on Thursday to New Hampshire to deliver a lecture. This was on top of editing the *North American* and, in December, raising funds to crank up the Loyal Publication Society again. No wonder Norton lamented to Godkin that "the life here is too crowded for one who is already a little tired." No wonder, too, that by the end of November he was sunk in another spell of debility.[65]

By this time he had also shepherded to publication a complete and elegant edition of his translation of the *Vita Nuova*. It not only contained the full *New Life* but substantially reworked, in a series of appendices, the scholarly material from Norton's privately printed 1859 essay. Longfellow had published his *Divine Comedy* the previous summer, and Norton's book was meant as a kind of pendant to Longfellow's three volumes.

Reviewing his friend's work gave Charles a chance to justify his (and Longfellow's) principle of "realism" in translation. Norton may have inherited a literalist bias from his father; the full rationale he had matured himself. A translation, he wrote, ought to give us a work "exactly as it is," not "remodelled according to modern ideas," for from old books we want "instruction" more than "delight." Though college classrooms were far from his mind, Norton was inching inadvertently toward a new conception of a liberal education:

> The deepest interest which a work of literary or any other art has for us, is not that which appertains to it as an isolated effort of human genius, but that which it possesses as one of a consecutive and allied series of monuments of thought and feeling, and as one of the records of the progress of the race in its slow development from age to age.[66]

Norton's version of the *Vita Nuova*, if itself no monument, met the standard of faithfulness to original meaning rather well. Whether his deliberately archaic diction reflected Dante's is another question altogether, though it was a respectable solution to an irresolvable conundrum. Francis Lieber, no bad judge and not given to gush, called the translation "exquisite." That pushed the limit. But nearly half a century later William Dean Howells, competent in Italian and not inexperienced in literature, still thought the version "joins the effect of a sympathy almost mounting to divination with a patient scholarship and a delicate skill unknown to me elsewhere in such work." Norton's *Vita Nuova* was a far from negligible piece of scholarship and literary craftsmanship.[67]

As such, it added a few more pounds to Norton's plumpening reputation. Around Harvard, the "social predominance of Shady Hill and the master there" was taken for granted. Around New England, Norton (whom local pride celebrated as "one of the finest scholars in America") made an obvious choice to preside over political meetings or lecture to civic groups. In 1864, when he and Lowell took over the *North American*, the *New York Tribune* credited him as a cultured and elegant scholar highly regarded around Boston but far "less prominent" than his co-editor; by 1867 the *Chicago Tribune* was calling Norton, not quite forty, "first among the younger representatives of New England culture." No one ranked him with Ruskin or Carlyle, but he began to get requests for his autograph. Even in Britain his name carried enough weight to be worth adding to public testimonials.[68]

Indeed, the name had by now grown almost as familiar to the English intelligentsia as to the broader circle of educated Americans. Editing the *North American* had helped, for the old lady still carried more prestige abroad than any other American periodical; and Norton's close association with the *Nation* had raised his stock still higher with liberal cognoscenti in England, who soon acknowledged it as the authoritative American voice of transatlantic liberalism. Its British readers even kept their upper lips stiff when Norton informed them that "to be in error in regard to American affairs is the normal condition of the educated Englishman." His was, after all, a moderate tone compared to that of some Northern writers these days. Ties frayed by the Civil War were being gingerly rewoven, as perhaps aptly symbolized in April 1866 by the success, at long last, in laying the Atlantic cable.[69]

War's end, at any rate, reopened the floodgates for British visitors to Shady Hill, a tide swelling in proportion to Norton's growing reputation in the United Kingdom. Besides MacKay and Dickens and the Russells, there appeared on the doorstep Britons ranging from the Reverend James Fraser, come to examine American education on behalf of the Schools Inquiry Commission, to Governor Musgrave of Newfoundland. At least, said Godkin after handing out one more letter of introduction to Norton (this one to the young journalist and aspiring politician John Morley), "you will have the consolation of knowing that nearly all the statesmen of the new régime in England have passed through your hands."[70]

How much consolation this gave their increasingly worn-down host may be doubted. Norton had once again assumed responsibility for Loyal Publication Society broadsides and, by the end of December 1867, had raised needed funds and planned the first issues. The renewed broadsides aimed to blast into oblivion the inflationary monetary policy promoted by western Republicans. Deliberately inflating the currency (still worse, paying off war bonds in these devalued paper "greenbacks") looked to Norton and other northeastern liberals little short of official robbery, an offense to "political morality & national honor." In crusading against a fiat currency, Norton's prominence in the nexus of Anglo-American liberalism did pay some dividend: he turned to no less a liberal god than John Stuart Mill to hurl a Jovian bolt across the Atlantic at "the deplorable doctrines now afloat in the United States."[71]

Trampling deplorable doctrines was gratifying, but it added to a load that would have burdened a healthier man than Charles. By early January his writing hand had gone lame: just "a touch of *paralysis scriptorum,*" he assured Godkin; but a month later he still had to baby it; two months later the debility lingered. His health "very much concerned" George Curtis— and Curtis knew where his friend's condition pointed. "I had no doubt when the word Europe was mentioned last year what the result would be!"[72]

When George wrote, at the end of January 1868, Europe only glimmered in prospect; within ten days it seemed likely; by March a July sailing was all but settled. Charles had for years thought vaguely of "prosecuting some literary work" in Italy. And a host of reasons besides his own flagging condition urged Europe on him now. Sue's health, too, needed bolstering, and the physicians thought Europe would do her good. With advancing age, Catharine's willingness to travel would falter, and Charles could not see leaving her (or, indeed, any of the family) behind. The children's youth argued likewise against delay: "we do not want them to be Europeanised, & we should wish to be at home with them as they grew old enough to be much affected by their surroundings, & by influences other than the domestic ones." However much their father yearned for the Old World, he still believed the New healthier. With Charles Sumner, he angled again, discreetly, for a diplomatic post: minister to Italy, should Marsh retire; failing that, minister to Belgium or Holland. All failed. So it was to be two or three years abroad as private citizen.[73]

Public travails clouded the remaining months at home. In May, Johnson came to trial before the Senate. Norton thought the whole business of impeachment impolitic and unnecessary. He had no taste for Johnson but preferred even him in the White House to Benjamin Wade, the president pro tem of the Senate who would succeed to the presidency were Johnson convicted and whose high-tariff, soft-money policies were exactly what the Loyal Publication Society and the *Nation* fumed at weekly. And not just Ben Wade bothered him. The Republican leadership in general seemed to Norton tempted by irresponsibility in national financial policy; he feared they would try "to outbid the Democrats on inflation, or repudiation." A cheerless outlook for any rentier. The Senate's narrow acquittal of Johnson in May relieved Norton but did nothing to lighten the shadow that the likes of Ben Wade cast over his politics.[74]

This distressing trend in Republican policy never ruffled Norton's faith in the future but perhaps did make the bright aftertime seem remoter. Norton remained confident "that the spirit of Christianity has become operative in civil & political affairs to a degree which makes certain a better time for mankind." A "philosophic student of history," he thought, could perceive "the distant, yet distinct, prospect" of "a society, self-governing under moral restraints, with laws founded on justice, & with institutions formed according to the rules of morality." He remained sure that the Civil War had made "practicable" the "approach" to that better time. America, with its democratic principles and institutions, certainly held out more hope than Europe, where progress could "only advance over the wrecks of many of the most venerable institutions, & must destroy much of beauty & excellence." But Norton was couching his confidence in more cautious words than a year or two earlier.[75]

Nonetheless, the country's most "threatening" problems seemed on their way to solution; and Norton's conscience gave him permission to withdraw temporarily from the fray. In late May he went to Ashfield to make arrangements for hay making and fruit harvesting on the Nortons' little farm during their absence; the house itself they let to the Curtises. Shady Hill was leased to E. W. Gurney, who was also taking charge of the *North American*—only till Norton returned, the publishers hoped. Norton gave them no ground for hope but did get the July issue to the printer. The Loyal Publication Society he placed in the hands of his longtime collaborator, James Thayer; it was winding down, anyway. Charles stored his "precious things," his finest pictures and rarest books, in Boston's new fireproof safe-deposit vault. The family's finances he deposited again with William Bullard, this time with Arthur Sedgwick as coadjutor.[76]

Charles somehow shepherded his mother, Grace and Jane, Sue, Eliot, Sally, Lily, and Rupert, their two nurses, and Sue's sister Sara aboard the New York train on Monday, 6 July. Two days later the *Scotia* carried them out into the Atlantic. "We fix no time for returning home, but shall let circumstances determine for us." After a miserable voyage, their ship docked in Liverpool on 18 July 1868, and the Nortons headed straight to Manchester. Charles would never see Mrs. Gaskell again, but her daughter Meta had arranged accommodations near the Gaskell house. She had taken care to have their rooms decorated with flowers and a portrait of Lincoln.[77]

NINE

Europe and Erudition, 1868–1872

He had escaped. He and Susan could delight together in picture galleries, swaddle each other in "associations," seek the health that eluded both. He had fled the constant pressure, the editing, the civic duties, his own imperious conscience, the stress of it all. Such evasion Norton could never confess to himself—nor entirely achieve.

For a while, the more imperative demands of ill health kept conscience at bay. "Rather poorly" during their days in Manchester, Charles mostly lay on the sofa reading newspapers and notes of welcome. The Liberal member of Parliament Mountstuart Grant Duff, a crony of Donald MacKay (the Scottish-Dutch diplomat who had sojourned at Shady Hill), came up from Oxford specially to make Norton's acquaintance; Grant Duff turned out "a most friendly person, full of intelligence and inquisitiveness," already at thirty-nine acquiring the reputation of knowing more about Continental politics than any other Englishman. On 25 July the Nortons retraced Grant Duff's steps, to while away a few amusing days around the university until Charles located some more permanent abode.[1]

Friends greeted them there—MacKay and Henry Acland, the physician who had treated Charles in Oxford in 1857. Charles and Susan of course mingled as well with collegiate icons: Henry Liddell, dean of Christ Church, and Robert Scott, master of Balliol (the "Liddell & Scott" whose Greek lexicon sat on every Harvard student's shelf); Friedrich Max Müller, bearer of comparative philology from Germany to England; Mark Pattison, rector of Lincoln, known for his writings on education as well as for classical scholarship. But the people Charles and Susan liked best were breaking the Oxford mold: a vigorous young chemist called Vernon Harcourt and Pattison's wife, Emilia (at twenty-eight, two years younger than Susan), the "cleverest woman" around the university, "a decided Positivist, altogether a femme emancipée, and as Susan well characterized her an Oxford high-bred grisette." Both the grisette, who shared art-historical interests with

Susan and Charles, and the chemist became friends. Then, during a dinner given by the vice-chancellor, Charles found himself seated close to the physician and public health reformer John Simon, in Oxford to receive an honorary degree. Simon, like Acland, ran in Ruskin's inner circle; finding out his neighbor's identity, he greeted Norton with un-English warmth.[2]

From Oxford, Charles took a train by himself to London to dine with their mutual and erratic friend at Denmark Hill. Conversation renewed the old warmth, and Ruskin's Turners looked better than ever. Ruskin remained standoffish about Sue, but Charles Dickens invited both Charles and Susan for a long weekend at his house near Rochester. Dickens led them through Rochester Cathedral, escorted them to Canterbury; his daughter Mamie, almost exactly Sue's age, began writing to "dearest Susan."[3]

All this made for great fun but did nothing to solve the housing problem. The idea was to rent a place where the family might settle till leaving for the Continent in mid-November, secluded from London's distractions yet not cut off from its attractions. After a frustrating week's search, Norton found a tolerable house in Kent. In the village of Keston, ten or fifteen miles south of London, the rectory was for rent. It was brick, old-fashioned, and ugly, the furnishings few and shabby, but the setting and scenery "truly delightful & most English." On 13 August the Nortons moved in and began to enjoy the neighborhood attractions: Roman remains in the field next door, a wild heathery common and a civilized park of oaks both within a few hundred yards, and a family called Darwin a mile down the road in the village of Down.[4]

And an easy train ride connected Keston with London. Two days after the move, Charles went back to pass a weekend with Ruskin and to stroll the National Gallery with him. Edward Burne-Jones, the painter whom Norton had met in 1856, came to dine at Denmark Hill and ended talking with Charles for hours. A weekend soon followed at the Burne-Jones's own house, the Grange, where another memory from the 1850s, William Morris, took flesh again.

But social life now centered on Keston. A week after the move, Ruskin came and saw Susan's dark eyes for the first time. It was also "the first time I've not been disappointed in a friend's wife," he conceded to Charles. He and Sue were soon writing chattily, and the Old Rectory's walls brightened with watercolors that Ruskin sent: Turners and Hunts and, indeed, Ruskins. The Darwins and Nortons also did a lot of to-ing and fro-ing; and Charles came to like Mr. Darwin immensely: his "simplicity, sweetness & strength," his "entire modesty," his "lively humour." Another neighbor, the Comtist author and public servant Frederic Harrison, thought Susan a paragon, exhibiting as she did qualities depressingly lacking in Englishwomen: "hearty frankness and independence" and "the suppleness, elasticity, and *dolcezza* of manner that we associate with a south European."[5]

Soon Norton's sociability was running again to excess: dinners out, lunches in, a nonstop succession of houseguests. He began to show strain. September had scarcely begun when weakness forced him to cancel a visit to his new friend Grant Duff. The widow of Norton's Anglo-Indian friend Richard Baird Smith then moved in for several days with her children, quickly followed by Vernon Harcourt, the Oxford chemist.

On 1 October, Norton joined Ruskin at Abbeville in Picardy, anxious for a little vacation, still more for Ruskin's restless but inspiriting fellowship. The visit did not disappoint. Of what they spoke one can only guess, but they talked long, plumbed depths, apparently conversing of Ruskin's innermost ambitions and speaking for the first time of his psychological torments, though evidently edging around the sexual side of his failed marriage and his pedophilia. "This last week has been a very happy one for me, a sad one too in many ways," Charles told Ruskin. "I cannot thank you aright for all you have given me. I am glad to know that these days have brought us nearer together than ever before."[6]

Back in Keston, news arrived that the Reverend Thomas Hill had resigned as president of Harvard—"an entirely unlooked for blessing" in Frank Child's view. Child mentioned, among the "very wild" suggestions for a successor being bruited about Boston, the name of Norton's cousin Charles Eliot. But Eliot's cousin worried more about the next round of dinner parties. One, on 18 October, included William Morris; Norton had a good time with Morris, but the guest thought his host looked peaked.[7]

Within a day or two, he became desperately ill. The nature of the attack is unclear; that death threatened is not. Ruskin, back in England, barraged Susan with frightened notes, hurried John Simon to Keston to consult. By 2 November, Sue breathed more easily; though still groggy from opium, Charles had turned the corner. By the seventeenth he could sit up to read and talk. He talked a lot with Simon, medical attendance having cemented friendship. One topic was the upcoming winter: Simon warned him to forget the Continent.

Toward the end of November, Charles was well enough for the family to relocate to London, which they did at 18 Queen's Gate Terrace, a monad in an infinite row of identical Regency houses; five-storied, white, and ample; a couple of blocks from the southeast corner of Kensington Gardens where the Albert Memorial waited to rise. Ruskin loaned more drawings to decorate the house. By 10 December, Charles dared again to venture out, for a quiet evening. The Nortons' Dutch bachelor Donald MacKay came over to spend Christmas with them. On the day itself they "lighted up a little Christmas tree which Susan had arranged for the children."[8]

Amusements proliferated that winter and spring: breakfasts and dinners more profuse even than the dinners and luncheons offered in return at Queen's Gate Terrace. (Housekeeping in London proved cheaper than in Boston, fortunately.) Charles fraternized a good deal, too, with other gentlemen amid the smokier atmosphere of London's clubs. "Everybody I have met," wrote Leslie Stephen (who had met the Nortons briefly in America in 1863) in January to a Boston friend, "has asked me whether I had yet seen the most charming people that ever were known & then proceeded to pour out panegyrics upon all the good qualities of the Norton's [sic]."[9]

The roster of hosts and guests reads like a roll call of Victorian worthies: older gentlemen of literary bent such as Arthur Helps and John Forster; rising political actors like Grant Duff, Frederic Harrison, and John Morley, Harrison's young positivist confrère and editor of the liberal *Fortnightly Review;* birds of an artistic feather like William Morris and Dante Rossetti; Americans popping in, like Francis Parkman, or settling down, like Henry James (for whom Norton opened "great doors" in London); occasionally a solid scholar of subfusc hue such as Norton's classmate Fitzedward Hall, now professor of Sanskrit at King's College; more often a figure of éclat like John Tyndall, the Irish physicist on his way to the presidency of the British Association; or Alexander Macmillan, the publisher; or Thomas Hughes, author of *Tom Brown's School Days* (whose role in workingmen's education gave him common ground with Norton); or John Acton, leader of liberal English Roman Catholics; or Fitzjames Stephens, the lawyer whom Norton thought "one of the best heads in England," with a mind like his body: "solid, ponderous in a good sense, & vigorous"; or Fitzjames's journalist brother Leslie, suppler in mind and more appealing to Norton; or the historian James Anthony Froude, whom Norton deemed a poseur, "anxious to produce an effect." And an album of others.[10]

An unkind observer might suspect Norton of collecting "eminent Victorians" as in his youth he had collected autographs. The observer would have failed to notice that eminence lay in the future for most of them. Yet Norton, in fact, did have a weakness for monuments. The tourist in Norton wished to observe Thomas Carlyle as well as Westminster Abbey—so he asked Grant Duff to arrange an evening with Carlyle, just as he had Dean

Stanley (married to his old friend, Augusta Bruce) lead a tour of the abbey. (The Carlyle evening led to Norton acting as go-between in Carlyle's bequest to Harvard of his books on Cromwell and Frederick the Great.) A weekend that Charles and Sue spent as the only houseguests at Earl and Lady Russell's country house was stimulating in its own right, Norton and Lord John having a "great deal of interesting talk" about Anglo-American relations; still, Charles did preen a bit in letters home because a former prime minister had singled him out for attention.[11]

Yet, original sin aside, Norton cast a pretty skeptical eye on the swishing and strutting about London. He knew that he judged harshly, inclined too much toward "fastidiousness & reserve." Yet, his own bias recognized, he still detected a basic artificiality, a corroding falseness, in social relations within what he called the comfortable classes of England. His ancient charge of "flunkeyism" had devolved into a subtler but equally acid critique. Most of the English seemed to play roles "in a sort of unreal external world, a little as if in a story where circumstances control character, & [w]here men do not know themselves very well." Even affections between husband and wife appeared "external," "matters of kindly relationship, of mere juxtaposition, rather than of essential sympathy & comprehensive intelligence." This was a crashingly blunt indictment, and Norton would have pointed to exceptions: Arnold, John Simon, the Darwins; the list would go on. Yet, the whole scene adjudged, in England the "regions of the soul are but little frequented"; and the alignment between inner and outer life had slipped badly awry. Norton did not charge hypocrisy, for a perfectly honest person might never look inward. Rather, he found England wanting by the standard of *sincerity*, a canon gaining in its appeal to the Victorian moral imagination.[12]

Respect for the "regions of the soul" did not imply contempt for the geography of convention. Whatever appreciative words he had uttered about *Leaves of Grass* in 1855, barbaric yawp was never much in Norton's line. He could admire, say, William Blake—and almost effusively did, in a review for the April *North American*—without wishing in all respects to emulate him. The problem was to hold the balance, and to sustain the flow, between the social conventions that made civilized life possible and the individual spirits that animated it.

A friendship that Sue and Charles struck up in London that winter illustrated the tension. On an afternoon late in January they went to dinner, tête-à-tête, at the house shared by George Lewes and the writer who styled herself "George Eliot." To dine there required on Susan's part some élan, because Mr. and Mrs. Lewes, as they called themselves, lived at the margin of proper society. Lewes was still legally wed to his first wife, and respectable women hesitated to visit the otherwise utterly bourgeois Lewes ménage. Charles did not find Lewes himself very impressive, except perhaps impressively ugly (Sue's friend Fanny Kemble remarked that he looked "as if he had been gnawed by the rats"). "Mrs. Lewes," however, struck him as "a person of strong mind who had thought much & who felt deeply," one who had knocked about in those regions of the soul. Not coincidentally, she had also kicked over the traces of convention. Norton puzzled over the dilemma she presented. People, he reported, did not think her immoral (certainly he did not); rather, her near ostracism arose from concern to avoid eroding the moral conventions that her relation to Lewes flouted. "I suspect society is right in this," though Charles and Sue dined again with the Leweses.[13]

Part of the reason that the Leweses could approach the world unconventionally, and part of the reason that the Nortons got on with them, lay in shared politics, broadly put. All four adhered to the loosely positivist, more or less utilitarian, wing of transatlantic liberalism, which paid obeisance to John Stuart Mill. (Later in the spring, the Nortons dined at Mill's house in Blackheath; there, Sue—once used to Mill's facial tic and constant shuffling of feet—"quite felt myself in the presence of a modern Plato.") *How* loosely positivist fixed one's location within the camp. Thoroughgoing positivists, consistent disciples of Auguste Comte, flourished better in English than American soil. As Comteans, the Leweses tended to heresy; coming head to head with the truly orthodox clarified the nature of Charles's own liberalism. Norton liked and respected John Morley and Frederic Harrison; the rest struck him as "doctrinaire" (a judgment that hardly makes one lurch in surprise), "cold & hard in their view of the poverty & distress which prevail around them." Norton's defense of American individualism made a "stumbling block"; "they will hardly admit that perhaps the best way to secure the ideal community is to secure first the best & largest development of the individual."[14]

To be sure, "ideal community" and "England" hardly belonged together in a sentence coming from Norton's mouth. He always measured the "old home" with the same calipers as America: Italy might seem a magical kingdom of art and antiquity; England was a factual land of politicians and poverty. Scarcely a month after landing in Liverpool, Charles was already telling Mill that "habits of thought & manner of expression" in England had greatly altered since his last visit, in a direction portending "still greater, even revolutionary changes." His vision refocused by the Civil War, Norton saw in England no longer "a real nation" but "simply a congeries of individuals divided into distinct & almost hostile classes." He could only shake his head at the *"appalling"* lack of "sympathy between the different classes." The conclusion seemed inescapable: "a new & better order can hardly arise without violent revolution"; with pauperism "beyond legal remedy," the country slid toward upheaval.[15]

This radicalized liberalism perfused two articles Norton wrote in spring 1869, one for the *North American,* the other for John Morley's *Fortnightly Review.* Both dwelt on the social divisions endangering England. They displayed not only his well-tested ability to gulp down official statistics in large draughts but also a new willingness to breach the sanctities of laissez-faire economics, at least in the matter of minimum wages. They not only invoked education (once again) as the ultimate answer to pauperism but also put a novel twist on this reflex: rubbing shoulders with the English upper crust had persuaded Norton that the prosperous needed educating as much as the poor.

Reform-minded liberalism like this found its clearest English voice in the middle-class, antiestablishment intelligentsia that matured during the first two decades of Victoria's reign. Norton had met a number of its insurgents in England in the 1850s and had come to know others when they made pilgrimage to the democratic republic across the sea. By now they dominated England's scientific, journalistic, and artistic life. This cultural and social group included Darwin and Huxley and Tyndall, Frederic Harrison and John Morley and Matthew Arnold, and in their own ways even Ruskin and Morris and Burne-Jones. Its worldview resembled that of the American crowd around the *Nation:* its politics mostly Millian, but not always, especially in matters of political economy; its stance toward orthodoxies of all kinds adversarial and sometimes arrogant. Yet it questioned not because of temperamental discontent (who could be less pugnacious than Darwin?) but because it saw the world as malleable and much in need of molding.

It also provided most of Norton's real friends in England. Charles Dickens, Aubrey de Vere, and John Acton made perhaps the only exceptions, the latter two doubly eccentric in being Roman Catholic. Norton might prove weak enough to drop Earl Russell's name, but it was Mountstuart Grant Duff's or Leslie Stephen's dinner table to which he constantly recurred. And, as the demand for his presence at tables of that kind shows, Grant Duff and Stephen esteemed his company as much as he theirs.

Comments by such English friends call attention to aspects of Norton

not so obvious in Boston. His "somewhat slow and emphatic speech" caught
Frederic Harrison's ear; and in Norton's precise but positive tones Harrison
heard "the guarded and balanced criticism of men and things, the detach-
ment of spirit and the freedom from all traditional and conventional formulas." Even the Comtists at the Reform Club admired Norton's earnest
effort to step back from the urgencies of the day not to evade commitment
but to make a sounder one. The dominating impression Norton gave was of
a "perfectly open mind, ready to weigh any new view, political, social, or
artistic, and yet not at all ready to pronounce judgment without a probing
kind of criticism all his own."[16]

Charles and Susan's closest friends in London, however, belonged to the
artistic rather than the political sector of the bourgeois intelligentsia. Only
one of them, John Simon, took deep interest in social and political reform as
commonly construed; and his ties to the Nortons owed more to Ruskin than
to reform. Little record remains of the blossoming of intimacy between the
Simons (John and his wife, Jane) and the Nortons, though one vignette
shows John bringing Susan "a great handful of spring flowers from Covent
Garden" for her birthday. As with Simon, Edward Burne-Jones attracted
Charles from the first: "a man of more culture & more force than most
painters possess, and of a sweetness & simplicity of life which would be rare
anywhere, & is most rare here"; his wife, Georgiana, shared in his charm for
both Charles and Sue.[17]

Their friendship occasioned one of Norton's few pieces of literary work
in London. The Burne-Joneses and William Morris spoke to him in the
highest terms of "an anonymous version of quatrains by Omar Khayyam,"
published to little notice a decade earlier. This was, in fact, Edward Fitzgerald's *Rubáiyát*, though none of Norton's circle knew the poet-translator's
name. Georgie lent Charles her copy, and the poem impressed him so
deeply that he composed a long review for the October *North American*,
including seven pages of excerpts in small print. (Faithful to his own theory
of translation, Norton noted that the anonymous English version was not
strictly a translation from the Persian but a recasting of the original into a
properly English mode of poetry.) Norton's review has commonly been
taken as what brought Fitzgerald's *Rubáiyát* to wide attention; without
question, it did that job for American readers.[18]

Burne-Jones, Simon, Norton—Ruskin supplied their common link.
And Ruskin remained for Norton in a special category: a friend of longer
standing and a specially worrisome one. There is no knowing how many

times that winter and spring Norton ambled up Denmark Hill along the high black fence, waited for the coachman to answer the gate bell, then walked up the avenue to the "perfect treasury of art." His relations with Ruskin became very intimate; Ruskin poured into Norton's ears confidences about his tangled, tumultuous inner life that would have grieved a friend far less devoted than Charles. Norton came to understand, to sympathize with, Ruskin's sense of isolation, the psychological hardships of his life. But Charles could scarcely talk of this to others, even to George Curtis. "I am so truly & deeply attached to him that I fear lest my words may not sound as tenderly as they are meant, & may not succeed in picturing a character so femininely delicate, sensitive, generous & lovable as his."[19]

Or one so unbalanced. Norton feared more and more Ruskin's "unreasonableness & moodiness." Up to 1865 his friend appeared "sane, cheerful, & for the most part reasonable." Sanity no longer seemed secure. Norton, his sense of privacy highly developed, recorded not a mention of Ruskin's unwholesome pining for little Rose La Touche; but he did protest Ruskin's divagations into political economy. He urged Ruskin not to unsettle himself with half-baked schemes to solve all the world's ills. Let him climb back on the solid foundation of art, where his mind could fix and find rest.[20]

Norton felt relieved when, in February 1869, his "dearest Ruskin" asked "my dearest Charles" to help him get a will drawn up and to act as his literary executor. This request—and Ruskin's ricocheting around it—set going a long, messy saga; but it gave hope of saving the man from the clutches of scoundrels. Ruskin's decision to depart for the Continent and get "again into a healthy train of art work" looked even more hopeful. He dumped the proof sheets for his latest extravagance, *The Queen of the Air*, into Norton's lap, with instructions to revise it and see it through the press, then left for the Continent on 27 April.[21]

The time approached for the Nortons to follow, though exact plans remained indefinite. Charles had once again whispered about a diplomatic post, once again too softly for Washington ears. The Nortons thought they might go to Switzerland for the summer. Meanwhile, Charles made contact, surprisingly late in his stay, with some leading English Dantists, Frederick Pollock, William Warren Vernon, and Giacomo (or James) Lacaita. On 11–12 May he and Sue journeyed up to Cambridge to see her distant and aged relative, the geologist Adam Sedgwick; the next weekend they took the train to Oxford, invited by Benjamin Jowett, the celebrated Balliol tutor much attacked for his contribution to the heterodox *Essays and Reviews*.

More than ever, Oxford impressed Charles as "a very delightful and very interesting *show* place." Jowett added to the "effect of unreality, for there is a sort of vagueness about his expression which corresponds with the confusion of his intellect; and it would hardly surprise you were he some day at the breakfast table to declare that he was a ghost, and so to vanish."[22]

On 25 May 1869, with few regrets, the Nortons left England, arriving in Lausanne a week later. There, news arrived that Harvard had elected as its president Charles Eliot, as dark a horse as one might bet on. Norton thought the college could scarcely have lit upon a better leader than his cousin. "He will be liberal & efficient,—& although of a somewhat positive & dogmatic temper his mind is quite accessible to ideas." This trait seemed only slightly eccentric in a Harvard president. After some searching, Charles rented a farmhouse called La Pacolte, near Vevey. Half an hour from town, high in the subalpine meadows above Lake Geneva, it commanded fine views of the lake, the Dents du Midi, and, far up the valley of the Rhone, the Grand Saint Bernard. Charles called the house "trop paysanne" for London tastes (probably true, with three cows sharing the same roof) but just large enough for the family.[23]

He felt relieved to "change the busy social life of England for a quieter life, with more opportunity for carrying on one's own special pursuits." Sue's relief was less palpable: "The quiet of this place after London is something extraordinary—good & pleasant in a way but for my personal taste a bit extreme." For Charles, a return to "consecutive study" gave real pleasure, "a pleasure of which I have tasted little" since the Civil War began. In the event, he managed no more than four or five hours daily of wrestling with German, "that intricate, invaluable & detestable language"; for his health gave way again, and he passed a lot of time lying listlessly in the shade staring at the views. Sue was pregnant once more.[24]

Even guests rarely ruffled the tranquility. Harry James came to dine two or three times; toward the end of August, Charles ran over to Thun for another stormy, exasperating, and loving visit with Ruskin; and, in early September, John and Jane Simon arrived for a welcome ten days. After they left, Charles attended a gathering of radical republicans at Lausanne—the International Congress of Peace and Liberty—reporting on it for the *Nation*.[25] Those made virtually the only breaks in a very domestic life. The children were "changing fast." Rupert was learning to talk, in a jumble of French and English. Sally and Lily, four and two, when not pulling each other's hair were learning their ABCs—and, inevitably, French from nurses who spoke nothing else. Eliot, a frail six-year-old, having conquered reading, began actual lessons during the quiet hours when his siblings napped. They were unusually cosmopolitan young Americans.[26]

Some evidence hints that their growing up pushed one step further their parents' thinking about religion. What ought Charles and Susan tell the children about God and death, right and wrong? Whatever the impulse, both parents had by this summer traveled beyond the remotest border of theism. "It does not seem to me," Charles wrote to Ruskin, "that the evidence concerning the being of a God, and concerning immortality, is such as to enable us to assert anything in regard to either of these topics." He acknowledged Christianity as the font of the "most enlightened" morality; and he still regarded Jesus as "the dearest saint of humanity,—but I would bind up the Gospels with Marcus Antoninus' Thoughts, and regard one as sacred as the other." Susan, "of her own mind," had come to share her husband's opinions. That very year Thomas Huxley coined a name for the Nortons' conclusion "that the question of the existence of God must be regarded as an open one": agnosticism.[27]

A name was needed. This form of unbelief (as distinct from aggressive and anticlerical atheism) was spreading in Norton's milieu. True, Lowell and Curtis clung to the fuzzy theism that Norton still shared with them only a year or two earlier: a comfort that his hard-edged sincerity no longer let him indulge. But Godkin and Olmsted drifted like Norton into agnosticism. And his English friends were more apt to be unbelievers than not— Leslie Stephen, George Lewes, George Eliot, Frederic Harrison—while Ruskin's and Matthew Arnold's stand-ins for the deity were so watery as to run through the fingers of anyone who tried to grasp them.

Unbelief affected profoundly the meanings and purposes in Norton's world. Most immediately the education of his children: "Can I give to them strong enough moral conceptions, without connecting these conceptions with religious sanctions, to make them strong against temptation, to develop upright, & virtuous characters?" Norton never doubted that moral rules existed independently of religion; he did worry that moral striving might falter without the ideal world created by Christianity. What could replace in human imagination the saga of creation and redemption, the story of the man who laid down his life for his friends, the epic, if not of saints and Virgin and angels, then at least of Oxford martyrs and Pilgrim feet and their stern impassioned stress? Ultimately, answering that question—not just for his children's education but for America's—led Norton to infuse new meanings into art and literature and put them to new uses. The loss of God required Norton to revise the meaning of culture, of history itself. His sturdy confidence in human progress had relied ultimately on the warrant that a loving God so ordained. The confidence never wavered; the warrant now badly needed repair.[28]

Progress was also running into more mundane problems. Norton had rejoiced at Grant's election in November 1868; now he fumed at the "disgraceful" men the new president named to office. "Grant's surrender, partial though it may be, to the politicians was an unexpected disappointment." It also gave more evidence of the fading in American politics of the Civil War idealism that Norton had cherished—or fantasized. In July he canceled his subscription to the *Boston Weekly Advertiser,* which "disgusted me once a week with my native land." Railroads buying legislatures, city bosses buying votes. "The trivialities, the meannesses, the dishonesties of American politics" hit Norton harder in Europe than they had at home; "for one feels here even more strongly than there the responsibilities we are under to mankind at large, & recognizes even more clearly our deplorable shortcomings."[29]

For that matter, Americans themselves he found pretty hard to endure in Europe. Herds of "rich vulgarians" almost sufficed alone to make Norton doubt American institutions and "look gloomily at the future of a society that can breed such vermin." A "vulgar stage" seemed inevitable in the development of democracy, he told Godkin; and America was "entering it now." Yet vulgarity, if inescapable, was also "the sign of the worst evils from which a national life can suffer,—and I do not believe it impossible for America to go down under their assaults." For now, Norton confided only to Godkin his nightmares of democratic Americans, there being no need to temper the wind to so thickly padded a lamb as Edwin.[30]

Susan took as acerbic a view of Germans. "To see them eat is a severe test of moral courage & to like them in spite of it implies a philosophy worthy of Mr. Mill." Her husband, however, was bent on wintering in Germany where he really could study the language—or at least he was in July. Whether four hours a day of the stuff dulled his taste for German or his health shook his resolve to endure rain and cold, by mid-August, Florence looked a lot better than Berlin. On 9 October the Norton caravan pulled out of Vevey. They traveled slowly—Sue being six months pregnant, Catharine seventy-six years old—over the Mont Cenis Pass to Turin, down to Genoa, through Lucca and Pisa.[31]

Toward the end of October their train chugged into Florence. They rented a roomy villa just outside the Porta San Gallo, not a mile from the duomo, planning to remain until summer, when Charles's ills usually grew worse, and then to remove to the higher, cooler neighborhood of Siena.

Charles settled down to old tomes and manuscripts. "I am just now in a state near despair at the vastness of human knowledge & the profundity of my own ignorance." To allay despair he relied on the new Biblioteca Nazionale on the second floor of the Uffizi, which combined the old Magliabecchiana and Palatine libraries. He "looked forward to doing a good deal of work there in the course of the winter" but on his first morning discovered the library to be so cold that his health could hardly allow regular days in it. Worse came, for his strength refused to make its usual winter recovery. Month followed month, and he remained "not positively ill" but "more than usually invalided, & out of vigor." Nor was Susan, at first, better off. "Good & sweet & patient" as she was, this pregnancy made her more "wretchedly uncomfortable" than any of the others.[32]

Neither wished much to see other people. Sue's friend Fanny Kemble spent some time with the Nortons in November 1869, and, in December, Charles finally made contact with George Marsh, the learned United States envoy. Marsh's erudition proved enormously useful "on difficult questions of language or history" in Norton's studies. But Marsh was "literally the only person speaking English" whom Norton saw before January, when he fell in with Pasquale Villari, a "most interesting" Italian his own age, professor of history at the university and secretary-general of the Ministry of Public Instruction. Social isolation seemed no grim fate from Charles's angle of vision. He wanted Florence, not dinner parties.[33]

True, he griped about the modernizing of Italy; but the same wonderful pictures remained in the Accademia: Filippino Lippi's *Annunciation* and Filippo's *Coronation of the Virgin* shining as brightly as ever. And the ever new pleasures of old-book dealers (he had his eye on a 1497 Dante) were sweetened by the publication, inspired by Italian nationalism, of several "precious inedited works of the trecento." Most of all he read. He immersed himself in Florentine history, studied Dante. "I am not idle, but I must busy myself more with learning a little than producing anything." Norton felt drawn to Michelangelo as never before, as much for his striving after the unattainable "full expression" of "the imaginations that possessed him" as for his achieved work.[34]

Norton in fact was thinking more and more about art, the imagination, and the relation of both to civilization—and to its sustenance. In January he lent an epistolary hand in persuading President Eliot to institute drawing classes at Harvard, taught by the painter Charles Moore. Few people, Norton lamented, understood "the nature & worth of art, as an instrument of expression of the higher faculties & emotions of man, and as a mode of culture without which all other education but imperfectly develops human character." Norton had long viewed art in Ruskinian terms as "not a product of a special faculty but of the whole healthy nature of man"; whatever "special gifts, or influences" made one person a painter and another a poet, one's art necessarily expressed one's whole nature. The habit of speaking of mental powers as if distinct entities obscured "the absolute unity of the spirit"; in fact "mind & heart, moral sense & artistic faculty" were "essentially inseparable." What was new was not this animating idea but Norton's growing conviction of its centrality for education. Living in Florence did encourage thinking about art.[35]

Life there got considerably better after Sue gave birth on 15 January 1870 to a third daughter, Margaret. Despite the difficult pregnancy, the birth proved uncomplicated; and Sue quickly recovered. Indeed, Charles told John Simon, she had not looked so well for years, "young & blooming." In April the two of them journeyed to Rome for Holy Week, passing through Assisi on the way. Susan loved the old town, and Giotto's frescoes in the great Franciscan basilica touched her deeply; she and Charles walked up to the Rocca Maggiore, the medieval citadel, to catch the last rays of the sun. Charles remembered it as "one of the best days in my life." Rome seemed more mundane, depressing with its modernization, though not so bad as Florence's; elating with its galleries, though not so good as Florence's.[36]

What attracted Norton most was the Vatican Council, opened by Pius IX on 8 December 1869, the pope's heaviest brigade in his war against liberalism. Not till July did the council formally approve the doctrine of papal infallibility, but Norton watched from the crowd at Saint Peter's when on 24 April the bishops made this a foregone conclusion by voting the constitution *De fide*. Norton sympathized with his friend John (now Lord) Acton's "painful position" as a leader of the outgunned liberal opposition and, indeed, believed the 24 April vote to contradict "the true interpretation" of the church's "own dogma viewed historically."[37]

At the same time, he could not help but think that Pio Nono had "in a worldly point of view" taken the shrewder line. As Norton reported to the *Nation*'s readers, the nineteenth century, "asserting the absolute authority of the reason and the right of free thought," had drawn a line in the sand "between the Church and the unchurched." Differences between Protestants and Catholics faded into irrelevance. The pope saw what Protestant myopia obscured: war had come, a world-historical combat "between the principle of authority and that of freedom in matters of opinion, between faith and scepticism, between supernaturalism and science, between obscurantism and intelligence." By focusing authority in its center, infallibility made the Church "a much more compact and united body," a far more formidable foe of its two deadly enemies, scientific intelligence and political freedom.[38]

Sue and Charles returned to Florence toward the end of April, departing a month later for Siena. Their new home, the Villa Spannocchi, topped a hill northwest of Siena, about a half-hour walk from the duomo and with a "glorious view" of it. A huge rectangular yellow pile, the house enjoyed a terraced garden and *bosco* in front, while red and brown buildings of the working farm attached to the villa clustered nearby. A half-hour's walk away, in the city center, just off the Campo, stood the Palazzo Piccolomini, now housing the recently formed Archivio di Stato di Siena, where Norton soon went to work. Although he feared that winter's poor health had left him ill fitted to endure "the season which always & everywhere pulls me down," a few days of Siena's "fresher & brisker air" perked him up. By late August he was spending virtually every morning buried in the Archivio di Stato—a routine varied by afternoons in "the Public Library" and the cathedral archive—digging out documents relating to the history of the duomo, hoping to fill the big gaps in "the printed works of Malavolti, Tommasi, & Gigli."[39]

This was no job for a dilettante. Merely locating documents posed mammoth problems. Gaetano Milanesi's *Documenti per la Storia dell'Arte Senese* provided hints; the Archivio di Stato itself had, a few years earlier, produced a limited general index; some handlists of predecessor collections survived from the seventeenth and eighteenth centuries. George Marsh sent from Florence an old manuscript history of Siena. In late September, Milanesi himself, now director of the Florentine archives, visited Siena; and a half-hour consultation with him gave Norton more clues. Inevitably, Charles turned up mostly "mere dust & rubbish"—but "now & then a fact worth hunting for." Norton's training in paleography came exclusively from turning the pages of old manuscripts, puzzling over strangely formed letters in cramped official hands, and decoding personal shorthands varying from official to official.[40]

He loved it. He even toyed, just briefly, with the normally unappetizing notion of becoming a professor. The archives, pace all pitfalls, proved "wonderfully full," few important documents after 1250 having disappeared. "It is surprising how near a feeling one gets to the men & women of these old times; how natural it seems to live with them," he mused to himself. By mid-September he had begun to write the story he was piecing together. A week of illness in October that kept him away from archives and pen ruffled his temper. By the end of autumn he had "got the history of the Duomo pretty well written out with many new documents." The story told not just of the building of a cathedral but also of "the political & social conditions of Italy during the Middle Ages."[41]

Those conditions seemed to Norton to have nurtured a different personality than his own time. The "immense energy" and "vigorous faith" expressed in Europe's cathedrals evidenced a "spirit & life" alien to the modern world. Norton's own perfected agnosticism left him more sensitive than ever to the importance—and the fragility—of what he called "ideal motives of action." These had weakened under the regime of "utilitarian reason"; America above all cultivated emotional constraint and social conformity. Compared to medieval man, his Victorian successor appeared "deficient in character, that is, in exercise of will, & play of motive, & susceptibility to passion."[42]

From America, Chauncey Wright wrote to challenge his friend's ardor for this "old and now impossible" sort of "nobleness" and "individual distinction." Norton replied that he did appreciate that modernity at its democratic best produced "a high general level of humanity." Yet he still felt dissatisfied with a "system of life" that "neither provides for nor desires the formation of marked individualities or high & strongly defined characters."

> No doubt "utilitarian reason must govern the modern world", but how can utilitarian reason supply to us that which makes up the poetry & highest delight of life? There is a delight beyond that of being reasonable, or of being generous;—it is the enjoyment of what is passionately desired, accomplished or felt. It belongs to a different range of spiritual conditions. . . . Now the sense of beauty is a part of human nature from which some of the purest, most refining & most elevating joys spring. It is wholly unscientific & for any direct result unutilitarian. It seems to belong in the highest degree only to passionate natures, or to natures readily susceptible to passion.

It also could be cultivated, but those charged with the nurture of American youth seemed neither to notice nor to care. In years to come Norton would labor to correct the defect.[43]

He never thought the sense of beauty a replacement for scientific rationality, nor Dante for the steam engine. But more and more clearly he distinguished between the sort of thinking appropriate to the spiritual domain and that fitted to the social. For problems of the spirit, beauty and passion held hope of solution; for the ills of society, utilitarian reason. Just as America needed to nurture the sense of beauty, so it must train utilitarian intellect, above all in its "best men." For, as Boston had taught him and journalism had confirmed, the influence of a relatively few cultivated leaders "frames a temper which by degrees becomes national."[44]

And just as Europe supplied Americans a school of beauty, so it furnished a laboratory for politics. The outcome of Italy's experiment in constitutional government Norton thought doubtful; indeed, the whole continent's future looked bleak. As he had perceived in England, politics itself had changed. Party divisions no longer arose merely from political disagreement but directly from social antagonism. The working classes "& those below them" had moved from murky discontent to clear "opposition to existing social institutions & arrangements." Norton did not blame them. He deemed property a legal institution justified only by results, and the results looked awful. He more than half believed that laws permitting "accumulation of capital in a few hands" were responsible for creating "a twofold class of the excessively rich, and the excessively poor." Certainly, no one who knew "what society at the present day really is" would think it "worth preserving on its present basis."[45]

This gloomy diagnosis informed Norton's reading of the Franco-Prussian War. France's declaration of war in July 1870 he regarded as wanton, criminal, and fraught with "appalling consequences." Prussian victory, on balance, served Europe well by destroying Napoleonism, discrediting "the system of standing armies," and replacing French with German principles: Protestantism, science, and free inquiry. For France itself he expected that defeat—confirmed at Sedan on 2 September—would bring chaos. Of this, too, he took a long view. France's wretchedness would launch the "long & trying period of revolution" inevitable before Europe could achieve a "social system which shall afford a solid basis for real progress, and be the commencement of a true social organization." He only regretted "that this revolutionary period should seem to be beginning in such a way as to give strength to the reactionary forces."[46]

One more hopeful sign appeared. On 20 September 1870, as Charles strolled outside Siena, he "heard the great bell of the city" celebrating the entry of Italian troops into the papal quarter of Rome. "The hope of centuries is accomplished"; "Dante should at last rest in peace." That night the tower and the fort were illuminated; the Nortons fired off rockets around the villa as its *contadini* shouted *"Viva Roma!"*[47]

The farmworkers did not quite exhaust the Nortons' social life. Ruskin visited in June; and Charles spent a couple of days with him in Florence before Ruskin came to Villa Spannocchi, then four days afterward in Pisa,

Lucca, Pistoia, and Prato. They admired together the Pisanis' pulpits in Pisa, and Norton introduced Ruskin to his beloved Lippis in the Accademia in Florence. Utterly converted to Filippo Lippi, Ruskin called his frescoes in the Prato duomo "the highest line of the true old Florentine school"; and Norton agreed: "The Renaissance brings in the supremacy of books, & abolishes that of painting."[48]

From Prato, Charles returned to the peaceful domesticity of Siena. The household's composition shifted slightly when Sara Sedgwick returned to America in August, replaced in November by Sue's other sister, Theodora; but its rhythms scarcely altered. That fall, Sue and Charles made "delightful" excursions to the monastery of the Osservanza, with its beautiful views and fine altarpiece by Luca della Robbia, and to the romantic little medieval city of San Gimignano, bristling with towers and girdled by walls. At the beginning of December the family moved back to Florence, into winter quarters in the Villa d'Ombrellino in Bellosguardo, across the Arno and high above the center of Florence but little more than a half-hour walk from the Ponte Vecchio. The Nortons settled again into solitude, broken only by an occasional guest. A piano and billiards table downstairs provided evening entertainment when cards and novels paled. Charles returned to his studies, work in Siena having sharpened his eyes for the duomo in Florence. Growing curiosity about medieval cathedral building perhaps motivated a trip in January 1871 to take another look at Orvieto.[49]

At the end of that month, Uncle Ticknor died, almost eighty. In adulthood, Charles had often quarreled with him about politics and social reform; but a younger Charley remembered happy romps and a powerful model of scholarship; and his death cut away a big piece of Norton's personal past.

Public affairs looked no cheerier. Norton's disenchantment with President Grant and the Republicans grew with every message to Congress and every new whiff of corruption; and, indeed, the stench arising from the Washington hog trough made many a less fastidious man worry about the future of the Republic. Meanwhile, in Europe the aftermath of the Franco-Prussian War confirmed the "worst in the national constitution and spirit of Germany": exemplified at Versailles on 18 January when the victors proclaimed a new German empire.[50]

A nasty head cold all through January did little to improve Norton's mood. He hated the Florentine climate, and in February he and Sue took off with her sister Theodora "in search of more genial airs." They headed for

Naples, for only in its vicinity could one "study Greece in Italy," as Charles wanted to do. (Norton's desire to "study Greece" would grow, culminating in one of the greatest monuments to his work.) Sue never having traveled south of Rome, they made the most of it: the Bay of Baiae, the Temple of Jupiter Serapis, the Arco Felice, Cape Misenum, Pompeii, Sorrento, Amalfi. Charles wished he could spend a month "studying the collections of ancient art" in the Naples museum; in fact, they returned to Florence around 10 March.[51]

Even as they traveled, Paris rose in desperate revolt against the reactionary new French Republic. The grim drama of the Paris Commune, its struggle against the so-called party of order, riveted Norton's gaze on the evil effect of a fattening plutocracy, concentrating ever greater wealth in ever fewer hands, sinking its talons into America as well as Europe, its distinguishing marks corruption in politics, exploitation in economics, vulgarity in culture. Norton dismissed the socialism embraced by many Communards as a quixotic attempt to repeal the laws of nature. Yet he agreed with the socialists that "our systems of individualism & competition" had "come pretty nearly to a deadlock." "We have erected selfishness into a rule of conduct, & we applaud the man who 'gets on' no matter at what cost to other men." He lumped venal American politicos like Boss Tweed, flashy capitalists like Jim Fisk, with Louis Napoleon "& the rest of that gang"— including Thiers, the new French president.[52]

Norton believed that "our present system" gave "unfair advantage" to capital over labor and that, as a result, poverty was growing disproportionately in both Europe and America. Socialism offered no answer; it would sap the motives "which ought to induce all men to feel that their happiness depends chiefly on their own qualities, on their intelligence, probity & industry & on their unselfishness." Whence, then, the redress? He speculated to Godkin that it would come through "violence of a very senseless character & of very destructive nature"; "after producing great & seemingly needless suffering," upheaval would "end in a partial readjustment of human relations in which the profits of labour will be more fairly, more equitably divided than they are at present." The feudal system, in its age the frame of society, became pernicious and had to fall, even though no one could imagine what would succeed it; the Roman Church grew corrupt and needed the Reformation, even though misery and warfare followed; so, now, a "social revolution" impended. It would "destroy many precious memorials, smash no doubt many painted windows." But it would also "make men more moral, more conscious of their duties to society." The Commune, blasting a few bricks from the crumbling foundation of the old order, marked a tiny step in man's "slow historic progress."[53]

By the same token, the violence and blindness on both sides of the barricades showed "the backward stage of his actual development." Norton, always an evolutionist of some stripe, inclined now "to believe in Darwinism as applied to man." "Monkeys can hardly have advanced more slowly into humanity; & no fight among gorillas was ever more irrational than this which is going on in Paris." (He also noted in passing that, in light of Darwin's new *Descent of Man*, the *Iliad* appeared to reflect "the dawning manhood of mankind," with Agamemnon and Achilles pawns of sexual selection: hardly Harvard's view of the classics, one closer to Jane Harrison's.) Jane Norton informed Godkin that her brother had grown "philosophical" about public affairs—"I might insert depressed in place of the longer word." His Darwinian turn implied much slower, more brutish, more disorderly ascent than the "progress of civilization" once imagined by Adam Ferguson and certified by Providence. And the United States, though still in advance of Europe in democratic practice, no longer appeared to him to have escaped the fetid poverty, arrogant wealth, and class divisions that bled the Old World.[54]

Yet disillusion did not crush Norton's faith in progress but only extended its already long time scale and suggested new priorities for the forces of light. In his homeland, where the long struggle against slavery had finally vindicated individual rights, the time had come to battle for community. To shore it up, Norton did not shirk "the compulsory action of government." With "intelligence & ignorance" at war, he warned Curtis, government must have "power to make education compulsory, to remove all hindrances to public health, to regulate some of the uses of property, and to take a larger share of accumulated wealth for general & public uses." But given the massive corruption of electoral politics, what mechanism could lift the civic consciousness of Americans?[55]

Norton fell back on what had always been his and Boston's panacea, education. But now he gave less thought to schooling the masses than to teaching the powerful: the plutocrats and their sons, the present and future opinion leaders. "Charles has got a stereotyped phrase lately," Jane wrote to Godkin, "which he delivers with unction, whenever he is discoursing upon America and American prospects": "'There are two institutions that will save America, if she is to be saved. The one is Harvard College, the other the New York Nation.'" Charles soon broadened this view—to include Yale.

These three, he told Godkin, his favorite sounding board on such issues, "seem to me almost the only solid barriers against the invasion of modern barbarism & vulgarity."[56]

Not only public affairs turned Norton "philosophical"; so did the damned Florentine climate, which played hob with his health. Indeed, the whole family seemed glad to shake off Tuscany's dust—or mud—and remove to genial Venice. Catharine's frailty made it prudent for her to travel ahead, with her daughters and the "devoted servant Antonio" to care for her. The rest of the crew abandoned Villa d'Ombrellino on 1 April 1871, arriving in Venice two days later. Charles griped that Venice, like the rest of Italy, was losing its "medievalism"; but even the acids of modernity had not really defaced its incomparable beauty. From rooms in a *pensione* near San Marco, the Nortons set out to enjoy it.[57]

Susan had never been healthier or happier; life had never given her more pleasure. Two years in Europe had quelled her recurrent fevers and "confirmed her health in every way." Europe, Charles reflected, "had enlarged all her resources of giving & receiving happiness." In early May she became pregnant once more but remained "uncommonly well." Sunday, 21 May, was their ninth wedding anniversary; the next week, in Santa Maria Mater Domini, they stood rapt together before Tintoretto's great *Finding of the Cross* (to whose merits, Charles thought, Ruskin had done "scant justice"); then Charles took Sue to San Marciliano to meet his old favorite, Titian's *Tobit and the Angel.*[58]

He doubtless talked to her of these paintings in words inflected by his recent researches, for these had firmed and deepened his understanding of the nature and end of art study. In the teeth of formalist theories of art then emerging in France and Germany, Norton's approach remained more resolutely than ever historical: almost, as it were, philological, textual, the orientation ultimately derived from Boston and Andrews. Charles cared about paintings less as expressions of individual minds (although he did insist that only genius could produce great art) than as records of a civilization. The archetypal Venetian pair, Titian and Tintoretto, appealed to him largely because they recorded with consummate skill and sensitivity their own cultural moment; Tintoretto, he avowed to Ruskin, had produced "the completest expression of the great qualities of Venice" at their apex. If all other records disappeared, a scholar might deduce the main lines of Venetian culture from his paintings.[59]

What treasures Venice offered! Norton bought "a fine copy of the original Surdino Dante," an incunabulum (Florentine actually) with illustrations by Botticelli; purchased "for a song" a little Veronese portrait; and came as close as a Norton could to salivating over the Rezzonico (Clement XIII) collection of engravings. He renewed acquaintance with Ruskin's friend Rawdon Brown, a deep well of Venetian lore, spending hours at Brown's home in the Palazzo Gussoni on the Grand Canal, examining old manuscripts that littered the tables and pictures of Venetian life that covered the walls. Tintoretto, San Marco, the schemes of the Doges, the argosies of the merchants—Brown answered Norton's most abstruse questions about Venice better than anyone else.[60]

Storm clouds shadowed this idyll in late May. In a blood-soaked week, troops of the Third Republic crushed the Paris Commune. Norton seethed at the "horrible cruelty" of its conquerors, thought "the saving of 'order' & of Paris by Thiers & the 'party of order' a calamity to the cause of order & civilization," and urged Godkin to "set the crimes of these men in the plainest light" in the *Nation*'s pages, "in order to account for the bitterness of the struggle that is to come." "I do not doubt," he told Frederic Harrison, that the "future belongs not to classes but to mankind"; but "that future is to be reached only through an infinitely long present of mistakes, confusion, misery, and bitterness."[61]

Almost simultaneously, a spasm of illness devastated Catharine. The disease appeared more debilitating than deadly, but it seemed best to get her out of Venice's muggy heat as soon as she could comfortably travel. Charles meant to winter in Germany, anyway; "for I must get rid of the German Dictionary"; and, besides, some aspects of the Middle Ages one could study deeply only there. So, on 16 June, Jane and Grace set out with their mother for Innsbruck, a way station where they would await the rest of the family. The next month passed for Charles and Susan in a last dream of Venice. On 19 July 1871 they left "with more regret than we ever left a city before,—with a true pang of grief at bidding it farewell probably never to see it again." In Austria they found Catharine "wonderfully improved in health."[62]

After a few weeks relaxing on an Alpine balcony, the family set out for Dresden, the elegant Saxon capital, where in early September they rented an apartment in the so-called English Quarter. There, they "comfortably established" the entire household once more, in what Sue called "this dullest & most respectable of cities." She was not the only Norton who found Dresden "langweilig"; her husband thought Germany "admirably suited to make one miss Italy." They adapted. Disappointed in the gallery (the "'restorations' have been terrible," he wrote Sam Ward), Charles took solace in music, "cheap & delightful." Jane became a "Wagnerianerinn"; seven-year-old Sally took up the violin. Sally and Eliot enrolled in a real school, until a scarlet fever epidemic drove them back to tutors. Eliot amused himself by collecting stamps and teasing Sally relentlessly. All the children got German lessons and dancing lessons, and Lily and Rupie kindergarten in its *Geburtsplatz*.[63]

Charles got mostly German—enough at least "to discourage myself thoroughly from time to time as I open new doors into unvisited chambers of learning." He perhaps did not utterly regret that children made such "great consumers of time, and interrupters of work." Still, a Holbein exhibition in Dresden that fall did prompt him to write an article arguing against the attribution to Holbein of the so-called "Dresden Madonna." The essay showed firm grasp not only of relevant documentary evidence but also of the technical details of painting.[64]

Norton was also preparing for the Leipzig art historian Albrecht von Zahn's *Jahrbücher für Kunstwissenschaft* a great wad of material he had unearthed on the building of the Duomo di Siena: eight long selections of previously unpublished documents from Sienese archives, arranged chronologically from 1260 to 1388 and interlarded with explanatory notes in German. These "Urkunden zur Geschichte des Doms von Siena" appeared in print the following May: Norton's first substantial publication of original research in art history, probably the first by any American.

The Nortons' life in Dresden usually had a lighter character than this. In October the historian John Lothrop Motley and his wife stayed with the Nortons; then Donald MacKay came to light the candles on the Christmas tree once more—and to whisk Charles away on a jaunt to Berlin. Just before Christmas, Norton had a private audience with Saxony's King John, a Dante scholar and an old friend of Uncle Ticknor, talking pleasantly of Dante, Ticknor, and the blooming university at Leipzig.

Some of the family's thoughts were turning homeward. The Nortons had always intended Germany as "a half way station," planning when summer arrived to travel to England, thence to Boston. Catharine, her health now restored, wanted to get back. But Shady Hill remained under lease until spring 1873; and, anyway, Charles and Sue felt no urgency. They tossed around the idea of letting Charles's mother and sisters return to live with the Bullards for a year, while they enjoyed more of Europe.[65]

They could, at least, still enjoy music in Dresden, though Susan's now enormous belly perhaps kept her away from the *Magic Flute* on the first of February. A week later she entered labor and, on the afternoon of 9 February, gave birth to her third son. They named him Richard, after the Nortons'

Anglo-Indian friend Richard Baird Smith. Despite a long, hard labor, Sue had no complications and went "on perfectly well."[66]

A week later she came down with pleurisy. The first attack, in the night of 15–16 February, did not alarm her doctors. Still, Charles wired Algernon Coolidge (the son of his old Parisian friend Mr. Coolidge), who was a physician and happened to be in Berlin. Charles met him at the station the next night around midnight and brought him back to the Nortons' apartment. Susan's condition looked hopeful; Coolidge, not wanting to excite her, decided to wait till morning to examine. Two hours later she lapsed into unconsciousness; Grace, at her side, called for Coolidge. The disease, he said, had begun to affect the heart. At seven in the morning, Charles joined them. Within five minutes an obvious change for the worse came over Susan. At eight o'clock, she died. Four days later, she would have celebrated her thirty-fourth birthday.

"With my whole heart I rejoice that if one was to be left I am chosen, and that the grief is mine not hers." Or so Charles said. The news hit James Lowell like "a heavy blow on the back of the head." The children, even Eliot and Sally, only dimly grasped the loss. Their father knew. "I have had ten years of exceptional happiness," he wrote to Longfellow. In that past, he took what consolation he could. Susan's death would not break him, he said, "because her love is still strong enough to support me. I can bear what I have to bear, for the thought of her is a comfort, and there is nothing but joy in the memory of her during those ten years in which her presence has blessed me." These were brave words—and nearly lies; for, in the end, there was no comfort. "One can but bear as silently & manfully as one may the unmitigated misery, & the ruin of life."[67]

Charles did not have a funeral to cauterize the wound. Susan's corpse was shipped back to Boston. Early in May, old Mr. Newell, the Nortons' retired pastor, conducted a service at Shady Hill. From there, her body was taken to Mount Auburn Cemetery, where patrician Boston buried its dead. An unusually bright spring had relapsed into winter, Harry James wrote Charles; and, as the mourners stood at the grave, heavy snowflakes began to drop from a silent, leaden sky.[68]

Interlude

Boston prescribed how a man should bear affliction: neither give way to grief nor deny it but get on with what had to be done. Charles gave Eliot his daily lessons, attended to the other children, tried to revive his researches on Venice. But he wanted to put Dresden behind him, to get "somewhere where occupation of mind may offer itself, & not be merely a hard effort." In early April the Nortons left, proceeding slowly westward, their goal England and then, in autumn, Shady Hill. On the way to Paris they stopped at Halle, so Charles could pass a day with the eminent Dantist Karl Witte. A spry seventy-two, Witte trotted his guest through the quiet old university town; they chattered away in Italian, examined the treasures of Witte's library: for Norton, a temporary distraction. Witte, about to publish a critical edition of the *Vita Nuova*, wanted to dedicate it to Norton. "It would have pleased me a little while ago," Charles glumly mused.[1]

The family stopped in Paris for a few weeks before crossing to England. In mid-May, Donald MacKay came from the Hague, to bring consolation and diversion; he and Charles went to see the controversial philologist Ernest Renan. The absence of dusty old folios and other scholarly apparatus in Renan's study surprised Norton at first, then reminded him of the value to scholarship of great libraries like the Bibliothèque Nationale, a resource he would miss in America. Although Charles saw a few faces from his past (notably Circourt), mostly he sat in the Louvre and the Bibliothèque Nationale, trying to get his mind off his pain, collating Dante manuscripts for Witte, collecting material for his own sketch of Tintoretto's life.

Such work seemed the sort of thing that might help to fill the empty days after he returned home. James Lowell had resigned his Harvard professorship, at least for a time; and President Eliot wrote to sound out cousin Charles about taking over Lowell's Italian classes. The thought of drilling verb forms left Norton cold, but an actual professorship could appeal, "for there are subjects," he wrote James, "on which I should be glad to speak to younger students." This prospect, however, looked pretty remote. Lowell had also intimated that Henry Adams might give up editing the *North American,* and Charles liked the idea of returning to that post. Whatever lay ahead, he wanted quickly to get behind him the pain of returning to Shady Hill without Sue and to end his children's separation from their mother's sisters.[2]

Bad news came in June. Shady Hill's tenant refused to give up the lease any earlier than its expiration in spring 1873. The family grimly redrew its plans, postponing England till the fall. Charles found a house to rent in Saint Germain-en-Laye, just west of Paris, where the children had a park and a forest to roam and where Charles had a train to the Bibliothèque Nationale.

In mid-September, preparing to remove to London, the Nortons abandoned Saint Germain for a Paris hotel, there to discover that Cambridge had descended on Paris, turning "the Quais & the Rue de Rivoli" into "mere continuations of Brattle Street." Charles and Harry James roved the Louvre together, where Norton's deepened expertise impressed James but left him ill at ease; his elder friend now took "art altogether too hard for me to follow him." "I feel less and less at home with them [the Nortons], owing to a high moral je ne sais quoi which passes quite above my head," James confessed to his sister. Chauncey Wright felt as easy as ever with Charles and came to chatter away the evening. Best of all, on 23 September, James and Fanny Lowell arrived, moving right into the Nortons' hotel. Their four years apart "faded away like a mist," for, with James, Charles still felt "more at home than with anyone in the world outside of my own household." To James he could talk of Sue.[3]

On 7 October the Nortons took the boat train for Folkstone and four days later moved into 33 Cleveland Square, a house that Burne-Jones had found for them in Bayswater. Only three blocks from Paddington Station, the location made it easy to run up to Oxford, where Ruskin, Slade Professor of Art since 1870, was lecturing that fall. Charles made the trip three or four times, finding Ruskin "never in a sweeter, less irrational mood."[4]

Mostly, though, life ran on in a quiet, domestic, almost retired groove, as compared with 1869; only the warmest of old acquaintances did Norton even tell of his return. He located a good school nearby for Eliot and a violin teacher for Sally, himself gave Sally and Lily lessons each morning, and committed the rest of the children's instruction to the German governess brought from Dresden. Eliot, now nine, needed a real playmate and discovered one in the Burne-Joneses' boy Phil. Jane and Grace made "most tender & faithful" surrogate mothers for all the children; Jane, still the General Blessing, commanded housekeeping. Every afternoon, at first, her brother took "a long & solitary walk."[5]

Yet isolation fitted Norton's nature poorly even in grief. Shortly after moving to Cleveland Square, Charles ran into Thomas Carlyle at a friend's house; upon leaving, the two strolled together toward Carlyle's home in Chelsea. The older man—Carlyle was closing in on seventy-seven—found the younger one sympathetic and invited Norton to join him on his afternoon walks whenever so inclined. Charles in turn appreciated in Carlyle the "tenderness of his sensibility, the quickness of his personal sympathies, and the sweet modesty of his inner nature." By December, Leslie Stephen, a famous pedestrian, was also companioning Norton weekly. By now Charles was seeing John Simon, William Morris, and of course, Ned Burne-Jones at least that often—and a fair amount of Frederic Harrison, Fitzjames Stephen, and John Morley. A day rarely passed without someone dropping in at Cleveland Square; MacKay came for a couple of weeks in January. Not everyone would have called this "a quiet life."[6]

Yet the comforting presence of familiars was hardly the London social whirl. In these long months of lonely nights, Norton took what cheer he could from real friends and serious talk. More exclusively than ever these came from the city's middle-class scientific and literary circles; outside his little circle of regulars, he saw once or twice Matthew Arnold, the Darwins, the Lyells, George Henry Lewes; that was about it. The bond with Leslie Stephen especially, rather slack before, tightened in this barren winter; a scholarly journalist with a taste for cultural history and a bent toward rationalist skepticism, Stephen could perhaps share more fully in Norton's world than even Burne-Jones and Ruskin. Mentally in mourning, Norton no longer had any use at all for the bejeweled pretensions of fashionable London. Even meeting the historian James Froude at Carlyle's gave him the shivers; when Carlyle asked why, Norton said that Froude "was a flatterer, and that flattery always implied insincerity." When Norton went out, it was to museums and galleries, not dinner parties. "The best of life lies behind me," he wrote to Lowell, "& I find it hard sometimes to look forward to the unending second best. I turn more & more to the past."[7]

He meant his own past with Susan, but he could well have included pasts far more remote. He haunted the dealers, buying old books and manuscripts. Carlyle got him made a member of the London Library, in aid of his Italian researches (in 1869 it had been the Athenaeum Club he needed); and Norton hired a research assistant to dig in the Florentine state archives.

Visiting Ruskin in Oxford made possible a search through medieval manuscripts in the Bodleian. Before Christmas Norton put the last touches on his
study of the building of the Siena duomo and handed it over to Ruskin for
comment. But mostly he studied the history of Venice, plugging away "at
Cicogna's bulky & close printed quartos, and at Muratori's still bulkier
folios." Their columns, he reported to Lowell, could not be skimmed as
quickly as the *Times;* "but one learns to skip here & there." He took a break
from folios to inspect the collection of artifacts excavated in Cyprus by Luigi
di Cesnola and destined for the new Metropolitan Museum in New York.
Norton reported on them for the *Nation:* America badly needed a basis for
serious study of ancient art, and the Cesnola collection's "archaeological
importance" equaled its "artistic interest," especially in "supplying the link
that has been wanting between the art of Egypt and Asia Minor and that of
Greece"—a shrewd comment. His own future lay in such pasts.[8]

This he could hardly anticipate; for now, antiquity offered respite from a
nearly unbearable present. Ruskin gave him a little sketch by Turner for his
birthday; it pleased him "because Sue saw it, four years ago, and liked it." "I
shall not be on even terms with life," Charles knew, "till I am at home once
more, & have faced the change." What home promised, he could not pre-
dict. Occasional breakdowns still caught him short, but he had taught himself to manage his frustrating mystery of a disease well enough to sustain
a career.[9]

To what end? He had amassed a store of erudition that only a handful of
Americans could equal in any field—and none in art history or medieval
studies.[10] What good was that, in a country with no serious university and
the tiniest appetite for learning? Five years of watching from afar the corruption of government in the United States, of seeing at firsthand the grinding down of the poor in Europe, had not destroyed his commitment to the
American Republic nor his faith in the ultimate success of democracy. What
did either matter for him, given the hopelessness of any foreseeable politicians and (an even grimmer thought) any foreseeable voters, given the victory of the plutocrats now rooting at will through every sty in Wall Street
and Washington? His brain had not softened to the point that he would go
back to preaching the gospel of democracy as he had done in the halcyon
days of 1864 and 1865; and he utterly lacked George Curtis's knack for real
politics. And the domestic life that he had always cherished, the home that
had provided a refuge in every storm, mocked him now, an empty shell, a
cruel mask. Only duty to his six children dragged him back to Shady Hill.

The Nortons booked passage for 15 May 1873. MacKay came from the

Hague to say good-bye, followed by James Lowell from Paris. Burne-Jones returned from Italy too late; he could only scribble a downcast farewell note. Carlyle gave Charles a cast of Cromwell's death mask; both knew they would never meet again. Leaving forever the old man of whom he had grown so fond numbered among Charles's "chief regrets"; for during this hard winter—so Norton recalled thirty-five years later—Carlyle's "sympathy was more comprehensive and more helpful than that of anyone else."[11]

Leslie Stephen "was more grieved" (he told Godkin) than seemed "reasonable at losing a friend whom I have only learnt to know well within six months." Tongue tied by English reticence, Stephen "could only growl" when he left Cleveland Square on the evening of 9 May. He sent a letter the next day: "You don't know what your friendship has been & will be to me." "It is really odd," he went on, "that, of all the men I know, you & perhaps Morley (I cant think of a third) are the only ones with whom I can be sure of finding thorough sympathy in such conversations as we used to have." Stephen's words merit a moment's reflection, as one more clue to that puzzling power of sympathy innate in Norton, which drew such different people to him and extended his influence over so many diverse minds.[12]

On Saturday, 10 May, the Nortons took the train to Oxford. Jowett, now master of Balliol, entertained Charles once more at breakfast; this time, Norton was alone: "I took Sally & Eliot to walk in the afternoon down the Long Walk & by Christ Church meadows, where their Mother liked to walk; and we looked into Christ Church itself, where the stones were full of memories." On Tuesday morning Norton and Ruskin breakfasted together. Charles would miss him a great deal. They parted at the gates of Corpus Christi, "the last friend to whom I bid farewell in England."[13]

"Left England & the past," recorded Norton's laconic diary for 15 May 1873. But as the *Olympus* steamed down the Mersey, it was the past that filled his mind, the voyage up the river five years earlier, with Susan. On 26 May the *Olympus* docked at East Boston after sunset. The drive to Cambridge with the children was all too familiar, painfully so; but America seemed different, wearier, to Norton. He could no longer accept "even American institutions as finalities." "I believe in a distant future not in the present as I used to do, & in this faith America is as good a home as another, perhaps a better than any other in some minor respects." He looked at himself and saw a man "vastly older in feeling & experience." "I have passed over the bounds of youth and have entered fairly within the limits of age."[14]

He was forty-five.

TEN

Beginning Again, 1873–1878

Almost five years had passed since the Nortons left for Europe, and Shady Hill swarmed with friends. Frank Child, Mr. Longfellow, Chauncey Wright—in his loneliness Charles leaned on comradeship, fed on its resources; he missed James Lowell badly. But no friendship could fill the hole in his life. Susan's ghost was everywhere at Shady Hill. The house itself seemed wraithlike, many of its furnishings still packed away or covered up. After a week or two, the Nortons moved on to Ashfield.

There, the people treated him as kindly, the memories as cruelly. Susan had walked every well-known path, sat in every room of their old farmhouse. Her sisters and their aunt Grace Ashburner rented a house near the Nortons: good for the children, pleasant companions for the adults, constant reminders of Sue. In July, Catharine fell seriously ill, sinking for a day or two into delirium. Charles had little hope of her recovery; a fog of mortality seemed to roll over every acre of his life. Yet Catharine did recover, though slowly; and the old friends of summer cheered Charles. The Curtises now lived only a field away; George, convalescing from a debilitating sickness of his own, had more time than usual for talking and walking. Godkin came for a long visit in August.

Yet Norton needed something constant to keep his thoughts off Sue in the long days to come, and he knew it. In July he again discreetly inquired about the editorship of the *North American;* in August, Charles Eliot asked him to lecture at Harvard during the upcoming academic year. That offer tempted, for Norton admired the new spirit animating the university under his cousin's leadership: Harvard had become "a real rallying-point for us all," Charles told Sam Ward: the "most essentially civilizing of our institutions" and "the breakwater against all the tides of plutocracy." But with only six weeks to prepare and meanwhile a new life to arrange, Norton could hardly say yes. Eliot understood, hoping that Charles would consider the lectures "only postponed."[1]

For the moment, Shady Hill preoccupied him. In early September, Charles returned, with only Sally for company, to ready the house; the family followed a week later. Over the next six weeks he unpacked crates from Italy and Germany: books for the Harvard library, souvenirs for friends, every object with some "precious memory & heartbreaking association." By the end he felt "worn & old." He looked it: his scholar's stoop had grown more pronounced; his hair had mostly fallen out, only a fringe of grey circling a bare pate, although the bushy side-whiskers and drooping mustache remained surprisingly brown. Money troubles added to his cares; taxes on forty-some acres of prime real estate in a growing city devoured the family dividends. In November, Charles met with the city engineer to discuss— "alas!"—laying out the streets that would, following Olmsted's plan, eventually break up Shady Hill. A governess took some of the load off Jane and Grace; Susan's Ashburner aunts and her sisters helped, having moved into the house built for them on the Kirkland Street edge of Shady Hill, next to Frank Child's. Life gradually settled into a simulacrum of normality. But "the mere effort to get through the days with tolerable composure, cheerfulness, & seeming indifference" strained Charles to his emotional limit.[2]

Never much given to introspection—not in any case cut much slack by New England for self-absorption—Norton resorted to burying his pain in busyness. By November he had started reviewing regularly for the *Nation,* excoriating with almost his old vigor "the insufficiency of American scholarship and the want of thoroughness of American discipline." (As a critic Norton always tended more to demolition than appreciation, a symptom perhaps of a scholarly disposition at bottom more trenchant than original.) About the same time he began to teach on Wednesdays an informal class of "half a dozen young men, professors in the college here, an architect, &c," who came to Shady Hill to hear of "the principles & history of Greek & Italian Art." Teaching helped to clarify his own researches, which he had resumed. He was preparing a paper on the duomo of Florence to match his study of Siena's, hoping to have in hand by spring a book on Italian cathedral building—the first note of optimism that fall. Although by December he had given up quick publication, he still wrote a little each day. This helped Norton to rein in his black thoughts; but, he knew, only compulsory steady work would keep them at bay.[3]

Charles Eliot had again offered such work at Harvard, now tentatively a professorship rather than temporary lecturing. But the proposal looked messy. The proffered chair (the Smith Professorship of Modern Languages and Belles Lettres, which Uncle Ticknor had first occupied) belonged to

James Lowell, still across the Atlantic playing cat-and-mouse with Harvard. Eliot hoped that Lowell would return to the chair or, if not, that Norton would take it. Molière could have written the farce-by-mail that ensued. Norton refused the professorship if Lowell wanted to keep it; Lowell wanted to resign so Norton could have it. In the end, Lowell decided to return to Harvard—once it became clear that Eliot had something else to offer Norton.

That something was a new line of teaching altogether. Harvard in 1874 remained in personal details familiar to Norton: his cousin was the president, his friend Ephraim Gurney was dean of the college, one of his father's pupils was head of the Divinity School, his classmates Frank Child and George Lane were long-serving professors, and five of his own teachers were still on the faculty. Yet in large the university had metamorphosed since Charles Eliot's accession in 1869. The new president sought to draw students from throughout the United States, breaking Harvard's orientation to Boston; he also aimed to raise the standard of instruction given them, chiefly by reverting to and extending the principle of free election of courses that Norton had known under President Quincy, thus freeing professors to teach sophisticated material to students interested in learning it. By 1874–75, "prescribed studies" still occupied all of freshman year but only a third of sophomore and junior courses, while seniors took nothing but electives. Eliot had already doubled the size of the faculty and increasingly made national scholarly distinction the criterion for staffing it.[4]

Harvard had thus staked out a position—along with the University of Michigan and the new Cornell University (joined in 1876 by an even more innovative foundation, Johns Hopkins University)—as a leader in reforming American higher education. The old classical college, starting to shake off its slumbers in Norton's student days, was now stumbling toward some as yet inchoate new model of liberal education; and institutions that a German might acknowledge as real universities (however different from the German type) were for the first time taking shape on American soil. President Eliot's cousin Charles applauded; Norton imagined that Harvard might even push American higher education beyond "the high-school level."[5]

Eliot wanted his cousin to do more than cheer. Under the elective system, for all its advantages, students lacked anything to glue their disparate courses together, to enlarge their perspective on their specialized studies, to situate knowledge within the business of living as a moral agent. In short, Harvard's young barbarians required cultivation, in the sense that Boston's Unitarian elite had come to understand that word. Offer culture, Eliot was convinced, and the parched young would flock to the fountain. And who better than America's most thoroughly cultivated scholar of art to turn on the tap? Ever since Norton's return from Europe, President Eliot and Dean Gurney had bruited some scheme "to secure your services to the College." Norton balked at a transient appointment (he was, after all, a middle-aged man of established distinction). Eliot and Gurney persuaded the Harvard Corporation to fund a one-year lectureship "with the avowed purpose" of creating a professorship if enough students elected the course, and Norton yielded.[6]

A handful of American universities had gingerly approached the "fine arts" before 1874. From the 1830s into the 1850s, Princeton offered extracurricular lectures on the history of architecture and in that last decade briefly employed a "Lecturer on the Fine Arts" (all likely concerned with practical technique rather than culture). Henry Tappan, president of the University of Michigan, meant to include "The Arts of Design" in his stillborn "University Course" in the 1850s; from 1867, Vassar's art teacher did lecture on great artists of the past to supplement his instruction in drawing and painting. Yale in 1869 and Syracuse in 1873 had actually opened schools of art: these, however, devoting themselves to training painters and sculptors rather than teaching liberal arts students. Harvard itself in 1871 (with Norton's urging) had hired Charles Moore, a disciple of Ruskin, to teach drawing in the Lawrence Scientific School; and in the *history* of art Harvard had induced Charles C. Perkins to deliver between 1871 and 1874—without pay—University Lectures on Michelangelo and Raphael and on the history of engraving. But before Norton no American college or university seems to have had a regular teacher concentrating on the history of art.[7]

Yet he did not teach art history as a self-contained discipline: that was the point. His title was "Lecturer on the History of the Fine Arts as connected with Literature"; and Eliot later stressed that he hired Norton (and endured complaints of nepotism) precisely because of his cousin's "unique combination of knowledge of *art and literature.*" The very idea would have seemed outlandish in American colleges a quarter century before. But as college students themselves, Norton and Eliot had enjoyed in Mr. Felton's Greek classes a unique foretaste of "culture" as an educational ideal; that fleeting experience must have left an impression on the two cousins, especially since it fitted so smoothly with the mind-set of Unitarian Boston while contrasting so sharply with the grammar grinding that dominated even their own privileged schooling. Now Norton's appointment fulfilled that brief promise—and gave an early glint of a new dawning in American college education: the rise of the humanities.[8]

Norton, like generations before him, had undergone an education centered on close attention to Greek and Latin grammar and calculated to impose "mental discipline" on the restless boys who inhabited classical (or "grammar") schools and colleges. But, by the time he began teaching at Harvard, even fairly traditional colleges distinguished in their educational goals between study of ancient languages and a newer "literary" or "liberal" culture. "The humanities" by the 1880s became the common name for this broadening "liberal culture," comprising a wide range of "culture studies," most new to the curriculum: literature, philosophy, art history, often general history as well. The humanities still included Greek and Latin, but even these traditional subjects acquired a novel literary orientation and cultivating aim. In this revolution in liberal education, Norton would become a recognized leader, the decisive innovator.[9]

In 1874 he already saw his novel teaching as mandated by "the increasing need for a truly liberal culture."

> In a complete scheme of University studies the history of the Fine Arts in their relation to social progress, to general culture, and to literature should find a place, not only because architecture, sculpture and painting have been, next to literature, the most important modes of expression of the sentiments, beliefs and opinions of men, but also because they afford evidence, often in a more striking and direct manner than literature itself, of the moral temper and intellectual culture of the various races by whom they have been practised, and thus become the most effective aids to the proper understanding of history.
>
> The study of history is very imperfectly pursued when the attention of the student is confined, as is too generally the case, to its political and legal sides. The history of culture has of late assumed new importance, and there is no branch of the subject more essential, as an element of a liberal education, than the study of the historic development of the Fine Arts.[10]

Norton's words implicitly argue against a better-known conception of culture as an educational ideal, that of his friend Matthew Arnold, articulated five years earlier in *Culture and Anarchy*. Arnold thought of culture as recurrence to "the best which has been thought and said in the world," a formulation in many respects congenial to Norton. But Norton further insisted that a cultivating education could not depend on any *timeless* "best," any point of reference outside of history. It required immersion *in* history.

His father before him had approached the Bible as shaped by the culture (using the word now in its anthropological sense) of its writers; Charles likewise taught as a philologist, an interpreter of texts. He sought to place texts in historical context, to tack from text to context, casting a bit more light on each with every oscillation, in the tradition of hermeneutics established in the Renaissance. Andrews took as texts the Gospels; Charles examined paintings or buildings as often as poems and charters. Andrews aimed always to clarify the text; Charles usually to illuminate the context. But the method did not essentially differ. Norton intended his students to interpret the Parthenon as expressing Athenian culture, to find in the temple, therefore, an aid to understanding the Athenians. His specific topic may have been "the historic development of the Fine Arts"; but his general subject was "the history of culture" with a lowercase "c." Thereby students might hope to cultivate their own minds and characters.

Their prospective teacher set to work on the next fall's lectures immediately upon his appointment, "reading hard at Greek history & antiquities." The same exacting standard of scholarship evinced in his reviews of others' books made Charles wince at his own ignorance. "The gulf to be filled is very deep, & too wide to be spanned by any suspension bridge." Nor did Harvard offer much in the way of pilings. Although the college library now held over 200,000 books (a fourfold increase since Norton's student days), he longed for the Bibliothèque Nationale and the Bodleian. Harvard held mere scraps relevant to Norton's teaching: his old friend Stillman's photographs of the Acropolis, a few maps of Athens, the pictures that Mr. Felton had brought back from his vacation in Greece twenty years ago. Norton's own bibliophilia filled a lot of gaps, but he still had to dig hard. And Charles, really, did not care; he wanted tough labor to take his mind off Susan. "Norton is pretty well physically," Longfellow reported to a mutual English friend that February, "but seems very, very sad and lonely. He bears up against his sorrow manfully."[11]

While preparing to teach, Norton also eased himself back into other public responsibilities. In early March 1874 he traveled to New York to conspire with Godkin and Olmsted about Republican politics and then returned to Boston to line up "the better sort of men" against the gubernatorial campaign of Benjamin Butler, the egregious exemplar, in Norton's eyes, of the irresponsible type of radical Republican. (Butler lost.) A very different sort of public duty engaged him more deeply. In April he organized a two-week exhibition to display to Boston "the range of Turner's genius." Norton had devoted hours in London to studying Turner's prints;

now he borrowed from other collectors to flesh out his own holdings, hanging Parker Fraternity Hall with etchings, engravings, and drawings in ink and watercolor by Turner and with copies of his work by other artists. Norton prepared a catalogue to guide viewers; and he opened the exhibition with a lecture on Turner, blasting "the prevalent taste & the prevalent modes of artistic study & discipline." About this time he also published a catalogue of Turner's *Liber Studiorum* (the plates of which Charles had purchased in London), including facsimiles of three plates and a heavy dose of Ruskin on Turner.[12]

In these months, Ruskin himself mattered more than ever, along with a handful of other English friends, collectively a mainstay in heavy emotional weather. True, their letters mostly jabbered about news and views, keeping Norton immersed in transatlantic intellect and politics, the Simons even forwarding weekly packets of the *Times*. But to these friends far away Norton could also unburden himself on paper, whereas to broach his loneliness and depression in person to Curtis or Godkin or Child evidently seemed to Charles ungracious, depressing, or even hazardous to his own stability. Not until Lowell returned home in July 1874 did Norton have a friend with whom he could fully let down his reserve face to face. Even then, ties to England remained strong. After his own wife died the next year, Stephen sighed that "the only good to be got out of such grief as we have known is that it helps to bind old friendships closer."[13]

From Ashfield that summer Charles often returned alone to Shady Hill, working up his Harvard lectures, relishing the solitude and the relief from keeping up a cheerful front. Yet, as he looked ahead to the autumn's busyness, "the simplicity of life" in Ashfield called him back. The idea entered his head of turning the Locusts into a retreat where he could live most of the year. Retreat preoccupied him. In September he made a will "for the benefit of my children"; only for their sake, he said, would he regret death. The "recuperative energies of life are so diminished with me, and the desire to live, except as the performance of a duty, so weak with me," he told Godkin, "that the chances of long life are not great." It was definitely time to meet the Harvard students.[14]

Norton began teaching on Friday morning, 2 October 1874—but not yet his own students. Frank Child had extended his summer vacation to hunt ballads in England; and Charles took his classes, two hours a day, for the first two weeks of the term. Norton's own lectures began that same afternoon: an hour every Monday, Wednesday, and Friday. With thirty-four students, mostly juniors and seniors, the class felt "too large for the personal relations I should like to establish with my students"; otherwise, "excellent." But the double load overstrained Norton's teetery health and sent him home till early November.[15]

Back on the dais, Norton showed firm ideas about his teaching. In the first place, he believed it a grave mistake to segregate the history of art from its practice; and it was probably he who engineered the transfer of Charles Moore's drawing instruction from the Scientific School to the College. From 1874, Moore's course became Fine Arts 1: "Principles of Design in Painting, Sculpture, and Architecture." Norton's (which required no skill with a pencil but "a fair knowledge of Greek, as well as facility in reading French") was Fine Arts 2: "The History of the Fine Arts, and their Relations to Literature."[16]

Across this ample plain, Norton roamed fairly widely but with fixed intention. After an introductory lecture on the "Purpose, value, relations of the study of the Fine Arts" and a second defining at length key terms like "beauty," "design," and "taste," Norton explained to his class that the "same principles" underlay art and literature and all modes of human expression, that no good poetry or painting could appear "unless men have something to express which is the result of long training of soul & sense in the ways of high living & true thought." Then, to give the students a sense of "the place of the arts in the history of culture," he took them on a five-week odyssey of the art and literature of ancient India, Assyria, Persia, and Egypt. (In the *Nation* the following spring Norton urged translations of Assyrian cuneiform and Egyptian hieroglyphics not as literature worth reading for its own sake but as "early records of our race" important to "all classical students.") On the last day of November they arrived in Greece.[17]

There they settled for the rest of the semester: twenty-two lectures, lasting till early February. In Greece the students got a stiff dose of political, intellectual, and social history—Norton wanting them to grasp "the moral & physical elements of the Athenian nature"—along with a thicket of detail about the buildings of the Acropolis. Indeed, given five lectures on Athenian culture followed by nine on the Parthenon, Propylaea, and Erechtheum, Norton's students may have conceived "Greece" and "Athens" as names for the same place, uttered distinctly only from some obscure professorial scheme to befuddle them. Their teacher, meanwhile, had not read so much Greek since his own student days; he found it "deeply interesting."[18]

He concluded the semester with a "Resumé," the elliptical notes for which bear quoting in full as a broad hint of what students had been hearing between descriptions of the horses on the Parthenon frieze:

Serious nature & broad relations of the study in which we have been engaged,—the study of the finest modes of expression of the most gifted race [the Greeks]. Such study has no tendency toward dilettantism. It invigorates the character while it refines & enlarges the intelligence. (Contrast with the study & pursuit of modern arts of fashion, drawing room or gallery sculpture & painting, and shop front architecture.) It tends to culture in a true sense, the harmonious training of the best qualities, a mental discipline that elevates the moral temper, and developes those sympathies and perceptions by which man is made more clearly conscious of his relation to men in past time, & in the future. Such a study leads to refinement without selfishness, to sensitiveness not sensuality, to delicacy but not effeminacy, to sound & active critical judgment, but not to petulant & feeble fastidiousness.

Use to Americans!! "Long may it wave."[19]

This jeremiad awakes interest on several points, not least Norton's adulation of fifth-century Greeks. Their elevation to "most gifted race" complicated, if it did not contradict, his lifelong belief in cultural evolution: only a few years' earlier he had located the ancestors of these same Greeks in "the dawning manhood of mankind." In truth, this homage to Athens was simply the obverse of Norton's now profound disillusionment with the art of his own era (leaving aside Turner and perhaps Burne-Jones), especially with the arts met in daily life. He wanted to make the young men at Harvard "see that we have in our days nothing to say, that silence befits us, that the arts of beauty are not for us to practise;—and seeing this to resolve so to live that another generation may begin to be happier than we." Blaming the decline of art on the rise of plutocracy, Norton regarded his Harvard work as combat against untrammeled wealth and the values it promoted. The unwashed masses threatened America far less direly than their well-scrubbed masters.[20]

More precisely, Norton's foes were materialism and plutocracy. Materialism meant the primacy of material aims in life; plutocracy was its political expression, holding democracy in thrall through bosses, patronage, and bribery. The evil did not flow from a defective political or social system (Norton's respect for American institutions held firm) but from corruption of values. Like the old revolutionaries of 1776 he dreaded corruption, silently corroding virtue: liberalism had not displaced the classical republican in Norton but, rather, developed it. But he had come to understand corruption as eating much deeper than politics. "The character of its intellectual men gives its character to a nation." So Andrews Norton had declared in 1819, and so his son still believed; or at least he believed that a people's values (as expressed in but also shaped by their art and literature) guided their communities to good or ill. If Norton had to tell students that studying art would not make them "feebly fastidious," he clearly thought that most Americans had lost any aspirations more enduring than yachts, mansions, and stockholdings. No speedy recovery was conceivable. American culture itself having grown sickly, the only antidote was cultural therapy; wealthy Americans being the principal carriers of the disease, healing could begin nowhere more efficaciously than in a Harvard classroom.[21]

It followed from all this that the traditional rationale for college education had lost force for Norton. To train individual mental faculties—the old "discipline of the mind"—no longer sufficed. If every human expression flowed from the whole person, as Norton believed, then students needed a new *kind* of "mental discipline": a "harmonious training" of *all* their perceptions and sympathies that would "elevate" their "moral temper" by giving them a broad sense of their place and purpose in the human story. Drawing on the strong tradition of self-culture in his Boston Unitarian upbringing, Norton pronounced in his classroom a fresh animating purpose for liberal education: "culture in a true sense." But such an education merely began in college; for, as he had reminded readers of the *Nation* earlier that year, "the imagination is a faculty not of youth but of maturity, perfected only by variety of experience and reflection." The continued use of the term "mental discipline," by Norton as well as other professors, camouflaged a radical shift in pedagogical theory, in which Norton proved seminal: a move from drilling individual mental skills to cultivating both intellect and attitudes. In years to come, Norton would think through this reformation, and its ramifications both in and out of classrooms, in greater detail and explicitness.[22]

The examinations he set already suggest his holistic approach to cultures and his push to inquire into the moral implications of civilization. He asked students not only to describe in detail the Parthenon sculptures but also to explicate generally "the chief characteristics common to all the fine arts of historic Greece"; not only to compare the arts of Greece "with those of Egypt and the East" but also to compare the arts of the Homeric period with those of historic Greece; not only to spell out what this comparison revealed about "the development of the true Hellenic race and spirit" but also to explain what Athenian sculpture implied about "the character and position of women at Athens." In breadth and intent, such questions marked a new epoch in American collegiate education.[23]

How much encouragement Norton got from the midyear examination on 20 February is unknown, but his teaching in the second term followed the same pattern as in the first. A brisk trot in four lectures through the arts of Rome laid a foundation for the Middle Ages. An outline sketch of medieval history then preceded basic instruction in the forms of Romanesque and Gothic architecture, followed by two or three weeks of general intellectual, social, and artistic history, until finally the students settled in Siena. There they ambled for a week and a half around the duomo and—after taking off one day for a bird's-eye view of "Italy in 13th century"—strolled for two more weeks through Florence. This brought them to the penultimate lecture, concerned with "general characteristics" of the fifteenth century. "The Renaissance. Architecture in Italy" got merely the last fifty minutes, on 10 May. What mattered for educational purposes seemed pretty clear.[24]

Outside of the classroom, however, Norton still dabbled eclectically. Although his teaching ignored everything past the Renaissance (mimicking in that respect general history courses at the time), he continued to take deep interest—odd though this taste at first seems in Norton—in William Blake. Norton found time in this crammed year to prepare an edition of Blake's illustrations of the Book of Job: both elegant (with twenty black-and-white heliotype plates) and expensive (ten dollars). The introduction and notes, leaning frankly on other works, showed Norton still committed to high-level popularization as well as original scholarship. He placed Blake at the head of the Romantic line leading to Carlyle, Tennyson, Ruskin, and Burne-Jones. Though wary of Blake's oracular and "impulsive genius," especially in his "more and more delirious and extravagant" later books, Charles believed the "depth of spiritual truth" in Blake's finest illustrations comparable only to "the early Italian masters,—to Giotto, to Orcagna": an observation that explained, or perhaps rationalized, Norton's enthusiasm.[25]

Enthusiasm really had returned to Norton's life, at least episodically; he seemed less restive and more cheerful than at any time since Sue's death. If nothing else, sharing Harvard Yard with three of his sweetest friends reduced the hours available for moping: Frank Child, himself a happier man since Eliot's reforms allowed him to dilute freshman composition with lectures on English literature; James Lowell, rambling on once again to advanced students about Dante and Old French; and, by lucky coincidence, Chauncey Wright, instructor this year in mathematical physics. Wright's alcoholism had worsened while Charles was in Europe, but his mind kept its keen edge. Friends beyond Harvard also helped in healing. William Dean Howells, who did not belong to Norton's inner circle, proved nonetheless very companionable. Godkin, who did, occasionally visited Cambridge, where his son was about to enter college; then in April his wife died, the blow making New York so painful that Godkin moved to Cambridge four weeks later.

Charles now had within a half-hour's walk all of his American intimates save Curtis; and Curtis stayed at Shady Hill in April when he came to orate for the centennial of the battles of Concord and Lexington. And Curtis's son would enter Harvard in September, guaranteeing paternal visits. In January, Norton was meditating England for the summer; by May he had abandoned the idea—because money had grown short, he told English friends. His need to flee America had also diminished.

The "compulsion to regular work" had done for Norton all he had hoped—and for Harvard all that Eliot hoped. Local esteem for Norton's teaching probably motivated an invitation in March to deliver another series of Lowell Lectures in 1875–76. (Norton chose for his topic church building in the Middle Ages, one more step toward the book he intended.) And Harvard had lived up to Norton's expectations as entirely as he to its. "Full of energy," the university seemed to Charles to be becoming "something like a *real*, & not merely nominal University," to be realizing what his father and Uncle Ticknor had dreamed five decades before: teaching and scholarship of a quality previously "unattainable in America." Given such mutual gratification, it surprised no one when on 8 March the Harvard Corporation voted to establish the envisioned professorship. On 24 March the Overseers concurred, and five days later the Corporation elected Norton professor of the history of art.[26]

Then the Overseers balked. No one questioned competence or character, but Norton's opinions in religion made people wary. Colleges were supposed, if not positively to inculcate Christian doctrine, at least to foster a Christian spirit and to mold Christian morals. Harvard already looked dubious: only vaguely Unitarian, "inclining toward too great laxity of opinions" in religion, and with a chemist not a clergyman as president. Hackles had risen, as all Cambridge knew, in 1870 when Eliot tried to hire the "atheist" John Fiske. (Fiske in fact believed vaguely in God and more precisely in Herbert Spencer.) Cambridge also knew that Norton himself had gone "astray." Should Harvard entrust an unbeliever with the education of the young, especially in a subject so powerfully charged with spiritual and moral voltage as art?[27]

The Overseers were right to suspect that Norton's agnosticism affected his teaching, wrong in the apparent drift of their suspicions. Norton was hardly some village atheist, biding his chance to loft a brick through the windows of Appleton Chapel. Openly to preach disbelief to callow young men not only would violate his implicit pledge to a college still nominally Christian but also might abet moral disorder, and Norton had no wish to push American degeneracy an inch further. Yet agnosticism did shape his aims as teacher. Unlike Clough and Arnold, Norton chanted no dirges over the death of faith; he resembled more closely another friend, Leslie Stephen. Like Stephen, Norton found unbelief liberating—and a goad to reconfiguring the moral nexus of human action.

Norton always believed that the only reliable road to knowledge ran atop the rational, empiricist methods of science that his father had employed to prove the genuineness of the Gospels. And the logic of science, he had concluded by 1869, could offer no knowledge of what transcended material reality, no assurance of a God. Yet neither could science ground human purposes. Human beings imposed their own aspirations on the world, rather than somehow drawing an ethic from their knowledge of it. In this sense, "religion"—that is, the commitments that ruled an individual's life—was intuitive, not empirical.

The truths by which we live, then, flow from human imagination. Ipso facto, these human truths do not compose knowledge; though leading us through objective reality, they remain distinct from it. "Science and imagination cannot quarrel," Norton wrote the following year, "because the imagination is supreme and absolute in its own domain." Given these views, it makes perfect psychological sense that, as Norton's belief in God waned, his commitment to art waxed. At the same time, he thought imagination far from subjective, in the sense of solipsistic. Great art and literature expressed ideals and aspirations to which any well-tuned person would resonate.[28]

And this agnostic conviction fixed the principal aim of his Harvard lectures. Imagination provided the necessary correlate to knowledge: if science was the ship to carry the human race safely through the shoals of the centuries, imagination was its helmsman. Literature and art were the supreme expressions of imagination, ergo, the clearest record of human aspiration. If Norton had his way, they would take the place in college education of the moral philosophy that the Reverend James Walker had taught him thirty years ago.

How deeply into these views, if at all, the Overseers peered is impossible to say. After debating the appointment during three meetings, they finally consented on 5 May 1875; in the final vote, only a single doubtful voice spoke. To have turned down a Bostonian *pur-sang* and President Eliot's cousin to boot would have required a bigger swallow of independence than usual for the Overseers. Yet the cracks in Harvard's Christian foundation gaped more visibly, and Andrews Norton's son had given academic knowledge one more push toward its eventual secularization. Eliot immediately proceeded to the secular rite of consecration for faculty in the modern university, appointing Norton to two committees: one to modernize the marking system, the other to oversee (inevitably) the library. Norton fled to Ashfield.[29]

The summer at Ashfield was quiet, devoted to the children, to groaning about politics with George Curtis, and to work: revising his Harvard course, writing a few reviews for the *Nation,* preparing next fall's Lowell Lectures. Chauncey Wright visited for more than a week in August, as every summer he did: he had become Charles's prime "agent for mental activity," a man to talk with "on all serious & difficult subjects." Charles saw him again at the end of the month when business required a brief trip to Shady Hill. In September, Luigi di Cesnola sent the manuscript of his book on the Cyprus temple excavations for a critical reading; by then Norton was also content-edly absorbed in English cathedrals, which he meant to add to his Italian studies for the Lowell Lectures.[30]

Dire news shattered the peace. On Sunday morning, 12 September, Chauncey Wright's landlady found him slumped over the desk in his Cambridge rooms; within minutes he was dead. Charles believed death "not unwelcome" to Wright; though he was only forty-five, his life was blighted by alcohol. Yet he was a great public loss—"the 'wisest' man we had, and the one who most truly represented the 'philosopher' "—and a profound private blow not just to Charles and his sisters but to the children who had grown so fond of their oversized playmate. Charles "had counted much on the unconscious influence upon them" of Wright's "simplicity of character & clear intelligence" and had hoped that he "might bye & bye give to the children some vivid personal impressions of their mother, for he had been much attached to her." A week or two after the funeral, Norton returned to Shady Hill, heart heavier than when he had left it.[31]

On the twenty-ninth, Norton attended his first faculty meeting, a watershed of sorts. The bents and accidents of his life had backed Norton, at the age of forty-seven, into a defined and seemingly permanent career. As professor, he now taught a pair of courses. Fine Arts 2 continued, with more attention promised to the Italian Renaissance than the cursory final lecture on architecture; it now enrolled eighty-four students, putting it among the college's largest classes. A new Fine Arts 3, "The Rise and Fall of the Arts in Athens and in Venice," developed in finer grain Norton's interest in those two exemplary sites of culture. A small class (seven juniors and seniors), it must have attracted serious students, for all books except *The Stones of Venice* were in French or German, ranging from the archaeologist Adolph Michaelis's treatise on the Pantheon to Jacob Burckhardt's *Kultur der Renaissance in Italien*. The course evidenced Norton's growing fascination with ancient Greece. About this time he began to fill scrapbooks with clippings about excavations of Greek sites—chiefly from British papers, there being scant American interest and no activity in classical archaeology. His own scholarship, however, remained rooted in medieval soil, and at the end of October he began his Lowell Lectures on church building in the Middle Ages.[32]

Two lectures into the series, they abruptly ceased. Once more, Norton's body rebelled. He had been expecting a collapse ever since Susan's death, although he failed to realize until actually breaking down that he had overloaded himself once more. For a month he could do nothing but "rake leaves, play with the children, read a novel or two." In the idle hours he solicited subscribers for a memorial to Chauncey Wright; having published in the *North American* Wright's first philosophical essay, Norton now prepared to edit his friend's *Philosophical Discussions*. By January 1876 he was well enough to settle down to that job and to get back to his teaching, but the Lowell Lectures he prudently postponed to autumn. The long convalescence, too many hours to think, left the world looking grim. Norton appreciated that better health would make him cheerier; but, as matters stood, he had neither Susan nor "mere physical pleasure in the days." Privately, he confessed to preferring death to life, wanting only "to live a few years longer for my children's sake."[33]

Norton could hardly wear this face in public: no weariness could justify retreating from the duties of life so long as he breathed; nor did he have the temperament to sit and mope for long. Late in January he jumped into a row in the *Nation* over Massachusetts's new method of teaching art in the common schools by copying geometric designs. Norton denounced it in Ruskinian terms; divorced from both forms in nature and "expression of individual thought, feeling, and fancy," the system turned children into copying machines. (The *Nation* featured another Norton that spring; Grace at last found an outlet for her intellectual disposition in reviewing books for its pages.) In April, Olmsted called his friend, as expert on the history of architectural styles, into another lengthy public set-to. Olmsted sat on a commission to oversee completion of the New York state capitol at Albany; the American Institute of Architects had condemned the design approved by the commissioners for incongruously mingling Renaissance and Romanesque. Norton judged the commission's plan the lesser of two uglies and weighed in on Olmsted's behalf, while privately advising him to modify the design. The gravity with which all parties received Norton's judgment was palpable. The Harvard appointment had sealed his letters patent as America's leading authority on art.[34]

Even authorities spend most of their hours living ordinary lives. Money was complicating Norton's; in May the need to "economize somewhat strictly" forced him to let the children's governess go. He was also feeling frazzled again, ready for a vacation; but, when the family went to Ashfield in mid-June 1876, he had to stay behind to clean up odds and ends of work and to consult with his colleague Charles Moore, who planned to collect during a study leave in Europe much-needed photographs and casts for the Harvard art department. Then Norton's old Indiana protégé Jonathan Harrison, now pastor of a liberal Unitarian congregation in New Jersey but still asking and receiving constant guidance from Charles, came for a second visit. Not till the end of June could Norton retreat to the western Massachusetts hills. There, the thermometer stayed high, as he liked, and the sky clear. He took seriously the warning that the November breakdown had given, for in large doses even enjoyable intellectual work now brought on at times tenacious headaches. He gave up steady reviewing for the *Nation*, fended off an invitation to lecture at the Yale School of Fine Arts in the early fall, and buckled down to a single task: "my stories of Church building" for the Lowell Lectures.[35]

When the Nortons returned to Shady Hill in September, he kept his prudent counsel. Even the presidential campaign did not lure him from his study. He agreed that Rutherford Hayes showed "a much higher type of character" than the Democrat Samuel Tilden, but at least Tilden's administration would not disgrace the country as Grant's had. Norton discovered that college work "shuts out the campaign"—and almost everything else. Aside from the Lowell Lectures and, in early December, the postponed lecture at the Yale School of Fine Arts, Norton did little besides college work that fall. It sufficed.[36]

Professor Norton had become one of the college's favorite lecturers and not just among undergraduates. Mature Bostonians, chiefly privileged women, often joined his crowded class. Among the regulars sat Isabella Stewart Gardner, a New Yorker who had married an exceptionally rich scion of the Boston patriciate. The rather flash Mrs. Gardner and the fastidious Norton made an odd pair; but she took art seriously, and the two gravitated to each other. Under his tutelage she began buying on the European market rare books, manuscripts, and paintings. From her purchases Norton got the thrill at secondhand of buying beautiful old paintings and the comfort of knowing that his mission to redirect American wealth toward aspirations higher than Worth gowns had made at least one convert.

The primary targets of his preaching remained the undergraduates. These came increasingly from across the country and even overseas, as Harvard's striving to transform itself from a New England college into a national university began to take hold. (One of Norton's students this year was Kaneko Kentaro, a young Japanese of the samurai class.) Most students knew Norton only as a lecturer and stood a little in awe of his "loathing of affectation and vulgarity," his "exquisite precision" of speech and knowledge (traits as susceptible to parody as productive of awe, he would come to discover). But Norton enjoyed interaction with students and encouraged relations beyond the classroom.[37]

For some students he developed into an enduring mentor. One was George Woodberry, class of 1877. Henry Adams and Norton between them dominated Woodberry's Harvard education; but, while Adams soon faded into memory, Norton remained a live influence. Right after graduating, Woodberry went to teach at the University of Nebraska; when he wrote bemoaning "exile" in "crude, raw" Lincoln, Norton told the boy to buck up. Norton never doubted the place was "odious" (he himself would "not willingly pass three days in Lincoln"); but he described his younger self freezing in the warehouses on India Wharf, reminded Woodberry that life might prove "worse than you expected," and pointed out that at least Nebraska offered a chance to observe "Primitive Institutions" at firsthand. Yet he also applauded Woodberry's poems, gently suggested improvements, and sent a piece of his own writing for Woodberry's comment—more to boost morale than in hope of learned critique. He tried to get Woodberry a Harvard fellowship and, failing at that, arranged a job on the *Nation* to bring him back east. Through his letters flowed a stream of advice about everything from Woodberry's ideal aspirations to tactics for managing Godkin. Doubtless all this gratified both Norton's ego and Woodberry's need for a hero to worship. It also helped the young man.[38]

Norton became a master not only to undergraduates and Bostonians hungry for culture but also to young assistant professors avid for advice on research programs or bibliographic arcana: long venerated in cultivated circles as expert on art and Dante, his professorship made him a specifically academic authority. He did not altogether like the transition, feeling uneasy in particular about the tendency to narrow "serious" knowledge to academic expertise. But, however he might kick against the traces, Norton could neither halt the segregation of academic knowledge from the public domain nor escape his own definition by the great world as academic expert.

And, in assuming this role, however ambivalently, he completed a transition that men such as his father had begun. Andrews and Uncle Ticknor had accomplished their scholarship mostly outside of any institutional framework: their research supported by private means, their books aimed largely at a general audience (though a well-educated one). Their public roles as university teachers had little to do with their private scholarship; indeed, both men completed their major works only after abandoning the academy. In all these ways they exemplified the scholars of their generation and of preceding ones. To the extent that one can identify a type of public intellectual authority in the first half of the nineteenth century, that figure remained the clergyman. Andrews's words commanded public respect probably as much from his quasi-clerical status as from his faculty position. Probably he and Ticknor reflexively modeled their own sense of scholarly authority on the clerical sway traditional in Boston.

At the same time, both the elder Norton and Ticknor appear now as transitional figures, almost as prophets of a new dispensation of knowledge. After all, both did wish for American colleges to become more like German universities; both wanted scholarship to make its home in the academy; both hoped that the academic could one day exercise authority qua professor. Andrews insisted in no uncertain terms that the *clergy* bow to academic expertise like his in their interpretations of the Bible.

And, as the cultural authority of the clergy did dribble away over the rest of the century, academic scholars and experts absorbed much of it. Religious faith remained potent in many respects, but it was losing its hold on the public intellectual domain. In consequence, the traditional public role of the minister as intellectual authority became, as it were, privatized. Into the space of high-cultural authority left void by the departing clergy stepped the gentleman scholars, their traditionally private role becoming correspondingly public. Charles Norton had already found himself in that position as Dante scholar, art expert, and editor of the *North American* in the 1860s. More and more after the 1860s, this public intellectual clout localized itself in the new, increasingly research-oriented universities. Nature, degree, and range of influence differed among the humanities, social sciences, and natural sciences; but the general phenomenon expressed itself in all fields. By 1890, for instance, an academic economist such as Richard Ely or Simon

Newcomb had a stronger claim to pronounce authoritatively on public policy than even a hyperactive social gospel minister like Lyman Abbot. Out of the eighteenth-century clergyman had developed the modern academic expert.

This, roughly, was the authority with which Charles Norton now found himself vested. He sometimes sniffed suspiciously at its academic odor. And, if in his laic preaching echoed faintly the old clerical style of community authority from which his role derived, he might have said that he had succeeded where his father had failed: Boston's most distinguished congregation, Harvard, had called him to its pulpit.

This was the last thing on his mind as 1876 drew to its end. Late that fall Jane had fallen sick, with cancer. There was nothing to do but hope and carry on. In February, Charles traveled with James Lowell and Frank Child for the launching of a lecture series Frank was giving at the new Johns Hopkins University in Baltimore. Child and Lowell stayed; Norton returned to take over Lowell's Dante class and to face the fifth anniversary of Sue's death. "Dear Charles," James wrote from Baltimore, "I know how sad a month this must always be to you, & I am almost glad that you find so much hard work before you on your return. It isn't a medicine—there is none—but it *is* an opiate & the only one." Norton was becoming addicted to work. He added two more to a full lot of jobs: raising money for a statue of George Sand in France and working (with Curtis) to try to get the old Sanderson Academy in Ashfield reopened, in hope of holding some of the town's brighter young men at home.[39]

And he took up politics again. Not that he cherished hope of any rebirth of civic virtue: in his study late at night with Lowell and Godkin, bosses and bribery blackened the talk; the groans of the three of them, Godkin said, "would make the very dogs of Rome to howl!" There did seem hope of cutting off one source of the swill that fed corruption, by turning the federal civil service from a patronage trough into a corps selected on merit. Norton had faith in President Hayes's commitment to civil service reform but not in his ability to escape the Republican party's political machinery, unless he moved quickly. George Curtis, active in civil service reform since the early 1870s, had Hayes's ear and shrewd political instincts. Probably under his tutelage, Norton, Lowell, Longfellow, and Eliot—the four icons of Cambridge culture—sent in March a telegram calculated to reinforce the good intentions Hayes had just expressed in his inaugural address. A few months later, Charles (coordinating with Curtis's lobbying) sent the president a pointed letter urging the cleansing of the Augean stables called the New

York Custom House. The long twilight battle against American materialism required of the dutiful soldier willingness to skirmish on electoral as
well as academic terrain.[40]

And to soldier on through personal travail. In late April, Lowell stopped
at Shady Hill to visit Jane and found her "as cheerful and affectionate as
ever." The next day she took to her room and never came out; in the early
afternoon of 12 May she died. The children were old enough to feel the loss
of a surrogate mother (Eliot would turn fourteen in July, and baby Richard was five); but Jane's death naturally hit her mother and Grace harder.
Charles, as usual, kept his feelings bound and his eye on his duty to the
family.[41]

A very different sort of loss, mixed with pleasure, followed. Lowell's
distinction as the country's "first literary man" had at last been crowned with
a diplomatic appointment (as used to be the quaint and charming custom of
American presidents); in July he sailed for Madrid. No friend could have left
a larger hole in Norton's life. Charles, at the Locusts keeping an eye on his
mother, could not see him off.

That summer, young Eliot spread his wings on a wagon trip through
New England, under the broader wing of a trusted Ashfield man. So, more
glumly, did Sara Sedgwick; twenty-seven years old and evidently unhappy
(though for no evident reason), she left for England to recover her equanimity. The family was slipping into new configurations. The country was,
too—and desperately. Economic depression struck hard and wide; labor
troubles multiplied, strikes turned violent, guns fired. Riot confirmed Norton's diagnosis of the modern condition: "we are face to face with difficult social questions which our institutions are not framed to meet & to
answer."[42]

As September faded, he turned back to the task of forming the young
men who might begin to develop fitter solutions. Along with his six fine arts
lectures he now had Lowell's Dante course as a permanent assignment, one
evening each week. It kept him busy, left him weary. His dense network of
English connections and his growing visibility as an intellectual tourist
attraction exacted their own cost. "The Englishmen begin to arrive," he
groused to Curtis in early October; and from now on the annual flood would
swell steadily in volume. The 1877 drifters at least proved "very pleasant
ones," including Darwin's friend, the botanist Joseph Hooker. From the
Darwins themselves a week or so later came news "absolutely unexpected"
and happy. Sara Sedgwick had engaged herself to William Darwin, Charles
and Emma's banker son; she would henceforth live in England. About the

same time, Godkin decided to return to New York. With Sara, Edwin, and James gone, Shady Hill began to look denuded. Norton found himself "far more solitary" in Cambridge than ever before, alone in his study with Turner's drawing of a Margate sunset and Ruskin's sketch of Schaffhausen Falls for company, the secluded scholar more often than the sociable companion.[43]

Certainly there remained social obligations enough—foreign visitors alone guaranteed that—and plenty of committee work at the university. Harvard had just appointed Norton its representative in supervising purchases for the collection of prints bequeathed by Francis Calley Gray. Still more time and thought was required by planning for Harvard's next step "toward the University of the future": the establishment of a "thorough, though at present, modest" program of graduate study, a move probably influenced by the new Johns Hopkins University's almost stunning commitment to graduate schooling.

> A Committee is working out the details of the scheme, and in a month or two I hope we may issue such a scheme as shall attract students who desire to lay deeper foundations of learning than is practicable in the undergraduate course, and may serve as a means by which the standard of professorial learning & labor shall be steadily raised.

It signified that Norton looked toward "deeper" foundations of learning, not more specialized ones.[44]

Respectably deep foundations underlay a project of his own, of a very new kind for him: a conjectural study of the proportions of the great ruined temple of Zeus at Olympia. He had worked on the paper through the summer, presented it to the American Academy of Arts and Sciences on 10 October 1877, and was now readying it for the press. "The Dimensions and Proportions of the Temple of Zeus at Olympia" appeared in the *Proceedings of the American Academy of Arts and Sciences* in December. First, Norton deduced from French and German surveys of the excavated ruins the likely dimensions of the temple in the unknown architect's plan: diameters at top and bottom of columns; length and breadth of cella; length, breadth, and height of the entire temple; and so forth. He then proceeded, drawing on ancient texts and modern German scholarship, to calculate that these dimensions reflected a rather simple scheme of proportion rooted in Pythagorean harmonies. Finally—after noting that no previous student had observed a Pythagorean schema in any Greek building—he argued that it was "not unlikely" that other Greek architects of Pythagorean persuasion, seeking to conform "their designs to the principles of the architecture of the world," had worked to the Pythagorean scale. From a single case study Norton had evolved a testable hypothesis of real import for classical research. Probably, in light of later information, he argued wrongly; but he argued plausibly within the expert knowledge of his day. The article was the tour de force of a ripened scholar.[45]

It also evidenced Norton's ever growing interest in ancient Greece. He now laid avid hands on photographs of objects unearthed by excavations in progress; he pulled strings to abet Cesnola's continuing dig in Cyprus. His Fine Arts 3, initially devoted to both Athens and Venice, became in 1876–77 "The Arts of the Age of Pericles" and in 1877–78 simply "Ancient Art." Yet Greece added to, rather than displaced, old interests; on top of his Harvard courses in the spring, Norton stacked lessons on Dante "to a class of ladies" in Boston.[46]

All this time, his mother worsened. In January an embolism caused a stroke, and Catharine lost much of her ability to speak. Louisa came every day from Boston; but, on the heels of Jane's death, the stroke still laid a great burden on Grace. At forty-three, she looked forward bleakly to sharing Shady Hill with no adult companion other than Charles; "the hardest experience in the lot of an unmarried woman," her brother vaguely understood, "the sense of essential loneliness."[47]

In March, Charles received a "most tender" note from Ruskin; but, putting it down, he picked up a newspaper and read a telegraphic report that Ruskin had fallen seriously ill; that evening news arrived of his death, "an unspeakable loss." For four days Charles grieved, before learning that the report was wrong.[48]

The truth proved grievous enough. John Simon wrote from Ruskin's home at Brantwood to tell Charles that his friend had gone insane; though he was recovering, it looked doubtful that he would ever write again. In these days a long-gestated plan came to appear almost a memorial to Norton's dearest English friend, though in fact it was simply one more of Charles's efforts to bring art seriously before his fellow citizens: a facsimile printing of his plates of Turner's *Liber Studiorum*, by the new autotype process. The edition was small, for Norton wanted no "great & immediate sale" but only to ensure that "serious students of drawing" had access to it. Nor did it turn into a memorial. Ruskin made an unexpectedly rapid recovery, though Charles continued to doubt his friend's ability to manage himself, unconvincing even in Ruskin's sanest moments.[49]

It had been a draining winter, and Norton hungered for the annual hills.

But as usual he had to stay at Shady Hill working when Grace took Cath-arine and the children to Ashfield. Labor was not uninterrupted. On Friday evening, 14 June, he gave a dinner for Howells and ten days later went to another at the Childs' for President and Mrs. Gilman of Johns Hopkins; the next morning the Gilmans came to see Norton's pictures "& were very pleasant." So were some of his academic chores, for Norton was hatching "a large plan for work in Greece." He was nonetheless glad to get to Ashfield when June exhausted itself.[50]

ELEVEN

Fresh Foundations of Learning, 1878–1882

All year Charles had "been conscious of growing old," but Ashfield's restorative powers softened the grip of age. His brood clustered round (except for Eliot, in nearby Amherst at "Dr. Saveur's summer school of languages"), the girls playing with visiting cousins, Rupie and Dick with the poultry. Their father read, wrote, made an occasional trip to Cambridge, and lounged on the grass watching Jupe fetch sticks thrown in the pond. George Curtis supplied a rejuvenative daily companion; as usual, friends like Frank Child came for a few days now and then. With Curtis only a summer comrade, Godkin back in New York, and Lowell in Madrid, Child alone among his intimates did Charles still see in everyday life. And Child and Norton, without at all cooling in their affection, seemed in middle age to navigate life on slightly different bearings.[1]

Charles hardly lacked friends, but he kept up with them mostly by letter. Not Ruskin; as he drifted in and out of sanity, his letters dwindled in apparent number and grew in eccentricity. The old affection shone through; sometimes the old give-and-take about books and buildings resurfaced; but Ruskin had become more worry than companion. Ned Burne-Jones made a poor correspondent, writing warmly but rarely and briefly. John Simon's letters did "efface the Atlantic with wonderful success," even more Leslie Stephen's—sinewy things, sharing news of intellectual affairs, personal life, politics. Yet the best letters hardly provide much of a matrix for an animating friendship: the give-and-take of daily intercourse, the burnishing that results from rubbing opinion against opinion, habit against habit, personality against personality.[2]

This being said, Norton's transatlantic links remained remarkably dense and supple. Longfellow wanted news of Fanny Lowell in Madrid: Norton forwarded a "letter from John Field which I received from Leslie Stephen this morning." His correspondents extended well beyond real friends such as Mountstuart Grant-Duff, Donald MacKay, and Edward Fitzgerald to ac-

quaintances ranging from the philologist F. Max Müller to the Master of
Balliol Benjamin Jowett, from Sir Frederick Pollock, the Dantist, to Arthur
Stanley, the dean of Westminster. Their letters left Norton longing for
Europe but also kept him fixed near the center of Victorian high culture.
Correspondence, though, was chiefly a summer pleasure; the college year
left little leisure for writing chatty letters.[3]

In 1878–79, with Lowell gone, Norton now handled instruction in
Dante, meeting on Tuesday evenings with eight "young graduates" and
seniors. This "picked set" studied "the Interpretation of the Divina Commedia, chiefly by means of Dante's Prose Works and the Commentators of
the Fourteenth Century." Norton listed this colloquium among the new
graduate courses in the catalogue: one more step toward realizing his father's
dream of grafting advanced study on to Harvard.[4]

His art history courses had grown so popular that probably a majority of
undergraduates now enrolled in one at some time during their four years. In
response, Norton retuned the courses to different levels of interest. Two
broad surveys—one covering ancient art, the other medieval and Renaissance art—led up to a pair of more specialized offerings, one in Greek art
and one in Romanesque and Gothic art, a survey and a higher-level course
to be given each year. All four still demanded "ability to use a German textbook," though for *what* the typical student used it makes a nice question,
since football and drinking left Harvard undergraduates few hours for foreign languages. Norton had no real alternative, since the new field of art
history lacked respectable texts in English. Before spring semester ended,
he found a partial remedy, arranging with Harpers to publish a translation
of Franz Reber's history of ancient art. One of Norton's bright young graduates, Joseph Thacher Clarke, agreed to do the job under his mentor's
supervision.[5]

This was the least of Norton's contributions to the new American universities that spring. He stood ready to launch an academic design of heroic
proportions: the "large plan for work in Greece" of which he had hinted the
previous June. The more deeply antiquity cast its spell on Norton, the more
irritated he grew that the United States took no part "in the vast and
stimulating increase of knowledge of early times." It grated on his patriotic
nerve that the "explorations of English, Italian, French, and German inves-
tigators" were "rapidly changing the face of the ancient world" while American scholars sat with their noses pressed against the window. Norton could
understand "lack of original work" in classical philology and art, given the
inadequacy of American libraries and museums. But archaeology—a field

that had fascinated him for thirty years—was another matter; it had become an "exact science" only within his own lifetime. Here, America "might labor on equal footing with others"; here, "she might do her part in the common interest of learning."[6]

Norton meant to egg her on. In 1878 he had asked the Greek government to allow a few recent Harvard graduates to excavate Delphi, then still buried. Happily for Delphi, the Greeks turned him down, while suggesting that other sites might be available to Harvard shovels. At this point, Norton's long experience with projects like the Loyal Publication Society showed itself. After mulling things over for several months, he enlisted a number of names resonant around Boston to promote the scheme. His old friend (and Loyal Publication Society collaborator) Martin Brimmer, president of the young Museum of Fine Arts, together with C. C. Perkins, the city's most visible entrepreneur of culture, helped to attach the local arts community. Augustus Lowell and Thomas Gold Appleton brought on board other monied Bostonians with no special interest in old statues. President Eliot and Dean Gurney gave Harvard's stamp. F. W. Putnam, curator of the Peabody Museum of Ethnology at Harvard, and William Watson Goodwin, Eliot Professor of Greek, provided a patina of expertise. These men, and a few others picked with equal finesse, put their names to a printed circular letter proposing a "Society for Archaeological Research."[7]

Over a hundred recipients—few hampered by poverty—showed interest; and a substantial fraction of them met in Boston's financial district on the morning of 10 May 1879 to organize the society. Its "chief objects," Norton told them, were "to increase the interest in Classical Studies by enabling competent persons to make investigations in Greece, Egypt and other countries and to stimulate interest in antiquity and the arts, which proceeded from it." But neither did Norton mean to ignore America's own antiquities. His youthful ardor for the Mound Builders possibly still flickered; and, anyway, Francis Parkman and F. W. Putnam stood at his elbow speaking up for American Indian archaeology. Norton wished across the board "to increase the knowledge of the early history of mankind, to quicken the interest in classical and biblical studies, to promote an acquaintance with the prehistoric antiquities of our own country, and to enlarge the resources of our universities and museums."

He envisioned ratcheting archaeological work in all spheres up to a level of serious research unknown in the United States. The new organization would assume the role of promoter and director of "archaeological investigation and research": sending out its own expeditions, assisting "independent explorers," publishing scholarly reports of these researches, seizing upon "any other means which may from time to time appear practicable." "Plenty" of people stood ready to pitch right in, Norton assured the meeting. His enthusiasm conjured up "several trained archaeologists" to lead the (more realistic) band of Harvard youngsters "who would prepare themselves with the best classical teachers for the work." If all this sounded slightly breathless, the veteran organizer revealed himself when it came to money: the first requisite was a rock-solid foundation. Norton wanted 250 members, ten thousand dollars in the bank to start, and five thousand dollars a year thereafter.[8] Then the new society might consider its first project.

Norton had one in mind. Joseph Clarke, the young translator of Reber's art history textbook, and his friend Francis Bacon, both trained as architects, had already set off in their own sailboat "to examine all the Doric ruins in Greece and its neighboring countries," hoping with charming naivete "to throw light on the many still unsettled questions of Doric Art." It says much about their commitment to classical archaeology that Clarke and Bacon's initial plan had been to raft down the Mississippi together.[9]

A week later, a second meeting adopted a constitution and unanimously elected Norton himself, who had at least published an article on Greek temples, as president. Parkman, Goodwin, and the architect William Ware (who taught at the Massachusetts Institute of Technology) brought to the executive committee the puny archaeological competence Boston had to offer. And the committee was very much a local one, seven of the nine members having graduated from Harvard within several years of Norton. Yet their president already aspired to something larger.

For Norton grasped the decisive fact that American scholarship of all sorts was drifting away from its old local moorings into new national and international seas. Any "narrow local interest" would capsize his aspirations. It was probably he who broke with the Boston elite's persistent inward-looking orientation and baptized the organization the Archaeological Institute of America; with that name, he argued, "our agents would then be considered as representing a national and not merely a local Society." Besides, he pointed out, "similar Societies abroad had similar titles." In succeeding months Norton strove to make the name a reality, while a broadside went out stressing the founders' desire to "include associates from all parts of the country." No American had a national network of acquaintance better suited to that purpose than Norton. Yet not only had Norton's friendships grown far beyond Boston, the center of gravity of American intellectual life had also begun to shift: it was college and university officers that Norton

strove especially to enlist. Scores of letters added to Norton's other obligations, slowing his writing on medieval church building. Normally, summer
provided uninterrupted hours for scholarship, but the work of building up
the AIA disturbed this one.[10]

So, too, did another recently assumed duty: that of helping to sustain
Ashfield as a viable little republican community by supporting its revived
Sanderson Academy. With Curtis's help, Norton organized a fund-raising
dinner to coincide with the opening of the school year in early September,
soliciting Massachusetts luminaries to lend their oratorical talents to the
cause. The thing turned out so successful that George and Charles decided
to repeat the dinner the next year. What began as a one-off affair of local
interest soon grew into an annual forum for political and social criticism
by renowned speakers, an event covered on the front pages of the New
York dailies.[11]

Behind the public activism personal anxieties built up. In Madrid typhus
struck Fanny Lowell; she almost died, rallied, then went violently mad.
Charles helplessly longed to join James—and would have but for Catharine's
state. In early August his mother took "a decided change for the worst"; she
grew confused, suffered hallucinations, and in lucid moments wept in "an-
guish at her own mental weakness." By early September, wildly delirious,
she no longer recognized her children; only opiates kept her manageable.
Somehow in the midst of all this Norton found time to peck away at his
scholarship; and, in mid-September, finally, he contracted with Harper to
publish *Historical Studies of Church-Building in the Middle Ages.*[12] Shortly
afterward, Charles and Grace brought their mother home to Shady Hill,
though she was long past knowing where she was. Just after midnight on the
twenty-fifth, her breathing quietly stopped. Everyone recognized it as a
"great blessing."[13]

His mother's death made Charles think how much of his own life had
slipped into the past, "on its way to dust." The children were growing up:
Eliot taller than his father, looking forward to college; Sally wearing a
woman's full-length dress; even Richard a schoolboy in long trousers. Nor
could Charles long stave off the breaking up of the Shady Hill estate. Rising
expenses strained "much reduced" means; hawking pieces of his art collection only postponed the inevitable. Norton still found comfort in the "cher-
ishing of ideal aims, in the clear recognition of the rarity and preciousness of
beauty and of joy"; but on the other side of that coin he saw as clearly "the
solitude, the weariness, the prosaic course of daily life"—life without Susan,
life without the reassurance of religion. Giving up hope of a life after death

left him, he thought, "gladder than other men in the gladness of the earth." But he knew this gladness to be fleeting and that in the end "life can afford no consolation."[14]

His personality was stiffening. The carapace he had exuded after Susan's death was now hardened by age and circumstance. Old friends were fading from his life: Ruskin erratically mad, Mr. Longfellow past seventy and ailing, Lowell (transferred in January 1880 from Madrid to the Court of St. James) far distant. New ones played nothing like the same roles; increasingly protégés and disciples surrounded Norton. Only Child remained as a daily close friend; only Grace challenged him at home. The ever adaptable and endlessly befriending young Charles Norton was becoming Professor Norton, crustier, less resilient, less able to listen. As sweet as ever to those who knew him best, the professor still helped many others with money, with books, with his fabled connections; but some generosity of spirit had slipped away. Accustomed now to accepting admiration, to speaking from authority, he became in his judgments a bit harsher, less pliant. Among people who remembered Andrews, Charles began to remind them of his father.

His activities had likewise settled into a pattern more defined, less fluid, than in earlier years. He still wrote for the *Nation* but only about art, classical studies, and Dante; tracts on foreign policy and unhealthy tenements vanished in favor of an annotated Michelangelo bibliography. In October 1879, Norton mounted in a local gallery an exhibition of Ruskin's drawings (successful enough to move to the Museum of Fine Arts in February and then on to New York); in November he went to New York himself to lecture to the American Institute of Architects. This potpourri hardly qualified as academic specialization *auf Deutsch;* far from it. Yet Charles now spent almost all of his own time nursing scholarship and high culture.[15]

For he had little faith left in politics or any other short-term hope for humankind. Culture had for Norton largely—not entirely—subsumed politics. One begins to see in him *in parvo* the detached scholars and alienated critics who came to dominate American intellectual life in the twentieth century. Aside from teaching, he poured most of his energy in the fall and winter of 1879–80 into the new AIA: in October pushing the executive committee to recruit young men from several colleges for an expedition to Greece, in December starting a long correspondence with the foremost American anthropologist, Lewis Henry Morgan, to get guidance for research into American Indian antiquities. Norton had not abandoned more traditional forms of citizenship; good republicans could yet plant the seeds of distant hope. In April 1880 he went to his district convention to elect delegates to the Republican National Convention, and he joined other reform-minded Independent Republicans in distributing tracts aimed at scotching the presidential candidacies of Grant and Blaine. But only left-over scraps of time went into politics.

With one revealing exception. Frederick Olmsted, still a good friend from the *Nation*'s early days, had for a decade agitated to get the New York state government to protect Niagara Falls. Pulp mills and factories, hotels, signboards, and hucksters despoiled more of its environs each year. At last in January 1879 an official inquiry began on both sides of the border, and the New York investigatory commission enlisted Olmsted to help draft a plan. In October he wrote asking Norton to aid in collecting names of "the really notable men of the time of all countries" on a petition in support of Niag-ara's preservation. Sheer weight of eminence, Olmsted hoped, would cow the Canadian and American authorities into submission.[16]

Few projects could have attracted Norton more strongly. The strategy fitted his belief in the power of cultural and social leaders; the assigned task exploited his organizing talent and his web of international acquaintance; the falls themselves had awed him since young manhood. Their preserva-tion appealed not only to his love of nature but also to his anxiety about the moral health of his countrymen. At a time "when wealth easily acquired is vulgarizing and impoverishing the spirit of the community," the Niagara campaign crackled with moral electricity. Forming the collective will to save this beauty from rapacious capitalism would amass some counterweight to materialism and hyperindividualism, striking a blow for the things of the spirit and the spirit of community. Politics could invigorate culture and culture assist a healthier politics. Norton put his pen to work; he scoured Massachusetts himself; he enlisted Mountstuart Grant Duff to collect names in London, Edward Childe to collect them in Paris, and Littré to collect them from the Académie Française. One thread in his transatlantic web led to another. Darwin asked Lord Derby; Derby suggested canvassing the House of Lords; it was done. Norton found himself as deeply involved as Olmsted.[17]

Meanwhile, the research begun nearly a decade before in the Sienese archives reached its end. In May, Norton put the final touches on *Historical Studies of Church-Building in the Middle Ages: Venice, Siena, Florence*, though Harpers withheld publication till fall. "If I have the leisure during the following year I mean to follow it up with further studies of the same sort of Cluny, St. Denis, and Chartres, for which I have most of the material ready."

In the event, the following year stretched into nine, and the study of Cluny never did appear.[18]

Church-Building itself confirmed a decisive turning both in Norton's life and in American erudition. For Norton, publication perfected his self-identification as a university-based scholar. He stopped pretending that research and writing served mainly to dull the pain of Susan's loss, tacitly conceded that the work itself had become a vocation. For American scholarship, the book, together with Henry C. Lea's studies in church history, established serious, document-based research in medieval history. *Church-Building,* moreover, broke with the institutional approach favored in Lea's work and in medievalist scholarship in Europe; its approach resembled more nearly that of a book just translated into English (though once assigned in Fine Arts 3 in the original German), the pathbreaking *Civilization of the Renaissance in Italy* (1860) by the Swiss scholar Jacob Burckhardt. Norton perceived in Italy's medieval cities "a close parallel" among the evolution of language, the development of literature and the arts, and political and social change. Uniting political and institutional developments, social and cultural history, art and literature, he staked out a broad field that a twentieth-century scholar might recognize as "medieval studies."[19]

For this was not the dabbling of a gentlemanly amateur. The chapter on Venice, relying on printed documents rather than archival research, was thinner than those on Siena and Florence; but in general Norton's footnotes evinced firm command of primary materials as well as of specialized scholarly literature in English, German, French, Italian, and Latin. In contrast to Ruskin, who believed himself able as "a gleaner and guesser" to comprehend intuitively an ancient Greek's mind, Norton swore allegiance to his father's philological ideal of expert erudition. (Now in a lucid period, Ruskin said that he "felt a chill from the tone" of *Church-Building.)* But neither did Norton succumb to the temptation to assimilate all science to natural science, which seduced Victorians as eminent as Herbert Spencer and Henry Adams. He distinguished sharply between the human sciences, with their interpretative approach and philological roots, and the very different methods fitted to the natural sciences seeking general laws. While admiring natural science, he disdained the fashion for explaining human affairs in terms of Darwinian evolution or thermodynamics. Such analogies "consist merely in terms, and not in any real similarity of relations," and only lead to "confusion of thought."[20]

At the same time, his philological approach opened a vista wide enough to satisfy any longing for breadth of vision. Believing that an "intrinsic similarity of spirit" had united medieval Europe, Norton thought the historian able to illuminate the whole by elucidating any part. (This contrast between medieval unity and modern fragmentation appealed to Henry Adams, who a quarter century later made it the mainspring of his great *Mont-Saint-Michel and Chartres.*) No scholar could adequately interpret the duomo of Siena without knowing the history of the city, but the duomo's story in turn helped to explain the city's. Forms of art—Gothic architectural structures, for instance—expressed deep cultural traits that resurfaced "in remote and varied fields of thought and of action"; studying its art therefore illumined a culture at large. But by the same token a student could not penetrate any art without knowing the culture that produced it. Here reappeared in different dress the hermeneutic circle basic to Andrews's scholarship and to all textual philology. Norton approached "church-building, not merely as a study of separate edifices, but as a clear and brilliant illustration of the general conditions of society, and especially of its moral and intellectual dispositions."[21]

And he argued that these "moral and intellectual dispositions" merited close attention from modern Americans. The medieval church's ideals of human equality and of reciprocal aid, however impotent in preventing the "oppression of the weak, the misery of the poor," still offered a salutary lesson to Americans besotted with social climbing and self-seeking. Likewise, the civic spirit of a proudly independent community, asserted in the cathedrals of Florence and Siena, might remind Americans of the republican virtue they, too, had once cherished. The vaunted individualism of the Renaissance became, in Norton's telling, a fatal expression of the "pride and wealth of special families or individuals," signaling the death of "the spirit and devotion of the whole community."[22]

Above all, Norton wanted his readers to observe the corrosion that material motives worked on a community. The engine of change in his story was the rise of wealth and luxury, depressing faith and art. When the "new thought of the Renaissance" sapped the "ancient faith," when the desire for "material prosperity" overwhelmed higher motives, the Italian city-states lost their communal spirit, their morality, their liberty, and in the end their artistic greatness—for art could not long survive the death of the ideal. The historian refrained from openly mounting the pulpit; Norton hardly needed to ape Savonarola to make his point.[23]

Having a moral point did not reduce *Church-Building* to a polemic, yet the melding of ethical sensitivity with advanced scholarship did suggest how the book carried the anima of the *North American Review* into the burgeoning domain of the research university. Norton's potential audience embraced New Englanders of literary bent, wanting amusement and instruction; but it stretched far beyond to include professors in Berkeley and Oxford, historians in Saint Louis and London, equipped to weigh and make use of his work. His own university now boasted a faculty of 150, six times larger than when he had gone to college, three times larger than when Charles Eliot had taken the helm a decade ago. And that faculty now taught graduate students, awarded the Ph.D. for demonstrated competence in research, and was itself increasingly apt to be judged on its own capacities to advance knowledge.

Norton grasped as fully as anyone this shift toward the research university, applauded it, promoted it. When he sent Ruskin the first volume of Francis Child's great *English and Scottish Popular Ballads*, Charles called it "a masterpiece of pleasant scholarship and character"; but he also warned him that it was "not a book for boys & girls, or for amusement, but a learned book, and it may not suit your fancy." Yet to say that Norton grasped as fully as anyone the character of the new university is not to say a great deal. Its character slipped and undulated, very much in flux, formless if not void, awaiting shaping hands. Even the distinction between graduate and undergraduate students remained foggy, the definition and boundaries of "research" unclear.[24]

Norton's reputation and connections put him near the heart of this inchoate complex of institutions and scholars. His Anglo-American intellectual network overlapped the newer scholarly one; and, despite its international scope, the academic nexus remained personal. Young scholars seeking advice or jobs "naturally" turned to Norton (as one wrote), while senior administrators wrote him for help in filling posts. Waldo Pratt illustrates the emergent system. In 1879 he applied for a graduate fellowship at Johns Hopkins University to pursue "aesthetic & archaeological studies." Its president, Gilman, forwarded Pratt's dossier to Norton with the gloss "We know of no one in this country so capable of advising him as you." Pratt's writing impressed Norton, and Hopkins duly awarded him a fellowship. On this fellowship Gilman sent Pratt to study for a few months under Norton. After Pratt returned to Baltimore, Norton loaned him books, sponsored publication of his essays, and probably helped him obtain a job at the Metropolitan Museum in New York in 1880. Norton's relation with Pratt resembled that with Woodberry, though far briefer; but, where Woodberry had met the professor in the traditional way, the new national university system had channeled Pratt to Norton. For all its novelty, nationalized scholarship absorbed older personal networks rather than devising new bureaucratic ones.[25]

The same pattern revealed itself in Norton's work for the Archaeological Institute, which ate up more and more of his time. By the time of the AIA's first annual meeting on 15 May 1880, Norton had given the Americanist work a strong initial shove, commissioning from Lewis Henry Morgan a survey of "the Houses of the American Aborigines" and, on Morgan's advice, engaging the anthropologist Adolph Bandelier to undertake investigations in New Mexico. Norton also persuaded the celebrated Western explorer John Wesley Powell, who had recently completed his influential *Report on the Lands of the Arid Region of the United States* and now directed the Smithsonian's Bureau of Ethnology, to address the annual meeting itself.[26]

Norton had expected Major Powell to inspire the troops with zeal for American archaeology; instead, his talk nearly provoked mutiny. Charles Perkins, a leader in the Museum of Fine Arts, rose to insist that the pressing need to buy classical antiquities for museums required postponing Americanist research indefinitely. Francis Parkman shot back that the AIA aimed at "the acquisition of Knowledge and not the acquisition of objects or works of art." The knowledge wanted, another member retorted to Parkman, "was not that of barbarians but that of cultivated races which had preceded us"; it would do no good to collect "all the pottery ware, kitchen utensils, and tomahawks" that the Indians ever made. This last gentleman, Parkman drily observed, "failed to comprehend the bearing of Ethnological investigation," which illuminated "the evolution of the human race" and "its civilization." Norton hastily lathered on soothing words; seeing "no reason for jealousy or division in the Society," he proposed raising eight thousand dollars immediately for two expeditions. The first would study pueblo life in New Mexico, a subcommittee chaired by Parkman being named to arrange this. The second would excavate either Epidaurus, in the Peloponnesus, or Assos, a Greek city in Asia Minor south of Troy; Crete appeared a third possibility.[27]

And, in truth, these last were the prospects that tickled the hairs on Norton's nape. "The occupied & the ruined Pueblos, & the Cliff dwellings" of the American Southwest did fascinate him; but the ancient Greek world commanded his attention. By July he had settled on Assos and decided to put Joseph Clarke, conveniently on the spot with his shipmate Francis Bacon, in charge of the excavation; by August, Norton was enlisting volunteers among the country's classically minded young college graduates. One of them, a Virginian with a recent Munich Ph.D. in philology, actually had qualifications. Charles also enrolled his old friend William Stillman from Newport days, now United States consul in Crete and an avid amateur archaeologist, as AIA "agent" to explore the unexcavated ruins at Knossos. Now remained only raising the money and securing permission from the Ottoman authorities. Norton was an old hand at fund-raising; dealing with Turkish ministers and pashas to get the required *firman* (official authorization) supplied a new and protracted agony. Month by month Norton's administrative correspondence swelled in volume; few college presidents handled more.[28]

Smaller jobs abounded, too, even after Norton reached the Locusts in early June. George Woodberry needed help with a history of wood engraving he was writing. ("For a wonder," said Woodberry several months later, "I have no favor to ask of you.") The English publisher Macmillan was bringing out an edition of Lowell's poems, and Charles advised James on selections, wielding the ax relentlessly: "The student of you will always be able to find the omitted pieces, the lover of the best in poetry will be thankful to you [or to Norton] for selecting your best for him." Only of Dante and Shakespeare, Charles judged, was "a part not better than the whole!" The annual Ashfield Academy Dinner came on 19 August; a couple of weeks later severe headaches began to torment Norton, hounding him back to Cambridge. There seemed no recourse but to abandon teaching that autumn. Finally, his physician relented, allowing Norton to offer his courses "on condition of giving up all other work."[29]

"All other work" had to exclude the AIA. The Assos expedition could scarcely await Norton's recovery, especially since his son Eliot had "caught the enthusiasm for the classics" and decided to join it. On 28 December a special meeting of the executive committee, with Joseph Clarke present, voted the expedition's funds and fixed its goal. Norton said "that the Committee laid no weight upon the prospect of finds"—so much for Perkins and the Museum of Fine Arts—but wanted "a more scientific result, giving us a distinct knowledge of the general characteristics of a site of Greek occupancy." A party at Shady Hill that same evening honored the young men setting out for Assos. Everything stood ready save for permission to dig. When Eliot boarded the *Rhein* in New York harbor in February, on his way to rendezvous with Clarke in Munich, a promised *firman* still eluded documentary reality.[30]

Norton's health had by that time improved enough for him to take on other projects. One had simmered for some time. Norton having spoken to the students in his advanced Dante course about the good work that an association to promote Dante studies might do, some of them offered to pitch in. Mr. Longfellow, though too decrepit for heavy duty, agreed to accept the presidency; and, at his home, Craigie House, he presided over the Dante Society's first meeting on 11 February 1881. Norton expected no great things; encouraging "a few of the better class of students" in the next generation to cherish Dante seemed justification enough.[31]

Only six days before the meeting, a dear friend and fellow-admirer of Dante, Thomas Carlyle, died. Charles helped to arrange a memorial meeting at Harvard, then handled the bequest of Carlyle's books to the college library arranged by Emerson and Norton a decade before. He had scarcely begun to sort out this business when a storm broke in England over the publication, within weeks of the death, of Carlyle's *Reminiscences* by his friend James Anthony Froude, a man whose character and judgment Norton had always suspected. The *Reminiscences* depicted Carlyle's troubled marriage all too clearly, outraged his niece, and incited (so Darwin told Charles) "more talk here than any book which has been published for many years." Norton, holding the privacy of intimate relations almost sacred, found Carlyle's frankness "honorable and precious" but troubling. He could hardly foresee how deeply he would be drawn into this storm.[32]

For now he got himself marginally involved in an extraordinary dramatic production. The previous fall, inspired by an Oxford performance of *Agamemnon*, a group of Harvard professors and students decided to stage *Oedipos Tyrannos* in Sophocles's Greek. Norton's health kept him from an active part; but he thought it "a great gain for culture that this interest in a classic work should be so strong" and opened his study at Shady Hill to a semipublic Saturday evening rehearsal on 29 January.[33]

The general enthusiasm for "the Greek Play," as it came simply to be called, says much about the resonance of Greek antiquity in Victorian culture. That classical Athens appeared the archetype of modern democracy supplied only a minor reason for Greece's appeal: republican Rome seemed closer to American institutions. Nor does the centrality of classical languages in education go far to explain it: Latin tags tripped off English-speaking tongues far more easily than Greek ones.

Rather, the secret lay in culture. Many of the political, epistemological, logical, and even artistic categories in which Europeans and Americans thought originated in classical Greece. True, the profoundly alien character of ancient Greece, especially its religion, was beginning to be glimpsed by a few. Nevertheless, Greece appeared *fons et origo* of what people such as

Norton were starting to conceive as the coherent intellectual and artistic tradition of European civilization, running from Herodotus to Harvard Yard. Norton tended to think of Greek architecture or statuary as embodying canons of taste rising above time and place, norms that expressed themselves again, more or less imperfectly, in later cultures that history produced in Florence and Rome, in London and Boston. The classical bias of education did certainly foster this way of thinking (and the tutelage of Rome to Greece directed the spotlight toward Hellas); but schools had for centuries dosed students with Homer. What changed in the nineteenth century was the larger cultural context. Christianity was contracting as a defining element in intellectual culture. Victorians looked for spirituality and timeless values elsewhere and nowhere more naturally than to the supposed source of their civilization.

Six thousand of them jammed the performances of *Oedipos Tyrannos* in Harvard's Sanders Theatre. Almost no one understood the words, yet scalped tickets sold for ten times their original price. New England's literary pantheon blessed opening night; every major American newspaper carried an account; telegraphed reports crossed the Atlantic. Norton thought the play "the most interesting event in College life and studies for years." In such a climate, an organization like the Archaeological Institute began life with cachet.[34]

Yet, while the AIA shared this general enthusiasm for Greek culture, it also advocated a specific scholarly approach to the ancient world, long established in Europe but novel in America. Hoping to "raise the scientific character" of American work on North American as well as European antiquity, Norton took as model for archaeological work such German expeditions as those to Samothrace and Pergamon. Classical texts—the "traditional modes of investigation"—had now to take second place to excavated artifacts; for "the fine arts" gave insight into "the life and thought of the ancient world" more "vivid, precise, and comprehensive" than the written word.[35]

The Ottoman government barred one source of insight in March when it refused a *firman* for Knossos (insuring that the discovery of Minoan civilization would await the excavations of Sir Arthur Evans two decades later). Norton barely kept his irritation under control. At last the sun broke through in May, the Turkish authorities granting the AIA permission to dig for two seasons at Assos. Clarke's "admirably made up expedition" already waited on the ground, Eliot included. His Papa dared not dream of "such magnificent discoveries" as the Germans had made at Pergamon; but he did expect "results of considerable interest" from "the thorough study of the temple, the theatre, the walls, and the tombs of the city."[36]

A scheme grander and more enduring than the dig at Assos now preoccupied Norton. From the institute's founding he had seen in his mind's eye "a permanent corps" of American classicists in the Aegean, a vision that soon developed into a concrete proposal for "an American School of Classical Literature, Art and Antiquities at Athens." The AIA annual meeting in May 1881 approved a committee to seek the cooperation of American universities in establishing such an entity. Professors composed a majority of its members. Norton never meant the Athens school as a place solely to train archaeologists and to mount expeditions, for he never conceived archaeology as an isolated discipline. Only one "branch of the study of antiquity," classical archaeology "could not be properly pursued without corresponding pursuit of the other great branch of the study," ancient languages and literature. Budding American scholars needed broad advanced training in the "single indivisible whole" of classical studies.[37]

Within weeks Norton and his associates had plotted their approach. He would try to raise twenty-five thousand dollars from the usual philanthropic individuals, while the institute would solicit leading Eastern universities— Harvard, Yale, Brown, Johns Hopkins, Cornell, Columbia—to support the school for an experimental decade, each supplying in rotation a professor of Greek to direct it. The AIA had by no means sidelined its enthusiastic amateurs, but even they could not miss the decisive shift of its center of gravity to an academic core: one more signal of the changing structure of knowledge in the United States and the rising power of university-based research in intellectual life.

The AIA, though certainly dominating Norton's horizon, did not blot out all other interests. Backed by the infant Dante Society, Charles had dusted off his almost twenty-year-old plan to publish Benvenuto da Imola's fourteenth-century *Comment* on the *Divina Commedia;* in early June he arranged for Marsh in Florence to have the Laurentian Library manuscript copied and himself began soliciting subscribers on both sides of the Atlantic to bear the cost of publication. Niagara, too, thundered for attention: New York's governor came out against preserving the falls, and Olmsted nearly lost hope. Norton superintended a last-ditch publicity campaign to last through the autumn, hiring a fluent former student to flood the press with articles and letters to the editor (shades of the Loyal Publication Society).

Charles had both Dante and Niagara in hand by 28 June, when George Curtis arrived to receive an honorary LL.D. at Harvard commencement, "an honor that pleased him greatly" and that his friend presumably played a part in arranging.[38]

At last the Locusts and exhausted relief. Norton had, as usual, to put some effort into signing up orators for the annual Academy Dinner (a little easier now that the platform had achieved national recognition); but he spent a good deal of time lounging with George Curtis and chatting with George Woodberry, come for his annual visit. There were two family home-comings—Eliot from his summer in Assos, Lily from a full year with Aunt Sara Darwin in England—and one unpleasant surprise.

Ever since Catharine's death, Grace had roamed restlessly, sometimes staying at the Locusts or Shady Hill, at other times visiting friends across the Northeast. In August she decided to move into her own house; "she has," her brother wrote to Lowell, "painful associations with the old home, and she fancies she will be happier in a new one." Charles thought not; separation from his children would merely bring her unhappiness—even though the distance totaled only several hundred yards down to the Kirkland Street edge of Shady Hill, next to the Childs. Separation from Grace certainly made her brother unhappy; more than ever the master of Shady Hill felt old and alone. That fall Eliot started college, at Harvard of course.[39]

Fortunately for his father there was rarely time to mope. Besides classes and committee meetings, the work of creating the American School of Classical Studies at Athens began in earnest. The organizing committee, chaired by Norton's colleague John Williams White, a professor of Greek at Harvard, met in early October. By then Norton had already commenced the arduous and familiar tasks of prying funds from wealthy pockets and cajoling university presidents into cooperation. He started to see, too, some results from his work for archaeology. A special general meeting of the AIA on 5 November heard reports on Bandelier's New Mexican expedition and on the first season at Assos. Clarke, back from Turkey for the winter, was invited to address the American Institute of Architects on his work. Maybe most satisfying of all to Norton's patriotism, the London *Athenaeum* held up the American work at Assos as an example for the English.

If archaeology satisfied, Dante frustrated. On 1 November a letter arrived from an English colleague warning that "another design is on foot" for printing Benvenuto's *Comment.* Baron Vernon (brother of the Dantist whom Norton had met in London in 1869), hearing of the Dante Society's project, had peevishly resurrected his late father's plan of publishing the manuscript: the very scheme that had scotched Norton's earlier attempt to print the *Comment* in 1864. Given the debt that Dante scholarship owed to Lord Vernon's father, Norton and Longfellow felt it "unbecoming" to interfere with a work in "honor of his memory," even with the copying of the Laurentian manuscript already under way. James Lowell in London railed; Vernon had robbed Charles "of the just honour of being the first to print what has so long been so great a *desideratum.*" Norton was resigned. At least the thing would be in print, and Harvard would have an exact copy of the manuscript.[40]

A storm swirling around the AIA blew away these comparatively small Dante clouds. In November attacks on Joseph Clarke's management of the Assos excavation from members of the expedition began to flood Shady Hill. Clarke was a mere digger, no scientist; he managed supplies badly; Frank Bacon really ran the show while Clarke played his banjo. He was "a libertine of the lowest tastes"; he abused his dog; he nearly drilled a co-worker with a pistol shot. William Stillman, by now at Athens, heard the tales, and with his wonted impetuosity joined the assault. That Clarke offended several of the Harvard boys is clear; that he was an untrained amateur, learning on the job, is equally sure; beyond that, the story grows obscure.[41]

Norton read all the letters, heard Clarke's defense, consulted with the other members of the executive committee. Eliot Norton supported his boss. And the excavation had, after all, succeeded: the temple completely uncovered, its ground plan and elevation deciphered, eleven new pieces of sculpture found. "An important addition to the knowledge of Greek art in one of its most interesting monuments has thus been made," Charles informed John Simon, "beside the acquisition of a considerable number of inscriptions and minor antiquities." Clarke would remain at the helm for the second season of the dig.[42]

Still, no wonder that by January 1882 Norton's head was "grumbling" again, making it difficult to work. He found relief in a friend from happier days: Henry James had come back to visit Cambridge for several months, dropping in often at Shady Hill. A less welcome visitor from England also showed up. Oscar Wilde had returned to Boston after touring the United States, "affectations" undamaged by contact with America, and was hunting Norton, a letter of introduction from Burne-Jones in his hand. Happily for Norton if not for his son, Charles had engaged himself to give four lectures on ancient and medieval architecture at Princeton University. At the end of January he dumped Wilde on a bemused and not exactly hospitable Eliot and fled south.[43]

"Heterodox as I am," Norton found himself "most kindly received" at staunchly Calvinist Princeton. His prime motive for accepting the invitation, he explained to Simon, sprang from

> my sense of the importance of binding together our Universities with a stronger sympathy than now exists in their common work as the chief nourishers and maintainers of the intellectual interests of the country, and as the strongest bulwarks against the tide of materialism which has risen of late years so fast and so high in the new world and in the old.

He also "succeeded beyond my hopes" in a secondary intention, enrolling the university as an underwriter of the American School at Athens. Even so, he felt glad to reach home. "I am too old to enjoy travel in America."[44]

He was, in fact, fifty-four; but ever larger chunks of his life were undeniably crumbling around him. Ruskin's memories mingled the actuality of Charles with "delirious dreams, and unkind hallucinations." Mr. Longfellow had grown so feeble that he had to spend his days in his chamber; on 24 March the tolling of the meetinghouse bell told Cambridge of his passing. Charles still treasured gifts Longfellow had given him "when I was younger than my own Richard." At the funeral Charles met Emerson, "his memory gone, his mind wavering"; a month later he too was dead. Between the two burials news arrived of Darwin's death. Charles told George Woodberry that he felt "suddenly old." The suddenness rings false; he often felt old now. He had long ago steeled himself to soldier on.[45]

The School at Athens required constant nurturing. In March it had run headlong into the skepticism of Columbia's old-fashioned president, Frederick Barnard. The New York Times hooted at Barnard (oh, yes, "American Greek" was "good enough for Americans"); but Norton still had to travel to New York in early April to mend fences, returning the next day sure of the support of all the "leading Colleges" and "chief classical scholars." He now expected the American School to open, ready to receive students, in the fall. European classical archaeologists were welcoming the American initiative. Norton pushed to get the Assos report through the press in time for the annual meeting in May, and the reaction to it proved just as gratifying. Adolf Michaelis, a leading younger German archaeologist, wrote to commend "the high interest and the thoroughness of Mr. Clarke's investigations." No wonder that Frederick Olmsted applauded Norton's "Grecian work" as a "real lift for the scholarship of the country—putting us on a higher plane."[46]

Olmsted's commendation would hardly have impressed an archaeologist; but it did suggest how the mantle of cultural leadership, until recently draped over Longfellow and Emerson, had fallen onto Norton's shoulders—and it also indicated how severely that garment had been retailored. The criticism that brought Emerson fame, the meditations on history that Longfellow essayed, now wore academic robes. When Norton turned away from planning the second season of the Assos dig, it was to attend the first meeting of a new Harvard faculty Committee on the Regulation of Athletic Sports and to work the academic network in hope (vain as it turned out) of landing George Woodberry a professorship at the University of California. Yet Norton's letter of recommendation for Woodberry showed that academic professionalism had not gelled into disciplinary molds. Woodberry's qualifications for a "chair of English literature" included not only competency in Early English and Anglo-Saxon but also "strong convictions" and the "tastes" of "a man of letters." "He has a remarkable gift of literary expression, fine critical faculties, and a wide acquaintance with literature. He has a solid judgment in matters of literary taste, and a keen appreciation of excellence." Cultural leadership and academic intellect could still walk hand in hand.[47]

Indeed, very soon Norton found himself again in the thick of the fight to save Niagara Falls—or rather "not so much to save the falls, as to save our own souls." "The growth of wealth and of the selfish individualism which accompanies it, (and corrupts many who are not rich), seems to weaken all properly social motives and efforts." Norton was helping to coordinate another press campaign; this time he enlisted his old protégé Jonathan Baxter Harrison. Harrison, now eking out a living as pastor of a little New Hampshire church, would get a much needed salary for two months of travel and writing; Niagara would get a well-schooled propagandist.[48]

July had arrived before Charles joined his children at the Locusts, and even Ashfield seemed an extension of his Cambridge study. The annual chore of the Academy Dinner loomed, this year luckily scheduled rather late in the dog days of August. Whatever the effort, Norton never doubted Ashfield worth it, for America needed examples of an older republic: "Men in cities & towns feel much less relation with their neighbors than of old; there is less civic patriotism; less sense of a spiritual & moral community."[49]

In Ashfield he began and largely finished a work of a new character for him. Years earlier, Emerson had handed over to Norton his letters from Carlyle, a decision seconded by Carlyle. Now, the two friends dead, their families wished Charles to edit both sides of the correspondence for publication. Norton meant to edit lightly (a "brief preface" and "a few explanatory notes"), the letters being interesting enough in themselves without dressing up. Still, it made a big job for one summer. Norton deleted matter he judged boring, excised comments apt to offend living persons, cleaned up vulgarisms, repaired punctuation, corrected spelling—did all that a Victorian editor normally did. But he did it with abnormal honesty and clarity, even marking deletions, foreshadowing new standards of editorial rigor. (Two reviewers criticized Norton for not bowdlerizing enough.) Tracking down personal details and missing letters required sheaves of correspondence—the search for one batch of early Emerson letters devolving into an English mystery, with Emerson's old disciple Moncure Conway playing detective in London for Norton. Then there were American and English publishers to negotiate with; an old hand at that, Norton struck a good deal for the heirs. By September insomnia and headaches had returned, always a sign of overwork, but the bulk of the job was over.[50]

And it had not kept him from his children; work never did. While Charles pored over manuscript, fifteen-year-old Rupert sat at a table close at hand working on Virgil (though "not yet finding much delight" in it), ten-year-old Dick across from him puzzling over fractions, twelve-year-old Margaret busy with her French. Eliot curled up nearby with Matthew Arnold's essays, while Sally and Lily (their German governess with them this summer) were "amusing themselves" with Freitag's *Aus einer kleinen Stadt.* Aunt Grace came to visit; she was finding "her independent life much to her taste," while Sally was "acquit[ting] herself admirably" at the head of the household. In the evenings Charles read aloud from Scott—his perennial favorite—and Dickens. Norton set his children a high standard; while protecting the special domain of childhood that he recalled so fondly, he never forgot that children were incipient adults.[51]

So he puzzled over child-rearing, especially the difficulty of nurturing intellectual and moral imagination: an anxiety that proved consequential for later generations. The friends his boys brought home seemed to talk of nothing but sports. Norton talked this over with a former student, G. H. Browne (class of 1878), who was interested in education; and at Norton's urging—initially "to provide opportunities for his own boys," Browne recalled—Browne started the Browne and Nichols School in Cambridge, intended to foster the culture of the imagination. One school made a good start, but merely a start. Colleges could only work with the raw material they received. Norton continued to ponder.[52]

As the autumn of 1882 approached, more immediate matters pressed. William Watson Goodwin, Norton's Harvard colleague, had already arrived in Athens to set up the American School; bookshelves were rising, chairs and tables entering the library. Goodwin visited Assos, where the work done on such small means astonished him. The handful of men still digging had about forty dollars left but expected a remittance from Norton any day. Goodwin loaned them ten pounds.[53]

TWELVE

Olympus Ascended, 1882–1886

Not only Athens and Assos were going well. In the early 1880s Charles seemed more comfortable with himself, with others, with his multiple roles, than at any time since Susan's death. Her absence still hurt, and from time to time smaller losses recalled and revived that supreme pain. Norton's aged Florentine friend, George Perkins Marsh, passed away in the summer of 1882, and Charles felt his death deeply, in part because it reminded him of Susan's. The loss of a spouse, Norton wrote to Marsh's widow in a letter of dubious consolation, brings "a trial which must make all remaining life a burden." But while the great wound still ached—and while cauterizing it made him more rigid—Norton had learned how to palliate the grief at the center of his being and to live at some ease with what remained.[1]

At ease: anything but at rest. As summer ended, he was chairing a committee to erect a memorial to Longfellow, swabbing up the residue of controversy surrounding Clarke's management at Assos, persuading the United States Navy to transport artifacts from that dig, weighing whether to continue the excavations for another year, selecting students for the first class of the American School at Athens, hurrying to finish the Emerson-Carlyle letters. Niagara also demanded attention. Harrison's summer of propaganda having alerted the public to the danger to the falls, now the only way actually "to accomplish anything," George Curtis advised, "is to enlist a few rich fanatics upon the subject." Howard Potter of New York, who had paid for Harrison's job, appeared the likeliest fanatic, and Norton schemed with Olmsted to induce Potter to form a Niagara Association to "take the work in charge." After returning from Ashfield to Cambridge, Norton met with Olmsted and Harrison to amplify the plot and to arrange to publish Harrison's Niagara letters between two covers.[2]

By then, Norton had taken up again the annual round of Harvard lecturing. This year he taught two courses back-to-back on Monday, Wednesday, and Friday afternoons: his big survey Fine Arts 4 (now covering all "art in

Italy from the Conquest of Greece by the Romans to the year 1600") and his smaller Fine Arts 5 on Greek art. Norton threw his limited energy into teaching and thought the expenditure worthwhile, for today's "ingenuous youth, full of good thoughts & aims," seemed to him "a better race, more manly & with larger outlook," than his own college generation. Still, lecturing always exhausted him, more than ever when he repeated the lectures for the young ladies of the new Harvard Annex, with which he had worked since its organization in 1879. Added to everything else, he knew the load was perilous to his health: "Six lectures a week & six proof-sheets are too much for any man." This did not deter him from new duties at the Boston Museum of Fine Arts. His old devil insomnia began to torment him.[3]

He had compensations. Greatest was the fulfillment of Norton's dream of an American School of Classical Studies at Athens, gratifying the lifelong patriotic craving, handed down from his father, for the United States to take her place in the vanguard of intellectual advance. Aided by a gratified Greek government, Professor Goodwin had rented a house, furnished it, fitted up a library, and welcomed the first seven graduate students. The proposed hundred-thousand-dollar endowment still eluded capture, and for now the school eked out a hand-to-mouth living on donations from the twelve cooperating colleges and universities. To later eyes the place looks a strange hybrid. It offered no degree, and some students apparently enrolled only to polish their Greek and indulge a taste for the exotic. Most seem to have meant to fit themselves for academic careers, and their director insisted on research of some sort from everyone. The American School did stand out as, among various less easily comprehensible things, the first American research institute in a humanistic field.[4]

Another compensation came from the Emerson-Carlyle correspondence. Norton toiled over this "record of forty years of admirable friendship" throughout the fall, finally putting it to bed in January 1883. He looked on the edition as a labor of love, love of two old friends who had touched his life deeply and sweetly, and he insisted, against the Emerson family's wishes, that all royalties go to the heirs. In the case of Carlyle's niece Mary, distraught over the image of her uncle in the "villain" Froude's biography, Norton hoped also for a nonpecuniary return: that Carlyle's side of the correspondence would "dispel some of the false impressions" of him broadcast by this supposed friend and disciple. The widespread notice that *The Correspondence of Thomas Carlyle and Ralph Waldo Emerson* got when it appeared in early March surprised and pleased Charles. His decision to keep his own voice out of the book, to let Carlyle speak for himself, had achieved the desired effect. The publication had also an unexpected result: Mary Carlyle asked Norton to edit all of her uncle's correspondence. This proposal Norton chose to mull over.[5]

He had, after all, other things to occupy a spare hour, should one miraculously manifest itself. The Niagara Falls Association materialized in January, with Harrison as corresponding secretary under Norton's and Olmsted's eyes. Success came quickly. By 30 April the governor of New York had signed a law authorizing a protective belt of land around the falls and creating a commission to select the acreage. But almost immediately Olmsted was pleading for help again: enemies had seized control of the commission. And Niagara was far from the only worthy cause clamoring for Norton's attention. Trying to get the fragments dug up at Assos out of Turkey, Norton found himself involved in protracted diplomatic negotiations with the Ottoman government; adjudicating which American would edit the inscriptions from the dig required scarcely less delicate ones. Meanwhile, he was up to his neck in deliberations about the format of the *Bulletin* and *Papers* that he wanted the AIA to publish in cooperation with the American School. Amid all this, he felt the duty to set aside time to write for the *Nation* in March an appreciation of his old friend Arthur Clough. For Americans needed badly to learn from Clough: his idealism, his sense of the complexity of truth, his acceptance of the limits of human knowledge—and his agnosticism in religion.[6]

Norton believed all these efforts worthwhile; that was the problem. He launched himself on marathons of work, sometimes forgetting he had a sprinter's body. All winter he teetered on the verge of collapse. A "heavy cold" in January 1883 turned into pleurisy; in March a New York newspaper reported him "rallying from a prostrating illness"; in April and May chronic insomnia and indigestion added to his exhaustion.[7]

In late May the doctor prescribed a vacation—in the Alps, where the air was pure, the villages calm, and clamorous demands three thousand miles away. "I do not want to go, but I am too tired," Charles wrote to James. To set foot in Europe must, he realized, rouse Susan's ghost. Dreading having only her shade for company, he enlisted his oldest son as bodyguard. Sally, almost nineteen, with the help of aunts and seventeen-year-old Lily, could manage the household. Papa booked passage on the 16 June steamer to Liverpool, for they could hardly skip the friends in England. The journey on 27 June to Ruskin's house, Brantwood, at Coniston in the Lake District, took them by way of Lancaster "with its fine old castle," along Morecambe Bay between misty mountains and solitary sea, then past the ruins of Furness Abbey. The contrast with America's raw landscape brought a half-forgotten pang. Probably so did the memory of Susan. The sky lowered "dull and grey" over their railway carriage; a light rain fell.[8]

Ruskin waited on the platform. Ten years and madness had taken their toll; he was sixty-four and looked it, with his pronounced stoop. All things considered, though, he appeared "well enough" in body, "as active and perhaps as vigorous as ever" in mind, as "perverse and irrational" in disposition yet with all his "old sweetness"—and as incomparably beautiful to Charles as the lakes among which he lived. The years vanished. Norton, Ruskin, and Flora Shaw, an "interesting and pleasing" young writer and Ruskin's guest, looked over medieval manuscripts, admired Turner watercolors, "and talked till dinner-time;—and then more talk, and more talk till half past ten and bed." The current of pleasure flowed over a bed of sadness; what had been would never be: Ruskin never fully himself again, and Susan never beside them where Miss Shaw now stood. For all its quiet joys, Brantwood struck a "pathetic" note; and Norton felt obliged to discuss with Ruskin's younger cousin and caretaker, Joan Severn, the disposition of her "Coz's" diaries after he died or went finally mad.[9]

London, reached on 2 July and departed two weeks later, the whole fortnight a reunion with Charles and Susan's old friends, likewise stirred emotions mixed of reawakened pain and almost forgotten happiness. Charles and his son settled into lodgings in Bolton Street, not far from Lowell's Lowndes Square house, where James—Uncle James to Eliot—welcomed them on arrival with the old smile. Ned Burne Jones took the first train back from Oxford the next day; Aubrey de Vere came down to see Charles on the eighth; Leslie and Julia Stephen had him to dinner that evening. Amid this swarm of old friends, Charles slipped away to Essex with Eliot to spend a day with his new one, Flora Shaw: a bright and independent young woman, it seemed, could yet revive the old genius for friendship.

The doctor had prescribed rest, not a whirl of hansom cabs and dinner tables. Stopping briefly in Paris, Charles and Eliot reached Geneva on 19 July for a long weekend of reminiscence with John and Jane Simon. Despite a steady rain, crossing the Simplon Pass into Italy brought all Norton's love for the country flooding back with physical immediacy: "the soft Italian speech, the gracious Italian manner, the pretty Italian villages, the colour, the landscape, the fertile and smiling hillsides and valley." At Domodossola the clouds lifted, the Italian sun shone. Among sun-flecked Alpine lakes Charles and Eliot meandered the next three weeks, Pallanza to Lugano to Monte Generoso to Bellagio. The "vast, conspicuous hotels" appalled Norton, "enormous democratic palaces"; and he scurried away to the beauty of mountains and water "undisturbed by inharmonious suggestions." "The imagination," he sighed to Sally, "has to exclude much of the intrusive life of the prosaic days in which we live." That was not all his imagination wished to exclude. Charles avoided his and Susan's beloved Italy south of the Alps, blaming this on the heat. In more than one sense, Florence, Siena, and Venice remained uncomfortably warm for him.[10]

In mid-August father and son turned reluctantly northward. The harness began already to tighten again on Norton in Switzerland, where he stopped to confer with Professor Lewis Packard of Yale, who was en route to Athens to replace Goodwin as director of the American School; afterward, visits to a few French cathedrals supplied more data for the projected sequel to *Church-Building*. At the end of the month the ferry moored in England. The unclouded pleasure of another day in the country with Flora Shaw relieved the complicated feelings of saying goodbye to older friends.

No affections swirled with more complexity than those surrounding Ruskin. On 7 September the Nortons arrived at Brantwood, where Ruskin seemed "steadier, less excitable, more equable than when I saw him nine or ten weeks ago." This was fortunate, for they had sober business. Froude's vile tale-telling about Carlyle (as Norton regarded it) had raised a warning flag about Ruskin. That erratic character had left a paper trail that made Carlyle look as prim as the Old Lady of Threadneedle Street. Discretion had never much inhibited Ruskin's epistolatory self-disclosure, and his disastrous stab at marriage had only whetted a predilection for pubescent girls; there was, to phrase the matter as favorably as possible, vast ground for misunderstanding. Ruskin himself in a rare moment of prudence had already scanned his old diaries and, to Norton's vast relief, decided that "Darling Charles" should govern "the burning of these things" after his death.[11]

Charles wanted authority over more than the diaries. Long discussions ensued, involving Norton, Ruskin, Joan and her feckless husband Arthur Severn, and Ruskin's disciple Alexander Wedderburn. In the end, Ruskin signed a will leaving control of published works to Joan Severn and Wedderburn jointly and management of unpublished manuscripts, far the more sensitive material, to her and Norton. Ruskin's reputation would have the wariest of guardians. Relief mingled with melancholy as Charles abandoned him to his "solitude."[12]

As his ship steamed out of the Mersey, Charles left behind most of his dearest friends, the scenes of his happiest memories, the paintings and churches of his richest moments—and for what? Naked landscapes, cities where one ugly building butted against another, politics putrefying with greed, a people enthralled by plutocracy. Even his own health had only "moderately" improved, although the headaches had gone, the dyspepsia abated, and the insomnia lessened.

By the time Charles attained Shady Hill in late September, he had reverted to his usual, more balanced comparison of Europe and his own land. "No present age, no actual age, was ever good" for "idealists" like himself. In Europe he felt "with pain the ill wrought by the progress of democracy,—the destruction of old shrines, the disregard of beauty, the decline in personal distinction, the falling off in manners." In the United States, "as we have less to lose, we have less to regret, and the spread of comfort, the superb and unexampled spectacle of fifty millions of human beings living at peace and in plenty, compensates in a certain measure for the absence of high culture, of generous ideals and of imaginative life." And, after all, had not Norton returned precisely to his own efforts to nudge some future America an inch closer to high culture, generous ideals, and imaginative life?[13]

He plunged back into the work with a vigor that belied his dubious health. He began by freshening his Harvard course offerings, leaving intact the big surveys of ancient and medieval art and the more specialized year-long course on Greek art but dividing "Art in Italy" into two new one-semester courses covering "Florentine Art" and "Venetian Art." The requirement that students read German quietly vanished from the catalogue, either a concession to reality, a result of Clarke's translation of Reber's text, or (most likely, since reality was hardly new and Clarke's translation had become available two years before) an attempt to make civilization more accessible to the unformed young who jammed his lecture room in ever larger masses.[14]

Lecturing did not drag him down as much as usual that fall, whether owing to the European vacation, better self-regulation, or blind luck. Although by mid-November winter had set in and the storm windows gone up at Shady Hill, Charles felt energetic enough to host within two weeks two dinner parties for Matthew Arnold and his wife, who had stopped to stay with him while on an American lecture tour. Norton had also taken on several extra tasks, including raising money to rebuild the Armenian monastery of San Lazzaro in Venice and renewing the perennial search for employment for Jonathan Harrison. Within weeks of return to Cambridge, he had again ignored the physicians' warnings and "immersed" himself "in a flood of occupations."[15]

The most demanding was editing. Soon after return he set out to revise his edition of the Carlyle-Emerson correspondence. Seventeen new letters had been uncovered; and drafts of others, previously known to Norton only in copies made on the new "type-writer," had turned up, requiring corrections in the printed versions. Norton was never a scholar to tolerate an inaccurate text, and the task stretched into May. Nor was he a merchant whose conscience rested easy with having sold flawed goods, and he persuaded the publisher to print a supplementary volume for purchasers of the first edition.

The Carlyle-Emerson correspondence had become prolegomenon to a vaster task, for he had acceded to Mary Carlyle's plea to edit all her uncle's letters. The previous spring James Froude had printed as *Letters and Memorials* a mélange of personal materials Carlyle had assembled in memory of his wife, Jane Welsh Carlyle, rending further the veil shielding the intimate relation of husband and wife, rendering blacker this particular husband's character; and this aggravation of Froude's sacrilege may have tipped the balance for Norton. Carlyle's own letters, he felt sure, would give a very different picture of the man than Froude had drawn. For the moment, vexingly, most of the putatively exculpatory documents remained in Froude's paws, pending completion of the second half of his biography of Carlyle.

So Norton had to content himself in the fall of 1883 with seeking out what letters he could, beginning with the young Carlyle's exchange of letters with Goethe. This would make a neat companion volume to the Emerson correspondence. Mary Carlyle held Goethe's letters to Carlyle, and by December, Norton had them in his desk. The other side proved elusive. Georg von Bunsen, visiting Shady Hill in October, warned him that Goethe's heirs "were a most dog-in-the-manger set," apt "even bluntly to refuse to say whether C's letters" still existed. Charles enlisted James Lowell to pull diplomatic strings; he was still tugging in spring. It took many months and the intervention of Britain's ambassador to Germany to locate the letters, which finally turned up in the Goethe Archives in Weimar under the more agreeable control of the grand duchess.[16]

Meanwhile, Norton was preparing another weapon to cut down Froude. Mary Carlyle complained that the "villain's" hasty edition of her uncle's *Reminiscences* was shot through with errors—and she had the manuscript to prove it. Without question, Froude had rushed the *Reminiscences* into print after inexcusably sloppy editing; his blunders distorted many of Carlyle's pronouncements but probably not the overall impression of the man, though neither Carlyle's niece nor his American friend would have concurred with that last judgment. Under Mary Carlyle's prodding, Norton set to work on a new edition, to be published, like Carlyle's correspondence, by James Osgood's Boston house. Norton meant his edition to compete head-to-head with Froude's, exposing the latter's shoddy execution of the master's trust.[17]

The venom that Norton spat at the hapless Froude contrasted bizarrely with the gentility and careful habits of speech that people had come to expect of him. His behavior startled and puzzled some of his English friends. Julia Stephen shared his animus, and pretty soon Leslie came around. But Edward Fitzgerald maintained that Froude had depicted Carlyle with accuracy and affection, admonishing Norton (in his last message before his death in June 1883) not "to heap more coals on Froude's head." Ruskin, who knew both Carlyle and Froude well (and revered the dead man), disagreed "in a chasmy manner" with Norton's estimates of both, siding with Froude "in all that he has done and said, about C, if it *had* to be said or done, at all." He added that he had never known "any one more deeply earnest & affectionate in trying to do right" than Froude. Ruskin was correct to point out that Charles did not really know Froude; but there was reason for this: Norton had never liked the man, suspecting him from their first meeting of toadyism and insincerity. Now Norton railed at Froude as a "humbug" and "falsifier," accusing him of an "attempt to blur and deface one of the loveliest pictures of the most sacred human relations that has ever been shown to the world."[18]

This last particular in the indictment dissolves some of the mystery of Norton's atypical vehemence and cranky judgment. A companion in the old man's walks during one winter several years after his wife's death, Norton hardly knew Carlyle well; those who did (except his worshiping niece) found in Froude's depiction of this rough-edged and self-centered personality both affection and truth to life. Carlyle's old friends differed as to the wisdom of Froude's candor about the discord that sometimes made the Carlyle marriage a hell but never doubted his accuracy. Though Norton was flatly wrong in thinking Carlyle's marriage peaceful and contented, in believing this he could not help but consider Froude a liar and a blackguard—and not just because Charles detested Froude and loved old Thomas.

For Norton needed an unscalable fence between public and private. He customarily burnt letters "to which no third person should be privy" and guarded the personal realm with special ferocity when privacy between man and woman was threatened. Letters from Ruskin that told "of sorrowful experience in love" went up in smoke, "for they were secrets between you &

me." Any Bostonian of Norton's breeding would have taken it for granted that marital relations offered no subject for public discussion, but for Charles this taboo was utterly inviolable. His own marriage seems to have come close to ideal; after Susan's death he certainly idealized it and erected an impenetrable wall to safeguard the sacred relation from profanation. With "tears blinding me," "I have burned some of the sweetest love letters ever penned, because I would make sure that no eye but mine should ever see them."[19]

To shield this enshrined memory, Charles could hardly stand imagining anyone's marital state as less than idyllic. As Ruskin told Charles, "Your entirely happy and unselfish life puts you out of court in judging of these mixed characters—C., or F., or me!" This got very close to the truth. Norton seems to have evaded detailed knowledge of Ruskin's unfortunate marriage, and he blithely ignored the abundant evidence of Carlyle's unhappy union. Froude, meanwhile, laid it out for public inspection. He thereby (Norton believed) contravened Carlyle's explicit injunction against publication, but this violation paled beside his blackest perfidy: Froude had violated "the confidences and intimacies of husband and wife."[20]

To turn from this bitter feud to the business of the AIA felt like walking out of a filthy yellow London fog into the pellucid sunlight of the Aegean. Still, relaxing on a beach it was not. Adolph Bandelier's first report on the pueblos needed shepherding through the press; Joseph Clarke's next one on Assos requiring sketching out. Clarke himself was dispatched to lecture on Assos, in hopes of rousing wider interest in the AIA; meanwhile, Norton wrote for *Harper's* (where Curtis perhaps pulled strings) an account of Sardis, puffing the institute. An enrollment crisis nearly scuppered the American School at Athens. At every step, maximum result had to be squeezed from minimal funds.

To ease that strain, the AIA undertook to reorganize itself in the spring of 1884. For all its national pretensions, the institute amounted to little more than a Boston dog wagging a New York–Princeton tail. It now subdivided into more or less independent local societies (beginning with Boston, New York, and Baltimore chapters) united in a loose federation, each electing members to a governing national council. The hope was to build, from the local ground up, a truly national membership and funding base. The name remained unchanged, as did the president. Day-to-day chores Norton often delegated to others; his Harvard colleague John Williams White, in particular, bore a heavy load as head of the American School's Managing Committee. But all major decisions and a buzzing cloud of gnat-sized ones came back to Norton's desk.[21]

His physician advised a year's leave from teaching to recharge his drained reservoir, but first came one more duty to Harvard. Cambridge University's Emmanuel College, alma mater of John Harvard and nursery of the younger Cambridge, was preparing to celebrate its tricentenary. Harvard could hardly fail to send ambassadors, and Charles Eliot asked his cousin Norton to join James Lowell in representing her. Lowell, as American minister to Britain, made an obvious choice; and Norton made another, having become by now the central figure in the web of personality and paper joining the United Kingdom and the United States into a single domain of intellect. Only a handful of American diplomats and expatriates rivaled his range of acquaintance in Britain, probably none his stature among the British intelligentsia. Norton was more apt to read the *Times* of London than the *New York Times*, and British scholars and writers visiting the United States called at Shady Hill as a matter of course. When James Bryce needed an American name to adorn a charitable appeal, Norton's came to mind; when the editor of the London *Athenaeum* wanted a report from America on "the tendencies of literature, the progress of learning, &c.," Norton seemed ideal; when Charles Eliot needed a man to send to Emmanuel—likewise.[22]

Norton groaned. He tried to talk Frank Child into the job, with no luck. The chance to help Sally see England, himself to see Lowell, tipped the balance. Charles committed the younger children to Grace and copy for the revised Emerson-Carlyle correspondence to the printer. When the *Cephalonia* steamed out of Boston harbor on 24 May 1884, Norton stood at the rail. Henry James welcomed him to London on 3 June; Lowell, Ned and Georgie Burne Jones, Jane and John Simon were not far behind.

Lowell traveled up to Cambridge with him for the Emmanuel tercentenary dinner on 18 June, where Norton delivered a pair of speeches. The next day, after a late morning service in Emmanuel's chapel, Norton walked to the Senate House and donned a scarlet robe to receive an honorary doctorate of letters. The Latin oration preceding the award singled out among his achievements the *Vita Nuova* translation, *Church-Building in the Middle Ages,* and his founding of the Archaeological Institute and the American School at Athens. Citation of both scholarship and institution building showed growing appreciation even outside the United States of Norton's multiple roles in the nineteenth-century reconstruction of humanistic learning. The praise he brushed off as "wonderfully graceful, ready, and well-turned flattery," even aside from the Ciceronian periods; but he transparently found an honorary degree from Cambridge highly acceptable unction.[23]

Edward Burne-Jones, sometime after 1874.

Georgiana Burne-Jones, sometime after 1874.

John Ruskin, with his younger friend and occasional caretaker,
Constance Hilliard, October 1879.

Norton and George W. Curtis, 1884 or 1885.

The Locusts, on Academy Dinner day, August 19, 1886. From left: Norton, William Dean Howells, Sally (seated), Eliot, Lily, Richard, unidentified man, Susan's aunt Anne Ashburner (seated), Margaret (seated), Susan's sister Theodora, Stephen Bullard (William's younger brother).

Norton and Sally (seated), with Princess Schalofsky (left),
and Mr. and Mrs. Wayne MacVeagh, Chicago, October 2, 1893.

Leslie Stephen with Richard Norton, early 1890s.

Norton in Oxford to receive an honorary degree, July 1900, with Sally
and Mr. and Mrs. Albert Venn Dicey.

Eliot and his son Charles Eliot Norton II (Tattoo),
with Grandpapa.

Norton's study at Shady Hill.

The second Susan Norton at Shady Hill.

With official business over, and after a day passed in the country with Flora Shaw, Charles gathered up Theo, Sally, and Sally's old playmate Margaret Burne Jones for a "campaign" of cathedral viewing, aiming to arrive in a week or so at Brantwood. Ruskin's condition confirmed in Charles "the conviction, which his letters had forced upon me, that he had never recovered his sanity, in the strict sense of the word, since the illness of '75." Back in London, other old comrades helped to chase away melancholy over Ruskin, but so did new friends. Matthew and Frances Arnold had grown very fond of Norton, and he of them; Norton had become a confidant for Flora Shaw, she something of the sort for him; James Bryce just wanted him for dinner. Charles, whose genius for friendship had atrophied in the grim aftermath of Susan's death, was recovering old warmth and sociability, more readily, it seemed, in England than at home. "Don't go back to America—stay here," pleaded Ned Burne Jones; and the temptation beckoned. Yet duty ran the length of Norton's spine; and, to tell the truth, at fifty-six he would have found it next to impossible to tear himself out of the house and the community where he had lived since birth. On July 26 he was home; three days later, at the Locusts.[24]

These last two English visits had forced him to recognize at what a fearsome rate his past was growing and how rapidly it was losing its vital connection with the present. John Simon was pushing seventy and losing his sight; Ruskin was hardly more than a cherished memory; even James Lowell had become less of a living presence: too long absent, worn down by his wife's illness, contemplating his own demise. In the fall, James made a will, naming Charles his literary executor: "I shan't haunt you if you leave me quiet in my grave." Another of Charles's oldest friends, John Field, had taken to summering in Ashfield; but Bright's disease left him feebler by the day. Godkin had just remarried, confirming his severance from Cambridge. Even in Cambridge, Norton's social life revolved around obligations to visitors and students, with seldom the luxury of intimate talk; late evenings long ago with Frank Parkman or Frank Child grew remote in memory.[25]

Younger companions came to fill more of an older Norton's hours. William Howells had known Charles from the days with Susan but now grew closer; he fell into visiting Ashfield regularly, and in 1886 Norton tried to talk him into buying a place there. George Woodberry had completed evolution from student into "amico." Epistolary friendship flourished with Flora Shaw. "Letters from you," she wrote, "have the charm of setting free currents of thought which have been still, and remind me of our pleasant talks." A set of mildly bohemian young Brahmins—as the heirs of Boston's old merchant princes were coming to be called—who founded the Tavern Club in 1884 drew Norton into their camaraderie.[26]

Inevitably, though, younger companions treated him with too much respect to allow uninhibited give-and-take. With Lowell preoccupied, Ruskin unstable, Godkin distant, Simon quietening, Burne Jones tongue-tied, and Child often too busy to talk, Leslie Stephen remained one of the few age-mates who really engaged Norton. Their regular exchange of letters swelled in bulk and in value to Charles. Of friends present in the flesh, only George Curtis seemed, during Ashfield's long summer days, a holdover from younger life. And George, however dear, could not talk literature and scholarship as Stephen and Lowell could. But he could talk politics better than any of them, and he and Charles loved to growl together.

A year earlier, Congress had enacted the Pendleton civil service law, which, despite manifest deficiencies, did at last set in place the principle of merit. In June 1884, as if to repent this lapse into purity, the Republican convention nominated for president James G. Blaine, "Continental Liar from the State of Maine," as an election jingle had it. Curtis used his pages in *Harper's* to bolt the party and endorse the Democrat, Grover Cleveland. To less public notice, Norton did likewise; and, as the November election approached, he admired the "manly way" in which Cleveland endured "by far the most disgusting political campaign we have ever had."[27]

Yet the narrowness of Cleveland's victory depressed Norton. "It displays the low average of moral sense in the people, which the defence of Blaine's course and the methods of his active supporters have done much to lower still farther." While Lowell believed that "the people are 'learning more & more how to be worthy' of their power," Charles found that faith "more questionable than it seemed ten or twenty years ago."

> It is not because I am ten or twenty years older that I say so, but because unfavorable influences, only nascent then, have, in recent years, been working with full force to affect the character & aims of the great body of the people. I have as strong a conviction as you that 'democracy' will work; but it may work ignobly, ignorantly, brutally; here, at least, it does not look as if the better elements of social life, of human nature, were growing & flourishing in proportion to the basest.

What did flourish were graft-ridden political machines in big cities and plutocratic greed in legislative chambers.[28]

Norton had not lost faith in "the quality of character in the average citizen," but he diagnosed it as "mostly latent & inoperative." The Republic had somehow to bring to life the character in its citizens and thus to reanimate the civic virtue dependent on character; the reformation of American democratic politics had to start not with corrupted practices but with weakened principles. Approval in March 1885 of funding for the Niagara Falls Reservation came as close to elating Norton as politics could; for New York's legislature had, *mirabile visu,* voted in behalf of "elevated sentiment and spiritual emotion." With each passing year, electoral candidates and immediate issues mattered less to Norton, and the long-term task of reviving the public morality and civic commitment essential to democracy mattered more. Success in that work depended less on the ballot box and more on the kind of cultural endeavor that he undertook in print and in the classroom.[29]

In 1884–85, with the classroom vacated for a year, he pursued more intensely than in a long time the scholarly side of this work. His interests were swinging back from their oscillation into ancient Greece toward their enduring center of gravity, medieval culture. That fall he drew together the materials on Cluny, which had been amassing since the early 1870s, and by December began to write the history of the great abbey church. He intended to wed Cluny with Saint-Denis and Chartres as a trilogy in French Gothic, counterpointed to the three Italian churches of *Church-Building.* He was still hard at work on Cluny in March.

Norton's interest in Dante had also grown active again. In February 1884 he had published in the *Century* magazine a brief " 'advertisement for readers' of Dante," urging them not to stop with the dramatic appeal of the *Inferno* but to savor the "full beauty and compass" of Dante's "extraordinary conception." Now he prepared for the *Nation* a review of two new translations of the *Divina Commedia,* laid groundwork for a published catalogue of Harvard's important Dante collection (largely built by him), and began supervising for the Dante Society the preparation by Edward Fay of a work of scholarship of internationally recognized import: a *Concordance of the Divina Commedia.* The Dante Society under Norton's leadership, like the AIA, was becoming sponsor of and venue for specialized scholarship; but, like the AIA, it resisted becoming a nest of professional specialists; its members remained mostly amateurs, its secretary a local attorney. Meanwhile, in the study at Shady Hill such amateurs met periodically to hear Norton read and discuss the *Divina Commedia.* This was far from the first time that Norton had offered small Dante classes like this, but he now had a new incentive.[30]

Sometime that spring he began a prose translation of Dante's epic. Why turn a poem into prose? Norton held no brief against versifying Dante in English—Longfellow had done just that—but even the best such attempts seemed to him to lose "too much of the directness & simplicity of the poem." So, whereas Andrews had tried to provide English readers with the exact meaning of the Gospels, his son now repeated the effort for Dante. Charles was not the only Victorian agnostic thirsting for spirituality who looked on the *Divina Commedia* as a gospel of sorts. Dante and Cluny "form the needed balance," he told Leslie Stephen, "to the more immediately practical affairs which occupy, of necessity, the greater part of one's time & thought."[31]

Occupying the greater part of Norton's time and thought in 1885 were the Carlyle letters. The previous autumn, Froude had completed his biography then scrupulously handed over to a seething Mary Carlyle all the letters he possessed. She packed them off to Norton, expecting him to burnish her uncle's tarnished halo. The actual "work of editing," Norton told Leslie Stephen, "is not difficult, but it takes a good deal of time"; and, besides editing *in se,* Norton had to track down and beg the use of letters in other hands, as well as to translate Goethe's German into English smooth enough for publication.[32]

Norton meant the several volumes to serve as a sort of biography in Carlyle's own words, to "dispel many of the false notions concerning him which Froude has done so much to propagate." James Osgood, publisher of the Carlyle-Emerson correspondence, won the rights to the new letters, then promptly went bankrupt, leaving Norton to negotiate a second contract with the British house of Macmillan. Besides a new edition of the *Reminiscences* to correct the errors in Froude's, Norton planned six volumes of selected letters: two of letters to family members, one of letters to early friends, one of letters to and from John Stuart Mill, and a final two to include the correspondence with Goethe and letters to Stirling, Browning, and others. In the end, six would prove a low estimate.[33]

His editorial principles and purposes, however, stayed firm. As with the Emerson-Carlyle letters, he edited lightly, intruding his own voice seldom—so seldom that Ruskin complained of its absence. But Norton held out; he meant "to let the letters speak for themselves" and limited himself to brief footnotes where a reader needed clarification and to just enough preface to explain the origin and context of each set of letters. The rare exceptions to this policy had two purposes: to refute and to excoriate Froude.[34]

In editing the Carlyle correspondence, Norton pioneered a novel type of scholarship. The "life and letters" of distinguished persons had by this time ripened into a venerable Victorian genre, cultivated with filial zeal in Boston, where each patrician generation paid literary homage to its predecessor. Uncle Ticknor had cobbled together from the letters of his friend, the historian William Prescott, just such a biographical tribute; Charles had helped Ticknor's widow and George Hillard produce a like memorial for Ticknor himself; one day Sally Norton and Mark Howe would do the same for Sally's Papa. In each case the pious editor interlarded carefully chosen chunks of letters with enough biographical commentary (the ratio of correspondence to narrative varying a good deal from book to book) to weave the letters into a coherent story exalting its hero: in the best instances, not merely worshipful but revealing of character, personality, and achievement. The generic filiation is with eighteenth-century epistolary novels rather than twentieth-century scholarly editions: hardly a surprise, since the early authors in this life-and-letters mode grew up reading eighteenth-century novels.

Other antecedents pushed the life-and-letters model in a new direction. Furthest back in time lay the great *Opera omnia* of Renaissance scholarship, the roster of worthy candidates for such collected works having expanded in the eighteenth century to comprehend writers freshly dead. More recent were the amassments of primary sources documenting near-contemporary history, such as the immense compilation published over twenty years by Peter Force (father of Norton's college pal Manning Force) and the issuance of more focused collections of letters bearing on politics, like the diplomatic correspondence of the American Revolution produced by Andrews Norton's friend and sometime collaborator Jared Sparks.[35]

Norton's editing echoed these traditions but aspired to something generically different. A thirst for authenticity, a wish to preserve the original voice of the author—desires spurred by what Norton regarded as Froude's distortions but not originating there—drove him to try to conserve the unvarnished thoughts and feelings of major intellectual and literary influences on the culture of his own time. Not *all* the thoughts and feelings, to be sure: his concern was to recover the public voice of a writer and its sources in private life, while omitting passages apt to embarrass the living or violate the sanctum of the dead. Nonetheless, it was the authenticity of direct revelation that Norton sought: the letters were to tell their own story. A century later, letters like Carlyle's and Emerson's would be compiled as a full primary record to subserve literary scholarship; Norton had that aim in mind—

though perhaps hypersensitive to the difference between scholarly curiosity and prurience—but also the goal of crafting something like an intellectual autobiography.

Like his contemporaries, he interfered more than later editors would with the manuscripts before him, silently correcting errors of grammar and slips of the pen; yet at the same time he displayed unaccustomed scholarly scruple, fastidiously indicating omissions in letters, striving to keep the printed text true to the writer's voice. One of his complaints about Froude's editorial sloppiness—and of that felony Froude was guilty beyond reasonable doubt—was that it often obliterated "the distinctive features of emphasis and punctuation, with which Carlyle gave such life and character to written words that they may be read almost as if with the tone, pause and inflection of speech." As a translator and the son of a translator, as a scholar and the son of a scholar, Norton lifted the life-and-letters genre to a plane of greater exactitude and thus played a large role in transforming it into the learned edition of a writer's correspondence.[36]

And, like Scaliger and other great savants before him, he used the text as a weapon of war. Froude's "carelessness & his virtual misrepresentations" outraged Norton—"worse even," Charles told Leslie Stephen, "than one could readily believe who had not the material before him which Froude himself possessed to draw from." "He does not often make a literal misstatement, but his statements are constantly falsely colored, so that their effect on the reader is much the same as if they were absolutely incorrect." Later literary historians, while conceding Froude's carelessness in editing the *Reminiscences,* have come down more on his side of this controversy than on Norton's; but it is important to understand that Norton's anger had scholarly as well as personal sources—recall his outrage when Bancroft's history of the United States omitted footnotes.[37]

To his damning prefaces to the Carlyle letters, Norton added in 1886 a "tremendous arraignment" in the *New Princeton Review* of Froude's editorial practices. This article, advertised "in the leading English papers," fell on Froude as the last straw. "Cursed up and down and accused of all the crimes in the decalogue," he begged Ruskin to use his influence to quiet Norton. Ruskin agreed: Norton's outrage, fed by deep scholarly and personal springs, did verge on the irrational. (Poor Ruskin, forced by mental breakdown to resign the Slade Professorship at Oxford in March 1885, was by now a far greater stranger to rationality than Charles even in his worst moments; he raved about Norton's abuse of Froude with much justice but growing irascibility and instability—though growling still to "dearest

Charles.") By August 1885 rumor circulated in London of Norton's forth-coming edition; at Christmas, Charles sent Macmillan the first batch of copy. Early in 1886 appeared simultaneously in London and New York two volumes of *Early Letters of Thomas Carlyle*, covering 1817 to 1825.[38]

Norton's doctors had intended his year of leave from Harvard in 1884–85 for recuperative leisure, but what peace the Carlyle business did not scotch vanished into the ravenous maw of the AIA. Wrapping up the Assos work and getting the excavated artifacts to the United States drew Norton into a diplomatic labyrinth worthy of Daedalus's original, pointlessly made yet more tortuous by Norton's sharp tongue, which irked General Lew Wallace, the American minister in Constantinople.[39] Not until April 1885 did the Sublime Porte nod. The lesson learned was not lost, and Norton and the AIA Council began to work to secure the appointment of sympathetic American consuls near key archaeological sites, particularly AIA workers themselves. More immediately, Joseph Clarke had begun to write the full report of the Assos expedition, and he needed periodic nudges from Norton.

At least American classical archaeology had made its first mark. (Mean-while, Americanist archaeology, never the AIA's highest priority and falling lower as Greek work absorbed more funds, became increasingly the prov-ince of government-sponsored expeditions, to Norton's regret.) The Ger-man Archaeological Institute welcomed the new player on the classical field by electing Clarke a corresponding member. However, the intended parent of America's archaeological future, the American School at Athens, teetered dangerously; much of March was spent scrambling to find a director willing to undertake the 1885–86 season. Notwithstanding, hopeful feelers went out for cooperation with a similar British school being set up in Athens. And in 1885 appeared *Papers of the American School of Classical Studies at Athens*, the first of a series of such publications that established the American School as a recognized center of classical research—though not one limited to profes-sional disciplinary scholarship, as the "amateur" authorship of many early archaeological reports showed.

Amid all this business, Norton's role was almost imperceptibly changing. Every consequential matter still ended on his desk, but no longer did he clearly hold the expertise that counted in many decisions. Joseph Clarke inadvertently put a finger on his mentor's dilemma in a letter home: "I am afraid that once I get drawn into general literary work, it will be the end of archaeological competency, which requires all one's intellectual labor!" Nor-ton remained primus inter pares in administration and fund-raising, where no one possessed his experience and skill or his range of contacts in the intellectual world. The later nineteenth century was the founding era of specialized learned societies in the United States; and, in an age of relatively primitive institutional arrangements, a well-connected, efficient individual like Norton was indispensable for the creation of any major academic enterprise.[40]

But when it came to running the School at Athens or overseeing an expedition into Mesopotamia, he had to lean on full-time classicists. This ceding of command resulted in part from other growing demands on his time, such as the Carlyle editing and the shift in his interests back toward the Middle Ages. More fundamentally, it reflected a change in the character of academic life. The expertise that the AIA nurtured encouraged a degree of specialization that began to raise questions about the limits of its founder's competence.

In 1885 a new periodical appeared under AIA auspices; and Norton's part in the venture clarifies this academic realignment and reveals his own newly unstable relationship to knowledge in America. The idea came from Arthur Frothingham, a Johns Hopkins archaeologist in his mid-thirties (who, as a specialist in medieval art, would himself soon be reclassified as art historian, not archaeologist). His proposed *American Journal of Archaeology* got an eager welcome in the inner circle but for curiously diverse reasons. Frothingham pined for something like the *Zeitschriften* of Germany, produced for professors, dominated by monographic reports of research. Henry Lea, the Philadelphia publisher, medieval historian, and AIA patron liked "very much Mr. Frothingham's idea of a periodical devoted to Art and Archaeology"—but because it would "bring together the lovers of art" and "stimulate the development of culture in that direction." Frothingham himself realized that America, only starting to breed a corps of professional archaeologists, could hardly yet sustain an *Archäologische Zeitung;* but he designed the *American Journal of Archaeology* to resemble one as closely as possible.[41]

Yet no AIA leader noticed any conflict between Frothingham's ideal of specialized expertise and Lea's ambition for general culture. All shared the goal of making "Art and Archaeology known and studied in America"; and Frothingham asked Norton, hardly a narrow-gauge specialist, to become general editor, "as it would add so much to the success of the Review." Norton declined (the offer was perhaps only a courtesy), and Frothingham took the post. But Norton would have made a plausible choice, for the general editor was to operate as coordinator rather than expert arbiter. Associate editors would be in charge of subfields and would exercise "authority over all the matters which pertain to their special department." Equally "specialist" seemed the practice of cramming page after page with abstracts of European learned journals, reviews of erudite books, and brief reports of archaeological finds.[42]

Yet specialized expertise appeared neither incompatible with general culture nor unpalatable to a broad (if well-educated) audience. The *American Journal of Archaeology* aimed to "make all the important work done in the field of Archaeology" available "in a convenient but scholarly form, to all who wish to inform themselves of the progress made in this branch of study." The first issue in January 1885 carried, in addition to field reports and boiled-down erudition, five articles. These ranged from an original monograph on inscriptions from Alexandrine sepulchral vases to syntheses of existing scholarship that were meant to illuminate large if somewhat technical issues in classical archaeology (such as the influence of crude-brick construction on the Doric style). Frothingham himself contributed "The Revival of Sculpture in Europe in the thirteenth century"; Norton a brief biography of John Izard Middleton (1785–1849), the first American to publish in classical archaeology. Though stressing Middleton's pioneering study of Cyclopean walls in ancient Latium, Norton's article qualified as scholarship only by an act of grace.[43]

At what did Norton qualify? No clear answer emerges. Had he chosen to write on medieval churches, he would surely have ranked as specialist, but he preferred to reserve such studies for general interest magazines like *Harper's!* Frothingham regarded him as sufficiently informed in classical archaeology to seek his advice repeatedly on an associate editor for that area. European classical archaeologists, too, treated Norton as a member of the club, though probably because he headed the AIA. The *Journal*'s editors and contributors trembled most obviously before him as an authority on English prose. In sum, specialized expertise remained jumbled up with general knowledge, the frontier between them befogged and Norton's fiefdoms in the kingdom of knowledge impressively wide if increasingly precarious.

Norton had more personal problems on his mind in the summer of 1885. James Lowell's wife Fanny had died in February, and a few weeks later the new Cleveland administration sacked Lowell in favor of a Democrat. He arrived home from London shortly after the middle of June, terribly lonely and with really no home to go to. James felt he could not bear living at Elmwood, and experience taught Charles to agree ("you could not lay the ghosts"); so James went to stay with his daughter in Southborough. In August, Lowell came to Ashfield, where clustered some of his oldest friends, Nortons and Curtises and Fields. There, he and Charles occupied their hours, as so many years ago, with translating Dante—only now it was Norton's new prose version. Charles persuaded James to take the podium at that summer's Academy Dinner on 27 August; perhaps he also talked him into accepting Charles Eliot's request to teach in the fall. James needed occupation. Charles knew all about that, and he left Ashfield sober even by Norton gauge.[44]

That winter the American School at Athens demanded almost as much time as the Carlyle editing: endless exchange of correspondence, an infinite series of meetings. Vigorous beating of dollar-laden bushes produced enough endowment by February to go ahead with plans for building; the managers of the new British School agreed to share some facilities; the business began of choosing an architect and builder and of negotiating with the Greek government for a site. In May a lot was selected on Mount Lycabettus, a remote mile from the Acropolis but next to the British School.

With Athenian correspondence flurrying around him and Carlyle's letters on his desk, Norton was also teaching again. Charles Eliot's elective system had by now completed its conquest of the Harvard curriculum, and students could select courses with virtually no constraint. More and more of them adopted Professor Norton's fine arts lectures, despite the subject's utter impracticality—or because of it. Fine Arts 4 on the arts of Florence (now enhanced by "large photographs" of art works bought for the lecture room at Norton's behest) enrolled about 125 of Harvard's 1,080 undergraduates this fall, putting it among the college's largest courses.[45]

Why so many students opted for fine arts poses a difficult question. The austere and slightly ethereal Norton, with his scholar's stoop and "the measured, accurate speech of the New England man of letters," never became the tweedy sort of Mr. Chips who attracted the affection of undergraduates. A felt need for "culture" motivated many of them to approach his lectern, though whether the need they felt was for spiritual enrichment or social polish is hard to say—probably a dab of both, in proportions varying by student. A felt need for an easy pass motivated maybe even more of them. Norton's courses had grown softer over the past few years, even notoriously so: apparently a deliberate strategy to lure into his lecture room the culturally malnourished. A smidgen of civilization might rub off even on the rich barbarians who never cracked a book, while a few of them would surprise themselves by discovering within their minds an aspiration never suspected. To get a gentleman's C from Norton was dead easy; "to win a mark of distinction was an exceedingly difficult thing."[46]

Yet grading policy goes very little distance in explaining his "enormous influence over the youth who sat under him." In 1921 the longtime editor of the Harvard alumni magazine ranked Norton's Fine Arts 4 as the most important course "given in modern days at Harvard." Whence this power? The two keys were the personal interest that he took in students and the ideals that he personified for them. The writer John Jay Chapman, a graduate of 1884 who did not warm to the way in which Norton looked down from Olympus upon the uncivilized masses below, conceded that he "gave to his students not only what he knew, but what he was."[47]

Norton did not simply teach art, literature, and culture: he embodied them. William Roscoe Thayer, class of 1881, who returned in 1885 for graduate work in literature and fine arts, encountered Norton only then. "The urbanity of his manner and the poise of his intellect" drew Thayer like a magnet, and he never shook off the spell. Another student that year, Bernhard Berenson, a Lithuanian Jewish immigrant, stood as far outside patrician Boston as a Harvard man could; yet he perceived in Norton's cultivation some glimmer of what he yearned to become—which was *not* a patrician Bostonian. As Berenson read Norton's beloved Dante under Norton's fastidious eye, "the Divine Comedy made me breathless as it loomed up before me, and I panted to reach up to it." Berenson's aesthetic path would diverge sharply from Norton's moralism, and he later came almost to despise his old teacher. Yet that teacher transformed Berenson's life, as much because of who he was as of what he said. It was not just Norton's "charm," undeniable though that was to a naive aesthete like Berenson; the old Berenson recalled Norton's "good and great influence not only over the young, breezy and not always high-bred barbarians who already were snobbizing Harvard, but over the marginals like myself, on the ragged edge of the social body, with nothing to recommend them but their Pandora's box of personal gifts and characteristics."[48]

John Jay Chapman, who graduated two years before Berenson, looking back thirty years later declared Norton "in some ways" the "most important man" at Harvard. "You heard about Goodwin; you heard about Lane; but you *knew* Norton. Every one knew him. He was an academic power of the first magnitude, a great individuality through which the best traditions of American college life were continued." "More men," Chapman went on, "have told me what Norton did for them in opening their understanding to the influence of art than have ever spoken to me of all the rest of Harvard professors put together." This from a man who did not much like the person of whom he wrote. As Norton delivered his lectures in the spring of 1886 he teetered on the brink of Harvard legend.[49]

Yet his reputation had long carried far beyond Harvard, and it now began to billow into national fame, for Norton answered a yearning felt by more than college boys. Around 1870 art museums started to crop up in cities across the land: the Metropolitan in New York (1870), the Museum of Fine Arts in Boston (1870), the Museum of Art in Philadelphia (1875), the Art Museum in Cincinnati (1877), the Art Institute in Chicago (1879), and many foundations less celebrated. By the 1880s this museum movement, and a parallel propensity to donate to colleges and universities, indicated some deeply felt aspiration, at least among the sorts of Americans who could afford to patronize such institutions.

This hunger, easy to reduce to caricature, probably will always elude precise delineation. It mingled envy of the trappings of European aristocracy, a desire to sanitize dubiously got wealth, and a craving for an ersatz public spirituality as religion began to disentangle itself from central institutions of national life. Nobler motives, too, compelled, chief among them a feeling that some meaning deeper than stocks and bonds, more universal than one's family and friends, inhered in life. All this was what "culture" signified. Religion had once provided such a sense of meaning and still did for many Americans. But, for others, Protestant Christianity began, in the later nineteenth century, to fade into a nebulous other world and a set of social rituals, or to seem slightly parochial in a country inhabited by well-tailored Jews and Catholics and agnostics, or even to evaporate altogether, as it had for Norton.

This supplied merely one of the qualifications that equipped him uniquely well to speak to and for these spiritually needy (and materially snug) Americans. He hobnobbed on terms of equality with celebrated masters of European culture. He sprang from about the closest thing to an American aristocracy, the Brahmin class of Boston.[50] And, unlike many fashionable preachers in actual churches, he did not hesitate to deliver to nouveaux riches the sermons denouncing their vices that many plutocrats believed, or half believed, they needed to hear. Moreover, he himself had deep faith in the morally strengthening and life-enriching effect of great art and literature. In the kingdom of the insecure the honest and fearless man is king.

Nor should one entirely discount the fact that by 1886 Norton simply knew more about a broader range of art and literature than any of his countrymen. The distinguished Italian archaeologist Rodolfo Lanciani labeled him "the father of American science" (meaning science in the broad sense of *Wissenschaft*). Visitors came to Shady Hill for the express purpose of seeing his pictures and hearing him talk about them as no other American could. Aspiring American collectors valued his advice on rare books and paintings. Even a successful businessman—should one say especially a successful businessman?—could see he was not bluffing.[51]

For years known as an expert in art, architecture, and literature, recognized as one of the country's soundest critics, Norton from the mid-1880s emerged as America's preeminent cultural arbiter. His voice in the Froude controversy resounded throughout the United States, not only across the Atlantic. As commentator on the health of his culture, he had before him the examples of his old friend Ruskin and his newer friend Matthew Arnold. Norton equaled neither in rhetoric, originality, or critical acuity; yet he was more deeply learned than Ruskin, more broadly learned than Arnold. He ranged more widely than Arnold in commenting on national life yet hewed persuasively closer to the mainstream of opinion than Ruskin. Most crucially, he wielded an organizational and strategic sense shrewder than either's. He knew how to embed a cultural critique in institutions as enduring as the Archaeological Institute, as occasional as the Ashfield Academy Dinners, as ingeniously targeted as the literary anthologies for youngsters that he proposed in autumn 1885 to the textbook publisher D. C. Heath.

The Victorians invented the intellectual as a social type. The writer once dependent on the patronage of wealthy men had become self-supporting; the clergyman once by virtue of his position a pillar of society had devolved into a secular and skeptical inquirer standing apart from any establishment (except perhaps a rather marginal academic one). Norton defined for this new creature a new role—cultural critic: arbiter of culture, censor of mores. Yet in doing so he hardly abandoned his Boston tradition. Just as the Puritan minister survived, transmuted, in the Boston Federalism of Andrews Norton, so the Federalist ideal of morally charged intellectual leadership took on new form, more angular, more acid, even alienated, in the criticism of Charles Eliot Norton.

THIRTEEN

Years That Bring the Philologic Mind, 1886–1891

The farther Norton sailed into the public eye, the more Ashfield's peaceful haven mattered. There, too, he found George's comradeship, dearer each year as seasoned friends grew fewer. By early June of 1886, Charles had settled quietly at the Locusts, not budging till October whistled him back to his Harvard lecture room. Ashfield, if not idyllic to every resident, seemed so to Norton: hay to gather, wood to chop, berries to pick, books to relax with, and agreeable visitors such as Matthew Arnold and his wife, who stayed twice that summer.

Controversy could pick a path even through the dense birch and maple of Franklin County. Any August, for instance, some famous orator at Norton and Curtis's Academy Dinner might gruffly speak his mind to the ever larger corps of reporters, avid for a dog-days story. This summer it was the American School at Athens that roiled Norton's pond and his old friend William Stillman who first troubled the waters. In June the *Nation* published a letter from Stillman denouncing the school's annual director for 1885–86, the Harvard classicist Frederic Allen. Allen had gone to Athens reluctantly and passed the winter there in poor health. Students complained that he neglected them, ignored important German archaeologists in town, and let his wife and her visitors use the school library as a private sitting room. Stillman's charges contained enough truth to force Norton and his colleagues to try to limit the damage; and the 1886–87 director, Martin D'Ooge of the University of Michigan, sailed in July under instruction to pacify the students.

This blowup speeded plans to cure the root defect: that each year a raw director started from scratch. Norton, John White, William Goodwin, and William Ware (the de facto managers for Athens) did not need Allen's ineptitude to realize the inadequacy of the system; but they also saw no easy solution. Their dilemma followed from the reason for founding the school in the first place—the United States had not a single experienced classical archaeologist—and from "the impolicy of employing anybody but an American." The amateur art lovers who largely populated the AIA and paid its bills sharpened the predicament by failing even to see the need for expertise. Norton thought the best way out to hire Charles Waldstein, head of the Fitzwilliam Museum at the University of Cambridge and at least American-born. Waldstein had flaws: he did not know modern Greek, and his expertise lay in ancient art rather than in archaeology. But, by October, White, Goodwin, and Ware had come round to Norton's view.[1]

By then Ashfieldian peace had ended anyway, and Norton faced the annual invasion of British visitors, as regular as the turning leaves. By now (as one Englishman observed) Shady Hill had become "a kind of literary consulate," its library a "literary museum" crammed with Norton's "almost unique collection of volumes, manuscripts, notes, and autographs," and Norton himself the celebrated "Proxenos, or Consul-General for British literature and men of letters" visiting Massachusetts. This year, with Harvard celebrating its 250th anniversary, British guests "all but swamped" Norton—"Five on Friday; two yesterday; two more today!" The delegate from Emmanuel College, the historian Mandell Creighton, and his wife stayed for a week at Shady Hill; and Norton returned Emmanuel's 1884 hospitality with a huge reception for them one evening and a formal dinner the next. The Harvard jubilee ended on 8 November, but the Creightons were scarcely out the door before the Italian archaeologist Rodolfo Lanciani arrived for a month of lectures in Sanders Theatre and of entertainment at Shady Hill.[2]

Fellow citizens also pestered Norton: for lectures, opinions, autographs. When one editor, hankering for the eminent name, asked out of the blue for an essay on (bizarrely) Tolstoy, Norton wearily replied that he had read too little of Tolstoy's work to judge it; and "even if I had read it all I have not the leisure to write what would be a difficult piece of criticism"—adding in acid, "The time of a man of letters is precious": "I am tempted to write a homily, but forbear." Even Christmas now passed publicly. Concerned about Harvard students too poor to return home for the holiday, Norton had begun inviting all the hangers-around to Shady Hill for Christmas Eve dinner. (The custom endured, folded into the Norton legend.) The New Year began with Charles Waldstein coming to stay for a week and be wooed for Athens. He returned off and on until March.[3]

What spare time Norton salvaged from the AIA and teaching went largely to literary work. In 1887 he published the Carlyle-Goethe correspondence and the revised *Reminiscences;* in 1888, two volumes of *Letters of*

Thomas Carlyle, 1826–36. As Norton's editing moved past the 1830s, with Carlyle advancing in fame and correspondents multiplying, the burden grew exponentially. Norton somehow got the job done by himself up to 1845. But in the fall of 1891 he hired his former student William Roscoe Thayer to choose, under Norton's oversight, letters "desirable to print" from the final thirty-five years of Carlyle's life; by February 1892 a selection stood ready for the editor's hand. Then Norton put off the project. Carlyle's family "had hoped and expected" him to finish the job; why he did not still puzzles. Perhaps the endless task simply interfered with work more urgent to Norton. Perhaps, having put Froude in his place, he had achieved his main end. Or perhaps Ruskin's anger over his attacks on Froude hurt too badly, for these ongoing editions sorely strained one of the two or three deepest friendships of Norton's life.[4] Although little comfort to Norton, others esteemed his Carlyle editions; and such literary work (though far from the only warrant) probably played a part in Harvard's decision to award her son an honorary LL.D. in June 1887.

In any case, gravitation toward more literary topics, away from art and archaeology, showed in Norton's teaching as well. In 1886–87 he retrieved Dante from a dispirited Lowell and, the next year, handed over his own upper-level course in Greek art to a former student (and student of the American School), Harold Fowler. Norton continued to teach the broad survey of ancient art (the celebrated Fine Arts 3), along with, in alternate years, a companion Fine Arts 4 covering medieval art. But the old treatments of Florentine and Venetian art devolved into a single course called "*Literature* and the Fine Arts in Italy during the Middle Ages and the Renaissance, with special study of Dante." This pattern—two big-scale art history surveys, a more specialized course centered on Dante—would continue to the end of Norton's classroom career.[5]

To avert breakdowns Norton had finally learned to cut back other business during term time, although even the abbreviated menu of public duties ran on and on, extended by private ones. On 31 March 1887, for instance, he presided over an authors' reading in behalf of the Longfellow Memorial Association, then two weeks later traveled to New York to represent Harvard at Columbia's centenary and to attend a fund-raising dinner for the American School. He returned just in time to greet his in-laws Sara and William Darwin and, a few days later, to give Lowell a farewell lunch before James's annual departure to summer in England, this year with Lily in tow. The three girls were growing into young women (even Margaret, who was seventeen), and they needed from their father a different sort of care as they began to attract from the Harvard students new attention. Sally, at twenty-two, had turned out decidedly a beauty, Lily attractive, Margaret very plain, and they had equally diverse tastes and talents. (Paradiso, Purgatorio, and Inferno, the undergraduates said—typically sensitive young males.) Their father seemed baffled about how to cope with any of them as they grew into Victorian sexual maturity, potentially into marriage, and certainly into new-felt urges to independence.

This year even Ashfield felt unsettled, restless. By early July, Sally had gone off to visit friends on the North Shore, leaving only the three younger children with Papa. And one of summer's most familiar faces had gone, John Field having at last succumbed to Bright's disease, just short of his seventy-second birthday. Except for George's company, Norton passed a "very solitary" summer, troubled again by insomnia and frustrated by the resulting inability to accomplish the work he had planned.[6]

More than physical ills or temporary irritation underlay his unease. "From year to year," he wrote James, "I seem to myself to grow more & more silent, and to express less of what is in my soul." Why quietude? The chill of age, coming over a man about to turn sixty? Was he confronting more honestly his own limitations, as sometimes happens when the great world applauds one's achievements? Charles Eliot Norton, prolific author, did tell Lowell that he yearned for "the power of expression"! He longed, but felt unable, "to give form and utterance to a few of the deepest conceptions of Life and its significance and uses which come to one as one grows old and draws the lessons from his own experience." Having Dante as constant companion did dish any illusions of one's own about saying something worthwhile. Returning to Shady Hill in late September, Charles "felt more keenly" than ever the "the lack of old friends, the burial of old memories in my heart." A few months later Georgie Burne Jones, no fool when it came to the human heart, commented on "a note of sadness" in a recent letter from Charles. "I think of you always as bearing a burden so heavy that you can only just carry it, but carrying it nevertheless in such a way that no one would exclaim that you were overladen—I take it that this is much what you would wish."[7]

The year passed. There were the students; the annual English herd to feed and water; visits from Godkin and Woodberry and Jonathan Harrison (now agitating for Indian rights); James Lowell to welcome home from England, just in time to celebrate Charles's sixtieth birthday on 16 November. And by following John Simon's prescription for daily rest Norton kept himself in tolerable health. In June 1888, Eliot graduated near the top of his class at Harvard Law School, though illness kept Rupert from his college commencement. On 13 June their father got a degree himself, an honorary doctorate of letters from Columbia. Then the trek to Ashfield: to garden, to read Dante, to watch from afar "the closing scenes of the life of the Republican party" gathered in convention at Chicago, "killed by swallowing its principles." To Norton's disappointment the dose did not prove fatal.[8]

Republican survival only showed how large a measure of corruption the nation's moral physiology had grown to tolerate—and made Ashfield correspondingly more precious in Norton's eyes. The little, old-fashioned country town, where each citizen knew every other and even the affluent lived without display, supplied an object lesson for America. Life there implicitly condemned the crass ostentation and corrosive poverty that disfigured the nation's large cities, the venality that infected its politics, the materialism and self-seeking that diseased its soul. America in the 1880s looked to Norton too much like the aristocratic England that had revulsed him in the 1850s.

He saw in Ashfield a republican simplicity, a muting of class division, a participatory democracy, a willingness of ordinary citizens to take up the burdens of self-government (and to follow the lead of wiser, more experienced heads, such as his) that bespoke an older, healthier America. A skeptic from a later era suspiciously wants to assume that Ashfield's lesser folk looked on things differently than its richest citizen, but nothing other than suspicion supports the assumption. Norton reported to Lowell a meeting of the Sanderson Academy trustees that August—"good men of the village all of them, excellent products of democracy."

> We discussed the questions of town schools, the town debt, town accounts, all with good sense & right purpose. Tonight "by request" I am to give a talk on Longfellow to the townspeople. Tomorrow night George is to preside at a general meeting of the taxpayers, for the discussion of some of the questions we had in debate last night.

At a moment in history when America choked in "a malarial political atmosphere," when its best leaders had to bend every effort barely to begin cleansing the Augean civil service, the nation needed to breathe the unpolluted air of a place like Ashfield.[9]

So Norton asked, "How can we save Ashfield and all that it stands for?"

> It stands for much. It is the image and type of towns that have been the wholesomest communities the earth ever bore, which by their intelligence have

shaped the institutions of the nation, and largely directed its course, and by their virtues have set high the standard of democratic civilization. How may these communities be saved, strong, vigorous, permanent, not for their sake alone, but for the sake of the nation?

How? In part by gracing the town with amenities that would dim the lure of the big city. This was why Norton raised money for and donated books to the town library. In larger part by giving Ashfield's children the intellectual advantages of the great world without their having to leave home. This was why Norton and Curtis year after year poured their efforts into sustaining Sanderson Academy—why in 1887 Norton sold some of his precious rare books to aid the academy; why he and Curtis each summer organized the Academy Dinner for its benefit.[10]

But the dinner had a larger purpose than fund-raising (though the hundreds of dollars it brought in each year did keep the academy going). For at its tables nationally prominent orators warned Ashfield of the needs and perils facing the nation, while Ashfield stepped forward to exemplify to the nation America's own best principles. Curtis and Norton always spoke themselves: in 1888 Curtis pleading "for independence from the tyranny of party"; Norton, for the cultivation of the imagination in schools and "the exercise of the imagination in daily life." "Without imagination"—as Charles had learned from his teachers almost a half century before—"there can be no true sympathy."[11]

Such oracles sprang increasingly often from Norton's tongue during these years, for without fully realizing it he was assuming the mantle of Anglo-America's most visible cultural critic. Ruskin had fallen silent by the end of the 1880s, though his body would live for another decade; and in April 1888 a heart attack cut down Matthew Arnold. Arnold's death hit Norton not only as a personal blow but as an "irreparable" loss to the anglophone world, "for he was doing work of which both America & England stood greatly in need, and there is no one left to continue it." In a eulogy Norton quoted with approval Arnold's idea of criticism as a "disinterested endeavor to learn and propagate the best that is known and thought in the world." Norton went on to stress that "subject, form, style" were "not the final object of criticism." "It is the criticism of life that underlies all true criticism of books, of manners, of institutions." He noted, too, that Arnold had "specially addressed the minds capable of receiving and propagating the highest influences."[12]

Norton's idea of the critic's role did not much differ from Arnold's, though he had absorbed its essentials from the culture of patrician Boston before either of them had taken his A.B. But Norton was no Boston Federalist, at ease in the land. Growing aversion to his country's plutocratic values and boss-ridden politics distanced him from the centers of power and alienated him from the drift of American life. Dissatisfaction engendered isolation, and isolation fed dissatisfaction. By the 1880s Norton exemplified more fully than either Ruskin or Arnold what would be the characteristic stance of that new social type, the intellectual: independent of the powers in the land, critical of their pretensions, opposed to their visions. Being tolerably rich oneself made the stance easier to sustain.

Going on twenty years, Norton had deplored the distinctive superficiality of "American talk about America," on which battened an endemic "national self-complacency." Even Cousin-President Eliot's speeches, he told Jonathan Harrison in 1888, lacked "that deeper view which sees beneath the surface of things." Norton took as his critical mission to speak frankly to his countrymen about precisely such foundational weaknesses and the corresponding overlooked potentials. He hardly expected converts in droves, and it is easy to see why.[13]

He told American architects that they "pander[ed] to the popular taste" because they knew as little, and cared as little, about "the principles of art" as their clients did. But he then reminded them that their craft exerted an "entirely peculiar and enormous power" on "the taste, and hence upon the morals of the community"; and he urged them to recall the civic responsibility thus laid upon them to cultivate "creative imagination and a keen sense of beauty." A former student, William A. Slater, Harvard 1881 (whom Norton liked because, "quite unspoiled by his enormous wealth," he made "no obtrusive display"), had endowed an art museum in Connecticut. This model capitalist invited his old professor to inaugurate the gallery in November 1888; in the event, this became a great public occasion, aswarm with reporters. Norton delivered what the *New York Times* described as "a very earnest but pessimistic lecture on the absence from Americans of the love and taste for art," feeding the crowd "many unpalatable statements."[14]

In that same month Norton published in the *Princeton Review* a widely read—or at least widely assailed—article, "The Intellectual Life of America," arguing that the American elite had allowed material progress to elbow aside intellectual development. Shaking a monitory finger, he warned that "our civilization" teetered on the brink of "degenerating into a glittering barbarism of immeasurable vulgarity and essential feebleness." The next year in *Scribner's* magazine he admonished Americans that their habit of moving restlessly from place to place in pursuit of "wealth and material comfort," their unconcern for family continuity and even for old houses, had stretched American individualism to a dangerous thinness, had weakened the feeling that each life forms "a link, however individual in its form, however different from every other, in a chain reaching back indefinitely into the past, reaching forward indefinitely into the future." The loss of this sentiment, he bleakly warned, "saps the main source of moral being." That in some quarters Norton began to acquire a reputation as a carping snob should come as no surprise.[15]

Neither should it be taken as gospel. Norton tried always to foster what he deemed the better elements in national life, not merely to rail at the worse. He took care to praise (with perceptible patriotic glow) American habits or institutions that he thought worthy of encouragement and emulation. In an 1890 *Harper's* article on Harvard, he applauded the new American university ideal, accurately noting (as not all commentators did, even a century later) that it departed fundamentally from both German and British models. While criticizing Harvard's defects—the "evil influence of wealth" on student attitudes, the excesses of college sports—he held up the university as "an institution in which an American may feel a legitimate pride." And he continued to develop his own projects to amend educational or artistic deficiencies, carrying over into the cultural arena the reformist activism of his model lodging houses and evening school of the 1850s. Most recently he had devised a scheme for "a Library of School Reading" to give young readers easy access to literature of merit. At first Harper Brothers' "educational man" had seemed intrigued, but for some reason he lost interest; by 1889 Norton was wheedling a resisting Century Company to take up the series.[16]

Yet, among Norton's roles, scholar and promoter of scholarship remained the leading ones, with Dante, once again, closest to his heart. Although Longfellow's death and Lowell's retreat had disbanded the original Cambridge Dante circle, Norton's own scholarship was entering its prime. As New England had regarded Andrews and Uncle Ticknor in their day as its most competent Dantists, so now the world recognized Charles—at infinitely higher level of expertise—as preeminent in America. One could press the analogy further, for Norton's special strength as scholar called his father to mind: like Andrews as a biblical critic, and unlike Longfellow and Lowell as Dantists, Charles was a "minute and indefatigable searcher of texts."[17]

He was also an indefatigable animator of other Dantists. In 1885 he had donated to the Harvard Library the bulk of the works by and about Dante that he had amassed over the decades: a capital resource for future researchers. Present ones relied on him in person, as Edward Fay did in preparing his important concordance to the *Divina Commedia* (1888). More generally, Norton's regular reviews of books in the field set for American scholars a critical standard equal to that prevailing in Europe. And under his leadership the Dante Society energized Dante studies in the United States. Beginning in 1887 the society's *Annual Report* included a comprehensive bibliography of the year's scholarship, American and European; within two or three more years the *Annual Report* had established itself as also a kind of *Jahrbuch* for American Dantists, a venue for even book-length monographs like Theodore Koch's pioneering historical survey, "Dante in America" (1896).

Norton's resurgent interest in Dante did not undermine his commitment to classical archaeology. Most urgently, the appointment of a permanent director for the American School still hung fire. In autumn 1887 Charles Waldstein stood on the verge of accepting; then he learned that funds to pay his salary might run short. There followed eighteen months of fiscal uncertainty and protracted negotiation before he agreed with the Managing Committee on a three-year appointment as "resident professor" for two months each winter. This arrangement at least gave the school some continuity of leadership.

And just in time, for the patriotic daydream that had flitted in and out of Norton's head since the seventies seemed at last in his material grasp: the chance for Americans to excavate that most alluring of Greek remains, the temple complex at Delphi, and thereby to vindicate the claim of American archaeology to stand on equal footing with European. In fall 1886 the AIA had begun actively wooing the Greek government for the franchise. The Ecole Française in Athens owned a prior claim, but this deteriorated as a result of Franco-Greek quarrels over a commercial treaty and of uncertainty whether the French could afford to buy out the owners of the ground at Delphi. Finally, in January 1889, the Greek authorities all but promised the site to the American School. "Things come round to those who wait," exulted Norton.[18]

Having waited over a decade, he wasted no time in setting out to raise the needed funds, almost a hundred thousand dollars; as a first step he assembled more than a hundred well-endowed New Yorkers in late January to hear him plead. But the French had no mind to yield; they, too, brought pressure to bear on the Greek government, and the struggle see-sawed for two years. Finally, on 19 November 1890, one of Norton's former students wrote to congratulate his old teacher on "the happy completion of your long cherished plan for the purchase of Delphi." The next day a letter arrived from Waldstein in Athens: the outcome was "by no means certain." On 10 March 1891, Waldstein cabled that the French had won; Norton's dream faded for once and all into the blue Greek skies.[19]

By that date Norton had left the AIA presidency. He resigned in May 1890: weary of letter writing and meetings; wanting more time for Dante and other literary pursuits; most of all, perhaps, feeling that in this field he had done what he could to make actual his vision of American scholarship. His co-worker Thomas Ludlow lamented that no one could fill Norton's shoes; and, in fact, even after Seth Low of Columbia took over the presidency, Norton remained for several years the éminence grise. But Ludlow also observed that the institute had matured to the point where "no one man, however great, is indispensable to its welfare." The AIA and the *American Journal of Archaeology* had supplied a nucleus around which classicists in American colleges coalesced into a profession that now stood on its own; and their coalescence, in turn, had given birth to an academic speciality new to America, classical archaeology. Scholars across the Atlantic "hailed with delight the entrance of America upon the old field of archaeological research," even the great Curtius calling the American dig at Icaria "epoch-making." In January 1890 the Deutsches Archäologisches Institut voted Norton himself honorary foreign member. European recognition, probably more than anything else, gratified the founder: a wounded patriotism always grimaced behind Norton's critiques of American culture.[20]

Yet scholarly nationalism never eclipsed scholarship *pur sang*. Even in striving to oust the French from Delphi, Norton worried less about "the credit for the Institute" than "the general interests of learning": a recent dig by French archaeologists at Delos, he thought, proved that they lacked the "thoroughness, accuracy, and respect for the ancient remains" that American excavators, emulating the Germans, did show. Norton treated the Archaeological Institute as a means to this larger international end of advancing erudition. This required nurturing among researchers a sense of mutual identity and common effort, and from the outset Norton had meant the AIA to be a national institution forging just such concert. He later boasted that, in uniting classicists throughout America, it had given them both "a hitherto unknown sense of independence" and a feeling "of equal brotherhood with the scholars of other lands."[21]

Linking scholars into such national and international networks therefore became one goal of Norton and his diverse collaborators—exemplified, for instance, in the AIA's links with the British Museum and in the Dante Society's broadening out from a Cambridge clan to a national body with international ties. More generally, Norton insisted, "our higher institutions of learning are closely bound together, and the prosperity of any one of them is matter of common interest to all." Yet the scholars in them, he warned, must not cluster together in order to isolate themselves from larger public concerns and the larger public; for "upon the character of our Universities the future civilization of America largely depends."[22]

Naturally, the institution that mattered most to him was Harvard. Norton's father and uncle had captained the first effort to turn Harvard toward serious scholarship; and Charles followed their example, aiding Charles Eliot as he steered the university further along the course their family had set. By the early 1890s, with some thirty-five full professors and more than seventy in lower faculty ranks, the university could sustain specialized postgraduate work across a range of fields. Such a program seemed to Norton as to others sine qua non for laying the "deeper foundations of learning." So he gladly taught the new courses "Primarily for Graduates," entangled himself in the modern business of advising graduate students about financial aid and courses of study, became one of the biggest old boys in the developing old-boy network for filling college teaching jobs, and served on the administrative board of Harvard's new Graduate School. For over a decade he had advocated a university museum to house collections for the advanced study of art. What he never did—curiously to later eyes—was to supervise a doctoral dissertation.[23]

His own scholarship on medieval church building had gone into dormancy while Norton built up the AIA, but it began to leaf out again in 1889. The October *Harper's* carried a long article on "The Building of the Church of St.-Denis," followed in November by one on Chartres. These French sequelae to Norton's Italian *Studies of Church-Building in the Middle Ages* seemed, however, comparatively stunted. His prose had grown cooler, his narrative more disjointed, his account of the buildings more superficial. In contrast to the *Atlantic* ten years earlier, *Harper's* allowed no footnotes. It appears that precious little of Norton's research found its way into these articles, that he "wrote down" to a "popular" audience newly redefined as lacking appetite for erudition. Norton always meant to rework these studies and add one of Cluny, making a book parallel to his earlier one on Venice, Siena, and Florence. Had he found the time to do so, one might venture a firmer judgment on his quality as historian.

What is transparent is that he did not fit into the mold of art history as the field defined itself in the two or three generations following him. He utterly ignored the formalist approach to criticism developing in Europe (and the analogous experiments of the Impressionists). Norton possessed a discriminating eye and an immense miscellany of detail about individual paintings and painterly techniques, about specific buildings and architectural methods: the basic tool kit of formalist connoisseurship. Yet he could not conceive art-historical scholarship as connoisseurship for its own sake, still less imagine teaching art history as the "appreciation" of individual objects abstracted from the gritty realities of bloodshed and avarice, of faith and ideals, that composed the milieu within which any painter took up a brush. But art history in the United States did just that in the decades after Norton, averting its gaze from history; not until the 1970s would the discipline wake up to the pastness of the past. So, paradoxically, the founder of the field of art history in America left almost no lasting impress on its practice. Rather, his scholarly influence worked in another way, by bending research in other domains of the humanities toward cultural history.

His student Woodberry credited Norton with two great contributions to historical scholarship in America. First, a book like *Church-Building* showed what research in the service of deeper understanding meant, providing a forceful "example of scholarly work such as I do not know of in our present publications,—an example which may have influence upon younger men, as it encouraged me like the flashing out of a new guiding light." Second, Norton treated "art *as a mode of history.*" Woodberry (in this, his master's disciple) regarded this approach to art as "of most importance, perhaps, for a people without art and accustomed to look on art as an appendix to life, so to speak." Later scholars might be more inclined to appreciate Norton's studies of medieval churches as pioneering the writing of integrated cultural history.[24]

However one specified Norton's strengths as historian, his great failing was patent. Venice, Florence, Saint-Denis remained isolated tales, not parts of a developed analysis of medieval culture. Why this should have been so is something of a puzzle. True, materials for the study of the Middle Ages remained scattered and fragmentary; but such a quandary did not stop Norton's younger contemporary, Henry Adams, from building a coherent study in *Mont-Saint-Michel and Chartres* (1904) nor his older one, Jacob Burkhardt, from seeing his vastly influential vision of *Die Kultur der Renaissance in Italien* (1860). Perhaps the positivist ex-Unitarian in Norton ultimately lacked enough respect for the culture he studied to see it as a compelling whole; perhaps the restless reformer and polymathic scholar had not the temperament to settle down long enough to weave all the threads into one tapestry; perhaps the moralist preferred the exemplary case over a less sharply pointed longer account. For whatever reason, Norton could not—or did not care to—cast his researches into a coherent, continuous narrative; they never added up to more than a loosely connected series of episodes with repeating themes.

As the 1880s ended, Norton faced fragmentation in his personal life, too—literal and metaphoric. Despondently, he watched the breaking up of Shady Hill, staved off for decades despite shrinking capital. In 1887–88, Charles Eliot's son (whom Norton had helped to guide into the new profession of landscape architecture) drew up a subdivision plan, running three new streets through the western, lower section of the estate. Norton had one comfort: the new neighbors he looked down on through the trees were mostly Harvard colleagues, among them William James, a friendly acquaintance for two decades.[25]

The passage of years also and inevitably sundered his family. In October 1888, Rupert sailed for Germany to begin medical studies, and Eliot moved to New York to set up a law practice. A year later he engaged himself to Margaret Meyer, a "pretty young lady" of that flashy city so alien to an old Bostonian. "So the young ones fly from the nest! They carry with them more than they know." In April 1889, Arthur Clough's son, also called Arthur, came to visit Shady Hill. Three weeks later, Arthur asked Sally to marry him. She wavered; he pressed his suit; she crossed the Atlantic to see him; and in September 1890, she returned, "taking," as Georgie Burne-Jones wrote Charles, "her heart back to you untouched." Sally had proved such "a thorough American," Georgie said, that she could not wed across the sea. Maybe. But in the end not one of Charles's three daughters (resembling in this two of Andrews's three) could pull away from the powerful magnet of their father.[26]

Especially, perhaps, when that father's loneliness grew painfully obvious. In October 1890, with Sally and Lily home from England and Rupert from Germany, Eliot and his new wife Margaret traveled up from New York for a reunion dinner. Not for three years had Papa got all six children together, nor would he again for a long time. And other vacancies threatened. In January 1890, James Lowell fell seriously ill, with internal bleeding of obscure origin; in February he hung near death. Though he rallied, he remained sickly and depressed all through the winter of 1890–91. Only a couple of months before Lowell's affliction, Leslie Stephen had collapsed from "nervous exhaustion." In this case the patient's need for prolonged rest paid a dividend to Charles: a three-week visit to America the following June and "a very good time" at Shady Hill. Even this was small change against the growing balance of lonely evenings in the big old house. Lowell disabled, Stephen back home, "whom have I to talk with in these wintry (spiritually wintry) days?" George Curtis still visited occasionally, as did one or two engaging ex-students; and Norton appreciated the virtues of the young "lawyers, doctors, artists" of Boston's Tavern Club—including "that of not forgetting us old men." In 1890 they remembered to elect Norton as their president. When all else failed, favorite authors filled the lonely dusk; in 1890 Charles rediscovered John Donne.[27]

The best antidote to loneliness was, as always, work. The spring of 1891 found Norton picking through selections for what were to be called the *Heart of Oak* books: a Boston schoolbook publisher, D. C. Heath, had finally committed his firm to the anthologies for young readers that Norton had long lobbied for. Helping in this job was Kate Stephens, an ex-professor of Greek at Kansas University who had fallen on hard times, adversity owed probably to her "extreme nervous" temperament, "ambitious disposition," and suspicious nature. For the next several years she became for Norton both an aide-de-camp and an object of charity.[28]

The *Heart of Oak* books were merely a sideline to Norton's great project; for five years now he had wrestled with canto after canto of the *Divina Commedia*. Perhaps the most precisely and limpidly written long poem in Western literature, Dante's epic is correspondingly the most maddeningly elusive to fit into words other than the ones its author chose. Despite the straitjacket of terza rima, there is, as Norton observed, "rarely a needless or forced word in Dante's lines." Inevitably, then, the contortion needed to twist them into English verse sacrificed Dante's "directness, simplicity, and naturalness," which were exactly the qualities that gave his poem its "distinction and permanence of effect." A prose translation sacrificed any hope of conveying the power and grace of Dante's poetry—but not the possibility (if truly a literal rendering) of representing faithfully its character and substance, "for the Italian verse is as direct as the English prose."[29]

During the winter of 1890–91, the Riverside Press in Cambridge began setting Norton's English prose version of the *Inferno* in type. By summer he was sending copy for *Purgatorio* while simultaneously, with what aid the ailing Lowell could give, revising proofs almost damp from the press, moving at the rate of two cantos a week. In November, Houghton Mifflin and Company published *Hell*, closely followed by *Purgatory* and a year later by

Paradise. A thorough revision of Norton's 1867 translation of the *Vita Nuova* appeared as a companion volume. As with all his books, Norton took care that these were elegantly designed and printed.[30]

The *Divine Comedy* made a literary event in America and won recognition on both sides of the ocean as among the most faithful translations of Dante's epic yet to appear. The *Nation*'s friendly reviewer deemed it unequivocally the best in English, whether judged for accuracy, lucidity, concision, or style; Norton had reproduced better than any predecessor even the shifting modulations in voices from episode to episode. The eminent British Dantist Paget Toynbee, while unenthusiastic about *Purgatory,* placed *Hell* atop the heap of prose translations. Other English critics tended to get sniffy about this American, though giving high marks for exactitude. As these disagreements suggest, the best parts of Norton's translation—notably *Hell*—read very well indeed, the worst parts clumsily, and all taken together maintain an unusually high average for fidelity to the letter of the original.[31]

Houghton Mifflin kept the *Divine Comedy* in print in its original three-volume format through 1928, then as a one-volume school edition from 1941 to 1958, also reprinting Norton's *Vita Nuova* as late as 1935. (Perhaps owing to the popularity of the translations, the old *Notes of Travel and Study in Italy* likewise remained in print into the twentieth century.) In the 1950s, Encyclopedia Britannica chose Norton's version for its series, Great Books of the Western World; other reprints appeared into the second half of the twentieth century. This durability bespeaks both the exactness and the fluency of the translation, and these qualities in turn resulted from Norton's careful scholarship and his minute attention to language. This compulsive care for language stretched back to the youth who modeled himself on his father.[32]

Yet the appeal of his Dante translations had deeper causes than their own comparative excellence, for Dante spoke with peculiar force to Victorians. The cult—and almost a cult it was—was recent. In 1812 George Ticknor could find only one copy of the *Divina Commedia* in Boston—which neither he nor the owner could read! Norton's friend Samuel Ward, a decade older than Charles, believed that "Dante has been invented in my lifetime." Yet by midcentury not only did "natural" *devotés* like Ruskin and the Rossettis adore Dante; so did people as unpredictable as the abolitionist senator Charles Sumner, the political economist Francis Lieber, and the South Carolina lawyer-diplomat Hugh Legaré.[33]

To understand the resonance of Dante among the Victorians, one must keep in mind two preliminary facts: first, that Dante, though famed for pioneering in the vernacular, remained part and parcel of a Latinate intellectual culture extending from antiquity through the seventeenth century; second, that classical schooling, a mere century or two removed from this true Latinate culture, still molded educated Victorians. (Not long after his *Divine Comedy* appeared, Norton wired birthday greetings to the elder Oliver Wendell Holmes; the telegram comprised in its entirety a moderately obscure Virgilian tag, in Latin.) Norton's students in the 1880s and 1890s represented the last American generation formed by this old-fashioned secondary education, the last to have some wraithlike familiarity with the intellectual culture behind the *Divina Commedia*. This was prerequisite.[34]

Given an ability to connect with Dante, what drew readers to him? Norton believed it was the spiritual cravings distinctive to his era. In the Turnbull Lectures delivered at Johns Hopkins in 1894, he attributed the vogue of Dante to a combination of "the materialism of our existing state of civilization" and "the general dissolution of the old forms of religious faith." Dante, the archetype of a great religious poet, proved superbly able to slake thirsts for larger meaning. "Antiquated, erroneous, or childish" theological debris cluttered the *Divina Commedia*; yet, Norton thought, it still spoke more powerfully to readers than any other work "of poetic art"—"alike because of the general truth of its fundamental proposition, the subjection of the whole world to the moral law, and because of the directness, vividness & power of the poet's application of this truth to the lives & destiny of individual men."[35]

Norton hit not far from the mark. To put the matter cynically, acquaintance with Dante was supposed to deepen his readers morally and emotionally; hence a fondness for the *Divina Commedia* put gratifying psychological distance between oneself and the money-grubbing *ignobile vulgus*, perhaps an especially nice feeling if one grubbed a bit oneself. (There is an analogy to the mugwump sensibility in politics, its purer-than-thou air.) A more charitable explanation probably explains better a larger number of readers. The United States underwent a phenomenal industrial expansion during the last third of the nineteenth century; this thrust into public view an unprecedently porcine greed, genuinely distressing many Americans, leaving them receptive to potent moral visions. Few could be more commanding than Dante's.

Yet these crude hypotheses scarcely begin to explain the specific character of the Dante cult. The *Divina Commedia* enriched the religious imagination in an era when for many in the educated classes the fund of Christian truth ran low, even approached bankruptcy. These were the decades when agnosticism first became a viable option for large numbers of people in

Britain and the United States. The number of out-and-out unbelievers, such as Norton, remained comparatively small; the number of those who worried whether God had really revealed the Bible, whether miracles could trump scientific laws, whether Christ (or oneself) could live after death, was large and growing. Yet the scientific vision of reality—by now more or less materialist in principle, more or less taken as an alternative to religion as a mode of explaining the world—did not entirely satisfy, for all its undeniable power and popularity. Hence the yearning that led readers confusedly to Dante. Compared even to lyric poetry or painting, Dante's highly symbolic, allegorical, even mystical art had the specific appeal of a counterweight to the hard-headed ethic of science. Most well-educated Victorians, like Norton himself, leaned toward utilitarianism in politics and social ethics, scientism in epistemology. But they rarely believed that pure rationality ought to reign in the domain of emotion, sympathy, and human purpose.

For human truths existed insusceptible to proof or disproof. Perhaps subjective in some absolute cosmic sense—for only the human species recognized such truths—they were objectively real for its members. The felt goodness of love, the allure of the beautiful, might no longer testify to universal divine law, might elude the experiments of science, but did nonetheless bind together all human beings. Thus an ethic of feeling countered the ethic of belief; an ethic of character, that of conscience; an ethic of art, that of science. Science penetrated to the truths behind forms; art, by veiling truth *in* form, revealed the outlines of truths in essence impenetrable.

Art drew boundaries around the cultural authority of science. It provided an alternative to the clear-sighted truthfulness that people like Norton associated with scientific reason. And no artist suggested this deeper, human reality more evocatively than the great allegorical poet of truths seen through a glass darkly, Dante Alighieri.

Publication of the *Divine Comedy* sealed Norton's scholarly reputation. By now his learning had become a Boston legend. William and Henry James's acidic sister Alice asked her diary in 1891, "Who, I should like to know, ever saw an over-educated Yankee!—save, always the egregious Norton." Much of his erudition converged on Dante, a field in which for two decades leading European scholars had treated Norton as a peer. In 1891 William Warren Vernon, a competent if flattering judge, declared him one of the three greatest Dantists alive. Few would have gone so far even at the time, and later generations of experts have not set Norton on a pinnacle. That being said, he did bring American scholarship up to an unprecedented level, a rough equality with the best European Dante literature.[36]

And, despite his suspicion of formal doctoral study, Norton raised up an entire generation of scholars to follow him. Even more than in the cases of classical archaeology and art history, the academic field of Dante studies in the United States owes its existence to him. (In all these cases, to be sure, another scholar would eventually have taken the lead had Norton not done so, though it is hard to imagine anyone else commanding the three different fields.) This act of institutional creation involved far more than his leadership of the Dante Society. He suggested lines of work, lent books, encouraged young scholars, helped them find their way to obscure sources. The first substantial works of American Dante scholarship—such as E. A. Fay's concordance to the *Divina Commedia* and Charles S. Latham's annotated *Translation of Dante's Eleven Letters*—would almost certainly never have seen the light without his aid. T. W. Koch, founder of the great Cornell Dante collection and author of the first survey of American Dante scholarship, was his student. Charles Grandgent, the preeminent Dantist of the early twentieth century, was first his student, then his colleague, finally his successor. This "new generation of American Dantists," the first rooted in universities, were right to look on Norton as their "spiritual father."[37]

Yet Norton's patriarchal role in Dante studies—as well as that in the teaching of art and the organizing of classical archaeology—raises a profound question about the history of learning. In 1844 Andrews Norton had encouraged the Boston dentist Thomas Parsons to continue his study and translations of Dante: a pursuit, he said, that might pleasantly and honorably occupy his *leisure* for years to come.[38] Such was pretty nearly the place that Dante occupied in Charles Norton's life; though he always enjoyed teaching Dante to Boston ladies or Harvard seniors, his Dante work, like his leadership in archaeology, bore scant relation to any professional commitment or academic position. Nonetheless, Norton did win eminence among university-based scholars in Europe, and he did largely found three professional academic specialities in the United States. How does this apparent paradox fit into the history of learning? Was he a genteel amateur? a new professional? some awkward transitional form in the evolution of the modern academic species?

Or are these even useful distinctions? Is the supposed "transition" from "amateur" to "professional" an artifact of a later era, a schema imposed anachronistically on a late-Victorian academic environment still plastic and undetermined, in order to make it fit into a neat story of the development of the twentieth-century idea of a university? Doubts about this simple tale of origins are in order. As late as the 1890s, long after the old generalist professor had in the leading colleges lumbered the way of *Stegosaurus*, the new ideals of "scholarship" and "research" pointed toward more than one academic future.

As Norton's own research deepened in the 1880s, as he concentrated more of his energy on translating Dante and on teaching art history, he might well have narrowed his scholarly purview. He might have addressed himself to a specialized audience, contracted the scope of his writings, spoken only to issues of immediate concern to other Dante scholars and art historians. He did not, in part because of temperamental intellectual restlessness, in part because of polymathic background and family heritage, in part because of hope that erudition might ultimately influence the mores of American democracy. Nor—and herein lies the larger point—did academic pressures push Norton to behave otherwise. Nothing seemed odd in his delivering a paper in May 1889 to the Harvard Philosophical Club, meeting at Shady Hill, no more than that the Harvard Classical Club should meet there in March 1891. University norms in 1890 did not yet mandate separating knowledge into distinct disciplines: that kind of specialization supplied one model of serious scholarship, but only one. And one about which Norton felt increasingly ambivalent—maybe *because of* his leadership in promoting research. Recall that, for all his advocacy of graduate education, Norton never directed a dissertation.[39]

Part of his ambivalence about the professional ideal of specialization arose from fear of cutting the tie between knowledge and character. Mere expertise—the pedantry of the Ph.D. mill—could not generate the morally deepening effect, the enlargement of sensibility and human sympathies, which growth in knowledge ought to bring, which indeed seemed to Norton the largest purpose of knowledge.

Also behind his ambivalence lay a measure of sensitivity to a profound change in the social structure of knowledge. The old intellectual culture of patrician Boston (like the cultures gravitating around other cities) had of necessity been relatively unspecialized; for the writers and savants who made up that culture had their reference points in the local community and therefore spoke in terms comprehensible to all educated Bostonians. Such a culture was not just locally oriented in space: it went deeper in time. Men of letters and men of science grew up together, went to school together, worked and argued together for a lifetime. They developed profound, growing, ripening intellectual-personal relationships that conditioned their intellectual work at every turn. These ties militated against fragmentation of knowledge, promoted fertilization across very different fields. At Harvard, George

Lane, Frank Child, to some extent even William James still sustained this kind of relation to Norton; so in the AIA did Frank Parkman, Martin Brimmer, and William Goodwin. But relationships like theirs grew rare in the nationalizing academic disciplines of Norton's later career, as a leading nationalizer like Norton knew well. The last of the men still at Harvard who had taught Charles as a college boy died or retired between 1886 and 1888.[40]

Such changes profoundly shaped the character of knowledge, but another epistemological question took scholars even closer to the groundwork. Largely unrelated to these previous ones, it posed a choice that would determine the next century of learning. At issue was not whether new, more scholarly modes of learning, based largely in universities, would displace older, more generalist forms, rooted in local communities (which is how historians often depict the situation). This transition, as such, raised scarcely a ripple, at least in the better colleges. As a matter of course, Norton applied a criterion of "original work" foreign even to so accomplished a historian as his old friend Parkman, routinely taking writers to task for failing to keep up with the latest research. Among serious scholars, such standards now went without saying (except on ritual occasions of public self-congratulation). What Norton and other professors in the new universities grappled with was how to structure this new knowledge.

No one slighted the depth of knowledge represented proverbially by German erudition; but many wondered how to absorb it, how to fit it with other ways of knowing. Norton's sporadic griping about mindless German fact grubbing or superficial French elegance arose from this concern. He worried especially about "the temptation, which attends the study of every science, to exalt the discovery of trifling particulars into an end in itself," to overlook "the distinction between pedantry and learning." Facts, "till ordered in their relation to some general truth, are nothing better than fragments in a heap of rubbish." Norton held up an ideal of a scholarship striving "for breadth of view, for intelligent marshaling of the facts and vivid presentation of them, for abundance of learning easily held in hand."[41]

Yet "breadth of view and abundance of learning" only begin to distinguish Norton's archetype of research; his own work, and his scholarly ideal, grew specifically from philology. In his father's day "philology" had referred to the study of language and literature in the broadest terms, comprehending everything from the comparative study of the evolution of languages, as essayed by Bopp, Rask, and Grimm, to literary criticism like Samuel Johnson's or Coleridge's, to emendation of classical texts, to Andrews's own biblical studies. By the later years of Charles's career, "philology" was migrating toward its more restricted twentieth-century meaning, principally referring to linguistic science (such as investigation of Indo-European) and to the study of old texts from a purely linguistic point of view.[42]

Behind these shifting usages, however, lurked a common methodology or mode of explanation. In its ancient origins and its Renaissance elaboration, philology had centered on improving understanding of an old text by contextualization: by comparing the words, or indeed stories, in the text to usages of the same words, or telling of similar tales, in other texts contemporary with the one under study. And philologists of whatever bent still strove to elucidate a "text" (which, in the case of comparative philology, might be an entire language) by such a process of comparison or contextualization. As Andrews Norton said in his first Dexter Lectures in 1813, the "circumstances in which a word is used" supply "a necessary commentary for defining its signification"; thus, the biblical interpreter must learn not only the characteristic style of the biblical writer and his period but also the conditions and outlook of the people to whom he directed his message, the historical circumstances under which he wrote, the social and economic character of his society, and so forth. This effort to elucidate and deepen meaning—of a text, an event, an idea, a painting—by appeal to historical and cultural context was the key to philology and its influence.[43]

That influence can hardly be overestimated. Charles Norton imbibed it direct from the paternal spring, but he need not have, for its different currents included the recovery of Indo-European by comparative philologists (the single most stunning triumph of scholarship in the nineteenth century); the so-called higher criticism of the Bible (which revolutionized Christianity); and history itself as a scholarly pursuit. From the early eighteenth century to the mid-nineteenth, philology reigned as queen of the sciences in the great German universities that exemplified learning for Europe and America. Darwinism bore its impress; anthropology acknowledged it as a parent.[44]

Yet the historicocultural method of philology produced stultifyingly narrow as well as breathtakingly broad scholarship. The German tradition in Norton's day pushed in both directions, notorious for fact grinders, celebrated for great humanists. In American college classrooms a philological approach could either anesthetize students by parsing Milton or fascinate them, as Lowell did, by telling tales of medieval Florence meant to help them understand Dante. Philology was, after all, in the first instance a work of recovery, the elucidation of lost meanings. As a recuperative discipline, philology could take an anti-interpretive stance; but recovering ancient texts also required interpretation. Setting a text—or a primitive custom or a medieval church—in historicocultural context could imply minute specificity or illuminating breadth. In teaching Dante, Norton aspired to both, explaining passages "fully from every side,—verbal, textual, literary, spiritual." In teaching art, his broad historicocultural contextualizing contrasted with both Ruskin's earlier formalism and Berenson's later aestheticism of technique. Always, the animating impulse was to reach out from the object of study and connect to a larger universe of knowledge.[45]

Philology provided the most important, but not the only, force pushing Norton in this direction. He had also absorbed in his youth the broad-gauged historicism that Unitarian Boston inherited from the Scottish Enlightenment (an outlook itself, by the way, ultimately rooted in philology). The Scots told a story of human progress as a single evolutionary history, implying that at least the historical and cultural sciences formed in the end a single field of knowledge, all being pieces of the one story of humanity. In so expansive a conception of learning, every piece must eventually link up with every other through longer or shorter chains of connection. Norton's own experiences in India, his early interest in the Mound Builders and Nineveh, his later work on the ancient world all conspired to reinforce this breadth of outlook, to dilate his scholarly perspective. And an impressive range of languages enabled him to put these epistemological principles to practical account. Before entering Harvard, Charles had studied Latin, Greek, German, French, and Italian; in 1849 he even added Hindi. Hindi soon dropped from the repertoire, but improving the others occupied him from college days until at least the early 1870s.

The aspired-to scope of erudition showed in Norton's amplitude of literary reference. His leisure reading ranged from Plutarch to Donne to Boswell to Théophile Gautier to Mr. Dooley; and this multiplicity of perspective, combined with a relational habit of mind, early gave him quick and accurate insight, often tossed off in almost epigrammatic classifications. Sir Walter Scott, he remarked in a letter of 1871, observed superbly "what is external & strongly marked in nature, character, & life" but lacked "penetrative" imagination "to reproduce intricate & obscurely defined characters." Norton measured writers of his own era against the whole canvas of European literature. William Morris, contrasted with the "Greeks and Shakespeare & Dante," lacked "sense of proportion of form"; Emerson was "not one of the Universal men in a large sense; but a man of some universal sympathies and relations curiously and instructively hampered by local, provincial, bonds." Such breadth of comparison led Norton not to denigrate but to appreciate contemporary writers: "Put the literature of this century into one scale and that of all preceding time into the other, and the balance would not hang very uneven."[46]

And it gave him a scale of similitudes, a set of criteria, to judge more securely, and to appreciate more deeply, the qualities of any artist or poet. Emerson reminded him not only, say, of Johnson or Hawthorne but also of an "Italian master in the 13th century." This long view explains Norton's easy inclination to cast aside the chaff in editing writers of his generation, rather than (as later editors would wish) to preserve every scrap of a poet's verse. Lowell's "ephemeral production" should "perish with the day to which it added a momentary charm"—as he told that poet more than once. Breadth of learning also accounts for his most remarkable strength as scholar, teacher, and academic innovator: the capacity to integrate erudition into a single great whole, even if that capacity was not exercised in any grand narrative. As the Italian historian William Thayer remarked, Norton held an "immense advantage" over every other British or American Dante scholar: "a specialist's knowledge of medieval art."[47]

Yet Norton was no freak of academic nature. He only exercised more impressively than most a common style of scholarship in the late nineteenth-century university. Rooted in the philological urge to link together pieces of knowledge, this mode of erudition resisted a competing impulse, rooted in physical science, to divide knowledge into discrete specialized "disciplines." Philological historicism—to give Norton's approach a label—displayed itself perhaps most clearly in the new field of comparative literature, itself a natural outgrowth from his kind of learning. Not coincidentally, a student and disciple of Norton's, Arthur Richmond Marsh, returned to Harvard in 1891 as the first professor of comparative literature in the United States. In a letter to his mentor, Marsh defined his new field as concerned with "the organic and consecutive growth of the conceptions which constitute civilization as contrasted with barbarism." His study of classical, medieval, and early modern literatures, he said, "made it possible for me to follow ideas from their genesis, through the Middle Ages, to the present." The program of the twentieth-century giants of comparative literature and the history of ideas—Erich Auerbach, Ernst Curtius, Arthur Lovejoy, J. B. Bury—rests here in embryo.[48]

Scholarship of this Nortonian scope resolved the dilemma haunting "scientific" erudition. In *The Gay Science* Nietzsche taunted academic specialism, the German-model pedantry that Norton similarly mocked.

Almost always the books of scholars are somehow oppressive, oppressed; the "specialist" emerges somewhere—his zeal, his seriousness, his fury, his over-estimation of the nook in which he sits and spins, his hunched back; every specialist has his hunched back. Every scholarly book also mirrors a soul that has become crooked.

But Nietzsche contrasted the scholar with the "man of letters who really *is* nothing but 'represents' almost everything": something akin to the polished superficies that Norton identified with a certain style of French *littérateur*. Nietzsche (a philologist) knew that scholars at least had what "men of letters" did not, commitment to "unconditional *probity* in discipline and prior training." "No, my scholarly friends, I bless you even for your hunched backs"—though hardly for their crooked souls. Norton had the hunched back—his "scholar's stoop" was a mobile Cambridge landmark—but philological historicism drew the specialist out of "the nook in which he sits and spins," opened to him spacious fields wherein to stretch his crooked soul.[49]

Yet such broadly integrated learning drew disdain in its turn: from some because it was broad, from others because it was learning.

Many professors oriented to research understood the "German model" to mandate just the sort of specialism that Nietzsche decried and they rejoiced in. Several of his Harvard colleagues shared Norton's broad-gauge, integrative idea of scholarship: William James, George M. Lane, Josiah Royce, George Herbert Palmer, among the better remembered. But others took a narrower view, believing that the true researcher could only dig deep by staying in one trench: most of the physical scientists but also eminent scholars in other fields, such as the economist J. Laurence Laughlin.

Their argument had force. George Lane might be admired for combining in his studies of Latin the "fine literary appreciation which characterizes the English school" with "the minute and exact knowledge of the Germans"; but even his admirers had to concede that he published little real scholarship. Norton at times spread himself too thin, lapsing from breadth of vision into sententiousness. Turned away one evening from a crowded public lecture by Norton, William James fumed, "Why can't one speak truth sometimes, and call C. E. N. publicly and without apology the infernal old sinner and sham that he is." "There isn't a genuine word in him," James exploded to his wife.[50]

In calmer moments James knew that his elder friend had quite a few genuine words in him, especially when talk turned to Dante or painting or

Greek architecture; and it is essential to realize that Norton's conception of scholarship not only made room for specialized knowledge but also depended utterly upon it. It was to Norton that his Latinist colleague Lane turned to get the correct form of Latin ordinal numbers for an inscription![51]

Such conspicuous erudition explains why the media of middle-class culture grew as uneasy with Norton's scholarly writing as did the professors of "Germanic" disciplinary specialization. For, in what almost amounted to a parallel movement, when many academic experts began to retreat into their nooks, magazines catering to educated readers began to expel scholarship from their pages. Tolerably well-schooled readers in the 1850s were still thought capable of digesting erudite discourse; by the 1880s magazine editors had decided that scholarship went over the heads of their audiences. As recently as 1878 the *Atlantic Monthly* had printed the articles based on Norton's *Church-Building* prominently, with footnotes. It was a sign of the times that in 1889 *Harper's* pushed their sequels to the back of the book and stripped them of notes.

Norton did *not* steer a middle course between popular culture and disciplinary specialism; he practiced a mode of learning different from either. His form of erudition demanded intimacy with original sources and modern research but denied that a scholar could acquire competence in only one area. Growing out of philological historicism, it saw knowledge as interrelated, expecting that the fruits of research in one domain would connect with other reaches of that whole. For only by setting scholarship in the context of larger human strivings and achievements, Norton and others like him believed, could the scholar illuminate broad human concerns. Even so technical a piece of research as Norton's article on the proportions of the Temple of Zeus at Olympia he mailed to his regular correspondents; the idea that Greek architectural principles might derive from religious belief, after all, did suggest implications broad enough to interest nonspecialists. Anyone who believes Norton unduly alarmist about the plague of fact grubbing ought to read the dissertations produced in his day—and not a few produced a century later. Norton thought pedantry toxic to the mind. A broadly humanistic scholarship he saw as integral to "the interests of high culture in America."[52]

Norton cherished high ambitions for the university. Within the matrix of a modern research ideal, he strove to foster a truly liberal scholarship. Liberal learning, in turn, he hoped might pump its regenerating serum through the arteries, veins, and capillaries of a general culture that badly needed to improve its health.

The true scholar is he who, avoiding useless specialism on the one hand, and loose inexactness on the other, never mistaking the roots of knowledge for its fruits, or straying from the highway of learning into its by-paths, however attractively they may open before him, holds steadily to the main objects of all study, the acquisition of a fuller acquaintance with life in all its higher ranges, of a juster appreciation of the ways and works of man and of man's relation to that inconceivable universe, in the vast and mysterious order of which he finds himself an infinitesimally small object.

Small wonder that the humanists of the early twentieth century—Irving Babbitt, Paul Elmer More—looked to Norton as model and mentor. They were not alone. Neither did they sway the future.[53]

FOURTEEN

To Make Democracy Safe for the World, 1891–1895

In August 1891 the blow fell, the heaviest since Susan's death. Lowell's condition had worsened as winter turned to spring; by July the doctor had diagnosed cancer, which had spread to the liver. Charles came from Ashfield to be with James. On Monday the thirteenth they shared a good long talk. When Charles returned to Elmwood on Tuesday, James lay stupefied by opium. The physician told Norton that he might as well go back to Ashfield: Lowell must stay drugged. In any case, his mind was beginning to wander; there was no point in Charles watching him die. The end came on 12 August. Norton, Curtis, and Child helped to carry the casket from the Harvard chapel.

For Charles, James's death "changes the balance of life as no other loss could have done; for no one is left who is so much of my own past as he was, or of whose past I have been so much." Norton neither had nor wanted the "delusive" consolation of religion; unbelievers stood "upon firmer ground for the meeting of sorrow": "To accept the irremediable for what it really is, not trying to deceive oneself about it, or to elude it, or to put it into a fancy dress, is to secure simple relations with life, and tends to strengthen the character without, I trust, any hardening of heart or narrowing of sympathies."[1]

There seemed these days a lot of the irremediable to accept. Impairments of age had just forced Leslie Stephen to hand over to other editors his great *Dictionary of National Biography;* heart pains had recently warned Child of his mortality. Charles himself claimed (to his old Oxford acquaintance Max Müller) not to mind "the approaching close of life," except for "a little curiosity as to the course which the thoughts of men are to take in the coming years, and as to the effect on conduct of the so-called loss of faith." "I know, indeed, that as old stars sink, new stars rise; and this is enough."[2]

Charles intended to say nothing of Lowell "for any journal or any public print." Others may "have been depraved by the reporter, and corrupted by

Froude and his tribe"; but to Norton "the sanctity and privacy of friendship" still mattered. He did mean to publish a selection of Lowell's letters, "strung on a brief thread of Memoir," to "serve as an autobiographical record"; and, as James's literary executor, he inherited the burdens of deciding what to do with the piles of Lowell's papers and of overseeing the inevitable collected works (this last job already begun by Lowell).[3]

These burdens proved enormous. Lowell's death engendered unprecedented competition in the American literary marketplace, with publishers hovering hungrily over so celebrated a corpse. After complicated negotiations, the contract for the collected works eventually went to Houghton Mifflin, Lowell's publisher at the time of his death, with whom Norton (acting for Lowell's daughter) drove a hard enough bargain to turn old H. O. Houghton red in the face. An astoundingly generous offer from Harper's won the rights to Norton's edition of the letters, while bits of unpublished manuscript ended in various magazines, each paying dearly for the dead poet's reputation. Houghton was not the only publisher taken unaware by the deftness with which his pocket had been picked by Norton. "I do not grow impatient with business details," the old East India merchant observed of himself, "for I have had enough to do with business to know their importance."[4]

While still bargaining with publishers, Norton began to assemble letters and reminiscences from Lowell's throng of correspondents, a chore complicated by the long diplomatic service in Madrid and London. Kate Stephens, the classicist manquée helping with the *Heart of Oak* books, had become a kind of literary factotum to Norton (living rent free at Shady Hill for the summer); and he hired her to index the letters. Soon enough it became clear that a biography was not to be avoided, and people naturally assumed that Norton would write it. On this personal front he pretty well held the line (conceding to *Harper's* only a brief appreciation of Lowell in connection with publication of the *Letters* in 1893); but finding a suitable biographer added to his load. In the end the job fell to Horace Scudder of Houghton Mifflin. Scudder also seems to have acted as chief editor of the *Works,* though Norton took an active hand. By November 1891 the first volume—a medley of literary essays—was in press. Simultaneously in progress was a New York "Brantwood Edition" of Ruskin's works, to the volumes of which Norton supplied introductions. To Charles the job must have felt eerily like the final duty he was carrying out for Lowell. Ruskin did live on, but as a sere husk. As with Lowell, all that remained to Charles was to help in embalming his friend for posterity.

These tasks he carried out with growing skill. He had begun by pre-serving Chauncey Wright's philosophic legacy, then the Emerson-Carlyle friendship and the younger Carlyle in his letters, now Lowell and a start on Ruskin. Norton was self-consciously converting his extraordinary group of friends into public memory. The received understanding of the so-called genteel tradition in American letters for the next half century owed much to his impress. "The way that man gets his name stuck to every greatness is fabulous," groused his neighbor William James—"Dante, Goethe, Carlyle, Ruskin, Fitzgerald, Chauncey Wright, and now Lowell!"[5]

Behind Professor James's palpable envy lurked also a distaste, bred in a younger, harder-edged, less idealistic generation than Norton's, for how the editor went about his job. Norton regarded Lowell, for instance, as "the best and most characteristic specimen of democratic manhood that New En-gland has produced; an American such as Americans should be." Taking his habitual view across a couple of millennia, Norton never confused Lowell's achievement with, say, Dante's; but he did see Lowell as among the finest flowers of his place and time. And he meant to present him as such to future generations, a study in character: "genius, faculties, acquisitions" all "under the control of his moral sense." This approach did not imply tampering with the evidence—it was Norton, after all, who brought a new canon of accuracy to American editions—nor ignoring Lowell's foibles but, rather, dressing him in his better clothes. Charles fretted over printing Lowell's weaker pieces, and left some in manuscript, trying to throw the spotlight on the "qualities which were characteristic of his writing at its best." The same principle would guide Norton's edition of the *Letters*. America needed to have held up before its eyes Lowell's "good sense and right feeling in public affairs," his "rare and exceptional grace and charm of genius added to character."[6]

This editorial labor fitted with a turning in Norton's work in the 1890s further away from archaeology and even art history and toward literature. It is not so clear whether this movement arose from a real shift in interest or mere force of circumstance, such as Lowell's death. Certainly, Italian paint-ings and Greek temples stayed close to Norton's heart. Even retired from its presidency he remained the great icon of the Archaeological Institute; but he devoted far more hours in 1891–92 to putting the final touches on his translations of the *Divina Commedia* and *Vita Nuova* than to anything else, while the Dante Society competed with the AIA for attention.

That winter and spring Norton also hewed the *Heart of Oak* books for young readers into something like final shape. Kate Stephens toted stacks of books to his study; he ransacked these for poems or stories apt to appeal to youngsters; sometimes she joined in the page turning. "There is no great literary merit in Cook's Voyages," Norton ruled; "More's Utopia is desirable but archaic; Southey's two poems are hardly likely to hold a permanent place in English literature"; so it went. By February, Norton had in hand a "rough draft" of the introduction to the first volume; by May, was fashioning the "final arrangement" of its selections. All this literary employment fitted into the interstices of Harvard business, a tighter squeeze than ever with Norton now serving on the college's administrative board as well as the Library Council.[7]

Companionship he found where he could. Will Howells came to visit in February. So did Godkin, a rare treat these days; Norton took him to the Saturday Club dinner, which Charles usually avoided: "too many ghosts." More often, younger friends chased the ghosts away from Shady Hill: George Woodberry regularly; but recently, too, a young novelist from Chicago, Henry Blake Fuller, who was fond enough of Norton to dedicate a revised edition of *The Chevalier of Pensieri-Vani* to his mentor. There were in the run of things family dinners as well—with Grace, Theodora Sedgwick, and the creaky Ashburner aunts all still living just down the hill. But Charles's children were mostly gone: the girls traveling, the boys busy with their careers. In June 1892 the youngest, Dick, graduated from Harvard and, a few days later, sailed for Europe to begin two years of archaeological training in Athens, Berlin, and Cambridge. Rupert was starting an internship at Children's Hospital in Boston; Eliot had by now staked out his turf as a Wall Street lawyer.[8]

At Ashfield that summer the routine business—reading proof for the *Paradise* and for Lowell's lectures on early English dramatists—went smoothly enough. The more complicated job of preparing Lowell's *Letters* dragged, though Norton still hoped to have the book in press by spring 1893. Bringing in the hay crop appealed more than sitting at a desk. "I am a farmer up here, and like it better than being a professor." A brief visit to Jonathan Harrison in New Hampshire brought home how desperately Norton's old friend and his wife were living. Harrison's writings, now in behalf of forest preservation, earned a pittance; Norton castoffs seem to have provided most of their clothing, and only a huge garden kept hunger at bay. Norton redoubled his efforts to find a publisher who would pay his friend better, pretty nearly a lost cause.[9]

And Harrison's sad plight was far from the most depressing scene of this dreary summer. "Our summer is deeply shadowed and saddened," Charles wrote to John Simon in July, "by the mortal illness of our very dear old friend George Curtis." A "frightful cold" the previous winter had developed into something genuinely dreadful. No one had the heart to stage the Academy Dinner that August. George died on the thirty-first, at the age of sixty-eight, too close behind James. Charles judged Lowell and Curtis more than friends; they were "the two men who during their generation had most truly represented the ideals of American culture and citizenship," the finest off-spring of the "conditions peculiar to our national institutions and life," of the large, generous "modern spirit of democratic society, in which each man has the opportunity and is consequently under the responsibility to make the best of himself for the service of his fellow-men." Their virtues "give reason for faith in the progress of man." That was Norton's public voice. It was one thing to face one's own approaching end with equanimity, quite another to watch one's two dearest friends die in quick succession. Early in October, Charles returned to an Ashfield of tolling bells, to play his ritual part in the town's memorial to George.[10]

As usual, Norton sank grief in work. Enrollment in his big fine arts course had swelled to over 350, the largest in the college. Crammed into the second floor of Massachusetts Hall, a huge but "entirely unfit" lecture room where some students could barely hear and their professor could show no pictures, the class, Norton thought, neared disaster. He threatened to stop teaching it until Harvard provided a proper room. As if by sympathetic magic, that room floated into view even as the young barbarians strained to catch his refined words. Mrs. William Fogg, widow of a wealthy New York merchant, bequeathed Harvard money to build the art museum for which Norton had yearned almost two decades. With galleries, lecture rooms, and staff offices, the college might at last have a facility adequate to the subject taught. Or it might not. Norton, always a cautious investor, wanted the Fogg bequest to accumulate interest until money sufficed for a building as substantial as needed. The Harvard Corporation bulled ahead—"without due consideration for the Fine Arts Department," Norton griped in December—choosing an unpromising site in the northeast corner of Harvard Yard. The world had not heard his last complaint about the Fogg Museum.[11]

For the present, Norton was mired in too deep an editorial swamp to worry overmuch about the siting of his new lecture room. He mailed the first bundle of copy for the *Letters of James Russell Lowell* to Harper's in December, while continuing to assemble letters, weave the connecting thread, and ship swatches through the winter. The *Letters* formed only one of his Lowell labors. Besides helping to edit the collected works, he was carving

out from James's unpublished lectures six articles for the *Century* magazine. And now Curtis had taken his place beside Lowell. Though George's
widow fretted that Charles was adding to an already unmanageable pile of
business, he could hardly decline to edit his friend's essays and speeches.
More negotiations followed with publishers, now striving to line up a
biographer.

Wading through the manuscript remains of his best friends made for a
pretty grim winter, and Norton may for once have welcomed the distractions of his massive social duties. As head of the Tavern Club, he presided
on 12 December 1892 over a dinner honoring the artists and architects of the
Columbian Exposition, the world's fair just opened in Chicago. The buzzing capital of the West inspired Norton with bemused admiration. In New
York three months later Norton appeared in his guise as the nation's arbiter
elegantiarum at another banquet, honoring the exposition's head architect,
Daniel H. Burnham—this feast taking over Madison Square Garden, in real
Chicago style. Burnham's classical designs for the fair's buildings appealed
to Norton, even more the "superb effect" achieved by the "successful group-
ing in harmonious relationships of vast and magnificent structures." At last
an American had arrived who, having "studied the work of the past," had
learned to build a true public architecture. Norton said so in his speech at
the dinner, which Burnham unsurprisingly thought "the most important
address of the night."[12]

By April 1893 the last of Lowell's *Letters* were in press (though Harper's,
sensing a hot seller, held the book for the more conspicuous autumn list).
Proof sheets of the first volume of Curtis's public addresses arrived at the
Locusts near the end of July, a temporary respite from wrestling with the
Heart of Oak series. Kate Stephens, living at Shady Hill for a third summer,
forwarded proof sheets for volume one, suggestions for the next. Norton
thought "Blue Beard" a good idea but wondered whether "the fastidious
moralists" would object. He vetoed "The Seven Champions of Christendom"; the tale "used to seem dull to me when I was a child." "Have you
thought of taking some further stories from Grimm, or have we got all the
best already?" He showed a soft spot for the soft-eared dog in Ruskin's
"King of the Golden River." Along with nursery rhymes and fairy tales,
essays by Lowell and addresses by Curtis, the annual backlog of correspondence had to be dealt with. For the first time Norton took a secretary with
him to Ashfield, one of his Harvard students.[13]

Two unusually agreeable visitors interrupted the editorial toils. First
came Flora Shaw, now a journalist making a trip round the world and

alighting at Shady Hill even before Norton left for Ashfield. She brought more than shared memories of Ruskin. Ever since coming to know Norton in England, Shaw had cherished "something special in my feelings" for the elder confidant, whose photograph sat always on her mantel; and three days of quiet walks gave a chance to talk over things not well said in letters. What the things were remains mysterious; a touch of June-December romance seems to have tinged the friendship.[14]

In September a nephew of Georgie Burne-Jones arrived. Having created a literary splash with tales of India, Rudyard Kipling had left England to settle in Vermont, where his brother-in-law owned property. Norton found Kipling a little rough on the outside but "at heart an excellent fellow." Rudyard reciprocated, and a friendship grew that might have surprised many who knew Professor Norton only by fastidious reputation. Inevitably, inequality in age conditioned the relationship (no matter how often Charles protested, Kipling never managed to stop calling him sir); but Kipling's stay at the Locusts made an auspicious start to autumn.[15]

And an exciting autumn it turned out to be. Probably guarding his health, Norton had decided to give up teaching for the year. The leave allowed him to accept an invitation from the organizers of the Columbian Exposition to visit the fair. Norton had traveled in four continents without journeying farther west than Niagara (unless Madras counts): an omission that throws a sudden and revealing light across the Bostonian's mental map of civilization. Taking Sally along for the experience, Norton approached the great metropolis of the West in early October with "the deepest interest," for he saw in Chicago "so much of the future of America for good or for evil."[16]

The auguries proved promising. He and Sally spent their days and nights in a whirlwind of sightseeing and dinners. The fair itself, in spite of "amazing incongruities" and an "immense 'border' of vulgarities" (the original Midway), showed "great promise." And whatever faults he detected in the booming city that bustled around the fair, Norton told Woodberry (perhaps still shivering at the thought of Nebraska) that no Eastern metropolis showed "so strong & wholesome a communal feeling." Norton admired, to be sure, not the *real* city, money hungry and poverty ridden, but "the ideal Chicago which exists not only in the brain but in the heart of some of her citizens."[17]

The brain in point belonged to the novelist Henry Blake Fuller, who had hesitated to send the eminence his latest novel, *The Cliffdwellers*. This told a sordid story of social climbing and peculation, centered in a Chicago skyscraper; and Fuller intuited in Norton "a real distaste for Chicago, if not a positive disgust." The hunch reflected an increasingly widespread impression of Norton, as the few who knew him well departed the scene, replaced by many who knew him only through glancing contact. His fastidiousness, aesthetic and moral, convinced most students and some colleagues that life's gritty realities revolted him.[18]

Fuller discovered that Norton's nice discriminations implied neither weak stomach nor prissy sensibility. A man who had lounged in the salons of Paris and hobnobbed with the seedier expatriates of Florence scarcely needed to avert his eyes from Chicago. In fact Norton praised *The Cliff-dwellers* as a great advance over Fuller's earlier, more idealistic novels of Europe, finding in it deeper penetration into human reality by the author's poetic imagination. Norton told Fuller that his fiction belonged "on the same shelf" with William Howells's (as tactful a phrasing of the comparison as one can imagine), reminding him that Howells "describes our American life with such insight & such truth" precisely because he "is essentially a poet." "It is the man of imagination, the poet, who alone sees things as they really are," whether "the charm of Italy, or the repulsiveness of that aspect of Chicago which you depict."[19]

From Chicago, Norton returned to the morbid parade of funerals, the first that fall "my old friend Parkman's" on 11 November. Two weeks later Susan's ancient aunt, Grace Ashburner, passed away after long illness. Her sister, Anne, followed in January. Of Susan's family, only her siblings remained: Theodora alone in the house down the hill, Sara Darwin in England, Arthur writing for the *Nation* in New York. Between funerals came more of the endless foreign guests. Prince Serge Wolkonsky, a Russian delegate to the Columbian Exposition, arriving in November to lecture at Harvard, stayed at Shady Hill. A young polymath, Wolkonsky impressed his host as "one of the finer products of that *terre vierge*"; and his departure began another lasting correspondence. As with so many European friends for so many years, Norton undertook to act as Wolkonsky's American literary agent, placing a magazine article, keeping track of a book publication. The French writer Paul Bourget arrived on Wolkonsky's heels, forwarded to Charles by Henry James: also *aimable*, less exotic, one more transatlantic connection forged. It had become second nature. Norton was also beginning to acquire transpacific friends among the Japanese who had begun to trickle through Harvard; but there hardly remained time to build *that* network.[20]

How few had the old friends become! Frank Child turned sixty-nine on 1 February. As the day approached he took up his pen to thank Charles "for fifty years." "How much of the richness of my life do I owe to you, and how faithful a friendship do I look back upon as I follow the years through from the beginning!" Charles could say the same.[21]

As much as Norton savored the pleasures of friendship, they had to compete for a share of the flagging energy of a sixty-six-year-old man against a rising tide of demands on his time. As "America's most distinguished fine art critic"—so declared the ladies in the Norton Art Club of Pueblo, Colorado—he paid the price of fame. (The regular reports from the earnest women of the Norton Art Club, Sally recalled, "amused my father.") The stream of requests for lectures, articles, or information never abated.[22]

The most attractive of the recent ones arrived from the young Johns Hopkins University in Baltimore. Its president, Daniel Coit Gilman, an amicable acquaintance since *North American Review* days, had written shortly after Norton's return from Chicago to ask him to deliver the annual Turnbull Lectures on poetry at the university, taking Dante for his subject. The invitation did great honor to the lecturer—the distinguished classicist Sir Richard Jebb had preceded Norton in the series—but Norton's rigorist agnostic conscience almost scuppered it. The Turnbull endowment required of the lecturer "an explicit and reverent recognition of God"; tactfully but firmly Norton refused any such recognition. Just as firmly Gilman quashed Norton's scruples. He would not concede "any control" to the donors: academic freedom was coming to imply the intellectual autonomy of the university from the community on which it otherwise depended. He said, moreover, that in fact Norton's appointment delighted the Turnbull family personally and Baltimore's "literary people" in general.[23]

All winter Norton pegged away at the lectures, aiming at a "mixed audience" rather than an academic one. He arrived in Baltimore in late March 1894, feeling a "little under the weather," fending off the excess of dinner invitations that blossomed like azaleas in the "genial, semi-Southern atmosphere" he knew of old. The six lectures themselves went smoothly. The first introduced the "function of poetry" and sketched Dante's cultural background, the next five dealt with the works individually, three with the *Divina Commedia* itself. In these popular lectures, Norton meant to do what "even" many "professed scholars" did not: "appreciate truly the nature of the poet and of his poem."[24]

This ambition to awaken his auditors to Dante's poetic imagination paralleled Norton's hope for the *Heart of Oak* books—which, even as he drafted the Turnbull Lectures in his neat merchant's hand, D. C. Heath was publishing. More precisely, publishing for the second time. The first issue, in autumn 1893, had turned Norton's face beet red. Kate Stephens failed to grasp the elementary requisites of the job that her overworked employer had left in her care—disastrously, it turned out. Sloppy transcription preceded careless proofreading. Errors riddled the text. The mortified senior editor agreed with the irate publisher; they had no choice but to suppress the books. They then hired George Browne, once a student of Norton's, now headmaster of the Browne and Nichols School in Cambridge, to ferret out the errata and establish accurate texts. That done, a proper—and to all appearances "first"—six-volume edition appeared in 1894 and 1895. The fiasco was as novel as it was embarrassing to Norton, normally as fastidious in book production as in his manners.[25]

Chagrin gotten over, he could take legitimate pleasure in the final outcome. The six-volume series meant to cultivate in children a "taste for good reading," which Norton believed most American children grew up without. He saw this defect as partly arising from "the fault or ignorance of parents and teachers" but also as the consequence of parents and teachers having at hand no "proper means of cultivation." This lack the *Heart of Oak* books aimed to remedy. Norton was the furthest thing from a Pollyanna, but he did believe that almost any child could develop *some* liking for reading if properly trained. The training, however, had to start "very early": a truism a century later but by no means a universal insight in 1894. Toddlers should hear lullabies and songs; early reading lessons should never aim to impart specific knowledge but to encourage enjoyment. Norton's own lifelong love of reading aloud showed through the first book: old nursery rhymes and simple traditional tales for parents to read to very young children.[26]

Early reading aloud having awakened the child's fancy, the next step led to the fables and fairy tales "which form the traditional common stock of the fancies and sentiments of the race." The second volume included not only fairy tales but also venerable standards of children's fiction (inevitably, *Goody Two-Shoes)* and verses "fitted to interest children who have already learned to read"; it ended with Charles Lamb's *Adventures of Ulysses.* The next volume introduced history and biography, mingled with more sophisticated poems and adventure stories and with "tales of heroic and romantic deed" drawn from Morte d'Arthur and old ballads. (One suspects in this last particular the invisible hand of Frank Child.) The final volumes advanced to "the best writing of the masters in English literature" that Norton judged interesting to young people. Authors ranged "from Sidney, Spenser, &

Shakespeare to Carlyle, Arnold, & Ruskin, to Emerson, Longfellow & Lowell": "ample variety for every taste, and for wide culture." And ample variety of the editor's friends.[27]

The *Heart of Oak* books superficially resembled school readers, but Norton insisted on a basic divergence in purpose. His anthologies were "meant not only as manuals for learning to read, but as helps to the cultivation of the taste, and to the healthy development of the imagination of those who use them, and thus to the formation and invigoration of the best elements of character." He wanted to educate "the moral sentiment" as well as "the intelligence," a goal descended from his own early education in the moral-psychological theories of the Scottish Enlightenment. The way to this end ran through the "imagination" with its empathetic powers: the "supreme intellectual faculty" yet the one most neglected "in our common systems of education." Good reading supplied "the most generally available and one of the most efficient means" for nurturing the imagination. "To provide this means" formed "the chief end" of the *Heart of Oak* series.[28]

The goal for the first volume animated them all: to enable every child "to share in the imaginative life of the English-speaking race." As obviously as the Turnbull Lectures, the *Heart of Oak* books strove to reach a popular audience (and in order to ensure that the material would appeal, Norton and Heath circulated bound proofs to teachers for criticism well in advance of publication). Less obviously but equally, the lectures and the anthologies flowed from Norton's scholarship, his broad erudition running under both.[29]

And both reflected his anxious passion that learning impregnate the public culture of democratic America. Norton had inherited his father's—and patrician Boston's—conviction of the formative power of ideas on any people's culture. Andrews had gone so far as to declare that the "character of its intellectual men gives its character to a nation." Charles no longer shared the easy confidence that every people would absorb its animating ideas from its clerisy. But he did still hope that "its intellectual men" *might* shape America: a leap of faith that inspired his commitment to Harvard. And he had inherited, too, old Boston's view of America's historic predicament. To his father, the Republic seemed an "experiment" to "determine what man may become when placed in the most favorable circumstances"; yet it also threatened to become "a sort of barbaric empire," with "a half-civilized population spread out over our soil, ignorant of all that adorns, and ennobles, and purifies the character of man."[30]

Almost exactly seventy-five years later his son wrote to Jonathan Harrison about "the character of our people":

I do not wonder at their triviality, their shallowness, their materialism. I rather wonder that, considering their evolution and actual circumstances, they are not worse. Here are 60 or 70 millions of people of whom all but a comparatively small fraction have come up, within two or three generations, from the lower orders of society. They belong by descent to the oppressed from the beginning of history, to the ignorant, to the servile class or the peasantry. They have no traditions of intellectual life, no power of sustained thought, no developed reasoning faculty. But they constitute on the whole as good a community on a large scale as the world has ever seen. Low as their standards may be, yet taken in the mass they are higher than so many millions of men ever previously attained. They are seeking material comfort in a brutal way, and securing in large measure what they seek, but they are not inclined to open robbery or cruel extortion. On the whole they mean "to do about right." I marvel at their self-restraint. That they are getting themselves & us all into dangerous difficulties is clear, but I believe they will somehow, with a good deal of needless suffering, continue to stumble along without great catastrophe.

"The world has never been a pleasant place for a rational man to live in," Norton added. "I doubt if it is a worse place for him now than it has been in past times. At any rate it is the only place we have got, & we must make the best of it."[31]

Like his father and his other teachers, Norton feared that an "ignorant" people would fall into "dangerous difficulties." The horrors of the Paris Commune lived in memory; now in his own country economic depression spawned Populist unrest and labor violence. Forty years earlier, he had tried to alleviate the "ignorance" and "misery" of Irish migrants through his evening school and model lodging houses; he fretted now about the corruption of politics by immigrant-based city machines, wondering in bad moments whether immigration threatened to divide America into antagonistic ethnoi. Part of Ashfield's allure was the absence of immigrants; it felt to Norton like the homogeneous New England village that Cambridge had seemed in his childhood. On the whole, though—and in sharp contrast to younger members of his caste, including a number of his own students— Norton looked on immigrants as "good but new neighbors." Given the prejudices around him and his own deep distrust of urban blights, he worried remarkably little about the alleged risks of foreigners flooding the land.[32]

Rather, the taproot feeding his anxieties ran all the way down to democracy itself. Not that Norton disapproved of democracy—far from it. The high optimism that the Civil War had fostered in him, that exuberant faith in the American people's special talent for self-governance, did prove a fragile flower, wilting under the hypocrisy of Reconstruction and the venality of the Grant years. But class-ridden aristocratic Europe, disfigured by "flunkeyism" and arrogance, endangered by envy and disdain, had not ceased to appall him; and his confidence that democracy represented "the true social development of mankind" never wavered.[33]

At the same time, he evolved in the 1870s and 1880s a much longer-range view of what was needed for a healthy democracy to mature. Democracy had transformed "social relations" by introducing "the principle of the moral equality of men, the elevation of the individual man, and the development of the greatest of all social forces, that of public opinion." This sea change, positive in the long run, produced negative effects as well. Democracies—at least those of the present day—tended to prefer mere material well-being to higher motives of action; to fall victim to plutocratic politics and corruption by money; to encourage the ignorant to think their opinions as valid as those of the well informed; to foster a kind of herd instinct rather than independence of character and judgment, yet also to forget the welfare of the community in pursuit of selfish interest; to erode the civility of manners that smoothes human relations in an impersonal world, but also to drag private relationships into the public sphere.[34]

Such problems, however, flowed not from democracy itself but from the values brought to it: from the materialism infecting modern civilization.

Materialism, in turn, resulted from a seismic shift in the intellectual basis of civilization. Just as democracy had transmuted "social relations," so had science transformed mental activity by liberating the "intelligence of man" from "many of the bonds of superstition and of ignorance." Christianity, Norton thought, had thus begun to lose its grip. Few had gone all the way to agnosticism; even fewer—in these democratic times—had the spunk to buck public opinion and avow their unbelief. Yet, like democracy, agnosticism seemed the wave of the future and in the end a very good thing. This conviction came easily when so many of one's admired friends professed some version of unbelief (Leslie Stephen, Jonathan Harrison, William James, Frederic Harrison, John Mill, Francis Parkman only began the list). Charles's classmate and colleague George Lane referred to the afterlife as "the Great Perhaps." Faith in God looked to Norton intellectually flabby and morally evasive, while the "new irreligion" not only freed the mind to explore the universe without inhibition but also increased the "sense of personal responsibility." Unbelief supplied "a better theory of life and a more solid basis for morality" than belief.[35]

Yet (again like the rise of democracy) the decline of belief brought evil side effects along with ultimate blessings. Christianity was slowly fading without any kind of noble aspirations replacing it for most people, so by default material desires filled the vacuum. "We are given over to the magazine & to science." Norton did "not doubt that the pendulum will in time swing back from the material to the spiritual side of life"; but a single oscillation of the pendulum "in the count of the world's hours" might take centuries. Meanwhile, only a cultivated few discovered new fonts of spirituality: in Dante and Emerson, in Turner's painting and Praxiteles's sculpture, in the temple of Olympian Zeus and even in a newly built, paradoxically Gothic temple of culture like the Oxford Museum. (This reliance on inherited relics to replace living religious conviction can seem as flimsy and sterile in Norton as in Arnold; but Norton had arrived at the barrenness by his own route, via the earlier Unitarian elision of Christianity and self-culture.) Because of his worry that ex-Christians would lose their high-mindedness along with their illusions, Norton valued the liberal clergy who treated religion as "a matter of sentiment not of intelligence"; evasive about doctrine, they preached moral lessons, which were more needed than ever.[36]

For democracy had handed power to the people just when they lost their spiritual compass; and, however flawed Christianity as a guide, selfishness was infinitely worse. The United States, with its advanced democracy, found itself on the leading edge of a wave sweeping the Western world, which seemed likely to leave in its wake moral barbarianism. The Irish bosses who bought votes in the streets of Boston mirrored the rich braggart Americans who promenaded in the *viali* of Bellagio—and who revolted the fastidious Norton even more deeply than the bosses did. He could hardly help contrasting the Boston mercantile princes in his memories of youth, living an ethic of service to their community and shuddering at overt display of wealth, with the nabobs who pillaged Wall Street like pirates, building with their booty the vast gilded "cottages" that deformed his old Newport. "A people wealthy, luxurious, vulgar in taste"—the nightmare of the old republicans of Andrews's boyhood came to life a century later in the mansions Charles visited along Central Park. Norton had long expected "to see luxury become more wanton, and politics more corrupt" in the United States; and the state of public affairs did seem only to darken as his years lengthened. "I can understand the feeling of a Roman as he saw the Empire breaking down, & civilization dying out."[37]

Plainly, democracy would lumber toward discord and disaster unless the values animating democrats were thoroughly renewed; plainly, too, Norton thought this a project for the centuries. "It will take much longer than we once hoped for the world to reorganize itself upon a democratic basis," he wrote to Leslie Stephen, "and for a new and desirable social order to come into existence." He meant this not as a cry of despair but a counsel of realism: "if we set our hope far enough forward we need not lose it."[38]

The only strategy fitted to the struggle (Norton having judged religion hors de combat) was education. At its most general level, this faith in education simply echoed the republican truism of the Founders and the universal opinion of Federalist Boston drummed into young Charley's head—from which it popped out again in the evening school and in his 1853 book, *Recent Social Theories*. During the Civil War and the early years of Reconstruction, Norton and his generation of liberal democrats had broadened the idea of how citizens might get educated, stressing that a relatively few men of "solid training" and "serious temper" could shape "a temper which by degrees becomes national." The *North American* under Norton and Lowell's editorship and the *Nation* had both explicitly targeted these opinion leaders.[39]

Yet by about 1870 Norton had evolved a still broader view of the education that democracy needed, and this long-range perspective framed the activities of his later years. If the Republic's disorder issued from materialism, if "wealth easily acquired" was "vulgarizing and impoverishing the spirit of the community," then not a cognitive but a moral and spiritual intellectual ailment plagued democracy. A moral and spiritual disease required a moral and spiritual remedy; that is to say, a culture that subordinated material goals to higher aims, a culture that broadened a narrow view of human needs and desires into a larger vision. Unhappily, in Norton's view, the modern world, with America in the van, was leaving behind precisely this sort of culture. The "reading of newspapers and magazines," for instance, "by the immense and distracting variety of their contents, tends rather to narrow than to enlarge the mind." The one-time editor bore no grudge against newspapers and magazines, regularly perusing several from both shores of the Atlantic; but "the street-dust of the newspapers, and the dry light of science" made it hard to see very far.[40]

Democracy needed a richer, deeper culture to help its citizens look beyond petty material desires. And, since materialism originated in modern times among the growing and prosperous middle classes, those archetypal readers of newspapers and magazines needed help where they could find it. Norton encouraged newspaper editors to print in each issue "some bit of literature of real excellence"; he urged architects to house office workers and college students in buildings that would work upon "the taste, and *hence* upon the morals of the community"; he asked his own students to learn each day a little poetry by heart. Regular encounter with poetry—broadly meant: what Norton liked to call the arts of expression—enlarged a person's comprehension of reality, strengthened sympathies with other human beings, set one's own aims higher. The "common charge that poetry has no practical relation to life" Norton indignantly rejected, for poetry "purifies and elevates the spirit."[41]

Not everyone would think elevating the spirit a matter of everyday practicality, but Norton did believe that culture shaped daily life. His argument was that revisiting the hopes and fears, victories and defeats, of other peoples, in other times and places, lifted one's eyes to questions more imperative than a fashionable dress or a higher salary—that breaking out of the narrow compass of American values circa 1890 helped one to develop a larger vision of what mattered in one's own life and in one's community—and that such a vision not only enabled individuals to navigate through life's sorrows and joys but also could inspire a larger sympathy and communal spirit, which might vitalize the public affairs of a democratic polity. "Woe to that nation which rejects the ideals that her poets, the instruments of her Imagination, have discerned for her."[42]

These opinions were not calculated to endear Norton to his fellow citizens. Those who took umbrage could dismiss him as a fanciful utopian. Odd though it may seem to say, this criticism scarcely held water; for Norton offered his politics of culture with the most chastened expectation of success—only, as it were, to edge America's rudder a degree or two to starboard. If not utopianism, cynics could place the project on the other end of the moral spectrum: a sanctimonious attempt to bypass democracy and impose on ordinary folk the values of an elite. In one sense, this charge comes close to tautology. Art, poetry, culture have no intrinsic contents; they must be constituted continually anew in discourse about them. Hence, any description even of aesthetic norms cannot help but try to impose values: to define morally a social order. This would remain true whether Charles Eliot Norton or Karl Marx did the job. And this truth no one realized more keenly than Norton. He understood his cultural work—whether promoting archaeological research or editing the *Heart of Oak* books—as a tiny share in the striving to give some conscious direction to the glacial creep of human moral evolution.

Was he thereby (if unconsciously) really trying to salvage the hegemony of his class, as many scholars might now suspect? Such a suspicion reveals a far more limited grasp of the world than Norton's. True, he inherited and sustained a social vision both hierarchical and universalizing. Its axioms blinded him to differences between the culture of an old rural town like Ashfield and the culture of his own patrician Boston, both of which he imagined as "traditional" New England. The same unitary principle made inconceivable to him a popular culture as worthwhile as the high culture that Dante inhabited. Yet these facts do not alter the authenticity of his distress that democracy excluded most citizens from the pleasures and enrichments of high culture. That a small elite should monopolize Dante and Titian contradicted his hopes for America.

Nor did his increasingly musty Boston elite stand to benefit if people besides themselves read Dante and looked at Titian. It is often and plausibly said that familiarity with Vivaldi and Heine serves to mark class distinctions in a world where even would-be aristocrats have given up wearing swords, where anyone can buy lace. If so, persuading clerks and machinists to spend their evenings with Shakespeare could only blur social pretensions. In any case, the matter was far more complex. For Norton, "taste" certainly provided a tool to make social and moral distinctions; and these were not utterly divorced from class distinctions. Neither, however, did they correspond easily to any extant class, including the debris of the Boston mercantile elite.

And, more to the point, Norton's version of cultural education—his training in taste—was a unifying move, of a specifically democratic sort. To say this is hardly to deny that culture can be put to antidemocratic uses, not even to deny that Norton's project was peculiarly prone to highjacking by plutocrats positioned to use their powers of patronage to seize control of culture as a way of validating their ascendancy. It is simply to note that Norton's work was far from exclusionary or socially discriminatory in outlook or intention. On one hand, he hoped to elevate the growing bourgeoisie and, ultimately, the newly literate masses (themselves starting to vanish into the middle classes). On the other, he wished to civilize *with the same code* the offspring of the "barbarous" capitalist elite. The distinctions, on the face of it, were far more moral than social.

And they had more to do with cultivating individual persons than imposing received norms. Following in the Boston Unitarian tradition, Norton understood culture as an activity, a process of development, not a collection of texts or a state of perfection. Though not influenced by the German concept of *Bildung*, Norton's views bore strong similarity to it; they thus overlapped, though inexactly, with his friend Matthew Arnold's notions of culture. Norton conceived culture more as a public transaction and also a historical process than did Arnold, and Norton's idea of public culture did not stand apart from his understanding of culture as an object of historical study. Rather, because he believed "poetry in the broadest sense" integral to the essence of all historical cultures, he was able to conceive poetry as a tool for shaping the personalities and values of individuals in his own culture. Put differently, if art did not express the moral substance of life—if art did not mirror some historical culture or cultures—it could not form a person's moral life: could not "culture" him or her.

And culture became fully public, a shared achievement of a community, when poet and people reacted upon one another. "It is not enough," Norton argued, that some "exceptional man of artistic genius" embody "his conceptions in forms of beauty." His fellow citizens "must be in such sympathy with him as to find delight in his work as the quickener of their own sensitive imaginations." The rarity of such an ideal state Norton readily conceded; its ideality he insisted upon. And such deep mutual sympathy explained how the artistic and political lives of a community could, ideally, meld into a unity. (Norton identified classical Athens, France from the eleventh to the fourteenth centuries, and Italy between 1250 and 1500 as sites of such unified cultures.) Certainly Norton himself never saw as essentially distinct his cultural role as teacher and his political duty as citizen. The scholar who delivered the Turnbull Lectures served as justice of the peace and head of the Cambridge Civil-Service Reform Association.[43]

He returned to Cambridge from Baltimore on 12 April 1894. Solicitations arrived to repeat or to print the Turnbull Lectures, but accretion of other business pushed them aside: Lowell's works rolling steadily through the press; the persistent drizzle of proof sheets from new printings of Norton's Dante translations; the Curtis volumes nearing completion. In June came the Harvard Commencement Dinner, a gala honoring cousin Charles on a quarter century as Harvard's president. Norton returned from Ashfield to preside. Even the Locusts provided scant vacation. Norton tangled with Harper's over the design of Curtis's essays: typeface too gaunt, page too short. He hurried away from the Academy Dinner on 15 August so he could speak on the sixteenth at the William Cullen Bryant centenary in nearby Cummington. And nowadays financial worries pestered incessantly. With his salary still hovering below $3,000 a year, not even $160,000 in securities returned enough during the great depression of the 1890s to offset the costs of Shady Hill and of three footloose daughters. Selling off pictures and books had become a routine device. Richard's homecoming after two years in Europe did bring one happy caesura, a September visit to Rudyard and Carrie Kipling in Vermont another. Even there, the omnipresent proof sheets pulled him away from amending Rud's verses. Meanwhile, the year of sabbatical drew rapidly to a close.

Back lecturing to packed classes, he still had to find time to assemble the *Last Poems of James Russell Lowell* and to complete extensive revisions for a new printing of his own *Purgatory* and *Paradise*. Perhaps it was emending his Dante that inspired Norton to set out on another scholarly project: compiling, for the Dante Society's *Jahrbuch* that spring, selections from the thirteenth-century chronicle of the Franciscan Salimbene di Adam corresponding to (and perhaps underlying) some twenty passages in the *Divina Commedia*. This was something of a jeu d'esprit.[44]

Norton committed far more time to a much more substantial literary project in 1894–95. For several years he had been reading John Donne with fresh appreciation. The taste hardly showed originality, for a revival of interest in the poet spread through the Atlantic world in the 1890s. Among the earliest devotees was Lowell, who in the 1850s had published a volume of Donne's poems, with which he tinkered through the following decades. After James's death, the Grolier Society of New York proposed to use his revisions in an elegant edition for the cultivated bibliophiles who composed its membership. Charles probably had a hand in this, for he knew that no "proper" edition of Donne's poems existed—their latest editor, Alexander Grosart, having made a hash of the job. At first, Lowell's daughter Mabel Burnett tried to sort out her father's "confused" scribblings. Norton having some expertise in seventeenth-century English literature, Mrs. Burnett naturally turned to her father's closest friend for assistance. Soon the whole business fell into his lap.[45]

Norton quickly discovered that extant texts of Donne wallowed in far greater confusion than he had guessed. Editing would require "minute comparison of all the editions of the poems in the seventeenth century." Norton already owned a number of Donne manuscripts and issues; he now assembled more and, tacking with a philologist's care among early printings and manuscripts, began to reconstruct the most reliable text, to place the more important variant readings in footnotes, and to compose an introduction and notes to guide readers. His Dante experience enabled him to work remarkably fast. By March 1895 he found himself "correcting the last proof-sheets" and "glad to have come to the end."[46]

He had not, it turned out, arrived there yet. Norton's and Lowell's combined erudition had produced the first reasonably accurate edition of Donne's poems. But Norton's speediness suggests loose ends left untied; and, indeed, in England the young E. K. Chambers immediately published one still better (itself outmoded by Grierson's in 1912). Preparing the Grolier edition had, in any event, piqued Norton's interest; and the next year he published a rather brief article, "The Text of Donne's Poems," in one of Harvard's scholarly journals. In it he sketched guidelines for establishing the text and summed up the state of scholarship on Donne. "The Text of Donne's Poems" marked an epoch, effectively beginning the modern era of Donne studies. No other American—and few European professors—came close to commanding the range of learning and the scholarly dexterity to pull off such a feat after a couple of years of work in spare hours.[47]

And Norton snatched the hours from more pressing engagements. Besides his regular classes, he had agreed to redeliver the Baltimore lectures on Dante to a Harvard audience. They began in March and ran into April. Every evening, crowds jammed Sanders Theatre, Harvard's largest auditorium. Frank Child could recall no "literary course in Cambridge being so well attended, and it is all sorts of people that go"; Will Howells reported from New York that, in the eyes of all knowledgeable observers, "you stand for Harvard in the humanities." This latter impression gained currency beyond Howells's circles: among the growing corps of art history teachers in American colleges who looked to Norton for a model, among the private collectors like Isabella Stewart Gardner who sought his expert advice.[48]

All the more angrily, then, did Norton grind his teeth at the new Fogg Museum, now ready to open. The building, designed by Richard Morris Hunt, struck Norton's cultivated eye as simply ugly. Worse, its spaces made it impossible to bring the university's architectural collections under the same roof as its paintings and drawings, which struck him as pedagogical lunacy. And the one thing any museum must have—good lighting—the Fogg did not. Even the acoustics of his new lecture room scarcely bettered the dead air of his old one. (As it happened, this turned out a consequential defect: the Harvard physicist Wallace Sabine, called in to see if something could be done about excessive reverberation in the new auditorium, was led to found the science of architectural acoustics.) Norton's student Edward Forbes, the Fogg's second curator, described his habitat as "a building with a lecture hall in which you could not hear, a gallery in which you could not see, working rooms in which you could not work, and a roof that leaked like a sieve." Had Norton not given up belief in God, he might have thought it divine justice that the architect died as the thing opened. He had, certainly, no wish to head the museum; and that job went to his longtime junior colleague in studio art Charles H. Moore.[49]

Norton's impress did shape the Fogg's collections—both positively and negatively: aggressive assemblage of late medieval art, relegation of American painting to a metaphorical if not literal basement. And, whatever poisonous thoughts the building inspired in him, Norton seized the propitious moment to lobby President Eliot for an additional teacher in fine arts, asking that Edward Robinson be appointed lecturer on Greek and Roman art. Norton's motives went beyond academic aggrandizement. The new position, he argued, would strengthen the links tying history, classics, and the fine arts together—fields only a German-style pedant would think distinct.

Norton's son Dick, despite some months of German training, was no pedant. He had returned from Europe with field training in Greece and museum study in England, both under Waldstein, in addition to seasoning in Berlin. And now he found a fiancée as well: Edith White, the daughter of Norton's colleague in classics John Williams White. In April, Richard found what may have been even more elusive than a wife, a job: Bryn Mawr College hired him as its first professor in a new department, "the History of the Fine Arts." "The work," Papa told his brother Eliot, "is just what he has been fitting himself for." Charles had a successor. And the last of his sons had put Boston behind him, though Dick stayed around Shady Hill for the rest of the year.[50]

By early January 1895 Norton had fallen into "too black a mood" even for writing to his old growling partner, Godkin. Whether the prospect of encroaching solitude, his country's growing seaminess, or something else pulled him down is hard to say—hard because only rarely and to his most intimate friends would he admit depression. To soldier through life with a cheerful face was a Norton principle older than Charles. But shadows lowered even over Ashfield that summer. Charles still swung an axe but was growing clumsier; the hair that remained on the sides had thinned and silvered; his face looked care drawn. A profound isolation was setting in. He told Mountstuart Grant Duff that the art of conversation had become extinct in America, but maybe the problem was more local. "I have," he admitted to Leslie Stephen, "no one to talk with in these days with whom I much care to talk."[51]

In May, Stephen's wife Julia had died; the loss devastated Leslie. Not until September could Charles bring himself to write the letter he wanted to write. This letter makes clear that Norton's growing isolation only deepened a far more primal loneliness, of far longer endurance. Charles had always been meticulous in reminding his children of the blessing of their mother's love and still did so in birthday notes. Otherwise, for two decades he had spoken of Susan only in the most superficial, glancing way. Yet she remained beside him, her ghost called from the grave by their children's features or "turns of expression."[52]

Now, responding to Leslie's loss, Charles spoke of his own.

Life divides itself more than ever into the external & internal, and I have found that the division grows wider as the years go on, and as the world in which she lived grows more remote to others, and in some ways to oneself. One's solitude becomes more & more intense, & one is really known to nobody, not even to one's children. One learns to keep up appearances, and in a sort to care for things, but I have found it difficult not to become too indifferent to everything. One cannot even suffer much from any new calamity.

In this half-life, work offered "the main resource, for it affords occupation of mind & one can do it as done for her." But there was no opiate to dull "the loss to her children," "no comfort," "no joy behind the pang." "However we may try we cannot make it good,—and we have to see them not only less happy but less good, less what we want them for her sake to be, because they lack her help. This is pure bitterness, and this too no one knows but ourselves." "Enough. It is almost twenty five years that these things have been in my heart, and I have not broken silence about them before. Your sorrow, dear friend, brings us closer than ever to each other."[53]

FIFTEEN

The Invention of Western Civilization, 1895–1898

A less personal sort of isolation menaced Norton as he neared seventy, for the better part of a new generation of American intellectuals deserted his standards. Younger, harder-shelled writers found prissy the language of high Victorian moralism that Charles had shared with the lengthening roster of his silenced friends. High among the proudly tough-minded sat, ironically, the late Dr. Holmes's own son and namesake, handing down a new "realism" from the Supreme Judicial Court of Massachusetts. The self-consciously modern disdain of men like Justice Holmes seemed as much mood as principle, but it left the ancestral linkage of knowledge and morality looking like one of Pollyanna's more fatuous daydreams. The phrase "value-neutral science" awaited coinage, but already, at Harvard and other American universities in the 1890s, an expanding cult gathered around this unnamed icon of the coming century.[1]

Norton recognized in these disciples the bastard children of nineteenth-century positivism, chanting off-key his own worldview. His confidence in science as criterion of knowledge never wavered; his fear of it as a destroyer of values deepened with each passing year. "Much that shelters itself under the name of science" reinforced the "increasing forces of semi-barbarism," which would rend knowledge apart from the ethical purposes that made it serve the moral development of the human race. He saw the Harvard faculty filling its ranks with dark doppelgänger even of his own beloved philology, mindless amassers of facts blind to the "distinction between pedantry and learning," narrow drillmasters "by whom our young students as well as old men, lovers of the beautiful, are wronged," German-model scholars "of the kind which is at present most approved, the kind that can plunge deepest into the sea of learning and come up driest."[2]

Seemingly on the opposite shore stood aesthetes like Norton's former student Bernhard Berenson. Berenson readily acknowledged his old master's influence, now "charged with a meaning that it has taken all these years to enable me to understand"—a meaning that gave the master a nasty shock, probably administered on purpose. For the charge that Norton's teaching now carried for Berenson flowed from the belief in art for art's sake with which Walter Pater had galvanized a generation of Epicureans: the polar opposite of Norton's doctrine. Berenson expunged morality from knowledge; and thus this renegade protégé's aestheticism proposed a "value-neutral knowledge" exactly parallel to that of the new social sciences and the cramped versions of philology, however different the flavor.[3]

Such oracles foretold for the life of the mind a strange and dissonant future, but they remained in 1895 Delphic in their obscurity. And, though these false prophets irritated Norton, they amounted now to little more than gadflies stinging a colossus. Respect for Norton continued to swell among the educated public, and he maintained among academic scholars of the humanities an organizing influence with no real analogue.

Its power showed in the mid-nineties, when a crisis of transition approached for the Archaeological Institute. Professional classicists such as John Williams White of Harvard and Francis W. Kelsey of Michigan had increasingly assumed the institute's governance, gently propelling to the sidelines both amateur businessmen and academic polymaths. Seth Low, Norton's successor as president, hailed from commerce, not scholarship, and palpably felt incompetent from the moment he took office. Yet the new professional order barely ruffled Norton's personal authority, and the governing coterie of specialists still revered the founder as leader. His advice proved key in the decision in May 1895 to establish a School of Classical Studies at Rome parallel to the one at Athens; and he, along with Thomas Seymour of Yale and Allan Marquand of Princeton, composed the ad hoc committee named at the same time to draw up a long-range plan for the AIA's future. True, his argument for more attention to Americanist archaeology fell on deaf ears; but, when Low resigned a year later, the specialists still looked to Norton to arbitrate the succession.

Such authority behind the scenes gained strength from general public esteem by now unmatched in American high culture. With Lowell dead, no American name carried more literary force. When the young poet Edwin Arlington Robinson published his first book, the slim volume went to Shady Hill for the sage's blessing; when the aged novelist Harriet Beecher Stowe died, Norton's endorsement certified the necessity of a major memorial. His name, though less potent in Britain, attracted homage there, too. In January 1896 Richard Garnett, keeper of printed books in the British Museum, gave Norton the "surprising pleasure" of dedicating to him a translation of the great sixteenth-century Portuguese poet Luis de Camoëns. Dr. Garnett's admiration pleased but did not really surprise. Indeed, English respect for Norton, of which Americans were well aware, partly explained his repute in the United States, which benefited from an obeisance to English culture now far more unqualified among the American bourgeoisie than ever at Shady Hill.[4]

Anglophilia, however, only erratically extended to politics; and in the summer of 1895 American jingoes spat in John Bull's face. The occasion arose from an ancient quarrel over the boundary between Venezuela and British Guiana, newly inflamed by the discovery of gold in the disputed region. The Cleveland administration, catering to the bellicose spirit of the American press, treated British "aggression" against Venezuela as violating the Monroe Doctrine, flouting the de facto protectorate of the United States over the Americas, and amounting to a casus belli. In December the altercation reached crisis. Leslie Stephen reported that the English papers "tell me that you are all in a state of Jingoism & it may be your duty & mine to cut each other's throats, by proxy at least."[5]

Norton stood appalled. He could hardly decide whether Cleveland's "course were the more foolish or the more criminal." Either way, "the war-spirit" had done enduring damage to "the national character." The old republicanism of the American Revolution lived in Norton; he fretted about the effect of warmongering on the people's civic virtue rather than the impact of war on their material state. Even if the United States escaped a devastating war, "we cannot escape from the far-reaching consequences of the excitement of brutal passions" and "the inculcation of false doctrine in regard to national greatness & duties." American democracy "in its present attitude" presented "a menace to civilization." With "a single cast," Cleveland had flung away the "best gains of a hundred years."[6]

This Caribbean storm dimmed for good Norton's political horizon, bleak enough already. He had long accepted that the material progress of the American people outstripped their "moral & intellectual progress"; but the "ignorance & semi-barbarism of the democracy" now seemed likely to retard for a very long time "the evolution of a better order of society." The political principles by which Norton judged the prospects of American democracy had altered little since *Considerations on Some Recent Social Theories* in 1853. (In fact, a couple of years later the old man inscribed in an admirer's copy of *Considerations* the injunction from Emerson's "Terminus": "Obey the voice at eve, obeyed at prime," a phrase he had lately grown excessively fond of quoting.) But, if Norton's tenets had not changed, America's mass democracy had—greatly—and, with it, his expectations.[7]

As winter neared amid rumors of war, Norton composed an article for the *Forum*, "Civilization in America" (completed, as it happened, the day before Cleveland sent a belligerent message to Congress in December 1895). He meant to warn of "the dangers from the growth of the barbaric elements in our national character and conditions." His warning evidently got heard, for the *Forum* article stirred greater public reaction than almost anything Norton had published. Predictably, a few sympathizers cheered while the rest of his own country honored him as prophets proverbially are. Samuel F. Clarke, professor at Williams College, wrote to say that "nothing, to my mind, has struck so directly to the root of the whole matter." The *Rochester Post Express* more typically fumed at "a mere closet philosopher," too cloistered to "touch the core of American manhood."[8]

American manhood took umbrage specifically at Norton's complaints about its crudity. Norton revealed himself more clearly than ever as a late-blooming cultivar of the old republican stock; and, as such, he saw manners, morals, and politics inseparably bound together in the problem of civic virtue or national character. Even thirty years before, in the rosy afterglow of Union victory, Norton had regarded the "prevailing ease of tone among us, the good-nature which degenerates into indifference to meanness and vulgarity," as "a sign of something very different from public virtue" and fussed over the "decline of manners owing to the spread of democracy." He did not blame individuals for their coarseness; far from it: a Barnum, rising from poverty, deserved more personal credit than he himself, starting with every advantage. But rawness on a continental scale boded ill for the Republic.[9]

This evil had now realized its threat, owing to mass immigration from Europe and mass emigration from the older states to the rude West. Unprecedented "equality of opportunity" and "the rapid rise to comfort and to power of the masses of men" gave good reasons for "her children" to hold America dear; but these very achievements encouraged "exaggerated self-confidence" and "the growth of popular delusions." A "long inheritance of ignorance and semi-barbarism" weighed down the mass of Americans, whether recent immigrants crowding the big cities or native-born Westerners living on the edges of civilization. To believe that public schools could overcome it in a generation or two was a snare and a delusion. Many children grew up with scant schooling; few schools offered competent training; and even the best school could only "give instruction," not truly educate.

"The education which shapes a child for his duties as a man and a citizen is mainly that which he gains from the influences of his home and of the community to which he belongs."

No wonder, then, that "ignorant and barbaric multitudes" pressed against American civilization. The civility needed to lubricate human interaction was declining everywhere but especially in the upper ranges of society. Parents neglected the training of children, and childish "wilfulness" blossomed into the evil flowers of "youthful lawlessness and resistance to restraint." The barbarity of inner-city street gangs mirrored that of college athletes. Newspapers, through "intellectual feebleness" or outright "pandering to the baser tastes and dispositions of the community," fostered these tendencies. And from such roots grew the political corruption sapping the Republic's institutions as well as the "deliberate appeal" by its leaders "to the most brutal instincts of the populace by advocacy of a policy of national aggression." The steady increase over the past century of "disrespect for rightful authority, whether that of law, of learning, or of experience," confirmed this "dangerous temper."[10]

Norton warned his fellow citizens that they had best look these perils in the face. "To deny or to undervalue the forces ranged against civilization is to increase their power." Yet he had no great expectation that Israel would heed Jeremiah. "It is hard to live in a land declining in civilization," he wrote to his old friend in Philadelphia, the Shakespearean scholar Horace Furness. "I have been reading 'Utopia' in these last days. I was driven to it by the newspapers."[11]

There were closer friends than Sir Thomas More to buck him up. Occasional visits from Will Howells and pleasant hours with Sarah Jewett supplied good literary talk; Grace might walk up the hill to chat of Montaigne, about whom she was writing, or to bring news of their old friend Henry James, her steady correspondent; Theodora came of an evening to read the *Nation* to her brother-in-law. In early June, with Richard finishing his first year of teaching at Bryn Mawr, his father traveled to Philadelphia to deliver the commencement address. They returned to Shady Hill to celebrate on the sixteenth Richard's wedding to Edith White. Over two decades later, the *New York Times* recalled it as "a notable society affair"; but it was more notably for Papa a family affair. For, with Rupert practicing medicine in the Washington area, Eliot law in New York, and their sisters often abroad, the wedding assembled Charles's offspring for a rare reunion. Richard and Edith went to honeymoon in Ashfield, and Papa turned to a celebration of his own.[12]

On 23 June the Harvard class of 1846 marked its fiftieth anniversary with a dinner at Young's Hotel. Twenty-five of sixty-nine original members survived, and twelve of them showed up at Young's to confront a dinner that might have staggered their younger selves: littleneck clams, green turtle soup, boiled salmon, fillet of beef with sauce béarnaise, green goose with potato stuffing, sweetbreads, frog legs, squabs, and desserts. A long Latin poem teasing the diners described inter alios a dank cloud spreading through Charley's "house," a *domus* that all assembled knew to mean the Fogg. After commencement, Richard and Edith returned to Shady Hill, since Richard was to teach at Harvard that summer; and Charles took their place in the western Massachusetts hills.[13]

There on 12 August in the Ashfield Town Hall he dedicated a bronze tablet honoring George Curtis. In the spirit of Curtis, Norton used the occasion to address the entire country "in its present confused and dangerous conditions of mind." Never was George's voice more missed, he said; for never was "there greater need than at this moment of enforcing upon the intelligence and the conscience of the people the truth that national safety and prosperity rest securely only upon the foundation of moral rectitude."

> The infuriate clamor for war, the eager cry for free silver and fiat money, the demand for subsidy under the name of protection may be suppressed, but they are only the symptoms of disease, and to suppress them is no more a remedy for the disease than to check a fit of coughing by an opiate is a remedy for consumption. The disease is the ignorance and the consequent lack of public morality of a large part of the people of our republic. To contend with this ignorance, to enlighten it, and in enlightening it to overcome it, is our task.

In this twilight struggle the soldiers of civilization wielded only the weapon of education. More and more, the voice of the warrior of Civil War and Reconstruction days reechoed.[14]

A month after the Curtis memorial the greatest loss since George's death struck Charles. In June, Frank Child had retired from teaching after fifty years as Harvard professor. That summer he worked to add glossary and indexes to his great compendium of ballads, completed in other respects two years before. But his heart condition had worsened; in August he fell seriously ill and, on 11 September, died. Charles felt the death at a primal level. Frank was the oldest of his dear friends and his last intimate in America. As for England, Georgie Burne-Jones had stopped asking when Charles would come. Along with Ned and Georgie, John Simon and Leslie Stephen survived, but only the latter kept in voluble touch.

In February 1897 Britain accepted arbitration of the Venezuela boundary dispute. This eased fears of war but inspired in Norton no larger hope for America's democracy. Still, he tried here and there to lay a pebble in the groundwork of a better future. Disgusted with Democrats and Republicans, he urged national leaders of political reform to launch a third party. He suggested that Jonathan Harrison write an autobiography of his career as freelance reformer, to serve as an instruction manual "of the actual situation of our people, of the stage of moral and intellectual development which they have attained."[15]

Most of his civilizing work was less overtly political. A medley of literary projects spread through the 1896–97 academic year. It began with publication of Norton's groundbreaking paper on the text of Donne's poems, which appeared as Charles's contribution to a volume honoring Frank Child on his retirement, turned unexpectedly into a memorial. Later that winter Norton helped Theodore Koch of Cornell to revise the galleys of *Dante in America,* a history initially proposed by Norton. His own Dante translations, steadily reprinted, required equally steady revision. Selections from these appeared in 1897 in a multivolume *Library of the World's Best Literature,* in which Norton prefaced them with a lucid thirty-three-page introduction summarizing Dante's works and setting them in historical and biographical context—the sort of easy essay possible only to a seasoned expert and experienced popularizer.

Norton had grown friendly with DeWitt Miller, a devotee of fine printing who headed a club of like-minded New Yorkers called the Duodecimos; for them Norton introduced an edition of the Puritan poet Anne Bradstreet. Bradstreet was his own remote cousin, but kinship got her nowhere; Norton frankly viewed her writing as of more historical interest than literary merit. For Rudyard Kipling he felt higher esteem and greater warmth; when Horace Scudder, the *Atlantic's* editor, asked for an assessment of Kipling's poetry, Norton readily agreed. He claimed for Kipling the status of a major poet (with admitted defects), who voiced the "conceptions and aspirations" of a "new generation," as the poets from Keats through Tennyson, Arnold, Clough, and Browning had expressed the ideals of the passing Victorian age. That disappearing Victorian "mood"—"its drifting creeds, its doubts, its moral perplexities, its persistent introspection"—fitted Norton far better than did Kipling's heartier humor; so Norton's bow to the younger era showed a certain generosity of spirit.[16]

In May 1897 the American School at Rome named Richard professor. The appointment specially gratified his father "because, so far as I can see, it was made on independent ground," with the committee choosing Richard "from a number of candidates as the one whom they deemed most likely to fill the position as they wanted it to be filled." Less than two months later, on commencement day, Charles's classmate and colleague George Martin Lane, a friend since schooldays, died. His death left only Wolcott Gibbs, retired for ten years, senior to Norton among living members of the Harvard faculty.[17]

Norton stood at the head of that faculty in other ways as well, having by the late 1890s grown into a Harvard legend. Only the geologist Nathaniel Shaler approached him in popularity among students, and even Shaler's courses never drew the mobs that filled Norton's. In 1897–98, 451 undergraduates—close to a third of the student body—packed Fine Arts 3.[18]

Their professor lured them with easy grades and a riveting show; and by no means all students took him seriously, especially in his last years of teaching. A graduate of 1892 told of returning several years later and watching a "line of students during a class hour descending the fire escape from the second story of Massachusetts Hall." Asking for an explanation, he heard "That's Norton's course." The alumnus could only shake his head; in his years Norton's "fiery denunciations of the vulgarity and corruption of modern society" had riveted the attention even of the most philistine clubmen. This oft-told tale was in fact grossly exaggerated: a less admiring piece of the Norton mythology. One suspects that Norton knew full well of occasional escapes and cared only that they not become routine.[19]

For to attract students within culture's circle of light mattered far more than to discipline them under its severer glare. Norton had inherited Andrews's feeble voice and perforce learned the tricks with which a lecturer overcame the handicap; his "exquisite precision" of bearing and speech exaggerated itself in the classroom, becoming a ripe subject for student satire but (for the same reasons) drawing hundreds to see the spectacle. When he wanted to capture the horde's attention, his carefully "modulated voice dropped off to something above a pensive whisper"; and several hundred young barbarian ears strained for his words. Theatrical extravagance became his stock in trade. The opening of one lecture passed into legend: "Young gentlemen—and as I speak these words the realization comes over me that no one here has ever seen a gentleman." A half century later a student remembered how, even on a warm spring day, "animadversions so preposterous" pulled restless eyes away from the butterflies fluttering "in and out of open windows" and back to the lecturer. Again, the legend distorts reality; students misunderstood their professor's reference to a "certain type" of European gentleman exemplified in the comte de Circourt, the savant at home in several languages, familiar with the classical authors in all the major European tongues. But the legend may capture the impression made better than the facts do.[20]

Snob, some hearers labeled this carping old man. And the expression of "abject pessimism" that chilled his features when something "annoyed and disappointed" him verified for a substantial minority of his students their picture of "an oversensitive malcontent" forever moaning about the ugliness around him. Yet apparently most recalled a second expression, "of warmth and something that could only be called sweetness," which glowed softly when he spoke of the "intimate, steadying experience" of the Arena frescoes or the *Vita Nuova*.[21]

For Norton's influence depended on far more than classroom sleight of voice. This professor did not peer about him with blinking eyes as if emerging from his study into unaccustomed sunlight. He had walked among the ancient ruins of India, enjoyed the hospitality of a British prime minister, lived in the galleries of Florence and Venice, merited the intimate friendship of Ruskin, of Curtis, of America's greatest poets.

> Beautifully academic as Mr. Norton showed himself in many ways to be, he yet moved in an aura that could scarcely escape even a moderately sophisticated undergraduate. He looked and spoke like a cross between a man of the world and a high, benign ecclesiastic. As this venerated man grew older, he became more and more a preacher to his students; but the preacher never ceased to be urbane.

Norton's neighbor and colleague, the philosopher Josiah Royce, remarked how Norton could embody his "whole personal influence" in "a word, a phrase, a tone of voice." Norton himself understood that, in any great teacher, worldview fused with persona, and persona weighed as heavily as any specific words uttered.[22]

To uncounted Harvard students this man proved decisive. One devotee of "the really important things of College life"—team sports, the glee club, amateur theatricals—recalled enrolling in Norton's course for the notoriously soft grade. A word Norton said or something in his manner "fascinated" the young man; "something clicked in the cavity where my mind was supposed to function, and gradually—not suddenly—but with steady and healthy progress I realized the joy of independent thinking." Emerson's grandson Edward Forbes registered in Norton's classes, fell under his sway, and found himself on a path that led to directing the Fogg Museum and helping largely to define the role of the university museum in the United States. Most Harvard students graduated into something less aesthetic, banking or manufacturing or insurance; yet Norton "very perceptibly affected" many of them "in the direction of art and public usefulness," such as Gardiner Lane, who found time in a full business career to serve as president of the Museum of Fine Arts. "It is hardly too much to say," testified another disciple, "that he brought to hundreds of our underdeveloped spirits a new universe."[23]

Undergraduates could feel the force of Norton's achievement, but perhaps only other academics could see its novelty. This was why so competent an observer as William Roscoe Thayer a quarter century later identified Norton's fine arts survey as the most significant course in Harvard's modern history. Norton imported into the curriculum (as a distinguished American historian a generation younger put it) "new interests, new enjoyments, and new appreciations"—"architecture, painting, the 'unapproachables' in literature." This in the end weighed far more heavily than Norton's persona in explaining his influence. The other key lesson that Norton impressed on teachers of the liberal arts was not new but perhaps pilfered from the ruins of the old moral philosophy courses that he had known in his own college days. This was to keep in the forefront of instruction "the relation to actual life & conduct" of what students learned in the classroom.[24]

Norton's distinctive doctrines had begun to root themselves in college classrooms across the nation, his example acquiring power because it provided a model around which an educational order thrown into chaos could partly reconstruct itself. By the 1890s American colleges, Harvard in the vanguard, had largely shed their old curriculum centered on drill in Greek and Latin and taught by classroom recitation. As Norton observed, this "rapid change in our educational systems" could hardly help but produce "a wide difference between the intellectual culture of the nineteenth and the twentieth centuries." The question was how to manage most effectively the transition, with greatest benefit and least damage to the culture. In his own student days, Charles had known the classical curriculum in its feeble late form, already in disintegration; by the time he joined the Harvard faculty, traditional classical education had collapsed into a dilapidated ruin of its Renaissance self.[25]

College leaders soon reached consensus that it needed either thorough rebuilding or complete demolition. At Harvard, Eliot's elective system dynamited what remained of the old edifice, replacing it with the hope that, if professors had no blueprint for what their students needed to know, the students might. Other institutions, notably the large and influential University of Michigan, traveled by different roads toward the same destination. Two principal alternatives challenged elective free fall: first, a required distribution of studies across a wide range of subjects unrelated to each other, such as history, a foreign language, English literature, chemistry or physics, mathematics; second, the preparation of students for practical work, an approach embodied most completely across the Charles River from Eliot's Harvard at the Massachusetts Institute of Technology. Ambiguities and ambivalence abounded: confusions compounded because the public commonly mistook any advocacy of languages and literature for "the old ideas of a classic education." Few undergraduate institutions made so clean a break with the past as Harvard or MIT; most mingled some concessions to "practicality," some degree of student election, and some insistence on variety of studies, including shreds of the old curriculum.[26]

Norton approved practical training for specific occupations and thought the elective system "a most valuable experiment" for "a period of such rapid change"; but neither approach satisfied him as an enduring core for collegiate education. He remained convinced that any hope for American democracy depended on an education both broader in scope and more specifically aimed at democracy's enemies. Only education could combat the materialism generated by science, by prosperity, and by democracy itself: materialism manifest in plutocracy, corruption, and self-seeking.[27]

Yet education supplied the feeblest of weapons. It could merely chip away at the foundations of materialism in a puny sapping operation extending over centuries. Unconquerable legions of professors never marched through Norton's insomniac dreams. For one thing, his Boston upbringing made him fully conscious of a fact many educators only dimly appreciated: a teacher just refined what home, family, and community had formed. He was naturally pleased to hear that young people "believe they have gained some good from me"; but he reminded grateful parents that "it is what a boy brings to the lecture-room that enables him to carry some good from it,— mainly what he brings from home." And, just as the home made an individual child receptive or impervious to teaching, so material circumstances "over which man has little control" limited the resonance of education among a whole people. In every generation, as Norton explained to his young admirer Paul Elmer More, "a few superior men" keep moral ideals pure; but "their influence depends greatly upon external circumstances which result from general conditions entirely apart from the faith actual or professed of a people." If overpowering luxury, grinding poverty, or sudden calamity break down morality, then "no ethical creed, however wise it may be, can stand against them."[28]

Yet, however frail and contingent its working, nothing but education could renew civilization on a broad democratic scale; toward that remote happier future Professor Norton bent his efforts. He remembered always that the real enemy was materialism and its political incarnation, plutocracy. Mass democracy might foster low behavior, but it could mature toward higher. The essential defect lay in values, not systems, the essential solution in culture, not polity. Norton's republican cultural politics of civil service reform and anti-imperialism—his tactics—dovetailed with his larger-scale, longer-term republican cultural education—his strategy. Even before delivering his Bryn Mawr commencement address, the "Position and Ideals of Educated Women in America," he tried (without success) to get it published in *Scribner's* in order to "reach a larger number of young women." He likewise meant his October 1896 memorial address for former Massachusetts governor William E. Russell (which was published) to "set forth Russell's character and career as an example for the youth just entering upon life."[29]

But youth entering upon life required more consistent formation than a scattering of speeches could provide. In earlier years moral philosophy courses had infused some coherence and sense of purpose into college education, starting from the axiom that one God had created a single universe and given His rational creatures the means to grasp it. In his own college days Norton had experienced how philosophy could pull knowledge into some approximation of a single thing. But in the elective system under President Quincy he had also seen the early shadows of its breakdown. Nostalgia could not disguise the blunt reality that efforts to integrate knowledge as a whole no longer carried credibility. Specialization and professionalization had undermined in practice the assumption of coherence in intellectual life, while God no longer commanded general assent as a theoretical unifying principle. "There is no worse school for the training of the intelligence," thought Norton, than metaphysics: "the investigation of the unknowable." The times demanded something novel to restore purpose to liberal education.[30]

Norton offered it under the name of "culture." In constructing this new model of education, he drew on his intellectual inheritance from Andrews Norton and patrician Boston, a legacy modified by a lifetime of reflection on his own experiences and intellectual encounters. There existed, he believed, "two superior sources of culture": the "history of what man has done" and "of

what he has thought." And the linked realms of ideas and of history structured his new version of liberal education. Its first principle was to acquaint
students with beauty, especially as manifest in literature and the arts. Norton
meant thereby to cultivate the sympathies that bound together human
beings, thus nurturing morality and molding character. No reader of Ruskin
or of Arnold would have showed surprise at this, though the emphasis on
sympathies as the operative tool of cultivation struck a distinctive note. The
second principle, more novel still, was to stress continuities linking the arts
and literature of one era to that of the next and ultimately to our own.
Norton meant thereby to root sympathies in an ongoing story of humanity,
as well as to give students the long perspective that he thought they needed
to judge their society's course and consequent needs. In brief, he replaced the
(vertical) ties between God and creature with the (horizontal) bonds among
people; and he invented Western civilization to strengthen them.[31]

His son Eliot half jokingly characterized his father's Harvard courses as
"Lectures on Modern Morals as illustrated by the Art of the Ancients"; and
the students who packed Sanders Theatre to hear them during Norton's last
years at Harvard understood what Eliot meant. Norton had inherited the
moral didacticism of the old-time college but utterly transformed it. Fifty
years later one student remembered how under Norton's tutelage "Beauty
became not aesthetic satisfaction merely but took her place high among
Moralities." And somehow morality elided into a kind of godless spirituality, for Norton "never divorced the spiritual from the beautiful."[32]

Norton directed this notion of "the humanities" (the plural form a neologism that he and others by now deployed as if traditional) against two foes
subverting American colleges. On one side lurked specialized studies that
narrowed "intellectual vision," on the other the spirit of practicality that
"would limit even the higher education mainly to the cultivation of the
faculties required for the attainment of material ends." He began Fine Arts 3
in 1897 by warning his students, "The great danger and difficulty in college
life today is the substitution of the lower interests for the higher interests of
life,—the substitution of material interests for spiritual interests." The humanities provided "the strongest forces in the never-ending contest against
the degrading influences of the spirit of materialism," hence "the knowledge
most useful for the invigoration and elevation of character." Such, in general, was what "culture" meant in Harvard Yard.[33]

In detail, the term needs dissection, best begun by anatomizing "beauty."
Beauty seemed to Norton "the ultimate expression & warrant of goodness,"

because without beauty "there can be no ideal aim." And "the better the ideal, whether shaped in visible form, or incapable of presentation to the dull senses, the more beautiful it is." All human beings shared, in however rudimentary a form, the same sense of beauty. Thomas Reid's doctrine of "the intuitions of the mind," taught to Norton in college, was not smothered by his embrace of the straiter empiricism of John Stuart Mill and Chauncey Wright but rather transformed into something less metaphysical.[34]

Norton certainly saw "no mysticism" in this universal human sense of beauty. Having toyed throughout his adult life with evolutionary explanations of human moral beliefs, he seems to have understood the "intuition" of beauty as a product of evolution. But "evolution" meant human cultural development, not Darwinian survival of the fittest: Norton owed far more to the Scottish Enlightenment's "progress of civilization," imbibed in youth, than to natural selection, absorbed in maturity. However he came to the conclusion, he did believe that an objective—though not strictly "natural"—hierarchy of values existed, formed by the human mind's development over millennia. Thus "beauty" as used by different persons and in different times and places "is a relative term," more or less remote from its evolving universal meaning, the one most clearly seen by the most developed persons. "That is, it will be one thing to you and one thing to me, according as we have cultivated ourselves, as we have made ourselves refined, and our perceptions true and accurate. A savage's idea of beauty would differ materially from ours." Since all human beings shared one sort of brain, the progress of civilization might conceivably bring all people to recognize one day a universal ethic. If they did, they would see their highest ideals as beautiful, and in beautiful objects they would see their highest ideals.[35]

For this was what "beauty" meant: the expression of the moral aspirations recognized by human beings as having the highest claim on them. So to cultivate in young men and women a taste for the beautiful was ipso facto to nourish in them a predilection to goodness. Just as the evolution of a sense of beauty was for the human race an education in self-control and moral salvation, so the study of art became for college students part of a similar developmental process, in which learning to view nature (and their own natures) in aesthetic terms fostered the highest morality.

Thus it made no sense for colleges to subdivide the humanities into different bins. Even in Norton's seminar for advanced students, "the study of Dante becomes a study of literature, of poetry, of religion, of morals." "The true conception of the Department of Fine Arts might be expressed," Norton argued to the Harvard Board of Overseers, "by giving to it the name of the Department of Poetry,—using the word 'poetry' in its widest sense as including all works of the creative or poetic imagination."[36]

And imagination was the key to unlocking a student's sense of beauty.

> For it is the imagination which lifts him from the petty, transient, and physical interests that engross the greater part of his time and thoughts in self-regarding pursuits, to the large, permanent, and spiritual interests that ennoble his nature, and transform him from a solitary individual into a member of the brotherhood of the human race.

The imagination achieved this effect not only because it widened sympathies with other members of the human race, past and present, but also because imagination interpreted experience, shaping "the fleeting and delusive shows of things into permanent forms of beauty accommodated to the ideals of the mind." And in the "attainment and enjoyment" of these ideal beauties or beautiful ideals one found "the true end of life." No aim of education, then, could matter more than fostering imagination.[37]

By "imagination" Norton meant "the faculty of inward vision which discerns under the show & outward form of things their reality and essence." This notion was not so Platonic as it seemed; for Norton regarded imagination as a "strictly intellectual" quality, based "on reflection, comparison, and reminiscence" of sense perceptions—not on the mere "accumulation of images," but "on ideas and principles derived from the recollection and classification, conscious or unconscious, of the impressions and images themselves." This way of understanding imagination bore clear relation to Norton's harping on "associations" in his earlier ruminations on relics of the past.[38]

Both ultimately derived from the psychological doctrine of associationism originated by Locke, developed in the Scottish Enlightenment, and delivered to Norton in his college years by Dugald Stewart's *Elements of the Philosophy of the Human Mind.* Stewart had explained imagination not as "a simple power of the mind, like attention, conception, or abstraction," but as "formed by a combination of various faculties": its strength and range dependent not on "the gift of nature" but on "acquired habits." To form these mental habits, Norton insisted, a student's thinking needed to be fertilized and pruned, "rightly nurtured and disciplined." To the old "mental discipline" touted by college presidents as the chief virtue of classical education Norton had given a new meaning. Like Frank Child's celebrated roses, imagination required, in a word, culture.[39]

The best culture of the imagination came from immersion in great "poetry" (in Norton's sweeping definition); for through poetry "we may most
easily quicken, and fully nourish our own feeble and undeveloped capacity
of imaginative vision." This was because "imagination is the source of the
poetic faculty" and the poet's own imagination "works more powerfully and
consistently than in other men." At the same time, "without culture of the
imagination we read poetry with a lack of appreciation." The more one
reflected on Shakespeare or Titian, the more powerful one's imagination
grew; and the more powerful one's imagination grew, the more susceptible it
became of cultivation through literature and art. This recursive upward
spiral, this progressive dialectic of improvement, resembled the philologist's
hermeneutic circle, the method of Norton's scholarship. At the deepest
structural level, Norton's type of erudition underlay his ideal of culture.[40]

Nothing in education mattered more than this culture; for "the wretchedness of the world" resulted mostly from selfishness, "and selfishness is
largely due to the lack, or the perversion of the imagination." Here again
Norton echoed the Scots he had read in his teens. Dugald Stewart had
taught him that imagination improves "human character and happiness" by
making us feel the pains and joys of others and thus take a livelier interest in
their lives. Now Norton put this doctrine to educational uses unimagined in
the Scottish Enlightenment: employing imagination to connect literary and
artistic culture with development of moral character.[41]

The link tying character to imagination was supplied by the correlate
and closely related Scottish idea of sympathy. Norton had imbibed it virtually with his mother's milk (though he might later have drunk also from
the *fons et origo*, Adam Smith's *Theory of Moral Sentiments*). "The imagination," Norton explained, "is the vital root of sympathy." A cultivated person
will thus sympathize with the "hopes, the desires, the ambitions, and the
labors" of all people, even if their interests seem objectively "of very little
worth," as "he sympathizes in those of all the living world." Indeed, with
God vanished from Norton's universe, "only through sympathy" could "a
man take much interest in life"; and "his prime duty" became "the cultivation of his sympathy with those whom he can in any wise assist." Even an
ancient art class made students feel that a "man who lives for self alone is an
outcast." Thus might cultivation of imaginative sympathy cultivate goodness as well; and the more cultivation, the more strongly would goodness
take root in character: "for it is only though the imagination that high and
just ideals are shaped."[42]

And thus back to beauty. For the "real value" that we grasp with "the rightly disciplined imagination" is goodness, and beauty is "the ultimate expression & warrant of goodness." Thus Norton could tell his History of Ancient Art students, "If you enlarge and invigorate the intellectual life, you are at the same time enlarging and invigorating the moral life." "Beauty is the end of all true life."[43]

Even so, the cultivated imagination needed to be fed on more than the "poetry" of one era; it needed to be stretched into sympathy with all human aspirations; it needed to be rooted in the long story of humanity. "For history deals with what is of peculiar interest to man,—the works of man, works of his brothers, with their passions and their emotions, and with their disappointments." The democratic imagination, in particular, needed also the long perspective that would permit citizens to judge rightly their society's course and consequent requirements. "Our provinciality" made Americans specially needy of "quickening our sense of relation with our fellows in past generations."[44]

So Norton invented Western civilization. (More precisely, he conceived the concept, not the phrase, typically speaking not of "Western" but of "our" civilization": "our" referring to Europeans and Americans.) To be sure, he hardly conjured Western civilization from thin air. Rather, he constructed it as Edison around the same time invented the incandescent lightbulb—by perfecting the earlier work of others, piecing together well-known materials into a new configuration that generated a brighter and longer-lasting illumination.

Norton's Western civilization rested on three founding assumptions. First, a common history had led the peoples of Europe (and their cultural descendants overseas) to share many beliefs and practices. These made of them a single civilization, the people of which, despite many differences dividing them, recognized themselves as distinct from the peoples of, say, Chinese or Egyptian civilization. Norton's travels in India long ago had crystallized in him the conviction that cultural history, not physical distinctions, separated "races" from each other. And on this point pivoted the idea of Western civilization: its most basic principle the primacy of culture over biology. Nor did Norton use "civilization" in a normative sense; he meant by it merely "the sum of the acquisitions,—whatever they may be, moral [or] material" of a people "at a given time." The "given time" matters. Ancient Greece, medieval Christendom, and modern Europe hardly composed a single civilization; and he spoke of them as distinct.[45]

Rather—and here is the second axiom—a chain of influences ran from the ancient Mediterranean through Rome and medieval Europe to the present. This linked modern European literature, art, and architecture with very different earlier forms from which the later evolved. As early as "the arts" of ancient Egypt and Mesopotamia lay "the beginnings of our own civilization." Yet, Norton believed, the Greeks had made the definitive breakthrough, initiating "a conscious study by man, of his own experience." Greek civilization was *not* our own, but it formed "the first rudimentary stages of it"; so "with the Greeks our life begins."[46]

And for this reason—the third axiom—modern students could best apprehend their own civilization by studying the influences that made it, by learning of "the historic evolution of our civilization." Learning "how to look at a statue" could, for instance, bring students "into very intimate connection" with Greek civilization and thus with key elements of their own. "You cannot know yourselves unless you know history," he told the mob in Fine Arts 3; and that meant all kinds of history. One student recalled Norton starting a lecture "with a few reminiscently thoughtful remarks on the place of the water closet in civilization." Even morality, primary in Norton's pedagogy, seemed to him "the result and expression of the secular experience of mankind."[47]

The idea of development supplied the motor of Western civilization. Like so much else in Norton's thinking, it had its ancestors in the Scottish Enlightenment; but Adam Ferguson had not invented Western civilization and could not have. Probably only someone with Norton's experiences and scholarly range—who had written about the Mound Builders, roamed India, organized classical archaeology, scoured medieval archives, publicized nineteenth-century painting—could have concocted Western civilization. And only then if he had filtered these materials through the sieve of college teaching during years of curricular anarchy. For Western civilization had a scholarly and pedagogical specificity about it. In small, it meant seeing Child's editions of old English plays as evidence of the state of English drama "immediately before its splendid manifestation in the works of the Elizabethan playwrights"; in large, it meant tracing a continuous development of values and conceptions from Greece through the present. It did not imply that ideas passed through history intact: such stasis would contradict the very principle of development. Nor did it suggest that Dante or Shakespeare saw himself as part of a developing civilization: Norton was too informed a scholar to swallow that.[48]

Nor, either, did development always imply progress: Norton was too chastened a moralist. He could specify ways in which the present improved the past, chiefly material; and he retained faith in a "very slow & irregular" rise "in the general morality of the race." But (like Arnold, though less sweepingly) he thought that the ancient Greeks in important respects surpassed all of their successors; hence Greek "teachings if properly understood would correct many of the faults of our own times." Eighteenth-century Edinburgh could hardly have taken this view of Athens, for the Scottish Enlightenment's "progress of civilization" could not logically conceive an enlightened present learning from a benighted past. Norton denied any such simple progressivism, arguing that "there is no secular development or evolution of the total body of human faculties"; the "faculties of the Englishman" were simply "very differently developed from those of the ancient Greek," not necessarily more finely or poorly as a whole. Therefore knowledge of antiquity "provides us with standards by which to measure our own capacities and performances," even while it "quickens our sympathies with the generations which have preceded us." Human beings exhibited enormous diversity in their evolution, but an essential human nature and basic human virtues would endure as long as humankind.[49]

In this long and manifold saga of human self-realization lay the whole point. The "great lesson" of Greek history was that every man should seek his own ideal development, should strive to "shape himself into the best that the material he possesses within himself, will allow." There existed no better "corrective" for American tendencies to dismiss "the ideal." Norton imagined Western civilization not as a historic reality but as an educational program grounded in history. It filled the vacuum in the curriculum left by the disintegration of the old form of moral philosophy. Western civilization gave students once again a way to integrate, or at least to form a broad understanding of, their education.[50]

This conception of liberal education, centered on the development of "our civilization," flowed in parallel with Norton's idea of liberal scholarship. After all, the same two copious springs, the Scottish Enlightenment and philological erudition, fed both. Advanced, expert learning of the sort that Norton advocated fitted into the same broad civilizational framework as this new notion of "undergraduate" education. The emerging great divide between general learning and specialized knowledge, between the aims and character of undergraduate and graduate education, he wished to erase.

Indeed, the whole domain of learning bore on his self-conscious goal: to reanimate the "conception of a liberal education." For, as the fin de siècle neared, Norton believed that the idea had "grown faint among us" of an education that enlarges the scope of mental vision, invigorates the understanding, confirms the reason, quickens and disciplines the imagination, and, instilling into the soul of youth the sense of proportion between the things of the spirit and the things of sense, animates it with ambitions that are safeguards of character not less than motives of action, strengthening it against the multiform temptations to worldliness, which means selfishness, and to acceptance of popular standards of judgment, which means superficiality, inspiring it with the love of what is best in thought, and in those arts which are the expression of the ideal conceptions and aims of men.

Such an education "needs revival and reinvigoration, not in the interest of the few, a select and eminent class, but in the interest of the many, of the whole community." And here the ideals of old patrician Boston spoke through its most eminent living son.

For the condition of healthy, progressive life in a democracy like ours, the condition on which order, confidence, credit, and stability permanently depend, is the existence of a reasonable correspondence between its spiritual and its physical elements, between its mental and its material development. This correspondence is to be secured only by means of the highest attainable level of education.

Norton conceded that "wise men" appeared without formal education, Lincoln being "the supreme example"; but "such endowment is as rare as it is precious" and no argument against the crying need for a renewed liberal education.

The education of the common school, even if universal, is not enough. Nor will the professional and scientific school, however excellent in its kind, supply what is needed. There must be a higher education still,—an education that shall train men to set a true value on things of the spirit, as compared with those of the flesh, and to seek for wisdom as better than wealth; "for wisdom is a defence and money is a defence, but the excellency of wisdom is that it giveth life to them that have it."[51]

Vigorous this program certainly was—but not *re*invigorated, for Norton's program of liberal education differed fundamentally from what he had known as a college student in the 1840s. Culture valued development of imagination and thus a broadening of sympathetic reach; the classical curriculum treasured discipline of the mind and thus a strengthening of intellectual grasp. Western civilization acquainted students with a "poetic" tradition constructed from literary, artistic, religious, and philosophical works; moral philosophy, with a gamut of sciences, human and natural. Norton held up to students "high ideals, noble ambitions, and the indescribable qualities that constitute character": the old college, divine law. Moral philosophy had wished students to know God and His creation. "Know thyself" Norton believed "the wisest and the most comprehensive maxim for the guidance of life that man has attained." And he was hardly blind to these essential distinctions, for he intended a new education fitted to a new era. And he substantially achieved it, the tendrils of his program infiltrating college curricula across the United States.[52]

Norton's hands had shaped into new form the ancient clay of liberal education. The introduction into the curriculum of the fine arts and an expansive poetry; the insistence on the practicality, the relevance to daily life, of the liberal culture defined around these new subjects; the replacement, through this culture, of ebbing religiosity with a new secular spirituality coaxed from art and literature; the setting up of these new humanities as a counterweight to American materialism; the use of the humanities to expand the sympathies of students beyond their own class and community, their own time and place; the invention of the idea of Western civilization to provide a matrix for such cosmopolitan sympathies—no American teacher had ever attempted, much less completed, so astonishing a work. Norton did not work alone; untold numbers of instructors in colleges across the country helped to craft component pieces. But he sculpted them into the whole.

It is not too much to say that his mark rests more heavily on the modern liberal arts college than any other's. His rendering of the humanities and their cultural meanings rooted itself widely in American collegiate education. True, the roots proved—and inevitably—shallow; and this point can hardly receive too much stress. For the larger structures of knowledge surrounding liberal education in the university—the modes of knowledge embodied in professorial research and housed in the graduate school—were simultaneously rejecting any vision of knowledge as integrated, rebuffing the value-laden learning that liberal education assumed, repudiating Norton's whole conception of liberal learning and scholarship. Nonetheless, Norton's wraith still haunts the college classrooms where freshmen once argued over "great books" and studied the origins of "our civilization." At least until the reforms of the 1960s, American liberal education executed his legacy; and professors still tussle over his bones.

The achievement was monumental, and an aging Norton could not but weary under the weight. He still looked a little younger than his years and was anything but feeble. When the college year ended and Ashfield arrived, he hefted his axe and marched out to thin the woods back of the Locusts—though, true, these days he often laid it down to watch "the squirrels, the woodchucks and the birds." And he remained capable of intellectual exercise as heavy as felling the swamp maples. Even while teaching almost five hundred students in 1897–98, he edited for the Grolier Society two of Thomas Carlyle's early notebooks, an edition showing the same scrupulous care as the larger-scale volumes of Carlyle correspondence—and taking one last slap at Froude.[53]

Still, Norton turned seventy in November 1897, and he had begun truly to look aged. Cambridge was coming to know him as "the stooped man with the side whiskers and the sharp, glancing eyes" and to call him affectionately "Old Norton." He had for many years "felt old" in moments of distress; but actual old age caught Charles, as it does all of us, by surprise: sometimes he still seemed to himself the boy sitting on a schoolroom bench, at other times "older than Methusaleh." He looked well but, as his doctor son, Rupert, noticed in January, tired easily. The eye troubles that had bothered him since boyhood grew more frequent, forcing him to resort to dictating to a typist. His memory started to warn him "that it is wearing out." He still endured a parade of visitors that would have exhausted younger hosts—and actually enjoyed having for houseguests in the autumn of 1897 the British jurist and historian James Bryce, Peter Kropotkin, "the mildest and gentlest of anarchists," and that "admirable Darwinian" George Darwin. But later that winter he did decline an invitation to dine with French visitors, no longer feeling the energy to keep up conversation in a tongue grown rusty.[54]

In June 1898 a sudden heart attack took Edward Burne-Jones—"Uncle Ned" to Lily and Sally, to their father a friend for more than forty years. "I had never thought of his dying before me," Charles grieved. "He is a great loss out of my life." Who was left? No one in the United States from the old days. Rarely these days did some feeble scratch arrive from John Simon; in Ruskin's wandering mind the memory of Charles flickered now and then. Only Leslie Stephen really remained. "How full our letters to each other of late years have been of the death of friends!" Charles wrote him in June, "and how solitary we are left!"[55]

In the deepest sense, Charles had lived solitary since Susan's death a quarter century before, and his own end he now awaited without "regret." "I am not impatient for it; I do not care whether it come soon or late,—provided only it come before I become a burden to others. There is a good deal which I should like to do, but I shall not be much disappointed if I have not time to do it." Norton insisted that existence had not yet become a burden to him; yet, his words echoing the old India days, he felt it "full time to furl the sails and make ready for entering port." He recalled how President James Walker smiled when the Harvard faculty asked him to reconsider his resignation "on the ground that no one saw the least reason" for it: "Do you suppose that I am going to wait until you do?"[56]

On his seventieth birthday Norton handed Charles Eliot his own resignation. The Corporation accepted it with an extraordinary resolution, recognizing the "great originality, broad scope, and enduring influence" of Norton's contribution to education and his impress on "thousands of students of different ages, dispositions, and tendencies." It also decided, given the gravity of the event in the life of Harvard, that public announcement had best be delayed a few months.[57]

This came on 18 February, and the next day newspapers around the country informed readers. Norton pulled his curtain of privacy aside long enough to permit an interview with a reporter from the *Boston Journal,* which other papers reprinted. Former students wrote: "Doubtless I was an indifferent student and learned all too little about the architectural beauties of Greece and Rome. But, sir, I learned one thing in that course, and learned it by a study from life, and that is how beautiful a thing it is to be a gentleman." So did their mothers:

> You do not at all know me, still I feel to-day so keen a sense of personal grief in your retirement from Harvard, that you will surely pardon this expression of it. Two of my sons have had the privilege of being led by you to a truer conception of beauty, and a higher ideal of character and purpose. Two others will miss the fair opportunity.

Even the *Lampoon,* the undergraduate humor magazine, laying aside its "jesting mantle," "sadly stands before the Grand Old Man of our University" to say "Good-bye, sir." "No one man," declared the student newspaper, the *Crimson,* "will ever fill the place in the esteem of the undergraduate which he has occupied." Even Norton might have felt satisfaction in work well done.[58]

Whatever satisfaction he took his country quickly blighted. Three days before the public announcement of Norton's retirement the battleship *Maine* exploded in Havana harbor, bringing to flash point a long-smoldering dispute between the United States and Spain over the independence of Spain's colony Cuba. In late April war began. To most Americans the Spanish War seemed a crusade to secure Cuban liberty, vindicating American honor. To Norton it seemed an imperialist adventure to impose American power, betraying republican principles. "My heart is heavy with anxiety lest the nation be entering on a path of calamity & disgrace," he wrote several days before the fighting started.[59]

He felt no sense of shock. "No clearsighted observer can have watched the course of our national life for the past thirty years without seeing that it was tending towards events of this kind." The Spanish war was the natural outcome of the jingoism displayed during the Venezuelan border dispute, of the slow erosion of civic virtue by selfishness and materialism, of the radiation of delusive ideals of national greatness through a democracy warped by ignorance. The victories of American arms—in Cuba, in Puerto Rico, in Guam, in the Philippines—were in actuality "calamities." "They rouse the lust of territorial expansion, the spirit of military aggression, & of national arrogance." They threatened to bring the traditional knell for any republic, "the establishment of a standing army."[60]

"It has seemed to me," Norton wrote to his old friend William Stillman, "as though I were witnessing the end of the America which we have loved,— and for which, in spite of all doubts, we have hoped."

> A new America is beginning; she has renounced the ideals of the old and, turning her back upon them, faces to the past instead of the future, and enters on the ways of ancient wrong. It is a bitter disappointment, for notwithstanding all the many signs of evil, it has been possible to believe that in the long run the better elements of the nation's life would prevail over the worse. But we made the mistake of believing that happier conditions than man had experienced elsewhere would work a change in human nature itself. We ought to have been wiser, and to have learned the lesson of history better. But our New England teachers all led us wrong,—and lo! the same old Adam has turned up in our Fool's Paradise.

Norton saw "no chance of saving the Old America." "We must make the best we can of the New."[61]

The republican idealism that had fired a younger Norton during the Civil War burned still in the old one, though the decades had battered his hopes. A new birth of freedom was not impossible, simply very far from the actual America. All that a patriot could now do was to resist materialism, to diminish ignorance in some small fraction, to keep alive the old ideals in a few young minds. These might, in some distant century, provide the seeds from which would germinate anew a democratic republic. And to this hope, after all, Norton had long dedicated his teaching. He used his first Harvard lecture after the declaration of war to address, to a hall overflowing with students, a few words "on the nature of true patriotism."[62]

SIXTEEN

Shady Hill Again, 1898–1908

It was as if the skies had opened. Newspapers throughout the country reported Norton's lecture, and there poured on his grey head a "hailstorm" of abuse. He had conceded to his students that war with Spain, once declared, had to be carried through; and he affirmed every American's duty to support his country. But he also advised that the young men "carefully consider whether the best use they could make of themselves in her service was to enlist in such a war," calling it "needless," "criminal," and—perhaps worst of all to patriot ears—"inglorious." His audience sympathized; and, when one among them rose to challenge their professor, the others started to hiss him down. Norton made them hear the dissenter out.[1]

Few jingoes granted Norton any such tolerance. "A Hoarse Croak from Harvard" ran a typical headline. "Proff Norton is a unamircan *ass,* one of those kind of animals that the Spanirds miss call *Pigs,*" one of the less literate among Norton's numerous new correspondents explained to him. An "Alumnus" redundantly advised him to resign ("Damn you"), declaring that his sons would "never be contaminated" by "such a fool." Ten days after the offending lecture, Norton imprudently repeated his views in a newspaper interview; somewhat garbled and widely reprinted, this stoked the fire. The *Los Angeles Times,* declaring "Nortonism" "another name for treason," labeled him a "miserable specimen of unpatriotic scrubs," who deserved to be "ducked into a swill barrel"; an Iowan suggested that he "find a hollow log and crawl into it, and stay there." In the interview Norton also rehearsed his well-known opinions on the shallow materialism of Americans and the dearth of gentlemen among them, giving outraged patriots the chance to vent more fury at the refined professor's fastidious distaste for their mores.[2]

For all the scurrility, many still revered Norton as a cultural icon, and not a few shared his antiwar sentiments. If many Americans classified him "in the line of the Tories of the Revolution and the Copperheads of the great Rebellion," the Harvard chapter of Phi Beta Kappa ostentatiously elected him president on 4 June. He himself tried to justify his ways in an address titled "True Patriotism" delivered three days later to the Men's Club of Prospect Street Congregational Church, which he handed over to the sympathetic *Boston Transcript* to print in full. So many requests for copies followed that the newspaper produced a slick-paper offprint, and a few weeks exhausted the stock of that.[3]

In this talk Norton insisted that republican principles, not some *Volkisch* identity or Anglo-American tradition, defined American nationality. These tenets included "the ideals of justice for all men, of independence, including free speech and free action within the limits of law, of obedience to law, of universal education, of material well-being for all the well-behaving and industrious, of peace and good will among men." The true patriot loved the United States *because* it stands for "these ideals"; this "deepest love for his country" indeed became the patriot's "religion," "the strongest motive of his life." The democratic nation forged in the Civil War thus perpetuated the old Republic of Andrews Norton's day, "the good citizen" still "always in arms" to defend its ideals at the price of life itself.

Yet since the 1870s the course of events had aroused increasing anxiety that the principles of democratic republicanism had lost "their power to control the direction of private and public conduct"; now the Spanish War brought "bitter disappointment to the lover of his country." Egged on by politicians and journalists "faithless to her noble ideals," spurning "the will of all her wisest and best," America "has been forced to turn back from the way of civilization to the way of barbarism." "With grief, with anxiety must the lover of his country regard the present aspect and the future prospect of the nation's life. With serious purpose, with utter self-devotion he should prepare himself for the untried and difficult service to which it is plain he is to be called in the quick-coming years." For only the defeat of American imperialism could save the American Republic. With the declaration of war against Spain, America "stood at the parting of the ways." Whether she now proceeded "downward to the darkness" depended entirely "on the virtue, on the enlightened patriotism of her children." "Nil desperandum de republica"—we must not despair of the Republic.[4]

So Norton said, but he himself teetered on the edge of despair. If human beings are "but little lower than the angels," he wrote to his daughter-in-law in October 1898, "the angels taken by and large must be a pretty poor lot." His decades-long combat to preserve the old Republic appeared now to be ending in defeat, for the moral force of cultivated leadership had proved helpless against the legions of materialism raised up by science and democracy. His fellow citizens more often called him a traitor than a patriot.[5]

A particularly stinging attack came from a classmate and occasional dinner companion at the Saturday Club, United States Senator George Hoar. "The trouble with Prof. Norton, who thinks his countrymen are lacking in a sense of honor," Hoar concluded in a speech in Worcester on 13 July, "is that there are two things he cannot in the least comprehend—he cannot comprehend his countrymen, and he cannot comprehend honor." Two days later, in an open letter from Ashfield published in the *Springfield Republican*, Norton shot back that Hoar had not only disregarded "our almost lifelong relations of friendliness" but distorted his actual opinions, which Norton saw "no reason to change." Hoar refused to apologize, defending the "general" accuracy of his speech and avowing that "the habit of bitter and sneering speech about persons and public affairs has so grown upon you that you do not yourself know, always, what you say." "All lovers of Harvard, and all lovers of the country, have felt for a long time that your relation to the University made your influence bad for the college and bad for the youth of our country. It was high time that somebody should say what I have said."[6]

Hoar could hardly have blundered more ineptly had he set out to prove Norton right in saying that manners in America had grown semibarbaric. In the following days letters supporting Norton inundated Shady Hill; the Harvard faculty and former students rallied around him. Even a stout backer of the war like the Reverend Lyman Abbott found Hoar's outburst appalling. Norton himself claimed to be unruffled, only regretting that someone of the senator's "abilities, position and influence should set an example of bad manners, and should foster the popular spirit of intolerance of independent opinion and freedom of expression." Charles's "chief new interest," he told his son Eliot, was "a little collie puppy," the "successor to old Jupe." "What a dear dog he was! I miss him still."[7]

Though Hoar's peevish misstep redounded to Norton's advantage, the tide of abuse continued to flow; and Norton found himself more in the public eye than ever. But he reserved his only other public utterance that summer for the Ashfield Academy Dinner on 25 August. By then the armed conflict had ended in Spain's utter rout. The featured speaker, Booker T. Washington, judiciously avoided mention of the war, knowing that it could only distract from his concern, the needs of southern Negroes; but the Reverend Philip S. Moxom of Springfield ringingly endorsed it—Norton having applied, even though painful, the principle of ventilating both sides at the dinners. His own wavering voice took the other.

"The actual conflict has ended; but less than one hundred days of War has resulted in revolution in the United States." The Spanish War, he said, had shaken the very foundations of the Republic. In acquiring colonies the United States had "undertaken obligations which neither our institutions nor our national character enable us properly to discharge." The country had thoughtlessly embraced the classic evils that endangered republics: a stand-ing army, a large debt, the entanglements of international affairs. The old America, before it had solved the "tremendous and magnificient experiment of a self-governing democracy," had transformed itself into an empire. But "the more threatening the dangers" and "more doubtful the issue, so much the more strenuous and steady must be the effort of the good citizen for the welfare of his country." The good folk of Ashfield listened to their first citizen with wonted respect but without sympathy; most newspapers showed neither. Norton "has had another fit of disloyalty," opined the *New York Sun*. The *Chicago Tribune* suggested confining "this venerable scold" to "a lunatic asylum until the present fit is over."[8]

A public career stretching back to the Civil War had inured Norton to abuse, but nothing assuaged his grief. "The bitterest disappointment in regard to America which I have had to bear in a life of more than seventy years," he wrote in a private letter, "is to find the conscience of the people so dead to the crime of war, and dull to its brutalizing horrors." His heart grew no lighter in the next three years, as he watched his government annex Puerto Rico, clamp a virtual protectorate on Cuba, and secure the Philip-pines by bloodily suppressing a popular rebellion. The Spanish War seemed to him to have brought greater disaster to the victors than to the vanquished, for it completed "the wreck of our old America."[9]

Norton had lost hope but not the will to carry on. As he had reminded the crowd at Ashfield, quoting his long-dead friend Clough, "If hopes were dupes, fears may be liars." Norton had always been able to take the long view, and he did so again in writing to a literary scholar at the University of the South. "How like is the conduct of our democracy on a vast scale to that of the Athenian democracy in the early years of the Peloponnesian war; and how analogous are many of the material & moral influences which have brought us to the present pass with those which shaped the fortunes of Athens!" If the American experiment had gone on the reef, the human race had not. The proportion of "civilized men," though still small, will be greater "a thousand years hence."[10]

Work remained for him at Harvard. Although the glory days of Fine Arts 3 and 4 had passed, Norton kept as professor emeritus his little advanced class in Dante. If he regretted the big lectures, he never hinted so. He did miss the faculty meetings, "for there," as he told his neighbor and former colleague William James, "more than anywhere else, are the humours of men displayed." But he found a new role at Harvard, which turned out to have its own rewards. He believed that the college, which had stagnated in recent years as Harvard's professional schools blossomed, needed bracing; he wished, too, to help President Eliot install a three-year undergraduate course. To advance these goals, he and his cousin agreed in September 1898 to put Norton on the Board of Overseers; at the next commencement the alumni duly elected him.[11]

Yet he had no intention of spending his remaining years hobbling around Harvard Yard. "There is much that I want to do," he told his old acquaintance, the historian Henry Lea; "I shall hope to do part of it." Even with lecturing off his back, he found himself with far more work than time—and with new demands constantly to ward off, as when his old friend Lord Acton asked him to contribute to the ambitious new *Cambridge Modern History*. For all that, retirement did allow Norton to indulge pleasures once postponed. Long a member of the Massachusetts Historical Society, he became an active one, regularly attending meetings (true, often to eulogize one more dead acquaintance) and developing a lively friendship with its president, and Norton's fellow Overseer, Charles Francis Adams. Scarcely half a mile from Shady Hill he found another satisfaction. Having for some years admired the devotion and good sense of the Roman Catholic nuns who staffed Holy Ghost Hospital for Incurables, he now went every week to read aloud (always a favorite pastime of his) to the patients and to organize other entertainments for them. He still gave occasional lectures—in December 1898 to the Boston Society of Arts and Crafts, on "the craftsman as an artist"—and still held his annual Christmas Eve party for the Harvard students stranded in Cambridge.[12]

Spells of illness did become more frequent and may have played some role in his decision at the end of March 1899 to resign as president of the Tavern Club, but he showed no sign of really flagging. He readily accepted a second term as president of Harvard Phi Beta Kappa and traveled to New York for meetings of the AIA Council and the American School's managing committee. When the Kiplings asked him to write a sketch of Rudyard's life to accompany a forthcoming edition of his works (aiming to counteract an inaccurate biography then circulating), he promptly agreed. On a larger scale, he undertook for Samuel Ward, his comrade long ago in the Loyal Publication Society and in recent years one of Norton's most voluble correspondents, to edit into a book the letters that Emerson had written to Ward years ago. (Having them appear in a magazine would have made Ward feel "like going into the street with my hat off," and he also wanted his name kept quiet.) The correspondence seemed to Norton important for understanding Emerson's mind. Working with his old speed, he had final proofs to the printer in early August; and Houghton Mifflin published in late September *Letters from Ralph Waldo Emerson to a Friend, 1838–1853.*[13]

That was one among many preoccupations. The mounting expenses of keeping up Shady Hill and the Locusts forced Norton to dispose of more of his treasures. He preferred when possible to sell to friends: keeping his precious objects, as it were, within the circle. His protégée Isabella Stewart Gardner being one of the few friends who could afford them, in May, Norton handed her one of his favorites: a 1445 manuscript book of devotions containing one of the earliest examples of a wood engraving print. In June 1899 Richard arrived home after almost two years abroad, carrying his own trophy: election to a five-year term as director of the American School of Classical Studies in Rome. This was "a great honor for such a youth" and a great source of pride for a father who may have felt that he had a real heir.[14]

Not that Papa was about to pass the baton. He turned his attention to the sorts of writing that time had rarely permitted in the last decade or two, beginning once more to review regularly for the *Nation*—not across his old range, for even the *Nation* had succumbed to the specialist, but on the subjects on which he ranked as America's leading expert: Dante and Donne. Otherwise, the routine of life altered little. Norton continued to ply his little personal charities—the regular check that kept J. B. Harrison alive, emergency funds for Harvard students: "just now a half-starving black man in our graduate school has stripped me, and a half starving white undergraduate has taken what was left." And he had the role of cultural monument to play, though increasingly with a retrospective attitude. Right after Christmas 1899 he opened in New Haven the first general meeting of a reorganized AIA by telling the founder's saga: "The Work of the Archaeological Institute of America."[15]

Charles looked back on his own life, too, as aged people do, meditating to other old men among his correspondents on the changes that had transformed the planet in his seventy-two years on it. "I find the heaviest burden of old age to be the disappointment, which these late years have brought, in steadily increasing measure, of the hopes for the advance of civilized man that we had some reason to indulge, up to perhaps twenty years ago." Material prosperity might prove to have a good effect in "a century or two"; but it "intoxicates for the time the rising horde of democracy, and makes the crowd arrogant, irresponsible, indifferent to the higher ends of life, while it diffuses a spirit of vulgarity, of essential selfishness & hardness of heart under an exterior of genuine kindliness throughout the community."[16]

There seemed no countervailing power to materialism. Protestantism had utterly failed. The "progress of science" had left it "vacant of spiritual significance, and a church of essentially insincere profession." However, Norton's immersion in medieval studies suggested an alternative to his ancestral faith, one made more comely by the Gray Nuns he had learned to respect at Holy Ghost Hospital. Might Rome, if "but a trifle more enlightened," offer a "spiritual influence with which to oppose the spirit of materialism"? If the Vatican came round to the Americanist "interpretation of Romanism," then "the Catholic church in this country would rapidly gain in spiritual power, and would render an enormous service in standing against the anarchic religion of the unchurched multitude." Even if, as seemed likelier, Rome stuck in its "obscurantism," Norton expected Catholicism to "gain strength among us." "For science has obviously nothing but a stone to offer to the ignorant and dependent masses who are always longing for bread," while Catholicism proffered "for those who like it, a wholesome substitute for bread." Andrews would have quaked. Yet the most enlightened Rome could do nothing but palliate the evil. "Materialism is but in the morning of its day; and, with the aid of science, its day promises to be long and stormy."[17]

Still, Charles neither repined nor repented, nor did he abandon the long hope that had infused his life. He did realize that his generation had overestimated "the capacity of human nature" to advance morally as rapidly as materially. But he thought "our misreadings of the lessons of history, and over-confidence in the effect of our new conditions upon character" to have been "natural," even "inevitable"; for "the conditions of the last fifty years are unparalleled in the history of man." No one could have predicted that the nineteenth century's great leap forward in technological control of nature would end "in corrupting and materializing the spirit of man." Norton took comfort in the "wide and delightful diffusion of prosperity" but feared even this happiness to be brittle, about to shatter on the jagged edge of greed, a victim of the growing inequality of wealth. Even so he never despaired, never believed "the old ideals" dead. They only slept; and "a time will come when they shall once more be reverenced and pursued." Charles

Norton really did, as he so often claimed, "obey the voice at eve, obeyed at prime."[18]

On 20 January 1900 a cable arrived to announce the final silencing of a voice Charles had heard at prime and, next to Lowell's, probably most loved. Ruskin was dead. Charles felt more relief than grief, for the dead man had suffered "essentially one of the saddest of lives." A few years later Norton reflected that Ruskin had never learned "to control the waywardness of his temperament, or to balance and correct the force of immediate impressions by recollection or comparison": an assessment that reveals as much about Norton's ideals as about Ruskin's disposition. At the time, Charles told Leslie Stephen that he had "never known a life less wisely controlled, or less helped by the wisdom of others than his." "The whole retrospect of it is pathetic; waste, confusion, ruin of one of the most gifted & sweetest natures the world ever knew. He was a kind of angel gone astray; meant for the thirteenth century he got delayed on the way and when he finally arrived was a white-winged anachronism."[19]

This angel had literary executors. Ruskin had entrusted to Norton the more sensitive decisions, those regarding unpublished manuscripts and correspondence. Charles at first doubted whether this required a trip to England but decided "reluctantly" to go, "only for the sake of fidelity to an old friendship." Never since Susan's death had he been able to think of visiting Europe without ambivalence. He settled on traveling in June, when both the Atlantic and the British Isles could be counted on for milder weather.[20]

The months between were not cheerful. Ruskin's relatives pressed Norton to write the expected official biography of his friend; nothing could have felt more distasteful. "If it depended upon me," Charles wrote to Leslie Stephen, "there would be no further word of Ruskin or about him given to the public." In April, Godkin suffered a stroke; and Charles journeyed to New York to spend a day or two chatting "of old times & new," helpless to do anything more for his "disabled and pathetic" old friend. He returned to Shady Hill only to have Will Howells plead with him to accept election to a new American academy meant to set apart a small body of American "immortals" like those of the Académie Française. To placate Howells, Charles gave in; but he found the thing repugnant, disliking "both the inclusiveness and the exclusiveness of its list, as I dislike all artificial distinctions." It was a relief to board the *New England* with Sally on 23 May and retreat for a few days into Charles Francis Adams's recent biography of his father, an old republican of sturdy stuff and no pseudoaristocratic pretension.[21]

The *New England* docked at Liverpool on the morning of 2 June, and that night found Norton at rest in a turreted bedroom at Brantwood. He would need rest, for the following two weeks proved as wrenching as anything since the deaths of Lowell and Curtis. Helped by Ruskin's niece Joan, Charles picked through the debris left by "the shipwreck of a great nature." Many, perhaps most, of Ruskin's letters fed a great bonfire in the garden of Brantwood, especially those that spoke most explicitly of his pedophilia and most wrenchingly of his periods of madness. Ruskin's urge to self-revelation Norton refused to indulge: if his dear friend had let the wall between public and private fall into disrepair, Charles would rebuild it. Norton judged Ruskin already to have "printed far more than he should have done"; little among remaining manuscripts warranted publication.[22]

On 15 June the twelve days of this ordeal ended, and Norton and Sally escaped to London—"far more stately & superb & spectacular than when I saw it last fifteen years ago" but without its "old charm." Most of the old friends were gone, too, but Charles got a strange and sober kind of pleasure in seeing the ones who remained, companions who had added so largely to those happiest years with Susan: John and Jane Simon, badly enfeebled; Donald MacKay (now Lord Reay); Frederic Harrison; other faces long blurred in memory. "Renewal of friendship with you," Lord Acton told him, "is like the renewal of youth." Leslie Stephen seemed weary, "depressed by his deafness." Charles reminded him later that summer that "you and I have known the best that life can give." Norton went down to Rye to stay with Henry James at Lamb House and then to Rottingdean to see Georgie Burne-Jones. On 25 June he left there for Oxford to receive an honorary degree and be feted by the Oxford Dante Society. With "tender affection" Georgie watched his departing back "and thought how unlikely it was that you and I should meet again in this world."[23]

Oxford had changed much, descending the same arid road as American universities. "Science has pretty nearly extinguished literature; erudition is substituted for culture." Leslie Stephen summed up in his career the good old cause of humane learning; and it gratified Charles to go with him to a luncheon given in London by the Lord Mayor to honor the completion of the *Dictionary of National Biography,* the great project of collaborative scholarship that Stephen had launched in 1882. Norton sat next to him, relaying the speakers' acclaim to Stephen's ear trumpet. Several days and many friends later, on July 5, a pleasantly exhausted Norton reboarded the *New England.*[24]

At the Locusts a congenial task awaited. Norton's version of the *Divina*

Commedia had secured a place as one of the two standard English prose translations, and Houghton Mifflin desired a new edition. After decades of translating, he still found the revision "an engrossing and endless task, for it has to do with the choice and aptness of words, 'the subtlest and delicatest instruments,' as I think Donne calls them, with which the spirit of man has provided itself to give form to immaterial things." Since the Locusts lacked a furnace, he reluctantly returned to Cambridge as September ended, to discover at Shady Hill that a mighty storm (the tail of the great Galveston hurricane of 1900) had ripped from the ground a grand old willow in front of the house, the tree he loved most on the old homestead. He plunged back into Dante and by December had reached *Paradise*.[25]

This New Year's Eve was exceptional, ending not only an old year but an old century. In a letter on 31 December remitting the quarterly check to Jonathan Harrison, Norton remarked how "these last hours of the century quicken the fancy and the memory." The old merchant kept now a different ledger.

> It is a good moment for summing up the Dr. & Cr. columns of one's own life, & of that of the world at large, and of striking, if possible, the balance. I cannot say on which side the balance would be. Much has been gained, but not all the gain has been profit; much has been lost, and some of the losses are grievous and irremediable. Is the character of so-called civilized men, in the mass, better than it was a hundred years ago[?] I hardly venture on a positive opinion. I think that we are sure of one enormous gain,—there is less physical suffering, and there is a greater proportion of the people of Europe & America raised above the level of material want.

"Well, the old century does not leave a very happy world for the new one to greet."[26]

In April 1901 Norton launched a last assault on one of his oldest foes. At least since admiring the Oxford museum in the 1850s, he had stressed the significance of public architecture; it ought both to express and to foster the ideals of its community. Collegiate architecture, in particular, should nurture high aspiration in young people by surrounding them with carefully designed intimations of moral ideals. Harvard Yard during Eliot's administration had sprouted a motley and ill-assorted aggregation of brick fungi, symbolizing only confusion. Norton now persuaded the Board of Overseers to pass a resolution requesting the Corporation to appoint a committee of five, including at least two Overseers and a faculty member, to vet "all plans and designs of permanent buildings for the University, previous to their adoption." Everyone knew the identity of one of the Overseers meant to sit in judgment.[27]

President Eliot, handicapped by the architectural equivalent of a tin ear, took a more utilitarian view of college buildings than his cousin; he certainly had no wish to bloat the budget with needless ornament. Attacked by the Overseers, he took shelter behind the stone walls of the governing Corporation. Norton laid siege for three years, and a public scolding in the *Harvard Graduate's Magazine* in March 1904 finally flushed his cousin from cover. After further months of skirmishing between Overseers and Corporation, the former hit upon the tactic of appointing Daniel Burnham, celebrated architect of the Columbian Exposition, to Norton's standing Committee on Fine Arts and Architecture. In a report in spring 1905 the committee excoriated Harvard for architectural incoherence, urging a campus plan to guide future building toward greater harmony. This appeared to jog mildly the Corporation's groggy aesthetic sense, and there Norton had to rest discontent.

Such campaigns, once a staple of Norton's public life, required more energy than he usually could muster these days. His eye trouble now came upon him more often, and perhaps this influenced his decision in the spring of 1901 to give up his last Harvard class. The next fall he handed it over to his pupil Charles Grandgent, well on his way to succeeding his mentor as the most distinguished American Dante scholar of his generation. Public appearances, too, grew sparser, though in June 1901 he did deliver the Radcliffe commencement address in Sanders Theatre, advising the young women, inter alia, "Whatever your occupation may be, and however crowded your hours with affairs, do not fail to secure at least a few minutes every day for refreshment of your inner life with a bit of poetry." This particular bit of advice caught the fancy of a newspaper editor, and for some time thereafter the *Boston Globe* and *Chicago Tribune*—probably other papers as well—ran daily poetry selections under Norton's dictum. The odium of the outraged imperialists was fading.[28]

Although he continued to speak every summer at the Academy Dinner, Norton had begun to retreat into more private satisfactions. Still largest among them was friendship, despite the loss of his real confidants. He kept in regular touch with longtime acquaintances like George Woodberry (now finally settled in the English Department at Columbia) and William Howells, each a good friend though not an intimate one. He also found in 1901 a new one: a woman of the younger generation, to whom Sally had grown close, a rising novelist named Edith Wharton. Mrs. Wharton, who lived in

New York but maintained a summer home near Louisa's in Lenox, took to visiting the Nortons at Shady Hill and, more often, Ashfield. Norton introduced her to Donne's poetry and sent rare old books to supply background for a novel of eighteenth-century Italy that she was writing, *The Valley of Decision*. Charles admired the book, published early in 1902, not so much as a story but as "a study of Italian thought and life"; he thought it placed "Mrs. Wharton among the few foremost of the writers (of fiction) in English today." Wharton more than reciprocated the esteem; and a genuine affection, tinged with reverence on her part, bloomed between them.[29]

Their relationship resembled Norton's older one with Isabella Gardner, though never as close. Norton still provided Mrs. Gardner expert advice in her pursuit of rare manuscripts and paintings; when Berenson tried to sell her a picture that he claimed as the only authentic portrait of Michelangelo, Norton warned her off, showing that "Michelangelo" looked nothing like Michelangelo but a lot like Baccio Bandinelli. Norton also disposed of more pieces from his own collection to her, as he kept lightening ballast: Venetian manuscripts, other Italian autographs, most spectacularly Tintoretto's *Marriage Feast at Cana*. He never charged what the market would bear—unlike Berenson he did not need to—in helping her to assemble one of the great American collections. To house these riches Mrs. Gardner constructed a vast Italianate palazzo in Boston's Fens, which she meant to serve the public as a museum as well as herself as a residence. On New Year's Eve in 1901 Norton stepped into the nearly finished Fenway Court with "amazing pleasure." Here, at least, one monument to his influence stood as a small but sturdy dike against the tide of materialist values.[30]

Acknowledgments of his influence accumulated with advancing years. At Yale's bicentennial festivities in 1901, Harvard's rival recognized Norton's achievements with one more honorary degree. When British art scholars founded the *Burlington Magazine* in March 1903, they chose him as one of two Americans on its small consultative committee.[31] The Archaeological Institute called on Norton to deliver the chief address when its twenty-fifth anniversary arrived in 1904. He arrived at that celebration as a newly dubbed *Grande Ufficiale della Corona d'Italia*, a high honor conferred by the Italian government for his Dante work. Ambivalence was the characteristic response. Enough of old Boston survived in Norton for public honors to make him uneasy.

He also had increasing reason to put such things in perspective. Just before the middle of April 1902 he collapsed with a serious illness, spent a week or two dosed with bromides, morphine, and belladonna, and did not recuperate until well into May. It was a forecast. He had barely recovered when, on 21 May, a stroke carried off Godkin. A few weeks later word arrived that Leslie Stephen had terminal cancer, followed immediately by news of Acton's death, never a close but a warm friend since youth. Also in May, however, Edith White Norton gave birth to Charles's first grandchild, a daughter; and a few days later Margaret Meyer Norton delivered a grandson. The parents named them Susan and Charles Eliot Norton. Always fond of children, Charles liked to watch these little ones playing around him when they came to visit; he smiled at "Tattoo"—Charles Eliot Norton II—sitting in the "same high chair in which I sat 75 years ago."[32]

The Christmas Eve party of 1903 brought 150 to 200 Harvard students to the house, from almost every one of the states and the Canadian provinces and from several foreign countries, to celebrate under Professor Norton's benign smile. Norton's pride in the "promiscuous" flavor of this crowd extended especially to the tiny delegation of Japanese students, for his grim view of the prospect of Western cultures heightened appreciation of East Asian ones. Civilization is "not as white people are apt to assume a possession exclusively theirs," he wrote to Sam Ward. "If the Chinese and Japanese civilization were in one scale, and the British and American in another, it is likely that they would more nearly balance each other, than the missionaries & the Christians generally have supposed." In a climate of intensifying xenophobia and rising hostility to immigration, Norton could still be relied on to oppose any form of "race proscription," such as the Chinese exclusion act. To enjoy the company of a couple of young men from Japan was one thing; to entertain 175 of their fellow students quite another for an old man. In 1904 Norton asked Charles Eliot to invite them henceforth to a Christmas Eve gathering in Harvard Yard. In subsequent years Norton went there instead, to read to the students, as he always had in his own house, the nativity story from Luke.[33]

He still found strength to write. Houghton Mifflin had published the revision of his *Divina Commedia* in March 1902, to sales far beyond expectation. Norton had no idea of stopping; the translation done, he regretted only that he could "accomplish but a very small part of what I desire to do before the end comes."[34] He busied himself through 1903 and 1904 with a revision of the Lowell letters, "a little tract of hardly twenty pages" on the poet Thomas Gray as a naturalist (printed by Berkeley Updike of the elegant Merrymount Press), an introduction to a selection of Ruskin's comments on Dante edited by George P. Huntington. More substantially, he decided to "give to the public a selection of Mr. Ruskin's very numerous letters to me."

This was not a concession to the despised craving for prying into private life but a strategy to thwart that urge, by controlling what got uncovered and by providing "a record of moods and mental conditions" to make Ruskin's thinking better understood. Norton flatly refused when Houghton Mifflin beseeched him to write his own recollections: "my mind is fixed upon that point: I shall not fall in with the contemporary taste for personal memoirs." There was, anyway, a vast heap of other literary work to get done.[35]

And Norton's ability to do it was beginning seriously to decline. Bouts of sickness confined him to his bedchamber for longer and longer periods. He often had there "a very quiet and pleasant time," reading, or having read to him, the novels of "the friend of mankind, Sir Walter"; but he was good for nothing else. Quietly, he began to prepare for the end. He gave the Loyal Publication Society's papers to the Boston Public Library; Lowell's manuscripts went, as he had wished, to Harvard. On 20 August 1903 Norton presided over the final Academy Dinner in Ashfield. Unlike the last few, it was a celebration rather than a scrap. The founder recalled the "wonderful procession" of "poets, novelists, statesmen, diplomatists, philosophers, divines, and lawyers" who had spoken there. Norton made a point of refusing to retract a single one of his unpopular words, but he spoke more feelingly of his joy in having spent in Ashfield "so large a portion" of his life: "Neighbors and friends, I thank you for all that you have been to me and have done for me." The rest of that summer and well into fall he spent "gently invalided" at the Locusts.[36]

When he did return to Cambridge, he could no longer "venture upon evening excursions." A cold snap now kept Norton shut up even during the day. Yet he insisted that he was "not conscious of old age yet in any lamentable way. Time is very gentle with me." In February 1904 Leslie Stephen died: "the best friend left to me in England." Charles kept at work, when able, on Ruskin's letters to him. A selection began to appear in the May *Atlantic,* continuing into the September issue. The July number evoked from William James, in a letter to Charles, one of the most celebrated Jamesian dicta: "Mere sanity is the most philistine and (at bottom) unimportant of a man's attributes." In May, Norton learned that one of the last friends whom he cared deeply about, Jonathan Harrison, was dying. Norton assured Harrison that his widow would still receive the sustaining checks— and that "so long as I have conscious existence I shall be glad to have known you, and grateful for what you have been to me."[37]

The summer of 1904 he declined invitations to visit friends, remaining at the Locusts working over Ruskin letters, aiming to have the book ready for the printer by 1 September. He beat his deadline by nearly a month—fortunately, for he had scarcely posted the copy when a new attack sent him to bed again. He seems to have recovered by late September, when the Nortons closed up the Locusts. That fall Henry James visited Cambridge and found "dear old C. E. Norton" pleasantly "ancient and mellow now." Norton still cherished plans—"if my life be prolonged"—to finish the long-contemplated volume on French church building and to turn "my Notes on Dante" into a book. And by early February 1905 he was at work on a second Donne collection, which Houghton Mifflin published later that year as *The Love Poems of John Donne*.[38]

Meanwhile his friends and former pupils were plotting a surprise that deeply touched Norton. He had built an enormous library atop his father's impressive collection; but his children had little use for precious first editions of British poets, Italian incunabula, German philological scholarship, or medieval manuscripts. Norton wanted to donate his library to Harvard but could hardly consider any option other than selling it, given the expenses that Shady Hill imposed. Some forty admirers clubbed together to raise fifteen thousand dollars to purchase the collection for the Harvard Library; well over five hundred more contributed to an endowment to buy additional books for Harvard in Norton's name. Norton could keep in his own hands whatever volumes he wished for the remainder of his life.

"The disposal of my library which has been arranged for with such affectionate consideration by my friends is the one of all others that I would have chosen," Norton wrote—and meant it. On 14 February, Harvard's librarian William Coolidge Lane and Professor Archibald Cary Coolidge came to Shady Hill to deliver the check. Ill in his room, Norton could not see them. But in May ten or fifteen of the leaders of this effort gathered in the library at Shady Hill, a fire in the hearth making the tobacco-brown wallpaper and crowded shelves glow, to present Norton with a parchment folder engraved by Berkeley Updike with the names of all 581 donors and a testimonial

TO

CHARLES ELIOT NORTON

FROM

HIS STUDENTS, ASSOCIATES, AND FRIENDS

IN APPRECIATION

OF HIS SERVICES TO HARVARD UNIVERSITY

DURING MANY YEARS

IN ADMIRATION

OF HIS LIFE-LONG DEVOTION TO HIGH IDEALS

IN LETTERS, ART, AND CIVIC DUTY

IN GRATITUDE

FOR HIS HOSPITALITY, COUNSEL, FRIENDSHIP

INSPIRATION

****

FELICE TE, CHE SÌ PARLI A TUA POSTA

MAY FIRST, 1905

His old student William Roscoe Thayer, now a well-known historian of Italy, made a presentation speech. Norton replied with "tears streaming down his face."[39]

That summer at Ashfield, now that the book of Ruskin letters to him was done, Norton read through the whole mass of them, "a very sad and melancholy task." When he finished he left a note for his executors: the letters written after Ruskin's derangement should be destroyed, the rest given to Harvard. Charles had probably destroyed several of the worst himself; he had no heart to burn the rest. Dick's wife Edith "& the little Susan" cheered the return to Shady Hill.[40]

Grandpapa got easily fatigued now. He enjoyed the family visits; other houseguests had become simply a burden. He went fairly regularly to the monthly Saturday Club dinners, kept an eye on the English rare book and manuscript markets in behalf of the Harvard Library, and "amused" himself with little literary projects such as the analysis of the vocabulary of the *Vita Nuova* that he eventually published in the Dante Society's annual report in 1907. Ashfield suffered through a "strange summer" that year, with "tropical heats & humidity" displacing the "clear mountain air" that Norton relied on; it was "a summer for keeping quiet." The elderly man "sat by the window day after day reading old books & new papers." The Nortons returned early to Shady Hill.[41]

They were back less than a week when news arrived that rocked Norton to his core. Richard intended to divorce Edith—"a grievous sorrow to me." The "stain & disgrace" of Richard's course weighed heavily on his Papa's mind but no more heavily than his son's uncertain future. It did not take Richard long to understand that he would have to resign as director of the American School at Rome and that he had no academic prospect in the United States. On Christmas Eve, Charles went to the annual Harvard party to read the Christmas story. His voice was weak; and, when he had done, he turned to President Eliot and said, "Charles, I shall never do that again."[42]

He roused himself in February 1907 to preside in Sanders Theatre over the celebration of the hundredth anniversary of Longfellow's birth, and he also attended a meeting of the Massachusetts Historical Society to speak of the poet. It was his last. Neither his "interest in the affairs of men" nor "delight in the familiar aspects of nature" had flagged, but his vigor had. Although the doctors reported his heart and arteries in good shape, he recognized that he could no longer "hope to be of much service to others." He could still be of some, taking that April a leading role at a special meeting of the Harvard Board of Overseers to consider Eliot's successor and the reorganization of the college, then delivering in June a eulogy at the funeral of Elizabeth Cary Agassiz, Radcliffe's founder and his longtime collaborator there.[43]

Norton endured a difficult summer and fall, shadowed by worry for Richard and by his own declining health. That summer he formed in Ashfield "a civic service committee," to provide "an organized, permanent body working for the general good of the town." It was past time to provide some successor in the work he had cherished so highly. In October 1907 Charles lost his favorite remaining correspondent with the death of Sam Ward. Also in October, however, the Museum of Fine Arts engaged Richard to collect in its behalf abroad; this got him appropriate employment and out of the country. Friends, not the museum, provided the salary: his father probably a quarter of it. On 1 November the prodigal sailed for Europe. Norton hoped that Richard had not been hired simply "out of kind regard for me." It appeared a slim hope.[44]

Two weeks after Richard's departure came Norton's eightieth birthday. Congratulatory letters choked the mailbox. Moorfield Storey, younger comrade in many battles for civil service reform and against imperialism, grouped Norton with Emerson, Lowell, Curtis, Schurz: "You are about the last of the generation from whom I learned my principles and my ideals." William Thayer, who edited the *Harvard Graduate's Magazine,* arranged a special Norton birthday issue. Its pages carried memories and appreciations contributed by eminences of Anglo-American intellectual life ranging from the British jurist and statesman James Bryce, just appointed ambassador to the United States, to the American historian and diplomat Andrew Dickson White, founding president of Cornell University and of the American Historical Association. It was no accident that these writers represented the zone where Norton had dwelt all his life, where erudition and political engagement overlapped and intermingled. Thayer's effort touched his old teacher, though Norton winced at the publicity and "wished that there had been a little more of Greek moderation in the celebration."[45]

On the day itself, 16 November 1907, a small delegation came to Shady Hill. Sidney Gunn, a graduate student of English literature, presented a book of vellum pages bound in dark red leather and inscribed with the names of hundreds of current Harvard students, who applauded "a life so distinguished by the unstinted though unobtrusive application of high powers to the common good." "Though included among us are prosecutors of every line of modern study and research, most of us know you as a scholar of distinguished achievement in our particular field, and all of us have learned to admire your personality and to find inspiration in your example." The rhetoric was, as Norton benignly complained, a shade overripe. But the sentiments were honestly felt and the summation of Norton's academic achievement remarkably close to the mark.[46]

For he had, indeed, founded in the United States three distinct academic fields. His teaching established art history as a university subject; his organization of the Archaeological Institute of America and the American School of Classical Studies at Athens laid the institutional foundation on which archaeology, especially classical archaeology, in the United States still stands; his Dante translations, his published criticism, his constitution of the Dante Society, and his advanced teaching at Harvard created Dante studies as an American academic speciality. He had also written probably the seminal essay in modern Donne scholarship; with Henry Charles Lea (and possibly Henry Adams) he had transformed American interest in the Middle Ages from romance into scholarship; one of his students, modeling his own work carefully on Norton's, had become the first professor of comparative literature in the United States.[47]

Yet a telling phrase in the encomium presented by Gunn hinted at Norton's larger failure: "most of us know you as a scholar of distinguished achievement in our particular field." Norton had carried into his late-arriving professorial career the baggage of his first forty-five years: the holistic culture of the early nineteenth-century Boston patriciate; his father's sense of scholarship as an integrating philology; his own fellowship in the Anglo-American world of letters, where Darwin's biology was no more sundered from Dickens's novels than London from Boston; his meanderings from the shades of ancient India through the politically charged editorship of the *North American Review*. He never divided learning into "particular fields"; he never separated erudition from the need for moral nutrition and the duty of republican citizenship. What had this vision to do with the resolutely compartmentalized new specialism?

Only in the new liberal education that Norton had constructed in Harvard's lecture halls did his legacy pass into the twentieth century in a form neither hideously mangled nor mockingly contrarian. Norton would have taken as greater tribute than Gunn's (and therefore blushed more deeply at) the epigraph that his "admirable pupil" Charles Grandgent later caused to be inscribed beneath his bust: "HE TAUGHT AN UNSEEING AGE TO SEE." This tribute pointed to more than the invention of Western civilization as a pedagogical method; it entailed the whole idea of liberal education as cultural formation rather than mental discipline, a conception that could evolve far beyond Western civilization. Yet to pretend that a liberal education broad in grasp and moral in intent could rest securely on a foundation of knowledge narrowly specialized and value-neutral was ludicrous. Only as an etiolated ghost did Norton continue to haunt American college classrooms.[48]

He already saw himself fading into a wraith, his long career as political and cultural gadfly about to slip from American memory. He knew that his broadly conceived humane scholarship was losing out to a different and narrower one. He accepted that his ideal of a principled democracy, resting on the virtue of its citizens and the liberality of its leaders, looked as hopeless as the ruined temples of ancient India. And he realized that his belief in the dependence of democracy on learning and learning on democracy meant nothing to most of his fellow citizens, to neither the half-schooled masses nor the self-seeking elites who battened on them. Whether his principles would survive to find new uses in later cultural contests, whether he had forged tools that generations yet unborn might take in hand to help in rebuilding democracy, or the academy, in some inconceivable future shape, he had no way of knowing.

He took all this in stride, always favoring the long view. In an article for the fiftieth anniversary of the *Atlantic Monthly* in November 1907, Norton assessed the changes during the past half century. He praised his old friend Darwin's theory of evolution not only as science but also for its "incalculable benefit in loosening the bonds of superstition from the minds of men." But he noted also that Darwinism's spectacular success had helped to pull the most vigorous intellects into science and had "indirectly exerted a powerful influence tending, through the rapid and intoxicating advance of control of the great forces of nature and of the boundless sources of natural wealth, to the subordination of spiritual to material interests."

Thus, both directly and indirectly, it has had a disastrous effect upon pure literature, especially upon the literature of the pure imagination, upon poetry, and upon romance. To-day the writing about material things and of the daily affairs of men, of politics and of society, history, biography, voyages and travels, encyclopaedias, and scientific treatises, far outweighs, in quality no less than in quantity, the literature of sentiment and the imagination. The whole spiritual nature of man is finding but little, and for the most part only feeble and un-satisfactory, expression.

"In poetry there is not to-day," he grieved, "a single commanding voice."

He did not despair; he never had. "The spirit in man is never wholly quenched"; so "the time shall come when the quest of the fruit of the Tree of Life shall be undertaken again in earnest and with fair promise."[49]

By January 1908 "muscular weakness of my hand" made it hard to write more than a few words. He still took an interest in the latest Dante scholar-ship and lent learned aid to an old acquaintance in deciding between variant readings in *Antony and Cleopatra.* But he was "steadily losing" the "little strength" he had "brought down from Ashfield in the autumn." "I am sliding downhill at rather an accelerated pace," he told Howells in March, "but with no objection to finding myself at the bottom."[50]

Still, at the end of February he awarded the first annual Longfellow Medals—probably his idea—to the schoolchildren of Cambridge. "Educa-tion can do nothing better for a man," he told them, "than to make him a lover of the poets." In March he enjoyed a conversation with the ancient historian J. B. Bury, visiting the American Cambridge from the English. On 19 May he presided over the Dante Society's annual meeting and the next day attended the semester's last meeting of the Board of Overseers.[51]

But in June he resisted the annual migration to Ashfield. Though his physician saw no reason for him not to go, "the journey and the risks of being ill at a distance from our old home" frightened Norton. Did he fear departing life away from the house where he had entered it? Certainly he had clung to continuity in his eight decades. How the ideas and values of Andrews Norton and of the Boston of his youth persisted in him was remarkable: no less remarkable how the rapidly mutating nineteenth cen-tury had utterly transformed their resonances. In late June Norton's favorite dog, old Taffy, died. "The loss of so constant a companion for nearly four-teen years and of such exclusive affection," he sighed, "leaves a large gap in one's sentimental interests."[52]

Otherwise he passed "a very peaceful and pleasant" summer "in my old home." He took some time to dictate to Sally a few of his overflowing memories—anecdotes of the journeys he had traveled, of the men and women he had known. In early July, to escape the "noises and confusions" of the Fourth, he and Sally went to spend four or five days at a house that Susan's sister Theodora was renting in Manchester, Massachusetts, "on the very edge of the sea." These were Norton's first real seaside days since the Newport house. When they returned, Howells, just back from Italy, paid "a delightful visit."[53]

At the beginning of August, Charles and Sally went back to pass a few more days with Theo. He sat quietly, remembering perhaps the *Milton* scudding the seas off Ceylon, gazing at "the wide ocean" stretching "illimitably before us." "The magic & mystery of the sea have their perennial charm, constantly shifting in aspect, but essentially always the same; & from here the view is always enlivened by a multitude of vessels; some starting on their distant voyage, some happily returning home. One wonders what message each vessel bears." By now he had lost the ability to write, and Sally took down his letters for him. Still, when Edith Wharton and Walter Berry visited Shady Hill soon after the Nortons returned, they thought Mr. Norton "absolutely like his normal self."[54]

Not much later—sometime around 20 August—he fell ill. There were ups and downs, "many hours of wretched discomfort." By early October 1908, though, the disease had passed off, leaving as Norton's "chief discomfort" an "extreme muscular feebleness which deprives me of the power of helping myself even in the simplest ways." His mind remained clear, and he had lost none of his "interest in the world and its affairs." The Ashfield Town Service Committee that he had formed the year before wrote to tell him of the various committees and other activities around Ashfield. "Happily my eyes are still good for reading," he informed his boyhood playmate Tom Higginson, "and I have fallen back, as always on similar occasions, on Shakespear and Scott, but I have read one or two new books also, the best of which, and a book of highest quality, is the last volume of Morley's essays."[55]

In fact there had been no "similar occasions." Friends turned his chamber into "a garden of roses." "I cared so much for him," Isabella Gardner told Sally. "He was a light in my life." His mind remained "absolutely clear," turning "with affection and interest to all his old friends and the things he has cared about." Holy Ghost Hospital sent a message, telling of the fondness that the sisters and patients felt toward Norton, "a monument to your benevolence." On the evening of 16 October, Charles was able to see William James, who assured him of "the deep and warm reverence and affection in which you are held."[56]

By then Rupert had joined his sisters at Shady Hill; Richard had managed to get back from Europe; Eliot stood ready to come on short notice. The newspaper reporters invested the house, their inquiries becoming so persistently intrusive that Dr. Stevens took to posting bulletins on the front door. The *Boston Record* reported the patient's state under banner headlines in extra editions. There was "no disease," the physicians said, "simply the infirmity of old age." Norton would hardly have been surprised that the newspapers had lost any sense of privacy. But by then his privacy had become secure.[57]

On Sunday the eighteenth he slipped into unconsciousness. On Tuesday, Howells arrived to say good-bye, too late to do more than hold his friend's hand once more.

When morning dawned on the twenty-first, one of the children, or perhaps a servant, extinguished the oil lamp in his chamber. Charles Norton had at last given up Shady Hill.

Notes

Notes have been kept to a minimum, limited in most cases to the sources of direct quotations. Nonetheless, even minor physical details in the foregoing narrative rest on specific evidence; and interested readers may find it in a longer, fully documented version of the present work deposited in both the Houghton Library and the Department of Special Collections, Hesburgh Library, University of Notre Dame. This manuscript is referred to below as CEN Long Version.

Quotations have been reproduced in the text as exactly as is practical, including peculiarities of spelling, syntax, and grammar. Except where its absence might confuse, the minatory sic is avoided. Oddities of handwriting can rarely be copied in type, and in adapting these I have tried to do justice to the writer's apparent intention. In particular, two eccentricities of CEN's hand need mention. The first is his haphazard use of single or double quotation marks and equally erratic placement of commas and periods within or without such marks. Unable to find reason behind CEN's inconsistency, and unwilling to burden the reader with pointless confusion, I have in these cases followed standard American usage of today. The second is his frequent practice of inserting tiny dashes after commas. CEN seems to have meant most of these as a sort of emphatic comma (for example, dividing clauses rather than a series of adjectives), a few as genuine dashes. I have judged which functioned as commas, which dashes, and reproduced each as such. An exact transcription into typeface of CEN's hand would have filled almost every quotation with dashes, giving a breathless quality far from the rhythm of CEN's writing.

In the following notes, works by authors other than CEN are cited by surname and year of publication ("James 1914"). This shorthand leads the reader to Sources Cited, which follows the notes. For works by CEN, a similar system of citation ("CEN 1865f") refers the reader to the Published Writings of Charles Eliot Norton, which follows Sources Cited.

ABBREVIATIONS

AIA: Archaeological Institute of America
AN: Andrews Norton
ANP: Andrews Norton Papers, Houghton
CEN: Charles Eliot Norton
CN: Catharine Eliot Norton

ELG: Edwin Lawrence Godkin
FJC: Francis James Child
FLO: Frederick Law Olmsted
GEW: George Edward Woodberry
GS: Goldwin Smith
GWC: George William Curtis
Houghton: Houghton Library, Harvard University
HUA: Harvard University Archives
HWL: Henry Wadsworth Longfellow
JBH: Jonathan Baxter Harrison
JR: John Ruskin
JRL: James Russell Lowell
LC: Library of Congress
Letters: Norton and Howe 1913, *Letters of CEN*
LS: Leslie Stephen
MHS: Massachusetts Historical Society, Boston
NAR: *North American Review*
NELPS: New England Loyal Publication Society
NP: Norton Papers, Houghton
SSN: Susan Ridley Sedgwick Norton

Prologue

1. This description of Shady Hill and the surrounding early nineteenth-century terrain is cobbled together from several sources, notably Marshall n.d., Whiting 1965, James 1914, p. 405, and CEN 1905c, pp. 12–13.

2. Morison 1921 remains standard for its subject; other important secondary sources are Dalzell 1987, Jaher 1982, pp. 15–156, and Green 1966; for fuller notes see CEN Long Version.

3. Morison 1921 notes (p. 24) that down to the Civil War "merchant" in Massachusetts meant, as in Johnson's *Dictionary*, "one who trafficks to remote countries." But, although sticking to this usage of "merchant," I use "mercantile elite" more broadly to name the entire intermarried group of elite Boston families, a usage reflecting the overwhelmingly predominant source (direct and indirect) of their wealth down to the late 1820s, when manufacturing money grew really significant.

4. Boston the Hub of the Universe,
The home of the bean and the cod,
Where Lowells speak only to Cabots,
And Cabots speak only to God.

5. Lowell, quoted in Dalzell 1987, pp. 145–46.

6. Simpson 1962, pp. 10–11; Quincy 1851, pp. 43–45, 68–71.

7. Greenslet 1947, p. 147; Goodman 1966, p. 444; Green 1966, p. 51.

8. Quincy 1851, p. 70.

9. "Memoir of the Athenaeum," in Quincy 1851, pp. 39–40.

10. See list in Story 1980, p. 34.

11. William Lawrence, *Life of Amos A. Lawrence, with Extracts from His Diary and Correspondence* (Boston), pp. 23–24, quoted in Dalzell 1987, p. 72.

12. Coleridge worked out his ideal of a "clerisy" or "national church" in *On the Constitution of the Church and State According to the Idea of Each* (1830). After developing the analogy to Coleridge's clerisy in a first draft of this prologue, I discovered that Lewis Simpson employed the same term in the title of his admirable essay on Joseph Buckminster: Simpson 1973, pp. 3–31.

13. Buell 1986, pp. 383–85.

14. McMurtry 1985, chap. 3; CEN 1897d and 1897e; and Kittredge 1898. FJC earlier almost married the daughter of Edward Everett: CEN to family, 30 April 1850, NP.

15. Higginson 1898, pp. 16–17.

16. It is true that Julia Ward Howe (1819–1910) and Isabella Stewart Gardner (1840–1924) flaunted their artistic self-sufficiency with considerable flamboyance. But they were New Yorkers who married into Boston and often grated on Boston nerves.

17. JRL to CEN, 15 February 1889, in NP (JRL got this story from Bancroft).

18. Harris 1970, p. 295.

19. CEN 1905c, p. 18; Samuel C. Thacher to AN, [c8] April 1806, box 9, ANP; James 1903, 1:12–13.

CHAPTER 1: SHADY HILL, 1786–1842

1. [Ticknor] 1869, pp. 201–3; [Whitmore] 1869; Eliot 1887, pp. 15ff.; Mott 1938, pp. 78–79. T. S. Eliot, a descendant of Reverend Andrew Norton and thus a remote cousin of Charles Eliot Norton (their lines becoming collateral with their great-grandfathers), memorialized the family's ancestral village in the *Four Quartets*.

2. [Ticknor] 1869, pp. 5–23; Eliot 1920–25, p. 60.

3. [Whitmore] 1859; *Hingham* 1893, pp. 92–94; Wilson 1984, pp. 39, 46; Lincoln 1827, pp. 106–10; Newell 1856, pp. x–xi; writ dated 15 January 1805, in 1796–1810 folder/box 1, Norton Papers, MHS.

4. Newell 1856, pp. x–xi.

5. Samuel Norton to AN, various dates, box 7, ANP; *Hingham* 1893, pp. 92–94; manuscript beginning "An account of the deaths in and of the family of Mr. Joseph Andrews . . . ," n.d. [post 1842], in 1838–41 folder/1830–92 box, Norton Papers, MHS.

6. Eliot 1910, 2:193–94; Lincoln 1827, p. 134. AN never grew close to his mother. Far and away the best biographical account of AN, though focusing on his role in the Unitarian controversy and ending about 1823, is Handlin 1989; see also the extended treatment of AN in CEN Long Version.

7. Newell 1856, p. xx; AN to Samuel Norton, 24 June 1803, box 2, ANP.

8. Eliot 1910, 2:193–94.

9. Simpson 1962, p. 3; [Norton] 1807, p. 44.

10. Tocqueville 1960, pp. 51, 57.

11. [Norton] 1807, pp. 41–43, 45; [Norton] 1810.

12. Henry Ware Jr., Journal, c. 1813, quoted in Ware 1846, 1:50–51.

13. Peabody 1888, pp. 74–76; Handlin 1989, pp. 58–64, 68.

14. AN to Samuel Norton, 17 June 1813, box 2, ANP; Palfrey [1836]; Wright 1954; Ahlstrom and Carey 1985, p. 67; Oliver Stearns, "The Divinity School," in Vaille

and Clark 1875, 1:201. The Divinity School was formally organized as a distinct entity within the university in 1819.

15. [Norton] 1812b, pp. 307–8; AN, Sketch of the first course of Dexter Lectures, undated MS. [1813], HUA.

16. George Ticknor to Stephen Higginson, 20 May 1816, in Higginson 1909, pp. 337–40; Norton 1819, pp. 35–37.

17. Turner 1993.

18. AN to William Eliot, 5 August 1816, box 13; AN, ms. fragment, n.d., box 12; and AN, Journal, 1 May–1 July 1819, Letterbook B; ANP.

19. [Norton] 1812b, p. 307.

20. John Ware to AN, 21 January 1820, box 6, ANP; Elizabeth Peabody to Maria Chase, May 1821, Sophia Smith Collection, Smith College.

21. AN to George Bancroft, 7 May 1821, box 1, ANP; Eliot 1920–25, p. 60; Downing, MacDougall, and Pearson 1967, p. 11. The building of the American Academy of Arts and Sciences now stands on the approximate site of the Norton house.

22. Oddly, the mother always spelled her name Catharine, while the daughter's was spelled Catherine.

23. AN's American peer was Moses Stuart of Andover Seminary; Charles Hodge of Princeton Theological Seminary would soon join them.

24. AN to Samuel Norton, 16 and 23 November 1827, box 3, ANP; Louisa Norton Bullard to CEN, 16 November 1907, NP; College Papers, 2d ser., HUA.

25. CN to Catherine Atkins Eliot, 28–30 May 1828, box 7, ANP.

26. *Letters*, 1:11–12; Anne Grant to Mrs. Hook, 2 February 1829, quoted in addendum to typed transcript of Anne Grant to AN, 27 February 1829, Manuscripts Dept., University of Virginia Library.

27. Remarks by CEN on AN, n.d., box 4, NP. The degree to which the sending back and forth of books occupied the letters in ANP forcefully recalls the conditions under which scholars worked prior to the building up of modern research libraries.

28. [Norton] 1824.

29. AN to Felicia D. Hemans, 8 July 1826, Letterbook C, box 13, ANP.

30. CN to AN, 27 March 1845, box 7, ANP.

31. AN to Miss Park, 3 August 1832, and to Samuel Norton, 20 December 1831, box 3, ANP; AN to J. G. Palfrey, n.d. [December 1831], Palfrey Family Papers, Houghton; AN to Samuel Norton, 13 February 1832, Grew Papers, Houghton; Baldwin 1914–15, 2:679.

32. Baldwin 1914–15, 1:520; CN to AN, [?]April 1845, Grace Norton to CN and Louisa Norton, 27 February 1845, NP.

33. AN to Samuel Norton, 20 December 1831, box 3, ANP; M. E. E. Jennison to CEN, 30 April 1833, Jane Norton to CN, 1–3 June [c. 1831], AN and CN to CEN, 18 May 1842, and Grace Norton to Louisa and Jane Norton, n.d. [1844?], NP.

34. CEN to Thomas Wentworth Higginson, 9 October 1865, and CEN to Charles Welsh, 8 February 1908, NP; CEN 1905c, p. 16.

35. Sara Norton to Kenneth McKenzie, 27 January 1921, Beinecke Library, Yale University; Pellico 1836, pp. vi–vii; Shields 1931, pp. 29–30; Silvio Pellico to CN, 5 October 1836, and to AN, 5 October 1836, unnumbered box, ANP.

36. Thomas W. Parsons to AN, 24 July 1843, unnumbered box, ANP; CEN to Sarah Orne Jewett, 24 December 1898, Huntington Library.

37. CEN to Thomas Carlyle, 24 March 1876, National Library of Scotland; Edward Everett Hale, "First Paper," in Hale et al. 1887 [unpaginated].

38. Charles Eliot Guild to CEN, 11 November 1897, NP. The relatives on the Norton side lived more remotely, not only geographically but apparently emotionally.

39. Henry Wadsworth Longfellow to CN, 24 July 1842, NP.

40. Dickens 1957, p. 60; Margaret Searle Curson to CN, n.d. [spring 1839?] and 18 August 1839, NP.

41. Henry Hart Milman to George Ticknor, 15 April 1844, quoted in Ticknor to AN, n.d. [May? 1844], box 9, ANP; Allen 1883, p. 68.

42. *Christian Register*, 15 April 1837, p. 58.

43. Channing 1838; quotations from pp. 10, 11, 32. I borrow the term "self-fashioning" from Greenblatt 1980, though one would of course look earlier than the period that Greenblatt treats for the coming together of various currents of thought into the notion of self-formation—most plausibly, perhaps, to Pico della Mirandola.

44. T. B. Macaulay to AN, 9 November 1840, unnumbered box, ANP; "Memoirs of Pellico," *NAR* 44 (1837): 122; CEN to AN, CN, and Louisa Norton, 29 May [1840], NP.

45. CEN to AN, CN, and Louisa Norton, 16 May [1840], NP.

46. CEN to Gardiner Martin Lane, 16 December 1907, NP; Morgan 1898, p. 2; Eidson 1951, pp. 16–17; CEN autobiography, Class of 1846 Class Book, HUA; CEN to AN, CN, and Louisa Norton, 16 May [1840], and CEN, Journal, 1842, box 15, Miscellaneous Papers, NP. For a more detailed account of CEN's schooling, see CEN Long Version.

47. Charles Folsom to AN, 12 May [n.y.], box 6, ANP.

48. Jane Norton to Dorothea L. Dix, 24 July 1836, and Jane Norton to CN, 1–3 June [c. 1831], NP; Higginson 1898, pp. 16–17; Henry Wadsworth Longfellow to Jane Norton, letters around 1841, in Hilen 1966–82, vol. 2, passim; CEN, Journal 1842, box 15, Miscellaneous Papers, NP.

49. Smith 1898, p. 10; CEN, Journal 1842, box 15, Miscellaneous Papers, NP; Hale 1899, p. 68.

50. Henry Wadsworth Longfellow to CN, 26 August 1842, and CEN, Journal 1842, box 15, Miscellaneous Papers, NP.

51. CEN, Journal 1842, entry for 11 March, box 15, Miscellaneous Papers, and CN to Henry Wadsworth Longfellow, 25 August 1842, NP; AN to John Norton, 17 May 1842, box 1, ANP; Harris 1970, pp. xxv, 29–30.

52. Certificate of admission, 23 August 1842, and steward's receipt, 26 August 1842, CEN Folder 1, HUA.

CHAPTER 2: CAMBRIDGE AND BOSTON, 1842–1849

1. *Catalogue 1842*, pp. 22–23; CEN c. 1905, p. 15. CEN Long Version, chap. 3, gives a full account of faculty and curriculum at Harvard in the 1840s, including the reforms of the Quincy era; scholars specifically interested in the histories of American higher education or of Harvard should consult it.

2. The 300 students did not include some 150 law and divinity students nor (in Boston) another 150 medical students.

3. J. A. Stevens to W. L. Ropes, 2 November 1908, Secretary's file, Class of 1846, and Class of 1846 Class Book, HUA; CEN, Journal 1843–45, box 15, Miscellaneous Papers, NP.

4. [Bancroft] 1824, 127; on "culture," see Winterer 1996, chap. 3. Material in the following paragraphs on freshman studies and life derive from *Catalogue 1842;* Hale 1893 and 1927; Higginson 1898; Hoar 1903; Morison 1936; Peabody 1888; [Quincy] 1844; Vaille and Clark 1875; undated clipping, reporting talk by CEN, "Harvard Recollections," 14 November 1901, CEN folder 1, HUA; and CEN, Journal 1843–45, box 15, Miscellaneous Papers, NP.

5. Palfrey, *The Worthy Student of Harvard College* (Cambridge: James Munroe and Co., 1834), p. 6, quoted in Yanikoski 1987, p. 137.

6. Undated clipping, reporting talk by CEN, "Harvard Recollections," 14 November 1901, CEN folder 1, HUA.

7. Eliot 1848, p. 118.

8. AN to CEN, 21 December 1842, NP.

9. CEN, College Journal, box 6, Miscellaneous Papers, and AN to CEN, 27 January and 10 February 1843, and HWL to CEN [29 January 1843], NP.

10. AN to CEN, 27 January, 10 and 15 February, and 14 March 1843, NP.

11. AN to CEN, 10 and 15 February 1843, NP.

12. AN to CEN, 10 February 1843, Grace Norton, AN, and CN to CEN, 23–25 February 1843, and HWL to Rufus Griswold, 13 April 1843, NP; *Letters,* 1:22–23; CEN to AN, n.d. [1843], Stockbridge (Mass.) Library Association; Scudder 1901, 1:109–14.

13. AN to CEN, 14 March and 24 May 1843, CEN, Journal 1843–45, entry for 26 April 1844, box 15, Miscellaneous Papers, and Louisa Norton to CEN, 19 May 1843, NP.

14. A. F. Hinchman and [illeg.] to CEN, 10 June 1843, and note to President and Faculty, 3 June 1844, in CEN folder 1, HUA; CEN 1905c, pp. 20–21.

15. CEN to family, 7 May 1844, NP; Winterer 1996, chaps. 2–3.

16. *Notice to Parents and Guardians in relation to Elective System,* 15 April 1843, Josiah Quincy Papers, HUA. Parents, not students, made the decisions, a significant difference from Harvard's later and more famous elective system.

17. The six were Joseph Lovering (physics), Asa Gray (botany), Jared Sparks (American history), Benjamin Peirce (mathematics and astronomy), Charles Beck (Latin), and Cornelius Conway Felton (Greek). Gray, Sparks, and Peirce count as major figures.

18. Goodwin 1906–7, 121–22, 124; Thomas Wentworth Higginson, in Hale et al. 1887; Winterer 1996, chap. 3.

19. Vaille and Clark 1875, 1:60; McKenzie 1908, p. 33; CEN to Elizabeth Sedgwick Child, 14 July 1906, NP. CEN unknowingly did listen to Harvard's most famous felon: Webster would hang in 1850 for the murder and dismemberment of his colleague George Parkman.

20. CEN to James Parton, 8 October 1864, NP; Whately 1846, pp. 179–80; Peabody 1888, p. 78. Whately 1846 was one of the assigned textbooks.

21. Keightley 1849, pp. 476–77; Smyth 1854; Heeren 1842. Francis Lieber's *Manual of Political Ethics*, read in senior year, was also strongly influenced by German ideas.

22. Paley 1827, pp. 67–68, 123, 151, 120; Stewart 1843, pp. 65–66; Butler 1852; Paley 1796.

23. Stewart 1843, pp. 315, 326–28.

24. Thomas Wentworth Higginson in Hale et al. 1887; Keightley 1849, chap. 4; Heeren 1842, esp. chap. 3 and p. 115.

25. CEN to GWC, 20 May 1877, NP; CEN to Francis Lieber, 13 April 1868, Huntington Library.

26. CEN to Mountstuart Grant Duff, 3 October 1894, Mountstuart Grant Duff Papers, courtesy of Shiela Sokolov Grant; McMurtry 1985, pp. 65–69; CEN 1897d, pp. 333–35; Hoar 1903, 1:105; FJC to CEN, "July" [prob. August] 1847 and 7 August 1846, NP. FJC ripened into one of the great scholars of the nineteenth century, and it is a scandal to American historiography that he lacks a full biography.

27. AN to Nathan Appleton, 11 November 1844, box 11, ANP; Grace Norton and AN to CN and Louisa Norton, 14 [15] March 1845, NP. This was before the outbreak of concern in Boston prompted by the Irish famine.

28. AN to Joanna Baillie, 1 August 1848, Letterbook B, box 13, ANP.

29. Desmond and Moore 1991, p. 359; AN to Joanna Baillie, 14 August 1844, Letterbook B, box 13, ANP.

30. CEN to Elizabeth Sedgwick Child, 14 July 1906, NP; Hale 1927, p. 204; Exhibition and Commencement Performances, 1844–45, HUA; Charging Records, 1845, Harvard College Library, HUA.

31. CEN to Grace Norton, 5 February 1846, NP; Stanton 1968, pp. 1–5, 225–38; Spalding 1989, pp. 137–38. Although CEN did not name the church, it can only have been St. Alphonsus, a Redemptorist parish dating from 1845. I am grateful to Jay Dolan, Philip Gleason, and especially Robert Louthan for information about the church. Although a handful of churches influenced by the Gothic revival had been built around Boston, at least some of which CEN must have seen, they were comparatively plain and simple structures.

It is worth adding that George Washington Doane, High Church Episcopal bishop of New Jersey and a key figure in introducing full-fledged Gothic Revival architecture into the United States in the 1840s (Stanton 1968, pp. 31ff.), was the stepfather of the Nortons' close friend Sarah Perkins Cleveland. CEN visited him on more than one occasion and became friendly with his son, though specific connection to CEN's interest in Gothic cannot be documented.

32. AN to CEN, 5 May 1843, NP.

33. Samuel A. Eliot to CEN, 27 May 1846, NP.

34. Class of 1846 Class Book, HUA; King 1884, pp. 33–34.

35. Pierce 1890, pp. 248–51; CEN, "Santa Croce," box 12, Miscellaneous Papers, NP; [Everett] 1847; Class of 1846 Class book, HUA.

36. CEN, Commonplace Book, September 1846, Miscellaneous Papers, box 3, and Samuel Eliot to CEN, 3 September 1846, NP. The lines are from "The Good Great Man" (1802).

37. Samuel Eliot to CEN, 3 September 1846, NP. The allusion to FJC is mine, not Eliot's.

38. Morison 1921, pp. 85–86, 252, 269–71, 282–85; CEN, Reminiscences 1846–59, box 6, Miscellaneous Papers, NP.

39. CEN, Reminiscences 1846–59, box 6, Miscellaneous Papers, NP; Morse 1905, pp. 407–9.

40. CEN, Reminiscences 1846–59, box 6, Miscellaneous Papers, and Samuel Eliot to CEN, 3 September 1846, NP.

41. CEN, Reminiscences 1846–59, box 6, Miscellaneous Papers, NP.

42. Ibid.; CEN c. 1905, p. 19.

43. CEN, Account of Personal Expenses, September 1846–December 1847, box 2, Miscellaneous Papers, NP.

44. Francis J. Child to CEN, 2 December 1846, and CEN to DeWitt Miller, 18 November 1899, NP.

45. *Literary World* 2 (22 January 1848): 608, cited in Harris 1966, p. 266; CEN, Account of Personal Expenses, September 1846–December 1847, box 2, and Account Book, 1848, box 15, Miscellaneous Papers, NP.

46. CEN's copy of *Specimens of the Table Talk of the Late Samuel Taylor Coleridge* (New York, 1835), Pierpont Morgan Library, New York.

47. CEN 1847, quotation p. 435.

48. Ibid., pp. 405, 416, 439.

49. Ibid., pp. 402, 440.

50. Abbot went on to become professor at Harvard Divinity School and a distinguished biblical critic.

51. CEN, Commonplace Book, August 1848, box 3, Miscellaneous Papers, NP.

52. CEN, Book of Verse, box 3, Miscellaneous Papers, NP.

53. *North American Review* 64 (1847): 266–68.

54. AN to Charles Sumner, 29 September 1846, Sumner Papers, Houghton.

55. Winthrop 1630, p. 83; CEN, typed reminiscence, 30 December 1902, box 11, Miscellaneous Papers, and CEN to Charles [Mills?], 5 May 1848, NP.

56. CEN to family, 11–13 June 1850, NP; Rufus Choate, quoted in Tyack 1967, p. 195.

57. CEN, Account Book, 1848, box 15, Miscellaneous Papers, NP.

58. Business Records, NP.

59. CEN, Account Book, 1848, box 15, Miscellaneous Papers, CEN to AN, 21 June 1848, AN to CEN, 26 April 1848, and George Livermore to CEN, 21 January 1850, NP; CEN 1848a; *NAR* 66 (1848): 110–45; Jared Sparks and AN, Circular letter, 25 May 1848, unnumbered box, ANP; *Athenaeum Centenary* 1907, p. 83. The title of the book reviewed translates as *Brief Account of the Most Important Church-Related Events occurring during the Voyage of the Royal Frigate Urania from 15 August 1844 to 4 March 1846.*

60. CEN, Reminiscences 1846–59, box 4, Miscellaneous Papers, NP; CEN 1897d, p. 335.

61. Doughty 1962, pp. 145–46, 150; Francis Parkman to CEN, 12 September 1848, CEN to Parkman, 18 April 1850, and CEN, Reminiscences 1846–59, box 4, Miscellaneous Papers, NP.

62. CEN 1848b; Francis Parkman to CEN, 12 September 1848, NP.

63. Bullard to CEN, 22 February 1849, NP.

64. J. Mackillop to Sir Thomas Turton, 1849 (letter of introduction for CEN), NP.

65. CEN to AN, 25–26 February and 26 August 1849, and Francis Parkman to CEN, 3 March 1849, NP; Francis Parkman to Ephraim George Squier, n.d. [February 1849], in Jacobs 1960, 1:58.

66. CEN to Manning Ferguson Force, 21 March 1849, Force Papers, University of Washington (microfilm at Library of Congress); CEN 1849b, pp. 495–96.

67. Samuel Eliot to CEN, 12 April 1849, and Rufus Anderson to Missionaries of the A.B.C.F.M., 16 July 1849, NP; Edward E. Salisbury to Charles E. Folsom, 19 May 1849, Boston Public Library.

68. Samuel Eliot to CEN, 8 May 1849, and passport in box 6, knife in box 9, Miscellaneous Papers, NP.

69. Nor 2847, Houghton; CEN to family, 6 February 1850, NP.

70. CEN to family, 21 May 1849, NP.

71. AN to CEN, 20 May 1849, NP.

72. CEN, Reminiscences 1846–59, box 6, Miscellaneous Papers, and CEN, Commonplace Book, November 1848, box 3, Miscellaneous Papers, NP (quoting *The Sketch Book)* "cloud *in* the horizon" is sic.

CHAPTER 3: THE WORLD, 1849–1851

There is no consistently satisfactory way to handle the spelling of Indian names in a nineteenth-century biography. My compromise has been to render the names of individuals as CEN spelled them (generally the same as the persons themselves did); to give the names of well-known places in their Victorian form (thus Cawnpore rather than Kanpur, Benares rather than Varanasi); and to spell lesser-known places in modern English forms (thus Saharanpur rather than CEN's Saharunpore, Dehra Dun rather than his Deyrah). I hope that this practice remains reasonably faithful to CEN's world while allowing readers to follow him on a map.

1. Morison 1921, pp. 254–56, 260; CEN to family, 1 June–31 August 1849, NP.

2. CEN to family, 1 June–31 August 1849, NP.

3. CEN to AN, 26 August 1849, and CEN to family, 1 June–31 August 1849, NP. Among his reading was the seaborne journal of another adventurous young Charles whom CEN would later come to know: Charles Darwin.

4. CEN to AN, 26 August 1849, NP.

5. CEN to family, 1 June–31 August and 8 September 1849, NP.

6. CEN to family, 8–15 September 1849, NP; Edwardes 1969, p. 37.

7. CEN to Sarah Cleveland, 12 September 1849, NP. I use the term Anglo-Indian as the Victorians did to refer to British residents of India, as distinct from its other reference to persons of mixed British and Indian ancestry.

8. CEN to Charles Guild, 13 September 1849, and J. Mackillop to Sir Thomas Turton, 1849, NP. The East India Company's name reflected its mercantile origins. Long before CEN arrived, it had become simply a well-reimbursed private government, which ruled India until the Sepoy Revolt of 1857 ("the Mutiny" to the British). Its army included some entirely European regiments and a far greater number of mixed regiments; a few regiments of the regular British army were on loan to the

company. The civilians, educated at the company's Haileybury College in Hertford-shire, had for subordinates a largely Eurasian civil service appointed in India. Aside from merchants with whom he did business in Madras and Calcutta, CEN's European acquaintances in India were almost entirely British officers (regular or company) and civilians.

9. CEN to Sarah Cleveland, 12 September 1849, and to Mary Eliot, 9–11 September 1849, NP.

10. CEN to Mary Eliot, 9–11 September 1849, NP.

11. CEN to William Greenough, 14 September 1849, Fales Library, New York University; CEN to William S. Bullard, 14 September 1849, and CEN to Charles Guild, 13 September 1849, NP.

12. CEN to family, 8–15 September 1849, and to CN, 21 September–8 October 1849, NP.

13. CEN to Charles H. Mills, 4 October 1849, and to AN, 9 October 1849, NP. "Ghat" refers both to a quay and to a stepped terrace on a riverbank, the former typically being the latter.

14. CEN to CN, 21 September–8 October 1849, and CEN to Sarah Cleveland, 16 September–5 October 1849, NP; Richard Lewis to CEN, 30 November 1850, Business Records, NP.

15. CEN to Jane Norton, 1 October 1849, and to Louisa Norton, 16–22 October 1849, NP. "Moonshee" (munshi) means secretary or writer.

16. CEN to Grace Norton, 24 October 1849, and CEN to Charles H. Mills, 4 October 1849, NP.

17. CEN to Thomas Wigglesworth Jr., 1 October 1849, Grew Papers, Houghton (copy in NP). Durga is Siva's consort Parvati, under her attribute as goddess of battle.

18. CEN to Louisa Norton, 16–22 October 1849, and CEN to Sarah Cleveland, 16 September–5 October 1849, NP; CEN to Thomas Wigglesworth Jr., 1 October 1849, Grew Papers, Houghton (copy in NP).

19. CEN to Louisa Norton, 16–22 October 1849, CEN to Edward Everett, 1 May 1850, and Rajinder Dutt to CEN, 7 January 1850, NP. Tippoo (Tipu) Sultan (1749–99) of Mysore was Britain's major opponent in the late eighteenth-century wars for control of India.

20. CEN to Louisa Norton, 16–22 October 1849, CEN to Anna E. Ticknor, 21 October 1849, CEN to Sarah Cleveland, 4 November 1849, and CEN to CN, 31 October–8 November 1849, NP. CEN said that Nondolal Shan meant "joyous disposition."

21. CEN to Thomas Wigglesworth Jr., 1 October 1849, Grew Papers, Houghton (copy in NP); CEN to CN, 21 September–8 October 1849, CEN to William S. Bullard, 20 October 1849, and CEN to AN, 29 October–8 November 1849, NP.

22. CEN to AN, 29 October–8 November 1849, CEN to William S. Bullard, 20 October 1849, and CEN to Charles H. Mills, 4 October 1849, NP.

23. CEN to CN, 31 October–8 November 1849, and printed India Post Office form, box 11, Miscellaneous Papers, NP. *Dak* bungalows varied from something approaching low-grade inns to mere shelters; although meant for the relays (*daks*) of

men and horses that transported mail across India, they were available to other travelers.

24. CEN to CN, 31 October–8 November 1849, CEN to Louisa Norton, n.d. [16–22 October 1849], and CEN to Francis Parkman, 21 October 1849, NP.

25. CEN to Jane Norton, 18–20 November 1849, NP. Variant spelling of "traveling" and "traveller" sic.

26. Ibid.

27. Ibid. Absence of question mark sic. The Latin phrase translates as "He changes his sky (or climate), not his soul (or disposition), who runs across the sea"— a well-known tag from Horace's *Epistles*, transposed by CEN from the original plural to the apposite singular.

28. Ibid.

29. Ibid.

30. Ibid., and St. George Tucker to CEN, 7 January 1850, NP.

31. CEN to Jane Norton, 18–20 November 1849, CEN to CN, 30 November 1849, and CEN to Sarah Cleveland, 2–5 December 1849, NP.

32. CEN to Sarah Cleveland, 2–5 December 1849, CEN to AN, 17 December 1849, and George Sim to CEN, 16 January 1850, NP.

33. CEN to AN, 17 December 1849, and CEN to sisters, 23–24 December 1849, NP; Keene 1897, pp. 107–8.

34. CEN to sisters, 23–24 December 1849, NP.

35. CEN to family, 6 February and 6–7 August 1850, NP.

36. CEN to Charles H. Mills, 9 February 1850, NP.

37. CEN to family, 6 February 1850, NP.

38. CEN to Charles H. Mills, 9 February 1850, and CEN to family, 6 February 1850, NP.

39. CEN to family, 6 February 1850, Richard Lewis to CEN, 19 December 1849, and CEN to CN, 21 September–8 October 1849, NP.

40. CEN to family, 6 February 1850, CEN to William S. Bullard, 11 February 1850, Rustamjee Jamsetjee to CEN, 1 February 1850, Sorabjee Jamsetjee to CEN, 23 May 1850, Montgomery Ritchie to CEN, 23 or 24 June 1850, and Frank Burlton to CEN, n.d. [10 January 1850?], NP.

41. CEN to family, 26 February and 13 March 1850 (with addenda dated 19 and 20 March), NP. The journey from India to Venice is detailed in CEN Long Version.

42. CEN to CN, 25 March–1 April 1850, CEN to Grace Norton, 5–10 April 1850, and CEN to William Dean Howells, 29 December 1907, NP.

43. CEN to CN, 25 March–1 April 1850, NP. The Palazzo Guistiniani lies just west of the Piazza San Marco and fronts on the Canal Grande, right at its mouth, directly across from the Dogana at the Punta della Salute.

44. Petrarch donated his books to Venice in 1362, when he came to the city fleeing plague in Padua; Doge Marin Falier was executed in 1355 for plotting to restore lost powers of his office.

45. CEN to Grace Norton, 5–10 April 1850, and CEN to CN, 25 March–1 April 1850, NP.

46. CEN to Grace Norton, 5–10 April 1850, NP.

47. CEN to family, 17–21 April 1850, and CEN to CN, 25 March–1 April 1850, NP.

48. CEN to CN, 25 March–1 April 1850, NP.

49. CEN to Charles E. Guild, 9 April 1850, NP.

50. CEN to Samuel Eliot, 9 April 1850, CEN to family, 17–21 April 1850, and CEN to Grace Norton, 5–10 April 1850, NP.

51. CEN to Francis Parkman, 18 April 1850, NP.

52. CEN to family, 17–21 April 1850, NP.

53. CEN to family, 30 April and 14–16 May 1850, NP.

54. CEN to family, 30 April 1850, NP.

55. CEN to William S. Bullard, 2 May 1850, and CEN to Edward Everett, 1 May 1850, NP.

56. HWL to CEN, 5 February 1850, AN to CEN, 14–16 March 1850, and CEN to Samuel E. Guild, 23 May 1850, NP.

57. CEN to family, 27–30 May 1850, and AN to CEN, 7 June 1850, NP.

58. CEN to family, 30 April 1850, NP.

59. CEN to family, 5–9 May and 14 May 1850, NP.

60. CEN to family, 5–9 May, 20–23 May, and 27–30 May 1850, and Charles E. Guild to CEN, 23 November 1853, Business Records, NP.

61. CEN to family, 5–9 May and 4–7 June 1850, NP. Childe was, as CEN noted, a daughter of General Henry "Lighthorse Harry" Lee, hero of the American Revolution. This also made her, as no one in 1850 had much reason to note, the sister of Robert E. Lee.

62. Adolphe, comte de Circourt, to CEN, n.d. [28 May 1850], and CEN to family, 5–9 May, 20–23 May, 27–30 May, and 4–7 June 1850, NP.

63. CEN to family, 14–16 May and 20–23 May 1850, and CEN to Sarah Cleveland, 16 May 1850, NP. Brem 1991 includes contemporary views of house and studio on the rue Chaptal (now the Musée de la Vie Romantique); a reproduction of *Saint Augustin et Sainte Monique* (1845), today in the Louvre, occupies p. 43.

64. CEN to family, 5–9 May, 14–16 May, and 27–30 May 1850, NP.

65. CEN to family, 27–30 May 1850, NP.

66. CEN to family, 14–16 May and 4–7 June 1850, NP. CEN always referred to Félix simply as "Rachel."

67. CEN to family, 20–23 May and 27–30 May 1850, and CEN to GWC, 15 January 1860, NP.

68. CEN to family, 14–16 May, 27–30 May, and 4–7 June 1850, NP.

69. CEN to family, 4–7 June and 11–13 June 1850, NP.

70. Quotation from CEN to family, 21 June 1850, NP. For details of these encounters, those in the next paragraph, and others, see CEN Long Version.

71. Quotations from Lady Beaufort to CEN, 14[?] June [1850], CEN to family, 11–13 June, and C. K. J. & F. W. Bunsen to CEN, 12 July [1850], NP. "Dr. Waagen" was G. F. Waagen, the first professor of art history in Germany and in 1850 at the height of his influence in guiding the picture buying of the monied classes in England; he organized (Steegman 1971, p. 234) the 1857 Manchester art treasures exhibition, which would provide the occasion for CEN's first published writing on art.

72. CEN to family, 27 June 1850, NP.

73. CEN to family, 27 June, 11–12 July, and 18 July 1850, NP.

74. CEN to family, 3–5 July and 27 June 1850, NP.

75. Francis Parkman to CEN, 22 September 1850, and CEN to family, 11–13 June 1850, NP.

76. CEN to family, 18 July 1850, NP.

77. CEN to family, 21 June and 18 July 1850, CEN to John Ware, 20 June 1850, and CEN to unknown correspondent (fragment), n.d. [1850], NP.

78. CEN to family, 3–5 July 1850, NP.

79. CEN to family, 18 July 1850, NP.

80. CEN to family, 11–12 July and 6–7 August 1850, NP.

81. GWC to William Wetmore Story, 12 August 1850, Harry Ransom Humanities Research Center, University of Texas, Austin; CEN to family, letters of 20–26 July through 1–6 September 1850, NP; Elizabeth C. Gaskell to Charles Bosanquet, 26 June [1861], in Chapple and Pollard 1966, pp. 662–63.

82. CEN to family, 7–13 September 1850, NP.

83. CEN to family, 31 July 1850, NP.

84. CEN to family, 1–6 September, 15–19 September, and 26 September–1 October 1850, NP.

85. CEN to family, 26 September–1 October 1850, NP.

86. CEN to family, 4–5 October and 7–12 October 1850, NP. La Flegere is CEN's spelling; I have not been able to identify it.

87. CEN to family, 16–18 October 1850, NP.

88. CEN to family, 19 October 1850, NP; CN to Jane Norton Wigglesworth, 1 October 1850, Society for the Preservation of New England Antiquities, Boston.

89. CEN to family, 28–31 October, 4–6 November, 10–14 November, 1–5 December 1850, NP.

90. T. W. Parsons to JRL, 2 January 1848, in Haraszti 1940(?), p. 39; CEN to family, 10–14 November 1850, NP. "My good sir, only a paolo"—an old Tuscan coin.

91. CEN to family, 16–21 November 1850, NP.

92. CEN to family, 16–21 November and 24–28 November 1850, and CEN, Journal, September 1850–January 1851, box 13, Miscellaneous Papers, NP.

93. CEN to family, 24–28 November and 6–7 December 1850, NP.

94. CEN to family, 13–19 December and 22–27 December 1850, CEN, Journal, September 1850–January 1851, box 13, Miscellaneous Papers, and Sophie Scheffer to CEN, 23 December [1850] and 21 April [1851], NP.

95. CEN to Manning F. Force, 19 March 1851, Force Papers, University of Washington (microfilm at LC).

96. CEN to family, 22–27 December 1850, NP.

97. CEN to family, 22–27 December 1850, NP. "And yet fifty years hence his name will hardly find a place even on the pages of the Biographie Universelle."

CHAPTER 4: A MERCHANT IN THE UNMAKING, 1851–1855

1. CEN to William S. Bullard, 18 January 1851 (telegram), and CEN to family, 13–19 December 1850, NP.

2. AN to Jane Norton, October 1851, Charles H. Mills to CEN, 15 May 1851, and

Grace Norton to Jane Norton and Louisa and William Bullard, 16 March 1851, NP; Dana 1968, 2:476; Jane Norton to HWL, 26 November 185[2?], HWL Papers, Houghton.

3. AN to John Gorham Palfrey, n.d. [1836], Palfrey Family Papers, Houghton; Newell 1856, p. xix.

4. CEN to HWL, 21 March 1851, HWL Papers, GWC to CEN, 29 March and 6 April 1851, GWC Papers, and JRL to CEN, 8 April [1851], JRL Papers, Houghton; HWL's journal, 22 March 1851, quoted in Longfellow 1886, 2:192.

5. CEN to Manning F. Force, 19 March 1851 and 13 April 1852, Force Papers, University of Washington (microfilm at LC); CEN to FJC, 22 April 1851, and Grace Norton to Jane Norton and Louisa and William Bullard, 12 April 1851, NP; CEN to Benjamin L. Walcott, 5 January 1853, Business Records (3), NP. For the general picture see Business Records, NP.

6. CEN to Charles Eliot Guild, 31 August–8 September 1851, Manuscripts Department, University of Virginia Library; Business Records, NP.

7. Grace Norton to Jane Norton and Louisa and William Bullard, 12 April 1851, Francis Bowen to CEN, 18 June 1851, American Ethnological Society to CEN, 20 June 1851, and CEN to Arthur Helps, 1 December 1851, NP; CEN 1851b.

8. CEN 1851a. I thank my former colleague Juan Cole for explaining Parsee naming practices.

9. Ibid., pp. 136–38.

10. Ibid., pp. 151.

11. HWL to John Forster, 7 December 1851, in Hilen 1966–82, 3:317.

12. CEN to family, 24–28 November 1850, CEN to FJC, 22 April 1851, and FJC to CEN, 4 June [1851], NP; GWC to CEN, 11 April 1851, GWC Papers, Houghton.

13. CN to CEN, 1 July 1854, and CEN to Arthur Hugh Clough, 22 August 1854, NP.

14. Notes, Nor 5257.25F, Houghton; CEN to Manning F. Force, 10 August 1858, Force Papers, University of Washington (microfilm at LC); CEN 1852a; E[mile]. Arnoult to CEN, 30 Aout 1853, in College Papers, 2d ser., 20: 158–61, HUA; Corporation Records, 8 November 1851, HUA; C. P. Curtis to CEN, 20 January 1852, NP.

15. CN to AN, 27 March 1845, box 7, ANP; Sutton 1976, p. 77; Handlin 1959, appendix table 7.

16. CEN to Arthur Helps, 1 December 1851, NP. I have altered the tenses of two verbs in this quotation to smooth the prose.

17. CEN, Reminiscences 1846–59, box 4, Miscellaneous Papers, NP; CEN to Manning F. Force, 13 April 1852, Force Papers, University of Washington (microfilm at LC); Francis Bowen to CEN, 25 February 1852; eulogy of CEN by Mayor Patrick McCarthy, *Providence Evening Bulletin*, 21 October 1908.

18. James 1930, 1:56; Higginson 1898, p. 129; Sutton 1976, p. 58.

19. CEN, Reminiscences 1846–59, box 4, Miscellaneous Papers, NP.

20. Jane Norton to CEN, n.d. [early October 1853?], and n.d. [early 1850s], NP.

21. CEN to FJC, "Wednesday" [January 1853], and 22 April 1851, NP.

22. Ballou 1970, p. 33; CEN 1897d, p. 335; McMurtry 1985, pp. 84, 101. There is some indication that CEN edited Keats, Shelley, or both for this series; but I think the (scant) evidence weighs against it.

23. CEN 1852b, pp. 464–66; CEN to CN, 30 October 1856, NP. Spelling sic.

24. CEN 1852b, pp. 467–68, 471, 473–80.

25. Ibid., pp. 481–87.

26. Fanny Appleton Longfellow to Emmeline Austin Wadsworth, 16 April 1852, in Wagenknecht 1956, p. 187; Francis Bowen to CEN, 28 April 1852, H. B. Rogers to CEN, 15 April 1852, and CEN to Elizabeth C. Gaskell, 7 February 1860, NP.

27. CEN, Reminiscences 1846–59, box 6, Miscellaneous Papers, and R. Baird Smith to Jane Norton, 17 June 1853, NP. I thank Barbara Doyle, historian of the Middleton Place Foundation, Charleston, for her assistance.

28. Charles E. Guild to CEN, 5 December 1852, Business Records, NP; CEN to Arthur Helps, 25 April 1852, Helps to CEN, 9 July 1852, Edward J. Pringle to CEN, 29 June, 19 and 31 July, 11 November, and 12 December 1852, William B. Pringle to CEN, 23 July 1852, and Harriet Beecher Stowe to CEN, 10 September [1852], NP; Accounts Current, September 1852, Business Records, NP. Both pamphlets were published anonymously, as the authors preferred.

29. Ralph Waldo Emerson to CEN, 4 September 1852, William Porcher Miles to CEN, 24 October 1852, CN to Jane Norton, 7 August [1852], and CEN to family, 18–21 August 1850, NP; *Letters,* 1:87n.

30. William Porcher Miles to CEN, 24 October 1852, and John Kenyon to CEN, 27 April 1852 and 14 March 1853, NP.

31. *Letters,* 2:428; Arthur Hugh Clough to Blanche Smith, "Sunday morning" [26 December 1852], in Mulhauser 1957, 2:318.

32. *Letters,* 2:442, 429.

33. Charles T. Brooks to CEN, 13 December 1852, and FJC to CEN, 24 January [1853], C. C. Felton to CEN, 13 October 1852, CEN, Reminiscences 1846–59, box 4, Miscellaneous Papers, CEN to Elizabeth C. Gaskell, 7 February 1860, and John Ware to CEN, n.d. [1852], NP; Arthur Hugh Clough to Blanche Smith, 29 December [1852], in Mulhauser 1957, 2:355; Class of 1846 Class Book, HUA; Dana 1968, 2:526. Whether the evening school continued after 1852–53 is not clear.

34. Allen 1981, pp. 510, 512, 515, 518, 565; Duberman 1966, p. 129; John Kenyon to CEN, 25 October 1852, NP. "The Bothie of Toper-na-Fuosich" was the original title, later altered to "The Bothie of Tober-na-Vuolich."

35. Arthur Hugh Clough to Blanche Smith, 15 November 1852, in Mulhauser 1957, 2:329; Lowell 1854, p. 53; HWL's journal, 30 December 1852, in Longfellow 1886, 2:230.

36. Arthur Hugh Clough to Blanche Smith, "Thursday" [18 November 1852] and "Tuesday" [26 April 1853], in Mulhauser 1957, 2:308, 419; Arthur Hugh Clough to CEN, n.d. [1853], NP.

37. Jane Norton to CEN, 4 March 1853, NP; GWC to CEN, n.d. [1853], GWC Papers, Houghton.

38. GWC to CEN, 17 March 1853, GWC Papers, Houghton; CEN 1853b.

39. CEN to Arthur Helps, 4 May 1853, NP.

40. CEN to family, 16–21 November 1850, NP; AN, unsigned article from Boston *Atlas,* box 11, ANP.

41. CEN to family, 16–21 November 1850, NP.

42. CEN 1853a, pp. 3, 157, 128.

43. Ibid., pp. 3–5, 7–8, 20.

44. Ibid., pp. 15, 20–21, 31, 43. *Recent Social Theories* has been called Burkean. CEN did share with Burke the belief that specific historical traditions or conditions determined the range of political possibilities. But, for a Burkean, the individual caught in a web of tradition was largely unconscious of the shaping forces, was motivated nonrationally, even antirationally; hence liberty depended on the power of traditional institutions such as the common law or of prescriptive habits such as respect for inherited political practices, *not* on so fickle and unreliable a quality as individual virtue.

45. Ibid., pp. 25–26.

46. Ibid., p. 26.

47. Ibid., pp. 27, 30, 53, 55, and chap. 5. There is no evidence that CEN knew anything of the *Bildungsidee*. Congruence of ideas presumably resulted from common roots.

48. Ibid., pp. 28–29, 136–38. The absence of a well-developed doctrine of the state in classical or Renaissance stoicism is hardly surprising, given the absence of a well-developed state. One could argue that heavy reliance on neo-Stoic sources helps to explain the feebleness of ideas about the state's role in American political thought. More specifically, it is easy to understand why the Boston patriciate from which CEN sprang would have been inclined to a Ciceronian-Senecan discourse of patronage, duties of office, and informal power rather than to a constitutional discourse of formal power.

49. Ibid., p. 119.

50. Cornelius C. Felton to CEN, 6 May 1853, Francis Bowen to CEN, 6 May 1853, and Edward J. Pringle to CEN, 10 May 1853, NP.

51. CEN to family, "Saturday morning" [25 June 1853], and to CN, 25 June [1853], NP; Jackman 1979, p. 90.

52. CEN to JRL, 28 June 1853, JRL Papers, Houghton; Arthur Hugh Clough to CEN, 29 June, 15 and 20 July 1853, NP.

53. CEN to Arthur Hugh Clough, 4 July, 2 August, and 25 September 1853, and FJC to CEN, "Friday Morning" [2 September 1853], NP; Newell 1856, p. xix.

54. Ephraim Peabody to CN, 10 January 1854, box 8, ANP; John Ware to CEN, 26 September 1853, NP.

55. I owe this formulation to Robert Sullivan.

56. CEN to JRL, 19 July 1854, JRL Papers, Houghton.

57. CEN, Reminiscences 1846–59, box 4, Miscellaneous Papers, NP.

58. CEN, Reminiscences 1846–59, box 4, Miscellaneous Papers, NP.

59. GWC to CEN, 24 February 1854, GWC Papers, Houghton; CEN to George Livermore, 19 March 1855, and CEN to FJC, 30 January 1855, NP; HWL to William Pitt Preble Longfellow, 13 July 1855, in Hilen 1966–82, 3:485.

60. Richard Lewis to CEN, 4 August 1854, Business Records, NP; CEN, Book of Verses, 1849–56, box 3, Miscellaneous Papers, NP.

61. CEN to FJC, 15 March 1855, and CEN to CN, 21 March 1855, NP; CEN to JRL, 6 April 1855, JRL Papers, Houghton.

62. CEN to JRL, 6 April 1855, JRL Papers, Houghton; CEN to CN, 15 April 1855, and to Arthur Helps, 4 June 1855, NP.

63. CEN to JRL, 6 April 1855, JRL Papers, Houghton.

64. Stillman 1901, vol. 1, passim; William James Stillman to CEN, n.d. [July 1855], NP; CEN to JRL, 18–23 September 1855, JRL Papers, Houghton.

65. William James Stillman to CEN, 2 July 1855, and William Delafield Arnold to CEN, 14 July 1855, NP; Richard Lewis to CEN, 22 January 1855, Business Records, NP; CEN 1855b; CEN 1855c. The notice of *Leaves of Grass* was reprinted, with an introductory essay by Professor Kenneth Murdock and CEN's own parody of the poem, to celebrate the centenary of his birth: *A Leaf of Grass from Shady Hill: With a Review of Walt Whitman's* Leaves of Grass (Cambridge: Harvard University Press, 1928).

66. CEN to FJC, 19 July 1855, and n.d. [late August 1855], NP; CEN to [Henry Barnard?], 3 October 1855, Henry Barnard Manuscripts, Fales Library, New York University.

67. FJC to CEN, 16 November 1872, NP.

Chapter 5: Adrift, 1855–1857

1. CN to Louisa and William Bullard, 23 October 1855, NP. "Or" sic.

2. CN to Louisa and William Bullard, 23 October 1855, NP; JRL to CEN, 11–12 and 28 October 1855, and CEN to JRL, 24 October 1855, JRL Papers, Houghton; JRL to William J. Stillman, 18 February 1856, in CEN 1893b, 1:256.

3. CN to Louisa and William Bullard, 23 October 1855, NP; Arthur H. Clough to FJC, 29 October [1855], in Mulhauser 1957, 2:448.

4. CEN to William S. Bullard, 24 October 1855, and to JR, "Wednesday" [31 October 1855], NP; CEN to JRL, 9 November 1855, JRL Papers, Houghton. When writing his autobiographical *Praeterita,* JR thought that he had first met CEN the following summer.

5. CEN to Arthur H. Clough, 28 November 1855, in *Letters,* 1:141; CEN to Thomas G. Appleton, 22 November 1855, NP.

6. CEN, Reminiscences 1846–59, box 4, Miscellaneous Papers, NP; Jane Norton to Louisa Bullard, 13 December 1855, NP; CEN to Arthur H. Clough, 28 November 1855, in *Letters,* 1:141.

7. CEN 1856; CEN to JRL, 21 December 1855, JRL Papers, Houghton. My thanks to Caroline Winterer for locating these issues of the *Crayon* for me.

8. CEN to JRL, 21 December 1855 and 13 January 1856, JRL Papers, Houghton.

9. CEN to JRL, 6 February 1856, JRL Papers, Houghton; Jane Norton to Louisa Norton, 1856 letters passim, NP.

10. Jane Norton to Louisa Bullard, 9 January 1856, NP.

11. Ibid.; CEN 1856, pp. 152–55; CN to Louisa and William Bullard, 14 January 1856, NP; *Letters,* 1:144n.

12. Jane Norton to Louisa Bullard, 9 January and 20 April 1856, and CEN to William S. Bullard, 11 March 1856, NP.

13. CEN to William S. Bullard, 8 January "1855" [1856], Jane Norton to Louisa Bullard, 17 February 1856, and CEN to William S. Bullard, 27 May 1856, NP.

14. Grace Norton to Louisa Bullard, 24 February 1856, NP.

15. CEN 1856, p. 206.

16. Ibid.; CEN to JRL, 13 January 1856, JRL Papers, Houghton.

17. CEN to JRL, 13 January 1856, JRL Papers, Houghton; and Grace Norton to Louisa Bullard, 8 March 1856, NP.

18. CEN to JRL, 6 February and 6 March 1856, and JRL to CEN, 27 February 1856, JRL Papers, Houghton; CEN 1859b, p. 101; Jane Norton to Louisa Bullard, 6–7 April 1856, NP.

19. CEN to Samuel Gray Ward, 5 August 1856, NP.

20. CEN to JRL, 6 March 1856, JRL Papers, Houghton.

21. Vance 1989, 1:229; Taylor 1957, p. 144; CEN to Samuel Gray Ward, 5 August 1856, and Grace Norton to Louisa Bullard, 30 March 1856, NP. Taylor 1957, plates 37 and 38, reproduces the painting. The Athenaeum initially rejected it, eventually yielded. Page painted more than one version, all virtually identical; the one that CEN saw probably no longer exists, a victim of the tendency of Page's experimental pigments and varnishes to disappear over time.

22. CEN 1859b, pp. 166–69; CEN to William S. Bullard, 15 May 1856, and Jane Norton to Louisa and William Bullard, 20 April 1856, NP.

23. CEN to CN, 23 April 1856, CEN to CN, Jane, and Grace Norton, 3 May 1856, NP.

24. FJC to CEN, 18 March 1856, NP.

25. CEN 1856, pp. 308–9; CEN to JRL, 13 June 1856, JRL Papers, Houghton. The three volumes of *The Stones of Venice* appeared in 1851–53.

26. Ruskin 1885–89, 3:41–42; CEN to JRL, 4 August 1856, JRL Papers, Houghton. "St. Martin" seems most likely to be Saint-Martin-Bellevue on the road to Annecy.

27. Ruskin 1885–89, 3:42; CEN to JRL, 4 August 1856, JRL Papers, Houghton. The first friend was John Brown.

28. CN to Louisa Bullard, 22 August 1856, and CEN to T. G. Appleton, "Monday morng" [25 August 1856], NP; CEN to JRL, 22 August 1856, JRL Papers, Houghton.

29. CN to Louisa Bullard, 22 August 1856, and Jane Norton to Louisa Bullard, 27 August 1856, NP.

30. CEN to FJC, n.d. [late August 1855], NP.

31. CN to Louisa Bullard, 3 October 1856, NP; CEN to John Gorham Palfrey, 27 August 1856, Palfrey Family Papers, Houghton.

32. CEN to JRL, 31 August 1856, JRL Papers, Houghton; CEN to John Gorham Palfrey, 14 September 1856, Palfrey Family Papers, Houghton.

33. CEN to Arthur H. Clough, 21 September 1856, in *Letters*, 1:149; Jane Norton to Louisa Bullard, 25 September 1856, NP.

34. CEN to William S. Bullard, 18 September 1856, NP.

35. CEN to CN, 16, 23, and 30 October 1856, and CEN to GWC, 20 June 1869, NP; [Burne-Jones]1906, 1:139; JR to CEN, October–November 1856 (six letters), NP.

36. CEN to Arthur H. Clough, "Sunday, 9th" [November 1856], NP; CEN to JRL, 9 November 1856, JRL Papers, Houghton. AN had been a High Federalist, and the New England disunionist tradition from the War of 1812 still echoed in his son's memory.

37. Arthur H. Clough to FJC, 13 November 1856, in Mulhauser 1957, 2:522; CEN

to CN, 19 November 1856, NP; CEN to Arthur H. Clough, 18 December 1856, in *Letters*, 1:156.

38. CEN, Reminiscences 1846–59, box 4, Miscellaneous Papers, and CEN to CN, 4 December, 5–11 December, and 28 December 1856, NP; CEN to Arthur H. Clough, 18 December 1856, in *Letters*, 1:157–58.

39. CEN to CN, 7–11 December and 14–18 December 1856, NP.

40. "Published" and "whole" are key words; translations of individual sonnets and canzoni appeared often enough in print, while Lyell translated the entire work but never published the prose portions. Emerson had produced a (bad) translation for his own delectation in the 1840s, and Longfellow had also fiddled with the text: LaPiana 1948, pp. 89–94. CEN knew of Garrow's translation by 1859: CEN 1859a, p. 101, n. 3.

41. CEN did *not* know in 1856–57 that Rossetti intended a complete translation of the *Vita Nuova:* CEN 1867a, p. 109.

42. La Piana 1948, p. 117; CEN to JRL, 1 January 1857, JRL Papers, Houghton.

43. CEN to CN, 7–12 February 1857, and CEN to John Simon, 15 May 1875, NP.

44. CEN to CN, 7–11 December 1856, and 5–6 April 1857, and CEN to Arthur H. Clough, 4 April 1857 (my emphasis), NP; CEN to JRL, 1 January 1857, JRL Papers, Houghton.

45. CEN to CN, 1 March 1857, and CEN to Arthur H. Clough, 4 April 1857, NP.

46. CEN to William W. Story, 26 October–1 November 1857, Harry Ransom Humanities Research Center, University of Texas, Austin; CEN to CN, 22 February 1857, NP. For clarity in reading, I have silently inserted a comma between "do nothing" and "as much" in Dr. Mutter's advice.

47. Meta Gaskell to CEN [fragment c. 1866–67], NP.

48. CEN to Elizabeth C. Gaskell, 5 June 1855, NP; CEN, Reminiscences 1846–59, box 4, Miscellaneous Papers, NP.

49. FJC to CEN, 30–31 January [1857], NP. These are conservative judgments, a fact that suggests how feeble American scholarship was in these areas. George Ticknor was at this point probably the best informed American Dantist; JRL, HWL, and conceivably Thomas W. Parsons were also CEN's superiors. The only other American versed in Dante studies had been Richard Henry Wilde of Georgia, who died in 1847. I can think of no American whose knowledge of Italian painting equaled CEN's, with the possible exception of James Jackson Jarves.

50. CEN to CN, 22 and 29 April 1857, and Meta Gaskell to CEN, n.d. [1857; two letters], NP.

51. CEN to CN, 22 and 29 April 1857, NP.

52. CEN to CN, 29 and 30 April 1857, NP. The basilica of San Marco was not a cathedral, a slip suggesting the still erratic character of CEN's expertise.

53. CEN to CN, 5 May 1857, and Rawdon Brown to CEN, 5 May 1857, NP; CEN to William W. Story, 26 October–1 November 1857, Harry Ransom Humanities Research Center, University of Texas, Austin. The others were, in order: (3) "our sunset place" in the *laguna* beyond Giudecca; (4) the Franciscan church of S. Miniato above Florence; (5) the Campo Santo at Pisa; (6) the Villa Celimontana, a park just south of the Colosseum (semirural in 1857); and (7) the Roman Campagna.

54. CEN to CN, 13 May 1857, NP.

55. CEN to CN, 5 June 1857, NP.

56. JRL to CEN, 22 May 1857, and CEN to JRL, 20 June 1857, JRL Papers, Houghton.

57. CEN to CN, 2 July 1857, NP.

58. CEN to Elizabeth C. Gaskell, 16 January 1865, NP; CEN 1857a.

59. CEN to CN, 16 June 1857, and CEN to FJC, 17 August 1857, NP.

60. CEN to JRL, 20 August 1857, JRL Papers, Houghton; Jane Norton to FJC, 9 August 1857, NP.

Chapter 6: A Literary Invalid, 1857–1861

1. Jane Norton to FJC, 9 August 1857, NP.

2. Fanny Appleton Longfellow to Mary Appleton Mackintosh, 2 November 1857, in Wagenknecht 1956, p. 211; CEN to William W. Story, 26 October–1 November 1857, Harry Ransom Humanities Research Center, University of Texas, Austin.

3. CEN, Reminiscences 1846–59, box 4, Miscellaneous Papers, NP; CEN to FJC, 28 October 1857, NP. CEN once or twice referred to the awkwardness of appearing fit while unable to work full-time, but in general he seemed unperturbed by playing what historians of Victorian culture would call the feminine role of prolonged invalidism. Indeed, I find not a shred of evidence to suggest that he or any of his acquaintance regarded his position as "feminine."

4. CEN to William W. Story, 26 October–1 November 1857, Harry Ransom Humanities Research Center, University of Texas, Austin.

5. CEN to JRL, 18 May 1858, and JRL to CEN, 25 March 1858, JRL Papers, Houghton; FJC to CEN, 18 March 1856, NP.

6. Grace Norton to "Patch" [FJC], 31 January 1858, and CEN to FJC, 13 December 1857, NP; CEN to JRL, 7 May 1858, JRL Papers, Houghton.

7. CEN to FJC, 17 August 1857, NP.

8. Richard Grant White to CEN, 28 October 1858, NP. Palfrey's pioneering historical scholarship appeared in five volumes, 1858–90, the author having predeceased the work. White's edition of Shakespeare was published 1857–66.

9. CEN to Francis H. Underwood, n.d. [January 1858], American Academy and Institute of Arts and Letters, New York; CEN to JRL, 30 January 1858, JRL Papers, Houghton; CEN, Reminiscences 1846–59, box 4, Miscellaneous Papers, NP.

10. Frances Appleton Longfellow to Mary Appleton Mackintosh, 2 November 1857, in Wagenknecht 1956, p. 211; CEN 1857a, pp. 36, 37, 43. I speak of JR's aesthetic theory as presented in the early volumes of *Modern Painters* and as CEN would have known it in 1857.

11. James's 1887 essay on John Singer Sargent, quoted in the *New York Times Sunday Book Review*, 24 August 1986; CEN 1857a, p. 38.

12. CEN 1857a, pp. 35–38, 44–46.

13. Frances Appleton Longfellow to Mary Appleton Mackintosh, 2 November 1857, in Wagenknecht 1956, p. 211.

14. Ezra Abbot to CEN, 27 July 1858, NP. My guess is that he decided not to publish because J. Spencer Northcote's *Roman Catacombs*, published in 1857, made the discoveries sufficiently available to anglophone readers.

15. CEN to Arthur H. Clough, 22 November 1858, NP; CEN to JRL, 23 June 1859, JRL Papers, Houghton. Ozanam, besides founding the Catholic Society of St. Vincent de Paul, was a scholar of major importance. I have not been able to identify Picchioni, showing perhaps that I am no scholar; the book in question treated allegory in the *Divina Commedia*. For someone like CEN with interests in medieval culture, the fourth-century grammarian Donatus (teacher of Jerome) would not have been an obscure figure, since his treatises became standard texts in medieval schools.

16. CEN to JRL, 7 May 1858, JRL Papers, Houghton.

17. CEN joined the Oriental Society in 1857: William D. Whitney to CEN, 22 December 1857, NP. Technically, FJC's Göttingen Ph.D. was honorary, not earned; but it was awarded (in 1853) in recognition of scholarly achievement.

18. Jeffries Wyman to CEN, 11 January 1860, NP. CEN admired "the patience of Mr. Darwin's research, the wide reach of his knowledge & his thought, and above all the honesty & manliness of his plain speech"; but he thought the "reasoning" not "as good as the science." "At any rate," he informed Elizabeth Gaskell, "I wait to be convinced that I am nothing but a modified fish." CEN to Elizabeth C. Gaskell, n.d. [25–27 December 1859], NP.

19. Foreign authors had no protection in the United States before 1891. (English-language authors still labored under onerous restrictions until 1955.) The more reputable American publishers printed authorized or "author's" editions of British works, on which they paid royalties and which more sensitive buyers preferred to purchase.

20. JR to CEN, n.d. [28 February 1858], JR to CEN, 15 August [1859], and CEN to Aubrey de Vere, 28 May 1860, NP.

21. CEN to JRL, 14 October 1858, JRL Papers, Houghton; CEN to Arthur H. Clough, 8 June 1858, NP.

22. CEN to Aubrey de Vere, 27 July 1858, NP; CEN to JRL, 7 May and 14 October 1858, JRL Papers, Houghton. Rossetti's version appeared in 1861 as part of his *Early Italian Poets*.

23. CEN to JRL, 14 October 1858, JRL Papers, Houghton; HWL to CEN, 14 March 1859, NP.

24. CEN to HWL, 14 March [1859], HWL Papers, Houghton; JRL to CEN, 26 July and 7 September 1859, and CEN to JRL, 29 June 1860, 19 and 26 May 1859, JRL Papers, Houghton; CEN to H. O. Houghton and Co., 27 May 1859, Butler Library, Columbia University.

25. CEN to William W. Story, 27 July 1859, Harry Ransom Humanities Research Center, University of Texas, Austin. The other artists of whom CEN saw much in this period were Samuel Worcester Rowse and Paul Akers.

26. JRL to CEN, 1 and 7 September 1859, JRL Papers, Houghton.

27. Jarves 1960, pp. xii and 12; CEN 1859c; Swan 1940, pp. 105–8.

28. CEN to Charles Sumner, 26 May 1860 and 29 November 1859, NP; CEN to James Jackson Jarves, 17 December 1859 [copy], Boston Athenaeum.

29. CEN to James T. Fields, 24 December 1860, Huntington Library; Richard G. White to CEN, 22 January 1860, NP; La Piana 1948, pp. 117, 120. Besides the discussion of the *Vita Nuova*'s structure, appendices included essays on the date of

composition and on inconsistencies between the *Vita Nuova* and the *Convito* as well as Charles T. Brooks's translation of Guido Cavalcanti's "Donna mi priega."

30. CEN 1859b, pp. 204–21, 246–67, 298–320.

31. *Atlantic Monthly* 5 (1860): 631.

32. CEN 1859g, pp. 767–68.

33. Ibid., p. 767; CEN 1860g, p. 628.

34. CEN 1860g, pp. 627–28.

35. Haraszti [1940?], p. 53; T. G. Appleton to CEN, n.d. [December 1859–January 1860], and Houghton Mifflin and Co. to CEN, 15 June 1897, NP; Jane LeCompte (Corporate Communications Manager of Houghton Mifflin) to author, 13 October 1994.

36. CEN to Manning F. Force, 31 January 1859, Force Papers, University of Washington (microfilm at LC).

37. CEN to H. W. Bellows, 21 September 1859, Bellows Papers, MHS; CEN to Manning F. Force, 13 October 1859, Force Papers, University of Washington (microfilm at LC).

38. CEN 1860k; CEN to Arthur Helps, 25 May 1858, NP.

39. CEN 1860f; CEN to Ellen Dwight Twisleton, 13 December 1859, NP.

40. CEN 1860g; CEN 1860c, p. 126; CEN to Arthur Helps, 25 May 1858, and CEN to Aubrey de Vere, 15 February 1860, NP.

41. CEN to Aubrey de Vere, 15 February 1860, NP.

42. O. W. Holmes to CEN, 29 August 1858, NP; JRL to CEN, 31 August 1858, JRL Papers, Houghton.

43. CEN to JRL, 29 June and 8 July 1860, JRL Papers, Houghton; CEN to Meta Gaskell, 19 August 1860, NP.

44. FJC to CEN, 21 August 1860, NP. Ruskin was, of course, now single again; but this was, to say the least, a special case.

45. CEN to FJC, 31 October 1860, NP.

46. CEN to H. C. Acland, 20 January 1861, Bodleian Library, Oxford University; CEN to Ellen Dwight Twisleton, 8 December 1860, NP.

47. CEN to Aubrey de Vere, 24 February 1861, NP.

48. CEN to William Porcher Miles, 22 December 1860, Miles Papers, Southern Historical Collection, University of North Carolina Library, Chapel Hill; CEN to GWC, 17 December 1860, NP.

49. CEN to GWC, 17 December 1860, and CEN to Aubrey de Vere, 24 February 1861, NP. The phrase "New Africa" pointed to a common Republican theme, which seeped briefly into CEN's thinking under the pressure of the secession crisis. In an *Atlantic Monthly* book review (CEN 1861d), CEN warned against the "africanization" of the United States by the extension of slavery, saying that the "black is in many of his endowments inferior to the white" and that "the qualities of race are so slowly affected by change as to admit of being called constant and permanent." This static view of "race" sharply contrasted with his deeply rooted historicist conviction, often expressed previously, that cultural development rather than innate characteristics explained the putative superiority of some peoples to others. The new, harder-edged position proved an aberration, never recurring.

50. CEN to Aubrey de Vere, 24 February 1861, and CEN to Charles Sumner, 22 March 1861, NP.

51. CEN to Charles Sumner, 22 March 1861, NP. I may be committing a slight anachronism: the Kingdom of Italy was not formally declared until 17 March 1861, so Marsh was probably initially appointed minister to its predecessor, the Kingdom of Sardinia. The secretary's post went to a man named Fry, against the wishes of Marsh, who unsurprisingly preferred CEN.

52. Blanche M. Clough to Jane Norton, 10 March 1861, and Samuel Eliot to CEN, 17 April 1861, NP.

CHAPTER 7: TOWARD "A SCIENCE OF IDEAL POLITICS," 1861–1865

1. CEN to GWC, 18 April 1861, NP.

2. Ibid.

3. CEN to JRL, 21 July and 8 August 1861, JRL Papers, Houghton; CEN to G. P. Marsh, 5 April 1861, University of Vermont Library, and Marsh to CEN, 2 June 1861, NP. The dictionary was the *New English Dictionary on Historical Principles*, now known as the *Oxford English Dictionary*.

4. A copy of de Vere's sonnet can be found at MS.52.63 in the Brown University Library.

5. CEN to GWC, 1 and 24 August 1861, NP; CEN to G. P. Marsh, 15 August and 9 November 1861, University of Vermont Library.

6. CEN to G. P. Marsh, 9 November 1861, University of Vermont Library; CEN 1861h, 364; Richard Baird Smith to CEN, 31 August 1861, NP.

7. George B. Emerson to CEN, 24 August and 16 September 1861, NP; CEN to JRL, 13 September 1861, JRL Papers, Houghton.

8. R. H. Dana Jr., to CEN, 18 November 1861, NP; CEN 1861i, 552–53, 556.

9. JRL to CEN, 25 October 1861, JRL Papers, Houghton; Blanche M. Clough to CEN, 29 November 1861, in Mulhauser 1957, 2:571; *The Englishman*, 16 December 1861; James 1930, 1:89.

10. While JRL and CEN were on bantering terms, HWL remained "My dear Mr. Longfellow." HWL was a close friend but almost a generation older than CEN; and their affection always included an element of almost paternal regard on HWL's part, filial respect on CEN's.

11. CEN to GWC, 1 August 1861, and JR to CEN, 25 February 1861, NP; CEN to JRL, 20 September 1875, JRL Papers, Houghton.

12. F. W. Palfrey to CEN, 5 December 1861, and CEN to GWC, 11 December 1861, NP; Nathaniel Hawthorne to Henry A. Bright, 8 March 1863, in Hawthorne 1984–88, 4:544.

13. John G. Palfrey, 16 December 1861, Palfrey Family Papers, Houghton; F. W. Palfrey to CEN, 26 December 1861, and Jane Norton to CEN, n.d. [late December 1861], NP; MS. in box 14, Miscellaneous Papers, NP.

14. CN to CEN, 19 December [1861], and Grace Norton to E. C. Gaskell, 18 May 1862, NP.

15. CEN to GWC, 1 and 19 March 1862, NP.

16. Grace Norton to Elizabeth C. Gaskell, 18 May 1862, NP. Theodore Sedg-

wick I, SSN's great-grandfather, served in the Massachusetts legislature, in both houses of Congress, and on the state Supreme Judicial Court. Her grandfather, Theodore II, was also a lawyer and a well-regarded writer on political economy. Her father, besides editing *Harper's Weekly*, wrote important legal treatises. Her great-aunt, Catharine Maria Sedgwick, wrote best-selling novels.

17. Grace Norton to Elizabeth C. Gaskell, 18 May 1862, NP; undated *New York Evening Post* clipping [c. 15 October 1863], in scrapbook at Cyc 1014F*, Houghton; HWL to Charles Sumner, 29 March 1862, in Hilen 1966–82, 4:272.

18. Grace Norton to Elizabeth C. Gaskell, 18 May 1862, CEN to GWC, 14 July and 7 September 1862, NP.

19. CEN to Aubrey de Vere, 7 February 1863, NP; C[atharine] M[aria] S[edgwick] to "My dear sister," 11 May 1862, Sedgwick Papers III, MHS.

20. FJC to CEN, "Friday, 2 o'clock" [March 1862], E. C. Gaskell to CEN, 22 April 1861, and JR to CEN, 28 April 1862, NP.

21. CEN to Meta Gaskell, 30 August 1862, NP.

22. JRL to CEN, n.d. [July 1862], JRL Papers, Houghton.

23. CEN to Meta Gaskell, 30 August 1862, NP.

24. GWC to CEN, 1 September 1862, GWC Papers, Houghton.

25. CEN to GWC, 7 September 1862, 30 January and 30 March 1863, and CEN to Meta Gaskell, 26 January 1863, NP; MHS, *Proceedings* 1st ser. 6:82–83; CEN 1863a.

26. CEN to G. P. Marsh, 27 April 1862, University of Vermont Library.

27. Ibid.; CEN to GWC, 17 May 1863, NP.

28. CEN to GWC, 23 September 1862, NP.

29. Ibid. and 12 November 1862, NP.

30. CEN to Meta Gaskell, 26 January 1863, and CEN to Aubrey de Vere, 7 February 1863, NP.

31. CEN to GWC, 10 January 1863, NP.

32. CEN to Meta Gaskell, 26 January 1863, CEN to HWL [3 Feb 63], 1 Mar 63, and [1863?], HWL Papers, Houghton.

33. Note inside portfolio in box 8, Miscellaneous Papers, NP.

34. Smith 1948, p. 292.

35. CEN to Sarah Forbes Hughes, 5 January 1899, NP; Circular letter, 9 March 1863, NELPS Papers, Boston Public Library.

36. CEN to J. M. Forbes, 6 February 1863, NP; Smith 1948, pp. 294–97.

37. JR to CEN, 10 February 1863, NP.

38. CEN to John Bright, 8 May 1863, 43391, f. 148, British Library; Thompson 1971, pp. 42 (13 July) and 66 (28 August, 6 September). In referring to a "hasty naval commander" CEN doubtless had in mind the 1861 hijacking by Captain Charles Wilkes of a British steamer in order to kidnap two Confederate diplomats on board.

39. CEN's contribution was "Forgotten Fame," CEN 1862a.

40. Thomas Hill to CEN, 9 March and 18 June 63, NP; Corporation Records, 28 March 1863, HUA.

41. CEN to G. P. Marsh, 9 May 1863, University of Vermont Library.

42. Ibid. I have inserted a comma inadvertently omitted by CEN after "slave-holding class."

43. CEN to J. M. Forbes, 25 September 1863, NP; CEN 1863b. The notion of "general opinion," "vulgar opinion," etc., was hardly novel; nor were attempts to use print to rouse enthusiasm for a cause (Thomas Paine's *Common Sense* being perhaps the most celebrated American example). But conceiving "public opinion" as a persisting and, as it were, free-standing entity, which could be and even needed to be steadily manipulated, was a nineteenth-century innovation, dependent on the huge multiplication of means for exchanging information.

44. JBH to CEN, 15 October 1863 and 12 December 1865, NP.

45. CEN to JBH, 2 October 1863, and JBH to CEN, 4 September and 15 October 1863, NP.

46. JBH to CEN, 20 January 1864, and CEN to JBH, 14 December 1863, NP.

47. Charles W. Eliot to CEN, 28 January 1864, and CEN to GWC, 21 September 1863, NP.

48. CEN to GWC, 3 September 1863, NP.

49. CEN to JBH, 14 December 1863, NP; report of speech by CEN to Unitarian Convention at Springfield, Massachusetts, 14 October 1863, undated *New York Evening Post* clipping [c. 15 October], in scrapbook, Cyc 1014F*, Houghton.

50. CEN to FLO, 24 January 1864, and CEN to GWC, 3 September 1863, NP.

51. CEN to FLO, 24 January 1864, and CEN to JBH, 14 December 1863, NP.

52. MHS, *Proceedings* 3d ser. 42 (1908): 32–33; CEN to FLO, 24 January 1864, NP.

53. CEN to FLO, 24 January 1864, NP; Armstrong 1978, pp. 62–64.

54. CEN 1904b, p. 253; LS's journal, quoted in Maitland 1906, p. 118.

55. R. W. Emerson to CEN, 30 October 1862, and CEN to Meta Gaskell, 20 March 1862, NP.

56. Undated *New York Evening Post* clipping [c. 15 October], in scrapbook, Cyc 1014F*, Houghton.

57. *New York Evening Post* clipping; Norton 1812a, rep. in Norton 1852, p. 27.

58. *New York Evening Post* clipping; CEN to JBH, 14 December 1863, NP.

59. JRL to J. L. Motley, 28 July 1864, in CEN 1893b, 1:335; CEN to FLO, 24 January 1864, NP.

60. CEN to FLO, 24 January 1864, and CEN to GWC, 16 October 1863, NP; contract at bMS Am 1236.2, Houghton.

61. CEN to Charles Sumner, 29 October 1863, Houghton.

62. CEN 1864n. Dime novels were what came to be called pulp fiction, roughly equivalent to Harlequin romances and Ace fantasy novels more than a century later. Despite his love of opera, music never figured much in CEN's cultural thinking, nor did he pretend to knowledgeability.

63. CEN 1864b; CEN to Richard Grant White, 28 December 1863, CEN–Grant White Letters, Houghton; CEN to William Dwight Whitney, 24 October 1867, Whitney Family Papers, Sterling Library, Yale University; CEN to James Parton, 8 October 1864, James Parton Papers, Houghton.

64. CEN to William Dwight Whitney, 24 October 1867, Whitney Family Papers, Sterling Library, Yale University; CEN to Daniel Coit Gilman, 29 October 1863, Milton S. Eisenhower Library, Johns Hopkins University. To be precise, Schuyler received one of three Ph.D.s awarded by Yale in 1861.

65. CEN to Caroline H. Dall, 8 February 1868, Dall Papers, MHS (microfilm at LC). "Mr. Marsh" is George Perkins Marsh.

66. CEN 1865i, p. 329.

67. *New York Daily Tribune,* 9 January 1864, and *New York Times,* 11 January 1864, *Boston Evening Transcript,* 25 January 1864, *Courier,* 23 January 1864, and *New York Observer,* 14 July 1864, clippings in scrapbook, Cyc 1014F*, Houghton; CEN to GWC, 23 January 1864, and E. G. Squier to CEN, 28 March 1864, NP.

68. *New York Evening Post,* 7 April 1864, clipping in scrapbook, Cyc 1014F*, Houghton; D. C. Gilman to CEN, 5 May 1864, O. B. Frothingham to CEN, 4 October 1864, and William Dwight Whitney to CEN, 5 November 1864, NP.

69. CEN to GWC, 18 October 1864, and J. T. Fields to CEN, 8 June 1865, NP. JRL seems to have handled the printer when CEN went away in summer.

70. Henry Adams to CEN, 28 June 1867, in Levenson et al. 1982, 1:538.

71. James 1914, p. 405; Edel 1953, p. 208
This may be the point to broach the snarled attitudes of the James family toward CEN: a tangle of affection, ambivalence, neighborliness, and distaste. The elder Henry privately found CEN off-putting, though no more off-putting than CEN found him; yet the two kept up rather close and evidently friendly relations. Daughter Alice displayed pretty nearly unrelieved contempt for the whole Norton clan (though it is fair to add that Alice had a lot of contempt to go around). William James, who spent the most hours with CEN over the decades, was utterly ambivalent, richoceting from what seems heartfelt fondness to bitterness tinctured with jealousy. The younger Henry, though never really intimate with CEN, also never really wavered in his affection for the older man, though even he found CEN's seriousness in facing life heavy weather at times. Henry also became quite friendly with CEN's sister Grace and brother-in-law Arthur Sedgwick, both closer to his own age.

72. Recollections by Arthur G. Sedgwick, c. 1912, box 11, bMS Am 1088.2, Houghton. Anonymity was pretty much a fiction by the time CEN and JRL took over.

73. Ticknor and Fields to CEN, 5 September 1865, NP. This increase in income fostered the emergence of a class of professional writers, which presented a more subtle and perhaps even deadlier challenge to the old quarterlies, not visible to CEN. The emergence of the professional author devalued the amateur writers—the lawyers, merchants, et al.—who had previously written most of what appeared in magazines. Higher pay and professionalization made a vicious circle; and, caught between the increase in cost of professional writers and the declining reputability and numbers of amateur authors, the weighty general-audience quarterlies like the *NAR* were slowly squeezed out. Buell 1986, p. 57, notes that compensation for literary journalism tripled between 1860 and 1880.

CHAPTER 8: THE *NORTH AMERICAN*, THE *NATION*,
AND THE *NATION*, 1865–1868

1. Howes c. 1911, p. 378; CEN to GWC, 23 February 1864, NP.

2. CEN to JRL, 7 July 1864, JRL Papers, Houghton. The house seems to have been built in the late eighteenth century.

3. CEN to GWC, 12 and 25 August 1864, and Ridley Watts to CEN, 5 August 1864, NP; GWC to CEN, 1 and 28 August 1864, GWC Papers, Houghton; CEN to JRL, 10 August 1864 and "Thursday evening" [1 September 1864], JRL Papers, Houghton.

4. CEN to GWC, 23 February 1864, NP; Child 1920, p. ix.

5. CEN to ELG, 3 December 1864, ELG Papers, Houghton; CEN 1865b, pp. 2–4.

6. CEN to William W. Story, 23 November 1864, Ransom Humanities Research Center, University of Texas, Austin; CEN 1865c, p. 233; CEN to Goldwin Smith [c. July 1864], printed in *Manchester* (Eng.) *Examiner and Times* (clipping in Goldwin Smith to CEN, 5 August 1864, NP); CEN to FLO, 24 January 1864, and CEN to Aubrey de Vere, 27 December 1864, NP; CEN to ELG, 24 February 1865, ELG Papers, Houghton.

7. CEN to JRL, 23 February 1865, JRL Papers, Houghton; CEN to Richard Grant White, 13 April 1865, CEN–Grant White Letters, Houghton.

8. CEN to ELG, 5 April 1865, ELG Papers, Houghton. Armstrong 1978, chap. 5, gives a concise and authoritative account of the *Nation*'s founding. For CEN's key role in the factional infighting that complicated the *Nation*'s first year, almost sunk the journal, and left ELG permanently grateful to CEN, see CEN Long Version, chaps. 11–12.

9. George L. Stearns to CEN (printed circular quoting advertisements for *Nation)*, 14 August 1865, and CEN to J. M. Forbes, 4 May 1865, NP. A second choice for editor, Whitelaw Reid, also declined.

10. CEN to Dante Gabriel Rossetti, 21 March 1865, Bodleian Library, Oxford; dedication in CEN 1865a. Happily for CEN's reputation, only fifty copies were printed, privately.

11. HWL's journal, 25 October 1865, quoted in Emerson 1918, p. 395; Howells 1910, pp. 154–56, 159–62.

12. CEN 1867w; JR to CEN, 15 August 1865, NP.

13. CEN to ELG, 15 June 1865, ELG Papers, Houghton; CEN to G. P. Marsh, 21 August 1865, University of Vermont Library.

14. CEN to JRL, 16 July 1865, and note by SSN appended to CEN to JRL, 11 August 1865, JRL Papers, Houghton; CEN to G. P. Marsh, 21 August 1865, University of Vermont Library; ELG to CEN, 3 August 1865, and Chauncey Wright to CEN, 18 August 1865, NP.

15. CEN to ELG, 10 and 23 December 1865, and 21 January 1866, ELG Papers, Houghton.

16. CEN to Goldwin Smith [c. July 1864], printed in *Manchester* (Eng.) *Examiner and Times* (clipping in Smith to CEN, 5 August 1864); CEN to ELG, 4 October 1865, ELG Papers, Houghton.

17. CEN to ELG, 5 April 1865 and 21 January 1866, ELG Papers, Houghton; CEN 1866a, p. 253; CEN to John A. Andrew, 19 January 1867, Andrew Papers, MHS (microfilm in LC).

18. CEN 1866a, p. 251; CEN to ELG, 14 April 1865, ELG Papers, Houghton; CEN to John A. Andrew, 19 January 1867, Andrew Papers, MHS (microfilm in LC); CEN 1865b, p. 3; CEN 1865x, p. 551. CEN did continue to distinguish, as he

had in *Considerations on Some Recent Social Theories*, between natural rights and civil (or as he said "political") rights. He still believed in principle that "there is no *natural right* to share in the government" and that the form of government is a matter of expediency. The United States had adopted the position—which CEN thought a good thing—that voting belonged as a *political* right to all who met "some low test" of competence: "No class of men have any political rights above those of any other class, excepting always the criminal & the ignorant." CEN to ELG, 5 March 1865, ELG Papers, Houghton.

19. CEN 1867c, pp. 150–51; John Stuart Mill to CEN, 26[?] November 1865, copy in NP (printed with date of 24 November in *Proceedings of the MHS* 3d ser. 50 [1916]: 11–12); CEN 1867y.

20. CEN to Goldwin Smith [c. July 1864], printed in *Manchester* (Eng.) *Examiner and Times* (clipping in Smith to CEN, 5 August 1864); CEN 1866w, p. 508; John Stuart Mill to CEN, 26[?] November 1865, copy in NP.

21. CEN 1865x, pp. 552–54.

22. Ibid., pp. 554–56. It followed, CEN argued, that the "idea of sovereignty" had "no moral weight in America" and should be dumped from political debate. The states themselves were "mere conveniences," arbitrary "geographical divisions"—not an odd position for a radical Republican to adopt in 1865—but the national government's institutions had no superiority in this respect. Indeed, in politics not even natural rights exist: "Natural rights exist only in morals, and inhere in the individual as a moral being." CEN broke pretty decisively with the predominantly constitutionalist or at least legalistic mode of political theorizing in the United States. Ibid., pp. 556–57. Emphasis on "ideas" added.

23. Ibid., p. 551.

24. Ibid.; CEN 1866w, pp. 507–8.

25. CEN 1864q, pp. 523–24.

26. CEN 1865x, pp. 550–52; CEN 1864q, p. 526; CEN 1865j, p. 344; CEN to Goldwin Smith [c. July 1864], printed in *Manchester* (Eng.) *Examiner and Times* (clipping in Smith to CEN, 5 August 1864).

27. CEN 1865x, pp. 561–62; CEN 1867c, p. 151; CEN 1867d, p. 249.

28. CEN 1865x, p. 558.

29. CEN to JBH, 20 March 1864, NP.

30. CEN to ELG, 13 March 1867 and 24 January 1866, ELG Papers, Houghton; CEN 1865s; CEN to Aubrey de Vere, 25 March 1867, NP.

31. CEN to ELG, 21 January 1866, ELG Papers, Houghton; CEN to FLO, 16 September 1866, FLO Papers, LC (typescript copy).

32. CEN to JBH, 20 March 1864, NP; CEN 1867y.

33. CEN to JBH, 20 March 1864, NP; CEN 1865i, p. 329; CEN 1865t; CEN 1865s.

34. CEN to HWL, 21 January 1866, HWL Papers, Houghton; CEN 1866e.

35. CEN to ELG, 4 February, 17 April, and 21 May 1866, ELG Papers, Houghton.

36. CEN to JRL, 2 August 1866, JRL Papers, Houghton.

37. James 1914, p. 257. Eventually the Ashburner-Sedgwick group bought its own house in Ashfield.

38. Ibid., p. 259.

39. CEN's recollections of Wright, in Thayer 1878, p. 90; Chauncey Wright to CEN, 18 August 1867, NP.

40. CEN's reminiscence of JBH, typescript, 20 July 1908, in box 4, Miscellaneous Papers, NP.

41. CEN to Henry C. Lea, 28 June 1866, Special Collections, Van Pelt Library, University of Pennsylvania; GWC to FLO, 6 September 1866, FLO Papers, LC.

42. Hall 1923, pp. 171, 174. The boy was G. Stanley Hall, later an eminent academic psychologist.

43. CEN to ELG, 1 November 1866, ELG Papers, Houghton.

44. CEN to JRL, 1 January 1867, JRL Papers, Houghton.

45. CEN to ELG, 17 December 1866, ELG Papers, Houghton.

46. CEN to George Perkins Marsh, 10 May 1864, University of Vermont Library.

47. CEN to FLO, 17 January 1867, and "Memorandum," 8 February 1868 (reproduced with the accompanying drawing and helpful notes in Olmsted 1992, pp. 257–61), FLO Papers, LC.

48. *New York Evening Post,* 14 October 1863, clipping in scrapbook at Cyc 1014F*, Houghton.

49. CEN to George E. Woodberry, 22 May 1881, and CEN to JBH, 19 March 1865, NP; CEN to JRL, 20–21 July 1867, JRL Papers, Houghton.

50. CEN to Meta Gaskell, 14 July 1867, NP; CEN to ELG, 8 February and 29 April 1867, ELG Papers, Houghton.

51. CEN to ELG, 4 February 1866, ELG Papers, Houghton.

52. CEN to Meta Gaskell, 27 May 1866, NP; CEN 1864q, p. 534 (quoting Goldwin Smith); CEN 1867k, p. 588.

53. CEN 1867k, p. 594.

54. Sin, of course, did regularly intervene, in consequence of Adam and Eve's obstinacy in the matter of the apple. This does not alter the point. Christianity traditionally involved getting reason and will (the two parties themselves inherited more or less from Stoicism) to cooperate toward a holy life. Christians differed over how this was to come about, not over whether both had a role. To say, as CEN did, that intellect had no role in religion (except to steer moral commitments clear of wackiness) broke with every version of Christianity, even those famously leery of creedalism: Quakers, for instance, still endorsed such doctrines as the existence of the Holy Spirit.

55. *NAR* 81 (1855): 281–82; CEN 1867k, p. 595.

56. CEN 1868b, pp. 378–79.

57. Ibid., pp. 378–79, 388.

58. CEN to JBH, 3 June 1866, NP.

59. CEN to James Parton, 11 April 1867, James Parton Papers, Houghton; CEN to ELG, 11 December 1866, ELG Papers, Houghton; CEN to Meta Gaskell, 27 May 1866, NP.

60. CEN to ELG, 22 October 1867, ELG Papers, Houghton; CEN to Meta Gaskell, 27 May 1866, NP; CEN to James Parton, 11 April 1867, James Parton Papers, Houghton.

61. CEN to Aubrey de Vere, 25 March 1867, NP; CEN to G. P. Marsh, 20 March 1867, University of Vermont Library; CEN to ELG, 22 May 1867, ELG Papers, Houghton.

62. CEN to ELG, 1 February 1867 and 24 January 1866, ELG Papers, Houghton.

63. CEN to JRL, 16 June and 20–21 July 1867, JRL Papers, Houghton; CEN to FLO, 22 June 1867, FLO Papers, LC; CEN to GWC, 24 July 1868, NP; CEN to ELG, 5 July and 15 April 1867, ELG Papers, Houghton.

64. CEN to ELG, 30 September and 13 October 1867, ELG Papers, Houghton; CEN to Meta Gaskell, 28 October 1867, NP.

65. CEN to ELG, 22 October and 3 November 1867, ELG Papers, Houghton.

66. CEN 1867r, p. 132.

67. Francis Lieber to Charles Sumner, 10 February 1868, NP; Howells 1910, p. 164. Victorian modes of translation have fallen so far out of favor as to make any such text hard to judge now.

68. James 1914, p. 257; T. W. Parsons to Mary A. Heard, n.d. [1866], Boston Public Library; *New York Daily Tribune*, 9 January 1864, clipping in scrapbook, Cyc 1014F*, Houghton; *Chicago Tribune*, 6 October 1867, clipping in HUA.

69. CEN 1866o, p. 457.

70. ELG to CEN, 4 December 1867, quoted in Ogden 1907, 1:303.

71. CEN to John Stuart Mill, 10 April 1868, Milton S. Eisenhower Library, Johns Hopkins University; John Stuart Mill to CEN, 18 March 1868, NP. Mill's short article arrived too late for the NELPS broadsides, which ceased publication at the end of August.

72. CEN to ELG, 9 and 31 January 1868, ELG Papers, Houghton; GWC to CEN, 26 January 1868, GWC Papers, Houghton.

73. CEN to Meta Gaskell, 25 March 1868, NP; CEN to Charles Sumner, 22 and 24 March 1861, Houghton.

74. CEN to ELG, 21 February 1868, ELG Papers, Houghton. By "repudiation" CEN meant partial repudiation of the national debt by paying it off in devalued greenbacks.

75. CEN to Aubrey de Vere, 29 March 1868, NP.

76. CEN to Meta Gaskell, 22 May 1868, and CEN to Charles H. Moore, 7 January 1870, NP. The safety vaults, just opened, were a brainchild and obsession of CEN's old boss Henry Lee.

77. CEN to Aubrey de Vere, 29 March 1868, NP.

CHAPTER 9: EUROPE AND ERUDITION, 1868–1872

1. CEN to GWC, 24 July 1868, NP; Reminiscences dictated by CEN, 15 July 1908, typescript, box 6, Miscellaneous Papers, NP.

2. CEN to ELG, 20 August 1868, ELG Papers, Houghton. Simon, who had French background, pronounced his surname as if French.

3. The excellent Bradley and Ousby 1987 make a rare error when (p. 108n) they put CEN with JR on 9 August (perhaps confused for 6 August); on the ninth he and SSN were staying with Dickens at Gad's Hill.

4. CEN to CN, 9 August 1868, and to Meta Gaskell, 14 August 1868, NP.

5. JR to CEN, 22 August 1868, and CEN to JR, 9 September 1868, NP; Harrison 1912, pp. 315–16.

6. CEN to JR, 9 October 1868, in Bradley and Ousby 1987, pp. 118–19. My conclusions about the topics of their conversation derives from later comments by CEN as well as contemporaneous correspondence.

7. FJC to CEN, 13 October 1868, and William Morris to CEN, 25 November 1868, NP.

8. Lease of 18 Queen's Gate Terrace, box 8, Miscellaneous Papers, NP; CEN to ELG, 25 December 1868, ELG Papers, Houghton.

9. LS to Oliver Wendell Holmes Jr., 3 January 1869, in Bicknell 1996, 1:68.

10. Edel 1953, p. 286; CEN to ELG, 8 June 1869, ELG Papers, Houghton; CEN to JRL, 1 January 1869, JRL Papers, Houghton.

11. CEN to ELG, 8 June 1869, ELG Papers, Houghton.

12. CEN to Henry James Jr., 11 April 1869, James Family Papers, Houghton; CEN to JR, 19 September 1868, NP.

13. GWC, 29 January 1869, NP; Fanny Kemble quoted in *New York Times Sunday Book Review,* 15 March 1992, p. 12. I avoid saying "Mary Ann Evans" because "George Eliot" did not use her birth name but "Mrs. Lewes"; yet to call her that without qualification short-circuits the issue here. That the focus on female rather than male behavior shows the historically typical double standard is, I suppose, so trite a point as to need no comment.

14. SSN to Chauncey Wright, 14 July 1869, NP; CEN to ELG, 13 January 1869, ELG Papers, Houghton.

15. CEN to John Stuart Mill, 29 August and 17 September 1868, Milton S. Eisenhower Library, Johns Hopkins University; CEN to JRL, 30 August 1868, JRL Papers, Houghton; CEN to Richard Grant White, 5 January 1869, NP. Emphasis CEN's.

16. Harrison 1912, pp. 315–17.

17. John Simon to CEN, 18 February 1872, NP; CEN to W. D. Howells, 10 January 1869, Howells Papers, Houghton.

18. CEN 1869e, p. 575; Fitzgerald 1980, 2:336–37 and 3:414–15.

19. CEN to GWC, 22 July 1869, NP.

20. Ibid.; CEN to Frederic Harrison, 6 August 1871, Frederic Harrison Papers, British Library of Political and Economic Science, London.

21. JR to CEN, 8 February 1869, CEN to Meta Gaskell, 28 April 1869, NP.

22. CEN to E. W. Gurney, 7 June 1869, copy in CEN Journal 1868–71, box 15, Miscellaneous Papers, NP.

23. CEN to FLO, 17 July 1869, FLO Papers, LC; CEN to Henry James Jr., 6 June 1869, James Family Papers, Houghton.

24. CEN to HWL, 17 June 1869, HWL Papers, Houghton; SSN to Chauncey Wright, 14 July 1869, NP; CEN to GWC, August 1869 ("unsent letter"), copy in CEN Journal 1869–73, box 15, Miscellaneous Papers, NP; CEN to ELG, 28 July 1869, ELG Papers, Houghton.

25. CEN 1869f and 1869g.

26. CEN to ELG, 8 June 1869, ELG Papers, Houghton; CN to Eliza Guild, 3 August 1869, NP.

27. CEN to JR, 8 October 1869, NP.

28. Ibid.

29. CEN to GWC, 22 July 1869, NP; CEN to ELG, 28 July 1869, ELG Papers, Houghton.

30. CEN to ELG, 30 August 1869, ELG Papers, Houghton.

31. SSN to Chauncey Wright, 14 July 1869, NP.

32. CEN to JRL, 15 November 1869, JRL Papers, Houghton; lease of Villa d'Elci, box 8, Miscellaneous Papers, and CEN to John Simon, 15 December 1869, NP; CEN to William Dean Howells, 4 June 1870, William Dean Howells Papers, Houghton.

33. CEN to George Perkins Marsh, 6 September 1870, University of Vermont Library; CEN to Chauncey Wright, 5 December 1869, NP; CEN to ELG, 16 January 1870, ELG Papers, Houghton.

34. CEN to JRL, 15 November 1869 and 16 January 1870, JRL Papers, Houghton. Filippo Lippi's *Incoronazione della Vergine* now hangs in the Uffizi.

35. CEN to Charles H. Moore, 7 January 1870, Autograph File, Houghton; CEN to D. G. Rossetti, 22 March 1867, Bodleian Library, Oxford (photocopy from Rossetti collection in British Columbia).

36. CEN to John Simon, 28 March 1870, and CEN to JR, 4 May 1874, NP. By no means all of the works in Assisi that CEN believed to be Giotto's are still attributed to the master himself, as distinct from followers or assistants.

37. CEN to John Dahlberg Acton, 29 April 1870, Cambridge University Library. That CEN should hold views on Catholic *Dogmengeschichte* may seem presumptuous; one needs to remember that by this time he had a pretty thorough grounding in medieval theology and that he had followed closely the arguments swirling around the council.

38. CEN to Sir John Dahlberg Acton, 29 April 1870, Cambridge University Library; CEN 1870.

39. CEN to D. G. Rossetti, 17 May 1870, Bodleian Library, Oxford; lease, box 8, Miscellaneous Papers, NP; Archivio di Stato di Siena, *Guida-Inventario dell'Archivio di Stato* (Rome, 1951), 1:xvii–xviii, and R[eale]. Archivio di Stato di Siena, *Indice Sommario delle Serie dei Documenti al 1.º Gennaio 1900* (Siena, 1900), pp. 1–3; CEN to John Simon, 22 May 1870, NP; CEN to William Dean Howells, 4 June 1870, Howells Papers, Houghton; CEN to G. P. Marsh, 6 September 1870, University of Vermont Library. I am very grateful to the staff of the Archivio di Stato for aid in the difficult task of identifying the building known in 1870 as the Villa Spannocchi (which had become in 1989 the Park Hotel, Siena's only five-star hotel).

40. Milanesi 1856; R[eale]. Archivio di Stato di Siena, *Indice Sommario delle Serie dei Documenti al 1.º Gennaio 1900* (Siena, 1900), pp. 1–3; CEN Journal 1869–73, 24 and 27 September 1870, box 15, Miscellaneous Papers, NP.

41. CEN Journal 1869–73, 23 September, 12 and 25 October 1870, box 15, Miscellaneous Papers, NP; CEN to JRL, 25 December 1870, JRL Papers, Houghton.

42. CEN to JRL, 16 June 1869, JRL Papers, Houghton; CEN to Chauncey Wright, 12 June 1870, NP.

43. Chauncey Wright to CEN, 21 March 1870, and CEN to Wright, 12 June 1870, NP.

44. CEN to Chauncey Wright, 13 September 1870, NP.

45. CEN to Chauncey Wright, 5 December 1869, NP; CEN to John Stuart Mill, 17 June 1870, Milton S. Eisenhower Library, Johns Hopkins University.

46. CEN to ELG, 24 July 1870, ELG Papers, Houghton; CEN to George P. Marsh, 25 August and 6 September 1870, University of Vermont Library; CEN to John Simon, 22 November 1870, NP.

47. CEN Journal 1869–73, 20 September and 16 October 1870, box 15, Miscellaneous Papers, NP.

48. CEN to Meta Gaskell, 12 July 1870, NP.

49. CEN Journal 1869–73, 26 October 1870, box 15, Miscellaneous Papers, NP.

50. CEN to M. E. Grant Duff, 4 January 1871, in the possession of Shiela Sokolov Grant.

51. CEN to Meta Gaskell, 25 January 1871, CEN to CN, 28 February and 4 March 1871, NP.

52. CEN to ELG, 3 November 1871, ELG Papers, Houghton.

53. Ibid. and 7 April 1871, ELG Papers, Houghton.

54. CEN to ELG, 7 April 1871, and Jane Norton to ELG, fragment, n.d. [1870–71], ELG Papers, Houghton.

55. CEN to GWC, undated fragment [late 1872/early 1873], NP.

56. Jane Norton to ELG, fragment, n.d. [1870–71], and CEN to ELG, 3 November 1871, ELG Papers, Houghton. I have silently capitalized "The" at the beginning of two sentences written with a lowercase "t" by Jane.

57. CN to Eliza Guild, 8 May 1871, NP; CEN to G. P. Marsh, 25 May 1871, University of Vermont Library; CEN to ELG, 7 April 1871, ELG Papers, Houghton.

58. CEN to S. G. Ward, 9 March 1872, Ward Papers, Houghton; CEN to FJC, 1 April 1872, NP; CEN Journal 1869–73, 21 and 29 May 1871, box 15, Miscellaneous Papers, NP.

59. CEN to JR, 26 July 1871, copied in CEN Journal 1868–71, box 15, Miscellaneous Papers, NP. CEN's insensitivity to formal-symbolic approaches to art surprises just a little, given JR's and his stress on art's spiritual meaning not to mention the importance of symbol and allegory in the *Divina Commedia*. Since Victor Cousin played a role in the development of this line of thinking, it is very unlikely that CEN was unaware of it.

60. CEN to JRL, 24 May 1871, JRL Papers, Houghton; CEN to CN, 25 June 1871, NP. The putative Veronese was a bust portrait of a woman, which CEN called "apparently the head of his wife when young."

61. CEN to ELG, 3 November 1871, ELG Papers, Houghton; CEN to Frederic Harrison, 6 August 1871, Frederic Harrison Papers, British Library of Political and Economic Science, London.

62. CEN to JR, 18 March 1871, and CEN to CN, 20 July 1871, and CEN to GWC, 29 July 1871, NP.

63. SSN to Emma Darwin, 20 November 1871, Cambridge University Library; CEN to G. P. Marsh, 15 November 1871, University of Vermont Library; CEN to S. G. Ward, 22 November 1871, Ward Papers, Houghton; CEN to GWC, 17 November 1871, NP.

64. CEN to JRL, 23 December 1871, JRL Papers, Houghton; CEN 1872a. The

article was meant for the *Fortnightly Review* but was never published, for reasons that are unclear.

65. CEN to S. G. Ward, 22 November 1871, Ward Papers, Houghton.

66. CEN to Meta Gaskell, 10 February 1872, NP.

67. CEN to S. G. Ward, 9 March 1872, Ward Papers, Houghton; JRL to CEN, 9 March 1872, JRL Papers, Houghton; Grace Norton to FJC, 19 February 1872, and Jane Norton to GWC, 17 February 1872, NP; CEN to HWL, 17 April 1872, HWL Papers, Houghton; CEN to Henry James Jr., 28 March 1872, James Family Papers, Houghton; CEN to Leslie Stephen, 13 December 1875, Berg Collection, New York Public Library.

68. Henry James Jr. to CEN, 6 May 1872, NP.

INTERLUDE

1. CEN to S. G. Ward, 9 March 1872, Ward Papers, Houghton; CEN Journal 1869–73, 11–12 April 1872, box 15, Miscellaneous Papers, NP.

2. CEN to JRL, 6 June 1872, JRL Papers, Houghton.

3. CEN Journal 1872–73, 20 April–10 May 1873, box 15, Miscellaneous Papers, NP; Henry James to Alice James, quoted in Strouse 1980, p. 157n; JRL to Mabel Lowell Burnett, 29 September 1872, in Lowell 1932, pp. 161–62; CEN to JRL, 13 November 1872, JRL Papers, Houghton.

4. Lease, box 8, Miscellaneous Papers, NP; CEN Journal 1872–73, 10 November 1872, box 15, Miscellaneous Papers, NP.

5. CEN to JRL, 19 November 1872, JRL Papers, Houghton.

6. CEN to Henry James Jr., 19 January 1873, James Family Papers, Houghton; CEN to ELG, 8 December 1872, ELG Papers, Houghton.

7. Reminiscences dictated by CEN, 17 July 1908, typescript, box 6, Miscellaneous Papers, NP; CEN to JRL, 13 November 1872, JRL Papers, Houghton.

8. CEN to JRL, Christmas 1872, JRL Papers, Houghton; CEN 1873a.

9. CEN Journal 1872–73, 16 November 1872, box 15, Miscellaneous Papers, NP; CEN to JRL, 13 November 1872, JRL Papers, Houghton.

10. In knowledge of the history of the medieval church, particularly the Inquisition, Henry Charles Lea of Philadelphia outclassed CEN; but Lea lacked CEN's breadth of expertise in the Middle Ages.

11. CEN to JRL, 20 April 1873, JRL Papers, Houghton; reminiscences dictated by CEN, 15 July 1908, typescript, box 6, Miscellaneous Papers, NP.

12. LS to ELG, 20 June 1873, in Bicknell 1996, 1:125; LS to CEN, 10 May 1873, NP. This extraordinary letter is printed in Bicknell 1996, 1:121–22.

13. CEN Journal 1872–73, 20 April–10 May 1873, box 15, Miscellaneous Papers, NP.

14. Entry for 15 May 1873, CEN's Notebook 1871–73, box 15, Miscellaneous Papers, NP; CEN to Henry James Jr., 13 March 1873, James Family Papers, Houghton; CEN to ELG, 8 December 1872, ELG Papers, Houghton.

CHAPTER 10: BEGINNING AGAIN, 1873–1878

1. C. W. Eliot to CEN, 15 August 1873, NP; CEN to S. G. Ward, 29 June 1873, Ward Papers, Houghton.

2. CEN to John Simon, 10 October 1873, NP; CEN to JRL, 24 November 1873, JRL Papers, Houghton; CEN to Henry James Jr., 5 December 1873, James Family Papers, Houghton.

3. CEN 1874g; CEN to JR, 10 January 1874, NP.

4. *Harvard University Catalogue, 1874–75.* The faculty remaining from CEN's student days were the botanist Asa Gray, the physicist Joseph Lovering, the mathematician Benjamin Peirce, the classicist Evangelinus Sophocles, and the historian Henry Torrey.

5. CEN to JRL, 24 November 1873, JRL Papers, Houghton.

6. E. W. Gurney to CEN, 14 January 1874, NP; Corporation Records, 30 January 1874, HUA.

7. *Catalogue of the College of New Jersey, 1855–56*, p. 19, and *Catalogue of the College of New Jersey, 1859–60*, pp. 5, 20; Turner and Bernard 1993, p. 75; Smyth and Lukehart 1993, pp. 58–60; Weir 1957, pp. 69–88; Galpin 1952, chap. 7; Morison 1930, p. 130; Corporation Records, 10 November 1873, 9 November and 25 May 1874, HUA. The closest thing to a survey of art instruction in American colleges up to 1874 (though superficial and at times uncomprehending) is Hiss and Fansler 1934, pp. 3–19, which, faute de mieux, scholars interested in the subject mistakenly take as authoritative.

8. Corporation Records, 30 January 1874, HUA; M. A. DeWolfe Howe, notes of conversation with Eliot, 23 May 1911, MS. notebook, Houghton (bMS Am 1826 [417]); Winterer 1996, chaps. 2–3. The word "humanity" was anything but new in education. In its academic meaning it appeared in English in the later fifteenth century, arriving via French and Italian from Latin *humanitas.* The neologism originally served to distinguish secular studies (principally of Greek and Latin texts: the *literae humaniores)* from theological ones; that is, "humanity" as opposed to "divinity." By Francis Bacon's time "humanity" had come to demarcate classical learning from both divinity on the one side and natural philosophy (science) on the other. The word in Bacon's sense was still current, though not frequently used, in American colleges prior to the mid-nineteenth century. Its now-predominant plural usage dates from the revolution herein discussed and makes a helpful flag for these profound changes.

9. Turner 1996 provides a fuller account of this educational revolution.

10. CEN to C. W. Eliot, 15 January 1874 [copy], Houghton (bMS Am 1826 [389]). This may be as good a point as any to warn against a tendency among art historians writing about CEN (e.g., Sybil Gordon Kantor, in Smyth and Lukehart 1993, pp. 161–66) to project back onto his teaching the formalist, object-oriented "Fogg Method" in art history, made orthodoxy at Harvard by his immediate successors but in fact alien to CEN. I do not believe that anyone who has actually studied the notes of CEN's Harvard lectures has made such a connection.

11. CEN to JR, 18 March 1874, NP; CEN to JRL, 23 February 1874, JRL Papers, Houghton; John Langdon Sibley, "Gore Hall," in Vaille and Clark 1875, 1:120; HWL to John Forster, 22 February 1874, in Hilen 1966–82, 5:717.

12. CEN to ELG, 12 and 30 March 1874, ELG Papers, Houghton; CEN to GWC, 3 April 1874, Vassar College Library; CEN to JR, 4 May 1874, NP.

13. LS to CEN, 27 December 1875, NP.

14. CEN to ELG, 18 September and 2 October 1874, ELG Papers, Houghton.

15. CEN to JR, 30 October 1874, NP.

16. *Harvard University Catalogue, 1874–75*, p. 62.

17. CEN 1875c. Most of the quotations in this paragraph and the following ones come from CEN, "Syllabus of Lectures, 1874–75," in Notebook 1874–75, box 2, Miscellaneous Papers, NP. The wish to advance his classes' study of Islamic art led Norton in 1877 to persuade the Yale Arabist Edward E. Salisbury to translate the Islamic section of Schnaase's *Geschichte der bildenden Künste,* to criticize the translation for Salisbury, then to help him to find a publisher.

18. CEN to JR, 10 February and 18 March 1874, and CEN to GWC, 28 January 1875, NP.

19. The old spelling of "developes" is sic.

Something ought to be said about the relation of CEN's teaching to the ideas of JR, whose disciple he is commonly taken to be. That JR much influenced CEN is without doubt, but there were great divergences between the two. Topically, CEN devoted far more attention to classical art than JR would have done. Methodologically, CEN's historicist approach owed far more to the philological tradition embodied in AN, his theory of culture more to the Unitarian tradition of self-culture, than either did to JR's writings.

20. CEN to ELG, 7 April 1871, ELG Papers, Houghton; CEN to JR, 10 February 1874, NP.

21. Norton 1819, p. 97.

22. CEN 1874d, p. 160.

23. Final examination in Fine Arts 4, 1880–81, HUC 7880.5, HUA. This is the earliest of CEN's examinations that survive; there is no reason to believe that it differed in approach from those given in 1875.

24. CEN, "Syllabus of Lectures, 1874–75," in Notebook 1874–75, box 2, Miscellaneous Papers, NP.

25. Ballou 1970, p. 236; CEN 1875a, pp. 11, 17–18, and 23. CEN cribbed especially from Alexander Gilchrist's two-volume *Life of William Blake* (London, 1863), completed by Dante Rossetti, and Algernon Swinburne's *William Blake, a Critical Essay* (London, 1863).

26. CEN to James K. Hosmer, 10 May 1875, Hosmer Papers, Minnesota Historical Society; J. A. Lowell to CEN, 19 and 23 March 1875, NP; Corporation Records, 8 and 29 March 1875, and Overseers' Records, 24 March 1875, HUA.

27. J. Elliot Cabot to CEN, 26 March 1876, and Chauncey Wright to CEN, 10 August 1870, NP. Fiske served as University Lecturer on philosophy in fall 1869; when the Overseers nearly blocked his appointment as acting professor of history in spring 1870, Eliot did not risk reappointment.

28. CEN 1876g, p. 117.

29. Overseers' Records, 14 and 28 April, 5 May 1875, HUA. This Committee on Marks developed the rank-group system that still prevails at Harvard.

30. CEN to John Simon, 15 May 1875, NP.

31. CEN to JRL, 20 September 1875, JRL Papers, Houghton; CEN to William Dwight Whitney, 17 December 1875, Whitney Family Papers, Sterling Library, Yale University.

32. Faculty Records, 29 September 1875, HUA; *Harvard University Catalogue, 1875–76*, p. 65.

33. CEN to GWC, 18 November 1875, NP; CEN to Leslie Stephen, 18 February 1876, Berg Collection, New York Public Library.

34. CEN 1876b.

35. CEN to GWC, 16 May 1876, NP; CEN to JRL, 16 August 1876, JRL Papers, Houghton.

36. CEN to M. E. Grant Duff, 18 July 1876, in possession of Shiela Sokolov Grant; CEN to GWC, 3 October 1876, NP.

37. Patton and Field 1927, p. 91. Harris 1970, p. 5, records that Harvard College students from outside New England comprised 13 percent of the total in 1850, 21 percent in 1860, 26 percent in 1870, 30 percent in 1880, and 37 percent in 1890.

38. GEW to CEN, 2 October 1877, and CEN to GEW, 11 October, NP. There seems a tinge of homoeroticism in GEW's letters to CEN in 1877 and 1878, not reciprocated by the older man.

39. JRL to CEN, 15 February 1877, Special Collections, Milton S. Eisenhower Library, Johns Hopkins University.

40. CEN to Katherine S. Godkin, 22 September 1906, ELG Papers, Houghton; JRL, HWL, C. W. Eliot, and CEN to Rutherford B. Hayes, 9 March 1877, Scrapbook 109:89, and CEN to Hayes, 22 July 1877, and GWC to Hayes, 22 July 1877, Incoming file, Hayes Papers, Rutherford B. Hayes Presidential Center, Fremont, OH.

41. JRL to Mabel Lowell Burnett, 5 June 1877, in Lowell 1932, p. 224.

42. CEN to JRL, 24 July 1877, NP.

43. CEN to GWC, 7 October 1877, NP; CEN to JRL, 31 October 1877, JRL Papers, Houghton.

44. CEN to GEW, 23 December 1877, NP; Cohn 1986, p. 260. In the matter of the Gray Collection, Charles C. Perkins spoke for the new Boston Museum of Fine Arts, ownership of the prints being ambiguous.

45. For expert advice on the plausibility of CEN's position, I thank Professor Joseph C. Carter of the University of Texas, who mentioned that similar claims about Pythagorean ratios have been made more than once concerning the Temple of Athena (or of "Ceres") at Paestum, south of Naples.

46. *Harvard University Catalogue, 1876–77*, p. 60, and *Harvard University Catalogue, 1877–78*, p. 83; HWL to JRL, 5 April 1878, in Hilen 1966–82, 6:346.

47. CEN to JRL, 20 January 1878, JRL Papers, Houghton.

48. CEN to John Simon, 3 and 6 March 1878, NP.

49. CEN to Ogden N. Rood, 13 August 1878, Butler Library, Columbia University; cf. CEN 1869a.

50. CEN to Eliot Norton, 24 June 1878, and CEN to GEW, 2 June 1878, NP.

CHAPTER 11: FRESH FOUNDATIONS OF LEARNING, 1878–1882

1. CEN to JRL, 19 May and 4 August 1878, JRL Papers, Houghton.

2. CEN to John Simon, 23 August 1879, NP. I say "apparent number" with respect to JR's letters because there is no way of knowing how many CEN destroyed.

3. CEN to HWL, 28 July 1879, HWL Papers, Houghton.

4. CEN to JRL, 22 February 1879, JRL Papers, Houghton; *Harvard University Catalogue, 1879–80*, p. 188.

5. CEN Long Version, chap. 15, n. 18 (enrollments); *Harvard University Catalogue, 1879–80*, p. 86; Contract Book, 4:9–12 and 5:241–44, and Memorandum Book, 5:70, Harper and Brothers Manuscript Collection, Butler Library, Columbia University. This course structure remained largely unchanged until 1883–84.

6. CEN 1900a, pp. 1–4. CEN's assessment of American scholarship (he made exceptions of two emigrés, E. A. Sophocles and Karl/Charles Beck) was pretty nearly on the mark, at least up to about 1870, when classical philology began rapidly to develop in the United States. As of 1879 no American had yet done anything worth mentioning in classical archaeology, though Norton might have noted the biblical archaeologist Edward Robinson (1794–1863), the only American before 1870 with international standing in archaeology. Dinsmoor 1943 surveys American studies in "Mediterranean archaeology" before 1879 (defining both "studies" and "archaeology" very broadly) while Sandys 1903–8, vol. 3, chap. 41, does the same for classical philology. The best general treatment of classical studies in the United States in the nineteenth century is Winterer 1996.

7. Minutes of General Meeting, 10 May 1879 and prefatory page, box 1, AIA Archives, Boston University.

8. Minutes of General Meeting, 10 May 1879, box 1, AIA Archives, Boston University; "Archaeological Institute of America," printed circular [June?] 1879, copy in CEN to Daniel Coit Gilman, 25 June 1879, Special Collections, Milton S. Eisenhower Library, Johns Hopkins University.

9. Minutes of General Meeting, 10 May 1879, box 1, AIA Archives, Boston University; Dinsmoor 1943, pp. 103–4.

10. "Archaeological Institute of America," printed circular [June?] 1879, copy in CEN to Daniel Coit Gilman, 25 June 1879, Special Collections, Milton S. Eisenhower Library, Johns Hopkins University; Minutes of General Meeting, 17 May 1879, box 1, AIA Archives, Boston University.

11. Gulick and Gulick 1990.

12. Contract dated 15 September 1879, in Contract Book, 4:13–15, Harper and Bros. Manuscript Collection, Butler Library, Columbia University.

13. CEN to JRL, 2 September 1879, JRL Papers, Houghton; CEN to FJC, 25 September 1879, NP.

14. CEN to John Simon, 25 September 1879, and CEN to GEW, 31 July and 25 December 1881, NP; CEN to JRL, 2 September 1879, JRL Papers, Houghton.

15. CEN 1879b(1); CEN 1879b(2); Bradley and Ousby 1987, p. 415n; CEN to GWC, 14 November 1879, NP; CEN 1880b.

16. Roper 1973, pp. 378–82, 395–97; FLO to CEN, 10 October 1879, NP.

17. Quotation (not about Niagara) from CEN to Mountstuart E. Grant Duff, 19 September 1882, courtesy of Shiela Sokolov Grant.

18. CEN to JRL, 27 June 1880, JRL Papers, Houghton.

19. CEN 1880a, p. 11.

20. JR to CEN [30 September 1870 (fragment)] and 20 January 1881, NP; CEN to John Fiske, 12 January 1880, Huntington Library.

21. CEN 1880a, pp. 10 and 56.

22. Ibid., pp. 13–16, 21–22, 177. This last judgment created some awkwardness for Norton's narrative, which was capped, so to speak, by Brunelleschi's admirable but obstinately Renaissance dome in Florence. Norton finessed the paradox by treating the dome as the literally ultimate expression of Italian civic art (p. 250).

23. Ibid., pp. 285–86.

24. CEN to JR, 3 April 1883, NP.

25. James MacAllister to CEN, 12 November 1879, and Daniel Coit Gilman to CEN, 20 May, NP.

26. CEN to Lewis Henry Morgan, 11 and 16 February, 7 and 14 March, 12 May, and 7 June 1880, Morgan Papers, University of Rochester Library; Morgan to CEN, 6 January 1880–15 January 1881, box 4A, AIA Archives, Boston University.

27. Minutes of General Meeting, 15 May 1880, box 1, AIA Archives, Boston University.

28. CEN to FLO, 22 July 1880, NP; CEN to James Longstreet [United States Minister in Istanbul], 6 December 1880, box 1, AIA Archives, Boston University (courtesy of Caroline Winterer). The Munich *Doktor* was J. R. S. Sterrett, who went on to a distinguished career in archaeology, ending as head of the Greek Department at Cornell.

29. GEW to CEN, 9 December 1880, and CEN to GWC, 13 October 1880, NP; CEN to JRL, 3 August 1880, JRL Papers, Houghton.

30. CEN to GEW, 31 January 1881, NP; executive committee minutes, 28 December 1880, box 4, AIA Archives, Boston University.

31. CEN to JRL, 11 February 1881, JRL Papers, Houghton. One of these eager students was Albert Bushnell Hart, later a distinguished American historian.

32. Charles Darwin to CEN, 30 April 1881, and GEW to CEN, 12 June 1881, NP.

33. CEN to GEW, 31 January 1881, NP.

34. Norman 1882, pp. 12–13, 62; CEN to GEW, 22 May 1881, NP.

35. CEN to George Perkins Marsh, 7 March 1881, University of Vermont Library; CEN 1882c, p. 547. This attitude helps to explain a certain distance, if not exactly coolness, between CEN and the great American classical philologist Basil Lanneau Gildersleeve.

36. CEN to George Perkins Marsh, 7 March 1881, University of Vermont Library.

37. Executive committee minutes, 24 May 1879, box 4, and minutes of General Meeting, 21 May 1881, box 1, AIA Archives, Boston University; CEN to Andrew Dickson White, 27 October 1881, White Papers, Department of Manuscripts and University Archives, Cornell University Libraries; Lord 1947, chap. 1; CEN 1900a, pp. 4–5.

38. CEN to JRL, 31 August 1881, JRL Papers, Houghton.

39. Ibid.

40. F. R. Pollock to CEN, 19 October 1881, NP; CEN to JRL, 1 December 1881, and JRL to CEN, 31 October 1881, JRL Papers, Houghton. The *Comment* was finally published in 1887, edited by James Lacaita.

41. Edward Robinson to CEN, 14 November 1881, William C. Lawton to CEN, 1 November 1881, Charles W. Bradley to CEN, 15 December 1881, box 1, AIA Archives, Boston University (courtesy of Caroline Winterer).

42. CEN to John Simon, 6 February 1882, NP.

43. CEN to GEW, 22 January 1882, and CEN to John Simon, 6 February 1882, NP.

44. CEN to John Simon, 6 February 1882, and CEN to GEW, 22 January 1882, NP.

45. W. G. Collingwood to CEN, 7 March 1882, and CEN to GEW, 1 June 1882, NP; CEN to JRL, 28 March 1882, JRL Papers, Houghton.

46. "The Proposed School at Athens," *New York Times,* 31 March 1882 (clipping), box 2, AIA Archives, Boston University (courtesy of Caroline Winterer); CEN to GWC, 16 April 1882, A[dolf]. Michaelis to CEN, 13 July 1882, and FLO to CEN, 17 July 1882, NP.

47. CEN to President Reid, 23 May 1882 (copy), NP.

48. CEN to J. B. Harrison, 23 July [1882], NP.

49. Ibid.

50. CEN to JRL, 3 August 1882, JRL Papers, Houghton; Slater 1964, pp. 65–68; CEN Long Version, chap. 15, nn. 208 and 209; Conway 1904, 2:407–13.

51. CEN to John Simon, 21 September 1882, NP; CEN to JRL, 6 August 1882, JRL Papers, Houghton.

52. Harvard *Crimson,* undated clipping [1927], in CEN folder 3, HUA.

53. W. W. Goodwin to CEN, 6–18 October 1882, NP.

CHAPTER 12: OLYMPUS ASCENDED, 1882–1886

1. CEN to Caroline Marsh, 5 August 1882, University of Vermont Library.

2. GWC to JBH, 10 August 1882, Beinecke Library, Yale University; CEN to FLO, 4 August 1882, NP.

3. *Harvard University Catalogue, 1882–83,* pp. 91–92; CEN to JR, 16 December 1882, and CEN to GWC, 7 November 1882, NP.

4. Veysey 1979, p. 89, identifies the American School as the first research institute in the humanities. Ironically, he refers on the preceding page to the "genteel amateurism" of CEN, apparently unaware of CEN's role in establishing what Veysey regards as a hard-nosed professional institution. Such confusion is common even among first-rate historians. It results from anachronistic projection into the late nineteenth century of mid- and late-twentieth-century ideals of research and the consequent dismissal of other models of research as amateurish.

5. CEN to John Simon, 21 September 1882, and Mary Carlyle to CEN, 9 August 1882, NP.

6. Charles Eliot Norton and Niagara Falls Collection, Misc. Manuscripts Collection, LC, 1:111–23, is the chief source for information about the Niagara Association. CEN 1883b was nominally a review of Samuel Waddington, *Arthur Hugh Clough: A Monograph* (London, 1883).

7. CEN to GEW, 10 and 28 January and 6 May 1883, CEN to JR, 3 April 1883, and CEN to John Simon, 13 August 1883, NP; GWC to CEN, 20 March 1883, GWC Papers, Houghton.

8. CEN to JRL, 22 May 1883, JRL Papers, Houghton; CEN to his children, 28 June 1883, in *Letters,* 2:148–49.

9. CEN to his children, 28 June 1883, in *Letters,* 2:149–50; CEN to JRL, 30 June 1883, JRL Papers, Houghton.

10. CEN to Elizabeth G. Norton, 27 July 1883, and to Sara Norton, 11 August 1883, in *Letters*, 2:150, 152, 154.

11. CEN to John Simon, 8 September 1883, and JR to CEN, 2 August 1883, NP.

12. JR's "Last Will and Testament," 1883, bMS Am 1088 (6207), and CEN to John Simon, 8 September 1883, NP.

13. CEN to Edward Lee-Childe, 29 September 1883, in *Letters*, 2:156–57.

14. *Harvard University Catalogue, 1883–84*, p. 92. CEN also settled on a standard biennial alternation, in Year A (starting with 1883–84) offering surveys of ancient art and medieval art, then in Year B more specialized courses on Florence (fall), Venice (spring), and Greece (both terms).

15. CEN to JRL, 17 November 1883, JRL Papers, Houghton.

16. CEN to JRL, 27 December 1883 and 10 February 1884, JRL Papers, Houghton; CEN 1887a, pp. v–vi.

17. Rollins 1958 is the most thorough and judicious study of the entire controversy. For the publishing aspect see CEN to J. R. Osgood, 7 April 1884, Manuscripts Department, University of Virginia Library; CEN to J. R. Osgood, 22 May 1884, Benjamin Holt Ticknor Collection, LC.

18. Edward Fitzgerald to CEN, 13 July 1882 and 12 May 1883, JR to CEN, 30 August 1882, and CEN to JBH, 22 April [1883?], NP; CEN to LS, 29 November 1884, Berg Collection, New York Public Library.

19. CEN to JR, 2 April 1873, in Bradley and Ousby 1987, pp. 285–86.

20. JR to CEN, 20 October 1885, NP; CEN 1886b, pp. 15–16; CEN to LS, 4 October 1885, Berg Collection, New York Public Library.

21. General Meeting minutes, 17 May 1884 and 11 October 1884, box 1, and Council minutes, 20 November 1884, box 4, AIA Archives, Boston University.

22. Norman MacColl to Henry Arthur Bright, 2[?] March 1883 (enclosed in Bright to CEN, 11 March 1883), NP.

23. Printed oration tipped into Houghton copy of *Letters;* CEN to Eliot Norton, 23 June 1884, in *Letters*, 2:160–62.

24. Georgie Burne Jones to CEN, 19 June 1884, NP; CEN to Frederic Harrison, 12 August 1901, Frederic Harrison Papers, British Library of Political and Economic Science, London School of Economics; Edward Burne Jones to CEN, "Saturday" [21 June 1884], NP.

25. JRL to CEN, 17 October 1884, JRL Papers, Houghton.

26. GEW to CEN, 31 October 1886, and Flora L. Shaw to CEN, 1 April 1885, NP.

27. CEN to JRL, 16 November 1884, JRL Papers, Houghton. The jingle played off the former senator and secretary of state's reputation for graft and generally a fairly distant acquaintance with honesty:
Blaine, Blaine, James G. Blaine,
Continental liar from the State of Maine.

28. CEN to JRL, 16 November 1884, JRL Papers, Houghton.

29. CEN to FLO, 5 March 1885, NP; JBH, "The Movement for the Redemption of Niagara," *New Princeton Review* 1 (1886): 245, quoted in Roper 1973, p. 396.

30. CEN 1884b. In 1884 CEN also recanted in print his attribution to Giotto twenty years earlier of the supposed portrait of the poet in the Bargello: CEN 1884c. Fay's *Concordance* was published in 1888.

31. CEN to Aubrey de Vere, undated fragment [summer 1885], NP; CEN to LS, 6 March 1885, Berg Collection, New York Public Library. CEN referred specifically to HWL's verse translation, of which he thought highly.

32. Cate 1982, p. 47; CEN to LS, 4 October 1885, Berg Collection, New York Public Library.

33. CEN to LS, 4 October 1885, Berg Collection, New York Public Library; CEN to Macmillan and Co., 13 August, 17 September, 9 November 1885, and Memorandum of Agreement, 1 December 1885, British Library Add. MS. 55033, ff. 65–72, 75–76, 88v.

34. JR to CEN, 10 March 1883, NP; CEN to LS, 13–24 December 1885, Berg Collection, New York Public Library; CEN 1886a, 1:v–vi, x–xii; CEN 1888a, vol. 1, preface.

35. It is characteristic that when Seth Ames published in 1854 a second edition of the *Works* of his father Fisher Ames (the Federalist politician), originally edited in 1809 by John Kirkland, he included a large selection of Ames's letters, the publication of which had evidently not crossed Kirkland's mind.

36. CEN 1886b, p. 17.

37. CEN to LS, 13–24 December 1885, Berg Collection, New York Public Library. Even Hyder Rollins failed fully to grasp how strongly CEN felt about scholarly accuracy (Rollins 1958).

38. William M. Sloane to CEN, 9 August 1886, J. A. Froude to JR, undated fragment [autumn 1886], enclosed in JR to CEN, 23 March 1887, NP. Simultaneity was necessary to ensure copyright in both countries.

39. The American minister was indeed the author of *Ben-Hur*.

40. J. T. Clarke to CEN, 5 April 1885, box 1, AIA Archives, Boston University (courtesy of Caroline Winterer).

41. H. C. Lea to CEN, 7 November 1884, *American Journal of Archaeology* file, box 4, AIA Archives, Boston University (courtesy of Caroline Winterer). In 1886 Frothingham moved to Princeton, where he spent the rest of his career.

42. A. L. Frothingham Jr. to CEN, 12 and 30 November 1884, *American Journal of Archaeology* file, box 4, AIA Archives, Boston University. The four "departments" planned were classical, American, "Christian" (medieval), and "Oriental" (Middle Eastern) archaeology.

43. CEN and A. L. Frothingham, "Circular to Literary Contributors," *American Journal of Archaeology* file, box 4, AIA Archives, Boston University.

44. CEN to JRL, 20 March 1885, JRL Papers, Houghton.

45. Charles H. Moore to CEN, 30 May 1886, NP. The Harvard *President's Reports* (available in HUA) show enrollments of around 75 in CEN's Fine Arts 3 and 4 in the early 1880s, rising to about 125 in the mid-1880s and to 250 by the end of the decade.

46. Patton and Field 1927, pp. 86–87, 91 (first quotation from John Jay Chapman).

47. Chapman, quoted in ibid.; William Roscoe Thayer, quoted in Hazen 1926, p. 37.

48. Hazen 1926, p. 37; diary entry for 12 June 1944, in Berenson 1952; Samuels 1979, p. 32.

49. Quoted in Patton and Field 1927, pp. 86–87.

50. The slightly more ancient and even more tightly interbred ruling class of Charleston, South Carolina, came closer to the ideal but, what with the Civil War, could hardly appeal to Yankees. The Quaker elite of Philadelphia put itself out of the running by its sectarian antecedents.

51. R. Lanciani to CEN, 24 June 1886, NP.

CHAPTER 13: YEARS THAT BRING THE PHILOLOGIC MIND, 1886–1891

1. W. R. Ware to CEN, 31 August and 4 October 1886, and J. W. White to CEN, 7 October 1886, box 2, AIA Archives, Boston University. During the First World War, Waldstein anglicized his Germanic surname to Walston; most references to him use this latter form.

2. Harrison 1912, pp. 315, 320; CEN to JRL, 26 October 1886, JRL Papers, Houghton; Sara Norton's scrapbook of social life, November–December 1886, fMS Am 1193.3, Houghton.

3. CEN to Bayard Wyman 9 August 1887, Manuscripts Department, University of Virginia Library. When CEN began the Christmas dinners is unclear.

4. Hazen 1926, pp. 76–77, 86–87; Carlyle 1904, 1:xii. Alexander Carlyle implicitly blamed the default on CEN's advancing age; this made sense in 1904 but hardly explained why publication ceased fifteen years before.

5. *Harvard University Catalogue, 1886–87,* pp. 105, 111; *Harvard University Catalogue, 1887–88,* p. 112. My emphasis.

6. CEN to JRL, 5 September 1887, JRL Papers, Houghton.

7. Ibid. and 17 October 1887, JRL Papers, Houghton; Georgiana Burne Jones to CEN, 9 March 1888, NP.

8. CEN to JRL, 24 June 1888, JRL Papers, Houghton.

9. CEN to JRL, 15 August 1888, JRL Papers, Houghton; CEN to JBH, 21 June 1888, NP.

10. CEN 1890 Ashfield Dinner address, quoted in Gulick and Gulick 1990, p. 26; CEN to James H. Weeks, 25 August 1888, Special Collections, Miami University Library.

11. *Greenfield* (Mass.) *Gazette,* 25 August 1888, and *Boston Post,* 24 August 1888, clippings in Sara Norton's scrapbook of social life, f. 48, fMS Am 1193.3, Houghton.

12. CEN to JBH, 21 June 1888, NP; CEN 1888b, pp. 349, 352.

13. CEN to JBH, 26 July 1888, NP.

14. CEN 1889e; CEN to GWC, 25 November 1888, NP; *New York Times,* 23 November 1888, clipping in Sara Norton's scrapbook of social life, f. 54, fMS Am 1193.3, Houghton. The institution was the Slater Museum in Norwich, Conn.

15. CEN 1888c, p. 324; CEN 1889c, pp. 636–38.

16. CEN 1895a, pp. 16, 22, 24; William Dean Howells to CEN, 15 December 1886, NP; CEN to R. W. Gilder, 20 March 1889, Huntington Library.

17. William Roscoe Thayer quoted in Hazen 1926, p. 40.

18. CEN to GWC, 13 January 1889, NP.

19. James Loeb to CEN, 19 November 1890, Seth Low to CEN, 21 November 1890, and William C. Lawton to "the Subscribers to the Delphi Fund," March 1891, NP; CEN 1889f.

20. Thomas W. Ludlow to CEN, 21 May 1890, and Ernst Curtius quoted in

W. R. Ware to CEN, 9 April 1888, box 2, AIA Archives, Boston University; W. H. Waddington to CEN, 31 August 1888, NP. The stepchild, Americanist archaeology, was never abandoned by the AIA but found other institutions for its chief support.

21. CEN to Seth Low, 16 January 1891, box 3, and F. J. de Peyster to CEN, 15 September 1881, box 2, AIA Archives, Boston University (courtesy of Caroline Winterer); CEN 1900a, pp. 8–9.

22. Martin Brimmer to CEN, 9 November 1887, NP; CEN to Provost of the University of Pennsylvania, 9 June 1888, Special Collections, Van Pelt Library, University of Pennsylvania.

23. Faculty: McCaughey 1974, pp. 321–24; courses: *Harvard University Catalogue, 1890–91,* p. 73. For examples of advising and the job network, see respectively CEN to ?Craven, 21 September 1888, Special Collections, Miami University Library, and same to same, 2 July 1889, Beinecke Library, Yale University; and CEN to ?Lawton, 26 August 1889, Amherst College Library. The Harvard Fine Arts Department gave its first Ph.D. in 1913: Shively n.d., p. 11.

24. GEW to CEN, 10 October 1880, NP. My emphasis.

25. Downing, MacDougall, and Pearson 1965, pp. 30–31; Whiting 1965, pp. 13–14. The streets were Irving, Farrar, and Scott; in 1889 James moved into 95 Irving, Josiah Royce into 103 Irving.

26. CEN to GWC, 2 October 1888, and Georgie Burne-Jones to CEN, 20 September 1890, NP. Within a short time Arthur had married "a rich wife" in England.

27. LS to CEN, 8 September and 3 December 1889, Julia Stephen to CEN, 10 July 1890, and CEN to GWC, 20 November 1887, NP; CEN to JRL, 23 January 1887, JRL Papers, Houghton. Harvard awarded LS an honorary degree during his visit, presumably at CEN's instigation.

28. CEN to W. P. Garrison, 22 April 1905, Bryn Mawr College Library. Kate Stephens later took umbrage at what she deemed Heath's and CEN's unfairness toward herself in the *Heart of Oak* business, publishing an extended, and so far as I can judge unfounded, even perhaps paranoid, attack on CEN long after his death.

29. CEN 1887c. CEN added that one seldom found in the *Divina Commedia* "such an inversion of the natural order of the words as to interfere with the plainness of the diction and the easy flow of meaning." This was certainly not true of English verse translations.

30. CEN's *Divine Comedy* showed in its apparatus the same restraint as his Carlyle editions: brief footnotes, only when needed to identify obscure characters and explain unclear metaphors.

31. *Nation* 53 (1891): 377; La Piana 1948, pp. 128–29.

32. Jane LeCompte, Houghton Mifflin Co. Corporate Communications Manager, to author, 13 October 1994.

33. Samuel G. Ward to CEN, 20 July 1902, NP.

34. CEN to O. W. Holmes, 30 August 1894, Oliver Wendell Holmes Sr. Collection, Manuscript Division, LC.

35. CEN, "Dante. Lecture I," typescript, box 13, Miscellaneous Papers, NP.

36. James 1934, p. 204; W. W. Vernon to CEN, 27 November 1891, NP; La Piana 1948, p. 130.

37. La Piana 1948, p. 130.

38. AN to [Thomas William Parsons], 7 June 1844, Houghton.

39. Josiah Royce to CEN, 22 May 1889, courtesy of Leslie J. Workman; invitation to Classical Club meeting in box 4P251, William James Battle Papers, Center for American History, University of Texas at Austin.

40. Asa Gray, Joseph Lovering, and Henry Torrey: Story 1980, pp. 214–15.

41. CEN 1900a, p. 11; CEN 1899f, p. 192; CEN to John Fiske, 6 April 1892, Huntington Library.

42. Compare *Oxford English Dictionary*, s.v. "philology," for instances both of the broad older usage and uncertainty about the late nineteenth-century meaning. The *OED*'s definition of "modern" (i.e., late Victorian) usage omits entirely the then (and now) common application of the word in "classical philology."

43. AN, Sketch of the first course of Dexter Lectures, undated MS. [1813], HUA. This is not to say that such efforts unambiguously improved understanding of the object of study. The choice of one context often tore a "text" out of another context; as Stephen Alter has reminded me, some Victorian philologists attacked the discipline of comparative grammar precisely for abstracting languages from their proper contexts. I have often had occasion to thank Dr. Alter for unambiguously improving my own understanding of Victorian philology.

Because of the fragmentation of philological enterprises into distinct disciplines during the later eighteenth and the nineteenth centuries, we lack a general history of the philological effort, although surveys of the large branches exist; for example, classical philology and linguistics. And substantial pieces have been very acutely examined in, for instance, the work of Arnaldo Momigliano on scholarship in classical antiquity, of Anthony Grafton on early modern philology, of Thomas Trautmann on the nineteenth-century connections between philology and anthropology, of Stephen Alter on nineteenth-century "science of language."

44. Alter 1999; Trautmann 1987.

45. William Roscoe Thayer quoted in Hazen 1926, p. 40.

46. CEN to Meta Gaskell, 25 January 1871, CEN to John Simon, 1 January 1871 and 21 September 1882, and CEN to GEW, 4 March 1883, NP.

47. CEN to GEW, 4 March 1883, NP; CEN to JRL, 27 June and 3 August 1880, JRL Papers, Houghton; CEN to R. U. Johnson, 13 April 1900, Huntington Library; William Roscoe Thayer quoted in Hazen 1926, p. 41.

48. Arthur R. Marsh to CEN, 26 December 1889 and 27 November 1888, NP. On Marsh, see CEN Long Version, chap. 17, n. 160. The origins of "disciplinary specialization," a subject far too complex to tackle here, are tentatively traced in Turner 1996.

49. Nietzche 1887, pp. 322–23 (bk. 5, sec. 366).

50. Morgan 1898, p. 7; William James to Alice G. James, 7–8 February 1888, James Family Papers, Houghton (courtesy of Deborah Coon).

51. George M. Lane to CEN, 21 and 25 March 1894, NP.

52. CEN to William Dwight Whitney, 25 February 1867, Whitney Family Papers, Sterling Library, Yale University.

53. CEN 1900a, pp. 11–12. I have silently removed a comma to smooth an awkward phrase.

CHAPTER 14: TO MAKE DEMOCRACY SAFE FOR THE WORLD,
1891–1895

1. CEN to Oliver Wendell Holmes, 4 November 1891, Oliver Wendell Holmes Sr. Collection, LC; CEN to LS, 2 May 1892, Berg Collection, New York Public Library.

2. CEN to F. Max Müller, 19 September 1892, Bodleian Library, Oxford.

3. CEN to Bliss Carman, 16 August 1891, Manuscripts Department, University of Virginia Library; CEN to Annie Adams Fields, 18 September 1891, Society for the Preservation of New England Antiquities, Boston (copy in JRL Papers, Houghton); CEN to Sydney C. Cockerell, 7 April 1892, Pierpont Morgan Library, New York; CEN to LS, 25 September 1891, Berg Collection, New York Public Library; CEN to William J. Stillman, 28 August 1892, William James Stillman Collection, Schaffer Library, Union College, Schenectady, New York.

4. CEN to Kate Stephens, 4 July [c. 1891–93], NP. For details of negotiations, see CEN Long Version, chap. 18, pp. 3–4, nn. 16–17.

5. Quoted in Ballou 1970, p. 383. I have silently corrected "Chauncy" to "Chauncey" in the quotation.

6. CEN to JBH, 18 November 1891, NP; CEN 1893c, p. 849; CEN to LS, 3 June 1892, Berg Collection, New York Public Library.

7. CEN to Kate Stephens, 9 October 1891 and 7 February 1892, NP; CEN to D. C. Heath, 9 March 1892, American Antiquarian Society.

8. CEN to Samuel G. Ward, 24 February 1892, Ward Papers, Houghton.

9. CEN to Kate Stephens, 16 July 1892, NP.

10. CEN to John Simon, 21 July 1892, NP; GWC to CEN, 18 February 1892, GWC Papers, Houghton; CEN 1893c, p. 846.

11. CEN to Frederic Coggeshall, 17 October 1892, and Martin Brimmer to CEN, 15 December 1892, NP; Forbes n.d., p. 4; CEN 1892c.

12. Howe 1934, p. 68; Hines 1974, p. 115; Daniel H. Burnham to CEN, 30 March 1893, NP.

13. CEN to ?Marsh, 3 August 1893, Princeton University Library; CEN to Kate Stephens, 15 and 27 July 1893, NP.

14. Flora Shaw to CEN, 20 July 1895, NP.

15. CEN to Eliot Norton, 14 September 1893, NP.

16. CEN to William Morton Payne, 5 March 1894, Payne Papers, Newberry Library.

17. CEN to Henry Blake Fuller, 30 October 1893, and CEN to GEW, 13 October 1893, NP.

18. Henry Blake Fuller to CEN, 30 October 1893, NP.

19. CEN to Henry Blake Fuller, 30 October 1893, NP.

20. CEN to GEW, 11 November 1893, NP; CEN to LS, 20 March 1896, Berg Collection, New York Public Library.

21. FJC to CEN, n.d. [late January 1894], NP.

22. Clipping from Pueblo, Colo., newspaper, in Sara Norton's scrapbook of social life, f. 71, fMS Am 1193.3, Houghton; programs of the Norton Art Club, with note in Sara Norton's hand, box 16, Miscellaneous Papers, NP.

23. CEN to Lawrence Turnbull, 4 December 1893, and Daniel Coit Gilman to CEN, 8 December 1893, NP.

24. CEN to Edward Moore, 6 March 1894, Bodleian Library, Oxford; CEN to Daniel Coit Gilman, 5 and 23 March 1894, Special Collections, Milton S. Eisenhower Library, Johns Hopkins University; CEN to Nathan Haskell Dole, 17 April 1894, NP.

25. The suppressed first printing (which apparently comprised only five volumes) survives in Houghton.

26. CEN 1894c, preface (in all volumes).

27. Ibid.; [CEN], "Contents & character of the *Heart of Oak* books," undated MS. [1893], box 6, CEN letters, NP (bMS Am 1088.2).

28. CEN 1894c, preface.

29. [CEN], "Contents & character of the *Heart of Oak* books," undated MS. [1893], box 6, CEN letters, NP (bMS Am 1088.2); Stephens 1927, pp. 14, 51–52.

30. AN, "Inaugural Discourse" (1819), in Norton 1852, pp. 96–97.

31. CEN to JBH, 13 March 1894, NP. For smoother reading I have twice modified punctuation in this quotation and added the word "place" in the phrase "a pleasant [place] for a rational man," where CEN clearly omitted an intended noun.

32. CEN to Arthur Helps, 1 December 1851, NP; CEN 1905b, pp. 13–14; Solomon 1956, passim.

33. CEN to JBH, 29 December 1879, NP.

34. CEN, "Art in America," January 1898, typescript, box 6, Miscellaneous Papers, NP.

35. CEN, "Art in America," January 1898, typescript, box 6, Miscellaneous Papers, NP; CEN to LS, 1 March 1893, Berg Collection, New York Public Library; George M. Lane to CEN, 25 March 1894, and CEN to Goldwin Smith, 31 January 1905, NP; CEN 1868b, pp. 381–82.

36. CEN to Richard Garnett, 6 March 1894, Harry Ransom Humanities Research Center, University of Texas; CEN to ELG, 29 January 1893, ELG Papers, Houghton.

37. CEN to Mountstuart E. Grant Duff, 19 September 1882, courtesy of Shiela Sokolov Grant; CEN to JBH, 29 December 1879, and CEN to LS, 3 September 1889, NP.

38. CEN to LS, 3 September 1889, NP.

39. CEN to Chauncey Wright, 13 September 1870, NP.

40. CEN to Mountstuart E. Grant Duff, 19 September 1882, courtesy of Shiela Sokolov Grant; CEN to Samuel G. Ward, 8 August 1900, NP; CEN to JRL, 15 August 1888, JRL Papers, Houghton.

41. CEN to JBH, 2 October 1863, NP; CEN 1889e; CEN, "Lectures on Roman & Mediaeval Art 1894. October 1894," manuscript notebook, box 1, Miscellaneous Papers, NP; CEN 1908b, p. 48.

42. CEN, "The Culture of the Imagination [1899]," typescript, box 1, Miscellaneous Papers, NP.

43. CEN, "Art in America [1898]," typescript, box 6, Miscellaneous Papers, NP.

44. CEN 1895f.

45. Haskin 1989, pp. 882–83; Scudder 1901, 2:102; CEN to Mary Aitken Carlyle,

4 March 1895, *Letters,* 2:224; CEN 1896d; Haskin 1985, p. 247; Mabel Lowell Burnett to CEN, n.d. [c. 1894], JRL Papers, Houghton. JRL never suffered the delusion that his early Donne collection (a "reader's" edition) answered the need for an adequate scholarly edition. I am grateful for much enlightenment from Professor Dayton Haskin about nineteenth-century Donne scholarship and CEN's role in it.

46. CEN to Mary Aitken Carlyle, 4 March 1895, *Letters,* 2:224.

47. Haskin 1989; CEN 1896d.

48. Child 1920, p. 143; William Dean Howells to CEN, 19 April 1895, NP.

49. Forbes quoted in Jones 1985, p. 24. After a new Fogg Museum was erected in the twentieth century, the old one was renamed Hunt Hall after its architect. The patina of age did not improve its looks. Harvard tore it down in the 1970s.

50. CEN to Eliot Norton, 14 April 1895, NP.

51. CEN to ELG, 7 January 1895, ELG Papers, Houghton; CEN to Mountstuart E. Grant Duff, 3 October 1894, courtesy of Shiela Sokolov Grant; CEN to LS, 8 July 1894, Berg Collection, New York Public Library.

52. CEN to John Simon, 21 July 1892, NP.

53. CEN to LS, 15 September 1895, Berg Collection, New York Public Library.

CHAPTER 15: THE INVENTION OF WESTERN CIVILIZATION, 1895–1898

1. Reuben 1996.

2. CEN to Samuel G. Ward, 3 July 1897, and CEN to George H. Palmer, 1 June 1899, NP; CEN 1899f, p. 192; CEN to William James, 12 December 1899, James Family Papers, Houghton. I refer not to the strict positivism of the Comtean cult but to the widespread scientistic epistemology associated with, for example, Mill.

3. Bernhard Berenson to CEN, 18 June 1898, folder of uncatalogued CEN correspondence, Boston Public Library.

4. CEN to Edwin Arlington Robinson, 14 December 1896, Special Collections, Colby College Library; CEN to Annie Adams Field, 24 October 1897, Huntington Library; CEN to Richard Garnett, 20 January and 6 June 1896, Harry Ransom Humanities Research Center, University of Texas at Austin. A handful of university presidents—Eliot of Harvard and perhaps Gilman of Hopkins, Angell of Michigan, White of Cornell, and Porter of Yale—enjoyed name recognition equal to CEN's; but their reputations, primarily as academic administrators, were narrower, their influence among the general populace more constricted.

5. LS to CEN, 21 December 1895, NP.

6. CEN to ELG, 22 December 1895, ELG Papers, Houghton; CEN to William Lloyd Garrison II, 1 January 1896 (typescript copy), Sophia Smith Collection, Smith College.

7. CEN to Richard Garnett, 20 January 1896, and Dewitt Miller's copy of CEN 1853a, Harry Ransom Humanities Research Center, University of Texas at Austin.

8. CEN to ELG, 22 December 1895, ELG Papers, Houghton; Samuel F. Clarke to CEN, 1 February 1896, and clipping from *Rochester Post Express,* 4 February 1896, NP.

9. CEN to ELG, 13 March 1867, ELG Papers, Houghton.

10. CEN 1896b, pp. 641–50.

11. Ibid., p. 651; CEN to Horace Howard Furness, 28 July 1896, Special Collections, Van Pelt Library, University of Pennsylvania.

12. *New York Times,* 4 August 1918 (Richard Norton obituary).

13. General folder, class of 1846, and Class Book, HUA.

14. CEN to Carl Schurz, 23 July 1896, Schurz Papers, LC; undated clipping [13 August 1896?], printing CEN's dedicatory speech, NP.

15. CEN to JBH, 4 March 1897, NP.

16. CEN 1897b; CEN to H. E. Scudder, 14 November 1896, Houghton Mifflin Co. Papers, Houghton; CEN 1897c, p. 111.

17. CEN to Charles W. Eliot, 13 May 1897, box 109, folder 126, Eliot Papers, HUA.

18. *President's Report for 1897–98,* p. 81 (copy in HUA).

19. Lovett 1948, p. 38, relates the old story; Forbes n.d., p. 4, corrects it.

20. Patton and Field 1927, p. 91; Sedgwick 1946, pp. 70–71; Howe 1946, 1:211; Forbes n.d., p. 8.

21. Sedgwick 1946, pp. 70–71; Brown 1948, pp. 146–47.

22. C. T. Copeland, "Norton in His Letters," *Harvard Bulletin,* 29 October 1913, clipping in HUA; Royce 1970, pp. 531–32.

23. Eliot 1941, pp. 32–33; Jones 1985, pp. 24–25; Howe and Adams 1914, p. 65; Sedgwick 1946, pp. 70–71. Lane was the son of George Martin Lane, which presumably mattered, but identified CEN as key.

24. Hazen 1926, p. 37; Albert Bushnell Hart to CEN, 28 May 1896, and Barrett Wendell to CEN, 20 October 1888, NP.

25. CEN 1901c, p. 307.

26. *New York Press,* 25 February 1898 (clipping in box 17, Miscellaneous Papers, NP). For an overview of this revolution, unaccountably neglected by historians, see Turner 1996. MIT, originally located in Boston, did not move to its Cambridge campus until 1916.

27. CEN's penciled notes on *Reports of the Joint Committee on the Organization of the University* (1907), HUG 1615.75, and lecture notes by F. B. Whittemore, lecture 1, Fine Arts 4, 1894–95, HUA.

28. CEN to William Lloyd Garrison II, 1 January 1896 (typescript copy), Sophia Smith Collection, Smith College; CEN to Paul Elmer More, 25 April 1898, Paul Elmer More Papers, Princeton University Library.

29. CEN to E. L. Burlingame, 15 and 20 May, 2 June 1896, Charles Scribner's Author Files, Princeton University Library; CEN to Charles F. Thwing, 9 November 1896, Records of the Office of the President, Office Files of Charles F. Thwing (1DB6), Box 6, Case Western Reserve University Archives; CEN 1896c.

30. CEN to LS, 19 June 1897, Berg Collection, New York Public Library.

31. CEN's penciled notes on *Reports of the Joint Committee on the Organization of the University* (1907), HUG 1615.75, HUA.

32. Howe and Adams 1914, p. 66; Sedgwick 1946, p. 71; William R. Thayer in Hazen 1926, p. 40. CEN's big courses moved from the unsatisfactory second floor of Massachusetts Hall into Sanders Theater, Harvard's largest venue, in 1893 or 1894: Forbes n.d., p. 5.

33. CEN 1900a, p. 8; "Notes on Fine Arts 3: Compiled from Stenographic Reports by W. E. Weaver" (typescript, 1898, Nor 5260.12F, Houghton), p. 1. On "the humanities" in its plural form as a neologism, see chap. 10, note 8, and, at greater length, Turner 1996.

34. CEN to William D. Howells, 28 July 1895, NP.

35. Ibid.; lecture notes by H. R. Gledhill, Fine Arts 3, 1890–91, HUA.

36. CEN to LS, 20–23 December 1897, Berg Collection, New York Public Library; [CEN], *Report of the Committee on the Fine Arts,* bound in *Reports of Visiting Committees of the Board of Overseers of Harvard College, I to CIX,* HUA.

37. CEN 1897a, p. 4315; CEN 1895d, p. 345.

38. CEN, "The Culture of the Imagination" (1899), typescript, box 1, Miscellaneous Papers, NP; CEN 1876h, p. 133.

39. Stewart 1843, p. 315; CEN, "The Culture of the Imagination" (1899), typescript, box 1, Miscellaneous Papers, NP.

40. CEN, "The Culture of the Imagination" (1899), typescript, box 1, Miscellaneous Papers, NP; CEN 1895d, p. 345; CEN 1897a, p. 4315; lecture notes by Harry Fletcher Brown, History of Ancient Art, 1888–89, vol. 1, lecture 1, HUA. The parallel to *Bildung* is unmistakeable. Though the German idea had no influence on CEN, there is good reason for the family resemblance; *Bildung,* after all, emerged from a culture in which philology supplied the great model of erudition.

41. CEN, "The Culture of the Imagination" (1899), typescript, box 1, Miscellaneous Papers, NP; Stewart 1843, pp. 326–28.

42. CEN 1901a(1); CEN to JBH, 17 November 1902 (typescript copy), NP; lecture notes by Harry Fletcher Brown, History of Ancient Art, 1888–89, vol. 1, lecture 1, HUA; CEN, "Bryn Mawr [graduation] Address," typescript, June 1896, box 1, Miscellaneous Papers, NP.

43. CEN, "Bryn Mawr [graduation] Address," typescript, June 1896, box 1, Miscellaneous Papers; CEN to William D. Howells, 28 July 1895, NP; lecture notes by Harry Fletcher Brown, History of Ancient Art, 1888–89, vol. 1, lecture 1, HUA.

44. "Notes on Fine Arts 3: Compiled from Stenographic Reports by W. E. Weaver" (typescript, 1898, Nor 5260.12F, Houghton), pp. 2–3.

45. Ibid., p. 12. I suppose it obvious that Western civilization is a product of the post-1450 age of European expansion and imperialism in the sense that one could only conceive "our civilization" in contrast to other civilizations. At the same time, CEN's teaching of Western civilization was not dismissive of others, merely silent about them. Personally, he never lost his low view of Indian civilization but developed a high one of Japanese, pretty conventional opinions around Boston in the late nineteenth century.

46. "Notes on Fine Arts 3: Compiled from Stenographic Reports by W. E. Weaver" (typescript, 1898, Nor 5260.12F, Houghton), pp. 46–47; CEN 1900a, p. 12.

47. CEN, "Dante. Lecture I" (typescript [1894?], box 13, Miscellaneous Papers, NP); lecture notes by F. B. Whittemore, lecture 1, Fine Arts 4, 1894–95, and lecture notes by George R. Noyes in Fine Arts 3, 1892–93, lecture of 23 February 1893, vol. 2, HUA; Lovett 1948, p. 38; CEN to Goldwin Smith, 14 June 1897, NP.

48. CEN 1897d, p. 335.

49. CEN to Goldwin Smith, 14 June 1897, and CEN to JBH, 6 August 1878, NP;

"Notes on Fine Arts 3: Compiled from Stenographic Reports by W. E. Weaver" (typescript, 1898, Nor 5260.12F, Houghton), p. 48; CEN 1900a, p. 15.

50. "Notes on Fine Arts 3: Compiled from Stenographic Reports by W. E. Weaver" (typescript, 1898, Nor 5260.12F, Houghton), p. 48. Because of its purpose as a tool of culture in CEN's sense, Western civilization required a list of "great books" for students to read. CEN hardly needed to compose this "canon"; he uttered conventional wisdom when he placed Homer, Dante, and Shakespeare above all others as repaying the student's attention. The canon as it descends to us, it scarcely needs saying, does not comprise some timeless crème de la crème but principally writers whose reputations happened to be high in the later nineteenth century, when Western civilization was conceived. This truism is sometimes bizarrely taken to mean that canonical texts have no enduring qualities setting them apart, as if it were an accident that late Victorians preferred Shakespeare to Tourneur or Dante to Cavalcanti.

51. CEN 1888c, p. 323.

52. W. L. Garrison Jr. to CEN, 30 December 1895, NP; CEN to Paul Elmer More, 25 April 1898, Paul Elmer More Papers, Princeton University Library.

53. CEN to William J. Stillman, 26 June 1898, William J. Stillman Collection, Schaffer Library, Union College.

54. Brown 1948, p. 156; CEN to LS, 20–23 December 1897, Berg Collection, New York Public Library; Rupert Norton to Charles W. Eliot, 3 January 1898, box 139, folder 1367, Eliot Papers, HUA; CEN to Clementina Dawes Nahmer, 8 February 1898 [1899?], Jones Library, Amherst, Mass.; CEN to S. G. Ward, 28 November 1897, NP; CEN to James Hazen Hyde, 12 February 1898, New York Historical Society.

55. CEN to LS, 24 June 1898, Berg Collection, New York Public Library.

56. CEN to LS, 20–23 December 1897, Berg Collection, New York Public Library; CEN to Henry C. Lea, 20 February 1898, Special Collections, Van Pelt Library, University of Pennsylvania.

57. Charles W. Eliot to CEN, 30 November 1897, NP; Resolution of President and Fellows of Harvard College, 20 December 1897, box 16, Miscellaneous Papers, NP.

58. Clippings, including *Harvard Lampoon*, 9 April 1898, in box 17, Miscellaneous Papers, NP; Samuel C. Bennett, 22 July 1898, and Mary Elizabeth Blake to CEN, 1 June 1898, NP; *Harvard Crimson*, 1 June 1898.

59. CEN to William G. Peckham, 13 April 1898, Manuscripts Department, University of Virginia Library.

60. CEN to Moncure D. Conway, 8 May 1898, Butler Library, Columbia University.

61. CEN to William J. Stillman, 26 June 1898, William J. Stillman Collection, Schaffer Library, Union College; CEN to Caroline H. Dall, 12 November 1898, Dall Papers, MHS.

62. CEN to LS, 24 June 1898, Berg Collection, New York Public Library.

CHAPTER 16: SHADY HILL AGAIN, 1898–1908

1. CEN to Moncure Conway, 8 May 1898, Butler Library, Columbia University; CEN, open letter to Senator George Hoar, 15 July 1898, in *Springfield Republican*,

19 July 1898, and interview with CEN, *New York Times*, 8 May 1898, clippings in "Records of the Hour," two-volume scrapbook, NP (fMS Am 1088.3). "Records of the Hour" is hereafter cited as "Records." CEN's son Rupert was "one of the first to offer his services to the Government in this war and has been working since the first of June at Fort McPherson, Georgia" (unidentified clipping in "Records").

2. Newspaper clippings; "Mass Soldier" to CEN [3 May? 1898]; "Alumnus" to CEN and Charles W. Eliot, n.d.; *Los Angeles Times* editorial, 19 May 1898, H. Jenkins to CEN, 20 May 1898; all in "Records."

3. James H. Burnham to CEN, 24 June 1898, NP; clipping from *Boston Transcript*, 8 June 1898 (with note in Sally's hand), and *Transcript* to CEN, 4 August 1898, in "Records."

4. "True Patriotism," reprint from *Boston Transcript*, 8 June 1898, in "Records."

5. CEN to Margaret Meyer Norton, 21 October 1898, *96MII(b), Houghton.

6. Clippings from *Springfield Republican*, 14 and 19 July 1898, in "Records." Ironically, Hoar soon came over to CEN's position on the war.

7. CEN to Lyman Abbott, 29 July 1898, Lyman Abbott Autograph Collection, Abbott Memorial Collection, Bowdoin College Library; CEN to Eliot Norton, 19 July 1898, NP.

8. Slip reprinting newspaper report of CEN's speech, *Springfield Republican*, 26 August 1898, and *New York Sun*, 26 August 1898, clippings in "Records"; *Chicago Tribune*, 31 October 1898, clipping enclosed in G. F. Westover to CEN, 3 November 1898, NP.

9. CEN to Lyman Abbott [manuscript draft, 6 August? 1898], NP; CEN to Moncure Conway, 28 November 1898, Butler Library, Columbia University.

10. Slip reprinting newspaper report of CEN's Ashfield speech, in "Records" (the quotation is from Clough's "Say Not the Struggle Nought Availeth"); CEN to William Peterfield Trent, 24 January 1899, in Trent Papers, Southern Historical Collection, Manuscript Department, Wilson Library, University of North Carolina, Chapel Hill.

11. CEN to William James, 12 December 1899, James Family Papers, Houghton.

12. CEN to Henry C. Lea, 20 February 1898, Special Collections, Van Pelt Library, University of Pennsylvania; CEN to D. Berkeley Updike, 25 April 1899, Providence (R.I.) Public Library. CEN also served on the hospital's board of directors; the lecture was partly reported as CEN 1899g.

13. Samuel G. Ward to CEN, 3 April 1899, NP. Howe 1934 gives an erroneous date of 1898 for CEN's resignation as Tavern president.

14. CEN to Isabella Stewart Gardner, 9 May 1899, Gardner Archives; CEN to LS, 8 July 1899, Berg Collection, New York Public Library.

15. CEN to Sarah Hammond Palfrey, 15 January 1900, Palfrey Family Papers, Houghton (punctuation sic); CEN 1900a.

16. CEN to Goldwin Smith, 20 February 1900, and CEN to Samuel G. Ward, 14 April 1901, NP.

17. CEN to Samuel G. Ward, 14 April 1901, and CEN to Goldwin Smith, 20 February 1900, NP.

18. CEN to Moncure Conway, 11 May 1900, Butler Library, Columbia Univer-

sity; CEN to ELG, 6 January 1900, ELG Papers, Houghton; CEN to Goldwin Smith, 20 February 1900, NP.

19. CEN to Samuel G. Ward, 8 August 1900, NP; CEN 1903a, p. xi; CEN to LS, 28 March 1900, Berg Collection, New York Public Library.

20. CEN to LS, 28 March 1900, Berg Collection, New York Public Library.

21. Ibid.; CEN to Samuel G. Ward, 24 April 1900, NP; CEN to William Dean Howells, 9 May 1900, William Dean Howells Papers, Houghton; CEN, Journal of trip to England, 1900, box 2, Miscellaneous Papers, NP.

22. CEN to Samuel G. Ward, 8 August 1900, NP. For fuller discussion of CEN's treatment of JR's *Nachlass*, see Bradley and Ousby 1987, pp. 7–10.

23. CEN to Samuel G. Ward, 23 July and 7 December 1900, and John Dahlberg Baron Acton to CEN, 2 July 1900, NP; CEN to LS, 3 August 1900, Berg Collection, New York Public Library; Georgiana Burne-Jones to CEN, 28 June 1900, NP.

24. CEN to ELG, 21 July 1900, ELG Papers, Houghton.

25. CEN to Samuel G. Ward, 19 September 1900, NP.

26. CEN to JBH, 31 December 1900, NP (punctuation sic).

27. Overseers Records, 10 April 1901, HUA.

28. CEN 1901a(1).

29. CEN to Samuel G. Ward, 10 March 1902, NP. Walter Berry, a former student of CEN's, was Wharton's closest companion; his admiration for CEN may help to explain hers.

30. CEN to Isabella Stewart Gardner, 8 January 1902, Gardner Archives. Gardner did purchase the Baccio portrait, under CEN's probable attribution to Sebastiano di Piombo; that Baccio was the subject is still regarded as correct, though the picture is now regarded as a self-portrait. With the *Marriage Feast at Cana* went a portrait attributed to Tintoretto, now regarded as a copy. In 1902 CEN gave her outright an eighteenth-century portrait of a Venetian nobleman, then attributed to Alessandro Longhi, now thought possibly by Pietro Uberti. Hendy 1974, pp. 12, 280–81.

31. The other American was Berenson, by now hostile to CEN and his view of art.

32. CEN to LS, 11 December 1903, Berg Collection, New York Public Library.

33. CEN to Eliot Norton, 27 December 1901, CEN to Samuel G. Ward, 7 October 1901, and William Lloyd Garrison to CEN, 14 December 1901, NP.

34. CEN to Goldwin Smith, 24 May 1902, Department of Manuscripts and University Archives, Cornell University Libraries.

35. CEN to Houghton, Mifflin and Co., 1 May 1903, Houghton Mifflin Co. Papers, Houghton; CEN 1904a, 1:6.

36. CEN to Samuel G. Ward, 9 March 1903, and CEN to William Dean Howells, 4 October 1903, NP; Gulick and Gulick 1990, p. 35.

37. CEN to GEW, 20 October 1903, CEN to Samuel G. Ward, 19 August 1902, William James to CEN, 30 June 1904, and CEN to JBH, 5 May 1904, NP.

38. Henry James Jr. to Edmund Gosse, 27 October 1904, Sir Edmund Gosse Papers, Perkins Library, Duke University; CEN to Houghton, Mifflin and Co., 1 November 1904, Houghton Mifflin Co. Papers, Houghton.

39. CEN to Katharine S. Godkin, 19 February 1905, ELG Papers, Houghton; CEN to William Coolidge Lane, 14 February 1905, and presentation folder, fMS Am 1088.4, NP; Constance Grosvenor Alexander, "A Evening in the Library of Charles Eliot Norton, 11 May 1905," typescript, MS Am 1088.7, Houghton. The quotation from the *Divina Commedia* (I.16.81) reads, in CEN's translation, "Happy thou that speakest at thy pleasure."

40. Note in CEN's hand, 26 August 1905, with copies of JR's letters (endorsed on margin in Elizabeth G. Norton's hand, "Read & destroyed as desired," January 1923), and CEN to Eliot Norton, 23 September 1905, NP.

41. CEN to Allain C. White, 5 October 1906, Watkinson Library, Trinity College, Hartford Conn. (I have silently altered "amuse" to "amused"); CEN to Samuel G. Ward, 23 August 1906, NP; CEN to Elizabeth Ellery (Sedgwick) Child, 22 September 1906, Francis J. Child Papers, Houghton.

42. CEN to Eliot Norton, 25 and 27 September and 28 December 1906, 31 May 1907, NP; M. A. DeWolfe Howe, notes of conversation with Charles W. Eliot, 23 May 1911, in MS. notebook at bMS Am 1826 (417), Houghton. The reasons for the divorce are almost entirely obscure, though CEN clearly thought Richard at fault.

43. CEN to Goldwin Smith, 27 March 1907, NP.

44. Howes 1911, p. 384; CEN to Eliot Norton, 17 October 1907, NP.

45. Moorfield Storey to CEN, 17 November 1907, and CEN to Eliot Norton, 18 November 1907, NP.

46. This item is in NP.

47. Lea's voluminous writings on the history of the Inquisition constituted far and away the most substantial American Victorian contribution to medieval *history* narrowly meant; CEN's scholarship on church building and Dante reflected a broader, less specialized conception of history as culture. One cannot but feel that the attention given in the later twentieth century to Henry Adams's brief foray into the Middle Ages reflects the afterglow of all Adams's brilliant writings rather than any actual influence on the shaping of medieval studies. Arthur R. Marsh, mentioned in chapter 13, was the professor of comparative literature.

48. Sedgwick 1946, p. 71.

49. CEN 1907c, p. 581.

50. CEN to Elizabeth Ellery (Sedgwick) Child, 19 January 1908, Francis J. Child Papers, Houghton; CEN to Eliot Norton, 15 February 1908, NP; CEN to William Dean Howells, 19 March 1908, William Dean Howells Papers, Houghton.

51. CEN 1908b, p. 48.

52. CEN to Meta Gaskell, 24 July 1908, and CEN to Eliot Norton, 24 June 1908, NP.

53. CEN to Thomas Wentworth Higginson, 6 October 1908, Thomas Wentworth Higginson Papers, Houghton; Elizabeth Ellery (Sedgwick) Child, 19 January 1908, Francis J. Child Papers, Houghton; CEN to Meta Gaskell, 24 July 1908, NP.

54. CEN to Elizabeth Ellery (Sedgwick) Child, 19 January 1908, Francis J. Child Papers, Houghton (words from an earlier visit to the house); Edith Wharton to Sara Norton, 25 August 1908, Beinecke Library, Yale University.

55. Edith Wharton to Sara Norton, 25 August 1908, Beinecke Library, Yale University; CEN to Eliot Norton, n.d. [late September or early October 1908], NP; CEN to Thomas Wentworth Higginson, 6 October 1908, Thomas Wentworth Higginson Papers, Houghton.

56. CEN to Owen Wister, 10 October 1908, and Sally Norton to Owen Wister, 10 October 1908, Wister Collection, LC; Isabella Stewart Gardner to Sara Norton, n.d. [October 1908], Gardner Archives; Nellie A. Danehy to CEN, 15 October 1908, and William James to CEN, 17 October 1908, NP.

57. *Boston Record,* 20 October 1908, clippings in CEN collection, HUA.

Sources Cited

Works by Charles Eliot Norton are listed in the separate bibliography of his writings. Newspapers are not listed here but are cited in full in the notes where they appear, as are magazines when the reference is only to a brief notice or incidental item. Other works, including periodical articles of more substantial relevance, are alphabetized by author's surname. The name appears in square brackets if the work was published anonymously. Works of unknown authorship are alphabetized by short title. N.d. signifies an unknown date of publication or composition. When a book lists two or more places of publication, only the first appears.

Ahlstrom, Sydney E., and Carey, Jonathan S. 1985. *An American Reformation: A Documentary History of Unitarianian Christianity.* Middletown, Conn.: Wesleyan University Press.

Allen, Gay Wilson. 1981. *Waldo Emerson: A Biography.* New York: Viking Press.

Allen, Joseph Henry. 1883. *Our Liberal Movement in Theology: Chiefly as Shown in Recollections of the History of Unitarianism in New England.* 2d ed. Boston: Roberts Bros.

Alter, Stephen G. 1999. *Darwinism and the Linguistic Image.* Baltimore: Johns Hopkins University Press.

Armstrong, William M. 1978. *E. L. Godkin: A Biography.* Albany: State University of New York Press.

Athenaeum Centenary. 1907. Boston: Boston Athenaeum.

Baldwin, Thomas W., ed. 1914–15. *Vital Records of Cambridge, Massachusetts, to the Year 1850.* 2 vols. Boston.

Ballou, Ellen B. 1970. *The Building of the House: Houghton Mifflin's Formative Years.* Boston: Houghton Mifflin.

[Bancroft, George]. 1824. "Value of Classical Learning." *North American Review* 19:125–37.

Berenson, Bernard. 1952. *Rumour and Reflection, 1941–1944.* London: Constable.

Bicknell, John W., ed. 1996. *Selected Letters of Leslie Stephen.* 2 vols. Columbus: Ohio State University Press.

Bradley, John Lewis, and Ousby, Ian. 1987. *The Correspondence of John Ruskin and Charles Eliot Norton.* Cambridge: Cambridge University Press.

Brem, Anne-Marie de. 1991. *L'atelier d'Ary Scheffer.* Paris: Musée de la vie romantique.

Brown, Rollo. 1948. *Harvard Yard in the Golden Age.* New York: Current Books.

Buell, Lawrence. 1986. *New England Literary Culture: From Revolution through Renaissance.* New York: Cambridge University Press.

[Burne-Jones, Georgiana]. 1906. *Memorials of Edward Burne-Jones.* 2 vols. London: Macmillan.

Butler, Joseph. 1852. *The Analogy of Religion, Natural and Revealed, to the Constitution and Course of Nature.* Orig. pub. 1736. New York: Harper and Bros.

Carlyle, Alexander, ed. 1904. *New Letters of Thomas Carlyle.* 2 vols. London: John Lane, the Bodley Head.

Catalogue. 1842 [et seq.]. *A Catalogue of the Officers and Students of Harvard University for the Academical Year 1842–43* [and *1843–44* et seq.; title varies]. Cambridge, Mass.: Metcalf.

Cate, George Allan, ed. 1982. *The Correspondence of Thomas Carlyle and John Ruskin.* Stanford: Stanford University Press.

Channing, William Ellery. 1838. *Self-Culture.* Reprint. New York: Thomas Y. Crowell Co., n.d.

Chapple, J. A. V., and Pollard, Arthur, eds. 1966. *The Letters of Mrs. Gaskell.* Manchester: Manchester University Press.

Child, Francis J. 1920. *A Scholar's Letters to a Young Lady.* Edited by Mark A. DeWolfe Howe. Boston: Atlantic Monthly Press.

Cohn, Marjorie B. 1986. *Francis Calley Gray and Art Collecting for America.* Cambridge: Harvard University Press for the Harvard University Art Museums.

Conway, Moncure Daniel. 1904. *Autobiography: Memories and Experiences.* 2 vols. Boston: Houghton Mifflin.

Dalzell, Robert F., Jr. 1987. *Enterprising Elite: The Boston Associates and the World They Made.* Cambridge: Harvard University Press.

Dana, Richard Henry, Jr. 1968. *The Journal of Richard Henry Dana, Jr.* Edited by Robert F. Lucid. 3 vols. Cambridge: Harvard University Press.

Desmond, Adrian, and Moore, James. 1991. *Darwin.* New York: Warner Books.

Dickens, Charles. 1957. *American Notes and Pictures from Italy.* Oxford: Oxford University Press.

Dinsmoor, William B. 1943. "Early American Studies of Mediterranean Archaeology." *Proceedings of the American Philosophical Society* 87:70–104.

Doughty, Howard. 1962. *Francis Parkman.* Pb. reprint. Cambridge: Harvard University Press, 1983.

Downing, Antoinette F.; MacDougall, Elisabeth; and Pearson, Eleanor. 1967. *Report Two: Mid Cambridge.* Survey of Architectural History in Cambridge. Cambridge, Mass.: Cambridge Historical Commission.

Duberman, Martin. 1966. *James Russell Lowell.* Pb. reprint. Boston: Beacon Press, 1968.

Edel, Leon. 1953. *Henry James: The Untried Years, 1843–1870.* Philadelphia: J. B. Lippincott.

Edwardes, Michael. 1969. *Bound to Exile: The Victorians in India.* New York: Praeger Publishers.

Eidson, John Olin. 1951. *Charles Stearns Wheeler, Friend of Emerson.* Athens: University of Georgia Press.

Eliot, Charles W. 1920–25. "Shady Hill: Notes of the Remarks of President Eliot at Shady Hill, June 7, 1924." *Proceedings of the Cambridge Historical Society* 17:60–62.

Eliot, Samuel A. 1848. *A Sketch of the History of Harvard College and Its Present State.* Boston: Charles C. Little and James Brown.

Eliot, Samuel A. 1941. "Some Cambridge Pundits and Pedagogues." *Publications of the Cambridge Historical Society* 26:13–35.

——, ed. 1910. *Heralds of a Liberal Faith.* Vol. 2: *The Pioneers.* Boston: American Unitarian Association.

Eliot, Walter Graeme. 1887. *A Sketch of the Eliot Family.* New York: Livingston Middleditch.

Emerson, Edward Waldo. 1918. *The Early Years of the Saturday Club, 1855–1870.* Boston: Houghton Mifflin.

[Everett, Edward]. 1847. *Twenty-First Annual Report of the President of the University at Cambridge to the Overseers, exhibiting the State of the Institution for the Academical Year 1845–1846.* Cambridge, Mass.

Fitzgerald, Edward. 1980. *The Letters of Edward Fitzgerald.* Edited by Alfred McKinley Terhune and Annabelle Burdick Terhune. 4 vols. Princeton: Princeton University Press.

Forbes, Edward Waldo. N.d. "History of the Fogg Museum of Art." Typescript in Fogg Museum Archives, Harvard University.

Galpin, W. Freeman. 1952. *Syracuse University.* Vol. 1: *The Pioneer Days.* Syracuse: Syracuse University Press.

Goodman, Paul. 1966. "Ethics and Enterprise: The Values of a Boston Elite, 1800–1860." *American Quarterly* 28:437–51.

Goodwin, William Watson. 1906–7. "Address of William Watson Goodwin [on C. C. Felton]." *Proceedings of the Cambridge Historical Society* 2:117–30.

Green, Martin. 1966. *The Problem of Boston: Some Readings in Cultural History.* New York: W. W. Norton.

Greenblatt, Stephen. 1980. *Renaissance Self-Fashioning: From More to Shakespeare.* Chicago: University of Chicago Press.

Greenslet, Ferris. 1947. *The Lowells and Their Seven Worlds.* London: Ernest Benn.

Gulick, Betty, and Gulick, Edward. 1990. *Charles Eliot Norton and the Ashfield Dinners, 1879–1903.* Ashfield, Mass.: Ashfield Historical Society.

Hale, Edward Everett. 1893. "My College Days." *Atlantic Monthly* 71:355–63.

——. 1899. *James Russell Lowell and His Friends.* Boston: Houghton Mifflin.

——. 1927. *A New England Boyhood.* New ed. Boston: Little, Brown.

——, et al. 1887. *The "How I Was Educated" Papers.* New York: D. Appleton.

Hall, G. Stanley. 1923. *Life and Confessions of a Psychologist.* New York: D. Appleton.

Handlin, Lilian. 1989. *"Babylon est delenda*—the Young Andrews Norton." In *American Unitarianism, 1805–1865,* edited by Conrad Edick Wright, pp. 53–85. Boston: Massachusetts Historical Society.

Handlin, Oscar. 1959. *Boston's Immigrants: A Study in Acculturation.* Rev. ed. Cambridge: Harvard University Press.

Haraszti, Zoltan, ed. N.d. [1940?]. *Letters by T. W. Parsons.* Boston: Trustees of the Public Library.

Harris, Neil. 1966. *The Artist in American Society: The Formative Years, 1790–1860.* New York: George Braziller.

Harris, Seymour E. 1970. *Economics of Harvard.* New York: McGraw-Hill.

Harrison, Frederic. 1912. *Among My Books: Centenaries, Reviews, Memoirs.* Facs. reprint. Freeport, N.Y.: Books for Libraries Press, 1970.

Haskin, Dayton. 1985. "Reading Donne's *Songs and Sonnets* in the Nineteenth Century." *John Donne Journal* 4:225–52.

Haskin, Dayton. 1989. "New Historical Contexts for Appraising the Donne Revival from A. B. Grosart to Charles Eliot Norton." *ELH* 56:869–95.

Hawthorne, Nathaniel. 1984–88. *The Letters.* 6 vols. Centenary Edition of the Works of Nathaniel Hawthorne. Vols. 15–20. Columbus: Ohio State University Press.

Hazen, Charles Downer, ed. 1926. *The Letters of William Roscoe Thayer.* Boston: Houghton Mifflin.

Heeren, Arnold H. L. 1842. *Ancient Greece.* Translated by George Bancroft. 2d American ed. Boston: Charles C. Little and James Brown.

Hendy, Philip. 1974. *European and American Paintings in the Isabella Stewart Gardner Museum.* Boston: Gardner Museum.

Higginson, Thomas Wentworth. 1898. *Cheerful Yesterdays.* Boston: Houghton Mifflin.

———. 1909. *Carlyle's Laugh and Other Surprises.* Boston: Houghton Mifflin.

Hilen, Andrew, ed. 1966–82. *The Letters of Henry Wadsworth Longfellow.* 6 vols. Cambridge: Harvard University Press.

Hines, Thomas S. 1974. *Burnham of Chicago: Architect and Planner.* Reprint. Chicago: University of Chicago Press, 1979.

Hingham. 1893. *History of the Town of Hingham, Massachusetts.* Hingham: Town of Hingham.

Hiss, Priscilla, and Fansler, Roberta. 1934. *Research in Fine Arts in the Colleges and Universities of the United States.* New York: Carnegie Corporation.

Hoar, George F. 1903. *Autobiography of Seventy Years.* 2 vols. New York: Charles Scribner's Sons.

Howe, Mark DeWolfe. 1934. *A Partial (and Not Impartial) Semi-Centennial History of the Tavern Club, 1884–1934.* [Boston]: Tavern Club.

Howe, Mark DeWolfe, and Adams, Charles Francis. 1914. "Memoir of Charles Eliot Norton." *Proceedings of the MHS,* 3d ser. 48:57–68.

Howe, Mark DeWolfe, ed. 1946. *Holmes-Pollock Letters: The Correspondence of Mr. Justice Holmes and Sir Frederick Pollock, 1874–1932.* 2 vols. Cambridge: Harvard University Press.

Howells, William Dean. 1910. *Literary Friends and Acquaintance: A Personal Retrospect of American Authorship.* Reprint edited by David F. Hiatt and Edwin H. Cady. Bloomington: Indiana University Press, 1968.

Howes, Frederick G. c. 1911. *History of the Town of Ashfield, Franklin County, Massachusetts from Its Settlement in 1742 to 1910.* Ashfield: Town of Ashfield.

Jackman, S. W., ed. 1979. *Acton in America: The American Journey of Sir John Acton, 1853.* Shepherdstown, W. Va.: Patmos Press.

Jacobs, Wilbur R., ed. 1960. *Letters of Francis Parkman.* 2 vols. Norman: University of Oklahoma Press.

Jaher, Frederic Cople. 1982. *The Urban Establishment: Upper Strata in Boston, New York, Charleston, Chicago, and Los Angeles.* Urbana: University of Illinois Press.

James, Alice. 1934. *The Diary of Alice James.* Edited by Leon Edel. Reprint. New York: Dodd, Mead, 1964.

James, Henry. 1903. *William Wetmore Story and His Friends.* 2 vols. Boston: Houghton Mifflin.

———. 1914. *Notes of a Son and Brother.* New York: Charles Scribner's Sons.

James, Henry. 1930. *Charles W. Eliot: President of Harvard University, 1869–1909.* 2 vols. Boston: Houghton Mifflin.

Jarves, James Jackson. 1960. *The Art-Idea.* Edited by Benjamin Rowland Jr. Cambridge: Harvard University Press.

Jones, Caroline A. 1985. *Modern Art at Harvard: The Formation of the Nineteenth- and Twentieth-Century Collections of the Harvard University Art Museums.* New York: Abbeville Press.

Keene, H[enry]. G. 1897. *A Servant of "John Company": Being the Recollections of an Indian Official.* London: W. Thacker.

Keightley, Thomas. 1849. *The History of Rome.* New York: Leavitt.

King, Moses. 1884. *Harvard and Its Surroundings.* 6th ed. Cambridge, Mass.: Moses King.

Kittredge, G[eorge] L[yman]. 1898. "Francis James Child." In *The English and Scottish Popular Ballads,* edited by Francis James Child. 5 vols., 1882–98. Facs. reprint. New York: Folklore Press, 1956.

Koch, Theodore W. 1896. *Dante in America: A Historical and Bibliographical Study.* Boston: Ginn for the Dante Society.

La Piana, Angelina. 1948. *Dante's American Pilgrimage: A Historical Survey of Dante Studies in the United States, 1800–1944.* New Haven: Yale University Press.

Levenson, J. C., et al., eds. 1982. *The Letters of Henry Adams.* Vols. 1–3. Cambridge: Harvard University Press.

Lincoln, Solomon, Jr. 1827. *History of the Town of Hingham, Plymouth County, Massachusetts.* Hingham: Caleb Gill Jr. and Farmer and Brown.

Longfellow, Samuel. 1886. *Life of Henry Wadsworth Longfellow.* 2 vols. Boston: Ticknor.

Lord, Louis E. 1947. *A History of the American School of Classical Studies at Athens, 1882–1942: An Intercollegiate Project.* Cambridge: Harvard University Press for the American School of Classical Studies at Athens.

Lovett, Robert Morss. 1948. *All Our Years.* New York: Viking Press.

Lowell, James Russell. 1854. "Cambridge Thirty Years Ago." In *The Writings of James Russell Lowell,* 1:43–99. 10 vols. Boston: Houghton Mifflin, 1896.

———. 1932. *New Letters of James Russell Lowell.* Edited by M. A. DeWolfe Howe. New York: Harper and Brothers.

Maitland, Frederic William. 1906. *The Life and Letters of Leslie Stephen.* London: Duckworth.

Marshall, Esther S. N.d. "Biographical Sketch of the Life of Elizabeth Gaskell

Norton." Typescript. Copy in Stockbridge, Mass., Public Library, Historical Room.

McCaughey, Robert A. 1974. "The Transformation of American Academic Life: Harvard University, 1821–1892." *Perspectives in American History* 8:237–332.

McKenzie, Alexander. 1908. "Some Cambridge Men I Have Known." *Cambridge Historical Society Publications* 3:19–36.

McMurtry, Jo. 1985. *English Language, English Literature: The Creation of an Academic Discipline.* Hamden, Conn.: Archon Books.

Milanesi, Gaetano. 1856. *Documenti per la Storia dell'Arte Senese.* 3 vols. Siena.

Morgan, Morris H. 1898. "Memoir of George M. Lane." *Harvard Studies in Classical Philology* 9:1–12.

Morison, Samuel Eliot. 1921. *Maritime History of Massachusetts, 1783–1860.* Boston: Houghton Mifflin.

———. 1936. *Three Centuries of Harvard, 1636–1936.* Cambridge: Harvard University Press.

———, ed. 1930. *The Development of Harvard University since the Inauguration of President Eliot, 1869–1929.* Cambridge: Harvard University Press.

Morse, John T., Jr. 1905. *Memoir of Colonel Henry Lee.* Boston: Little, Brown.

Mott, Frank Luther. 1938. *A History of American Magazines.* Vol. 1: *1741–1850.* Cambridge: Harvard University Press.

Mulhauser, Frederick L., ed. 1957. *The Correspondence of Arthur Hugh Clough.* 2 vols. Oxford: Clarendon Press.

Newell, William. 1856. "Biographical Notice of Mr. Norton." In Norton 1856, pp. ix–l.

Nietzsche, Friedrich. 1887. *The Gay Science.* Translated by Walter Kaufmann. New York: Random House, 1974.

Norman, Henry. 1882. *An Account of the Harvard Greek Play.* Boston: James R. Osgood. (Copyright date 1881.)

[Norton, Andrews]. 1807. "Epistles, Odes, and Other Poems, by Thomas Moore, Esq." *Monthly Anthology and Boston Review* 4:41–45.

[———]. 1810. [Report of the inauguration of President Kirkland of Harvard]. *Monthly Anthology and Boston Review* 9:350.

[———]. 1812a. "A Defence of Liberal Christianity." *General Repository and Review* 1:1–25.

[———]. 1812b. "Character of Rev. Joseph Stevens Buckminster." *General Repository and Review* 1:306–14.

———. 1819. *Inaugural Discourse, Delivered before the University in Cambridge, August 10, 1819.* Cambridge, Mass.: Hilliard and Metcalf.

[———]. 1824. "On the Future Life of the Good." *Christian Examiner* 1:350–57.

———. 1827–29. "On the Author of the Epistle to the Hebrews." *Christian Examiner* 4:495–519, 5:37–70, 6:198–225.

———. 1837–44. *The Evidences of the Genuineness of the Gospels.* Vol. 1. Boston: John B. Russell, 1837. Vols. 2–3. Cambridge, Mass.: John Owen, 1844.

———. 1852. *Tracts Concerning Christianity.* Cambridge, Mass: John Bartlett.

———. 1853. *Verses.* Cambridge, Mass.: Privately printed.

———. 1856. *A Statement of Reasons for Not Believing the Doctrines of Trinitarians,*

Concerning the Nature of God and the Person of Christ. 3d ed. Edited by Ezra Abbot. Boston: Walker, Wise for the American Unitarian Association.

Norton, Sara, and Howe, Mark DeWolfe, eds. 1913. *Letters of Charles Eliot Norton with Biographical Comment.* 2 vols. Boston: Houghton Mifflin.

Ogden, Rollo. 1907. *The Life and Letters of Edwin Lawrence Godkin.* 2 vols. New York: Macmillan.

Olmsted, Frederick Law. 1992. *The Papers of Frederick Law Olmsted.* Vol. 6: *The Years of Olmsted, Vaux & Co., 1865–74.* Edited by David Schuyler and Jane Turner Censer. Baltimore: Johns Hopkins University Press.

Paley, William. 1796. *A View of the Evidences of Christianity.* 2 vols. Facs. reprint. Westmead, Hants.: Gregg International Publishers, 1970.

———. 1827. *The Principles of Moral and Political Philosophy.* Orig. pub. 1785. Bridgeport, Conn.: M. Sherman.

Palfrey, John Gorham. [1836]. *Divinity School of the University of Cambridge.* Cambridge, Mass.

Patton, Cornelius Howard, and Field, Walter Taylor. 1927. *Eight O'Clock Chapel: A Study of New England College Life in the Eighties.* Boston: Houghton Mifflin.

Peabody, Andrew Preston. 1888. *Harvard Reminiscences.* Boston: Ticknor.

Pellico, Silvio. 1836. *My Prisons: Memoirs of Silvio Pellico of Saluzzo.* [Translated by Catharine Norton.] Edited by Andrews Norton. Cambridge, Mass.: Charles Folsom.

Pierce, John. 1890. "Some Notes on the Commencements at Harvard University, 1803–1848 [diary of Rev. John Pierce]." *Proceedings of the MHS,* 2d ser., 5:168–263.

[Quincy, Josiah]. 1844. *Eighteenth Annual Report of the President of Harvard University, to the Overseers, on the State of the Institution for the Academical Year 1842–43.* Cambridge, Mass.: Metcalf.

———. 1851. *The History of the Boston Athenaeum, with Biographical Notices of its Deceased Founders.* Cambridge, Mass.: Metcalf.

Reuben, Julie A. 1996. *The Making of the Modern University: Intellectual Transformation and the Marginalization of Morality.* Chicago: University of Chicago Press.

Rollins, Hyder E. 1958. "Charles Eliot Norton and Froude." *Journal of English and Germanic Philology* 57:651–64.

Roper, Laura Wood. 1973. *FLO: A Biography of Frederick Law Olmsted.* Baltimore: Johns Hopkins University Press.

Royce, Josiah. 1970. *The Letters of Josiah Royce.* Edited by John Clendenning. Chicago: University of Chicago Press.

Ruskin, John. 1885–89. *Praeterita.* 3 vols. In *Complete Works.* New York: Kelmscott Society, n.d.

Samuels, Ernest. 1979. *Bernard Berenson: The Making of a Connoisseur.* Cambridge: Harvard University Press.

Sandys, John Edwin. 1903–8. *A History of Classical Scholarship.* 3 vols. Facs. reprint. New York: Hafner Publishing, 1964.

Scudder, Horace Elisha. 1901. *James Russell Lowell: A Biography.* 2 vols. Boston: Houghton Mifflin.

Sedgwick, Ellery. 1946. *The Happy Profession*. Boston: Little, Brown.

Shields, N[ancy]. C. 1931. *Italian Translations in America*. New York: Institute of French Studies.

Shively, Charles. N.d. "Harvard Fine Arts Department." Unpub. ms. [1960s]. In possession of author, courtesy of Professor Shively.

Simpson, Lewis P. 1973. *The Man of Letters in New England and the South: Essays on the History of the Literary Vocation in America*. Baton Rouge: Louisiana State University Press.

——, ed. 1962. *The Federalist Literary Mind: Selections from the* Monthly Anthology and Boston Review, *1803–1811, Including Documents Relating to the Boston Athenaeum*. Baton Rouge: Louisiana State University Press.

Slater, Joseph, ed. 1964. *The Correspondence of Emerson and Carlyle*. New York: Columbia University Press.

Smith, George Winston. 1948. "Broadsides for Freedom: Civil War Propaganda in New England." *New England Quarterly* 21:291–312.

Smith, Harriette Knight. 1898. *The History of the Lowell Institute*. Boston.

Smyth, Craig Hugh, and Lukehart, Peter M., eds. 1993. *The Early Years of Art History in the United States: Notes and Essays on Departments, Teaching, and Scholars*. Princeton: Princeton University, Department of Art and Archaeology.

Smyth, William. 1854. *Lectures on Modern History; from the Irruption of the Northern Nation to the Close of the American Revolution*. 2 vols. Orig. pub. 1839. London: H. G. Bohn.

Solomon, Barbara Miller. 1956. *Ancestors and Immigrants: A Changing New England Tradition*. Pb. reprint. New York: John Wiley and Sons, 1965.

Spalding, Thomas W. 1989. *The Premier See: A History of the Archdiocese of Baltimore*. Baltimore: Johns Hopkins University Press.

Stanton, Phoebe B. 1968. *The Gothic Revival and American Church Architecture: An Episode in Taste, 1840–1856*. Baltimore: Johns Hopkins University Press.

Steegman, John. 1971. *Victorian Taste: A Study of the Arts and Architecture from 1830 to 1870*. Orig. pub. 1950 as *Consort of Taste 1830–1870*. Cambridge: MIT Press.

Stephens, Kate. 1927. *A Curious History in Book Editing: Inclosing [sic] Letters of the Senior Editor Charles Eliot Norton*. New York: Antigone Press.

Stewart, Dugald. 1843. *Elements of the Philosophy of the Human Mind*. Orig. pub. 1814. Boston: James Munroe.

Stillman, William James. 1901. *The Autobiography of a Journalist*. 2 vols. Boston: Houghton Mifflin.

Story, Ronald. 1980. *The Forging of an Aristocracy: Harvard and the Boston Upper Class, 1800–1870*. Middletown: Wesleyan University Press.

Strouse, Jean. 1980. *Alice James: A Biography*. Boston: Houghton Mifflin.

Sutton, S[tephanie]. B. 1976. *Cambridge Reconsidered: 3½ Centuries on the Charles*. Cambridge: MIT Press.

Swan, Mabel Munson. 1940. *The Athenaeum Gallery, 1827–1873: The Boston Athenaeum as an Early Patron of Art*. Boston: Boston Athenaeum.

Taylor, Joshua C. 1957. *William Page: The American Titian*. Chicago: University of Chicago Press.

Thayer, James Bradley. 1878. *Letters of Chauncey Wright, with Some Account of His Life*. Cambridge, Mass.: Privately printed.

Thompson, Henry Yates. 1971. *An Englishman in the American Civil War: The Diaries of Henry Yates Thompson, 1863*. Edited by Christopher Chancellor. London: Sidgwick and Jackson.

[Ticknor, Anna Eliot]. 1869. *Samuel Eliot, 1739–1820*. Cambridge, Mass.

Tocqueville, Alexis de. 1960. *Journey to America*. Translated by George Lawrence. Edited by J. P. Mayer. New Haven: Yale University Press.

Trautmann, Thomas R. 1987. *Lewis Henry Morgan and the Invention of Kinship*. Berkeley: University of California Press.

Turner, James. 1993. "Religion et langage dans l'Amerique du XIXème siècle: le cas étrange de Andrews Norton." *Revue de l'histoire des religions* 210:431–62.

———. 1996. "The Relocation of Religion and the Invention of the Humanities." Paper delivered at Princeton University Conference on Higher Education, March 1996.

Turner, James, and Bernard, Paul. 1993. "The 'German Model' and the Graduate School: The University of Michigan and the Origin Myth of the American University." *History of Higher Education Annual* 13:69–98.

Tyack, David B. 1967. *George Ticknor and the Boston Brahmins*. Cambridge: Harvard University Press.

Vaille, Frederick O., and Clark, H. A., eds. 1875. *The Harvard Book: A Series of Historical, Biographical, and Descriptive Sketches*. 2 vols. Cambridge, Mass.: Welch, Bigelow.

Vance, William L. 1989. *America's Rome*. 2 vols. New Haven: Yale University Press.

Veysey, Laurence. 1979. "The Plural Organized Worlds of the Humanities." In *The Organization of Knowledge in Modern America, 1860–1920*, edited by Alexandra Oleson and John Voss, pp. 51–106. Baltimore: Johns Hopkins University Press.

Wagenknecht, Edward, ed. 1956. *Mrs. Longfellow: Selected Letters and Journals of Fanny Appleton Longfellow*. New York: Longmans, Green.

Ware, John. 1846. *Memoir of the Life of Henry Ware, Jr.* Reprint of 1846 "New Edition." 2 vols. Boston: American Unitarian Association, 1874.

Weir, John Ferguson. 1957. *The Recollections of John Ferguson Weir, Director of the Yale School of the Fine Arts*. Edited by Theodore Sizer. New York: New York Historical Society.

Whately, Richard. 1846. *Elements of Rhetoric*. Orig. pub. 1828. Facs. reprint. Delmar, N.Y.: Scholars' Facsimiles and Reprints, 1991.

Whiting, Charles F. 1965. "Development of the Communities of Francis Avenue and the Norton Estate in Cambridge, Massachusetts." Typescript. Copy in Harvard University Archives.

[Whitmore, William Henry]. 1859. *A Genealogy of the Norton Family, with Miscellaneous Notes*. Boston: Henry W. Dutton & Son. (Repr. from *New England Historical and Genealogical Register*, July 1859.)

[———]. 1869. *Andrew Elliot, of Beverly, Mass., and his Descendants*. Boston.

Wilson, Robert J., III. 1984. *The Benevolent Deity: Ebenezer Gay and the Rise of Rational Religion in New England, 1696–1787*. Philadelphia: University of Pennsylvania Press.

Winterer, Caroline. 1996. "The Classics and Culture in the Transformation of American Higher Education, 1830–1890." Ph.D. diss., University of Michigan.

Winthrop, John. 1630. "A Model of Christian Charity, Written on Board the *Arbella* on the Atlantic Ocean." In *The Puritans in America: A Narrative Anthology*, edited by Alan Heimert and Andrew Delbanco, pp. 82–92. Cambridge: Harvard University Press, 1985.

Wright, Conrad. 1954. "The Early Period (1811–1840)." In *The Harvard Divinity School: Its Place in Harvard University and American Culture*, edited by George Huntston Williams, pp. 21–77. Boston: Beacon Press.

Yanikoski, Richard Alan. 1987. "Edward Everett and the Advancement of Higher Education and Adult Learning in Antebellum Massachusetts." Ph.D. diss., University of Chicago.

The Published Writings
of Charles Eliot Norton

This list comprises all works known to have been published or privately printed by CEN. I have certainly failed to uncover some, especially ephemera and brief reviews. Deliberately excluded, except in special cases, are (1) newspaper reports of talks or lectures by CEN, (2) bureaucratic items such as reports of committees chaired by CEN, (3) New England Loyal Publication Society broadsides (available in the NELPS collection at the Boston Public Library), and (4) letters to newspapers or magazines. Unsigned articles are ascribed to CEN only when there seems to be good evidence, such as references in correspondence or attributions in magazine indexes. Asterisks mark a handful of items that I have been unable to locate but for which evidence indicates CEN's authorship.

Under any given year, books or parts of books are listed first (regardless of when actually published during the year), followed by the articles of that year in chronological order. Where texts include no title, I use the running title; absent a running title (most commonly in book reviews), I give in square brackets subjects of articles or reviews. I do not indicate which works were published anonymously. When a title page or copyright page gives two or more cities as places of publication, only the primary location is cited. Occasional annotations appear where clarity seems to require.

1847. "Reminiscences of Coleridge." *North American Review* 65:401–40.
1848a. "Capobianco's *Brief Narrative.*" *North American Review* 66:245–47. (Critical notice of Raffaele Capobianco, *Breve racconto delle cose chiesastiche più importanti, occorse nel viaggio fatto sulla real fregata Urania, dal 15 Agosto, 1844, al 4 Marzo, 1846.*)
1848b. "The Life of William Tyndale." *North American Review* 67:322–53.
1849a. "George Samuel Emerson." *Christian Examiner* 46:343. (Obituary.)
1849b. "Ancient Monuments in America." *North American Review* 68:466–96.
?1850. "Emerson's *Representative Men.*" *North American Review* 70:520–24. (Critical notice, at least once attributed to CEN, probably wrongly.)
1851a. "Sir Jamsetjee Jeejeebhoy: A Parsee Merchant." *North American Review* 73:135–52.
1851b. "Parkman's *History of Pontiac's War.*" *North American Review* 73:495–529.
1852a. (Editor.) *Five Christmas Hymns.* Cambridge: Privately printed.
1852b. "Dwellings and Schools for the Poor." *North American Review* 74:464–89.

1853a. *Considerations on Some Recent Social Theories*. Boston: Little, Brown.

1853b. "The St. Nicholas and the Five Points." *Putnam's Monthly* 1:509–12.

1853c. [Five letters on poverty and charity in Cambridge]. *Cambridge Chronicle*, July–August.

1853d. "Canals of Irrigation in India." *North American Review* 77:439–66.

1853e. "A Cambridge Man on Slavery." *North American Review* 77:528–30.

1854a. (Editor.) *A Book of Hymns for Young Persons*. Cambridge: John Bartlett.

1854b. "The Palankeen." *Putnam's Monthly* 3:654–60.

1855a. "Sketches of India." *Crayon* 2:127–28, 143–44, 160–62, 192–93, 223–24, 239–40.

1855b. [Walt Whitman, *Leaves of Grass*]. *Putnam's Monthly* 6:321–23.

1855c. "The Opening of the Ganges Canal." *North American Review* 81:531–43.

1856. "Italy in 1855–56." *Crayon* 3:85–87, 118–20, 151–55, 179–81, 206–9, 246–47, 274–76, 306–9, 338–40, 371–72.

1857a. "The Manchester Exhibition." *Atlantic Monthly* 1:33–46.

1857b. "The Indian Revolt." *Atlantic Monthly* 1:217–22.

1857c. [A. de Vere, *May Carols*]. *Atlantic Monthly* 1:256.

1858a. [J. C. Peabody, *Dante's Hell*]. *Atlantic Monthly* 1:382–83.

1858b. [J. S. Harford, *Life of Michael Angelo Buonarotti*]. *Atlantic Monthly* 1:510–12.

1858c. "The Catacombs of Rome." *Atlantic Monthly* 1:513–22, 674–85, 813–21; 2:48–58, 129–39.

1858d. [G. F. Waagen, *Galleries of Art in Britain*]. *Atlantic Monthly* 1:765–66.

1858e. [P. H. Gosse, *The Aquarium*, and J. G. Wood, *Common Objects of the Seashore*]. *Atlantic Monthly* 2:253–55.

1859a. *The New Life of Dante: An Essay, with Translations*. Cambridge: Privately printed. (Enlarged from 1859d; printed by Riverside Press, H. O. Houghton.)

1859b. *Notes of Travel and Study in Italy*. Boston: Ticknor and Fields. (Later printings by Houghton Mifflin.)

1859c. *Letters Relating to a Collection of Pictures Made by J. J. Jarves*. Cambridge: Privately printed.

1859d. "'The New Life' of Dante." *Atlantic Monthly* 3:62–69, 202–12, 330–39.

1859e. "Despotism in India." *North American Review* 88:289–312.

1859f. [*Memoirs and Letters of Thomas Seddon*]. *Atlantic Monthly* 3:648–50.

1859g. [H. W. Acland and J. Ruskin, *The Oxford Museum*]. *Atlantic Monthly* 4:767–70.

1860a. [A. H. Clough, *Plutarch's Lives*]. *Atlantic Monthly* 5:110–19.

1860b. [W. S. R. Hodson, *A Soldier's Life in India*]. *Atlantic Monthly* 5:124–25.

1860c. [A. Helps, *Friends in Council*, new ser.]. *Atlantic Monthly* 5:125–26.

1860d. [C. T. Brooks, *Simplicity of Christ's Teaching*]. *Atlantic Monthly* 5:250–51.

1860e. [A. Trollope, *West Indies and Spanish Main*]. *Atlantic Monthly* 5:375–78.

1860f. [J. Redpath, *Captain John Brown*]. *Atlantic Monthly* 5:378–81.

1860g. [*Le Prime Quattro Edizione della Divina Commedia*]. *Atlantic Monthly* 5:622–29.

1860h. "Model Lodging-Houses in Boston." *Atlantic Monthly* 5:673–80, 762–63.

1860i. [*Mademoiselle Mori*]. *Atlantic Monthly* 5:754–55.

1860j. "Pasquin and Pasquinades." *Atlantic Monthly* 6:395–405.

1860k. [*Essays and Reviews*]. *Atlantic Monthly* 6:633–35.

1860l. [J. S. Brewer, ed., *Rogeri Bacon Opera*]. *Atlantic Monthly* 6:746–59.

1861a. *The Soldier of the Good Cause.* Army series 2. Boston: American Unitarian Association.

1861b. [E. G. Squier, *Documents concerning the Conquest of America,* vol. 1]. *Atlantic Monthly* 7:122–23.

1861c. [Fisher, *The Laws of Race, as Connected with Slavery*]. *Atlantic Monthly* 7:252–54.

1861d. [*Il Politecnico*]. *Atlantic Monthly* 7:508–9.

1861e. "Original Memorials of Mrs. Piozzi." *Atlantic Monthly* 7:614–23.

1861f. [G. Tambarini, trans., *Benvenuto da Imola . . . Comento sulla Divina Commedia*]. *Atlantic Monthly* 7:629–37.

1861g. "Journal of a Privateersman." *Atlantic Monthly* 8:353–59, 417–24.

1861h. "The Advantages of Defeat." *Atlantic Monthly* 8:360–65.

1861i. "Alexis de Tocqueville." *Atlantic Monthly* 8:551–57.

1862a. "Forgotten Fame." In *Only Once: Original Papers by Various Contributors, Published for the Benefit of the New York Infirmary for Women and Children.* New York: John F. Trow, p. 9. (Copy at Nor 1862, Houghton.)

1862b. (Editor.) *The Poems of Arthur Hugh Clough. With a Memoir, by Charles Eliot Norton.* Boston: Ticknor and Fields. (Memoir revised and expanded from 1862c.)

1862c. "Arthur Hugh Clough." *Atlantic Monthly* 9:462–69.

1863a. [George Livermore, *An Historical Research respecting Opinions of the Founders on Negroes as Slaves, Citizens, and Soldiers*]. *Atlantic Monthly* 12:263–64.

1863b. [S. H. Smothers, ed., *Students' Repository*]. *North American Review* 97:557–59.

1864a. "Immorality in Politics." *North American Review* 98:105–27.

1864b. "Gillett's Life and Times of John Huss." *North American Review* 98:282–85.

1864c. "My Farm of Edgewood." *North American Review* 98:288–89.

1864d. "The Two Legacies." *North American Review* 98:294–95.

1864e. "The New Path." *North American Review* 98:303–4.

1864f. "Dream Children." *North American Review* 98:304.

1864g. "St. Louis and Joinville." *North American Review* 98:419–60.

1864h. "Hunt's Life of Edward Livingston." *North American Review* 98:592–94.

1864i. "Clark's Daleth." *North American Review* 98:604–6.

1864j. "The Poems of Robert Lowell." *North American Review* 98:617.

1864k. "Our Soldiers." *North American Review* 99:172–204.

1864l. "Notices of Gillett's Huss." *North American Review* 99:269–74.

1864m. "Parton's Life and Times of Benjamin Franklin." *North American Review* 99:302–3.

1864n. "Beadle's Dime Books." *North American Review* 99:303–9.

1864o. "My Cave Life in Vicksburg." *North American Review* 99:309.

1864p. [H. W. S. Cleveland, *Hints to Riflemen*]. *North American Review* 99:310.

1864q. "Goldwin Smith." *North American Review* 99:523–39.

1864r. "Scudder's Life and Letters." *North American Review* 99:629–30.

1864s. "Maine's Ancient Law." *North American Review* 99:630.

1865a. *On the Original Portraits of Dante.* Cambridge: Privately printed. (50 copies.)

1865b. "Abraham Lincoln." *North American Review* 100:1–21.

1865c. "Chittenden's Report of the Peace Conference [of February 1861]." *North American Review* 100:233–38.

1865d. "Wilson's Anti-Slavery Legislation." *North American Review* 100:238–41.

1865e. "McPherson's Political History." *North American Review* 100:241–42.

1865f. "The Works of Francis Bacon." *North American Review* 100:266–67.

1865g. "Felton's Familiar Letters." *North American Review* 100:287–88.

1865h. "Tennyson's Enoch Arden." *North American Review* 100:305–7

1865i. "The Semi-Centenary of the North American Review." *North American Review* 100:315–30. (Possibly written by, or jointly with, JRL; but style suggests CEN.)

1865j. "America and England." *North American Review* 100:331–46.

1865k. "Martin's History of France." *North American Review* 100:594–600.

1865l. "Perkins's Tuscan Sculptors." *North American Review* 100:602–4.

1865m. "Harper's Weekly." *North American Review* 100:623–25.

1865n. "Johnson's Family Atlas." *North American Review* 100:625–26.

1865o. "Vanity Fair." *North American Review* 100:626.

1865p. "Hall's Arctic Researches." *North American Review* 101:272–74.

1865q. "Friswell's Familiar Words." *North American Review* 101:291–93.

1865r. "White's Shakespeare." *Nation* 1:23–24.

1865s. "The Paradise of Mediocrities." *Nation* 1:43–44.

1865t. "Education at the Great English Public Schools." *Nation* 1:149–50.

1865u. "A Melancholy Poet." *Nation* 1:152.

1865v. "Mr. Parkman's Historical Narrative." *Nation* 1:344.

1865w. "Mr. Draper's Civil Policy of America." *Nation* 1:407–9.

1865x. "American Political Ideas." *North American Review* 101:550–66.

1865y. "Merivale's Conversion of the Roman Empire." *North American Review* 101:608–10.

1865z. "Burke's Works." *North American Review* 101:624–25.

1865aa. "Michelant's Voyage de Jaques Cartier." *North American Review* 101:628.

1865bb. [A. J. Downing, *Theory and Practice of Landscape Gardening*]. *North American Review* 101:629.

1865cc. "Atalanta in Calydon." *Nation* 1:590–91.

1866a. "The President's Message." *North American Review* 102:250–60.

1866b. "Saadi's Gulistan, or Rose Garden." *North American Review* 102:260–64.

1866c. "Alexander's Sunday Book of Poetry." *North American Review* 102:315–16.

1866d. "Allingham's Ballad Book." *North American Review* 102:316–18.

1866e. "Tuscan Sculptors." *Nation* 2:116–17.

1866f. "Waste." *Nation* 2:301–2.

1866g. "Dante, and His Latest English Translators." *North American Review* 102:509–29.

1866h. "The Works of Philip Lindsley." *North American Review* 102:573–74.

1866i. "Doolittle's Social Life of the Chinese." *North American Review* 102:574.

1866j. "Lady Wallace's Letters of Mozart." *North American Review* 102:609–14.

1866k. "Harper's Weekly." *North American Review* 102:637–38.

1866l. "Palfrey's History of New England." *North American Review* 102:638–40.

1866m. "Martin's History of France." *North American Review* 102:640–41. (Further volumes beyond those reviewed in 1865k.)

1866n. "Sabin's Reprints." *North American Review* 102:641–44.

1866o. "The American Lectureship at Cambridge, England." *Nation* 2:457–59.

1866p. "Good Manners." *Nation* 2:571.

1866q. "Ecce Homo." *North American Review* 103:302–7.

1866r. "Beardsley's Episcopal Church in Connecticut." *North American Review* 103:307–8.

1866s. "Sir Alexander Grant's Ethics of Aristotle." *Nation* 3:106–7.

1866t. "More Poetry of the War." *Nation* 3:187–88. (Reviews Melville's *Battle Pieces.)*

1866u. "Venetian Life." *Nation* 3:189.

*1866v. "The Soldier's Cause." *The Soldier's Friend,* September.

1866w. "Harvard Memorial Biographies." *North American Review* 103:498–509.

1866x. "Lea's Superstition and Force." *North American Review* 103:583–86.

1866y. "Wight's National Academy of Design." *North American Review* 103:586–89.

1866z. "Laugel's United States during the War." *North American Review* 103:599–602.

1866aa. "Report of the Board of State Charities." *North American Review* 103:602–4.

1866bb. "International Policy." *North American Review* 103:608–9.

1866cc. "Howell's Venetian Life." *North American Review* 103:610–13.

1866dd. "Coloney's Manomin." *North American Review* 103:613–19.

1866ee. "Brace's Short Sermons to Newsboys." *North American Review* 103:621–22.

1866ff. "Sarmiento's Las Escuelas." *North American Review* 103:622–23.

1866gg. "Smith's Lectures on the Study of Modern History." *North American Review* 103:624–25.

1867a. *The* New Life *of Dante Alighieri.* Boston: Ticknor and Fields.

1867b. "Portraits of Dante." In *The Divine Comedy of Dante Alighieri,* translated by Henry Wadsworth Longfellow, 1:347–53. Boston: Ticknor and Fields. (Reprinted from 1865a.)

1867c. "The Work of the Sanitary Commission." *North American Review* 104:142–55.

1867d. "Partridge's Making of the American Nation." *North American Review* 104:247–52.

1867e. "With Sheridan in Lee's Last Campaign." *North American Review* 104:252–54.

1867f. "Lady Wallace's Translation of Beethoven's Letters." *North American Review* 104:297–99.

1867g. "Dana's Household Book of Poetry." *North American Review* 104:303–4.

1867h. "Whitmore's Elements of Heraldry." *North American Review* 104:304–5.

1867i. "Bartlett's Literature of the Rebellion." *North American Review* 104:305–6.

1867j. "Randolph's Hopefully Waiting." *North American Review* 104:308.

1867k. "Religious Liberty." *North American Review* 104:586–97.

1867l. "Parton's Biographical Writings." *North American Review* 104:597–602.

1867m. "The Book of the Sonnet." *North American Review* 104:626–30.

1867n. "Felton's Greece, Ancient and Modern." *North American Review* 104:658–60.

1867o. "Stone's Life and Times of Red Jacket." *North American Review* 104:660–61.

1867p. "Mr. Longfellow's Translation of the Divine Comedy." *Nation* 4:369–70.

1867q. "Mr. Emerson's Poems." *Nation* 4:430–31.

1867r. "Longfellow's Translation of the Divine Comedy." *North American Review* 105:124–48.

1867s. "Swinburne's Song of Italy." *North American Review* 105:324–25.

1867t. "Emerson's May-Day and other Pieces." *North American Review* 105:325–27.

1867u. "Turgenef's Fathers and Sons." *North American Review* 105:328–29. (Review of first U.S. translation of Turgenev, by Eugene Schuyler.)

1867v. "Critical and Social Essays." *North American Review* 105:329–30. (Review of essays reprinted from *Nation.)*

1867w. "The Harvard and Yale Memorial Buildings." *Nation* 5:34–35.

1867x. "The Life and Death of Jason." *Nation* 5:146–47.

1867y. "Female Suffrage and Education." *Nation* 5:152.

1867z. "Compulsory Education." *Nation* 5:191–92.

1867aa. "Mr. Longfellow and His Critics." *Nation* 5:226–28.

1867bb. "Mr. Matthew Arnold's New Poems." *Nation* 5:228–29.

1867cc. "Arthur Hugh Clough." *North American Review* 105:434–77.

1867dd. "Freeman's Norman Conquest of England." *North American Review* 105:640–45.

1867ee. "Memoirs of the Long Island Historical Society." *North American Review* 105:653–59.

1867ff. "Plain Dealing, or News from New England." *North American Review* 105:659–61.

1867gg. "Church's History of King Philip's War." *North American Review* 105:662–64.

1867hh. "Reid's After the War." *North American Review* 105:695–96.

1867ii. "Dr. Parson's Translation of the Inferno of Dante." *Nation* 5:269–71.

1868a. "Ehninger's Legende of St. Gwendoline." *North American Review* 106:335–36.

1868b. "The Church and Religion." *North American Review* 106:376–96.

1868c. "Charles Dickens." *North American Review* 106:671–72.

1868d. "Biddle's Musical Scale." *North American Review* 106:734–36.

1868e. "John Hookham Frere." *North American Review* 107:136–66.

1868f. "Jarves Collection of Early Italian Painters." *North American Review* 107:371–73.

1868g. "Hassaurek's Spanish Americans." *North American Review* 107:373–75.

1868h. "Stone's Invasion of Canada in 1775." *North American Review* 107:375–76.

1868i. "Whitmore's American Genealogist." *North American Review* 107:376.

1869a. "The Autotype or Carbon Process in Photography." *Nation* 8:47.

1869b. "Blake's Songs and Poetical Sketches." *North American Review* 108:641–46.

1869c. "The Poverty of England." *North American Review* 109:122–54.

1869d. "On Emigration." *Fortnightly Review* 12 [new ser. 6]:189–99.

1869e. "Nicolas's Quatrains de Khèyam." *North American Review* 109:565–84. (First U.S. publication of portions of Fitzgerald's *Rubaiyat.)*

1869f. "The International Congress of Peace and Liberty." *Nation* 9:313–15.

1869g. "The Congress of Peace and Liberty at Lausanne." *Nation* 9:336–37.

1870. "The Crisis at Rome." *Nation* 10:350–51.

1872a. *The Holbein Madonna*. London?: Privately printed. (Copy in Harvard University Library.)

1872b. "Urkunden zur Geschichte des Doms von Siena." *Jahrbücher für Kunstwissenschaft* 5:66–90. (Journal edited by A. von Zahn at Leipzig [title sic]; copy in Fine Arts Library, Harvard.)

1873a. "The Cesnola Collection of Antiquities from Cyprus." *Nation* 16:62–63.

1873b. [Note on Dante translations by the late King John of Saxony]. *Nation* 17:306–7.

1873c. "Sara Coleridge." *Nation* 17:425–26.

1874a. *List of the Drawings, Engravings and Etchings by Turner, and from his Designs, shown in Connection with Mr. Norton's Lectures on Turner and his Work. . . . April 23–May 5, 1874*. Cambridge: University Press.

1874b. *Catalogue of the Plates of Turner's Liber Studiorum. With an Introduction and Notes*. Cambridge: Welch, Bigelow, University Press.

1874c. "Laugel's England." *Nation* 18:13.

1874d. "Rossetti's Translations from the Early Italian Poets." *Nation* 18:159–60.

1874e. "Popularizing Art in America." *Nation* 18:170–71. (Signed letter.)

1874f. [Note and query re the poet Samuel Rogers]. *Nation* 19:8.

1874g. "Brigham's Cast Catalogue of Antique Sculpture." *Nation* 19:28.

1874h. "The Montpensier Gallery." *Nation* 19:255–56.

1874i. "John Hookham Frere." *Nation* 19:270–71.

1874j. [N. D'Anvers, *Elementary History of Art*]. *Nation* 19:307.

1874k. [Availability of Michelangelo's writings]. *Nation* 19:319.

1874l. [H. W. Longfellow's *Hanging of the Crane*]. *Nation* 19:402–3.

1874m. [Illustrations to Ruskin's Works]. *Nation* 19:439.

1874n. [Morris Moore's alleged Raphael painting]. *Nation* 19:439–40.

1874o. [A. P. Putnam, *Singers and Songs of the Liberal Faith*]. *Nation* 19:443.

1875a. *William Blake's Illustrations of the Book of Job. With Descriptive Letterpress, and a Sketch of the Artist's Life and Works*. Boston: James R. Osgood.

1875b. "Massachusetts Hall." In *The Harvard Book: A Series of Historical, Biographical, and Descriptive Sketches*, edited by Frederick O. Vaille and H. A. Clark, 1:53–57. 2 vols. Cambridge: Welch, Bigelow.

1875c. "Records of the Past—Assyria and Egypt." *Nation* 20:176–77.

1875d. [Death of Sir Arthur Helps]. *Nation* 20:191.

1875e. [*Records of the Past*, vol. 3]. *Nation* 20:192.

1875f. [C. W. Horton, *Architecture for General Students*]. *Nation* 20:194.

1875g. [H. A. Bright, *Account of Glenriddell MSS. of Burns's Poems*]. *Nation* 20:208.

1875h. [H. M. Ladd, *Essay on the Madonna in Christian Art*]. *Nation* 20:300–301.

1875i. [Current magazine poetry]. *Nation* 20:362.

1875j. [Henry Maine's Rede Lecture]. *Nation* 20:411.

1875k. [J. Ruskin, *Proserpina*]. *Nation* 20:411. (Probably by CEN.)

1875l. [Rajon's etching of Watts' portrait of Mill]. *Nation* 20:411.

1875m. [Henry Maine and Bentham]. *Nation* 21:9.

1875n. [Mafia]. *Nation* 21:42.

1875o. [Beatification of Columbus]. *Nation* 21:42.

1875p. "Recent Poetry." *Nation* 21:44.

1875q. [W. S. Baker, *William Sharp, Engraver*]. *Nation* 21:46.

1875r. "Tennyson's Queen Mary." *Nation* 21:60–61.

1875s. [H. H. Morgan, *Representative Names in English Literature*]. *Nation* 21:61–62.

1876a. "Some Recent Volumes of Poetry." *Nation* 22:14–15.

1876b. [Editorial reply to letter on "Art Instruction in Massachusetts"]. *Nation* 22:62.

1876c. [Death of John Forster]. *Nation* 22:97.

1876d. [W. S. Baker, *American Engravers and Their Work*]. *Nation* 22:104.

1876e. [S. S. Crosby, *Early Coins of America*]. *Nation* 22:104.

1876f. [Hogarth's engravings]. *Nation* 22:114.

1876g. "Stedman's Victorian Poets." *Nation* 22:117–18.

1876h. "Feminine Poetry." *Nation* 22:132–34.

1876i. "The Life of George Ticknor." *Nation* 22:148–49.

1876j. "The Massachusetts System of Instruction in Drawing." *Nation* 22:252–53.

1876k. [Editorial reply to letter on art instruction in schools]. *Nation* 22:306–7.

1876l. [Sidney Lanier on poetry and music]. *Nation* 22:336.

1876m. [P. G. Hamerton, ed., *Portfolio*]. *Atlantic Monthly* 37:762.

1876n. "A Flock of Songsters." *Nation* 22:353–55.

1876o. "O'Hara and His Elegies." *Nation* 22:417–18.

1876p. [St. George Mivart and Chauncey Wright]. *Nation* 22:60.

1876q. [*Verses from the "Harvard Advocate"*]. *Nation* 23:139–40.

1877. "The Dimensions and Proportions of the Temple of Zeus at Olympia." *Proceedings of the American Academy of Arts and Sciences* 13:145–70. (Presented 10 October 1877.)

1878a. "Biographical Sketch of Chauncey Wright." In Chauncey Wright, *Philosophical Discussions*, edited by CEN, pp. vii–xxiii. New York: Henry Holt. (Date on title page is 1878, copyright date 1876.)

1878b. "Venice and St. Mark's." *Atlantic Monthly* 41:202–17. (Reprinted with minor emendations in *Historical Studies of Church-Building*, 1880a.)

*1878c. [Annotated Michelangelo bibliography]. *Bulletin of the Library of Harvard University*, March, June, October 1878, January, March 1879. (Reprinted as book, 1879a.)

1878d. [Death of William Cullen Bryant]. *Nation* 26:404–5.

1878e. "Florence, and St. Mary of the Flower." *Atlantic Monthly* 42:564–75, 657–69. (Reprinted with substantial additions and revisions in *Historical Studies of Church-Building*, 1880a.)

1879a. *List of the Principal Books Relating to the Life and Works of Michelangelo; with Notes.* Number 3, Bibliographical contributions of the Library of Harvard University. Edited by Justin Winsor. Cambridge: John Wilson & Son. (Reprinting of 1878c.)

1879b(1). *Notes of Drawings by Mr. Ruskin, Placed on Exhibition by Professor Norton in the Gallery of Messrs. Noyes & Blakeslee, 127 Tremont Street, Boston. October 1879.* Cambridge: John Wilson and Son, University Press.

*1879b(2). *Notes of Drawings by Mr. Ruskin Placed on Exhibition at the Museum of Fine Arts, Boston, February, 1880.* Cambridge.

1879c. [W. G. Rawlinson, *Turner's Liber Studiorum*]. *Nation* 28:169–70.

1879d. [*Tanagra Figurines*]. *Nation* 29:248.

1880a. *Historical Studies of Church-Building in the Middle Ages: Venice, Siena, Florence.* New York: Harper & Bros. (Reprinted at least once, 1902.)

1880b. "Painting and Sculpture in Their Relation to Architecture, as Illustrated by the Practice of the Italian Artists of the Thirteenth and Fourteenth Centuries." *American Art Review* 1:192–95, 249–53. (A paper read before the American Institute of Architects, 19 November 1879.)

1880c. [Restoration of S. Marco, Venice]. *Nation* 30:13.

1880d. [Abridged edition of *Stones of Venice*]. *Nation* 30:75–76.

1880e. "Recent Works on Fine Art and Artists." *Nation* 30:123–24.

1880f. [C. H. Moore's mezzotints and the art of mezzotint]. *Nation* 30:418–19.

1880g. "Butler's Translation of Dante's Purgatory." *Nation* 31:397–98.

1880h. "Newton's Essays on Art and Archaeology." *Nation* 31:449–50.

1881a. "Turner's Drawings for the Liber Studiorum." *Nation* 32:8.

1881b. "Muntz's Life of Raphael." *Nation* 32:208–9.

1881c. "Murray's History of Greek Sculpture." *Nation* 32:444–45.

1881d. "The Greek Play at Harvard." *Atlantic Monthly* 48:106–10.

1882a. *Address at the Celebration of the Two Hundredth Anniversary of the Building of the Old Meeting-house at Hingham, August 8, 1881.* Cambridge.

1882b. "Remarks of Mr. Norton at the Annual Meeting of the Dante Society, May 16, 1882." In *First Annual Report of the Dante Society, May 16, 1882,* pp. 17–25. Cambridge: John Wilson and Son, University Press.

1882c. "Perry's History of Greek and Roman Sculpture." *Nation* 34:547–48.

1882d. "Early Mention of Assos." *Nation* 35:11.

1882e. [English editions of Mai's *De re publica* of Cicero]. *Nation* 35:113.

1882f. "Major di Cesnola's Salaminia." *Nation* 35:138.

1883a. (Editor.) *The Correspondence of Thomas Carlyle and Ralph Waldo Emerson.* 2 vols. Boston: James R. Osgood.

1883b. "Clough." *Nation* 36:259–60.

1884a. (Editor.) *The Correspondence of Thomas Carlyle and Ralph Waldo Emerson.* Rev. and expanded. 2 vols. Boston: James R. Osgood.

1884b. "On the Reading of Dante." *Century* 27:629.

1884c. "Dante's Portrait in the Bargello." *Century* 27:956.

1884d. "A Visit to Sardis." *Harper's New Monthly Magazine* 68:672–79.

1885a. "The First American Classical Archaeologist [J. I. Middleton]." *American Journal of Archaeology* 1:3–9.

1885b. "Two Recent Translations of the Divine Comedy." *Nation* 40:524–25.

1886a. (Editor.) *Early Letters of Thomas Carlyle.* 2 vols. London: Macmillan.

1886b. "Recollections of Carlyle, with Notes Concerning His 'Reminiscences.'" *New Princeton Review* 2:1–19.

1886c. "Omissions by Mr. Froude in Carlyle's 'Reminiscences.'" *Nation* 43:74.

1886d. "A Gift of Dante." *Nation* 43:251.

1887a. (Editor.) *Correspondence between Goethe and Carlyle.* New York: Macmillan.

1887b. (Editor.) *Reminiscences by Thomas Carlyle.* 2 vols. New York: Macmillan.

1887c. "Dean Plumptre's Translation of the Divine Comedy." *Nation* 44:102–4.

1887d. "Time References in the Divina Commedia." *Nation* 44:322–24.

1887e. "The Excavations at Crotona." *Nation* 44:386.

1887f. [G. A. Scartazzini, *Handbook to Dante*]. *Nation* 44:454–55.

1888a. (Editor.) *Letters of Thomas Carlyle, 1826–36.* 2 vols. New York: Macmillan.

1888b. "Matthew Arnold." *Proceedings of the American Academy of Arts and Sciences* 23 [new ser. 15]:349–53.

1888c. "The Intellectual Life of America." *New Princeton Review* 6:312–24.

1889a. "A Definition of the Fine Arts." *Forum* 7:30–40.

1889b. "Mr. Cole's Woodcuts in the *Century.*" *Nation* 48:267.

1889c. "The Lack of Old Homes in America." *Scribner's* 5:636–40.

1889d. "Rawdon Brown and the Gravestone of 'Banished Norfolk.'" *Atlantic Monthly* 63:740–45.

1889e. "The Prospects of Architecture as a Fine Art in the U.S." *Technology Architectural Review* 2:19.

1889f. "A Last Word on the Excavations at Delphi." *Nation* 49:169–70.

1889g. "The Building of the Church of St.-Denis." *Harper's* 79:766–76.

1889h. "The Building of the Cathedral at Chartres." *Harper's* 79:944–55.

1890a. "Harvard University in 1890." *Harper's* 81:581–92. (Reprinted in *Four American Universities*, 1895a.)

1890b. [J. A. Symonds, *Introduction to the Study of Dante*]. *Nation* 51:271–72.

1890c. "The Early Biographers of Dante." *Nation* 51:307–9.

1891a. (Translator.) *The Divine Comedy of Dante Alighieri.* 3 vols. Boston: Houghton Mifflin, 1891–1892. (Rev. ed. 1902.)

1891b. (Co-editor in part.) *The Writings of James Russell Lowell.* 10 or 12 vols. Boston: Houghton Mifflin, 1890–92, and later printings. (The question of editorship is complex. The edition began to appear in 1890 under JRL's supervision; after JRL died and perhaps even during his last illness, CEN seems to have collaborated with Horace E. Scudder in final editing of the first edition and then in continuing revision but with no clear distinction among editions. CEN to Scudder, 24 December 1896, Special Collections, Wellesley College Library, names Scudder "editor," while CEN's correspondence with Houghton Mifflin shows his own editorial role. The *Writings* appear in the initial printing to have comprised ten volumes, but CEN 1891c and 1892b were quickly added as volumes 11 and 12.)

1891c. (Editor.) *Latest Literary Essays and Addresses of James Russell Lowell.* Boston: Houghton Mifflin.

1891d. Introductions to John Ruskin, *Works.* Brantwood edition. New York: Charles E. Merrill, 1890–92.

1891e. Preface to Charles Sterrett Latham, *A Translation of Dante's Eleven Letters, with Explanatory Notes and a Biographical, Historical, and Critical Comment to the First, Second, Third, Ninth, and Eleventh Letters.* Edited by G. R. Carpenter. Memorial edition. Cambridge: Riverside Press. (Latham died before publication. Evidently a cheaper student's edition was also published by Houghton Mifflin.)

1892a. (Translator.) *The New Life of Dante Alighieri.* Boston: Houghton Mifflin. (Revision of 1867 edition.)

1892b. (Editor.) James Russell Lowell, *The Old English Dramatists.* Boston: Houghton Mifflin.

1892c. "The Department of Fine Arts and the Fogg Bequest." *Harvard Graduate's Magazine* 1:118–19.

1893a. Preface to Thomas William Parsons, translator, *The Divine Comedy of Dante Alighieri.* Boston: Houghton Mifflin.

1893b. (Editor.) *Letters of James Russell Lowell.* 2 vols. New York: Harper and Brothers.

1893c. "James Russell Lowell." *Harper's* 86:846–57.

1893d. "The Letters of James Russell Lowell." *Harper's* 87:553–60.

1893e. (Editor.) [Unpublished lectures of JRL, individually titled]. *Century,* new ser. 25:125–31, 223–24, 432–39, 515–16, 716–21; new ser. 26: 24–28. ("Prefatory Note," *Century,* new ser. 25:124.)

1894a. (Editor.) *Orations and Addresses of George William Curtis.* 3 vols. New York: Harper and Brothers.

1894b. (Editor.) George William Curtis, *Literary and Social Essays.* New York: Harper and Brothers. (The volume indicates no editor, but CEN's correspondence with Harper's shows that he edited it.)

1894c. (Editor.) *The Heart of Oak Books.* 6 vols. Boston: D. C. Heath, 1894–95. (A five-volume edition showing Kate Stephens as co-editor, published in 1893–94, was suppressed owing to gross errors by Stephens in the textual editing; a copy of this earlier edition survives in Houghton. The preface (printed in all volumes but volume 1) was abstracted as "A Taste for Good Reading," *School Review* 2:448–50.

1894d. Introduction to *The Complete Poetical Works of Sir Walter Scott.* New York: Thomas Y. Crowell.

1894e. [Syllabus of] *Lectures on Dante: Percy Turnbull Memorial Lectureship of Poetry, Johns Hopkins University.* [Baltimore]. (No publication information in pamphlet; presumably published as bulletin of the university.)

1895a. "Harvard." In *Four American Universities: Harvard, Yale, Princeton, Columbia.* New York: Harper & Bros.

1895b. (Editor.) *Last Poems of James Russell Lowell.* Boston: Houghton Mifflin.

1895c. (Co-editor, with JRL.) *The Poems of John Donne.* 2 vols. New York: Grolier Club. ("From the Text of the edition of 1633, revised by James Russell Lowell, with the various readings of the other editions of the seventeenth century, and with a preface, an introduction, and notes by Charles Eliot Norton." 383 copies printed.)

1895d. "The Educational Value of the History of the Fine Arts." *Educational Review* 9:343–48.

?1895e. [Bernhard Berenson's *Lorenzo Lotto*]. *Athenaeum* [London], no. 3520, p. 481. (Samuels 1979, pp. 212–13, identifies CEN as author but without citing evidence. It seems clear that Berenson came to believe that CEN wrote this review; but the particular style of sarcasm, and the style more generally, strike me as not CEN's.)

1895f. "Illustrations of the Divine Comedy from the Chronicle of Fra Salimbene." In *Fourteenth Annual Report of the Dante Society (Cambridge, Mass.), May 15, 1895,* pp. 21–34. Boston: Ginn for the Dante Society.

1896a. (Editor.) *The Power of Sound: A Rhymed Lecture, by James Russell Lowell.* New York: Privately printed.

1896b. "Some Aspects of Civilization in America." *Forum* 20:641–51.

1896c. "The Public Life and Services of William Eustis Russell." *Harvard Graduate's Magazine* 5:177–94. (Printing of memorial address delivered by CEN at invitation of city of Cambridge, 26 October 1896. Reprinted in 1908a.)

1896d. "The Text of Donne's Poems." *Studies and Notes in Philology and Literature* 5:1–19. Child memorial volume. Boston: Ginn for Harvard University, Modern Language Departments. (Printed at pp. 19–22 as an appendix is a variant version, found in a ms. of Donne's poems, of a poem by Francis Beaumont, "Mr. Francis Beaumont's Letter to Ben Jonson," together with a brief note on it by CEN.)

1897a. "Dante." In *Library of the World's Best Literature, Ancient and Modern,* edited by Charles Dudley Warner, 11:4315–78. New York: International Society.

1897b. Introduction to *The Poems of Mrs. Anne Bradstreet (1612–1672); Together with her Prose Remains.* New York: Duodecimos.

1897c. "The Poetry of Rudyard Kipling." *Atlantic Monthly* 79:111–15.

1897d. "Francis James Child." *Proceedings of the American Academy of Arts and Sciences* 32:333–39. (Reprinted, with additions, as 1897e.)

1897e. "Francis James Child." *Harvard Graduate's Magazine* 6:161–69.

1898. (Editor.) *Two Note Books of Thomas Carlyle, from 23d March 1822 to 16th May 1832.* New York: Grolier Club.

1899a. Introduction to *Il Pesceballo: Opera in One Act.* Italian words by F. J. Child. English version by J. R. Lowell. Chicago: Caxton Club. (210 copies printed.)

1899b. Biographical sketch in Rudyard Kipling, *Plain Tales from the Hills.* New York: Doubleday & McClure.

1899c. (Editor.) *Letters from Ralph Waldo Emerson to a Friend, 1838–1853.* Boston: Houghton Mifflin.

1899d. "The Purport of the Divine Comedy." *Roma letteraria* 7:149–51.

1899e. "Rudyard Kipling: A Biographical Sketch." *McClure's Magazine* 13:282–85. (Advance publication of 1899b.)

1899f. "Recent Works on Dante." *Nation* 69:191–92, 210–12.

*1899g. [The craftsman as an artist]. *Architectural Review* 5:81.

1900a. "The Work of the Archaeological Institute of America." *American Journal of Archaeology,* 2d ser. 4:1–16. (Reprinted in *Archaeological Institute of America Bulletin,* 1903?).

1900b. [Temple edition of Dante's Paradiso]. *Nation* 70:91.

1900c. "Gosse's Life of Donne." *Nation* 70:111–13, 133–35.

1900d. [Edmund Gardner's *Dante's Ten Heavens* and *Dante*]. *Nation* 70:376–77.

1900e. [P. H. Wicksteed's translation of *Paradiso*]. *Nation* 70:377.

1901a(1). *Commencement Address* [to Radcliffe graduates]. [Cambridge]: Privately printed.

1901a(2). "Address to Radcliffe Graduates." *Harvard Graduate's Magazine* 10:38–45.

1901b. [Frederic Whitmore's translation of Tasso's *Amyntas*]. *Nation* 73:232.

1901c. [H. F. Tozer, *An English Comment on Dante's Divina Commedia*]. *Nation* 73:307–8.

1902a. (Translator.) *The Divine Comedy of Dante Alighieri.* Rev. ed. 3 vols. Boston: Houghton Mifflin. (Revision of 1891a.)

1902b. "The Life and Character of George William Curtis." In *Memorials of Two Friends: James Russell Lowell, 1819–1891, George William Curtis, 1824–1892.* New York: Privately printed. (50 copies printed.)

1902c. "The Worth of the Child's Own Book." Introduction to *The Story Teller,* edited by Thomas Bailey Aldrich. The Young Folks' Library, vol. 1. Boston: Hall and Locke.

1902d. "Epitaph of Dietzmann, Landgrave of Thuringia, Ascribed to Dante." *Twentieth Annual Report of the Dante Society (Cambridge, Mass.), 1901,* pp. 3–13. Boston: Ginn for the Dante Society.

1902e. "Tribute to William W. Story." *Proceedings of the Massachusetts Historical Society,* 2d ser. 15:368–71.

1902f. "William Wetmore Story." *Harvard Graduate's Magazine* 10:351–54. (Printing of CEN's MHS memorial address.)

1903a. Introduction to *Comments of John Ruskin on the Divina Commedia,* edited by George P. Huntington, pp. ix–xiv. Boston: Houghton Mifflin.

1903b. *The Poet Gray as a Naturalist, with Selections from His Notes on the Systema Naturae of Linnaeus and Facsimiles of Some of His Drawings.* Boston: Charles E. Goodspeed. (Printed by D. B. Updike at his Merrymount Press in Boston.)

1903c. "Address of Charles Eliot Norton." In *The Centenary of the Birth of Ralph Waldo Emerson,* pp. 45–58. Concord: Social Circle in Concord.

1903d. "Tribute to Mr. James Elliot Cabot." *Proceedings of the Massachusetts Historical Society,* 2d ser. 17:163–67.

1903e. "The Price Letters, 1767–1790." *Proceedings of the Massachusetts Historical Society,* 2d ser. 17:262–377. (Letters to the English dissenting minister Richard Price by various well-known Americans, 1767–90. These were sent to CEN by SSN's relative Walter Ashburner of London and then supplied by CEN to the MHS for printing. What editorial role CEN played, if any, is unclear.)

*1903f. "The Work of the Archaeological Institute of America." *Archaeological Institute of America Bulletin* 1:251–66. (Reprinted from *American Journal of Archaeology.)*

1903g. "Il n'y a que le premier pas qui coûte." *Atlantic Monthly* 91:572–74.

1903h. "The Founding of the School at Athens." *American Journal of Archaeology,* 2d ser. 7:351–56.

1904a. (Editor.) *Letters of John Ruskin to Charles Eliot Norton.* 2 vols. Boston: Houghton Mifflin. (Partly printed in 1904d.)

1904b. "Tribute to Sir Leslie Stephen." *Proceedings of the Massachusetts Historical Society,* 2d ser. 18:252–54.

1904c. "A Criticism of Harvard Architecture Made to the Board of Overseers." *Harvard Graduate's Magazine* 12:359–62. (Printing of CEN's annex to the report of the Harvard Overseers' Committee on Fine Arts and Architecture.)

1904d. (Editor.) "Letters of John Ruskin." *Atlantic Monthly* 93:577–88, 797–806; 94:8–19, 161–70, 378–88. (Reprinted and expanded in 1904a.)

1905a. (Editor.) *The Love Poems of John Donne.* Boston: Houghton Mifflin.

1905b. *Ashfield Children's Exhibit and Prize Day.* Leaflet no. 2. Boston: Massachusetts Civic League.

1905c. "Reminiscences of Old Cambridge." *Cambridge Historical Society Publications* 1:11–23.

1906a. (Translator.) *Sonnets from the Vita Nuova of Dante.* Brookline: Privately printed. (From CEN's translation. 30 copies printed by hand by Daniel Edwards Kennedy. Copy in Houghton.)

1906b. *An Appeal to Reason as Well as to Compassion.* N.p. (Leaflet supporting euthanasia. Nor 5259.06.2 in Houghton.)

1906c. *Henry Wadsworth Longfellow: A Sketch of His Life, Together with Longfellow's Chief Autobiographical Poems.* Boston: Houghton Mifflin.

1906d. "The New Humanistic Type." *Printing Art* 6:273–82.

1907a. "Note on the Vocabulary of the Vita Nuova." *Twenty-Fifth Annual Report of the Dante Society (Cambridge, Mass.), 1906,* pp. 1–17. Boston: Ginn for the Dante Society.

1907b. [Tribute to Carl Schurz]. *Proceedings of the Massachusetts Historical Society,* 2d ser. 20:402–3.

1907c. "The Launching of the Magazine." *Atlantic Monthly* 100:579–81.

*1908a. "William Eustis Russell." In *Sons of the Puritans.* Boston: American Unitarian Association. (Reprinted from *Harvard Graduate's Magazine,* December 1896.)

1908b. "Remarks of Charles Eliot Norton [on awarding Longfellow Prize, 27 February 1908]." *Cambridge Historical Society Publications* 3:47–49.

1908c. "A Note on 'The Pleasant Art of Reading Aloud.'" *Nation* 86:32. (Letter to editor.)

1908d. "The Japanese Point of View." *Nation* 86:257. (Letter to editor.)

Charles Eliot Norton's immediate family members are shown with parenthetical relationships. Other parenthetical notations include life dates to distinguish between persons with the same name, e.g., Oliver Wendell Holmes. Minor appearances of some characters have been eliminated from the index; substantive discussions remain. The following abbreviations are used in index entries: AN (Andrews Norton); CEN (Charles Eliot Norton); HWL (Henry Wadsworth Longfellow); JRL (James Russell Lowell).

Library of Congress Cataloging-in-Publication Data

Turner, James, 1946–

The liberal education of Charles Eliot Norton / James C. Turner.

p.   cm.

Includes bibliographical references and index.

ISBN 0-8018-6147-0 (alk. paper)

1. Norton, Charles Eliot, 1827–1908.   2. Journalists—United States—
Biography.   3. Authors, American—19th century—Biography
4. United States—Intellectual life—19th century.   5. Criticism—
United States—History—19th century.   6. Nation
(New York, N.Y. : 1865)   I. Title.

PN4874.N66   1999

818'.409

[B]—DC21   99-11498 CIP